Sunset
Recipe Annual
1990 EDITION

Every *Sunset Magazine* recipe and
food article from 1989

By the *Sunset* Editors

Fruit Taco (page 156)

Sunset Publishing Corporation ■ **Menlo Park, California**

A Decade of Fine Food

Double Pea Soup (page 51)

Completing a decade of delicious culinary adventures, all of *Sunset Magazine's* food articles for 1989 are collected in the pages of this third edition of *Recipe Annual*. From January's marinated cheeses and Andalusian-style fish to December's gingerbread people, every morsel that appeared in the 1989 issues is here for you to savor.

If you've tried recipes from earlier editions, you'll know what a marvelous banquet awaits you in this book. It covers every kind of appetizing occasion—from breakfast and picnic lunches to barbecues and elegant dinner parties.

You'll find here what people expect from *Sunset*—plenty of fresh, light ingredients carefully combined to produce tempting dishes. Included, too, are all of 1989's popular monthly features: *Sunset's Kitchen Cabinet*, *Menus*, and *Chefs of the West*.

While cooking with a variety of wholesome foods has been an ongoing practice at *Sunset*, in 1989 you may notice even more recipes that are lean in fat and calories, yet rich in natural flavor. A nutritional analysis (see page 5) accompanies every recipe to guide you on specifics.

Front cover: Shrimp and scallops take on international flair when paired with Middle Eastern pasta in Shellfish Couscous (page 116). Design by Susan Bryant. Photography by Tom Wyatt. Food styling by Tori Bunting. Photo styling by Susan Massey-Weil.

Back cover: Pour vibrantly colored and flavored fresh fruit purées side by side to create dramatic-looking, delectable, and simple fruit soups. Recipes appear on page 178. Photography by Peter Christiansen.

Sunset Magazine
 Editor: William R. Marken

Sunset Books
 Editor: Elizabeth L. Hogan

Fourth printing June 1991

All material in this book originally appeared in the 1989 issues of *Sunset Magazine* and was created by the following editors, illustrators, and photographers:

Food and Entertaining Editor
Sunset Magazine
Jerry Anne Di Vecchio

Food Staff
Sunset Magazine
Linda Anusasananan, Special
 Assignments Editor
Sandra Bakko Cameron
Paula Smith Freschet
Bernadette Hart
Elaine S. Johnson
Annabel Post
Betsy Ann Reynolds
Christine Weber

Illustrations
David Broad (*Chefs of the West*)
Alice Harth (*Sunset's Kitchen Cabinet*)
Lois Lovejoy (*pages 28–29*)

Photography
Glenn Christiansen
Peter Christiansen
Norman A. Plate
Darrow M. Watt
(*See page 304 for individual credits.*)

Recipe Annual was produced by *Sunset Books*.

Contributing Editors
Cornelia Fogle
Gregory J. Kaufman
Helen Sweetland
Susan Warton

Design
Williams & Ziller Design

Contents

A Letter from *Sunset*

DEAR READER,

Capping one of *Sunset's* most delectable decades in 60 years of publishing, this edition of *Recipe Annual* collects every food article and recipe published in *Sunset Magazine* in 1989. This year's articles give special emphasis to well-balanced meals, fresh foods low in fat, exotic produce, elegant vegetables and salads, and simple family fare from foreign cuisines. We expect that these themes will gain momentum as the coming decade approaches the next century.

But as important as ever in 1989 are the traditions Westerners have come to expect from *Sunset. Kitchen Cabinet*, a showcase of reader-submitted recipes, has turned up faithfully every month since the 1930s. *Menus*, recipes that are either quick to prepare or require minimal attention once under way, pays special attention to the busy cook's timetable. Finally, the monthly column *Chefs of the West* presents a lighthearted look at what men like to cook.

In **January,** we toast the new year with a taste of perishable stone fruits transported from orchards in the Southern Hemisphere. Apricots, peaches, nectarines, and cherries dress up kuchen, savarin, and compote in "Summer-winter desserts." **February** features fish in an update of our 1982 article "Fish market revolution." This year's report introduces some less familiar species now available and describes five easy cooking methods that can be used with most market fish.

Sunset food editorial staff includes, left to right (seated), Linda Anusasananan and Jerry Anne Di Vecchio; (standing) Paula Smith Freschet, Sandra Bakko Cameron, Betsy Ann Reynolds, Annabel Post, Bernadette Hart, Christine Weber, and Elaine S. Johnson.

Starting with The Best of Sunset in 1987, each Recipe Annual that followed has been a keepsake edition of the previous year's food articles and recipes.

March boasts one of *Sunset's* favorite foods—a beautiful bread. This one, a version of Venice's *panettone,* is a sugared loaf that bakes tall in an unpretentious paper bag. **April** announces that "The stylish wardrobe of a well-dressed salad depends on accessories." Just coordinate quality basics with good-tasting oils, vinegars, and seasonings as you follow the four simple, judge-as-you-go steps to variations on the splendid green salad.

May promises perfect picnic weather for the "Take-it-anywhere spring feast." Forget the forks—all you need are fingers and napkins for the seasoned artichokes, steeped shrimp, crisp vegetables, and crusty bread. Another outdoor adventure is **June's** *rijsttafel,* a Dutch-Indonesian rice table that's a lively spectacle of color, texture, and tastes. Our simplified version keeps the essence of this Southeast Asian classic with only a fraction of the work.

July celebrates the summer's bounty of fresh fruits and vegetables with fruit-filled "taco" cookies and pretty-as-a-picture salads that are almost too beautiful to eat, but pleasingly light and nutritious if you do. **August** relaxes with a stunning patio party featuring Hawaiian appetizers called *pupus.*

September transports us to Italy, where climate and produce are similar to ours in the West. Italian family favorites, including a Florentine mixed grill, individual pizzas, a trio of frittatas, and wine-glazed pears, brighten this nine-page story. Also on September's bill of fare are three exquisite low-fat dinner entrées, featuring chicken, shrimp, and rice combined with beans.

October heralds the beginning of the baking season with blue-ribbon muffins, selected by a *Sunset* taste panel from a multitude of reader-submitted recipes. Sample any of our half-dozen choices, including blueberry, spicy apple, and peanut butter and bran.

November, of course, means Thanksgiving dinner, which at *Sunset* we celebrate differently—but always deliciously—each year. For 1989, we present a truly indigenous American feast that features such unexpected delights as quinoa with wild rice and a salad of green beans and jicama, as well as the traditional roast turkey, cranberries, and sweet and white potatoes. And don't overlook the plump and tender miniature pumpkins. Use them as decorative—and edible—containers for a spicy squash mixture, a chutney relish to accompany meat or turkey, or a pumpkin pie filling.

TO USE OUR NUTRITION INFORMATION

Sunset recipes contain nutrition information based on the most current data available from the USDA for calorie count; grams of protein, carbohydrates, and total fat; and milligrams of cholesterol and sodium.

This analysis is usually given for a single serving, based on the largest number of servings listed for the recipe. Or it will be for a specific amount, such as per tablespoon (for sauces), or by a unit, as per cooky.

The nutrition analysis does not include optional ingredients or those for which no specific amount is stated (salt added to taste, for example). If an ingredient is listed with an alternative—such as unflavored yogurt or sour cream—the figures are calculated using the first choice. Likewise, if a range is given for the amount of an ingredient (such as ½ to 1 cup butter), values are figured on the first, lower amount.

Recipes using regular-strength chicken broth are based on the sodium content of salt-free homemade or canned broth. If you use canned salted chicken broth, the sodium content will be higher.

December brings smiles at the design and taste of cooky people, including a tennis player, sunbather, and skater with headset. The whimsical ginger-kids are made from a 24-year-old *Sunset* recipe given back to us this year by a reader, with personalized revisions, whose family has been baking them annually for three generations. Another recipe modified and returned to us after three generations of use is the loaf of tender, sculpted Christmas tree bread, perfect for a holiday breakfast.

As always, all of our recipes have been tested, tasted, and evaluated by our food editors in our test kitchens. We expect our dishes to be delicious, attractive, nutritious, and achievable in as few steps and as little time as possible (with occasional exceptions on time and complexity if the reward is worth the extra effort). The next time you're near our headquarters in Menlo Park, California, we hope you'll stop by during the week for a tour of our editorial offices and a chance to observe our test kitchens in action.

Until next year,

Jerry Anne Di Vecchio
Food and Entertaining Editor
Sunset Magazine

JANUARY

Lemon Savarin with Peaches (page 10)

Bring a taste of summer
to midwinter meals with one of our handsome desserts using
stone fruits grown in the Southern Hemisphere. For another
intriguing treat, we marinate cheeses in flavorful oils or
liquor saturated with herbs or spices. Add fresh interest to
your January menus with a hearty vegetable or meat soup
and salad for lunch or supper, a substantial cioppino or fish
entrée featuring freshly caught seafood, or one of our
adaptable potato side dishes.

Marinated Cheeses

Customized cheeses, *bathed in a flavorful oil marinade or saturated with a variety of herbs and liquor, make handsome presentations.*

These embellishments add more than intriguing tastes and good looks; they extend the life of the cheeses, allowing ample time to enjoy them.

As an appetizer, scoop herb-scented feta, chèvre, or breakfast cheese from oil onto crackers and eat with salty olives.

To end a meal, try breakfast cheese or camembert in spiced oil spread thickly on gingersnap cookies.

(Use the flavorful marinade left from cheeses to dress salads.)

Blue-veined cheese with cognac or port is good before or after dinner, served on crackers and accompanied by toasted nuts and lady apples or ripe pear wedges.

CHEESE IN OLIVE OIL

- ½ pound feta cheese or an unripened goat cheese like Montrachet, or 3 slightly soft whole breakfast cheeses (3 oz. each)
  About 5 sprigs (each about 3 in. long) fresh or dry marjoram, rosemary, oregano, or thyme (or 2 tablespoons of the dry, crushed herbs)
- 3 cloves garlic, peeled
- 5 or 6 niçoise or salt-cured olives, or Spanish-style green olives
  About ½ cup olive oil

Cut feta into large chunks. Cut goat cheese into 1½-inch-thick slices. Leave breakfast cheeses whole.

Fit cheese compactly into a jar or crock, about 1½-cup size. Add herbs, garlic, and olives. Fill jar with oil to cover cheese; cover jar.

Chill cheese at least 5 days (oil congeals, but melts at room temperature).

Serve at room temperature. Store in refrigerator up to 6 weeks. Makes 6 to 8 appetizer servings.

PER SERVING, DRAINED OF OIL: 125 calories, 4.2 g protein, 1.8 g carbohydrates, 11 g fat, 25 mg cholesterol, 376 mg sodium

CHEESE IN SPICED NUT OIL

- 3 slightly soft whole breakfast cheeses (3 oz. each) or 2 slightly soft whole camembert (4 to 5 oz. each)
- 1 tablespoon whole cloves
- 1 cinnamon stick (about 3 in. long)
- 1 long strip (8 to 10 in.) orange peel, orange part only
- 1 long strip (8 to 10 in.) lime peel, green part only
- 1 to 2 cups walnut oil, almond oil (the kind that smells like almonds), hazelnut oil, or salad oil

Stud top and bottom of cheeses evenly with cloves. Place cheeses in a jar or crock, 3- to 4-cup size; add the cinnamon stick and drape the orange and lime peels around the cheese.

Pour oil into container to cover cheese; cover container. Chill at least 5 days (oil congeals, but melts at room temperature).

Serve at room temperature. Store in refrigerator up to 6 weeks. Makes 8 to 10 dessert servings.

PER SERVING, DRAINED OF OIL: 107 calories, 4.5 g protein, 0.7 g carbohydrates, 9.6 g fat, 16 mg cholesterol, 192 mg sodium

POTTED BLUE CHEESE

- 1 fresh or dry bay leaf
- 1 sprig (about 5 in.) fresh rosemary, or 1 teaspoon of the dry herb
  About ¾ pound blue cheese such as Danish blue, Gorgonzola, or Stilton
  About ¼ cup cognac or port

Place bay leaf and rosemary (if using fresh) against inside of a jar or crock, 1½- to 2-cup size.

Trim off any wax or dried edges from cheese; break cheese into 1- to 1½-inch chunks. Pack half the cheese into container (put dry rosemary on cheese).

Pour half the cognac over Danish or Gorgonzola cheese; use port with Stilton. Pack remaining cheese into jar. Pour cognac over cheese to cover it.

Serve at room temperature. Store in refrigerator up to 6 weeks. Makes 16 to 18 appetizer servings. —*Martin Cohen, Hollywood, Calif.*

PER SERVING: 98 calories, 5.4 g protein, 0.7 g carbohydrates, 7.2 g fat, 19 mg cholesterol, 352 mg sodium

Spread cracker with pungent feta and a bit of the olive oil and marinating herbs.

Add cinnamon stick and orange and lime peels to clove-studded breakfast cheeses in jar. Add enough walnut oil to cover.

Pour port over big chunks of Stilton cheese packed into a crock with herbs.

Easy-to-make marinated cheeses are ready to use or give (left to right): breakfast cheese with citrus peel, spices, and nut oil; feta with herbs and olive oil; Stilton with port and herbs.

Summer-Winter Desserts

A TASTE OF SUMMER *in the height of winter used to be a rare treat. But this luxury is no longer hard to come by, as stone fruits grown in the Southern Hemisphere's reverse-season climate show up in our markets.*

The fruits, mostly from Chile and New Zealand, are the same as or similar to varieties we grow here. They can be costly, though prices have become more moderate as imports increase. Quality of the fruit, usually firm to firm-ripe, is often surprisingly good.

Here, we pair imported apricots, peaches or nectarines, and cherries with domestic citrus fruits (now entering their peak winter harvest). The first and last recipes work well for dessert or brunch; all the dishes have make-ahead steps.

APRICOT GINGER KUCHEN

    ½   cup (¼ lb.) butter or margarine, at
        room temperature
    ¾   cup firmly packed brown sugar
    4   large eggs
    1   teaspoon vanilla
    1½ cups all-purpose flour
    2   teaspoons ground ginger

    1   teaspoon ground cinnamon
    ½   teaspoon ground nutmeg
        About 1 tablespoon finely
        shredded orange peel (orange
        part only)
    14 to 16 firm-ripe apricots (about 2 lb.
        total), cut in half and pitted
    2   tablespoons granulated sugar
    1½ tablespoons finely chopped
        crystallized ginger
        Powdered sugar

In the small bowl of an electric mixer, beat butter with brown sugar until smoothly blended. Add eggs, 1 at a time, beating well after each. Stir in vanilla, flour, ground ginger, cinnamon, nutmeg, and 1 teaspoon orange peel.

Butter and flour-dust an 11-inch tart pan with or without removable bottom. Spread batter evenly in the pan. Arrange apricots, cut side up, on batter, pressing fruit slightly into it. Sprinkle granulated sugar evenly over fruit and batter, then sprinkle with crystallized ginger.

Bake the kuchen in a 350° oven until firm when touched in center and just beginning to pull away from the pan, about 35 minutes. Let cool at least 30 minutes on a rack, then dust with powdered sugar and sprinkle with remaining peel. Remove pan rim, if possible. Cut into wedges; serve warm or at room temperature. If made ahead, cover when cool and let stand up to 8 hours. Serves 10 to 12.

PER SERVING: 255 calories, 4.7 g protein, 38 g carbohydrates, 9.9 g fat, 112 mg cholesterol, 107 mg sodium

LEMON SAVARIN WITH PEACHES OR NECTARINES

Bake the savarin on page 19, omitting the wine syrup; instead, saturate the cake with this lemon syrup.

        Savarin, warm, released but in
        pan (recipe page 19)
        Lemon syrup (recipe follows)
    6   medium-size firm-ripe peaches or
        nectarines (1¼ to 1½ lb. total)
        Whipped cream

With a fork, pierce warm savarin deeply about every ½ inch over surface. Set aside ½ cup syrup; pour remainder over savarin. Let stand until at room temperature. If made ahead, cover and chill until next day; let come to room temperature.

Up to 2 hours before serving, immerse peaches (not the nectarines) in boiling water to cover for about 30 seconds, then pull off skins. Discard pits and thickly slice fruit. Mix fruit with reserved syrup.

Invert savarin onto a wide, rimmed plate. Spoon peaches around cake; ladle fruit juices on savarin. Spoon whipped cream into cake's center, or serve from a bowl. Slice the savarin and top with fruit; add cream to taste. Makes 14 to 16 servings.

PER SERVING: 252 calories, 3.8 g protein, 37 g carbohydrates, 8.6 g fat, 85 mg cholesterol, 82 mg sodium

Lemon syrup. In a 2- to 3-quart pan, combine 1½ cups **sugar,** 1½ cups **water,** 2 teaspoons grated **lemon peel,** ½ cup **lemon juice,** and ¼ teaspoon ground **coriander.** Bring to a boil on high heat; boil, uncovered, for 5 minutes. Let cool slightly, then stir in ¾ cup **rum.** Pour through a fine strainer. Use warm or cool.

CHERRY & PINK GRAPEFRUIT COMPOTE

    5   medium-size pink grapefruit
        (about 4¼ lb. total)
    1   pound sweet, dark cherries, pitted
    ⅓   cup orange-flavor liqueur
        About 2 tablespoons sugar
    1½ tablespoons honey

Fresh apricot kuchen, flecked with orange peel and candied ginger, is good warm or cold. Prepare it in advance to serve for dessert or brunch.

Winter meets summer: lemon syrup bathes fresh peaches and soaks savarin, a tender yeast cake. Serve with whipped cream.

With a vegetable peeler, pare only golden part of peel from 1 grapefruit. Cut peel into very thin, long slivers.

With a knife, cut and discard remaining peel and white membrane from each grapefruit. Hold fruit over a bowl and cut parallel to membrane to release segments into bowl. Squeeze juice from membrane into bowl; discard membrane. Drain off juice and reserve.

To fruit, add cherries, ¼ cup liqueur, and sugar to taste. Mix gently. If made ahead, cover and chill up until next day.

In a 1½- to 2-quart pan, combine slivered peel and 1 cup water. Bring to a boil over high heat; drain. Repeat step. To the peel, add reserved juice, remaining sugar, and honey. Boil, uncovered, over high heat; stir often to prevent scorching. Cook until the peel is translu-

cent and the syrup is reduced to about 2 tablespoons. Stir in remaining liqueur; remove from heat. If made ahead, cover and let stand up until next day.

Ladle fruit and juices into individual bowls and top equally with peel and syrup. Makes 6 to 8 servings.

PER SERVING: 125 calories, 1.3 g protein, 27 g carbohydrates, 0.6 g fat, 0 mg cholesterol, 0.3 mg sodium

Soup & Salad

SIMMERING SOUPS *rarely require much attention. And when paired with a salad, they make a satisfying, quick-to-assemble meal. Here, we offer three choices. The first two are vegetable based and cook in less than 30 minutes. The third requires long, slow simmering to tenderize the meat and blend the flavors.*

CURRIED CARROT & ONION SOUP

Serve with a salad of butter lettuce, Roma-type tomatoes, and green onions.

- 2 **tablespoons olive oil**
- 1¼ **pounds carrots, thinly sliced**
- 2 **medium-size onions, chopped**
- 2 **teaspoons minced fresh ginger**
- 1 **fresh jalapeño chili, stemmed, seeded, and minced**
- 2 **teaspoons curry powder**
- 1 **tablespoon mustard seed**
- 1 **teaspoon** *each* **coriander seed, cumin seed, and cardamom seed (pods removed)**
- 1 **teaspoon fresh thyme leaves or ½ teaspoon dry thyme leaves**
- ⅓ **cup long-grain white rice**
- 8 **cups regular-strength chicken broth**

In a 5- to 6-quart pan over medium-high heat, combine oil, carrots, onions, ginger, chili. Cover and stir often until vegetables begin to brown, 12 to 15 minutes. Add curry, mustard seed, coriander, cumin, cardamom, thyme, and rice; mix well. Add broth and bring to a boil. Reduce heat and simmer, covered, until rice is tender to bite, 20 to 25 minutes. Serves 6.

PER SERVING: 164 calories, 5.3 g protein, 19 g carbohydrates, 7.5 g fat, 0 mg cholesterol, 91 mg sodium

FRESH MUSHROOM & SPINACH SOUP WITH GARLIC CROUTONS

Get extra spinach and enoki mushrooms when you make the soup, then use them in a salad with toasted almonds and blue cheese dressing.

- 2 **tablespoons butter or margarine**
- 1½ **pounds common mushrooms, thinly sliced**
- 1 **large onion, chopped**

Aromatic seeds and spices flavor carrot and onion soup. Accompany with a butter lettuce salad dressed with oil and vinegar.

Enoki and common mushrooms give broth mellow richness. Spinach adds color to soup and forms base of salad.

4 cups regular-strength beef broth
1 tablespoon dry sherry
½ package (3½ oz. size) enoki
   mushrooms
⅛ teaspoon ground nutmeg
¼ teaspoon ground white pepper
4 cups packed spinach leaves,
   washed, drained, and cut into thin
   strips
   Garlic croutons (recipe follows)

Melt butter in a 4- to 5-quart pan over medium-high heat. Add sliced mushrooms and onion; stir often until all but about ½ cup liquid has evaporated, 8 to 10 minutes. Add broth, sherry, enoki mushrooms, nutmeg, and pepper. Bring to a boil; reduce heat and simmer, covered, to blend flavors, about 15 minutes. Serve; or cover and chill up to 3 days, then reheat.

To serve, stir spinach into soup, then ladle equally into 4 bowls; top each portion with a garlic crouton. Accompany with remaining croutons. Serves 4.

PER SERVING WITHOUT CROUTON: 148 calories, 6.9 g protein, 18 g carbohydrates, 7.6 g fat, 16 mg cholesterol, 117 mg sodium

Garlic croutons. Combine 2 tablespoons **olive oil** with 1 clove **garlic,** minced or pressed. Cut 1 (8 oz.) **baguette** into ½-inch slices. Place slices in a 10- by 15-inch baking pan; brush tops equally with garlic oil. Bake in a 300° oven until crisp and golden, 25 to 30 minutes. Serve hot or at room temperature. Makes 24 to 26.

PER CROUTON: 35 calories, 0.8 g protein, 4.9 g carbohydrates, 1.3 g fat, .26 mg cholesterol, 51 mg sodium

WINTER BEEF VEGETABLE SOUP & SALAD

About 3½ pounds beef shortribs
1 to 2 pounds soup bones (optional)
8 cups regular-strength beef broth
3 cups water
1 cup dry white wine
1 can (15 oz.) stewed tomatoes
1 large onion, chopped
¾ pound carrots, chopped
2 stalks celery, chopped
½ cup firmly packed parsley sprigs
4 cloves garlic
1 dry bay leaf
½ teaspoon *each* dry basil leaves,
   dry rosemary leaves, and dry
   thyme leaves
   Salt and freshly ground pepper
   Grated parmesan cheese
   Beef salad (directions follow)

Shortribs, tomatoes, onion, carrots, and celery make a flavorful soup that's a hearty meal in itself. After simmering meat, you shred it to mix with salad greens.

Place shortribs in an 8- to 10-quart pan over medium-high heat; brown well on all sides. Add soup bones, broth, water, wine, tomatoes, onion, carrots, celery, parsley, garlic, bay leaf, basil, rosemary, and thyme. Bring to a boil; reduce heat, cover and simmer until meat is very tender when pierced, about 3 hours. Lift out and discard soup bones. Lift out shortribs; when cool enough to handle, discard bones and fat. Tear meat into bite-size pieces; reserve for beef salad.

Pour broth through a fine strainer into a bowl; skim off and discard fat. Whirl vegetables in a food processor or blender until coarsely puréed. Return vegetables and broth to pan. Bring to a boil over high heat; stir often. Ladle into bowls. Season to taste with salt and pepper; offer cheese to sprinkle over individual portions. Accompany with beef salad. Serves 6 to 8.

PER SERVING: 57 calories, 1.7 g protein, 11.8 g carbohydrates, 0.9 g fat, 0 mg cholesterol, 161 mg sodium

Beef salad. In a large bowl, mix together **reserved beef** (preceding), ¼ cup **balsamic** or red wine **vinegar,** ½ cup **olive oil.** Add 1 small **red onion,** thinly sliced and separated into rings; 3 or 4 **red radishes,** thinly sliced; and 8 to 10 cups washed, crisped, bite-size pieces mixed salad greens such as **red** or green **leaf lettuce** and **watercress.** Spoon onto salad plates. Offer additional **vinegar** and **oil,** and **salt** and **pepper** to add to taste. Makes 6 to 8 servings.

PER SERVING: 306 calories, 17 g protein, 1.8 g carbohydrates, 23 g fat, 50 mg cholesterol, 41 mg sodium

Fresh-Catch Cioppino

IMAGINE HAVING TWO DOZEN *chefs over for dinner. What could you serve that would satisfy their discriminating tastes?* Leonard Cohen of the Olde Port Inn in Avila Beach, California, faces this challenge when he hosts his annual dinner for chefs and winemakers who participate in his Sea Fare and Wine List Preview.

His delicious answer—cioppino filled with freshly caught seafood.

To flavor the cioppino base, use either dry white or red wine. White wine creates a lighter, more delicate broth; red a deeper, mellower one. Or try some of each.

COHEN'S CIOPPINO

- ½ cup olive oil
- 2 large onions, thinly sliced
- 6 leeks (1½ lb.), ends trimmed, cut in half lengthwise, rinsed, and diagonally sliced ½ inch thick
- 3 cloves garlic, pressed or minced
- ¼ cup chopped parsley
- 4 dry bay leaves
- ½ teaspoon dry oregano leaves
- ½ teaspoon dry thyme leaves
- ½ teaspoon pepper
- 1 teaspoon saffron threads
- 2 cans (28 oz. each) diced tomatoes; or 6 cups ¾-inch-diced firm-ripe tomatoes
- 2 cans (16 oz. each) tomato sauce
- 1 quart dry white or dry red wine (or some of each)
  Salt and liquid hot pepper seasoning
- 2 dozen clams (about 2 in. wide), suitable for steaming, well scrubbed
- 2 dozen small mussels (about 3 in. long), well scrubbed and beards trimmed
- 1 to 1½ pounds extra-jumbo shrimp (16 to 20 per lb.), shelled and deveined
- 1½ pounds firm, light-flesh fish steaks such as shark or swordfish, cut into 1½-inch chunks
- 2 cooked Dungeness crab (about 4 lb. total), cleaned and cracked

Shrimp, mussels, clams, crab, and chunks of fish flavor cioppino broth made with either white or red wine.

In a 12- to 14-quart pan, combine oil, onions, leeks, garlic, parsley, bay leaves, oregano, thyme, pepper, and saffron; cook over medium-high heat, stirring occasionally, until onion is limp. Add tomatoes and juice, tomato sauce, and wine. Cover and boil gently until flavors are blended, about 15 minutes with canned tomatoes, 45 minutes with fresh tomatoes. Add salt and hot pepper seasoning to taste. If made ahead, cool, cover, and chill until the next day. To continue, heat until simmering.

Add clams, mussels, shrimp, and fish chunks; cover and simmer 10 minutes.

Add crab and simmer, covered, just until crab is hot and clams and mussels open, about 10 minutes longer. Ladle cioppino into wide bowls. Makes 10 to 12 servings.

PER SERVING: 334 calories, 33 g protein, 21 g carbohydrates, 14 g fat, 111 mg cholesterol, 933 mg sodium

Fish Baked the Andalusian Way

T HIS SIMPLE FISH DISH *reflects the regional bounty of Andalusian Spain. A mild-tasting Mediterranean fish, very similar to our Western rockfish, is gently baked, then seasoned and served with sherry, olives, capers, and garden vegetables that flourish in Andalusia (and in the West). The result is a hearty, easy-to-like country dish.*

Although it's more dramatic if you use a whole fish, which you may need to order ahead, fillets are a convenient option.

BAKED SPANISH-STYLE FISH

Use the smaller amounts of ingredients for a 3-pound fish; use full amounts for a larger fish or fillets.

- 2 **tablespoons butter or margarine**
  About 3 tablespoons olive oil
- 2 **or 3 medium-size (1 to 1½ lb. total) russet potatoes, scrubbed and cut into 1-inch chunks**
- 1 **large onion, thinly sliced**
- 2 **or 3 cloves garlic, minced or pressed**
- 2 **or 3 tablespoons chopped parsley**
- 2 **or 3 tablespoons drained capers**
- 1 **jar (5 or 8 oz.) pimiento-stuffed Spanish-style olives, drained**
- ½ **to ¾ cup dry sherry**
- 1 **whole (3 to 4 lb.) firm-textured, white-flesh fish such as rockfish or striped bass, scaled, gutted, and rinsed; or 2 to 4 equal-size fillets (about 2 lb. total) of any of these fish, rinsed**
- 2 **to 3 medium-size, firm-ripe tomatoes, cored and cut into ¼-inch-thick slices**
- 1 **lemon, cut into wedges**

In a 10- to 12-inch frying pan, melt butter with 2 tablespoons oil over medium-high heat. Add potatoes, cover, and cook until browned and tender when pierced, about 15 minutes total; turn as needed with a spatula. Lift potatoes from pan; set aside.

Add onion to pan and cook, stirring often, until limp and golden, 10 to 15 minutes; add 1 to 2 teaspoons more oil if needed to prevent sticking. Set off heat; add garlic, parsley, capers, olives, and

sherry. Stir to loosen browned bits in pan and set aside.

To bake whole fish, lay a 12- by 24-inch piece of foil in a rimmed baking dish or pan that is long enough to hold the fish; the tail can extend beyond the edge of the pan (support it with foil). Brush foil generously with oil and lay fish on top. Cover tightly with another sheet of foil. Bake in a 400° oven until fish is opaque in thickest part (cut to test), about 30 minutes.

To bake fillets, brush a 9- by 13-inch baking dish or pan with oil. Lay fillets in pan, thick sections at opposite ends; overlap fillets to make as evenly thick as possible. Cover tightly with foil. Bake in

a 400° oven until fish is opaque in thickest part (cut to test), 15 to 20 minutes.

Lift foil with fish from pan; drain juices into frying pan. Slide whole fish onto a platter or transfer fillets to platter with a wide spatula; keep warm.

Return potatoes to frying pan and boil on high heat until juices reduce to about ½ cup if you started with ½ cup sherry, ¾ cup if you used ¾ cup sherry.

Arrange tomato slices around fish, then spoon the hot vegetable mixture onto tomatoes and pour liquid over fish. Accompany with lemon to add to taste. Makes 4 to 6 servings.

PER SERVING: 365 calories, 34 g protein, 22 g carbohydrates, 16 g fat, 66 mg cholesterol, 789 mg sodium

An Andalusian medley of flavors—dry sherry, olive oil, capers, green olives, tomatoes, lemon, potatoes, onion, garlic, and parsley—gives a Spanish accent to whole baked fish.

Potatoes: Vegetable Chameleons

VERSATILE POTATOES *take on the personality of any seasoning and adapt to any part of the meal.*

Bake small, creamy-textured potatoes with apples and onions to make a splendid accessory to roast pork or ham—or offer slivers of them in a brandy-flavored cream sauce as a first course. Or combine more crumbly russets in a salad balancing the tang of yogurt, orange, and cilantro; serve with beef.

Small, thin-skinned potatoes bake with sweet onion and apple wedges, in a flavorful combination that goes well with a pork roast.

BAKED NEW POTATOES & APPLES

    2 pounds thin-skinned potatoes
       (1½ to 2 in. wide), scrubbed
    2 medium-size onions, cut into
       1-inch wedges
    2 tablespoons olive or salad oil
    1 pound red apples, such as Empire,
       Jonathan, or Winesap
 1¼   cups regular-strength beef broth
    ¾ cup apple juice
    2 tablespoons cornstarch
    ¾ teaspoon ground allspice

Place potatoes in a 9- by 13-inch baking dish. Break apart onion wedges and sprinkle over potatoes. Add oil and mix well. Bake, uncovered, in a 400° oven for 25 minutes; stir occasionally.

Rinse apples; quarter, core, and cut into ¾-inch wedges. Mix together broth, apple juice, cornstarch, and allspice.

When potatoes have cooked 25 minutes, mix in apples and juice mixture. Return to oven, spooning juices occasionally over apples and potatoes. Bake until potatoes are very tender when pierced and juices begin to form thick bubbles, about 25 minutes longer. Makes 8 or 9 servings.

PER SERVING: 161 calories, 2.6 g protein, 31 g carbohydrates, 3.5 g fat, 0 mg cholesterol, 8.1 mg sodium

BRANDIED CREAM POTATO BATONS

 1½   pounds thin-skinned white
       potatoes, scrubbed
    2 tablespoons butter or margarine
    ½ cup *each* brandy and regular-
       strength chicken broth
    1 cup whipping cream
    4 green onions, ends trimmed
       Freshly ground black pepper
       Freshly grated nutmeg

Cut potatoes into ¼-inch-thick sticks.

In a 10- to 12-inch frying pan over medium-high heat, melt butter and add potatoes. With a wide spatula, occasionally turn potatoes, gently, just until they begin to turn pale gold, about 10 minutes.

Add brandy and broth; cover and simmer until potatoes are tender when pierced, about 15 minutes. Add cream. Gently turn potatoes over with the spatula. Cook over high heat until boiling vigorously, about 5 minutes. Spoon equal portions of potatoes onto 4 salad plates and place a green onion alongside. Sprinkle generously with pepper and nutmeg. Serves 4.

PER SERVING: 367 calories, 5.4 g protein, 33 g carbohydrates, 25 g fat, 82 mg cholesterol, 96 mg sodium

PESTO-ORANGE POTATO SALAD

    2 pounds cold, cooked russet
       potatoes
    2 medium-size oranges
    ½ cup *each* lightly packed parsley
       and fresh cilantro (coriander)
       leaves
    ¼ cup grated parmesan cheese
    ¾ cup unflavored yogurt
    1 teaspoon sugar
    ½ cup walnut halves
       Salt and pepper

Peel and discard skin from cooked potatoes. Cut potatoes into ½-inch chunks and place in a large bowl.

Grate enough peel from oranges to make 2 teaspoons. Cut remaining peel and white membrane from oranges. Over a small bowl, cut segments free from membrane, catching juices. If done ahead, cover and chill segments up to 4 hours.

In a blender or food processor, combine orange juice, the grated orange peel, parsley, cilantro, parmesan cheese, yogurt, and sugar. Whirl until smoothly blended.

Pour the dressing over the potatoes and gently mix. If made ahead, cover and chill up to 4 hours. Spoon potato salad onto a serving dish. Garnish with orange segments and walnuts. Add salt and pepper to taste. Serves 6 to 8. — *Marie Mitchell, Lake Oswego, Ore.*

PER SERVING: 171 calories, 5.4 g protein, 27 g carbohydrates, 5.2 g fat, 3.2 mg cholesterol, 72 mg sodium

Quick Winter Warmups

ON A CHILLY DAY, *sipping a steaming beverage is a soothing way to warm your bones, particularly when you're settled in front of a crackling fire.*

Here are three quick ways to fill your cup. The first is a ruby-colored fruit punch scented with orange, lemon, raspberry, and cranberry. Second is a blend of puréed dried apricots, apricot nectar, and tangerine juice; brandy is optional. Last is a freshly brewed espresso, dressed up with almond and chocolate syrup, whipped cream, and almond cookies.

CRANBERRY-CITRUS COCKTAIL WITH RASPBERRY SWIZZLE

- 1 package (12 oz.) frozen unsweetened raspberries, partially thawed
- 1 bottle (64 oz.) cranberry juice cocktail
- 1 *each* medium-size orange and lemon, thinly sliced

Select 24 of the best-looking raspberries. Thread 3 to 4 berries on each of 6 to 8 thin wooden skewers. Lay skewers on a flat pan and put in freezer until berries are firm, about 45 minutes. (If made ahead, cover and store up to 5 days.)

When remaining raspberries are thawed, press through a fine strainer into a 4- to 5-quart pan; discard seeds and pulp. To pan, add juice and slices of orange and lemon. Stir over medium heat until steaming, 10 to 15 minutes. Ladle juice (no slices) into 6 to 8 tall glasses; add a swizzle to each. Makes 6 to 8 servings, 1- to 1½-cup size.

PER SERVING: 168 calories, 0.5 g protein, 42 g carbohydrates, 0.5 g fat, 0 mg cholesterol, 5.3 mg sodium

WARM APRICOT JEWEL

- ½ cup firmly packed dried apricots
- 1½ cups water
- 1 can (46 oz.) apricot nectar
- ¼ cup thawed frozen tangerine juice concentrate
- 3 tablespoons lemon juice
- ½ cup brandy (optional)

Smoothly purée dried apricots and water in a blender. Rub purée through a fine strainer into a 3- to 4-quart pan. Add apricot nectar, tangerine concentrate, and lemon juice. Stir over high heat until steaming. Add brandy, if desired. Pour into mugs. Makes 8 cups, 6 to 8 servings.

PER SERVING: 136 calories, 1.1 g protein, 35 g carbohydrates, 0.2 g fat, 0 mg cholesterol, 7.7 mg sodium

Dried apricots and their fragrant nectar give this warming drink a vivid yellow-orange hue. Serve with more of the dried fruit.

ESPRESSO ALMOND TORTONI

- About 2 cups tiny Italian-style amaretti (crisp almond macaroons)
- 6 to 8 strips lemon peel (yellow part only), each about ⅛ inch wide and 3 inches long
- ¼ cup *each* sugar and water
- ½ cup semisweet chocolate baking chips
- ½ teaspoon almond extract
  Hot espresso (directions follow)
- ¾ cup whipping cream, softly whipped

Coarsely crush enough cookies to make 3 tablespoons; set aside.

Tie each strip of peel in a knot; set aside.

In a 1- to 1½-quart pan, stir sugar, water, and chocolate over low heat until chocolate melts; stir in almond extract. Add chocolate mixture to espresso; mix well.

Pour coffee into 6 to 8 espresso cups or demitasse (3- to 4½-oz. size). Top each serving equally with whipped cream and crushed cookies. Offer peel to add to coffee, and cookies to nibble. Serves 6 to 8.

PER SERVING: 155 calories, 1.2 g protein, 15 g carbohydrates, 11 g fat, 26 mg cholesterol, 15 mg sodium

Hot espresso. Measure 1 cup **finely ground espresso** or other dark-roast coffee into a strainer or cone lined with a paper coffee filter. Pour 5 cups boiling **water** through filter into a pitcher. Or put grounds in a filter-plunger coffee pot, add water, push down plunger. Use hot.

More January Recipes

OTHER JANUARY RECIPES *featured savory mushroom crêpes with fresh asparagus, a springy cornbread, and a light savarin soaked in spicy wine syrup.*

MUSHROOM CRÊPES WITH ASPARAGUS

A sophisticated mushroom sauce folded into tender crêpes makes an ideal party presentation.

   Three-mushroom sauce
   (recipe follows)
   Crêpes (recipe follows)
24 thin asparagus spears, tough ends
   snapped off

Distribute 2 tablespoons mushroom sauce over 1 half of pale side of each crêpe. Fold plain side over filling, then fold each crêpe again to make a triangle.

Lay triangles slightly apart in a 9- by 13-inch pan. If made ahead, cover and chill up to 24 hours. Bake, uncovered, in a 450° oven until hot, about 8 minutes.

Meanwhile, in a 10- to 12-inch frying pan on high heat, cook asparagus, uncovered, in 1 inch boiling water until just tender when pierced, 4 to 6 minutes; drain. If made ahead, immerse at once in ice water. When cold, drain, cover, and chill up until next day. To reheat, immerse in boiling water until warm, about 2 minutes. Or cover with plastic

wrap and cook in microwave oven at full power (100 percent) until hot, 1 to 2 minutes.

Arrange crêpes and asparagus on plates. Spoon warm mushroom sauce onto crêpes and asparagus. Makes 4 light entrées or 8 first-course servings. — *Philippe Padovani, Halekulani, Hawaii.*

PER ENTRÉE: 369 calories, 10 g protein, 26 g carbohydrates, 27 g fat, 155 mg cholesterol, 118 mg sodium

Three-mushroom sauce. In a bowl, soak 1 ounce (about 1 cup) **dried shiitake mushrooms** and ½ ounce (about ⅔ cup) **dried morels** in 2½ cups hot water until soft, about 20 minutes. Squeeze mushrooms frequently to release any grit. Lift mushrooms from water and squeeze the

Crêpe triangle, filled with three-mushroom sauce, goes with asparagus topped with more sauce. Serve as a warm dinner starter, or serve two crêpes as a light entrée.

water in them back into the bowl. Gently pour water into a 2-cup glass measure; take care not to disturb sediment in bottom. Measure water and add enough to make 2 cups. Discard sediment.

Cut off and discard tough stems from shiitakes; mince caps and set aside.

Rinse ½ pound **common mushrooms** and finely chop. In a 10- to 12-inch frying pan over high heat, combine 2 tablespoons **butter** or margarine, ¼ cup **minced shallots,** and chopped mushrooms. Stir often until mushrooms are lightly browned, about 6 minutes.

Add shiitakes and morels to pan. Stir in reserved mushroom water and 1 cup **whipping cream.** Boil on high heat, uncovered and stirring occasionally, until shiny bubbles form and sauce is reduced to about 2 cups, about 10 minutes. Use hot. If made ahead, let cool, cover, and chill up to 24 hours. Stir over medium heat until hot.

Crêpes. In a blender or food processor, whirl 1 **large egg** with ⅓ cup **all-purpose flour;** add ½ cup **milk** and whirl until smooth. Place on medium heat a 6- to 7-inch crêpe pan or other flat-bottom pan that measures 6 to 7 inches across bottom. When hot, add ¼ teaspoon **butter** or margarine and swirl to coat pan surface. Stir batter and pour 2 tablespoons into pan; quickly tilt so batter coats bottom.

Cook until surface is dry to touch and edge is lightly browned. Turn out onto plate. Repeat to cook remaining crêpes; stack as made. Use, or package airtight and chill up to 4 days; freeze to store longer. Bring to room temperature to avoid tearing when separating crêpes. Makes 8.

Yeast Cornbread

The light and springy texture yeast brings in baking provides the ideal foil for other ingredients. Here, this texture contrasts with the crunch of cornmeal.

About 5½ cups all-purpose flour
1 cup yellow cornmeal
¾ teaspoon salt
2 packages active dry yeast
2 cups hot water (120° to 130°)
¼ cup (⅛ lb.) butter or margarine, cut up and at room temperature
⅓ cup honey

If using an electric mixer, stir together 2½ cups flour, cornmeal, salt, and yeast. In another bowl, stir together hot water, butter, and honey. Stirring, add water mixture to flour. Beat at medium speed for 2 minutes. Stir in another ½ cup flour; beat at high speed for 2 minutes longer.

With a heavy spoon, add 2¼ cups more flour and stir until moistened. Scrape onto a floured board and knead, adding flour to prevent sticking, until dough is smooth and elastic, 8 to 10 minutes. Turn dough over in an oiled bowl.

If using a dough hook, combine 5¼ cups flour with dry ingredients. Add liquid ingredients (combine them as above) and mix at low speed until moistened; then beat at high speed until dough pulls cleanly from bowl sides and is no longer sticky, 8 to 10 minutes; add more flour, if needed, 1 tablespoon at a time.

Cover bowl (either method) with plastic wrap. Let dough rise in a warm place until doubled, about 45 minutes. Punch dough down to expel air, divide in half, and shape each into a loaf. Place each in a greased 5- by 9-inch loaf pan. Cover lightly with plastic wrap; let rise in warm place until almost doubled, 20 to 30 minutes.

Bake, uncovered, in a 375° oven until well browned, 40 to 45 minutes. Remove from pans; cool on racks. If made ahead, package airtight up to 1 day; freeze to store longer. Makes 2 loaves (1½ lb. each). —*A.J. Stefani, Cobb Mountain, Calif.*

Per Ounce: 70 calories, 1.6 g protein, 13 g carbohydrates, 1.1 g fat, 2.4 mg cholesterol, 42 mg sodium

Four-spice Wine Savarin

Spicy wine syrup is poured over the light, porous savarin in this dessert. Or, if you prefer, use the lemon syrup on page 10.

1 package active dry yeast
¼ cup warm water (about 110°)
3 tablespoons sugar
About ½ cup (¼ lb.) butter or margarine
4 large eggs
½ cup warm milk (about 110°)
½ teaspoon vanilla
½ teaspoon lemon peel
2 cups all-purpose flour
Four-spice wine syrup (recipe follows)
Vanilla bean ice cream

In a small bowl, sprinkle yeast over water; let stand until softened, about 5 minutes.

In the large bowl of an electric mixer, beat together sugar and ½ cup of the butter. Add eggs, 1 at a time, mixing well after each. Add milk, vanilla, lemon peel, yeast mixture, and flour; beat until well blended. Cover with plastic wrap and let rise in a warm place until doubled, about 1½ hours. Stir vigorously to expel air.

Heavily butter and flour-dust a 10-cup ring mold. Pour batter into pan. Cover with plastic wrap; let stand in a warm place until puffy-looking and almost doubled, about 30 minutes.

Bake savarin, uncovered, in a 375° oven until browned and just pulling from pan, about 30 minutes. Let stand on a rack about 10 minutes. Invert rack onto top of pan; hold pan and rack together and invert to release savarin, then tip cake back into pan (so cake comes out easily later).

With a fork, pierce hot savarin deeply about every ½ inch over its surface. Pour syrup over cake. Let stand until warm or room temperature. If made ahead, cover and chill until next day; serve at room temperature. Invert savarin onto a wide, rimmed plate. Cut into slices and accompany with scoops of ice cream. Makes 14 to 16 servings.

Per Serving: 223 calories, 3.7 g protein, 35 g carbohydrates, 7.6 g fat, 85 mg cholesterol, 82 mg sodium

Four-spice wine syrup. In a 4- to 5-quart pan, combine 1½ cups **sugar,** 2 cups **dry white wine,** 2 teaspoons grated **orange peel,** 1 cup **orange juice,** 3- to 4-inch **cinnamon stick,** 1 teaspoon **coriander seed,** ½ teaspoon **whole cloves,** and ¼ teaspoon freshly grated or ground **nutmeg.** Bring to a boil on high heat and boil, uncovered, until reduced to 3 cups; stir occasionally. If made ahead, let stand, covered, up until next day. Pour syrup through a fine strainer to use; reserve spices as garnishes, or discard.

SWEET & SOUR ONION SPREAD

Low-fat appetizer features sweet onions with yogurt. Serve with pumpernickel toast, tomatoes.

3 large onions, thinly sliced
2 tablespoons salad oil
1 cup unflavored yogurt
1 tablespoon rice vinegar or cider vinegar
Salt
Coarse-ground pepper

In a 12-inch frying pan or 5- to 6-quart pan, combine onions and oil; cook over medium-high heat, stirring frequently, until onions are limp, 10 to 15 minutes. Reduce heat to medium-low and continue cooking, stirring occasionally, until onions are golden and sweet tasting, 15 to 30 minutes longer. Let onions cool. (If made ahead, cover and chill until the next day. To continue, let warm to room temperature.)

Shortly before serving, stir together cooked onions, yogurt, vinegar, and salt to taste. Spoon onion mixture into a serving bowl. Cover mixture generously with pepper. Makes 2 cups, 8 to 10 appetizer servings. — *Roxanne Chan, Albany, Calif.*

PER SERVING: 55 calories, 1.8 g protein, 5.2 g carbohydrates, 1.4 g fat, 0 mg cholesterol, 16.9 mg sodium

SPICED SPINACH & POTATOES

Ground coriander and ginger fragrantly spice diced potatoes and shredded spinach.

¼ cup salad oil
About 1¼ pounds russet potatoes (2 large), peeled and cut into ½-inch cubes
2 cloves garlic, pressed or minced
2 teaspoons ground coriander
½ teaspoon ground ginger
About ½ cup water
¾ pound spinach, stems and any yellow and wilted leaves discarded
Salt and cayenne

Pour 3 tablespoons oil into a 12-inch frying pan or 5- to 6-quart pan set over medium-high heat. Add potatoes; stir occasionally until browned on most sides, 10 to 15 minutes. Over low heat, add 1 tablespoon oil, garlic, coriander, and ginger. Stir for 2 to 3 minutes. Add ½ cup water, cover, and simmer until potatoes are tender when pierced, 5 to 10 minutes; add a little water if needed to prevent sticking.

Meanwhile, cut spinach leaves crosswise into ½-inch strips. Wash and drain strips. Add spinach and stir often over high heat until wilted and most of the liquid evaporates, about 2 minutes. Add salt and cayenne to taste. Spoon into a bowl. Makes 4 servings. — *Betty Buckner, Port Angeles, Wash.*

PER SERVING: 241 calories, 4.4 g protein, 26 g carbohydrates, 14 g fat, 0 mg cholesterol, 59 mg sodium

SHRIMP & SAUSAGE ON MEXICAN RICE

Rice bakes with tomatoes; salsa-seasoned shrimp and sausage go on top.

1 cup long-grain white rice
1 can (14½ oz.) Mexican-style stewed tomatoes
½ cup *each* water and regular-strength chicken broth
½ pound bulk pork sausage
1 clove garlic, pressed or minced
1 small onion, chopped
1 teaspoon cumin seed
¾ pound tiny cooked shelled shrimp
2 tablespoons chopped fresh cilantro (coriander)
½ cup purchased fresh salsa

In a shallow 2-quart baking dish, mix rice, tomatoes, water, and broth; cover tightly. Bake in a 350° oven until rice is tender to bite, 50 to 60 minutes.

About 15 minutes before rice is done, crumble sausage into 1-inch chunks in a 10- to 12-inch frying pan over medium-high heat. Stir occasionally until sausage browns, 5 to 10 minutes. Discard all but 2 tablespoons of fat from pan.

Add garlic, onion, and cumin; stir until onion is limp, about 5 minutes. Add shrimp, cilantro, and salsa; stir until hot, about 3 minutes. Spoon over hot rice. Makes 4 or 5 servings. — *Carol Byng, Coupeville, Wash.*

PER SERVING: 354 calories, 22 g protein, 36 g carbohydrates, 13 g fat, 156 mg cholesterol, 913 mg sodium

CHICKEN BREASTS MARIANNA

4 boned chicken breast halves
  (about 5 oz. each), skinned
1 large egg, lightly beaten
  Crumb mixture (recipe follows)
  About ¼ cup salad oil
½ cup shredded mozzarella cheese

Place chicken between sheets of plastic wrap. Evenly pound with a flat mallet to make each piece about ¼ inch thick. Dip chicken in egg, then press into crumb mixture to coat.

Pour ½ of the oil into a 10- to 12-inch frying pan on medium-high heat. When oil is hot, place chicken in pan; do not crowd. Cook until golden on both sides, 2 to 3 minutes total. When chicken is almost done, sprinkle each piece with ¼ of the mozzarella. Cover pan; cook until cheese melts, about 1 minute. Transfer to plates. Cook remaining chicken, adding more oil if it sticks. Serves 3 or 4. —*Mary Ann West, Eureka, Calif.*

PER SERVING: 395 calories, 41 g protein, 13 g carbohydrates, 19 g fat, 166 mg cholesterol, 514 mg sodium

Crumb mixture. Tear 4 slices **white bread** into pieces; in a blender or food processor, whirl into coarse crumbs. On a sheet of waxed paper, mix crumbs with ¼ cup *each* grated **parmesan cheese** and chopped **parsley,** and about ¼ teaspoon *each* **salt** and **pepper.**

Shredded mozzarella melts over golden chicken breasts that were pounded, breaded, and pan-fried.

CRISP RED CABBAGE & BEETS

2 slices bacon, diced
6 cups shredded red cabbage
  (about 1¼ lb.)
1½ cups shredded peeled beets
  (about 6 oz.)
1 medium-size red onion, cut into
  thin slivers
1 large Red Delicious apple, cored
  and shredded
⅓ cup cider vinegar
2 tablespoons firmly packed brown
  sugar
¼ teaspoon ground allspice
  Salt and pepper

In a wok or 12-inch frying pan, stir-fry bacon over high heat until crisp, about 2 minutes. If there are more than 2 tablespoons fat, discard excess.

Add the shredded red cabbage, beets, and onion slivers; stir-fry over high heat just until cabbage begins to wilt, 2 to 3 minutes.

Add shredded apple, vinegar, brown sugar, and allspice. Stir-fry just until apples are hot, about 1 minute. Add salt and pepper to taste. Pour cabbage mixture into a serving dish. Serve hot. Makes 8 servings.—*Charlotte E. Bunnell, Brinnon, Wash.*

PER SERVING: 91 calories, 1.8 g protein, 14 g carbohydrates, 3.6 g fat, 3.7 mg cholesterol, 70 mg sodium

Stir-fry traditional combination of apples, beets, and cabbage for crisp texture.

CHOCOLATE CHIP PEANUT MELTAWAYS

1 cup (½ lb.) butter or margarine, at
  room temperature
1¼ cups powdered sugar
1 teaspoon vanilla
¼ teaspoon almond extract
2¼ cups all-purpose flour
¾ cup chopped salted roasted
  peanuts
½ cup finely chopped semisweet
  chocolate
2 tablespoons unsweetened cocoa

Beat together butter and ½ cup powdered sugar until creamy. Beat in vanilla and almond extract. Add flour; mix until blended and dough forms. Stir in peanuts and chocolate.

Roll dough into 1-inch balls; place about 1½ inches apart on ungreased 12-by 15-inch baking sheets.

Bake in a 375° oven until cookies are pale gold, 8 to 10 minutes. (If baking more than 1 sheet at a time, switch pan positions in oven halfway through.)

Meanwhile, mix ¾ cup powdered sugar and cocoa in a small bowl. Roll warm cookies, a few at a time, in cocoa mixture to coat. Cool on racks. Serve warm or cool. Store airtight up to 5 days. Makes about 40 cookies.—*Bea Schauer, Milwaukie, Ore.*

PER COOKY: 105 calories, 1.6 g protein, 10 g carbohydrates, 6.8 g fat, 12 mg cholesterol, 58 mg sodium

Peanuts and chocolate flavor these delicately tender sugar- and cocoa-dusted cookies.

ALTHOUGH NO SINGLE LABEL *can describe the philosophy of the Western chef,* syncretism *comes close. The syncretist is one who attempts to reconcile various schools of thought; he would be happiest if he could prove that all cooking sprang from one primordial dish—barbecued or otherwise—varied through the ages by time, the confusion of tongues, and the availability of local produce.*

This culinary evolution gets some help from Robert Ronald, who has brilliantly grafted Latin American seasonings—chilies of varying degrees of heat, and tomato—onto a Middle Eastern understock of couscous, olives, and raisins. Serve when you're not pining for the latest stage in primordial barbecue.

COUSCOUS OLÉ

> 2 **tablespoons butter or margarine**
> 2 **tablespoons olive oil or salad oil**
> 1 **medium-size onion, chopped**
> 1 **large clove garlic, minced or pressed**
> 1 **large red bell pepper, stemmed, seeded, and chopped**
> 1 **large fresh Anaheim (California) chili, stemmed, seeded, and chopped**
> 1 **fresh jalapeño chili, stemmed, seeded, and finely chopped**
> 1 **tablespoon** *each* **ground cumin and chili powder**
> 1¾ **cups (or 1 can, 14½ oz.) regular-strength chicken broth**
> ¼ **cup water**
> 2 **tablespoons lime juice**
> 2 **cups couscous**
> ¼ **cup golden raisins**

> ½ **cup frozen petite peas, thawed**
> 1 **large firm-ripe tomato, cored, peeled, seeded, and chopped**
> ¼ **cup sliced ripe olives**
> **Salt and pepper**
> **Chopped fresh cilantro (coriander)**
> **Sour cream or unflavored yogurt**

Melt butter in oil in a 5- to 6-quart pan over medium heat; add onion, garlic, red pepper, Anaheim chili, and jalapeño. Stir occasionally until onion is golden, about 15 minutes. Stir in cumin and chili powder. Pour broth, water, and lime juice into onion mixture. Bring to a boil over high heat. Add couscous and raisins; stir well. Cover, remove from heat, and let stand until liquid is absorbed, 5 to 10 minutes. Mix in peas, tomato, and olives. Cover until flavors are blended, about 3 minutes. Season to taste with salt and pepper.

Spoon couscous onto a platter. Garnish with cilantro. Offer sour cream or yogurt to add to individual portions. Makes 8 to 10 servings.

PER SERVING: 185 calories, 4.9 g protein, 28 g carbohydrates, 6.4 g fat, 6.2 mg cholesterol, 86 mg sodium

Robert C. Ronald

Pullman, Wash.

ONE DEFINITION OF TRAGEDY *is the fall of a noble personage from a high estate to ruin. By this definition, the fate of the holiday turkey—in its feastable glory so shortly ago—is truly a tragedy. Plump, glisteningly brown, breathing savory vapors, it is the center of attention—for an hour. By the time dessert is served, the bird is a melancholy hulk, its keel and ribs showing bare as those of a shipwreck on a desolate reef.*

Still (and again this fits in with tragic theory), its ghost lurks behind, leaping from refrigerator or freezer to affright the family as turkey hash, turkey noodle casserole, turkey sandwiches, even turkey croquettes. The bird is simply seeking the respect it had when it first came to the table. Bring rest to its troubled spirit as Don Drew does, by serving the leftovers in turkey quiche. Your family will love it, and the turkey will haunt you no more.

TURKEY QUICHE

> 5 **large eggs**
> 2½ **to 3 cups leftover bread stuffing or ½ package (6-oz. size) bread stuffing mix, prepared according to package directions**
> 1 **cup (4 oz.) shredded Swiss cheese**
> 1 **cup diced cooked turkey or chicken**
> ¼ **cup thinly sliced green onions, including tops**
> ½ **cup sliced mushrooms**
> 1 **cup half-and-half (light cream)**
> **Salt and pepper**

In a bowl, beat 1 egg until blended, then add stuffing and mix well. Press stuffing over bottom and up the sides of a

"The Western chef attempts to reconcile various schools of thought."

greased 10-inch pie pan or deep quiche pan or dish. Bake on the lowest rack in a 425° oven until stuffing is crisp and dry to the touch, about 15 minutes. Remove pan from oven; lower oven temperature to 350°. Sprinkle cheese over bottom and sides of stuffing crust, then evenly top with turkey, onions, and mushrooms.

In the same bowl, beat remaining 4 eggs to blend, then stir in half-and-half and season to taste with salt and pepper. Pour over turkey and vegetables.

Bake on the lowest rack in a 350° oven until liquid mixture looks firm and set when pan is gently shaken, 30 to 35 minutes. Let stand at least 10 minutes, then cut into wedges and serve hot or lukewarm. Makes 4 to 6 servings.

PER SERVING: 343 calories, 21 g protein, 14 g carbohydrates, 23 g fat, 297 mg cholesterol, 398 mg sodium

Don C. Drew

San Jose, Calif.

CHUCK PLOOF'S BABY BACK *ribs owe their distinction to their creator's uncommonly good basting sauce. With 14 ingredients, it is not the simplest of sauces, but neither is it the most complex. Like most barbecue sauces, it contains sweet, sour, and spicy ingredients—in this case, the right ingredients in the right proportion. Essential to your complete enjoyment of these ribs are finger bowls and paper napkins.*

Baby back ribs, in case you wonder, haven't anything to do with the age of the pig but are actually the bones that parallel the pork loin. With much pork loin being sold as boneless roasts, these succulent bones are more frequently available.

CHUCK'S BABY BACK RIBS

2 tablespoons butter or margarine
1 medium-size onion, chopped
½ cup *each* water, catsup, and tomato-based chili sauce
¼ cup cider vinegar
2 tablespoons lemon juice
½ cup firmly packed brown sugar
2 tablespoons Worcestershire
½ cup dark molasses
2 teaspoons dry mustard
½ teaspoon *each* pepper and paprika
2 teaspoons liquid smoke
3 to 4 pounds pork baby back ribs

"Baby back ribs, in case you wonder, haven't anything to do with the age of the pig."

Melt butter in a 10- to 12-inch frying pan over medium heat; add onion and stir often until onion is limp, about 10 minutes. Then stir in water, catsup, chili sauce, vinegar, lemon juice, brown sugar, Worcestershire, molasses, mustard, pepper, paprika, and liquid smoke. Bring to a boil, then reduce heat and simmer, uncovered, until reduced to about 2¼ cups, about 30 minutes.

Meanwhile, trim and discard excess fat from ribs; place ribs in a 6- to 8-quart pan. Add water to cover bones. Place over high heat; when boiling, cover and reduce heat. Boil gently for 5 minutes.

Drain ribs and arrange in a single layer in roasting pan or broiler pan that is at least 12 by 14 inches. Brush ribs generously with sauce, then cover pan. Bake in a 400° oven for 15 minutes. Uncover, baste generously again, and continue to bake, basting generously every 15 minutes until ribs are very tender when pierced and all the sauce is used, about 1 hour longer. Makes 4 or 5 servings.

PER SERVING: 831 calories, 43 g protein, 57 g carbohydrates, 48 g fat, 184 mg cholesterol, 934 mg sodium

Charles T. Ploof

San Rafael, Calif.

A NEWSPAPER WE KNOW OF *has an annual contest in which children are awarded prizes for growing the largest and heaviest zucchini. If this were a just world, in which reason prevailed, the children would be punished for letting the zucchini grow so big. Making them eat these huge zucchini (boiled plain, without salt, pepper, or butter) would be appropriate.*

These summer squash are at their best when they are just a few inches long—finger-size or a little bigger. Their will to live is so strong, though, that a few manage to hide among the leaves until they have passed optimum size. These are still salvageable if you stuff them, and quite delightful if you stuff them according to this recipe submitted by John Rockwell.

Despair not that it's winter. Zucchini not only persist among the leaves, they also manage to hang around markets, which offer up squash of varying sizes all year.

STUFFED ZUCCHINI ELEGANTE

4 zucchini, each 6 to 7 inches long
¼ pound mild Italian sausage
¼ cup chopped onion
1 clove garlic, minced or pressed
1 teaspoon dry oregano leaves
½ cup corn kernels, fresh or frozen
1 small firm-ripe tomato, peeled, cored, seeded, and diced
1 cup (4 oz.) shredded sharp cheddar cheese

Split zucchini in half lengthwise. Place, cut side down, in a 12- to 14-inch frying pan. Add about ½ inch water, cover, and place over high heat. Bring to a boil, reduce heat, and boil gently until zucchini are slightly soft when pierced, 4 to 5 minutes. Lift zucchini from pan and drain, cut side down.

Discard water, wipe pan dry, and place over medium heat. Remove sausage casing; crumble meat into pan. Add onion and garlic; stir often until sausage is browned and onion is limp, 10 to 15 minutes. Discard fat. Add oregano, corn, and tomato; stir often for about 2 minutes. Remove from heat; stir in ⅔ cup cheese.

With a spoon, scoop out and discard zucchini seeds. Evenly mound sausage mixture in zucchini halves. Set side-by-side in an 8- by 12- or 9- by 13-inch baking dish or pan. Sprinkle with remaining cheese.

Bake, uncovered, in a 375° oven until stuffing is heated through, 12 to 15 minutes. Makes 8 servings.

PER SERVING: 120 calories, 7.4 g protein, 6.6 g carbohydrates, 7.6 g fat, 23 mg cholesterol, 190 mg sodium

John Rockwell

Anchorage

January Menus

UPER BOWL DOMINATES *the sports scene this month; bring together the loyal fans at home with a super sandwich supper.*

For breakfast and supper, we propose meals easy enough for weekdays, dressed-up enough for weekends.

SUPER BOWL SUPPER

Giant Baked Hero Sandwich
Broccoli, Cauliflower & Radish Basket
Seasoned Garbanzo Dip
Frozen Yogurt Bars
Tangerines   Green Grapes
Beer or Soft Drinks

As light refreshment on this long day of football, try some of the flavorful, non-alcoholic beers available in markets now.

Make dip the day before. While sandwich rises, rinse and cut up vegetables, then mound them in a basket. Use vegetables to scoop up dip.

GIANT BAKED HERO SANDWICH

   2 **loaves (1 lb. each) frozen white bread dough, thawed**
       Garlic oil (recipe follows)
   ½ **pound** *each* **thinly sliced dry salami and cooked ham**
   ¼ **pound thinly sliced dry coppa (optional)**
   ½ **pound thinly sliced fontina or jack cheese**
       Grilled onion (recipe follows)
   1 **jar (7¼ oz.) roasted red peppers, drained well on paper towels**

Pat loaves together. On a lightly floured board, roll dough into a 12- by 18-inch rectangle. Brush surface with 2 tablespoons of the garlic oil. Cover half the dough lengthwise with overlapping layers of salami, ham, coppa, cheese, onions, and peppers. Lift plain half of dough over filling (if dough sticks, loosen with a spatula). Press edges firmly together to seal.

Super-size baked hero sandwich holds thinly sliced cured meats, sliced cheese, grilled onions, and roasted red peppers.

Using 2 wide spatulas, transfer packet to an oiled 12- by 17-inch baking sheet; tuck ends of dough under to fit on pan. Brush dough with remaining oil. Let rise in a warm place until puffy, about 20 minutes. Bake in a 400° oven until richly browned, 15 to 20 minutes. Cut sandwich lengthwise in half, then crosswise into 3-inch slices. Makes 6 to 8 servings. —*Bernice Merslich, San Mateo, Calif.*

PER SERVING: 659 calories, 29 g protein, 58 g carbohydrates, 34 g fat, 78 mg cholesterol, 1,507 mg sodium

Garlic oil. Combine 3 tablespoons **olive oil** with 2 cloves **garlic**, minced or pressed; and ½ teaspoon *each* **dry basil leaves, dry oregano leaves,** and **dry thyme leaves.**

Grilled onion. In an 8- to 10-inch frying pan over medium-high heat, combine 1 tablespoon **olive oil,** 2 tablespoons **bal-** samic or red wine **vinegar,** and 1 large **onion,** sliced. Stir often until onion begins to brown, 8 to 10 minutes; set aside.

SEASONED GARBANZO DIP

In a blender or food processor, smoothly purée 1 can (15 oz.) **garbanzo beans** with ¼ cup of their **liquid** (add more if needed), 2 tablespoons **mayonnaise,** 1 tablespoon *each* minced **shallots** and **anchovy paste,** and ⅛ teaspoon **crushed dried hot red chilies.** Serve, or cover and chill up until next day. Makes about 1⅔ cups.

PER TABLESPOON: 93 calories, 3.3 g protein, 12 g carbohydrates, 3.5 g fat, 3.2 mg cholesterol, 261 mg sodium

This simple yet substantial breakfast goes together in about 30 minutes.

As the tomato sauce simmers, brown the Canadian bacon in another frying pan, then cover and keep warm until breakfast is ready. Also, make the cinnamon butter—or just offer cinnamon sugar to sprinkle on buttered toast. While the bread is toasting, cook the eggs.

SKILLET EGGS IN HERBED TOMATO SAUCE

- 2 tablespoons olive oil
- 1 clove garlic, minced or pressed
- 1 can (28 oz.) tomatoes
- 1½ tablespoons minced parsley
- 1 teaspoon rubbed sage leaves
- ½ teaspoon *each* dry rosemary leaves and sugar
  Salt and pepper
- 8 large eggs

In a 12- to 14-inch frying pan over medium heat, combine oil, garlic, tomatoes with their juice, parsley, sage, rosemary, and sugar. Boil, uncovered, until reduced to 1¾ cups, 20 to 25 minutes; stir often, breaking up tomatoes with a spoon. Add salt and pepper to taste.

Increase heat to medium-high. Break eggs onto sauce. Cover pan and cook until eggs are set the way you like; allow 3 to 4 minutes for soft yolks with firm whites. Spoon eggs with sauce onto plates. Add salt and pepper to taste. Serves 4 to 8.—*Charles Buchignani, San Carlos, Calif.*

PER SERVING: 175 calories, 9.4 g protein, 7.1 g carbohydrates, 12 g fat, 365 mg cholesterol, 308 mg sodium

WHIPPED CINNAMON-PECAN BUTTER

Beat together until fluffy ½ cup (¼ lb.) room-temperature **butter** or margarine, 1 teaspoon **ground cinnamon**, 1 table-spoon firmly packed **brown sugar,** and ¼ cup chopped **pecans.** Serve, or cover and chill up to 2 days. Makes about ¾ cup.

PER TABLESPOON: 88 calories, 0.3 g protein, 1.7 g carbohydrates, 9.2 g fat, 21 mg cholesterol, 78 mg sodium

Let the oven take charge; rice cooks without stirring, fish bakes without fussing.

Put the rice in to bake, then make the sauce for the fish. As the fish bakes, make the salad and set the table.

For dessert, serve fresh pears, or bake them alongside the rice in the 350° oven. Just cut ripe pears in half, core, and put cored side up in a close-fitting pan. Sprinkle with brown sugar, dot with butter, and bake until hot and lightly browned, about 20 minutes.

BAKED LEMON RICE PILAF

In a deep, 1½- to 2-quart baking dish, stir together 2 cups **regular-strength chicken broth**, 1 cup **long-grain white rice**, 2 teaspoons grated **lemon peel**, 2 tablespoons **lemon juice**, ¼ cup chopped **green onion**, and 1 tablespoon **butter** or margarine. Stir to mix; cover tightly.

Bake in a 350° oven until rice is tender to bite, 45 to 50 minutes. Serves 4.— *Linda Bailey, Woodinville, Wash.*

PER SERVING: 212 calories, 4.4 g protein, 39 g carbohydrates, 3.8 g fat, 7.8 mg cholesterol, 60 mg sodium

(Continued on next page)

On a wintry morning, serve eggs poached in herbed tomato sauce with Canadian bacon, cinnamon-pecan butter, and raisin toast.

LINGCOD IN MUSHROOM-TARRAGON SAUCE

- ¼ cup (⅛ lb.) butter or margarine
- ½ pound mushrooms, thinly sliced
- ¼ cup all-purpose flour
- 2 cups milk
- 1½ teaspoons dry tarragon leaves
- ¼ teaspoon ground white pepper
- ⅓ cup dry white wine
- ½ cup grated parmesan cheese
- 4 lingcod steaks, ¾ to 1 inch thick (6 to 8 oz. each)
- 1 tablespoon minced parsley

Melt 1 tablespoon butter in a 10- to 12-inch frying pan over medium-high heat; add mushrooms and stir often until lightly browned, 8 to 10 minutes. Reduce heat to medium and add remaining butter and flour; stir until bubbling, about 2 minutes. Gradually blend in milk, tarragon, and pepper; stir until sauce boils. Add wine and cheese; mix well. Remove from heat; use hot or warm.

Rinse fish and pat dry. Arrange in a single layer in a buttered shallow 2-quart baking dish. Pour sauce over fish. Bake, uncovered, in a 350° oven until fish is opaque in thickest part (cut to test), 15 to 20 minutes. Top with parsley. Serves 4.

PER SERVING: 412 calories, 40 g protein, 15 g carbohydrates, 21 g fat, 144 mg cholesterol, 468 mg sodium

Fish market update (page 28)

What's new in the West's fish markets? Our February issue features a timely report for fish shoppers and five easy, versatile techniques for cooking fish. Fresh ideas to brighten midwinter entertaining include a three-course dinner from the Italian Riviera and a dessert-tasting party for a crowd. To brighten winter's dark, chilly days, we suggest a trio of satisfying vegetable soups and two aggressively seasoned dishes from the Chinese province of Sichuan.

Fish: A Market Update

SINCE WE REPORTED on the "Fish Market Revolution" in October 1982, new species have been introduced, and the availability of others has changed. The health benefits of eating fish, now widely recognized, have kept demand for it high, despite higher prices.

Americans aren't the only ones eating more fish (and paying more for it). In what is still largely a wild harvest, world demand and the dollar's value in relation to other currencies directly influence which fish are available here day by day—and at what prices.

Even with its sizable fishing industry, the United States now depends on imports for nearly two-thirds of its seafood supply. Transported by jet aircraft, fresh fish from around the world can get to market almost as fast as the local catch can.

Many of the sea basses are among kinds now in very short supply. But there's good news about some local fish. Runs of California barracuda have been good the last few seasons. And the famous Pacific sardine, which disappeared mysteriously in the 1940s, has recently been showing up in promising numbers along the central California coast.

Widespread use of aquaculture techniques has significantly increased the world's supply of salmon and shrimp. And farm-raised sturgeon, tilapia, steelhead trout, and striped bass are now being offered to home cooks.

Larger and more modern fishing boats are in use in many areas. Some are equipped to bring up fish—orange roughy is one example—from greater depths than were reachable before. Others can process and freeze fish at sea; operating in remote areas, these factory ships are harvesting species (Alaska pollock among them) too perishable to be brought to market in the past. Some of the best-quality mahi mahi is now frozen at sea.

Freshly caught fish that are filleted, then individually quick-frozen (called IQF in

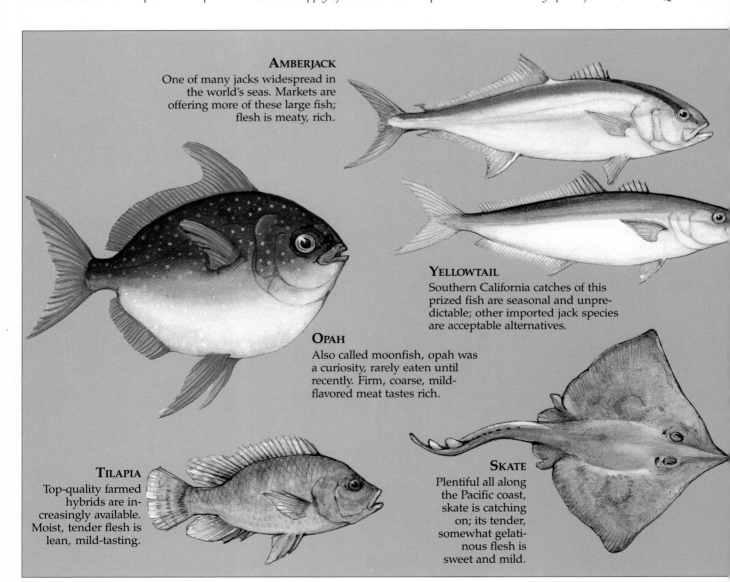

AMBERJACK
One of many jacks widespread in the world's seas. Markets are offering more of these large fish; flesh is meaty, rich.

YELLOWTAIL
Southern California catches of this prized fish are seasonal and unpredictable; other imported jack species are acceptable alternatives.

OPAH
Also called moonfish, opah was a curiosity, rarely eaten until recently. Firm, coarse, mild-flavored meat tastes rich.

TILAPIA
Top-quality farmed hybrids are increasingly available. Moist, tender flesh is lean, mild-tasting.

SKATE
Plentiful all along the Pacific coast, skate is catching on; its tender, somewhat gelatinous flesh is sweet and mild.

Here's a sampling of today's market fish, some new, some more widely available. (Illustrated fish are not all drawn to same scale.)

the trade) are changing the image of frozen fish. Although many markets still routinely defrost fish before displaying it, you can usually ask for and get the still-frozen product. Well-frozen fish, cooked without defrosting, matches or exceeds the quality of fresh fish that's been stored on ice.

With fish selection constantly changing and expanding, it's a challenge for consumers to know what to buy and how to cook it. To add to the difficulty, market names for fish can be confusing, overlapping, and sometimes downright incorrect.

The best approach is to arm yourself with the information you need to ask the right questions about the fish you're being offered. (You can often judge the quality of a market by how well informed its fishmongers are about the seafood they sell.)

To help you decide how to cook any fish, the listings on pages 32 and 33 classify fish according to their cooking characteristics. The listing for each group of fish tells you which cooking methods usually give the best results; it will also help you make substitutions if the fish you planned to buy is unavailable. On pages 34 and 35, we describe five easy and versatile techniques for cooking fish. Here, we provide an introduction to some of the newer fish, as well as updated information on several familiar species.

CALIFORNIA BARRACUDA

Although some species of barracuda are susceptible to a dangerous toxin, the California one is not only safe to eat, but also delicious. This fish migrates into Southern California waters from Mexico in spring and summer; although not plentiful, barracuda is worth watching for. Its tender-firm flesh is moderately oily but surprisingly mild-tasting.

COD-RELATED FISH

Several members of the cod family are newly available here. Very few of Alaska's *Pacific cod* or *pollock* were sold here

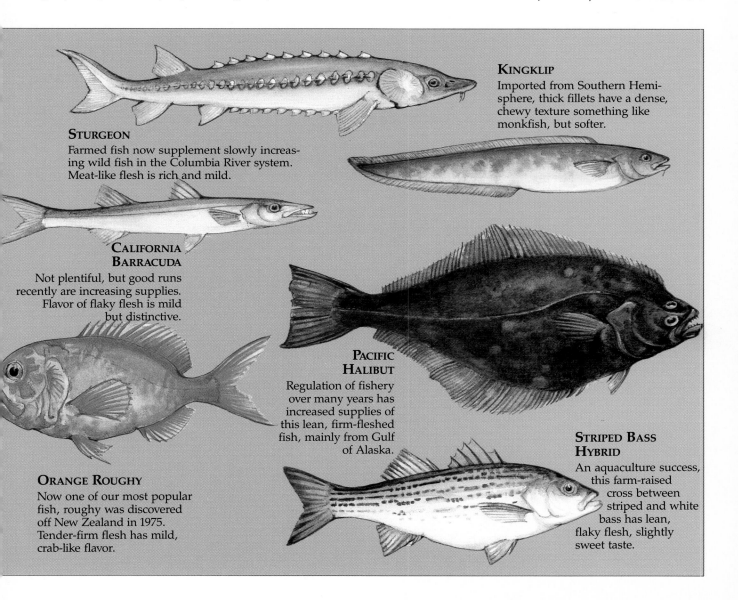

STURGEON
Farmed fish now supplement slowly increasing wild fish in the Columbia River system. Meat-like flesh is rich and mild.

CALIFORNIA BARRACUDA
Not plentiful, but good runs recently are increasing supplies. Flavor of flaky flesh is mild but distinctive.

ORANGE ROUGHY
Now one of our most popular fish, roughy was discovered off New Zealand in 1975. Tender-firm flesh has mild, crab-like flavor.

KINGKLIP
Imported from Southern Hemisphere, thick fillets have a dense, chewy texture something like monkfish, but softer.

PACIFIC HALIBUT
Regulation of fishery over many years has increased supplies of this lean, firm-fleshed fish, mainly from Gulf of Alaska.

STRIPED BASS HYBRID
An aquaculture success, this farm-raised cross between striped and white bass has lean, flaky flesh, slightly sweet taste.

Fish is sold in various forms. At top (from left) are whole sole, cleaned trout, and whole fresh-water drum. Fillets (middle row) are orange roughy and rockfish. On bottom row (from left) are swordfish slice, salmon steaks, tuna chunk.

before, but now they're being caught and frozen at sea. Almost identical to the well-known Atlantic cod, skinless fillets of Pacific cod make an excellent frozen product. Fresh Alaska pollock doesn't keep well, but the inexpensive frozen-at-sea fillets are good value.

Two imported cod-related fish are also worth trying. Antarctic whiting is usually sold here as *Antarctic queen;* caught off the southern coast of Chile, it yields large, snow-white fillets. *Hoki* is taken off the New Zealand coast; its flaky white flesh compares in flavor with Atlantic haddock. You can use any of these lean, mild-flavored fish as you would cod.

HALIBUT

The only true halibut in our markets is *Pacific,* also called northern or Alaska halibut. But in California, it's often confused with *California halibut,* a large flounder that resembles the Pacific species in shape but not in texture. Pacific halibut has firm, meaty flesh, while the California species is coarser and softer.

True halibut is sold fresh sporadically during spring and summer, but most of the catch is frozen. If you're offered fresh halibut during the fall or winter, it's probably the California species.

JACK FAMILY

Although *yellowtail* (the best-known Western jack) is scarce, this family has many members worldwide, and some are showing up in our markets. One, the *amberjack,* is taken in the Gulf of Mexico; another amberjack, *kahala,* is caught in Hawaii; and *Japanese yellowtail* is known to sashimi aficionados as *hamachi.*

Jack crevalle is sold by various names, including *cavally, cavalla, toro* (in Mexico), *trevally,* and *jackfish.* Hawaii has about 10 species of jack, among them the *ulua,* or giant trevally, and the smaller *papio,* or trevally.

Most jacks have firm to very firm, meaty flesh; only the papio has softer, flakier flesh. If properly bled and handled, jack meat is moderately rich-tasting. For best flavor, remove skin and as much of the red muscle underneath as possible. With papio, you can simply scale it and cook it with the skin on.

KINGKLIP

A plentiful fish in southern oceans, kingklip is sold as fillets in some markets now. *Golden kingklip* is the most abundant and best of the four species. Avoid darker, less tender *South African* and *black kingklip*.

The meat has an unusual dense, chewy texture somewhat like monkfish, but softer and with loose flakes. It's lean and bland-tasting, with a hint of sweetness.

MACKEREL

Although Pacific mackerel has staged a comeback since the 1970s, when it practically disappeared, not everyone appreciates its rather assertive flavor. *Jack mackerel* (actually a jack), looks much like Pacific mackerel but is leaner and milder in flavor. You can recognize the jack by a row of tiny, shallow surface bones along each side.

The choicest mackerel of all is *wahoo*; its Hawaiian name, *ono*, means sweet and delicate, a fitting name for this fish found worldwide in tropical and subtropical seas. It has a fairly high oil content and a firm, meaty texture. Good frozen-at-sea wahoo is also available.

OPAH

(Also called *moonfish*.) Now gaining acceptance with those who appreciate its unique texture, this exotic fish resembles a garbage can lid in shape and size. Most opah is taken in Southern California as an incidental catch, and in Hawaii.

An opah has four types of firm, coarse-textured flesh, each a different color: amber-red behind the head and along the back, pale pink and slightly stringy toward the belly, red in the cheeks, and ruby red inside the breast-plate. The breast meat cooks up brown and tastes something like beef; meat in other areas cooks white, and is rich and fairly mild in flavor (compare it to chicken).

If you buy skin-on fillets, remove the thick scales or cut away the skin and fatty layer underneath before or after cooking.

SEA BASS

No fish name causes more confusion in markets. The sea bass family itself, which includes groupers, is the largest and most diverse group of fish in the world. And fish from other families are also often called by the name. Sea bass usually has a mild flavor but dramatic differences in texture and fat content (species fall into four different categories in our listings on the next two pages).

The kind of sea bass sold here in the past has become rather scarce. The most commonly available species now is *Chilean sea bass*; its flesh is white and mild, as might be expected, but much softer and oilier than other sea basses.

White sea bass (actually a drum) is still taken in Southern California, but it's becoming rare. There's also some *baquetta* (a grouper) available in Southern California. And some Hawaiian black sea bass, called *hapu'upu'u*, is now sold on the Mainland.

Two other sea basses are imported from New Zealand—the *bluenose* (actually a sea bream) and *New Zealand groper* (a true grouper). Both New Zealand and Hawaiian fish have firm, meaty flesh.

SKATE

This unusual-shaped fish is becoming more common in markets. Only the tri-angular wings are eaten. Each yields two fillets divided by cartilage (there are no bones). It's sold both as skinned whole wings and as fillets.

When cooked, the deeply ridged fillets are tender and somewhat gelatinous. To eat skate cooked with the cartilage attached, anchor the fish with a fork and scrape off the cooked meat. The meat is lean and tastes sweet and delicate.

STRIPED BASS HYBRID

Commercial fishing for stripers is banned now in most Eastern states as well as in California. But hybrid bass, being farmed in geothermally heated tanks in the California desert and in ponds elsewhere, is beginning to supply demand for this popular fish.

Most farmed fish are in the 1- to 3-pound range now, but fish up to about 5 pounds are coming; they'll be a perfect shape and size to bake or poach whole.

STURGEON

In the wild, sturgeon grow slowly; females are more than 6 feet long and may be 19 years old before spawning.

By contrast, aquaculturists can now produce white sturgeon weighing 8 to 10 pounds in about two years.

Sturgeon is firm and meaty, almost like veal; it's firm enough to cube and cook on skewers. The flavor is mild but distinctive. Try barbecuing or smoking a whole, skin-on fish as you would salmon.

TILAPIA

Native to Africa, these little fish can thrive almost anywhere, and they're easily interbred to produce new hybrids. Tilapia's quality depends on the water in which it grows, and it hasn't always had a good reputation. But high-quality fish, some of it farmed in the West, is now available. At its best, the flavor of tilapia is mild and sweet. Buy it from a reliable market and you won't be disappointed.

Fish: The Four Groups

S IZE, TEXTURE, FLAVOR *intensity, and fat content are to a large extent the factors that determine what cooking methods will be most successful for a particular type of fish.*

On these pages we divide fish into four basic groups and indicate some of the best ways of preparing and cooking each type of fish.

Within each group, fish may vary widely in quality, but usually they can be substituted for one another in recipes. Ask your fishmonger for cooking suggestions if you are uncertain.

A few one-of-a-kind fish, such as monkfish, skate, and smelt, have not been included because they don't fit into the basic groups.

Lean: Less than 2.5 percent fat
Moderately lean: Less than 5 percent fat
Oilier: More than 5 percent fat
(These differences are not significant nutritionally.)

*See pages 34 and 35 for description

GROUP 1
THIN & DELICATE

Small flatfish yield fillets less than ½ inch thick and flexible (they can be rolled). Whole fish are too thin to cut into steaks. Smallest species (rex sole and sanddab) are sold whole or deeply trimmed (pan-ready). Tender meat is delicate to mild in flavor. All are lean. Dusting with flour aids browning when pan-frying.

All the small soles and flounders, including English sole, petrale sole, rex sole, sanddabs, and Eastern fish such as gray sole and winter flounder (also called lemon sole).

Best ways to cook

Fillets. Pan-fry or pan-poach*; roll fillets to poach.

Small whole fish. Oven-brown*, pan-fry, pan-poach*, or poach.

A quick way to produce deliciously cooked fish, such as this salmon, is to pan-poach in a small amount of seasoned liquid. Then you reduce the liquid to make a tasty sauce. For pan-poaching directions, see page 34.

GROUP 2
MEDIUM-DENSE, FLAKY

Small to medium-size fish with moist, tender meat. Steaks and fillets are usually ½ to 1 inch thick and sturdier than those of fish in Group 1, but they need to be supported on foil or in a hinged broiler if grilled. Crumb coatings usually add flavor and texture. Group includes small pan-size fish and larger fish sold whole for baking or poaching.

2A LEAN; MILD FLAVOR

Bass, striped
Cods and related fish, including Antarctic queen, Pacific whiting, haddock, hoki, and pollock
Flounder (large)
Halibut, California
Kingklip
Lingcod
Perch, walleye and yellow (fresh water)
Pike, northern (fresh water)

Rockfish, including Pacific ocean perch and Pacific snapper
Snapper, red (Florida) and Hawaiian ta'ape, opakapaka, onaga, and uku
Tilapia (fresh water)
Tilefish

Best ways to cook

Steaks and fillets. Bake in sauce*, broil with moist heat*, deep-fry, oven-brown*, pan-fry, pan-poach*, or poach.
Small whole fish. Bake in sauce*, broil with moist heat*, oven-brown*, pan-fry, pan-poach*, or poach.

2B MODERATELY LEAN; MILD FLAVOR

Catfish (fresh water)
Salmon, chum and pink
Sea bream, including porgy, sheepshead, New Zealand snapper (tai)
Sea trout, spotted, gray weakfish, and shortfin corvina
Trout, rainbow (fresh water)

To pan-fry thin sole fillets, turn when tops look milky white. You'll soon need to remove them from the pan.

Best ways to cook

Steaks and fillets. Bake in sauce*, barbecue, broil with dry or moist heat*, deep-fry, oven-brown*, pan-fry, pan-poach*, or poach.

Small whole fish. Bake in sauce*, barbecue, broil with dry or moist heat*, oven-brown*, pan-fry, pan-poach*, or poach.

2C OILIER OR DISTINCTIVELY FLAVORED

Oilier and mild in flavor

Buffalo (fresh water)

Carp (fresh water)

Greenland turbot

Lake trout (fresh water)

Sablefish (black cod, butterfish)

Sea bass, Chilean

Shad (fresh water)

Whitefish, lake (fresh water)

Distinctively flavored

Barracuda, California

Herring and sardines, fresh

Mackerel, Atlantic, jack, Pacific, and Spanish

Mullet, striped

Pompano, Florida

Salmon, Atlantic, king (Chinook), silver (coho), and sockeye

Best ways to cook

Steaks, fillets, and small whole fish. Bake in sauce*, barbecue, broil with dry heat, oven-brown*, pan-fry, pan-poach*, poach, or smoke.

When barbecuing soft-textured fish, such as this sablefish, place pieces on a sheet of perforated foil.

Stir-frying cubes of fish with vegetables (see page 35) is a quick way to cook the firm-fleshed fish in groups 3 and 4.

GROUP 3
MEDIUM-DENSE WITH EXTRA-FIRM FLAKES

Medium-size to large fish with firm, compact flakes. Thick cuts are sturdy enough to put directly on a greased grill. Fish hold their shape well when cooked. Steaks and fillets are generally at least ¾ inch thick and usually don't need a coating for good browning. Some species are sold whole; they're a good size to bake, barbecue, or poach. As a group, they're lean (except orange roughy, which is about 8 percent fat, but it's a unique type of fat that doesn't taste oily) and light to moderately pronounced in flavor.

Drum, black and red

Mahi mahi

Orange roughy

Papio (Hawaiian jack)

Sea bass, white

Best ways to cook

Steaks and fillets. Bake in sauce*, barbecue, broil with moist heat*, deep-fry, oven-brown*, pan-fry, pan-poach*, poach, or stir-fry*.

GROUP 4
DENSE & MEATY

Large fish with the fewest small bones of all fish. Meat holds its shape very well, so these are the best choices for skewer cooking. Fish are usually cut into thick steaks, fillets, or boneless pieces at least 1 inch thick; they brown well when pan-fried without a coating. Fish range from lean and mild-tasting to oily and rich-tasting.

4A LEAN; MILD FLAVOR

Grouper, large species such as giant, Nassau, and Warsaw

Halibut, Pacific (Northern, Alaska)

Sea bass, baquetta, bluenose (New Zealand sea bream), and Hawaiian (hapu'upu'u)

Shark

Best ways to cook

Steaks, fillets, and boneless slices. Bake in sauce*, barbecue, broil with moist heat*, cook on skewers, pan-fry, pan-poach*, poach, or stir-fry*.

4B MODERATELY LEAN TO OILIER, DISTINCTIVELY FLAVORED

Cobia

Jack, amberjack, California yellowtail, Hawaiian ulua, jack cravelle, and trevally

Mackerel, king and wahoo

Opah

Sturgeon

Swordfish

Tuna, including albacore

Best ways to cook

Steaks, fillets, and boneless slices. Bake in sauce*, barbecue, broil with dry or moist heat*, cook on skewers, pan-fry, pan-poach*, poach, smoke, or stir-fry*.

Broiling with moist heat (see page 34) produces delicious results with lean fish, such as these shark fillets.

Fish: Five Cooking Techniques

THINK FISH IS TRICKY *to prepare? In truth, it could hardly be simpler. Here, we equip you with five easy and flexible cooking methods that give reliable results with most market fish. Each method has several variations you can try. And two of the techniques can be used with undefrosted frozen fish.*

On pages 32 and 33, you'll find listings of fish grouped by characteristics such as size, texture, fat content, and flavor intensity. Check those lists to see which cooking methods are recommended for the fish you've selected.

MOIST-HEAT BROILING

Broiling the usual way, with dry heat, is best reserved for fish with enough natural oil to keep them from drying out, but this technique gives delicious results with lean fish, such as those in groups 2A, 3, and 4A (see pages 32 and 33). Use it for steaks or fillets ½ to 1¼ inches thick, or for small whole fish, such as trout.

FISH BROILED WITH MOIST HEAT

1½ to 2½ **pounds lean fish steaks or fillets, or 4 to 6 cleaned small fish (6 to 10 oz. each)**
    About 1 cup regular-strength chicken broth or dry white wine
2 **tablespoons melted butter or margarine**
1 **teaspoon dill weed or dry thyme leaves**
    Salt and pepper
    Almond or caper sauce (recipes follow), optional

Rinse fish and pat dry; cut into serving-size pieces. Arrange fish in a single layer in a greased baking pan (about 10 by 15 in.) that can be used under the broiler. Adjust oven rack so heat will be 3 inches from pieces ½ to ¾ inch thick, 4 inches from pieces 1 to 1¼ inches thick. Remove pan from oven and heat broiler.

Pour broth around fish to a depth of ⅛ inch. Combine butter with dill and brush part of it over fish.

Broil fish (do not turn), basting once or twice with remaining butter mixture, until just slightly translucent or wet-looking inside when cut in thickest part, 3 to 6 minutes for fish ½ to ¾ inch thick, 6 to 10 minutes for fish 1 to 1¼ inches thick.

Transfer fish to a warm platter and season to taste with salt and pepper. Serve with sauce. Makes 4 to 6 servings.

PER SERVING MADE WITH PACIFIC HALIBUT STEAKS AND NO SAUCE: 141 calories, 20 g protein, 0.3 g carbohydrates, 6 g fat, 40 mg cholesterol, 98 mg sodium

Almond sauce. In an 8- to 10-inch frying pan, heat ¼ cup (⅛ lb.) **butter** or margarine over medium-high heat until it foams. Add ¼ cup **sliced** or slivered **almonds** or chopped filberts; stir until nuts begin to brown. Remove from heat and add 2 tablespoons **lemon juice.**

Caper sauce. Follow directions for **almond sauce,** omitting almonds. When butter foams, add 2 tablespoons drained **capers.** Heat just until capers are hot. Omit lemon juice.

PAN-POACHING

This short-cut poaching technique is a quick way to prepare any fresh or frozen fish steaks or fillets (¼ to 1½ in. thick), or small whole fish, such as trout. The fish steams in a small amount of seasoned liquid inside a covered frying pan. Then you reduce the cooking liquid to make a sauce that can be enriched with cream, if you choose.

PAN-POACHED FISH

1 **to 1½ pounds fresh or individually frozen fish fillets or steaks, or 3 or 4 cleaned small whole fish (6 to 10 oz. each)**
2 **tablespoons butter or margarine**
3 **shallots or 3 green onions (roots trimmed), with about 4 in. of the tops, finely chopped**
1 **teaspoon grated fresh ginger, or ¼ teaspoon dry tarragon leaves**
⅔ **cup regular-strength chicken broth, or ⅓ cup *each* broth and dry white wine**
    Salt, pepper, and lemon or orange wedges (optional)

Rinse fish and pat dry. In a 10- to 12-inch frying pan, melt butter over medium heat. Add shallots and ginger and cook, stirring, until limp, about 3 minutes. Add broth and bring to a boil.

Arrange fish in pan in a single layer. Reduce heat, cover, and simmer until just slightly translucent or wet-looking inside when cut in thickest part, 3 to 4 minutes for fresh fish ¼ to ½ inch thick (4 to 6 minutes if frozen), 4 to 6 minutes for fresh fish ½ to ¾ inch thick (6 to 10

minutes if frozen), 8 to 12 minutes for fresh fish 1 to 1½ inches thick (13 to 22 minutes if frozen).

With a wide spatula, lift fish from pan and arrange it on a warm platter; cover and keep warm.

Over high heat, boil pan juices, adding any liquid that accumulates on platter, until reduced and thickened slightly; spoon over fish. Season to taste with salt and pepper and serve with lemon wedges. Makes 3 or 4 servings.

PER SERVING IF MADE WITH CHINOOK SALMON STEAKS: 265 calories, 23 g protein, 1.5 g carbohydrates, 18 g fat, 90 mg cholesterol, 122 mg sodium

POACHED FISH WITH CREAM SAUCE

Follow preceding recipe. After removing fish, add ¼ cup **whipping cream** to juices in pan. Boil as directed until reduced to about ½ cup.

PER SERVING IF MADE WITH CHINOOK SALMON STEAKS: 309 calories, 24 g protein, 1.9 g carbohydrates, 22 g fat, 107 mg cholesterol, 127 mg sodium

OVEN-BROWNING

In this method, a flavorful crumb coating keeps the fish moist while it bakes to a crusty brown. This is a good way to cook lean or oilier fish steaks or fillets in groups 2 and 3, and small whole fish in groups 1 and 2 (see pages 32 and 33), such as rex sole or trout. Start with fresh or frozen fish. Steaks and fillets should be ½ to 1¼ inches thick.

OVEN-BROWNED FISH

1 **to 1½ pounds fresh or individually frozen fish steaks or fillets, or 3 or 4 cleaned small whole fish (6 to 10 oz. each)**
    Crumb coating (choices follow)
3 **tablespoons melted butter or margarine, or olive oil**

Rinse fish and pat dry. Spread crumb coating on waxed paper. Pour butter into a shallow bowl. Coat fish pieces in butter, then turn in the crumb mixture to coat thickly. Place pieces in a foil-lined, rimmed shallow baking pan, large enough so pieces can be at least 1 inch apart.

Bake, uncovered, in a 425° oven until browned and just slightly translucent or wet-looking inside when cut in thickest part, 10 to 20 minutes for fresh fish, 30 to 40 minutes for frozen fish. Transfer to a warm platter. Makes 3 or 4 servings.

PER SERVING IF MADE WITH PACIFIC ROCKFISH FILLETS AND CHEESE CRUMBS: 203 calories, 22 g protein, 3.3 g carbohydrates, 11 g fat, 64 mg cholesterol, 198 mg sodium

Cheese crumbs. Crumble 1 slice **firm-textured bread** into a blender or food processor and whirl to make soft crumbs. Mix crumbs with ½ tablespoon **grated parmesan cheese** and ½ teaspoon *each* **dry thyme leaves** and **paprika**.

Nut crumbs. Combine ½ cup minced or ground **almonds** or filberts with ¼ cup **fine dry bread crumbs** and 1 teaspoon grated **lemon peel**.

Crouton crumbs. Whirl in a food processor or crush 1 cup **seasoned croutons** to make fine crumbs.

BAKING

Fish can be cooked more slowly in the oven than by other methods, so there's less chance of overcooking it. Choose from two different sauces to bake and serve with the fish. Start with fillets or steaks at least ¾ inch thick, or small whole fish, such as trout or mackerel.

FISH BAKED IN SAUCE

> 1½ to 2 pounds fresh or thawed frozen fish steaks or fillets, or 4 to 6 cleaned small whole fish (6 to 10 oz. each)
> Baking sauce (choices follow)
> Salt and pepper

Rinse fish and pat dry. Place fish in a single layer in a greased baking pan just large enough to hold fish without crowding. Pour sauce over fish.

Bake, uncovered, in a 375° oven until fish looks just slightly translucent or wet inside when cut in thickest part, 15 to 25 minutes. Transfer fish to a warm platter; spoon sauce around it. Season to taste with salt and pepper; garnish as directed with sauces. Makes 4 to 6 servings.

PER SERVING WITH LINGCOD FILLETS AND CITRUS-SHALLOT SAUCE: 175 calories, 20 g protein, 2.6 g carbohydrates, 8.8 g fat, 80 mg cholesterol, 148 mg sodium

Citrus-shallot baking sauce. In a 6- to 8-inch frying pan, melt ¼ cup (⅛ lb.) **butter** or margarine over medium heat. Add 4 chopped **shallots** or green onions (ends trimmed, with green tops); cook, stirring often, until limp, about 5 minutes.

Remove from heat and add ¼ cup **orange juice**, 2 tablespoons **lemon juice**, and ½ cup **dry white wine** or regular-strength chicken broth. Add to fish as directed. After fish is on platter, pour sauce back into frying pan. Boil, uncovered, on high heat until reduced to about ⅓ cup. If desired, garnish fish with **toasted almonds** and serve with **orange wedges** to squeeze over individual servings.

Tomato-caper baking sauce. In a 10- to 12-inch frying pan over medium heat, melt ¼ cup (⅛ lb.) **butter** or margarine. Add 1 medium-size chopped **onion** and 1 clove minced **garlic**. Stir often until onion is limp, about 5 minutes.

To pan, add 1 tablespoon drained **capers** and 1 can (about 14 oz.) **pear-shaped tomatoes** and their liquid. Break up tomatoes with a spoon. Bring to a gentle boil; then simmer uncovered, stirring often, about 5 minutes. Stir in 1 tablespoon **lemon juice**. Add to fish. Garnish with minced **parsley** and serve with **lemon wedges**.

STIR-FRYING

Stir-frying is a quick way to cook the firm-textured fish in groups 3 and 4 (see page 33), as well as nonflaky fish such as monkfish. Serve the fish and vegetables with rice to complete a meal.

You need to have everything ready to add to the pan—there's not time to assemble ingredients once the cooking begins. Fish and vegetables should be cut into uniform-size pieces.

STIR-FRIED FISH WITH EDIBLE-POD PEAS

> 2 teaspoons sesame seed
> 1 to 1¼ pounds boneless, skinless firm-fleshed fish
> 1 clove garlic, minced or pressed
> 1 tablespoon minced fresh ginger
> ½ pound edible-pod peas
> 2 tablespoons salad oil
> Cooking sauce (recipe follows)

Toast sesame seed in a 6- to 8-inch frying pan over medium-high heat, shaking pan frequently, until golden, about 2 minutes; set aside.

Rinse fish, pat thoroughly dry, and cut into 1-inch chunks. (If monkfish is used, remove membrane.) In a bowl, combine fish with garlic and ginger.

Remove ends and strings from peas. Cook in 1 quart boiling water over high heat, uncovered, just until color turns a brighter green, about 1 minute. Drain and cool at once in ice water; drain again.

Place a wok or 10- to 12-inch frying pan over high heat. When hot, add 1 tablespoon of the oil. When oil is hot, add half the fish mixture; stir-fry gently with a wide spatula until fish looks just slightly translucent in center when cut, about 2 minutes. Slide out of pan and set aside. Add remaining 1 tablespoon oil and cook remaining fish; add to cooked fish.

Stir sauce with any accumulated juices from fish and add to pan. Bring to a boil, stirring. Add fish and vegetables and cook, stirring gently, until hot, about 1 minute. Transfer to a warm platter and sprinkle with sesame seed. Makes about 4 servings.

PER SERVING IF MADE WITH MAHI MAHI (DOLPHIN FISH): 237 calories, 24 g protein, 8 g carbohydrates, 12 g fat, 83 mg cholesterol, 622 mg sodium

Cooking sauce. Combine ¼ cup regular-strength **chicken broth**, 2 tablespoons *each* **dry sherry** and **soy sauce**, 1 tablespoon *each* **lemon juice** and **Oriental sesame oil**, and 2 teaspoons **cornstarch**.

STIR-FRIED FISH WITH ASPARAGUS OR BROCCOLI

Follow preceding recipe, omitting edible-pod peas. Remove tough ends from ¾ pound **asparagus** or broccoli.

Cut asparagus into ½-inch slanting slices; or peel broccoli stems and cut crosswise into ¼-inch slices, and cut flowerets ½ inch thick. Cook either vegetable in boiling water as directed until tender-crisp, about 2 minutes; drain and cool in ice water as directed.

PER SERVING IF MADE WITH MAHI MAHI (DOLPHIN FISH): 223 calories, 23 g protein, 5.6 g carbohydrates, 12 g fat, 83 mg cholesterol, 620 mg sodium

A Dessert Tasting Party

DESSERT LOVERS REJOICE! *Here is a party made for you. Built around six show-stopping desserts, this lavish but surprisingly easy buffet is perfect for a late-evening party.*

Collectively, the desserts serve 50 to 60. For those who want to try them all, tiny portions of each are more than adequate. For fewer guests, offer fewer desserts.

Designed to be decorative but not complicated, each dessert can be made ahead. Cooking solo, you can make them all in a few days; better yet, invite several friends to participate. Last-minute details include a few simple but effective garnishes. Since guests help themselves, serving chores are at a minimum.

The desserts please multiple tastes. A light sponge cake is the base for two desserts—a marzipan-cloaked lime-curd loaf and a pinwheel pastry filled with white chocolate mousse. Chocolate lovers will enjoy the petite mocha cups and the dark chocolate torte, scented with raspberry brandy. The nut torte has a soft, caramel-like filling loaded with pecans and dried apricots. Golden nut brittle crowns an unusually creamy cheesecake.

With the desserts, offer coffee and a slightly sweet sparkling wine, such as Asti Spumante or extra-dry champagne. If you like, also provide fresh fruit for anyone with a less developed sweet tooth.

WHITE CHOCOLATE PINWHEEL TORTE WITH CRANBERRY SAUCE

    Sponge cake (recipe follows)
    Kirsch syrup (recipe follows)
⅓ cup raspberry jam
    White chocolate mousse (recipe follows)
    Cranberries, fresh or frozen (optional)
    Cranberry-raspberry sauce (recipe follows)

Smoothly line a 3-quart mixing bowl with plastic wrap; set aside.

Unroll sponge cake and slowly spoon kirsch syrup evenly over it until all the syrup is absorbed. Spread cake with raspberry jam. Starting at a short end, reroll cake; set aside for about 15 minutes.

Cut cake roll crosswise into ½-inch-thick slices. Reserve 4 or 5 slices. Fit remaining slices into lined bowl, arranging neatly from the bottom of bowl upward in an even layer; cut some pinwheels in half to make an even top rim.

Pour mousse into cake-lined bowl, gently pushing mousse into any gaps between cake pieces. Spread top to make smooth and level. Top filling with reserved cake slices and push slightly down into filling. Cover with plastic wrap and chill at least 4 hours, or for up to 2 days.

To unmold, uncover cake and invert a flat plate on bowl. Hold plate and bowl together; invert. Lift off bowl and peel plastic wrap off cake. Garnish cake with cranberries. Slice into thin wedges no more than 30 minutes after removing from refrigerator or torte will squash when you cut. Top portions with cranberry-raspberry sauce. Makes 18 to 20 servings.

PER PIECE: 212 calories, 2.2 g protein, 27 g carbohydrates, 11 g fat, 64 mg cholesterol, 41 mg sodium

Sponge cake sheet. Butter a 10- by 15-inch baking pan. Line the pan with waxed paper. Make batter for sponge cake as directed for marzipan box on page 38.

Pour batter into prepared pan and spread evenly. Bake in a 350° oven until golden and cake springs back when lightly touched, about 10 minutes.

Invert cake onto a towel; carefully peel off paper. Turn cake over. Starting at a short end, gently and snugly roll cake in towel. Let stand until cool, or up to 4 hours.

Kirsch syrup. In a 2- to 3-cup pan, bring ⅔ cup **sugar** and ⅓ cup **water** to a boil over high heat. Remove from heat and add 2 tablespoons **kirsch**. Use, or cover and hold up until next day.

White chocolate mousse. Melt 9 ounces finely chopped **white chocolate** and 5 tablespoons **water** in a 1½- to 2-quart pan over lowest heat; stir until most of chocolate is melted. Remove from heat and stir until remaining chocolate melts smoothly; cool to room temperature.

With an electric mixer, beat 1½ cups **whipping cream** until soft peaks just begin to hold. Fold cream into cooled chocolate. Use at once.

Cranberry-raspberry sauce. In a covered 1½- to 2-quart pan, cook 1½ cups **fresh** or frozen **cranberries** and ⅔ cup **sugar** on low heat until cranberries are translucent, about 30 minutes; stir occasionally until sugar dissolves. Remove from heat and let stand until cranberries absorb most of the remaining syrup, at least 15 minutes. Stir in ½ cup **raspberry jam**. Use, or let stand at room temperature until next day.

PER TABLESPOON: 43 calories, 0.1 g protein, 13 g carbohydrates, 0 g fat, 0 mg cholesterol, 0.9 mg sodium

MOCHA BROWNIES IN SILVER CUPS

    2 ounces unsweetened baking chocolate
½ cup (¼ lb.) butter or margarine
      About ¼ cup roasted coffee beans
    2 large eggs
    1 cup sugar
    1 cup all-purpose flour

Put chocolate and butter in a 1- to 1½-quart pan. Cover and warm on lowest heat, stirring occasionally, until melted, 5 to 10 minutes; set aside.

In a coffee grinder or blender, grind or whirl 1 tablespoon of the coffee beans to a fine powder.

With an electric mixer, beat eggs until light and lemon colored; mix in sugar, chocolate mixture, and ground coffee. Blend in flour.

Set 48 baking cups (silver or gold foil, or paper), each about 1 inch wide, in a 9- by 13-inch baking pan. Pour batter into cups in equal portions; top each with a coffee bean. Bake in a 375° oven until brownies are firm but still feel slightly soft when pressed, about 10 minutes. Let cool in pan. If made ahead, cover and let stand up until next day; or wrap airtight and freeze up to 1 month. Makes 48.

PER PIECE: 52 calories, 0.7 g protein, 6.5 g carbohydrates, 2.8 g fat, 17 mg cholesterol, 23 mg sodium

(Continued on page 38)

Stunning collection of six desserts tempts all palates. Choose from (top, clockwise) mocha brownies in silver cups, caramel nut torte, white chocolate pinwheel with cranberry sauce, star-stenciled chocolate torte, marzipan lime-curd loaf, and pine nut brittle cheesecake.

Caramel Nut Torte

- 1 cup firmly packed brown sugar
- 2 large eggs
- 1 large egg yolk
- ½ teaspoon baking powder
- ½ teaspoon grated orange peel
- ½ cup all-purpose flour
- 2 cups coarsely chopped pecans
- 1 cup dried apricots, chopped
  Nut crust (recipe follows)
- ¾ cup whipping cream
- 1 tablespoon powdered sugar
  Thinly shredded orange peel
  (orange part only), optional

Beat together sugar, eggs, egg yolk, baking powder, and grated orange peel until smooth. Mix in flour until blended. Stir in pecans and apricots. Pour into crust. Bake in a 350° oven until medium golden brown all over, 25 to 30 minutes. Cool in pan on rack. If made ahead, cover and hold at room temperature up to 1 day.

Up to 1 hour ahead, whip cream with powdered sugar until it holds stiff peaks; cover and chill. To serve, remove pan sides, put tart on a plate, and mound cream in center of tart. Sprinkle with shredded peel. Makes 12 to 16 servings.

Per Serving: 359 calories, 4.1 g protein, 31 g carbohydrates, 26 g fat, 75 mg cholesterol, 75 mg sodium

Nut crust. In a food processor or blender, whirl 1¾ cups coarsely chopped **pecans** until finely ground. If using a blender, pour nuts into a bowl. To nuts, add ⅓ cup **all-purpose flour**, 3 tablespoons **sugar**, and 6 tablespoons **butter** or margarine, cut into chunks. Whirl or rub with your fingers until mixture holds together. Spread dough evenly over bottom and sides of a 9-inch tart pan with removable bottom.

Marzipan Box

Top cake with a pretty blossom, such as a pale green cymbidium orchid.

  Sponge cake (recipe follows)
  Lime syrup (recipe follows)
- 1 cup whipping cream
  Lime curd (recipe follows)
  Powdered sugar
  Tinted marzipan (recipe follows)

After you remove sponge cake from the pan, wash and dry pan. Line bottom with waxed paper. Nestle bottom layer of cake on pan bottom, cut side up. Moisten cake evenly with ½ the lime syrup.

With an electric mixer, whip cream until it holds soft peaks. Fold lime curd into whipped cream. Pour mixture onto cake in pan. Gently top filling with remaining cake layer, cut side down. Moisten cake evenly with remaining syrup. Cover with plastic wrap; chill at least 8 hours or up until next day.

Uncover cake and run a knife around pan sides. Invert a serving plate on pan; invert together, then lift off pan. Cover lightly and put in the refrigerator.

Lightly coat a sheet of waxed paper (at least 12 by 18 in.) with powdered sugar. Form marzipan into a flat, square patty and set on sugar. Sprinkle marzipan lightly with more sugar, then top with another sheet of waxed paper. Roll marzipan to form a rectangle about 11 by 15 inches. If paper wrinkles and gets embedded in marzipan, peel off and replace.

Just before serving, remove lime curd–filled cake from refrigerator and uncover.

Peel top sheet of paper off marzipan. Gently pull and lift marzipan off bottom paper sheet, supporting marzipan over your hand and arm, as needed. Carefully center marzipan atop cake, draping edges down cake sides. Tuck in marzipan at corners to fit snugly against cake. Let ends fall, then fold excess up and under itself to make flush with bottom of cake. Cover and chill at least 1 or up to 4 hours.

Slice cake no more than 30 minutes after you remove it from the refrigerator, or it will squash when you cut it. Make about 1-inch-wide slices, then cut slices in half crosswise. Makes 18 to 20 servings.

Per Piece: 287 calories, 4 g protein, 43 g carbohydrates, 11 g fat, 122 mg cholesterol, 92 mg sodium

Sponge cake. Butter a 5- by 9-inch loaf pan, then line with waxed paper.

With an electric mixer, rapidly beat 3 **large egg yolks** until about double in volume. Beating, slowly add ½ cup **sugar.** Add ¾ teaspoon **vanilla.** In a small bowl, stir ½ teaspoon **baking powder** with ½ cup **cake flour;** beat into yolk mixture.

With clean beaters, whip 3 **large egg whites** on high speed until they hold stiff peaks. Stir about ¼ of the whites into yolk mixture. Pour yolk mixture into remaining whites; fold gently just to blend. Pour into prepared pan.

Bake in a 350° oven until cake is golden and springs back when lightly touched, 12 to 15 minutes. Invert cake onto a rack and carefully peel off paper; let cool. With a serrated knife, slice cake horizontally in half. Use, or return to pan, wrap airtight, and store up until next day.

Lime syrup. In a 2- to 3-cup pan, bring ½ cup **sugar** and ¼ cup **water** to a boil over high heat. Remove from heat and add 2 tablespoons **lime juice.** Use, or cover and chill up until next day.

Lime curd. In a 3- to 4-quart pan, melt ½ cup (¼ lb.) **butter** or margarine. Add ½ cup **lime juice,** 1¼ cups **sugar,** and 4 **large eggs,** beating to blend thoroughly. Cook over low heat, stirring, until thick enough to coat the back of a metal spoon in a thick, velvety layer, about 20 minutes.

In a 1- to 2-cup pan, mix 1 teaspoon **unflavored gelatin** with 2 tablespoons **water;** set aside until gelatin is moistened. Place over low heat until melted. Thoroughly stir gelatin into warm lime curd. Cover and let cool to room temperature. If made ahead, cover and chill up to 2 days; use at room temperature.

Tinted marzipan. With your hands, knead 1 drop *each* **green** and **yellow food coloring** into 14 to 16 ounces (about 1½ cups) **marzipan** (sweetened almond paste) until evenly colored pale green. If made ahead, wrap airtight and chill up to 2 days. Use at room temperature.

PINE NUT BRITTLE CHEESECAKE

- ¾ **cup pine nuts or slivered almonds**
- 1½ **cups sugar**
- 3 **large packages (8 oz. each) cream cheese, at room temperature**
- 4 **large eggs**
- 1 **teaspoon grated lemon peel**
- 3 **tablespoons amaretto (almond-flavored liqueur) or lemon juice**
- 2 **teaspoons vanilla**
- 1 **cup sour cream**
  Lemon crust (recipe follows)

In a 10- to 12-inch frying pan, toast nuts over low heat, shaking pan often, until nuts are light gold, about 12 minutes. Remove from pan and set aside. Add ¾ cup sugar to pan; shake pan often over medium-high heat until sugar liquefies and turns golden, 5 to 8 minutes. Stir in nuts, then immediately pour onto a buttered sheet of foil. With a buttered spoon, press mixture to flatten slightly. Let cool, then break into about ½-inch chunks. If made ahead, store airtight up to 3 days.

In a bowl, beat until smooth cream cheese, remaining sugar, and eggs. Add lemon peel, amaretto, vanilla, and sour cream; beat until smooth. Pour half the mixture into crust and sprinkle evenly with ½ of the brittle (store remainder). Spoon remaining cheese mixture over brittle. Bake in a 325° oven until center of cake jiggles only slightly when gently shaken, 50 to 60 minutes. Cool. If made ahead, cover and chill up to 2 days.

Up to 30 minutes before serving, remove pan sides; set cake on a platter. Pile remaining nut brittle in center of cake. Makes 16 to 20 servings.

PER SERVING: 296 calories, 6.2 g protein, 22 g carbohydrates, 22 g fat, 104 mg cholesterol, 150 mg sodium

Lemon crust. In a food processor or blender, combine 32 **vanilla wafers** (2-in. size, broken into chunks) and ¼ cup **pine nuts** or slivered almonds; whirl until mixture forms fine crumbs. Pour into a bowl. Add 1 teaspoon grated **lemon peel** and 3 tablespoons melted **butter** or margarine. Press mixture evenly over bottom and about 1 inch up sides of a 9-inch cheesecake pan with removable bottom.

SCENTED CHOCOLATE TORTE

- 6 **ounces semisweet or bittersweet chocolate, chopped**
- ¼ **cup (⅛ lb.) butter or margarine, cut into small pieces**
- ¼ **cup framboise (raspberry brandy) or orange-flavored liqueur**
- 3 **large eggs, separated**
- ¼ **teaspoon cream of tartar**
- ¾ **cup granulated sugar**
- ¾ **cup cake flour**
  Powdered sugar

Butter a 9-inch-diameter cake pan; line bottom with baking parchment or waxed paper. Butter paper; dust with flour.

In the top of a double boiler, combine chocolate and butter. Place over simmering water. When soft, stir until blended. Mix in brandy. Remove from heat.

In a small bowl, combine egg whites and cream of tartar. Beat with an electric mixer until soft peaks form. Gradually add ¼ cup granulated sugar, beating until whites hold stiff, moist peaks; set aside.

In a large bowl, beat ½ cup granulated sugar and egg yolks until thick and pale yellow. Stir in warm chocolate mixture. Add egg whites, sift flour over them, and fold gently to blend. Pour into pan.

Bake in a 350° oven until top is dry and crusty and a toothpick inserted in center comes out almost, but not completely, clean, 20 to 25 minutes. Let cake cool in pan on a rack until lukewarm, about 45 minutes. With a knife, cut around pan sides. Invert cake onto a flat plate. Peel off paper and brush off crumbs. If made ahead, cover and store at room temperature up until next day, or wrap airtight and freeze up to 2 weeks; thaw to use.

With your hands, press sides of cake toward the center to make straight sides. Up to an hour before serving, place decoratively cut pieces of paper (we made large stars), a stencil, or a doily on cake. Sift powdered sugar over cake. Carefully lift off cutouts. Wrap a 1¼- to 1½-inch-wide ribbon snugly around side of cake. Secure ribbon ends with a decorative sticker or tape. To serve, break ribbon free and cut cake into wedges. Serves 12 to 16.

PER SERVING: 158 calories, 2 g protein, 22 g carbohydrates, 7.7 g fat, 59 mg cholesterol, 43 mg sodium

Three-Course Dinner from the Italian Riviera

Lots of fresh sage, *marjoram, and vegetables share the limelight in this three-course dinner for eight. The menu features specialties of Liguria, a region of the Italian Riviera. Sonia Siccardo and her mother-in-law, Piera, both natives of the area, prepared the meal.*

The first course is pansotti—"little paunches"—plump, ravioli-like pasta triangles filled with herbs and four greens.

For the entrée, sautéed artichokes and marjoram-seasoned brains accompany chicken with olives and pine nuts. If you like, follow these foods with a green salad before presenting the simply prepared apricot tart.

Ligurian wines—Cinque Terre with pansotti, Gavi with the main dishes, Muscato with dessert—make fitting accompaniments. Or choose domestic dry Sauvignon Blanc and a muscat-flavored wine.

For the most carefree preparation, shape and chill pansotti a day ahead, or freeze up to several months. Enclose the filling in fresh pasta (made by hand or in a food processor) or purchased won ton skins.

A day before serving, you can also cook the chicken and tart, and clean salad greens. About 1½ hours before dinner, start artichokes and brains (keep warm, as browned, in the oven). Cook and serve the pasta; as you eat it, reheat chicken.

GREENS- & RICOTTA-FILLED PASTA (Pansotti)

Try this as an entrée for another meal.

½ pound *each* escarole, curly endive, dandelion greens, and spinach
2 tablespoons butter or margarine
1 large clove garlic, minced
3 tablespoons fresh marjoram leaves, minced, or 2 teaspoons dry marjoram leaves
¼ teaspoon ground nutmeg
1 cup ricotta cheese
1¼ cups (about 6 oz.) grated parmesan cheese
1 large egg
   Salt
   Fresh pasta (recipe follows) or about 70 won ton skins (3- by 3½-in. size)
   Sage butter (recipe follows)
   Fresh sage sprigs (optional)

Trim ends from escarole and endive, and tough stems from dandelion greens and spinach. Discard bruised, yellowed, or tough leaves. Measure greens; you should have 2 packed cups of each. Separately, rinse greens well; drain.

In a 5- to 6-quart pan over high heat, bring ¾ inch water to a boil. Push escarole and endive into water, cover, and cook, stirring occasionally, until stems are very tender to bite, about 12 minutes. Lift out with a slotted spoon; drain. Add dandelion greens and spinach to pan; boil, covered, until dandelion stems are very tender to bite, 7 to 9 minutes. Drain; let cool; squeeze out as much water as possible.

In the same pan, melt butter over medium-high heat. Add garlic and greens; stir for 5 minutes to dry greens somewhat. Remove from heat; let cool.

In a food processor or with a knife, very finely mince greens. Whirl or mix in a bowl until smoothly blended with marjoram, nutmeg, ricotta, ½ cup of the parmesan, and egg. Season to taste with salt.

To shape pansotti, work with 1 strip of

To make pansotti, spoon vegetable- and cheese-based filling onto sheets of fresh pasta; enclose, and cut triangles apart. Serve with sage butter as a first course. A short cut to the pasta: instead of making the dough and rolling it out, use won ton skins.

pasta (or 6 won ton skins) at a time. Along strip's center, mound 1-tablespoon lumps of filling at 2-inch intervals, 2 inches in from each end (or put about 2 teaspoons in center of each won ton skin).

Starting at one end of pasta strip, fold dough over first filling mound to form a triangle with sides about 4 inches long. (If using won ton skins, moisten edges with water and fold skins over filling, making edges flush.) With fingers, press pasta's cut sides around filling to seal and form ½-inch rims (¼ in. for won ton skins). With a pastry wheel or knife, cut filled triangle from strip along pressed edges.

Repeat for all pasta and filling. Place filled pansotti slightly apart on generously floured baking sheets. Gather any pasta scraps into a ball, reroll, and fill.

If made ahead, cover pansotti airtight and chill up to 1 day. Or freeze on baking sheets, then package airtight and store in freezer up to 3 months.

To cook pansotti, fill a 5- to 6-quart pan ⅔ full with water and bring to a boil over high heat. Drop ½ of the pansotti (fresh or frozen) into water and boil, uncovered, until dough is barely tender to bite, 10 to 14 minutes for pasta, 3 minutes for won tons. During cooking, gently push pansotti down into water several times.

Drain well; transfer pansotti with a slotted spoon to a bowl and mix gently with ½ of the sage butter. Arrange on a platter. Repeat with remaining pansotti and butter. Garnish with sage sprigs; add remaining parmesan to taste. Makes about 45 with pasta, 70 with won ton skins, enough for 8 first-course or 4 entrée servings. —*Sonia Siccardo, Sunnyvale, Calif.*

PER PANSOTTI WITH FRESH PASTA: 93 calories, 3.9 g protein, 9.5 g carbohydrates, 4.4 g fat, 23 mg cholesterol, 107 mg sodium

Fresh pasta. You will need about 3½ cups **bread flour,** 1 **large egg,** and ¾ cup **water.**

If using a food processor, whirl flour, egg, and water until dough forms a ball; whirl 45 seconds longer. If dough is sticky when pinched, whirl in 2 tablespoons more bread flour until dough forms ball, at least 30 seconds. Cover with plastic wrap.

By hand, mound flour in a bowl, make a well in center, pour in egg and water. Stir with a fork until evenly moistened.

Second course for festive Italian meal includes sautéed artichokes and brains with lemon, and chicken with green olives and pine nuts.

Pat into a ball and knead on lightly floured board until dough feels smooth (add flour as required to keep from sticking), 10 to 15 minutes. Cover with plastic wrap.

To roll with a pasta machine, set rollers on widest opening. Cut dough into 4 pieces. Feed 1 portion at a time through rollers, then fold dough in thirds crosswise. Repeat rolling and folding until dough feels smooth and supple, 10 to 20 times. If dough gets sticky, brush with flour; shake off excess. Roll dough through at successively thinner settings until it's as thin as possible; if dough gets too long to handle easily, cut in half. Lay rolled sheets in a single layer on a flat, floured surface.

To roll by hand, divide dough in 8 pieces. Roll 1 portion at a time on a lightly floured board into a 4- by 20-inch sheet.

Sage butter. In a 1- to 2-quart pan over medium-high heat, melt ½ cup (¼ lb.) **butter** or margarine with ¼ cup coarsely chopped **fresh sage leaves** or 1½ tablespoons dry sage leaves.

CHICKEN WITH OLIVES & PINE NUTS
(Pollo con Olive e Pignoli)

⅔ cup pine nuts
1 tablespoon *each* olive oil and butter or margarine
8 *each* chicken legs and thighs (3 to 3½ lb. total), skinned
2 cups drained unpitted Spanish-style olives
At least 5 fresh sage leaves or 1 teaspoon dry sage leaves
¼ cup water

In a 10- to 12-inch frying pan over medium heat, toast nuts about 10 minutes; shake often. Remove from pan; set aside. Increase heat to medium-high. Add oil and butter to pan; brown half the chicken at a time; this takes about 10 minutes total. Discard fat from pan. Return chicken and nuts to pan; add olives, 5 sage leaves, and water.

Simmer, covered, over medium-low heat until meat is no longer pink at bone (cut to test), about 25 minutes. If made ahead, let cool, cover, and chill until next day. Return to simmering, covered, over medium heat. Garnish, if desired, with sage leaves. Makes 8 servings.

·PER SERVING: 252 calories, 26 g protein, 2.2 g carbohydrates, 16 g fat, 93 mg cholesterol, 921 mg sodium

(Continued on next page)

SAUTÉED ARTICHOKES & BRAINS
(Carciofi e Cervella Fritta)

You may need to order the brains ahead.

2½ pounds small artichokes (1- to 1½-in. diameter)
1 quart water
⅓ cup vinegar
½ cup all-purpose flour
About ¾ cup olive oil
5 large eggs
1½ tablespoons fresh or 1 teaspoon dry marjoram leaves
⅔ cup fine dry bread crumbs
1 to 1¼ pounds beef brains (transparent outer sac-like membrane pulled off), rinsed and cut into 1- to 2-inch pieces
Fresh marjoram sprigs (optional)
Salt and pepper
Lemon wedges

Pull off and discard artichoke leaves down to tender, all-edible pale green ones; peel stem ends and cut off thorny tips. Put artichokes in a bowl with water and vinegar to reduce darkening.

Drain; slice lengthwise ¼ inch thick. Coat with flour; shake off excess (coated artichokes can stand up to ½ hour).

Heat 3 tablespoons oil in a 10- to 12-inch frying pan over medium heat. In a bowl, beat eggs to blend. Dip a few artichoke slices at a time in egg; lift out, drain briefly, and put in pan. Without crowding, cook, turning once, until golden, 2 to 3 minutes. Add oil as needed. Keep cooked artichokes warm in a 200° oven.

Mix marjoram leaves and crumbs. Dip brains in egg, drain briefly, then roll in crumbs. Add more oil to pan; cook brains, turning once, until deep golden, about 3 minutes. Arrange on platter with artichokes. Garnish with marjoram sprigs; season to taste with salt, pepper, and lemon. Serves 8.

PER SERVING: 629 calories, 13 g protein, 19 g carbohydrates, 57 g fat, 1,121 mg cholesterol, 209 mg sodium

Golden apricot tart shines at dessert time; just fill press-in crust with jam. Enjoy with espresso and muscat wine.

APRICOT TART
(Crostata)

2 cups all-purpose flour
⅔ cup sugar
½ teaspoon baking powder
¼ teaspoon salt (optional)
½ cup (¼ lb.) butter or margarine
1 large egg
1 large egg yolk
1 cup apricot jam
¼ cup water

In a food processor or bowl, mix flour, sugar, baking powder, and salt. Add butter and whirl or rub with your fingers until mealy. Add egg and egg yolk; whirl or mix with a fork until evenly moistened.

Gather dough into a ball. Press ¾ of it over bottom and ¾ of way up side of a 10- to 12-inch tart pan with a removable bottom. Mix jam and water; spread in crust.

With your fingers, roll remaining dough into long, ¼-inch-thick logs. Crisscross logs on top of jam to form 3 big and 2 small Xs (see picture above). Bake in a 350° oven until crust is deep golden, about 45 minutes. Let cool on a rack for 30 minutes, then remove pan side. Serve tart warm. If made ahead, store airtight up to 2 days; reheat in a 325° oven for 10 minutes. Makes 8 servings.

PER SERVING: 407 calories, 4.7 g protein, 67 g carbohydrates, 13 g fat, 99 mg cholesterol, 159 mg sodium

Tofu Dishes from Sichuan

MILD, ABSORBENT TOFU *soaks up aggressively hot seasonings in these dishes from the Chinese province of Sichuan.*

The soup is a vegetable version of the classic pork or chicken hot and sour soup. Chili oil and white pepper add heat.

The second dish describes its creator, a pock-marked old woman. Its legendary heat comes from four forms of chili or pepper—cayenne, hot bean paste, crushed dried hot red chilies, and curiously numbing Sichuan peppercorns. Together they produce a complex spiciness.

Shop at Asian markets or some supermarkets for Sichuan peppercorns, black beans, or bean paste. Or omit them for milder flavors.

HOT & SOUR TOFU SOUP

    8 medium-size dry shiitake
       mushrooms (about ¾ oz. total)
    1 tablespoon salad oil
    1 clove garlic, minced or pressed
    1 tablespoon minced fresh ginger
    1½ quarts regular-strength chicken
       broth
    1 pound soft or regular tofu,
       rinsed, cut into ½-inch cubes,
       and drained well
    3 tablespoons rice vinegar or cider
       vinegar
    1½ tablespoons soy sauce
    3 tablespoons cornstarch
    ¾ to 1 teaspoon white pepper
    ½ to 1 teaspoon chili oil (optional)
    4 green onions (ends trimmed),
       thinly sliced
       Crisp noodles (recipe follows)
       Crisp-creamy peas (recipe follows)

Soak mushrooms in hot water to cover until soft, about 20 minutes. Drain; cut off tough stems and discard. Cut caps into thin strips; set aside.

Pour oil into a 4- to 5-quart pan. Place over medium heat and add garlic and ginger; stir until garlic is light gold. Add broth and mushrooms; bring to a boil on high heat. Add tofu; cover and simmer until tofu is hot, 3 to 5 minutes. Mix rice vinegar, soy sauce, and cornstarch until smooth; stir into soup. Cook, stirring, until soup boils. Add white pepper and chili oil to taste. Stir in onions. Pour into a tureen. Offer noodles and peas to add to taste. Makes 6 servings.

PER SERVING: 141 calories, 9.2 g protein, 11 g carbohydrates, 7.4 g fat, 0 mg cholesterol, 317 mg sodium

Crisp noodles. Pour about 1 inch **salad oil** into a 2½- to 3-quart pan. Heat oil to 350°. Add a handful of **fresh Chinese noodles** or fresh tagliarini (you'll need 3 oz. total) to oil; fry, turning, until crisp and golden, about 1 minute. Lift out; drain on paper towels. Repeat to fry remaining noodles. Serve, or let cool and store airtight up to 5 days. Makes 3 cups.

Or omit this step and use 1 can (5 oz.) chow mein noodles.

PER ½ CUP: 113 calories, 1.8 g protein, 11 g carbohydrates, 7 g fat, 0 mg cholesterol, 0.3 mg sodium

Crisp-creamy peas. Rinse and drain 1 can (16 oz.) **black-eyed peas.** Spread out on a double layer of paper towels and pat dry. Place beans in a 10- by 15-inch baking pan. Add 1 tablespoon **salad oil** and mix to coat beans. Bake in a 400° oven until beans are lightly browned and crisp on outside, about 15 minutes; stir occasionally. Serve hot or warm. Makes 1 cup.

PER TABLESPOON: 78 calories, 3.6 g protein, 10 g carbohydrates, 2.7 g fat, 0 mg cholesterol, 226 mg sodium

MA PO TOFU

    2 tablespoons salad oil
    ⅓ pound ground lean pork
    1 tablespoon hot bean paste or
       sauce (optional)
    2 tablespoons salted fermented
       black beans, rinsed, drained, and
       chopped (optional)
    3 cloves garlic, pressed or minced
    1 tablespoon minced fresh ginger
    ¾ to 1 teaspoon crushed dried hot
       red chilies
    ¼ to ½ teaspoon cayenne
    1½ cups regular-strength chicken
       broth
    1 tablespoon soy sauce
    1 pound soft or regular tofu, rinsed,
       cut into ¾-inch cubes, and
       drained well
    1½ tablespoons cornstarch
    3 tablespoons water
    ½ cup thinly sliced green onion
       Ground Sichuan peppercorns
       (recipe follows), optional

Add crisp fried noodles and black-eyed peas to hot and sour soup with tofu.

Place a wok or 10- to 12-inch frying pan over high heat. When pan is hot, add oil and swirl over surface. Add pork; stir-fry until lightly browned and crumbly, about 2 minutes. Add bean paste, black beans, garlic, ginger, chilies, and cayenne; stir-fry until spices are very aromatic, about 30 seconds. Add broth, soy sauce, and tofu; bring to a boil. Simmer, uncovered and stirring occasionally, until tofu is hot, about 3 minutes.

Mix cornstarch and water. Add to pan along with onion; stir until boiling. Pour into a bowl and sprinkle to taste with Sichuan peppercorns. Makes 4 servings.

PER SERVING: 238 calories, 18 g protein, 7.6 g carbohydrates, 16 g fat, 25 mg cholesterol, 315 mg sodium

Ground Sichuan peppercorns. Put 2 teaspoons **Sichuan peppercorns** into a 6- to 8-inch frying pan. Pick out and discard any debris.

Cook peppercorns over medium heat, shaking pan often, until they are fragrant and lightly toasted, 2 to 3 minutes. Finely crush with a mortar and pestle (or whirl in blender). Makes 2 teaspoons.

Vegetable Soups for Winter

SOOTHE THE CHILL *of winter with light, satisfying vegetable soup. The process is simple, and the results are colorful and refreshing. In the first soup, onions cooked slowly to sweetness go with carrots and bright green okra. The second smoothly combines canned garbanzos and barley, while the third mixes golden squash, hominy, cauliflower, and mustard greens.*

Ladle onion soup, studded with okra and carrot, into bowls; serve with parmesan toast.

ONION SOUP WITH OKRA

2 tablespoons butter or margarine
3 medium-size onions, thinly sliced
8 garlic cloves, minced or pressed
5 cups regular-strength chicken broth
1 cup thinly sliced carrots
2 cups (about 9 oz.) frozen sliced okra
   Parmesan bread (recipe follows)

In a 5- to 6-quart pan over medium heat, cook butter, onions, and garlic; stir often until onion is golden and sweet-tasting, about 45 minutes.

Add broth and carrots to pan. Bring to a boil over high heat, cover, and cook until carrots are tender to bite, about 5 minutes. Stir in okra; heat until hot.

Ladle soup into 4 to 6 bowls and serve with parmesan bread. Makes 4 to 6 servings, 1¼- to 1¾-cup size.

PER SERVING WITHOUT BREAD: 110 calories, 4 g protein, 12 g carbohydrates, 5.4 g fat, 10 mg cholesterol, 95 mg sodium

Parmesan bread. Mix together 6 tablespoons **butter** or margarine, at room temperature, and ½ cup grated **parmesan cheese;** set aside. Diagonally cut 1 slender **baguette** (8 oz.) into ½-inch-thick slices.

Spread butter mixture onto 1 side of each baguette slice; place slices, buttered sides up, in 2 pans, each 10 by 15 inches. Broil 1 pan at a time, about 6 inches from heat, until golden, about 4 minutes.

PER ½-OUNCE SLICE: 91 calories, 2.4 g protein, 7.9 g carbohydrates, 5.5 g fat, 14 mg cholesterol, 173 mg sodium

CREAMED GARBANZO SOUP WITH TOASTED SESAME SEED & GREEN ONION

2 tablespoons olive or salad oil
1 medium-size onion, chopped
⅓ cup pearl barley
1 teaspoon cumin seed
5 cups regular-strength chicken broth
2 cans (15½ oz. each) garbanzo beans, drained
¼ cup sesame seed
6 green onions (ends trimmed), thinly sliced
   Lemon wedges (optional)

To a 5- to 6-quart pan over medium-high heat, add 1 tablespoon oil, onion, barley, and cumin; stir until barley is opaque and onion is translucent, about 5 minutes.

Add broth, bring to a boil, cover, and simmer until barley is tender to bite, about 25 minutes. Add garbanzo beans; simmer until they are hot, about 10 minutes. Pour ½ of mixture into a blender; whirl until smoothly puréed. Pour back into pan.

Meanwhile, in a 6- to 8-inch frying pan over medium-high heat, combine remaining oil and sesame seed; stir often until golden, about 4 minutes. Add onions and stir until bright green, about 1 minute. Spoon sesame mixture into a small bowl.

Ladle soup into 6 bowls; add sesame mixture and squeeze juice from lemon wedges to taste into individual portions. Makes 6 servings, 1-cup size.

PER SERVING: 321 calories, 12 g protein, 46 g carbohydrates, 11 g fat, 0 mg cholesterol, 485 mg sodium

WINTER VEGETABLE SOUP

1 pound banana squash
6 cups regular-strength chicken broth
1 ounce fresh ginger (about 1 by 1½ in.), peeled and thinly sliced
½ pound mustard greens
1 medium-size (about 1½ lb.) head cauliflower, cored and separated into flowerets
1 can (14½ oz.) yellow hominy, drained

Cut rind from banana squash and discard; cut squash into ½-inch cubes.

In a 5- to 6-quart pan, combine squash, broth, and ginger. Bring to a boil on high heat; cover, and simmer until squash is tender when pierced, about 10 minutes.

Meanwhile, rinse mustard greens, discard tough stems, and sliver leaves.

To soup, add cauliflower and hominy. Turn heat to high and bring soup to a boil; cover and boil gently until cauliflower is tender when pierced, about 15 minutes. Stir in greens. Ladle soup into 6 bowls. Makes 6 servings, 1½-cup size.

PER SERVING: 124 calories, 6.6 g protein, 22 g carbohydrates, 2 g fat, 0 mg cholesterol, 271 mg sodium

More February Recipes

ADDITIONAL DISHES FEATURED *in February include a succulent goose with a sweetened cabbage stuffing, a barbecue chicken pie for family suppers, and an easy but elegant dessert.*

GREAT GOLDEN GOOSE WITH CABBAGE-APPLE STUFFING

Rich flavor, more than beauty, is what gives the goose its high standing. Like duck, this gangly bird is all dark meat. Both fowl have a wealth of fat which you release by pricking the skin.

Light cabbage stuffing, slightly sweet from apples and raisins, provides a fine balance to the goose's succulence.

You may need to order the goose ahead. If it comes frozen, allow a couple of days for thawing in the refrigerator.

- 1 **goose (8 to 12 lb.), thawed if frozen**
- 2 **medium-size lemons**
- 1 **tablespoon olive oil or salad oil**
- 1½ **pounds green cabbage, cored and finely shredded**
- 4 **cups peeled, cored, and coarsely chopped Golden Delicious apples**
- 1 **cup golden raisins**
- ¾ **cup chopped parsley**
- ½ **teaspoon** *each* **dry marjoram leaves, dry thyme leaves, dry chervil leaves, rubbed sage, and ground allspice**
- ½ **cup white grape juice or apple juice**
  Pepper
  Parsley sprigs
  Lemon wedges (optional)

Remove the giblets from goose and reserve for other uses. Pull off and discard lumps of fat. Rinse bird inside and out, and pat dry. With a small metal skewer, pierce skin all over at about 1½-inch intervals. Cut 1 lemon in half; rub and gently squeeze ½ lemon all over inside of goose. Set remaining lemons aside.

Place oil, cabbage, and apples in a 5- to 6-quart pan over medium-high heat. Cover and cook, stirring occasionally, until cabbage is wilted, about 8 minutes. Remove from heat and stir in raisins, chopped parsley, marjoram, thyme, chervil, sage, and allspice.

Grate peel from the remaining whole lemon and stir into cabbage mixture. Ream juice from this lemon and stir into grape juice; set mixture aside.

Stuff body and neck cavities of bird with cabbage mixture; skewer cavities closed. Rub outside of goose with remaining ½ lemon; sprinkle all over with pepper. Place bird, breast down, on a V-shaped rack in a 12- by 17-inch roasting pan. Cover goose with a tent of foil, sealing foil to pan edges.

Roast goose in a 350° oven for 1 hour. Uncover, and siphon fat from pan. Turn goose breast side up and insert a thermometer into thickest part of a drumstick. Continue to cook, uncovered, siphoning fat and basting bird with juice mixture every 30 minutes, until thermometer reaches 175°, 1 to 2 hours longer.

Lift goose onto a large platter. Remove skewers, then spoon stuffing next to bird. Garnish with parsley sprigs and lemon wedges, and carve the meat. Serves 6 to 8. —*Marlene Brooks, San Jose, Calif.*

PER SERVING MEAT (WITHOUT SKIN OR BONES) AND STUFFING: 522 calories, 49 g protein, 32 g carbohydrates, 23 g fat, 157 mg cholesterol, 142 mg sodium

BARBECUE CHICKEN PIE

Flavored like Southern-style barbecue, this family supper pie uses cooked chicken and cheese in an easy pizza crust.

- 1 **package (10 oz.) refrigerated pizza dough, or 1 package (1 lb.) frozen white bread dough, thawed**
- 2 **cups diced or shredded cooked chicken**
  Barbecue sauce (recipe follows)
- 1 **large yellow bell pepper, stemmed, seeded, and thinly sliced**
- ½ **pound jack cheese, plain or seasoned with chilies, shredded**
- ½ **cup lightly packed fresh cilantro (coriander) sprigs**

Press dough over bottom and up sides of an ungreased 10- by 15-inch rimmed pan or a 14-inch-diameter pizza pan. Pierce dough with a fork at 2-inch intervals. Bake on the bottom rack of a 400° oven until light golden, 10 to 15 minutes.

Mix chicken with barbecue sauce. Spread mixture evenly in baked crust. Arrange pepper slices over sauce, then cover evenly with cheese. Bake on the bottom rack of a 400° oven until cheese bubbles, about 15 minutes. Garnish with cilantro. Cut into rectangles or wedges. Serves 6.

PER SERVING: 450 calories, 27 g protein, 40 g carbohydrates, 20 g fat, 92 mg cholesterol, 1,130 mg sodium

Barbecue sauce. In a 10- to 12-inch frying pan over medium heat, combine 2 tablespoons **butter** or margarine and 1 large **onion,** thinly sliced. Stir occasionally until onion is golden brown, 25 to 30 minutes. Add ½ cup **catsup,** ½ cup **tomato-based chili sauce,** ¼ cup **cider vinegar,** 1 tablespoon **molasses,** and 1 tablespoon **Worcestershire.** Simmer, uncovered, until reduced to 1½ cups, about 10 minutes. Use; or cool, cover, and chill up to 2 days.

PORT WINE FOAM WITH STRAWBERRIES

A golden foam of port-flavored eggs, known as zabaglione in Italy, flows over whole strawberries in this elegant dessert.

Zabaglione takes only minutes to prepare. Just whip egg yolks with wine and sugar over heat until the mixture holds soft peaks. For a dramatic presentation, cook it at the table in a classic round-bottom zabaglione pan, or you can use a double boiler in the kitchen.

- ½ **cup whipping cream, softly whipped**
- 12 **to 16 large strawberries, rinsed and hulled**
- ⅓ **cup port**
- 3 **tablespoons sugar**
- 3 **large egg yolks**
  Fine strands of lemon peel (yellow part only), optional

Spoon equal portions of cream into 4 wide glasses or bowls. Set 3 or 4 berries, stem end down, in each glass.

In a round-bottom zabaglione pan or in a double-boiler top, beat together port, sugar, and egg yolks. Place round-bottom pan directly over medium gas heat or high electric heat; set the double boiler over simmering water. Beat rapidly with a whisk or electric mixer until foam is just thick enough to briefly hold a slight peak when whisk is lifted, 3 to 5 minutes. At once pour warm port foam over berries. Garnish with lemon peel. Serve at once. Serves 4. —*Ulla Pironi, Belmont, Calif.*

PER SERVING: 184 calories, 2.8 g protein, 14 g carbohydrates, 14 g fat, 237 mg cholesterol, 19 mg sodium

Lemon-glazed rolls, filled with poppy seed and nuts, start with frozen bread dough.

POPPY SEED BREAKFAST ROLLS

¼ cup poppy seed
1 teaspoon grated lemon peel
¼ cup finely chopped pecans
¼ cup (⅛ lb.) butter or margarine, melted
1 large egg white
½ cup sugar
1 loaf (1 lb.) frozen white bread dough, thawed
Glaze (recipe follows)

Mix poppy seed, lemon peel, pecans, 3 tablespoons of the butter, egg white, and sugar. Set aside.

On a lightly floured board, roll dough into a 10- by 14-inch rectangle. Spread filling over dough to within ½ inch of edges. From a long side, roll dough into a smooth log. Pinch edges to seal. Cut log crosswise into 12 equal pieces. Brush 2 cake pans, 8-inch-diameter size, with remaining butter. Set 6 rolls, cut side up, in each pan. Cover with plastic wrap and let rise in a warm place until puffy, about 30 minutes; uncover. Bake in a 350° oven until golden brown, 25 to 30 minutes. Invert from pans; drizzle tops with glaze. Serve hot or warm. Makes 12.—*Vera Harmon, Louisville, Colo.*

PER SERVING: 232 calories, 3.8 g protein, 36 g carbohydrates, 8.6 g fat, 12 mg cholesterol, 227 mg sodium

Glaze. Mix well 1 cup sifted **powdered sugar** and 2 tablespoons **lemon juice.**

Winter salad includes greens, sliced pears, candied walnuts. Blue cheese goes on last.

PEAR, WALNUT & BLUE CHEESE SALAD

4 cups lightly packed rinsed and crisped watercress sprigs (5 to 6 oz. untrimmed)
4 cups rinsed and crisped, bite-size pieces butter lettuce (about ½ lb. untrimmed)
2 small firm-ripe pears, cored and cut into thin slices
Candied walnuts (recipe follows)
Shallot dressing (recipe follows)
½ cup crumbled blue cheese
Salt

In a large bowl, combine watercress, lettuce, pears, and walnuts. Add dressing and mix gently. Spoon mixture onto 6 salad plates. Sprinkle with cheese. Add salt to taste. Serves 6.—*Carmela Meely, Walnut Creek, Calif.*

PER SERVING: 305 calories, 4.9 g protein, 14 g carbohydrates, 27 g fat, 8.4 mg cholesterol, 171 mg sodium

Candied walnuts. Pour 2 tablespoons **sugar** into a 7- to 8-inch frying pan over medium-high heat; shake often until sugar melts and turns amber color. Add 1 tablespoon **water** (sugar hardens); cook, stirring, until sugar melts. Add ½ cup **walnut halves.** Stir until syrup clings to nuts. Spread nuts out on foil; cool.

Shallot dressing. Mix together 2 tablespoons **lemon juice;** ½ cup **olive** or salad **oil;** 1 large **shallot,** minced; ½ teaspoon *each* **pepper** and **sugar.**

Mellow sauce on tortellini features sautéed mushrooms, garlic, basil, and cream cheese thinned with milk.

TORTELLINI WITH MUSHROOM-CHEESE SAUCE

1 tablespoon butter or margarine
1 pound mushrooms, finely chopped
3 cloves garlic, minced or pressed
1 tablespoon minced fresh basil leaves, or 1 teaspoon dry basil leaves
6 ounces (⅔ cup) cream cheese
¾ cup milk
1 package (12 oz.) frozen tortellini
Parsley sprigs

Melt butter in a 10- to 12-inch frying pan over medium-high heat. Add mushrooms, garlic, and basil; stir often until all liquid has evaporated and mushrooms begin to brown, 10 to 12 minutes. Add cheese and milk; stir until cheese melts and sauce begins to boil.

Meanwhile, in a 5- to 6-quart pan, bring 4 quarts water to boiling over high heat. Add frozen tortellini and cook, uncovered, until just barely tender to bite, 15 to 20 minutes. Drain and pour into a bowl; add mushroom sauce and mix well.

Spoon tortellini and sauce equally onto 4 to 6 heated dinner plates; garnish with parsley sprigs. Makes 6 first-course servings, 4 entrée servings.—*Linda Lum, Tacoma.*

PER FIRST-COURSE SERVING: 325 calories, 14 g protein, 29 g carbohydrates, 18 g fat, 41 mg cholesterol, 319 mg sodium

ZUCCHINI-SAUSAGE BAKE

1 pound hot or mild Italian sausages, casings removed
1 large onion, chopped
1 large red bell pepper, stemmed, seeded, and chopped
1 can (14½ oz.) tomatoes
About ¾ pound zucchini, ends trimmed, thinly sliced
½ teaspoon dry oregano leaves
1 cup regular-strength beef broth
½ cup long-grain white rice
½ cup grated parmesan cheese

Crumble sausage into a 10- to 12-inch frying pan. Stir often over medium-high heat until lightly browned, 8 to 10 minutes. With a slotted spoon, lift out sausage and set aside. Drain off and discard all but 2 tablespoons fat.

To pan, add onion and bell pepper; stir often until vegetables begin to brown, 8 to 10 minutes. Add tomatoes with their liquid; break up with a spoon. Add zucchini, oregano, and broth. Simmer 5 to 10 minutes to blend flavors; mix in rice. Pour sauce into a shallow 2-quart baking dish. Sprinkle with sausage. Cover tightly. Bake in a 350° oven until rice is tender to bite, 50 to 55 minutes. Sprinkle with cheese. Serves 4 to 6. — *Neva Rawling, Salt Lake City.*

PER SERVING: 334 calories, 17 g protein, 21 g carbohydrates, 20 g fat, 51 mg cholesterol, 771 mg sodium

Brown sausage first for casserole dish; then make a vegetable sauce, add rice.

STUFFED CHICKEN BREASTS WITH CHUTNEY

3 tablespoons olive oil
2 cloves garlic, minced or pressed
1 large onion, chopped
2 cups lightly packed spinach leaves, rinsed and chopped
8 boned, skinned chicken breast halves (each about 4 oz.)
Salt and pepper
2 teaspoons balsamic or red wine vinegar
¼ cup *each* water and chopped chutney

In a 12- to 14-inch frying pan on medium-high heat, stir 1 tablespoon oil, garlic, and onion until onion is slightly browned. Add spinach; set aside.

With a flat mallet, pound breast halves between sheets of plastic wrap until ¼ inch thick. Sprinkle with salt and pepper. Spoon spinach mixture equally in center of each chicken piece. Roll to enclose filling; fasten with toothpicks.

Add remaining oil to pan. Brown rolls on medium-high heat. Add vinegar, water, and chutney. Cover and simmer until meat is white in center (cut to test), 8 to 10 minutes. Remove rolls. Boil sauce on high heat until reduced to ½ cup; pour over chicken. Serves 8.—*Constance Chaplin, Seal Beach, Calif.*

PER SERVING: 202 calories, 27 g protein, 7.5 g carbohydrates, 6.6 g fat, 66 mg cholesterol, 104 mg sodium

Pounded chicken breast halves have spinach stuffing. Brown in olive oil, then simmer in a sauce seasoned with chutney.

TOASTED ALMOND–MOCHA BLENDER TORTE

4 large eggs
¾ cup sugar
Toasted almonds (directions follow)
¼ cup all-purpose flour
2½ teaspoons baking powder
Mocha cream (recipe follows)

In a blender, whirl eggs, sugar, and 1 cup almonds until nuts are very finely ground. Add flour and baking powder; whirl until mixed well. Pour batter into a buttered 9-inch-diameter cake pan.

Bake in a 350° oven until cake feels set in center when lightly touched, 20 to 25 minutes. Let cool 10 minutes (cake will settle), then invert cake onto a plate and cool completely. Spread torte with mocha cream. Sprinkle with remaining nuts. Serves 8.—*Suzanne Peschelt, Newport Beach, Calif.*

PER SERVING: 386 calories, 7.8 g protein, 36 g carbohydrates, 25 g fat, 187 mg cholesterol, 185 mg sodium

Toasted almonds. Place 1¼ cups **sliced almonds** in an 8- or 9-inch-wide pan. Bake in 350° oven until lightly toasted, 8 to 10 minutes; shake often. Cool.

Mocha cream. In a blender, combine 1½ cups **whipping cream,** ⅓ cup **sugar,** ¼ cup **unsweetened cocoa,** 1 tablespoon **instant coffee powder,** and 1 teaspoon **vanilla.** Whirl mixture to whip.

Almond-topped torte is frosted with a mocha cream. Mix both cake and frosting in a blender.

WE'VE TALKED BEFORE *about syncretism, and our remarks certainly apply to Bob Stewart's Chicken or Pork Burros—a Mexican dish prepared using a Chinese stir-fry technique in a wok. Another Chinese touch, heating a hot pepper in cooking oil until it begins to blacken, is the Szechuan kung pao treatment for spicing the oil, which in turn flavors other ingredients.*

While the Chinese cook would leave the pepper in the food—letting the wise diner eat around it—Stewart removes the pepper early in the process, saving anyone the unpleasant surprise of encountering it hidden in the tortilla.

Note that the sauce is a mild one; this is traditional in northern Mexico, as are the flour tortillas.

CHICKEN OR PORK BURROS

> Salad oil
> 1 clove garlic, minced or pressed
> 1 small dried hot red chili
> 1 whole chicken breast (about 1 lb.), skinned, boned, and cut into ½-inch cubes; or 4 pork loin chops, boned, fat trimmed off, and meat cut into ½-inch pieces
> 1 tablespoon dry sherry
> ½ cup finely chopped celery
> 2 green onions (ends trimmed), thinly sliced
> 4 medium-size mushrooms, sliced
> Burro sauce (recipe follows)
> 4 large flour tortillas, each about 10 inches in diameter
> 4 slices (1 oz. each) cheddar cheese, each cut into strips

Heat 2 tablespoons oil in a wok or 12-inch frying pan over medium-high heat; add garlic and chili. Stir until chili turns almost black. Discard chili and reduce heat to medium. Add meat and sherry; stir-fry just until meat is white in center and liquid has evaporated, 4 to 5 minutes for chicken, 6 to 8 minutes for pork. Lift meat from pan and set aside.

Add 1 more tablespoon oil to pan, then add celery and stir-fry for 2 minutes; add onions and mushrooms and stir-fry for 2 minutes longer. Return meat to pan, add sauce, and stir over low heat until hot. Remove from heat.

"Chicken or Pork Burros—a Mexican dish prepared using a Chinese stir-fry technique in a wok."

To shape each burro, lay 1 tortilla flat, spoon ¼ of the stir-fry mixture near 1 edge, and top with ¼ of the cheese strips. Fold tortilla edge up over filling, then fold in sides and roll to enclose filling.

Rinse wok and wipe dry. Heat 2 more tablespoons oil in wok over medium-high heat; add 1 burro and cook until browned on both sides. Repeat to fill and cook remaining burros, adding more oil to pan as needed. Makes 4 servings.

Burro sauce. Stir together ¼ cup **catsup**, 1½ teaspoons **honey**, 1 teaspoon **Worcestershire**, ¼ teaspoon **garlic powder**, and 2 to 3 drops **liquid hot pepper seasoning**.

PER SERVING: 545 calories, 38 g protein, 34 g carbohydrates, 28 g fat, 96 mg cholesterol, 667 mg sodium

Bob Stewart

Scottsdale, Ariz.

ARTHUR VINSEL CAN ALWAYS *be relied on to send in recipes of considerable originality, often with names of startling originality. We don't always use the names, some of which might be libelous. This one we are calling Brown Rice à l'Orange. (If you must know, Chef Vinsel calls this dish Brown Rice au Snakenavel McCune.)*

The orange and other seasonings give the rice distinction without making it so strongly flavored as to dominate the dish it accompanies. It would go well with a barbecued or broiled chicken.

BROWN RICE À L'ORANGE

> 1 cup long-grain brown rice
> 1 cup orange juice
> ⅓ cup dry white wine
> About ⅔ cup water
> 2 strips pared orange peel (orange part only), each about 2 inches long
> 3 sprigs fresh sage or marjoram, each about 4 inches long, or ¼ teaspoon of the dried herb
> 2 tablespoons butter or margarine
> Prepared teriyaki sauce (optional)

In a 3- to 4-quart pan, combine rice, orange juice, wine, water, orange peel, and sage. Bring to a boil over high heat; cover, reduce heat to low, and cook until rice is tender to bite (add water, 2 to 3 tablespoons at a time, if needed to prevent sticking), 55 to 60 minutes. Remove the rice from heat and let stand, uncovered, for 5 minutes.

Discard orange peel and sage sprig; stir butter into rice until melted. Offer teriyaki sauce to add to taste. Makes 4 servings.

PER SERVING: 247 calories, 3.9 g protein, 43 g carbohydrates, 6.7 g fat, 16 mg cholesterol, 64 mg sodium

Arthur R. Vinsel

Costa Mesa, Calif.

FLOURLESS MUFFINS? *It seems an impossibility, but read this recipe. They're made with grain in a different guise: breakfast cereal and graham cracker crumbs. (The graham cracker, by the way, was first baked 160 years ago by Sylvester Graham, whose advocacy of a vegetarian diet and home-baked bread earned him the enmity of butchers and bakers.) Greg Levin's muffins also contain raisins, walnuts, maple syrup, and yogurt, but the chief flavoring ingredient is peanut butter. Don't let all these healthful ingredients put you off; the muffins taste great.*

PEANUT BUTTER BREAKFAST MUFFINS

- 2 cups wheat-rye-flax breakfast cereal
- 1 cup graham cracker crumbs
- 1 teaspoon *each* baking powder and baking soda
- ¼ cup firmly packed brown sugar
- 2 large eggs
- ½ cup cream-style peanut butter
- ½ cup unflavored yogurt
- ¼ cup maple or maple-flavor syrup
- 2 tablespoons butter or margarine, melted
- 2 cups buttermilk
- 1 cup raisins
- ½ cup chopped walnuts

In a large bowl, stir together breakfast cereal, graham cracker crumbs, baking powder, baking soda, and brown sugar.

In another bowl, with a whisk or a rotary beater, beat eggs and peanut butter until smoothly mixed. Mix in yogurt, maple syrup, butter, and buttermilk.

Add egg–peanut butter mixture to dry ingredients and stir just until well moistened. Stir in raisins and nuts. Spoon batter into greased 2½-inch muffin cups, filling each about ¾ full.

Bake in a 375° oven until a toothpick inserted in the center comes out clean, 20 to 25 minutes. Lift from muffin cups and serve warm. Makes about 2 dozen.

PER SERVING: 154 calories, 4.8 g protein, 20 g carbohydrates, 6.5 g fat, 27 mg cholesterol, 149 mg sodium

Bellingham, Wash.

THE FRENCH, TOO, *have a pizza; it is called* pissaladière *and is usually associated with the Riviera, especially the city of Nice. Its broad crust is usually topped with onions, anchovies, and olives, and it is often known in English as onion or anchovy tart. When he speaks of French tart, Grayson Taketa is thinking of a derivative of this dish—not Mademoiselle from Armentières or any of her historic sisterhood.*

Taketa's tart nods toward Italy in its use of mozzarella cheese and tomatoes, but the Dijon mustard saves it for the French. This kind of tart invites fussing, and you might want to try anchovies, olives (salty green Spanish-style or green or black ripe), bell peppers, or any of the thousand natural amendments that pizza is heir to.

FRENCH TART

- 1 package (10 oz.) refrigerated pizza crust
- ¼ cup Dijon mustard
- ¾ cup thinly sliced green onions, including tops
- 1 teaspoon dry Italian herb mix
- 3 cups (¾ lb.) shredded mozzarella cheese
- 4 to 5 Roma-style tomatoes (about ¾ lb.), thinly sliced

Unroll crust and with your fingers press into a greased 10- by 15-inch baking pan. Evenly spread dough with mustard, sprinkle with onions and herbs, then top evenly with cheese and tomato slices.

Bake on the bottom rack in a 425° oven until cheese is bubbly and crust is golden brown around the rim, about 20 minutes. Cut into squares. Makes 6 servings.

PER SERVING: 306 calories, 16 g protein, 27 g carbohydrates, 16 g fat, 44 mg cholesterol, 746 mg sodium

Los Altos Hills, Calif.

LINGUINE WITH CLAMS (con vongole) *is commonplace—delightfully commonplace—on Italian restaurant menus. If it works with clams, reasons Steve Harrison, why wouldn't it work with oysters? He was able to prove that it works very well indeed—if you like oysters. Despite a hot bath in butter, wine, cream, and a variety of seasonings, the oyster emerges triumphant, its scent and flavor evocative of low tide in a quiet estuary.*

LINGUINE WITH PACIFIC OYSTERS

- 1 jar (10 oz.) small Pacific oysters
- 2 tablespoons butter or margarine
- 1 small red bell pepper, stemmed, seeded, and chopped
- 2 cloves garlic, minced or pressed
- 1 can (2¼ oz.) sliced ripe olives, drained
- ½ cup dry white wine
- ¼ cup dry vermouth
- 1 teaspoon dry basil leaves
- ½ teaspoon dry oregano leaves
- ½ cup whipping cream
  Salt and pepper
- 1 tablespoon chopped parsley
- 8 to 9 ounces fresh linguine

Lift oysters from jar (reserving any liquid) and cut into bite-size pieces. Melt butter in a 10- to 12-inch frying pan over medium-high heat; add oysters and cook just until edges curl, 1 to 2 minutes. With a slotted spoon, lift from pan; set aside.

Add bell pepper and garlic to pan and stir often until pepper is limp, about 5 minutes. Add olives, wine, vermouth, basil, oregano, oyster liquid, and cream. Turn heat to high and stir often until liquid is reduced by half, about 10 minutes. Return oysters to sauce, season to taste with salt and pepper, and heat through.

Meanwhile, bring about 3 quarts water to boil on high heat in a 5- to 6-quart pan. Add linguine and boil, uncovered, until tender to bite, 4 to 5 minutes. Drain well and pour into a shallow serving bowl; pour oyster mixture onto pasta and add parsley; lift with 2 forks to mix well. Makes 3 or 4 servings.

PER SERVING: 362 calories, 11 g protein, 39 g carbohydrates, 18 g fat, 113 mg cholesterol, 220 mg sodium

Stan R. Harrison

Portola Valley, Calif.

February Menus

OLD STANDBYS *get dressed up this month for dinner, the most demanding meal. These reliable favorites cook quickly and make use of many ingredients you can keep on hand.*

Eggs go into classic omelets that fill the bill for a quick but romantic meal for two.

Dry split-pea soup has a new look with the addition of tiny frozen peas. Accom-pany with freshly baked pastry twists made from frozen dough. Both come together in about an hour. You can tailor recipe sizes to your family and possibly make two meals from one.

For the third menu, present hamburgers with accouterments designed to please either simple or adventurous tastes. The choices are All-American and Asian.

VALENTINE'S SUPPER FOR 2

Blue Cheese Omelet
Asparagus Salad
Multigrain Rolls
Chocolate Truffles
Asti Spumante with Campari

Even if you get home late, or are exhausted after putting the children to bed, this pretty, light dinner is no challenge.

Cook the asparagus before you start the omelets; also warm the rolls. Buy two of the most elegant chocolate truffles you can find for dessert. When you serve dinner, splash some bitter, herbal Campari into a slightly sweet version of the Italian sparkling wine to give it a tang and pale, rosy hue.

BLUE CHEESE OMELET

- 4 large eggs
- 2 tablespoons water
- 2 to 4 teaspoons butter or margarine
- 2 tablespoons crumbled blue cheese
  Salt and pepper

In a bowl, beat eggs to blend with water. Set a 7- to 8-inch omelet pan on medium-high heat. When pan is hot, add ½ the butter and swirl on the heat until melted. Pour in ½ the egg mixture.

Lifting cooked egg to allow uncooked mixture to flow beneath, cook until eggs are set. Sprinkle ½ the cheese down center of omelet. With a spatula, lift ½ the omelet and fold over cheese. Shaking pan, slide omelet onto a warm dinner plate; keep warm. Repeat steps to make the second omelet. Add salt and pepper to taste. Makes 2 servings.

PER SERVING: 222 calories, 14 g protein, 1.4 g carbohydrates, 17 g fat, 566 mg cholesterol, 295 mg sodium

ASPARAGUS SALAD

- ½ pound asparagus
- 2 tablespoons olive oil or salad oil
- 1 tablespoon lemon juice
- 1 tablespoon finely shredded parmesan cheese
  Salt and pepper
- 2 lemon wedges

Cut tough ends from asparagus; discard. If desired, pare spears with a vegetable peeler.

For a special valentine, offer blue cheese–filled omelet, parmesan cheese–seasoned asparagus, and sparkling wine flavored with Campari; truffles for dessert come last.

In a 10- to 12-inch frying pan on high heat, bring 1 inch water to boiling. Lay spears in water. Cook, uncovered, until asparagus is tender when pierced, about 6 minutes. Drain; serve warm.

Arrange asparagus on dinner plates. Mix oil with lemon juice and spoon over asparagus, then sprinkle with parmesan. Add salt and pepper to taste. Garnish with lemon wedges. Makes 2 servings.

PER SERVING: 151 calories, 3.3 g protein, 4.3 g carbohydrates, 15 g fat, 2.4 mg cholesterol, 60 mg sodium

---

SOUP & BREADSTICK SUPPER

Double Pea Soup
Unflavored Yogurt   **Lemon Wedges**
Quick Salt Sticks   **Dijon Mustard**
Chicory Salad with Pecans
Edam Cheese   **Pears**
Dry Sauvignon Blanc   **Apple Cider**

For a warming family meal, soup made of split peas without the typical ham bone is lighter, leaner, and faster. Caraway seeds speckle the flaky salt sticks.

While the soup simmers, shape and bake the puff pastry salt sticks. Offer yogurt and lemon to add to the soup to taste, and mustard to spread—fat pretzel–style—on the bread (or buy the pretzels, too).

Make salad of rinsed, crisped curly chicory; roasted and salted (or not) pecans; and an oil-and-vinegar dressing.

Other cheeses that go well with ripe winter pears include gouda, jarlsberg, and cheddar.

DOUBLE PEA SOUP

If you expect only a few for dinner, make the full soup recipe and save part of it for another meal. Or make half the recipe and cook the soup in a 3- to 4-quart pan.

  2 pounds yellow or green split peas
  4 cloves garlic, minced
  1 tablespoon butter or margarine
 10 cups regular-strength chicken broth
  1 package (10 oz.) frozen petite peas
    Salt and pepper

Sort through split peas and discard any debris. Rinse and drain peas.

In a 5- to 6-quart pan on medium-high heat, stir garlic in butter until golden,

Cozy supper features thick but lean pea soup with hot pastry sticks. A no-cook option instead of bread: big pretzels.

about 2 minutes. Add split peas and chicken broth; bring to boiling on high heat. Cover and reduce heat to a simmer; cook until peas are tender when mashed, 45 minutes to 1 hour. Add frozen peas; stir often until hot, about 5 minutes. If made ahead, let cool, then cover and chill up to 3 days, or freeze for longer storage; reheat to serve. Makes about 3 quarts, 8 servings.

PER SERVING: 463 calories, 32 g protein, 75 g carbohydrates, 4.7 g fat, 3.9 mg cholesterol, 146 mg sodium

QUICK SALT STICKS

To make half a recipe, use only half the ingredients; keep the extra pastry frozen.

  1 package (17 oz.) frozen puff pastry
1½ teaspoons caraway seed
  1 egg white, slightly beaten
  1 teaspoon coarse salt (such as kosher salt)

Separate sheets of pastry and let thaw. Cut each pastry sheet into quarters; then cut each quarter into 2 triangles. Sprinkle evenly with caraway seed.

Roll each triangle into a stick, starting with the longest side and rolling toward opposite angle or point. Place sticks, center point down and several inches apart, on an ungreased 12- by 15-inch baking sheet. Brush sticks lightly with egg white; sprinkle evenly with salt.

Bake in a 400° oven until golden brown, about 15 minutes. Serve hot. (If made ahead, let cool on racks, wrap airtight, and chill up to 1 day. To reheat, place on baking sheet in a 400° oven until hot, about 5 minutes.) Makes 16.— *Herman Plate, Redwood City, Calif.*

PER PIECE: 132 calories, 1.7 g protein, 11 g carbohydrates, 8.5 g fat, 0 mg cholesterol, 240 mg sodium

(Continued on next page)

VERSATILE HAMBURGER DINNER

Hamburgers with Buns or Rice
Mayonnaise   Catsup   Mustard
Teriyaki Mustard Sauce
Cucumber Slices
Napa Cabbage Salad
Fresh Pineapple   Gingersnaps
Green Tea   Apricot Nectar

Ground beef patties—broiled, grilled, or pan-browned to taste—are the foundation of this meal. Serve ballpark-style toppings for simple tastes, Asian toppings for the more daring.

Put rice on to boil before you start the hamburgers. Delicate napa cabbage salad holds up if you want to make the salad several hours ahead.

TERIYAKI MUSTARD SAUCE

¼ cup *each* Dijon mustard, soy
sauce, and sugar

In a bowl, blend mustard with soy sauce and sugar. Use, or cover and chill up to 2 weeks. Makes ¾ cup.

PER TABLESPOON: 25 calories, 0.3 g protein, 5.3 g carbohydrates, 0.3 g fat, 0 mg cholesterol, 493 mg sodium

NAPA CABBAGE SALAD

4   medium-size carrots
4   cups finely slivered napa cabbage
⅓   cup white wine vinegar
2   tablespoons sugar
1   clove garlic, minced
1   teaspoon minced fresh ginger
    Salt

Finely shred carrots. In a salad bowl, gently mix together carrots, cabbage, vinegar, sugar, garlic, ginger, and salt to taste. If made ahead, cover and chill up to 4 hours. Makes 6 cups, 6 servings.

PER SERVING: 48 calories, 1.1 g protein, 11 g carbohydrates, 0.2 g fat, 0 mg cholesterol, 22 mg sodium

Venetian-style Panettone (page 54)

Spring often brings an urge
to try fresh ways with food. Creating a festive centerpiece on
Easter morning is our Venetian-style Panettone, a tall
handsome sweet bread encrusted with sugar crystals and nuts
and baked in a brown paper bag. For elegant dinners we
transform plain roasts with fresh herbs and create an
intriguing make-ahead dessert. Sharing our March pages are
dishes featuring pungently flavored greens and tropical fruits,
and some new ideas featuring old favorites.

Italian "Brown Bag Bread"

A JEWELED CRUST, *lavishly set with crystals of sugar and golden nuts, crowns this citrus-flavored, honey-colored bread from Venice. Much like the popular and beloved panettone of Milan, this holiday sweet bread has a similar butter- and egg-enriched dough, but it lacks the characteristic jumble of candied fruit and raisins. Instead, this version is lightly laced with candied orange peel.*

Although the bread is traditionally baked in a paper-lined mold, we've improvised by baking the dough in doubled-up paper lunch bags, to give the panettone its tall stature and rustic simplicity.

Serve this handsome loaf Easter morning or as an afternoon snack with coffee or cappuccino. Many Italians also eat this rich, sweet bread as cake for dessert.

The buttery dough does take time to rise. If you like, you can bake the bread ahead, then thaw, if frozen, and reheat to serve.

VENETIAN-STYLE PANETTONE
(*Veneziana*)

- 2 packages active dry yeast
- ¾ cup warm water (110° to 115°)
- ½ cup granulated sugar
- ½ teaspoon salt
- ½ cup (¼ lb.) butter or margarine, at room temperature

Drop ball of soft, egg-rich dough into buttered double-thick brown paper lunch bag supported in a loaf pan.

- 1 large egg, separated
- 3 large egg yolks
- 2 teaspoons vanilla
- ¾ teaspoon grated lemon peel
  About 3¼ cups all-purpose flour
- 1 tablespoon melted butter or margarine
- ¾ cup diced candied orange peel
- ¼ cup whole blanched almonds
- 6 sugar cubes (½ in.), coarsely crushed
  Powdered sugar (optional)

In a large bowl, combine yeast and water; let stand about 5 minutes to soften. Add granulated sugar, salt, the ½ cup butter, the 4 egg yolks, vanilla, lemon peel, and 2 cups of the flour. With an electric mixer, beat at low speed until the flour is moistened, then at high speed until the dough is smooth, stretchy, and glossy, 5 to 10 minutes. Add 1¼ cups flour.

To knead with a dough hook, beat at low speed until flour is moistened, then at high speed until dough is smooth and pulls cleanly from side of bowl. If dough still sticks, add flour 1 tablespoon at a time and continue kneading until dough pulls free (dough will be soft and slightly tacky), 5 to 10 minutes total.

To knead by hand, stir dough with a heavy spoon until flour is moistened. Then scrape dough onto a well-floured board. Knead lightly until smooth and elastic, adding as little flour as possible to prevent sticking (dough will be soft and slightly tacky), 5 to 10 minutes. Return dough to the bowl.

After kneading by either method, cover bowl with plastic wrap and let stand in a warm, draft-free place until the dough has about doubled in volume, 1½ to 2 hours.

Meanwhile, line 1 brown paper lunch bag (about 3½ by 5 in. on bottom) with 1 more bag of the same size. Fold top edges down to form a cuff on the outside; shortened bag should be about 6½ inches tall. Brush inside of bag generously with the melted butter. Set bag upright in a 4- by 8-inch loaf pan.

Punch dough down, then scrape onto a lightly floured board. Sprinkle candied orange peel over dough, a portion at a time, and knead to distribute peel.

Shape dough into a ball and drop into buttered bag. Cover lightly with plastic

Cut panettone into wedges so every piece has a bit of the sugary crust. Inside view reveals porous texture and bits of candied orange peel.

wrap and set in a warm, draft-free place until dough has almost doubled in size, 45 minutes to 1 hour.

Reserve ½ of the nuts for garnish. Finely chop remaining nuts. Gently brush top of risen loaf with reserved egg white, then lightly press reserved whole nuts into top of loaf. Sprinkle with chopped nuts and the coarsely crushed sugar cubes.

Bake in a 350° oven for 30 minutes. (If top browns too fast, cover lightly with foil.) Reduce heat to 325° and continue baking until a long, thin wooden skewer inserted into thickest part comes out clean, 25 to 30 minutes longer. Cool in pan on rack about 10 minutes. Lift out of pan and set on rack to cool further.

Serve warm or cool. (If made ahead, let bread cool, then wrap airtight up to 1 day, or freeze for longer storage; thaw wrapped. Reheat, lightly covered, in a 350° oven until warm, 15 to 20 minutes.) If desired, sift powdered sugar lightly over top of loaf. Tear off bag to serve bread. Cut into wedges or slices. Makes 1 loaf (2 lb. 6 oz.), 8 to 10 servings.

PER OUNCE: 102 calories, 1.9 g protein, 14 g carbohydrates, 4.2 g fat, 37 mg cholesterol, 63 mg sodium

Tear off paper to reveal nut- and sugar-crusted Venetian holiday bread. Bag acts as a mold for soft dough as it bakes, giving it a tall, rustic profile. Offer sweet bread on Easter morning with fruit and coffee.

Taming the Bitter Greens

A TASTE FOR BITTER FOOD *is an acquired pleasure. While some relish the sharp, jolting pungency and the soothing, almost medicinal note that follows, others push the same distinctive morsels to the side of the plate.*

But not the Italians. They savor bitter flavors with a passion, from their Campari apéritif and salads exploding with tongue-tingling sensations to cooked dishes enlivened with acrid accents. Often the bitterness can be traced to the chicory family—Belgian endive, curly endive, escarole, frisée, and radicchio. They all have the same underlying nip.

For maximum effect, use these chicories raw in salads. To tame and mellow their bite, cook them as a vegetable, in risotto, or for pasta. If you're less adventurous, consider the milder greens—escarole, curly endive, or frisée (a fine-leafed variety of curly endive); they acquire a balancing sweetness when cooked.

Escarole, Belgian endive, and curly endive are commonly available in most supermarkets. Look for radicchio and frisée in markets with specialty produce.

Pour shreds of curly chicory cooked in seasoned broth over hot vermicelli.

CHICORY RISOTTO

2 tablespoons olive oil
3 cups shredded Belgian endive (12 oz.) or radicchio (6 oz.); or 5 cups shredded escarole (10 oz.), curly endive (6 oz.), or frisée (10 oz.)
1 tablespoon lemon juice (optional)
3 tablespoons butter or margarine
1 small onion, finely chopped
1 small clove garlic, pressed or minced
1 cup medium-grain white rice or Italian short-grain white rice (such as arborio)

3½ cups regular-strength chicken broth
   Grated parmesan cheese
   Whole leaves of Belgian endive, radicchio, escarole, curly endive, or frisée, rinsed and crisped

Place 1 tablespoon of the olive oil in a 3- to 4-quart pan over high heat. Add shredded chicory (and lemon juice if using radicchio). Stir over high heat until wilted, about 2 minutes. Remove from pan with a slotted spoon and set aside.

Add remaining tablespoon olive oil, 2 tablespoons of the butter, onion, and garlic to pan. Stir occasionally over medium heat until onion is golden, about 5 minutes. Add rice and stir until it looks milky, about 3 minutes. Mix in broth and bring to a boil, stirring often. Adjust heat so rice boils gently; cook uncovered, stirring occasionally, until rice is tender to bite, 15 to 20 minutes. Lower heat and stir more often as mixture thickens.

Stir in cooked chicory. Remove from heat and add remaining butter and ⅓ cup grated parmesan cheese; mix gently. Scoop into warm serving dish. Garnish with whole chicory leaves. Offer additional cheese to add to taste. Makes 4 to 6 servings.

PER SERVING WITH BELGIAN ENDIVE: 238 calories, 4.2 g protein, 29 g carbohydrates, 11 g fat, 15 mg cholesterol, 95 mg sodium

VERMICELLI WITH CHICORY

1 pound dry vermicelli
3 slices (2 to 3 oz. total) pancetta or bacon, thinly slivered
¼ cup olive oil
2 green onions (ends trimmed), thinly sliced
3 parsley sprigs
1¾ cups regular-strength chicken broth
1 teaspoon grated lemon peel
8 cups shredded curly endive (8 oz.), escarole (12 oz.), or frisée (1 lb.); or 6 cups shredded radicchio (12 oz.) or Belgian endive (1½ lb.)
2 tablespoons lemon juice (optional)
   Salt and pepper
   Lemon wedges

Cook the vermicelli in about 3 quarts boiling water, uncovered, until just barely tender to bite, 7 to 9 minutes. Drain and place in a warm serving dish; keep warm.

Meanwhile, in a 12-inch frying pan or 5- to 6-quart pan, stir pancetta over high heat until lightly browned, 2 to 4 minutes. Add oil, green onions, and parsley. Stir until onions are limp.

Radicchio leaf cradles creamy risotto laced with shreds of this mildly bitter red chicory. Present as a first course or as a complement to meats.

Curly endive

Belgian endive

Escarole

Frisée

Radicchio

Add a pungent nip to raw salads with one of these members of the chicory family. Varying in flavor from mild to bitter, they can also be cooked to moderate their acrid bite. Our Italian-inspired recipes use them in risotto, with pasta, and braised as a vegetable.

Add broth and lemon peel. Boil, uncovered, until liquid reduces by about ⅓, about 5 minutes. Remove and discard parsley sprigs. Stir in shredded chicory (and lemon juice if using radicchio). Stir until greens wilt, 2 to 3 minutes. Pour over hot vermicelli.

Add salt, pepper, and lemon to taste. Makes 6 to 8 servings.

PER SERVING WITH CURLY ENDIVE: 342 calories, 8.9 g protein, 45 g carbohydrates, 14 g fat, 7.1 mg cholesterol, 89 mg sodium

BRAISED CHICORY

1 head escarole (¾ to 1 lb.) or curly endive (8 to 12 oz.); or 2 heads frisée (8 oz. each), radicchio (4 oz. each), or Belgian endive (4 oz. each)
  Extra-virgin olive oil
  Salt and pepper
  Lemon wedges

Cut escarole and curly endive lengthwise through the core into quarters. Cut frisée, radicchio, and Belgian endive in half lengthwise. Rinse gently between leaves, keeping quarters or halves of the heads intact. Drain.

To a 10- to 12-inch frying pan over medium-high heat, add 2 tablespoons olive oil. Place chicory, cut side down, in pan. Add 3 tablespoons water. Cover and cook until thickest stems are barely tender when pierced, chicory is lightly browned on bottom, and water has almost evaporated, 3 to 6 minutes. Transfer to serving dish. Add salt, pepper, olive oil, and lemon to taste. Makes 4 servings.

PER SERVING WITH ESCAROLE: 75 calories, 1.1 g protein, 2.9 g carbohydrates, 7.2 g fat, 0 mg cholesterol, 19 mg sodium

Good Old Teleme: A Classic Western Cheese

A WESTERN CLASSIC and a California exclusive, teleme is a creamy white cheese made from whole milk. Once ranked as the best-selling specialty cheese in California, it slipped from attention in the late '60s, when some early producers stopped making it.

The invention of teleme is credited to a Greek cheese maker in Pleasanton, California. Shortly thereafter, production was begun by others, including one California family of Italian heritage, the Pelusos. The Pelusos began commercial distribution in 1925 and, three generations later, still supply Westerners with this distinctive cheese.

Authoritative classifications group teleme with feta. But it's much more like Italy's stracchino in taste and texture. Both cheeses have a mild but refreshingly smooth-tart flavor (without feta's saltiness). Teleme, however, is smoother and creamier throughout; when heated, it melts into a delicate sauce—a property of which these recipes take advantage.

The process of making teleme and feta starts the same way, but feta turns out firm and crumbly; teleme goes the opposite direction, in an operation that's more difficult to control. Not surprisingly, it was an unexpected development in a batch of feta that created teleme.

Teleme is made in 10- to 12-pound blocks. The cheese is ready to eat in about 10 days but can age up to two months. As it ages, it develops more complex flavor and creamier texture.

The cheese is finished in three styles, sometimes identified, sometimes not.

Easiest to recognize is "flour teleme." Blocks of the fresh curd are dusted with rice flour, then aged exposed to air. The surface dries, forming a crust that darkens somewhat as the center ripens to the ideal creaminess. The floured exterior may develop mold, which can be trimmed off. Try flour teleme with fresh fruit, as shown above.

The other ways to finish the cheese both start by sealing blocks of curd in plastic bags. If it gets no further aging, it is sold just as "teleme." If the cheese is then aged, it becomes "semisoft teleme." Compared with the younger cheese, aged teleme is

Creamy, ultrasoft interior shows this teleme cheese is perfectly ripe. Serve with slices of fresh pear and grapes for a delightful dessert.

more flavorful and softer overall. (If you like, you can age young teleme in your refrigerator.) Both forms are crust-free, of uniform color throughout, and protected from surface mold.

To store teleme several days, wrap airtight and chill. Past its prime, teleme gets bitter and has an acrid-stale smell. Frozen teleme keeps longer; it's inclined to crumble, but melts smoothly.

An ounce of teleme has 77 calories, 4.98 grams of protein, 5.87 grams of fat, 1.06 grams of carbohydrates, 150 milligrams of sodium, and 5.1 milligrams of cholesterol. (Cheddar cheese has about a third more calories and twice as much fat.)

Though teleme is widely sold in California supermarkets, cheese shops, and Italian delicatessens, availability elsewhere in the West is spotty—look in Italian delis or cheese shops. But you can order teleme (in cool months, for best quality) from Peluso Cheese: 429 H St., Los Banos, Calif. 93635, or telephone (209) 826-3744. Call to check current price and shipping charges. If you're passing through Los Banos (about 10 minutes east of I-5. 45 minutes east of U.S. 101), you can visit Peluso's retail shop and also see the cheese made. Hours are 10 to 4 weekdays, 10 to 2 Saturdays (no cheese is made on weekends).

Melted Teleme with Brandy & Lemon

- ½ **pound teleme, semisoft teleme, or flour teleme cheese, sliced**
- 1 **baguette (8 oz.), cut into ½-inch diagonal slices**
- 1 **teaspoon coarse-ground pepper**
- 1 **lemon, cut in half or wedges**
- 2 **tablespoons brandy**

Lay teleme slices in a shallow baking dish (about 1½ cups). Also arrange baguette slices in a single layer on a 12- by 15-inch baking sheet.

Bake cheese in a 400° oven until melted and bubbly at edges, 8 to 10 minutes. At the same time, bake bread until crisp and toasted; turn slices for even color and remove from oven as lightly browned, after about 10 minutes.

Set cheese on a heatproof platter, sprinkle with pepper, and place toast and lemon alongside.

In a 2- to 3-cup pan, warm brandy over medium heat until hot. Ignite brandy (not beneath a fan or near flammables) and pour over cheese. When flames die, scoop cheese with a spoon, a portion at a time, onto toast and add squeezes of lemon juice. Makes 4 to 6 appetizer servings or 2 entrée servings.

PER APPETIZER SERVING: 217 calories, 10 g protein, 25 g carbohydrates, 9 g fat, 7.9 mg cholesterol, 420 mg sodium

Teleme with Roasted Vegetables & Chicken

- 2 **medium-size eggplants (about 2 lb. total), stems trimmed off**
  About ¼ cup olive or salad oil
  Roasted vegetables and chicken (directions follow)
- 1 **pound teleme, semisoft teleme, or flour teleme cheese, cut into ½-inch slices**

Cut eggplant into ½-inch-thick rounds. Brush 2 baking pans (each 10 by 15 in.) lightly with oil. Arrange eggplant slices in a single layer. Brush tops of slices lightly with oil. Bake in a 425° oven until slices are well browned and very soft when pressed, about 45 minutes. After 20 minutes, turn slices over and alternate pan positions in oven.

With a wide spatula, transfer all slices to 1 of the pans and set aside. Use the remaining pan to roast the vegetables and chicken.

In a 10- by 12-inch (or 9- by 13-in.) baking dish, arrange half the eggplant slices. Gently spread vegetable-chicken mixture over slices, then top evenly with remaining eggplant. Cover tightly with foil. (If made ahead, cover and chill up until next day.) Bake in a 425° oven until mixture is hot, about 25 minutes.

Lay cheese evenly over vegetables and bake, uncovered, until cheese is melted and hot in center, about 10 minutes. Let stand about 5 minutes, then serve. Makes 6 to 8 servings.

PER SERVING: 387 calories, 21 g protein, 10 g carbohydrates, 27 g fat, 39 mg cholesterol, 420 mg sodium

Roasted vegetables and chicken. In a 10- by 15-inch pan used to bake eggplant, combine 2 tablespoons **olive oil** or salad oil; 2 medium-size **green bell peppers,** stemmed, seeded, and chopped; 1 large **onion,** chopped; 6 medium-size **Roma-style tomatoes** (about ¾ lb. total), cored and cut in half; ½ cup **garlic cloves** (about 20); ½ cup chopped **parsley;** 2 tablespoons **fresh oregano leaves** (or 1 tablespoon crumbled dried oregano leaves); and 1 teaspoon **pepper.** Mix well. Bake in a 425° oven until vegetables are soft and beginning to brown, about 45 minutes; stir with a wide spatula about every 20 minutes. Push vegetables to side of pan.

Lay 4 **chicken thighs** (about 1¼ lb. total) in open space. Continue to bake until thighs are no longer pink in center of thickest part, about 25 minutes. Let cool. Pull chicken from bones; discard bones and chop meat.

In a food processor or blender, combine vegetable mixture and 2 tablespoons drained, **oil-packed dried tomatoes;** whirl until coarsely puréed. Mix with chicken.

Baked teleme, creamy-smooth and flaming with brandy, makes a superb appetizer.

Fresh Herbs Transform a Plain Roast

LIKE GOOD ACCESSORIES, *fresh herbs can transform a plain roast into a stylish and well-dressed star. The make-over process is minimal, and the results are handsome and delicious.*

Coat a pork loin with minced sage and rosemary. Then cloak the back with strips of pancetta (an Italian-style bacon) and sprigs of the fresh herbs. After roasting, the pancetta and herb sprigs turn appealingly crisp and golden.

Cover a split, boned turkey breast with minced fresh thyme, prosciutto, and cheese; then roll, tie, and garnish with sprigs of fresh thyme. When roasted, the herb flavor permeates the meat and also adds a pretty heart of green.

Both roasts can be completely assembled ahead, ready for the oven.

Place sprigs of fresh sage and rosemary on bacon- and herb-coated pork loin roast; tie in several places to secure.

PORK RIB ROAST WITH HERBS

1 center-cut pork loin roast (about 4 lb.)
2 tablespoons olive oil
1 tablespoon minced fresh rosemary or 2 teaspoons crumbled dry rosemary
1 tablespoon minced fresh sage or 1½ teaspoons dry rubbed sage
2 cloves minced garlic
½ teaspoon pepper
¼ teaspoon salt (optional)
5 or 6 slices pancetta or bacon (4 to 5 oz. total)
2 or 3 sprigs (3 to 4 in.) *each* fresh rosemary and sage
Lemon wedges (optional)

Trim excess fat from pork. Mix olive oil, minced rosemary, minced sage, garlic, pepper, and salt. Rub all over roast.

Lay 3 cotton strings, each about 24 inches long, on a board, parallel to each other and about 2 inches apart. Set roast, bone side down, perpendicular to and across center of strings. Lay pancetta slices lengthwise in a single layer over meaty side of roast. Lay sprigs of rosemary and sage over pancetta. Bring strings up and around roast and tie. If needed, tie in a few more places to secure. (If made ahead, cover and chill up until next day.)

Place pork, bone side down, on a rack in a 10- by 15-inch roasting pan. Roast pork in a 325° oven until a thermometer inserted against bone in thickest part reaches 160°, 1½ to 1¾ hours. Transfer roast to serving platter and remove strings. Keep warm and let rest about 10 minutes. Offer lemon to add to taste. Makes 5 or 6 servings.

PER SERVING: 417 calories, 43 g protein, 1.2 g carbohydrates, 26 g fat, 136 mg cholesterol, 164 mg sodium

TURKEY ROAST WITH HERB HEART

1 whole turkey breast (4 to 5 lb.), boned
¼ cup chopped parsley
2 tablespoons minced fresh thyme leaves or 2 teaspoons dry thyme leaves
Salt and pepper
2 ounces thinly sliced fontina cheese
2 ounces thinly sliced prosciutto
3 or 4 sprigs (each 3 to 4 in.) fresh thyme or parsley
1⅓ cups regular-strength chicken broth
½ cup dry white wine
1½ tablespoons cornstarch mixed with 3 tablespoons water

Lay 3 cotton strings, each about 24 inches long, on a board, parallel to each other and about 2 inches apart. Set turkey breast, skin side down, lengthwise and perpendicular to the strings and about 3 inches from one end of strings.

Sprinkle turkey evenly with parsley, minced thyme, and salt and pepper to taste. Lay fontina and prosciutto over surface, overlapping slices. Fold over breast side closest to ends of strings, then turn whole breast over, so top side faces up. Tuck any excess skin under the roast.

Arrange thyme sprigs on top of turkey. Bring ends of center string over roast and tie to secure; tie remaining strings. Also tie lengthwise and crosswise a few more times to make neat and compact. (If done ahead, cover and chill until next day.)

Place roast, skin side up, on a rack in a 10- by 15-inch roasting pan. Roast in a 325° oven until a thermometer inserted in center reads 170°, 1½ to 2 hours. Place on a serving platter and remove strings. Keep warm and let rest 10 to 15 minutes.

Add broth and wine to drippings in roasting pan; set over high heat. Cook, scraping browned bits free. Add cornstarch mixture and stir until boiling. Pour sauce into serving bowl; offer to spoon over slices of meat. Makes 8 to 10 servings.

PER SERVING: 300 calories, 39 g protein, 2.1 g carbohydrates, 14 g fat, 116 mg cholesterol, 219 mg sodium

Layer boned turkey breast with slices of prosciutto and fontina cheese and minced fresh thyme, then fold and tie roast securely. Garnish with additional herb sprigs for extra flavor. When sliced, roasted turkey reveals vein of green herbs and pink prosciutto.

Exotic Tropical Fruits

RECITE THEM QUICKLY *and they sound like a Gilbert and Sullivan patter song: litchi, longan, mangosteen, rambutan. In reality, they are the names of four Asian and Southeast Asian fruits in or closely related to the family Sapindaceae; they have in common a distinctive texture, white color, and range of flavors best defined as exotic.*

About June, litchis and longans occasionally appear fresh in a few markets. Both fruits are grown in Hawaii and Florida. Fresh rambutans and mangosteens from Asia are not allowed in this country; if grown in Mexico, they can be imported.

But all four of these tropical to subtropical fruits are available and quite satisfactory canned; look for them in Asian—Chinese, Filipino, and Thai—food markets. A 1¼-pound can of any of the four kinds of fruits costs about $1.50.

The pictures on the labels don't hint at how good most people agree they taste.

Litchis *(litchees, lychees), by general acclaim, have the best flavor; their taste and crisp-soft-succulent texture are somewhat reminiscent of a peeled muscat grape. Fresh, the round fruit is about 1½ inches in diameter, encased in a thin, leathery brown shell. Inside, the translucent, pearly white fruit surrounds a large, shiny brown pit; the pit is removed before eating or canning.*

Four Asian fruits (mangosteens, rambutans, litchis, and longans) have similar translucent white flesh and intriguing sweet-tart flavor.

Longans *are very much like litchis, except smaller, coarser textured, not quite as flavorful, and often somewhat less expensive. They have another popular and quite descriptive name: dragon's eyes.*

Rambutans, *native to Malaysia and very popular in Southeast Asia, look rather fearsome fresh. Like a litchi, a rambutan has a thin leathery shell, but it is covered with soft, bright red or sometimes yellow spines. The shell peels easily, revealing a white fruit about the size of a litchi; it has a single seed and tastes like a litchi.*

Mangosteens, *also native to Malaysia, are about the size and shape of a small Fuyu persimmon when fresh—with a thick, smooth, brownish purple, leathery hide. Inside, the white fruit is segmented like an orange; each segment may have a small, smooth seed, even when canned.*

You can use these fruits interchangeably in these recipes, but for the most attractive results, we've specified choices.

SHRIMP & LITCHI SALAD

1 **pound medium-large shrimp (36 to 42), shelled except for last section of tails, and deveined**

1 **can (1 lb. 4 oz.) litchis, longans, or rambutans, packed in syrup**

¼ **cup salad oil**

2 **tablespoons lemon juice**

2 **cups sliced European-style cucumber**

4 **cups lightly packed watercress sprigs, washed and crisped**
   Salt
   Freshly ground pepper

Rinse shrimp. Bring 3 quarts water to boiling on high heat in a 5- to 6-quart pan. Add shrimp to boiling water, cover, and remove from heat. Let stand until shrimp are opaque in center (cut to test), 2 to 3 minutes. Drain; let cool.

Drain and reserve fruit syrup. In a bowl, mix oil, 2 tablespoons fruit syrup (save balance of the syrup for other uses), and lemon juice.

If desired, cut fruit pieces in half.

To the bowl add fruit, shrimp, cucumber, and watercress; mix lightly. Divide

Refreshing salad: pink shrimp, white litchis, green watercress and cucumbers.

between 4 dinner plates; add salt and pepper to taste. Makes 4 entrée salads.

PER SERVING: 331 calories, 20 g protein, 30 g carbohydrates, 16 g fat, 140 mg cholesterol, 203 mg sodium

PORK STIR-FRY WITH MANGOSTEENS

1   **can (1 lb. 4 oz.) mangosteens or longans, packed in syrup**
    Teriyaki sauce (recipe follows)
¾   **pound boneless pork, such as loin shoulder, or shoulder or butt**
2   **to 3 tablespoons salad oil**
4   **green onions (ends trimmed), thinly sliced**
1   **whole green onion, ends trimmed**

Drain fruit; reserve syrup for teriyaki sauce. If made ahead, cover fruit and syrup and chill up to overnight.

Trim off and discard most fat and tough connective tissue from pork. Slice meat across the grain into ¹⁄₁₆- to ⅛-inch-thick strips about 3 inches long. Mix meat strips with teriyaki sauce; cover and chill at least 1 hour, or up to overnight.

Place a wok or 10- to 12-inch frying pan over high heat. When hot, add 2 tablespoons oil. Lift ½ the meat from teriyaki sauce with a slotted spoon; add to pan. Stir-fry until meat is lightly browned, about 2 minutes. Lift out with slotted spoon and set aside. Repeat to cook remaining pork; add oil to prevent sticking.

Add marinade, all meat and juices, fruit, and sliced onion to pan. Stir gently until boiling. Spoon onto a platter; garnish with whole onion. Warn your guests that mangosteen sections may have seeds. Makes 4 servings.

PER SERVING: 412 calories, 17 g protein, 30 g carbohydrates, 26 g fat, 60 mg cholesterol, 1,126 mg sodium

Teriyaki sauce. Stir together ¼ cup **soy sauce,** ½ cup reserved **fruit syrup** (preceding; save balance for other uses), 2 tablespoons minced **fresh ginger,** and 1 **garlic clove,** minced or pressed.

RAMBUTANS & BERRIES

1   **can (1 lb. 4 oz.) rambutans or litchis, packed in syrup**
2   **cups strawberries, hulled, rinsed, and drained**
    Toasted almonds (directions follow)

Pour rambutan syrup into glass with canned rambutan and sparkling water. Add a squeeze of fresh lime; sip, then eat the fruit.

Drain fruit and reserve syrup. Cut 4 strawberries in half and set aside.

In a blender or food processor, whirl remaining strawberries, adding ½ cup fruit syrup (reserve extra for other uses), until puréed. Pour purée equally onto 4 rimmed dessert plates. Set equal amounts of rambutans in the center of each plate, and garnish with strawberry halves. Sprinkle fruit with almonds. Makes 4 servings.

Toasted almonds. In a 7- or 8-inch frying pan, gently stir ¼ cup sliced almonds over medium heat until lightly toasted, about 4 minutes. Use warm or cool.

PER SERVING: 158 calories, 1.9 g protein, 34 g carbohydrates, 3.6 g fat, 0 mg cholesterol, 50 mg sodium

PEARL FRUIT COCKTAIL

1   **can (1 lb. 4 oz.) litchis, longans, or rambutans, packed in syrup**
    Ice cubes
    About 2 bottles (28 oz. each) or 7 cups cold sparkling water or mineral water
2   **limes, each cut into 6 to 8 wedges**
    Mint sprigs (optional)

Drain fruit syrup into a small pitcher. Put fruit in a small bowl. Into each glass (6- to 8-oz. size), drop pieces of fruit and several ice cubes.

Fill glasses with sparkling water and add fruit syrup to taste. Squeeze and drop a lime wedge into each glass; add a sprig of mint. Sip liquid, then eat fruit. Makes 6 to 8 servings.

PER SERVING: 55 calories, 0.3 g protein, 15 g carbohydrates, 0.2 g fat, 0 mg cholesterol, 24 mg sodium

Surprisingly Mild Garlic Soups

THE LARGE QUANTITY *of garlic in these soups may startle you. But rest assured: long cooking of even the strongest clove humbles it to a mellow sweetness.*

For a light meal, consider a broth generously flecked with garlic and onion, then topped with toast and a poached egg.

Or for a richer choice, try the creamy soup. New Orleans chef Susan Spicer shared this recipe at the Masters of Food and Wine at the Highlands Inn in Carmel, California.

SPANISH GARLIC SOUP WITH EGG

- 4 slices (½ in. thick, about 3½ in. wide) French bread
- 3 tablespoons olive oil
- ½ cup chopped garlic
- 1 large onion, chopped
- 5 cups regular-strength chicken broth
- 1 dry bay leaf
- 4 large eggs
- ¼ cup chopped parsley
  Salt and pepper

Brush both sides of bread lightly with oil, using about 1 tablespoon total. Place in a single layer on a rack in a 10- by 15-inch pan. Bake in a 325° oven until firm and golden, 20 to 25 minutes.

Meanwhile, in a 3- to 4-quart pan, combine remaining 2 tablespoons oil, garlic, and onion. Stir often over medium heat until onion is very limp, about 15 minutes. Add broth and bay leaf. Cover and simmer 15 to 20 minutes.

Crack eggs carefully into simmering broth, adding 2 at a time. Cover and simmer just until whites are barely set and yolks are still soft, about 3 minutes. Lift out eggs with a slotted spoon and set each egg on a piece of toast. Repeat with remaining eggs. Ladle equal portions of soup into 4 bowls. Set a piece of toast with egg in each bowl, then sprinkle equally with parsley. Add salt and pepper to taste. Makes 4 servings.

PER SERVING: 325 calories, 13 g protein, 26 g carbohydrates, 19 g fat, 275 mg cholesterol, 286 mg sodium

CREAMY GARLIC-THYME SOUP

- 1 cup chopped garlic
- 4 tablespoons olive oil
- 3 large onions, coarsely chopped
- 6 cups regular-strength chicken broth
  Herb bundle (directions follow)
- ⅓ pound French bread, cut into about 1-inch chunks (about 4 cups)
- 2 tablespoons chopped fresh thyme leaves or 1½ teaspoons dry thyme leaves
- ½ cup whipping cream
  Salt and pepper
  Fresh chives or fresh thyme sprigs (optional)

In a 3- to 4-quart pan, combine 3 tablespoons garlic and 2 tablespoons of the oil. Cook over medium heat, stirring, just until garlic is golden, about 5 minutes. Lift out garlic and set aside.

Add remaining garlic, oil, and onion. Stir often over medium heat until mixture is a light gold, about 30 minutes. Add broth, herb bundle, bread, and thyme. Simmer, covered, 20 to 30 minutes. Lift out and discard herb bundle.

In a blender or food processor, whirl soup, a portion at a time, until smoothly puréed. Return to pan and add cream. Stir over medium heat until hot. Add salt and pepper to taste. Ladle into a large tureen or 6 to 8 bowls. Add equal amounts of the fried garlic and chives to each portion. Makes 6 to 8 servings.

PER SERVING: 231 calories, 5.7 g protein, 23 g carbohydrates, 13 g fat, 17 mg cholesterol, 158 mg sodium

Herb bundle. Tie together or wrap in a piece of cheesecloth 10 sprigs (3 to 4 in. each) **parsley**, 5 sprigs (3 to 4 in. each) **fresh thyme**, and 1 **dry bay leaf.**

Egg poached in broth floats on toast in surprisingly mild-tasting, garlic-laden soup. To remove garlic skin easily, first crush cloves slightly with flat edge of knife.

Simple but Hearty Beef Stews

ON A COLD EVENING, *succulent hot stew is inviting fare. Its rich and simple flavors are warm and satisfying. Like most stews, these two are hearty. Both center on beef.*

In the first recipe, oxtails (actually beef, not from oxen) bake alongside an assortment of vegetables. Oven cooking makes these bulky ingredients easy to handle and serve. A splash of red wine finishes the full-flavored sauce. In the second dish, beef chuck simmers to tenderness with a generous dose of onions, dark beer, and a touch of herbs.

BAKED OXTAIL & VEGETABLE STEW

 6 pounds disjointed oxtails, fat trimmed
 1 quart regular-strength beef broth
 3 tablespoons all-purpose flour
 6 cloves garlic, minced or pressed
 2 tablespoons tomato paste
 1 teaspoon dry thyme leaves
 1 dry bay leaf
 12 small (1½-in.-diameter) thin-skinned potatoes, scrubbed
 12 small (1½-in.-diameter) onions, peeled if desired
 6 small turnips (2-in. diameter; 1 lb. total), ends trimmed, peeled if desired
 12 small carrots (1 lb. total), peeled
    About ¼ cup dry red wine
 1 package (10 oz.) frozen petite peas
    Salt and pepper

Set oxtails in a single layer in an oiled, deep, 12- by 17-inch roasting pan. Roast, uncovered, in a 475° oven for 30 minutes, then turn oxtails over. Continue to roast until juices around meat begin to brown, about 30 minutes longer. Spoon out and discard fat.

Mix broth with flour, garlic, tomato paste, thyme, and bay leaf. Add to meat; scrape browned bits free. Cover pan with foil and bake at 425° for 1 hour.

Turn oxtails over; push to 1 side of pan. Add potatoes, onions, and turnips to cleared end of pan. Bake, covered, for 30 minutes. Turn meat and vegetables over. Add carrots; cover and bake until meat and vegetables are very tender when pierced, about 45 minutes longer.

Turn vegetables and meat in sauce, then lift out and arrange separately on a large platter; keep warm. Skim and dis-

card fat from sauce; add enough wine to make 1¾ cups. Place over high heat and bring to a simmer, stirring to loosen browned bits. Add peas; stir just until hot, then lift peas with a slotted spoon to platter. Pour sauce into a bowl; serve with stew. Add salt and pepper to taste. Makes 6 servings.

PER SERVING: 526 calories, 46 g protein, 41 g carbohydrates, 21 g fat, cholesterol not available, 397 mg sodium

FLEMISH BEEF STEW

 2 pounds boned beef chuck (fat trimmed), cut into 1½-inch pieces
 ¼ pound salt pork, diced (or 4 slices bacon, chopped)
 3 cups dark beer, ale, or stout
 3 large onions, sliced
 2 tablespoons all-purpose flour
 1 dry bay leaf
 1 teaspoon dry thyme leaves

 ⅓ cup minced parsley
    Parsley or celery sprigs, optional
    Toast triangles
    Salt and pepper

Place beef, pork, and ½ cup of the beer in a 5- to 6-quart pan. Cover and simmer over medium heat for 30 minutes. Add onions. Cook uncovered, stirring occasionally, until liquid evaporates and juices and onions are brown and stick to pan, 30 to 35 minutes. Add flour; stir gently for 30 seconds. Add remaining beer, scraping browned bits free. Stir in bay leaf, thyme, and minced parsley.

Cover and simmer over low heat, stirring occasionally, until meat is very tender when pierced, about 1 hour longer. Garnish with parsley sprigs. Serve with toast triangles and season to taste with salt and pepper. Makes 4 to 6 servings.

PER SERVING: 454 calories, 32 g protein, 13 g carbohydrates, 30 g fat, 115 mg cholesterol, 395 mg sodium

Glazed with sauce, stew combines oxtails, potatoes, turnips, onions, peas, and carrots.

It's Rhubarb Time

ROSY-COLORED RHUBARB *is most tender and pink when hothouse grown —the only choice in the market now. Although a vegetable, rhubarb is treated like a fruit. It's intensely tart and crisp, so it needs cooking to make it soft and sweetening to make it palatable. The tender coffee cake and creamy pudding use rhubarb this way. But raw, sour rhubarb, used discreetly, is also interesting, as in the salsa for the orange salad.*

Select crisp, brightly colored, unblemished stalks trimmed of leaves. The dark green leaves are dangerously toxic.

Cooked strawberry-rhubarb filling peeks through chunky streusel topping on butter-tender coffee cake. Serve with coffee or tea.

ORANGE SALAD WITH RHUBARB SALSA

- ¾ cup finely diced rhubarb
- 2 tablespoons sugar
- ¾ cup finely diced peeled jicama
- 6 large red radishes, finely diced
  Ginger dressing (recipe follows)
- 6 large butter lettuce leaves, washed and crisped
- 3 large oranges, peeled, with white membrane cut off

In a bowl, combine rhubarb and sugar; let stand until juices form, about 30 minutes. Add jicama, radishes, and ginger dressing; mix well. Set salsa aside.

Line each of 6 salad plates with a lettuce leaf. Thinly slice oranges crosswise; arrange equal portions on lettuce. Spoon salsa onto oranges. Serves 6.

PER SERVING: 98 calories, 1.3 g protein, 24 g carbohydrates, 0.4 g fat, 0 mg cholesterol, 7.8 mg sodium

Ginger dressing. Stir together 3 tablespoons **rice wine vinegar**, 2 tablespoons finely minced **crystallized ginger**, and 1 tablespoon finely shredded **orange peel**.

STRAWBERRY-RHUBARB COFFEE CAKE WITH CRUNCH TOPPING

- 2 cups all-purpose flour
- ¾ cup sugar
- 1 tablespoon baking powder
- ½ teaspoon baking soda
- ½ cup (¼ lb.) butter or margarine, cut into small pieces
- 2 large eggs
- 1 cup buttermilk
- 1 teaspoon vanilla
  Strawberry-rhubarb filling (recipe follows)
  Crunch topping (recipe follows)

In a large bowl, stir together flour, sugar, baking powder, and baking soda. Using a pastry blender or your fingers, cut or rub butter into flour mixture until coarse crumbs form.

Beat eggs to blend with buttermilk and vanilla; stir into flour mixture just until evenly moistened.

Spread batter in a buttered 2-inch deep 7- by 11-inch or 9- by 13-inch baking dish. Evenly spoon filling onto batter; coarsely crumble topping over filling.

Bake in a 350° oven until a toothpick inserted in center (not in filling) comes out clean, 50 to 60 minutes. Serve warm or cool. Cut into 8 to 10 pieces. Makes 8 to 10 servings. —*Carol Van Brocklin, Port Angeles, Wash.*

PER SERVING: 423 calories, 6.2 g protein, 62 g carbohydrates, 17 g fat, 97 mg cholesterol, 366 mg sodium

Strawberry-rhubarb filling. In a 2- to 3-quart pan over medium heat, combine 2½ cups **rhubarb,** cut into ½-inch pieces; 1½ cups **strawberries,** rinsed, hulled, and sliced; and ½ cup **sugar.** Cover and cook, stirring occasionally, until rhubarb is soft when pierced, about 5 minutes. Combine 2 tablespoons **cornstarch** with 2 tablespoons **water;** add to rhubarb mixture. Bring to a boil, stirring. Let the mixture cool.

Crunch topping. Combine ¾ cup **all-purpose flour** and ¼ cup **sugar.** With a pastry blender or with your fingers, cut or rub ⅓ cup **butter** or margarine into flour mixture until fine crumbs form.

With your hands, squeeze the mixture into large lumps.

RHUBARB CREAM

- 1½ cups rhubarb, cut into ¼-inch pieces
- 5 tablespoons sugar
- ¼ cup water
- 1 tablespoon grated orange peel
- 1 tablespoon orange-flavor liqueur
- 1 large egg white
- ½ cup whipping cream

Combine rhubarb, ¼ cup sugar, water, and 1 teaspoon of the orange peel in a 1- to 1½-quart pan over medium-high heat; cover. Bring to a boil; reduce heat and simmer until rhubarb is very soft when pierced, 5 to 7 minutes. Stir in liqueur, then cover and chill rhubarb until cold, about 2 hours.

Whip egg white until foamy. Gradually add remaining sugar, beating until white holds stiff, moist peaks. In another bowl whip cream with same (unrinsed) beaters until it holds soft peaks. With rubber spatula, gently fold rhubarb mixture and egg white into cream, blending only until purée runs through cream in streaks. Spoon mixture into 4 stemmed dessert glasses (8- to 10-oz. size). Garnish with reserved orange peel. Serve, or cover and chill up to 6 hours. Makes 4 servings.

PER SERVING: 173 calories, 1.9 g protein, 20 g carbohydrates, 9.3 g fat, 33 mg cholesterol, 25 mg sodium

Lace Eggs

IT LOOKS LIKE DELICATE FILIGREE, *but this egg is actually squiggles of melted chocolate piped over a styrene foam form. When the chocolate hardens, the curlicues become a shell. Fill shells with chocolate mousse for a make-ahead Easter dessert.*

Look for the styrene foam eggs at crafts supply stores.

CHOCOLATE LACE EGGS

White chocolate varies widely in how it melts. For this recipe, the small baking chips work best (the larger deluxe baking pieces do not melt smoothly).

1¼ cups (8 oz.) **white or semisweet chocolate baking chips**
   Chocolate mousse (recipe follows)

1 cup **raspberries**, rinsed and drained

Place chocolate in the top of a double boiler. Set pan over hot (not simmering) water and stir occasionally until chocolate is melted and smooth, about 4 minutes. Remove from water, then let chocolate cool to lukewarm, about 100°.

Meanwhile, cut three 3½-inch- or four 3-inch-long styrene foam eggs in half lengthwise. Wrap each half tightly in plastic wrap, pulling excess wrap over flat (or cut) side of egg; secure with tape. Curved side of egg should be smooth.

Line a 12- by 15-inch baking sheet with plastic wrap. Set eggs, flat side down and about 2 inches apart, on pan. Fill a pastry bag fitted with an ⅛-inch plain tip with chocolate (or use a spoon); drizzle chocolate over eggs in a thick lacy pat-

White chocolate egg holds a delicious surprise—white chocolate mousse and tart raspberries.

Pipe melted chocolate over wrapped styrene foam form, crossing lines often.

tern to within ¼ inch of cut edges of egg. Chill until firm, about 10 minutes.

Carefully remove form from shell by pulling on excess plastic wrap on back; or use a fork inserted in flat side of form. If made ahead, cover and chill up to 3 days.

To serve, fill half of the shells with equal portions of mousse; top with a few berries. Set each filled shell on a plate. Cover with remaining chocolate shells. Garnish with remaining berries. Makes 3 large or 4 medium servings.

PER MEDIUM SERVING: 551 calories, 6.6 g protein, 60 g carbohydrates, 32 g fat, 36 mg cholesterol, 101 mg sodium

Chocolate mousse. In the top of a double boiler, stir ⅔ cup (4 oz.) **white** or semisweet **chocolate baking chips** over hot (not simmering) water until smooth. In a small bowl, beat 2 **large egg whites** until foamy. Gradually beat in 2 teaspoons **sugar,** beating until stiff peaks form. Fold in melted chocolate. In a small bowl, beat ⅓ cup **whipping cream** until stiff; fold into egg white mixture. Cover and chill at least 1 hour or up to next day. Makes 1¾ cups.

Sour cream swirled into hot broccoli and potato soup makes a pretty finish; stir cream first to soften.

CREAM OF BROCCOLI SOUP

- 1 small onion, chopped
- 1 tablespoon salad oil
- 3 cups water
- 2 cups milk
- 4 chicken bouillon cubes
- ¾ pound thin-skinned potatoes, peeled, cut into 1-inch chunks
- 1½ pounds broccoli, rinsed
  About 1 cup sour cream

In a 4- to 5-quart pan on medium heat, stir onion in oil often until lightly browned, about 10 minutes. Add water, milk, bouillon, and potatoes. Bring to a boil on high heat; cover and simmer until potatoes are almost tender when pierced, about 10 minutes.

Peel broccoli stems; slice ⅛ inch thick. Add stems and flowerets to broth. Simmer until vegetables are tender when pierced, about 15 minutes longer.

Scoop half of the vegetables into a blender; whirl with enough broth to smoothly purée. Set mixture aside, then purée remaining vegetables. Return mixture to pan (if made ahead, cover and chill up to overnight; reheat to continue). Ladle soup into bowls. Add sour cream to taste. Makes 2 quarts, 6 to 8 servings. —*Paula Bohlman, Loma Linda, Calif.*

PER SERVING: 174 calories, 6.6 g protein, 16 g carbohydrates, 10 g fat, 21 mg cholesterol, 623 mg sodium

Greek-style meat loaf makes good sandwiches with mint leaves, onion, tomato, feta cheese, and cucumber.

GYROS MEAT LOAF

- 2½ pounds ground lean lamb
- 1 can (8 oz.) tomato sauce
- 1 cup *each* minced onion and green bell pepper
- ½ cup fine dry bread crumbs
- 2 large eggs
- ¼ cup chopped fresh mint leaves
- 2 teaspoons *each* pepper, dry oregano leaves, and dry basil leaves
- 1 teaspoon dry rosemary
- 2 cloves garlic, minced
  Salt (optional)

In a bowl, combine lamb, tomato sauce, onion, bell pepper, crumbs, eggs, mint, pepper, oregano, basil, rosemary, garlic, and ½ teaspoon salt. Squeeze mixture with your hands to mix very well.

Firmly press meat into a 5- by 9-inch loaf pan. Bake, uncovered, in a 350° oven until well browned on top, about 1½ hours. Let stand until lukewarm. Tilt pan and drain off juices. Invert loaf onto a plate and turn brown side up. Serve warm or cold. If made ahead, cover and chill up to 1 day. Add salt to taste. Makes 8 to 10 servings. —*Andrea Libberton, Mill Valley, Calif.*

PER SERVING: 228 calories, 25 g protein, 7.8 g carbohydrates, 10 g fat, 140 mg cholesterol, 246 mg sodium

Browned bacon bits, pine nuts, and shallots dress warm asparagus.

ASPARAGUS WITH BACON & PINE NUTS

- 1 to 1½ pounds asparagus, tough ends trimmed off
- ¼ pound bacon, chopped
- 1 tablespoon olive oil (optional)
- 2 tablespoons pine nuts
- 2 tablespoons minced shallots
- ¼ teaspoon *each* pepper and ground nutmeg

In a 10- to 12-inch frying pan on high heat, bring 1 inch water to boiling. Lay asparagus in water. Cook, uncovered, until spears are tender when pierced, 4 to 6 minutes; drain. Remove asparagus and set aside. (If made ahead, immerse in ice water to cool; drain and let stand up to 4 hours.)

In the frying pan on medium heat, stir bacon often until nearly crisp. Discard all but 1 tablespoon fat; or discard all the fat and add olive oil. Add pine nuts, shallots, pepper, and nutmeg. Stir often on medium heat until nuts are golden, about 3 minutes. With a slotted spoon, remove mixture from pan and set aside.

Turn heat to high; add asparagus and shake until hot, about 1 minute. Pour asparagus onto a platter and top with bacon mixture. Serves 4 to 6. —*Carmela M. Meely, Walnut Creek, Calif.*

PER SERVING: 73 calories, 3.6 g protein, 2.6 g carbohydrates, 5.9 g fat, 6 mg cholesterol, 97 mg sodium

FIVE SPICE ROAST CHICKEN

1 teaspoon salad oil
1½ teaspoons Chinese five spice, or ½ teaspoon *each* anise seed and ground ginger and ¼ teaspoon *each* ground cinnamon and ground cloves
3 tablespoons soy sauce
1 tablespoon *each* sugar and dry sherry
1 clove garlic, minced
1 broiler-fryer chicken (4½ to 5 lb.)
3 tablespoons minced green onion

In a 2- to 3-cup pan, stir oil with five spice on medium heat until hot. Add soy, sugar, sherry, and garlic.

Rinse chicken and pat dry; reserve giblets for other uses. Put chicken, breast up, on a rack in a 9- by 13-inch pan; rub generously with five spice mixture. Pour remaining sauce into cavity of bird. Roast, uncovered, in a 375° oven until chicken is no longer pink at thigh bone (cut to test), about 1 hour.

Drain juices from chicken cavity into pan, then put bird on a platter. Stir juices to free browned bits; pour sauce into a small pitcher and skim off fat; add onion. Offer sauce with chicken. Makes 4 servings. —*Doreen Holton, Maui, Hawaii.*

PER SERVING: 573 calories, 62 g protein, 5.7 g carbohydrates, 32 g fat, 198 mg cholesterol, 957 mg sodium

Chinese seasonings flavor crisp roast chicken; serve with its own drippings and fresh cilantro sprigs.

STRAW & HAY PASTA

4 ounces *each* green and white dry vermicelli or other thinly cut dry pasta (or all green or all white pasta)
1¼ cups half-and-half (light cream) or 1½ cups whipping cream
⅓ to ½ cup thinly sliced cooked ham, cut into slivers
⅓ cup frozen petite peas
⅓ to ¾ cup grated parmesan cheese

In a 4- to 5-quart pan over high heat, bring 1 to 2 quarts water to boiling. Add pasta and cook, uncovered, until tender-firm to bite, about 6 minutes.

Meanwhile, in a 4- to 5-quart pan, combine half-and-half, ham, and peas. Stir often on medium-high heat until steaming. (Or pour whipping cream into pan and boil, uncovered, on high heat until reduced to 1¼ cups. Stir in ham and peas; simmer 1 to 2 minutes to thaw peas.) Remove from heat.

Drain pasta and pour into cream mixture. With 2 forks, lift pasta to mix with cream; do this several times for 3 to 4 minutes. Pasta will absorb much of the liquid. Then add ⅓ cup of the cheese and mix well. Serve pasta, adding more cheese to taste. Serves 4. —*Gladys Kent, Port Angeles, Wash.*

PER SERVING: 374 calories, 16 g protein, 47 g carbohydrates, 14 g fat, 67 mg cholesterol, 355 mg sodium

White and green pastas (straw and hay) are classic duo; here the sauce is light.

QUEEN MAUD'S NORWEGIAN PUDDING

1 cup milk
5 egg yolks
⅓ cup sugar
1 teaspoon vanilla
2 cups whipping cream
3 ounces semisweet chocolate, grated
Sweet marsala (optional)

In a 1- to 2-quart pan, warm milk over medium-high heat until steaming. In a bowl, beat together egg yolks and sugar; whisk in ¼ cup hot milk. Return egg-milk mixture to pan. Stir on medium-low heat until mixture is thick enough to smoothly coat the back of a metal spoon, 10 to 12 minutes. Remove from heat; stir vanilla into custard. Cover lightly and chill until cold, about 1½ hours.

Whip the cream until it will hold stiff peaks. Gently fold custard into cream. Pour half the custard mixture into 8 dessert bowls or wine glasses (at least ¾-cup size). Sprinkle desserts evenly with ¾ of the chocolate. Top evenly with remaining custard, then sprinkle with remaining chocolate. Serve, or cover lightly and chill 2 to 6 hours. Offer marsala to pour onto individual desserts. Makes 8 servings. —*Jan Sheldon, San Lorenzo, Calif.*

PER SERVING: 320 calories, 4.5 g protein, 18 g carbohydrates, 27 g fat, 241 mg cholesterol, 41 mg sodium

Norwegian cream and custard pudding is velvety smooth; chocolate and marsala embellish.

THE LOVE AFFAIR *between chili and the Chef of the West continues to smolder (and occasionally flare into a case of heartburn). It's a wonder that no artistic or literary monument—a painting, a statue, an opera, a play, or a sonnet cycle—exists to celebrate this pure passion. But there are problems: what would a statue of chili look like in bronze, marble, or wood? And what would rhyme with garlic or cilantro?*

Perhaps the easiest way out would be a painting—part historical and part allegorical—of The Birth of Chili. *It might best be done in the style of Sir Lawrence Alma-Tadema's classical processions—with appropriate adjustments for time (the present) and place (the Southwest): maidens in shawls lead a sacrificial steer toward a temple; the steer is decked in chili pods, which garland his neck and drape in a swag between his horns; and from crowded balconies people pelt the participants with cilantro sprigs.*

At the left, wearing his chef's hat and holding a knife, stands the priest, flanked by a cauldron and an altar, and holding a can of tomatoes and a can of beer. If the beer strikes you as a discordant element here, don't tell Jack Carmody. His chili employs a can of beer as its liquid ingredient—and to very good effect.

HAVE-A-BEER CHILI

1 pound mild or hot Italian
    sausages, casings removed
1 pound boneless lean beef chuck,
    cut into 1-inch cubes
1 pound boneless lean pork
    shoulder or butt, cut into
    1-inch cubes
2 medium-size onions, chopped
2 cloves garlic, minced or pressed
1 can (28 oz.) tomatoes
¼ cup dehydrated masa flour (corn
    tortilla flour)
1 can (12 oz., or 1½ cups) beer
2 tablespoons chili powder
1 tablespoon paprika
1 teaspoon *each* dry oregano leaves
    and ground cumin
⅛ teaspoon cayenne
½ cup chopped fresh cilantro
    (coriander)
3 tablespoons lemon juice
1 can (7 oz.) green chili salsa

"It's a wonder that no artistic monument exists to celebrate chili."

1 medium-size fresh jalapeño chili,
    stemmed, seeded, and chopped
1 large green bell pepper, stemmed,
    seeded, and chopped
    Condiments (suggestions follow)

Coarsely chop or crumble sausages and put into a 6- to 8-quart pan. Stirring often, cook over medium-high heat until sausages are well browned, about 15 minutes; lift out meat and set aside. Discard all but 2 tablespoons of the drippings. Add beef and pork to pan, a portion at a time, and stir often until browned, about 20 minutes; set aside as browned. Add onions and garlic to pan and stir often until onions are limp,

about 10 minutes. Stir in tomatoes (break up with a spoon) and their liquid, masa, beer, chili powder, paprika, oregano, cumin, cayenne, cilantro, lemon juice, salsa, jalapeño, and bell pepper.

Return meats and any juice to pan. Bring to a boil over high heat; reduce heat, cover, and simmer until meats are very tender when pierced, about 2 hours. Stir occasionally.

Skim off any fat, then ladle chili into serving bowl. Offer condiments to add to individual servings. Makes about 10 servings, 1-cup size.

PER SERVING WITHOUT CONDIMENTS: 371 calories, 25 g protein, 12 g carbohydrates, 24 g fat, 92 mg cholesterol, 660 mg sodium

Condiments. Offer in separate bowls: 1 or 2 large **avocados,** peeled, pitted, and sliced; about 1 cup **sour cream;** 1 to 1½ cups (4 to 6 oz.) shredded **cheddar cheese.**

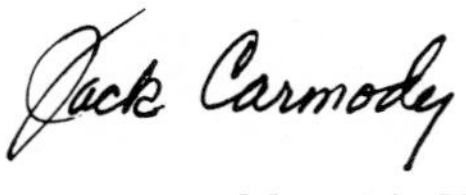

Jack Carmody

Mountain View, Calif.

S OME LITTLE MASOCHISTIC *streak in our taste buds makes them want to live dangerously, to seek thrills by daring fire. Why else would we try the incredibly sour, salty, and hot Indian pickled limes, the sour and salty Japanese pickled plums, the corrosive horseradish and jalapeño? John Endresen has a relish that will satisfy the thrill seeker's tongue without disabling it. Try this on sausages or hamburgers.*

PIQUANT RELISH

    3 tablespoons Dijon mustard
    2 to 3 tablespoons minced jalapeño
       chilies
    ⅓ cup finely chopped mild onion
    1 tablespoon lemon juice
       Grilled sausages, frankfurters, or
       hamburgers

In a small bowl, stir together mustard, jalapeños, onion, and lemon juice. Serve, or cover and chill up to 2 days. Spoon onto meats to taste. Makes about ⅔ cup.

PER TABLESPOON: 8.2 calories, 0.1 g protein, 1.2 g carbohydrates, 0.3 g fat, 0 mg cholesterol, 135 mg sodium

John A. Endresen

Bothell, Wash.

Q UICK BREADS—*biscuits, cornbread, muffins, and their kin—have always been favorites of mainstream America. Homey and comforting, as opposed to haute cuisine, they are not likely to appear with your average $45 prix fixe dinner. Nevertheless, muffins have recently become rather fashionable—not as a mainstay but rather as a less sweet, less caloric alternative to dessert cakes with tea or coffee. Muffin shops sell them in a wide variety of flavors and seem to vie with each other for the largest possible muffins with the highest, broadest hats.*

Richard Schock's Oat Bran Muffins are high in flavor and fiber, relatively low in sugar and cholesterol.

OAT BRAN MUFFINS

    2½ cups oat bran
     2 cups buttermilk
     1 cup nonfat milk
     ½ cup raisins
     1 large egg
     ⅓ cup olive oil or salad oil
     ½ cup firmly packed brown sugar
    1½ cups whole-wheat flour
     1 teaspoon *each* baking soda,
        baking powder, and ground
        cinnamon
     ½ teaspoon ground allspice
     ½ teaspoon salt
     ½ cup chopped walnuts (optional)

In a large bowl, stir together oat bran, buttermilk, milk, and raisins. Let stand 20 minutes; stir once or twice. Add egg, oil, and sugar; stir until well blended.

In another bowl, stir together the flour, soda, baking powder, cinnamon, allspice, and salt. Add to oat bran mixture and stir until blended. Mix in nuts.

Spoon batter into 18 paper-lined 2½-inch muffin cups, filling each flush with top. Bake in a 400° oven until muffins are well browned and top springs back when lightly pressed, 30 to 35 minutes. Makes 1½ dozen muffins.

PER MUFFIN: 170 calories, 5.5 g protein, 25 g carbohydrates, 5.7 g fat, 17 mg cholesterol, 173 mg sodium

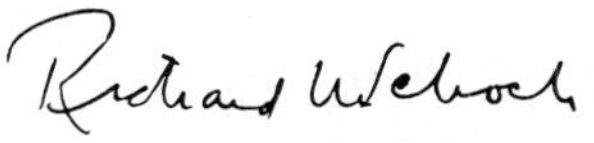

Richard Webock

Escondido, Calif.

I N THE CUISINE OF INDIA, *the making of curries is an art of great complexity. The cook prepares a complicated blend of spices for each meat, fish, or vegetable by following regional tradition and family preference. Curry powder is a compromise for those who have neither the time, the tradition, nor maybe even the spices for the ancient way. It is a worthwhile compromise, since curry powders are generally of high quality; they also enable you to vary the intensity by altering the amount of powder used.*

This curry is mild and does not overpower the delicate shrimp. Coconut milk contributes considerable character to the dish, too, with its mellowing sweetness. The condiments you serve alongside lend

visual excitement, a variety of flavors, and a sense of audience participation.

HAWAIIAN SHRIMP CURRY

    6 tablespoons butter or margarine
    1 medium-size onion, chopped
    6 tablespoons all-purpose flour
    2 teaspoons chopped fresh ginger
    2 tablespoons curry powder
   1½ cups *each* canned coconut milk
       and regular milk
   1½ pounds shelled cooked tiny
       shrimp
       Salt
       Hot cooked rice
       Condiments (suggestions follow)

Melt butter in a 4- to 5-quart pan over medium heat. Add onion; stir often until limp, about 10 minutes. Add flour, ginger, and curry powder, stirring for 1 to 2 minutes. Remove from heat and add coconut and regular milk; stir to blend smoothly with flour mixture. Return to medium heat; stir until just simmering. Add shrimp and mix gently until hot. Salt to taste. Serve curry with rice and condiments to add to taste. Serves 6 to 8.

PER SERVING CURRY WITHOUT RICE AND CONDIMENTS: 302 calories, 21 g protein, 9.5 g carbohydrates, 20 g fat, 196 mg cholesterol, 308 mg sodium

Condiments. Offer 3 or 4 of the following: about ¼ cup chopped **Major Grey chutney;** 4 to 6 slices crisply cooked and crumbled **bacon;** 1 **lime,** cut into wedges; about ½ cup thinly sliced **green onion;** 2 chopped hard-cooked **large eggs;** about ½ cup **salted peanuts;** 1 medium-size ripe **banana,** peeled and sliced; about ¼ cup **raisins;** ½ cup fresh **cilantro** (coriander) **leaves.**

John Young

Scottsdale, Ariz.

"The curry is mild and doesn't overpower the delicate shrimp."

March Menus

THE EBBING OF WINTER *and the promise of spring make it difficult to plan menus in March. We've split the choices. The first is a warming, substantial, slow-cooked oven meal. The second is a lighter, grill-cooked dinner, which goes together quickly for the occasional warm evening.*

Breakfast comes from a jar full of chunky, wholesome, fruit-laden cookies that make hand-held substitutes for cereal.

**RIB SUPPER
FROM THE OVEN**

Country-style Ribs with Sauerkraut,
New Potatoes & Mustard Greens
Applesauce
Hot Fudge Ice Cream Sundaes
Gamay   Milk

When you expect to be home for a 3-hour stretch, be a lazy cook. Tuck meaty country-style pork ribs and sauerkraut in to bake. Add potatoes later, then cook the greens in the roasting juices, making a one-dish meal for hearty appetites.

Add potatoes to pan after ribs have cooked 1½ hours. Buy or make applesauce. Warm fudge sauce, homemade or purchased, to flow over ice cream.

COUNTRY-STYLE RIBS WITH SAUERKRAUT, NEW POTATOES & MUSTARD GREENS

- 1 **large can (27 oz.) sauerkraut, drained**
- 3 **pounds country-style pork ribs**
- 1 **tablespoon coarse-ground pepper**
- 8 **small thin-skinned potatoes (about 1½-in. diameter; about 1 lb. total), scrubbed**
  About 1 pound mustard greens
- 1 **tablespoon prepared horseradish**

Pour sauerkraut into a colander and rinse with cool, running water; let drain. In a 10- by 14-inch roasting pan, evenly spread sauerkraut. Lay the pork ribs on sauerkraut down the center of the pan; sprinkle with pepper. Tightly cover pan with foil. Bake in a 375° oven for 1½ hours.

Remove foil, turn ribs over, and tuck the potatoes into sauerkraut around the ribs. Bake, uncovered, until ribs are browned and meat and potatoes are very tender when pierced, about 50 minutes.

Meanwhile, rinse mustard greens. Cut or tear off tough stems and discard. Cut into strips about ½ inch wide.

With a slotted spoon, gently transfer ribs, potatoes, and sauerkraut to a platter; keep warm. Set pan with juices over medium-high heat; add mustard greens and horseradish. Stir until greens are limp and a darker green. Spoon greens and juices into a bowl, or alongside ribs. Makes 4 servings. —*Iris Harris, Carmel, Calif.*

PER SERVING: 611 calories, 31 g protein, 31 g carbohydrates, 41 g fat, 117 mg cholesterol, 549 mg sodium

Baked together, country-style pork ribs, sauerkraut, and small potatoes go with mustard greens and applesauce.

Small chunks of chicken breast, skewered, cook fast on the barbecue. To save time, buy boned and skinned breasts.

The quickest route is to first season the chicken, then heat the barbecue. Next, make the yogurt sauce, and skewer the chicken while bringing broth to boil for the couscous. This tiny pasta doesn't need cooking; it warms and swells in hot broth. Then, as the chicken grills, slice the vegetables and fruit.

CHICKEN-ON-A-STICK WITH COUSCOUS

1¼	**pounds boned and skinned chicken breasts**
⅓	**cup lemon juice**
⅓	**cup olive or salad oil**
¼	**cup dry white wine**
6	**cloves garlic, minced or pressed**
2	**dry bay leaves, crumbled**
	Couscous (recipe follows)
	Salt and pepper

Rinse chicken, pat dry, and cut into about ¾-inch chunks. In a bowl, combine chicken, lemon juice, oil, wine, garlic, and bay leaves; mix to blend ingredients. Cover and chill 15 minutes to 4 hours.

Lift meat from marinade; reserve marinade. Divide meat into 8 equal portions. Thread each portion on a slender skewer (you'll need 8, each at least 6 in. long). Lay skewered chicken on a grill 4 to 6 inches above a solid bed of medium-hot coals (you should be able to hold your hand at grill level only 3 to 4 seconds).

Cook chicken, basting with marinade and turning as needed, until meat is lightly browned and no longer pink in center of thickest piece (cut to test), about 10 minutes. Place 2 skewers of

Ladle cumin-garlic yogurt sauce onto barbecued chicken, couscous, and vegetables.

chicken on each dinner plate. Serve with couscous and salt and pepper to taste. Makes 4 servings. — *Amy McClure, Bozeman, Mont.*

PER SERVING: 531 calories, 43 g protein, 55 g carbohydrates, 15 g fat, 90 mg cholesterol, 168 mg sodium

Couscous. In a 2- to 3-quart pan over high heat, bring to a boil 2½ cups **regular-strength chicken broth** and 1 tablespoon **butter** or margarine. Stir in 10 ounces (1⅔ cups) **couscous**. Cover and remove from heat; let stand until liquid is absorbed, about 5 minutes. Stir in ½ cup sliced **green onion** and **pepper** to taste. You can cover couscous and keep warm up to 15 minutes; stir with a fork and serve.

CUMIN-GARLIC YOGURT SAUCE

1½	**cups unflavored yogurt**
2	**tablespoons minced fresh cilantro (coriander)**
1	**clove garlic, minced or pressed**
1	**teaspoon cumin seed**

In a bowl, mix together yogurt, cilantro, garlic, and cumin seed. Cover and refrigerate at least 15 minutes or until next day. Makes about 1½ cups.

PER TABLESPOON: 9.4 calories, 0.7 g protein, 1 g carbohydrates, 0.2 g fat, 0.8 mg cholesterol, 10 mg sodium

(Continued on next page)

COOKY JAR BREAKFAST

Cereal & Fruit Cookies   Milk
Raspberry-Cranberry Juice Cocktail

These chewy cookies are good for a family with varied schedules and little time.

For a fast, high-energy breakfast or snack, supplement nutrient-dense cookies with a glass of milk or a bowl of yogurt. You can even pack a breakfast to go, with milk, yogurt, or juice in cartons.

CEREAL & FRUIT COOKIES

2 large eggs
½ cup honey
¼ cup (⅛ lb.) butter or margarine, melted and cooled
1 cup grated carrot
1 cup chopped walnuts
½ cup *each* raisins, finely chopped dried apricots, and finely chopped pitted dates or pitted dried prunes
1 cup *each* all-purpose flour and regular rolled oats
½ teaspoon baking soda
¾ teaspoon *each* ground cinnamon and ground nutmeg
1½ cups ring-shaped toasted oat cereal

In bowl, beat together eggs, honey, and butter until well blended. Stir in carrot, nuts, raisins, apricots, and dates.

In another bowl, mix together flour, oats, baking soda, cinnamon, and nutmeg. Add flour mixture and oat cereal to fruit mixture; stir until ingredients are well mixed.

Shape dough into 2-tablespoon-size balls and place about 1 inch apart on ungreased 12- by 15-inch baking sheets. Bake in a 350° oven until cookies are firm when lightly pressed, about 15 minutes; if 2 pans are in 1 oven, alternate positions halfway through baking.

Transfer cookies to racks; serve warm or let cool. Store airtight. Chill up to 1 week; freeze to store longer. Makes about 3 dozen. —*Fran Hamburg, Seattle.*

PER COOKY: 95 calories, 1.8 g protein, 14 g carbohydrates, 3.8 g fat, 19 mg cholesterol, 41 mg sodium

Cornhusk Muffins (page 76)

R

ustic flavors of
Southwestern cooking—corn, chilies, cheese, and sage—
inspire this month's desert brunch menu from Santa Fe. For
salad chefs we share the keys to a perfectly dressed salad. Our
suggestions for company entertaining include an elegant
seafood and pasta entrée and a rich chocolate cherry cake.
Other April articles feature ways to cook with cherimoya, lean
pork on the barbecue, speedy microwave pizzas, and quick-to-
prepare desserts using unbaked pie shells.

Santa Fe Brunch

THE STRENGTH OF SOUTHWEST *cuisine comes from the region's complex blend of people—Spanish, Indian, Mexican, and Anglo—and how they use their local ingredients. Corn and chilies are woven into many meals. Sometimes cheese and wild sage work their magic, too.*

Inspired by these rustic flavors, this handsome, easy-to-assemble brunch menu reflects the cultural heritage of this area.

Drop cornmeal batter laced with chili cheese into muffin cups lined with cornhusks; top with more cheese and bake.

DESERT BRUNCH

**Chili Relleno Custard
with Sage Cheese
Cornhusk Muffins   Butter
Papaya Wedges with Lime
Hot Chocolate or Coffee
Orange Juice**

Dry cornhusks, soaked in water, frame corn muffins. Many supermarkets and Mexican groceries sell the husks.

The egg casserole contains mild green chilies filled with a blend of mild neufchâtel cheese, tangy goat cheese, and sage. Baked under a blanket of custard, the dish makes a simple brunch entrée.

If you need a head start, you might fill the chilies and mix up the dry ingredients for the muffins the night before. The muffins and chilies can bake at the same time. While they cook, cut the papayas and make hot chocolate or coffee. Serve the chilies right from the oven; the puffy egg portion settles slightly as it cools.

CHILI RELLENO CUSTARD WITH SAGE CHEESE

       2 **cans (7 oz. each) whole green
          chilies, drained
          Sage cheese (recipe follows)**
       8 **large eggs**
       2 **cups milk**
     ½ **cup all-purpose flour**
     ¼ **teaspoon salt (optional)**
     ¼ **cup grated parmesan cheese
          Prepared chili salsa**

Slit chilies lengthwise; pat dry with paper towels. Fill chilies with cheese mixture, using all. Lay chilies in a single layer in a well-buttered 2½- to 3-quart shallow casserole. (If made ahead, cover and chill until the next day. Warm to room temperature to continue.)

In a blender, combine eggs, milk, flour, salt, and parmesan cheese; whirl until smooth. Pour evenly over chilies.

Bake in a 375° oven until top is lightly browned and a toothpick inserted in center (not in cheese) comes out clean, about 45 minutes. Serve at once. Scoop out portions and add salsa to taste. Makes 8 to 10 servings.

PER SERVING: 244 calories, 13 g protein, 12 g carbohydrates, 16 g fat, 283 mg cholesterol, 526 mg sodium

Sage cheese. In a small bowl, combine 1 large package (8 oz.) **neufchâtel cheese** or cream cheese, at room temperature; 4 ounces (⅓ cup) **chèvre cheese** or cream cheese, at room temperature; 1 **large egg;** 2 tablespoons minced **fresh sage leaves** or 1 teaspoon dry rubbed sage; 1 clove **garlic,** pressed or minced; and 3 tablespoons minced **green onions.** Beat with an electric mixer until blended. Add **salt** and **pepper** to taste.

CORNHUSK MUFFINS

       6 **to 8 dry cornhusks (6 to 8 in. long)**
       2 **cups all-purpose flour**
     ¾ **cup yellow cornmeal or
          dehydrated masa flour (corn
          tortilla flour)**
       1 **tablespoon baking powder**
     ½ **teaspoon salt**
    1⅓ **cups (about 5 oz.) shredded jack
          cheese with chilies**
       1 **large egg**
     ¼ **cup (⅛ lb.) melted butter or
          margarine**
       2 **tablespoons honey**
       1 **cup milk**

Separate cornhusks. In a large bowl, pour boiling water over husks to cover; let soak until soft and pliable, about 10 minutes. Drain husks and pat dry. Tear lengthwise into 1½- to 2-inch-wide strips.

In a bowl, mix flour, cornmeal, baking powder, salt, and ¾ cup of cheese. Make a well in center. In another bowl, beat egg, butter, honey, and milk until blended. Pour into well of flour mixture. Stir just enough to moisten dry ingredients.

In each of 12 greased 2½-inch muffin cups, place 2 or 3 strips of husk, crossing centers in bottom of each cup, so husk ends fan out around sides. As each cup is lined, fill with batter. Sprinkle tops with equal amounts of remaining cheese.

Bake in 375° oven until tops are golden, about 25 minutes. Lift out of pan; cool on rack. Serve warm or cool. Store at room temperature up to 12 hours, or wrap airtight and freeze up to 2 weeks (thaw unwrapped). Reheat in a 350° oven until warm, about 7 to 10 minutes. Makes 12.

PER MUFFIN: 215 calories, 6.7 g protein, 27 g carbohydrates, 8.8 g fat, 49 mg cholesterol, 337 mg sodium

Sample favorite flavors of the Southwest in this oven-baked brunch: Menu features sage-scented chilies rellenos baked in custard and topped with chili salsa, cornhusk muffins spread with butter, and wedges of papaya garnished with lime.

A Perfect Salad Every Time

THE STYLISH WARDROBE of a well-dressed salad depends on accessories—flavorful oils and vinegars, and perhaps some mustard. Coordinating them with quality basics—crisp leaves and tender vegetables—is simple.

You need choices, not a recipe, to dress a salad well; below, we explain the process in four easy steps. Select good-tasting, fresh oils for smoothness, and distinctive vinegars for tang; start a collection. Pick and choose among them, combining to your own taste with other seasonings, such as Dijon or other fancy mustards, capers, anchovy paste, fresh and dried herbs, and mixtures such as pesto.

THE BASIC GREEN SALAD

1. Start with cold, crisp greens, enough for one person or a crowd. If you like, rub the salad bowl with a cut clove of garlic before adding greens. Mix in some minced **fresh chives,** other fresh or dried herbs, thin cucumber slices, or any favorite salad condiments. Have ready **olive oil, red** or white **wine vinegar, Dijon mustard** (optional), **salt** (or seasoned salt), and **pepper** (preferably freshly ground).

2. Add oil, a spoonful at a time, and mix to coat salad. The amount depends on

Keys to creating a perfect salad: Start with cold, crisp greens or vegetables, add oil and vinegar with a light hand, and finish with your favorite seasonings. To add intriguing new flavors, experiment with various mild-flavored oils and unusual vinegars or citrus juices.

your taste and diet. About 1 tablespoon oil per serving gives rich flavor to most salads, but if you're watching calories, you can dress a salad with much less oil; just see that everything has a shiny coat.

3. Add vinegar, a little at a time, to taste. Start with about 1 teaspoon per serving; vinegars vary in acidity, and it's easy to get too much, especially in green salads (starchy ingredients such as potato need more acid, as well as more seasonings). This is also when you can add paste mixtures, such as prepared mustard; just put a little mustard (try about ¼ teaspoon per serving) in the spoon of your salad servers, dilute it with a little vinegar, then mix into salad. Start tasting, mixing in more vinegar

and mustard until the acidity and flavor suit you perfectly.

4. Season to taste with salt and pepper. While you're at it, decide if your salad needs more oil or vinegar; it's not too late to add a dash of either one.

Moving beyond the basic mixed green salad, you'll discover many other combinations can be dressed with the same oil-and-vinegar formula. To trigger your imagination, use the three salads below as the framework for salads of your own design.

SHOPPING FOR OIL & VINEGAR

A mild salad oil and olive oil are basic. Extra-virgin olive oil is worth the cost, but the flavors vary, so you may want to

taste several. Experiment with unusual mild-flavored oils, such as avocado or grape seed. As you expand your repertoire to other kinds of salads, try some of the more distinctively flavored oils, such as Oriental sesame oil, the various nut oils (some have a roasted nut flavor), and oil that dried tomatoes come packed in. Freshness is important for all oil, so don't buy too much at once. Store in a cool, dark area, and keep tightly covered.

In addition to wine vinegars, your collection might include Oriental rice vinegar (seasoned or unseasoned); fruit-, garlic-, and herb-flavored vinegars; or malt, balsamic, and sherry vinegars. Fresh lemon, lime, orange, or grapefruit juice can stand in for all or part of the acid.

Greens with fruit. *A sweet step forward from a green salad: try butter lettuce with orange slices, red onion rings, and toasted walnut pieces (optional); dress with walnut oil, raspberry vinegar (mix to taste with honey or sugar).*

Other options: romaine or red-leaf lettuce; thin slices of apple, Asian pear, crisp persimmon, or halved grapes; roasted filberts, almonds, or pecans; avocado slices. Dress with any mild oil and enliven with another berry-flavored or white wine vinegar.

Potato and other vegetables. *A substantial base begins with sliced cooked thin-skinned potatoes, lightly cooked cut green beans, chopped shallots or green onion, and diced red bell pepper (optional); dress with olive oil and balsamic vinegar mixed with Dijon mustard.*

Delicious alternatives: cooked dry beans (or canned ones) or cooked pasta for the potato; cooked broccoli flowerets, sliced carrots, or peas for the green beans. Dress first with olive oil, salad oil, or oil from dried tomatoes (add a few tomato slivers to salad). Then add spark with vinegar (sherry, malt, or red wine).

Chinese meat, crunchy greens. *It's enough to make the main course: strips of roast beef, finely shredded cabbage and carrot (optional), sliced green onions, fresh cilantro (coriander) leaves, and toasted almond slices; dress with Oriental sesame oil and salad oil (using about equal parts) and seasoned rice vinegar.*

Or use another roast or barbecued meat; shredded cooked chicken, duck, or turkey; chunks of cooked firm-fleshed fish (such as monkfish); or cooked and shelled tiny shrimp. Try other roasted nuts such as peanuts or cashews.

Cooking with Cherimoya

I**T TASTES LIKE PARADISE!** *This is a typical reaction to the cherimoya, an odd-looking fruit that originated in the cool mountain valleys of Peru. The cherimoya is considered the tastiest of a large family of tropical American fruits called* anonas; *it has a pleasing, sweet-tart flavor and a heady aroma reminiscent of banana, cherry, pineapple, strawberry, and vanilla. To some, it's simply the "ice cream fruit," so named for its custard-like texture and rich flavor.*

But for all its intriguing assets, this fruit tends to intimidate shoppers, and not just because it looks a little strange—some say reptilian. First, cherimoyas are expensive: $5 to $8 a pound (an average fruit weighs ¾ to 1 lb.). And cherimoyas must be handled properly or they'll never ripen and will rot.

Two types: White cherimoya (foreground) is bumpy and greenish tan; bay (rear) is smooth with green skin. They ripen differently but are similar in taste.

Why are cherimoyas so pricy? Because they take time to grow: flowers must be hand-pollinated, fruits take about six months to mature, and the delicate fruits must be individually harvested.

In the past, cherimoyas came from Florida or Mexico. Now, Western growers also produce the fruit found in our markets. Harvest runs January through May, with peak supply in the spring.

You'll find two varieties for sale: Bays and White. They are rarely labeled as such, but their shapes make them easy to tell apart (see picture at lower left).

Bays are round, with a smooth, green skin that stays the same color as fruit ripens. White cherimoyas are conical, with a rougher skin that takes on a tan tone as fruit ripens. Both types have soft, creamy flesh with large black seeds.

When ready to eat, fruits of either variety should give when gently squeezed, like a ripe peach.

If you must select an underripe cherimoya, it should be an even green color with no soft spots (splits near the stem end shouldn't affect fruit). Let fruit ripen, unwrapped, at room temperature. A wrapped fruit will decay—the flesh darkens and sours. Never chill an unripe cherimoya; cool temperatures stop its maturing process.

For best flavor, eat fruit as soon as it is ripe. Ripe fruit can be refrigerated up to three days.

You can check ripeness by making a tiny slit in your fruit and testing its taste and texture. If it isn't ready, don't worry: the slit will seal itself and the fruit will continue to ripen.

Cherimoyas taste delicious unadorned, split in half and scooped out with a spoon. But they also add an exotic aura to these simple dishes. Both the appetizer salad and main-dish salad take advantage of a cherimoya's sweet-tart flavor. The desserts make use of the fruit's ice cream–like qualities.

CHERIMOYA APPETIZER WITH PEPPER-LIME SALSA

  6 tablespoons lime juice
  ½ cup minced red bell pepper
  1 fresh jalapeño chili, stemmed, seeded, and minced
  1 tablespoon minced parsley
  2 teaspoons minced fresh ginger
  1 ripe cherimoya (about ¾ lb.), cut into 4 lengthwise wedges
     Parsley sprigs (optional)

In a bowl, combine lime juice, bell pepper, jalapeño chili, minced parsley, and ginger. If made ahead, cover salsa and chill up to 2 days.

Place a cherimoya wedge on each of 4 salad plates. Spoon salsa onto fruit. Garnish with parsley sprigs. Makes 4 appetizer servings.

PER SERVING: 80 calories, 1.2 g protein, 20 g carbohydrates, 0.4 g fat, 0 mg cholesterol, 4.8 mg sodium

CHERIMOYA CHICKEN SALAD

  ¾ pound boned and skinned chicken breasts
  ¼ cup *each* olive oil or salad oil and lemon juice
  1½ teaspoons *each* grated lemon peel and sugar
  ½ teaspoon pepper
  1 piece (about 7 in. long, ½ lb.) European-style cucumber, quartered lengthwise, then thinly sliced
  3 green onions (ends trimmed), thinly sliced
     About 8 medium-size butter lettuce leaves, washed and crisped
  1 ripe cherimoya (about ¾ lb.), cut into 4 lengthwise wedges
     Lemon wedges
     Salt

In a 4- to 5-quart pan, bring 3 quarts water to a boil over high heat. Add chicken, cover, and remove at once from heat. Let stand until chicken is no longer pink in thickest section (cut to test), about 20 minutes; drain. If made ahead, cover and chill up until next day.

In a large bowl, mix together oil, lemon juice and peel, sugar, and pepper; spoon out 2 tablespoons and reserve. When chicken is tepid or cool,

Shiny black seeds stud wedge of creamy cherimoya. Fruit's exotic sweetness pairs well with tartly dressed chicken salad.

holds soft peaks; stir in vanilla. Add to cherimoya mixture and fold gently together. Spoon into 4 to 6 dessert dishes (about 7 oz. each). Cover airtight; don't let wrap touch surface. Chill until cold, at least 2 hours or up until next day. Garnish each serving with a few seeds (they are inedible). Makes 4 to 6 servings.

PER SERVING: 148 calories, 3.2 g protein, 21 g carbohydrates, 6.3 g fat, 22 mg cholesterol, 33 mg sodium

CHERIMOYA ICE

- 1 ripe cherimoya (about ¾ lb.)
- 1 cup orange juice
- 2 tablespoons sugar
  Thin orange slices and/or mint sprigs (optional)

Cut cherimoya into 8 lengthwise wedges. Trim off and discard peel. Cut or scoop out seeds and discard.

In a blender or food processor, smoothly purée pieces of cherimoya, orange juice, and sugar.

Freeze mixture in a self-refrigerated ice cream maker or a frozen ice cream cylinder; follow manufacturer's directions. Freeze until almost firm; serve at once while softly frozen.

Or pour mixture into an 8- to 10-inch-square metal pan; cover and freeze until mixture is solid, at least 4 hours or up to 1 month. Break into small chunks and whirl in a food processor or beat with an electric mixer until it forms a smooth slush. Serve at once, or cover and freeze about 1 hour. To store the ice, cover and freeze up to a maximum of 1 month. Ice gets very hard; to serve, break into chunks and beat to a smooth slush in a food processor or with an electric mixer. Garnish scoops with orange slices and/or mint. Makes 4 servings, about ½ cup each.

PER SERVING: 121 calories, 1.4 g protein, 31 g carbohydrates, 0.3 g fat, 0 mg cholesterol, 0.1 mg sodium

tear it into bite-size pieces and add to bowl. Stir in cucumber and green onions.

Arrange lettuce on 4 dinner plates; fill leaves with equal amounts of salad. Set a cherimoya wedge on each plate and drizzle with reserved dressing. Garnish with lemon wedges; offer salt to add to taste. Makes 4 entrée servings.

PER SERVING: 313 calories, 22 g protein, 25 g carbohydrates, 15 g fat, 49 mg cholesterol, 63 mg sodium

CHILLED CHERIMOYA SOUFFLÉ

- 1 teaspoon unflavored gelatin
- ½ cup orange juice
- 1 ripe cherimoya (about ¾ lb.)
- 3 large egg whites
- 3 tablespoons sugar
- ½ cup whipping cream
- ¼ teaspoon vanilla

In a 2- to 3-cup pan, or in a glass measuring cup, sprinkle gelatin over juice; let stand until softened, about 5 minutes. In pan over direct heat, or in measuring cup in a microwave oven, warm juice until gelatin melts. Let mixture cool until slightly warm.

Meanwhile, cut cherimoya into 8 lengthwise wedges. Trim off and discard peel. Cut or scoop out seeds; rinse and set aside.

In a blender or food processor, smoothly purée cherimoya with gelatin mixture. Pour into a large bowl and set aside.

With an electric mixer on high speed, whip egg whites until foamy. Gradually add sugar and whip until whites hold stiff, shiny peaks. Scoop into bowl with cherimoya. With unwashed beaters, whip cream in the same bowl until it

Appetizer Nuts with a Chinese Twist

A CRISP GLAZE *cloaks these appetizer nuts from China. Cayenne and numbing Sichuan peppercorns speckle peanuts' candied coats, making an intriguing combination; look for the fragrant peppercorns in Asian markets. Sugar and soy sauce melt into dark, glossy skins on walnuts.*

SICHUAN SPICED PEANUTS

- 1 teaspoon Sichuan peppercorns or black peppercorns
- 2 cups salted roasted peanuts
- ½ cup sugar
- ½ teaspoon cayenne

Toast peppercorns in a 10- to 12-inch frying pan over medium-low heat, shaking often, until they are very fragrant, 4 to 5 minutes; do not scorch. Remove from pan. Crush with a mortar and pestle or place peppercorns in a plastic bag and crush with a heavy flat mallet until very finely ground. Pour through a fine strainer back into pan. Discard coarse pieces.

Add peanuts, sugar, and cayenne to pan; mix well. Stir over medium heat until sugar melts completely, then reduce heat to low and continue stirring until sugar coats nuts with a shiny glaze, about 10 minutes. Pour nut mixture onto a piece of oiled foil. Cool. Break nuts apart. Serve, or store at once (nuts absorb moisture quickly) airtight up to 2 weeks. Makes 2 cups.

PER TABLESPOON: 65 calories, 2.4 g protein, 4.9 g carbohydrates, 4.4 g fat, 0 mg cholesterol, 39 mg sodium

Intriguing nibbles to serve with an apéritif: sweet-hot peanuts cloaked in Sichuan spices and candied walnut halves with a glossy soy and sugar glaze.

CANDIED WALNUTS

- 2 cups (about 7 oz.) walnut halves
- 1 tablespoon soy sauce
- ¼ cup granulated sugar
- ¼ cup powdered sugar
  Salad oil

In a 3- to 4-quart pan, bring about 2 quarts water to boiling. Add nuts and boil, uncovered, 3 minutes. Drain well. Return to pan and mix nuts and soy. Add granulated and powdered sugars; mix well.

Pour 1 to 1½ inches oil into a wok or deep 10-inch frying pan. Place over medium heat until oil reaches 275° on a thermometer. With a slotted spoon, transfer nuts to hot oil. Stir nuts often and carefully maintain oil temperature. Cook until nuts turn deep golden brown, 5 to 7 minutes.

Lift out nuts with a slotted spoon and place on a chilled 10- by 15-inch baking pan. Using oiled chopsticks or forks,

immediately separate nuts. Let cool until glaze is hard. Blot excess oil off nuts with paper towels. Break apart nuts, if needed.

Serve, or store at once (nuts absorb moisture quickly) in an airtight container in a cool place up to 1 week. Makes 2 cups.

PER TABLESPOON: 57 calories, 0.9 g protein, 3.7 g carbohydrates, 4.7 g fat, 0 mg cholesterol, 33 mg sodium

Seafood & Pasta in Parchment

EFFORTLESSLY ELEGANT *describes this dinner entrée. Its preparation is minimal, but the results are handsome and delicious.*

Wrap seafood and a tomato caper sauce in parchment to make a neat cooking and serving package. In the oven, clams, mussels, shrimp, and scallops quickly steam to succulence in the packet's moist environment. As the seafood cooks, you boil fresh pasta. At the table, open each packet and add some of the hot noodles, dressed in olive oil and parsley, swirling them through the flavorful sauce.

You might start the meal with a salad of mixed baby lettuces and buttered baguette toast. Accompany the baked seafood packets with a fruity Beaujolais or a crisp Chardonnay. For dessert, consider offering a purchased or homemade fruit tart or crème brûlée with fresh raspberries.

Cooking parchment is essential to this presentation; look for it in the same area where waxed paper is sold in supermarkets. The packets can be assembled up to 2 hours ahead. If you need more of a head start, clean the seafood and make the sauce the night before.

SEAFOOD IN PARCHMENT PACKETS

- 6 tablespoons olive oil
- 1 clove garlic, minced or pressed
- 1 can (15 oz.) tomato purée
- ½ cup dry white wine
- 2 tablespoons drained capers
- ½ cup chopped parsley
  Salt and pepper
- ½ pound sea scallops, rinsed, drained, and cut crosswise into ½-inch-thick slices
- 12 large shrimp (31 to 35 per lb.), peeled and deveined
- 12 clams in shells (1½ to 2 in.), suitable for steaming, scrubbed
- 12 mussels in shells (2 to 2½ in.), scrubbed and beards pulled off
- 4 sprigs parsley
- ½ pound fresh or dry linguine

In a 2- to 3-quart pan, stir 2 tablespoons oil and garlic over medium-high heat until garlic is soft. Add tomato purée, wine, capers, and ¼ cup chopped parsley. Simmer, uncovered, until sauce thickens slightly, about 10 minutes. Add salt and pepper to taste. Let cool. (If made ahead, cover and chill until the next day.)

Cut 4 sheets cooking parchment, each 15 by 24 inches. Lay ¼ of scallops and shrimp in center of each paper, then flank with ¼ of clams and mussels. Pour ¼ of the tomato sauce over each portion of scallops and shrimp; top each with a parsley sprig. To seal each packet, bring together short ends of paper and fold over 1 inch twice, then fold under ends 2 or 3 times and tuck under seafood. Transfer packets to 12- by 15-inch baking sheets.

Bake in a 425° oven until clams and mussels pop open, about 15 minutes (open 1 end of packet to check; reseal if not done and continue baking). If using 1 oven, switch pan positions halfway.

Meanwhile, cook linguine in a 5- to 6-quart pan in about 3 quarts boiling water until just barely tender to bite, 3 to 4 minutes for fresh pasta, about 8 minutes for dry pasta.

Drain noodles and place in a warm serving bowl. Add remaining ¼ cup olive oil and chopped parsley; mix lightly. Keep warm.

Transfer packets, seam sides up, to 4 dinner plates. At the table, open each packet, folding back parchment and tucking excess under. Add about ¼ of the noodles to each packet alongside seafood. Makes 4 servings.

PER SERVING: 587 calories, 34 g protein, 56 g carbohydrates, 25 g fat, 145 mg cholesterol, 777 mg sodium

Add linguine to individual packets of oven-steamed seafood. Swirl the pasta through tomato sauce enriched with shellfish juices.

Lean Pork on the Barbecue

LESS INTRAMUSCULAR FAT *makes to-day's pork leaner. And, when trimmed of surface fat, certain cuts—like the center loin and tenderloin—are particularly lean and make ideal choices for lighter eating. These cuts are very similar in calories, fat, and cholesterol to skinned chicken thighs.*

To capitalize on the lean benefits, here we barbecue boned chops and tenderloins. The chops, seasoned with a Thai-inspired chili paste, are pounded thin for quick cooking. The grilled tenderloin, marinated in raspberry-herb dressing, is sliced to serve with mixed salad greens.

For succulent pork, cook it to an internal temperature of 155°. While the meat may look slightly pink in the center, it will fade right away. The trichina parasite, rarely present, is destroyed at 137°.

Raspberry-herb marinade flavors both barbecued pork tenderloin and salad of mixed greens. Meat is sliced thinly across grain to serve.

THAI-SEASONED LOIN CHOPS WITH CILANTRO PESTO & HOT SWEET MUSTARD

    8   boneless center-cut pork loin
        chops, each ½ inch thick (about
        1½ lb. total)
        Thai chili paste (recipe follows)
        Cilantro pesto (recipe follows)
        About ½ cup purchased hot sweet
        mustard

Trim and discard surface fat from chops. Spread 1 teaspoon of chili paste on each side of chops. Place chops, well apart, between sheets of plastic wrap. With a flat mallet, pound evenly and firmly until meat is about ¼ inch thick. If done ahead, cover and chill up until next day.

Peel off wrap and place chops on a grill 4 to 6 inches above a solid bed of hot coals (you should be able to hold your hand at grill level only 2 to 3 seconds). Cook, turning once, until meat is still moist and looks faintly pink to white in the center (cut to test), 5 to 7 minutes total. Offer cilantro pesto and mustard to add to taste. Serves 4 to 6.

PER SERVING: 284 calories, 24 g protein, 4.6 g carbohydrates, 19 g fat, 78 mg cholesterol, 368 mg sodium

Thai chili paste. In a blender or food processor, combine 1 teaspoon grated **lemon peel;** 4 cloves **garlic;** ¼ cup *each* chopped **fresh ginger** and **shallots;** 1 tablespoon **chili powder;** ½ teaspoon *each* **ground coriander, pepper,** and **crushed dried hot red chilies;** 1 teaspoon **anchovy paste;** and 3 tablespoons **water.** Whirl until a smooth paste forms; scrape

down sides of container often. If made ahead, cover and chill up until next day.

Cilantro pesto. In a blender, purée 3 cups lightly packed **fresh cilantro** (coriander) **leaves,** 1 clove **garlic,** and 3 tablespoons **olive oil.** Add **salt** to taste. If made ahead, cover and chill up until next day. Makes about ½ cup.

PER TABLESPOON: 31 calories, .12 g protein, .2 g carbohydrates, 3.4 g fat, 0 mg cholesterol, 1.3 mg sodium

GRILLED PORK TENDERLOIN IN RASPBERRY-HERB MARINADE

    2   pork tenderloins (each about
        ¾ lb., 1½ lb. total)
        Raspberry-herb marinade
        (recipe follows)
    6   tablespoons olive oil
    8   to 10 cups washed, crisped, bite-
        size pieces mixed salad greens,
        such as purchased mesclun or
        a combination such as red- or
        green-leaf lettuce, radicchio,
        watercress, and escarole
        Salt

Trim and discard surface fat and silvery membrane from pork. Set meat aside.

Pour ½ cup of the marinade into a heavy plastic bag; add tenderloins, seal bag, and rotate to coat meat with marinade. Set bag in a pan and chill 2 hours or up until next day; turn meat over occa-

sionally. Add oil to remaining marinade; mix well. Cover and set aside until ready to use.

Lift meat from marinade; drain briefly. In a barbecue with lid (uncovered), ignite 50 charcoal briquets on fire grate. When briquets are lightly covered with gray ash (25 to 30 minutes), push half the coals to each side of the grate. Position grill 4 to 6 inches above the coals.

Place tenderloins in center of grill. Cover barbecue and open dampers. Cook, basting often, until a meat thermometer inserted in center of the thickest part (parallel to length of the tenderloin) registers 155° (or cut into center to test—meat will look slightly pink, but will fade when removed from heat), 20 to 30 minutes.

Meanwhile, mix reserved marinade with salad greens. Thinly slice meat across grain. Serve pork with salad, adding salt to taste. Serves 4 to 6.

PER SERVING: 274 calories, 25 g protein, 6.5 g carbohydrates, 17 g fat, 74 mg cholesterol, 144 mg sodium

Raspberry-herb marinade. In a small bowl, combine ½ cup **raspberry vinegar,** 2 cloves **garlic** (minced or pressed), 1 tablespoon *each* **Dijon mustard** and **honey,** 1 teaspoon *each* minced **fresh leaves** of **marjoram, sage,** and **thyme** (or ¼ teaspoon *each* of the dry herbs), and ½ teaspoon **coarse-ground pepper.**

After You Land That Salmon . . .

FRESHLY CAUGHT SALMON, properly bled, dressed, and iced, is as fine a fish for eating as you can find. The process, while simple, can't be delayed and isn't for the squeamish. It preserves the quality of the flesh by reducing bacteria and bruises and slowing rigor mortis.

You need a thin-bladed, very sharp knife (such as a boning knife or a salmon-cleaning knife), a teaspoon, and a pair of textured rubber gloves. As soon as you grasp the fish, hit it on the head to stun it. Immediately reach in on one side of the head and cut the gills (step 1) so the fish will bleed; the sluggish flow lasts 5 to 20 minutes. Scaling is unnecessary; an unscaled fish resists bacterial activity better and stays fresh longer.

Lay fish on its back in a cleaning trough (a wedged tray that braces the fish) if you have one, or improvise bracing with clean, heavy towels. Hold knife with the cutting edge up and at a 45° angle and neatly slit belly open (step 2) from anus to throat latch (between gills on belly) if you want to keep the head; with palm up, reach in behind gills, twist them, and pull free. *If you don't want the head,* cut on through the chin, then reach in and pull gills free.

Cut through the esophagus (just in front of innards mass—step 3). Gripping firmly but gently, pull innards toward tail and out. If desired, set aside skein of golden-red eggs or long, cream-colored milt sac if present in cavity. In a sockeye, a translucent membrane lines the stomach; in other species, a membrane may cover the kidney along the spine; pull out any membrane you find.

Make parallel cuts down the spine along each side of the dark kidney (step 5). Use a spoon to scoop out this dark material.

With cool water, rinse fish well, but gently (to protect scales), from head to tail.

Put fish on ice at once, in a chest that drains; cover with more ice. Draining ice keeps bacteria washed off fish. For best texture, ice the fish before it enters rigor mortis (gets stiff); on ice, the process is slower and causes less tissue breakage, resulting in firmer and moister fish. At home, fish kept in chest in draining ice will be in excellent condition up to one week, until ready to cut up for cooking.

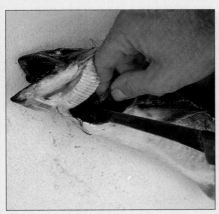

1 *Reach inside to gills and make one or two deep cuts close to the throat latch on the bottom of the fish; let the blood drain away.*

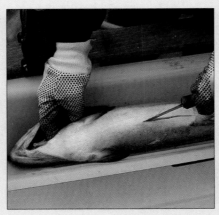

2 *Cut salmon open from anus to throat latch; to avoid cutting innards, hold knife, cutting edge up, at a 45° angle. You can cut through throat latch if you plan to remove head.*

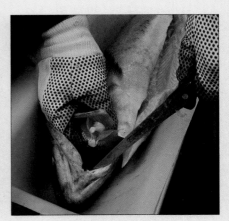

3 *Cut through esophagus where it joins stomach; especially at this step, textured gloves help grip.*

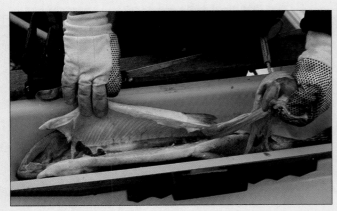

4 *To remove innards, pull firmly; save salmon roe for caviar or bait and milt sac to sauté in butter.*

5 *Cut along each side of dark kidney that lines fish's backbone. Scoop out with a spoon and discard.*

Speedy Microwave Pizza

PIZZA IN LESS THAN 5 MINUTES? *It's possible with these short-cuts—flour tortillas for the crust, ready-to-use toppings, and a microwave oven for cooking.*

Start by crisping the tortilla: first brush it lightly with water and then heat between sheets of paper towels. Next, add toppings and cook again until the cheese melts. To save more time, use packaged shredded or sliced cheese.

These quick microwave pizzas use no pans and are easy for young cooks to assemble for nutritious snacks. However, keep in mind that a microwave oven cooks differently from a conventional one, and the tortilla base will be chewier and firmer than a crisp-crusted oven-baked pizza.

If you prefer crisper results or plan to make more than one pizza, use a conventional oven to bake them. You'll need to allow extra time for the oven to get hot.

FIVE-MINUTE MICROWAVE PIZZA

1 flour tortilla (8 in.)
2 ounces thinly sliced or ½ cup shredded cheese (choices included with the following recipes)
Toppings (choices included with the following recipes)

Pierce flour tortilla with a fork in several places. Brush lightly with water on both sides. Place tortilla between 2 sheets of paper towels and set on a dinner plate.

Cook in a microwave oven at full power (100 percent) until tortilla is dry to touch and almost crisp (do not overcook or tortilla may become too hard; it firms as it cools), 45 seconds to 1½ minutes. Remove from oven and discard towels; wipe plate dry. Return tortilla to plate.

Lay cheese slices (tearing if needed) or sprinkle shredded cheese over tortilla to cover. Distribute toppings evenly over cheese. Return to microwave oven and cook at full power (100 percent) until cheese melts, 1 to 1½ minutes. Cut into wedges, if desired. Makes 1 serving.

To cook in conventional oven. Prick tortilla with a fork and brush lightly with water. Omit paper towels; set tortilla on a 12- by 15-inch baking sheet. Bake in a 500° oven until tortilla is almost crisp, about 4 minutes.

Remove from oven; add cheese and toppings. Return to oven and bake until cheese melts and browns slightly, about 2 minutes longer. (You can bake 2 pizzas at a time on the pan, if desired.)

TOMATO BASIL PIZZA

Use **mozzarella cheese.** Core 1 medium-size **Roma-type tomato** and cut it crosswise into ¼-inch-thick slices. Over cheese evenly distribute tomato, 2 tablespoons minced **fresh basil leaves** (or 2 teaspoons dry basil leaves), 1 tablespoon *each* **extra-virgin olive oil** and grated **parmesan cheese,** and **salt** and **pepper** to taste.

PER PIZZA: 427 calories, 17 g protein, 28 g carbohydrates, 28 g fat, 48 mg cholesterol, 518 mg sodium

ARTICHOKE PEPPER PIZZA

Use **provolone cheese.** Over cheese lay ¼ cup drained **marinated artichoke hearts** and 2 tablespoons drained **roasted red peppers,** cut in strips and blotted dry in paper towels. Sprinkle with **crushed dried hot red chilies** to taste, if desired.

PER PIZZA: 374 calories, 19 g protein, 31 g carbohydrates, 20 g fat, 39 mg cholesterol, 1,003 mg sodium

BEAN & SALSA PIZZA

Use **jack cheese.** Over cheese sprinkle ⅓ cup rinsed and drained **canned kidney beans** or black beans and 2 tablespoons chopped **green onions.** After the cheese melts, add **salsa** and **sour cream** (optional) to taste.

PER PIZZA: 397 calories, 22 g protein, 38 g carbohydrates, 18 g fat, 50 mg cholesterol, 807 mg sodium

REUBEN PIZZA

Use **Swiss cheese.** Over cheese spread 2 teaspoons **Dijon mustard** and ¼ cup rinsed, drained, and squeezed dry **sauerkraut.** Sprinkle with 1½ ounces thinly sliced **corned beef** or pastrami, cut into slivers, and ½ teaspoon **caraway seed.**

PER PIZZA: 456 calories, 28 g protein, 29 g carbohydrates, 25 g fat, 94 mg cholesterol, 1,275 mg sodium

Easy to assemble and quick to cook, microwave pizza uses tortilla for base, toppings of thinly sliced mozzarella, tomato rounds, and finely chopped basil.

Learning How Eggs Work: Recipes for Young Chefs

EGGS ARE GOOD FOOD, *teaches Linda Fairfield to the young cooks in her Sun Valley, Idaho, kitchen. She explains how eggs are made of water, protein, minerals, and fat to provide nutrition and flavor, and act in wondrous ways in cooking.*

Some recipes call for whole eggs; others use eggs separated into whites and yolks, so children see what happens each way. The warm eggnog shows how yolks thicken, the chewy macaroons how whites bind ingredients together. The quiche recipe uses eggs for both these reasons.

HAM & CHEESE QUICHE

 ¾ cup chopped cooked ham
1½ cups (6 oz.) shredded Swiss cheese
    Pat-in crust (recipe follows)
 3 large eggs
1½ cups half-and-half
 ¼ teaspoon salt (optional)
 ¼ teaspoon white pepper
 ¼ teaspoon dry dill weed
 2 tablespoons grated parmesan cheese

Scatter ham and Swiss cheese in crust. In a small bowl, beat eggs, half-and-half, salt, pepper, and dill until blended. Pour into crust; sprinkle with parmesan cheese. Bake on bottom rack in a 375° oven until center of custard barely jiggles when gently shaken, 40 to 45 minutes. Cool 20 minutes. Cut into wedges. Serves 6.

PER SERVING: 527 calories, 22 g protein, 28 g carbohydrates, 36 g fat, 284 mg cholesterol, 602 mg sodium

Pat-in crust. In a 9-inch pie pan, combine 1½ cups **all-purpose flour** and ½ cup (¼ lb.) **butter** or margarine, in chunks. Rub with fingers until fine crumbs. Add 1 **large egg** and stir until dough clings together. Then press evenly over bottom, sides, and rim of pan. With your fingers, pinch dough rim to crimp. Bake on the bottom rack of a 375° oven until pale gold, about 10 minutes.

Conquering the art of separating eggs, young cook is careful to keep the yolk in its half-shell cup as egg white drops into mixing bowl.

WARM EGGNOG

2½ cups milk
 3 large egg yolks
 ¼ cup sugar
 1 tablespoon vanilla
   Ground nutmeg

In the top of a double boiler, mix 1½ cups milk, yolks, and sugar. Blend well. Set container over (not in) simmering water in bottom of double boiler. Stirring, cook until custard thickly and evenly coats the back of a metal spoon, 8 to 10 minutes. Stir in remaining milk and vanilla. Serve warm or hot. Or cool, cover, and chill. Serve in cups; sprinkle with nutmeg. Makes about 3 cups, 4 to 6 servings.

PER SERVING: 133 calories, 4.7 g protein, 14 g carbohydrates, 6.2 g fat, 150 mg cholesterol, 54 mg sodium

QUICK MACAROONS

 3 large egg whites
 ½ cup sugar
 1 teaspoon lemon juice
1½ teaspoons all-purpose flour
 1 cup sweetened flaked dry coconut

In a small bowl, beat whites with an electric mixer at high speed until foamy. Add sugar, 1 tablespoon at a time, beating until whites hold stiff, glossy peaks. Add lemon juice and flour; fold in gently with a spatula until blended. Fold in coconut.

Line 12 muffin cups (2½ in. wide) with paper liners. Drop equal portions of the coconut mixture into each cup. Bake in a 300° oven until golden brown, 30 to 35 minutes. Cool on racks. Makes 12.

PER SERVING: 67 calories, 1.1 g protein, 12 g carbohydrates, 2 g fat, 0 mg cholesterol, 29 mg sodium

Leaves Upon Leaves

LEAF-CRADLED LEAVES—*with a few seasonings—describes these showy and quickly prepared vegetable dishes. They're dressy companions for simply cooked meats, poultry, or fish.*

Start each dish with either cabbage, mustard greens, or lettuce, reserving some of the large, pretty leaves. Then cut, sauté, and flavor the remaining leaves and serve them upon the reserved whole leaves to make an attractive presentation.

SAUTÉED CABBAGE & PINE NUT CUPS

½ cup distilled white vinegar
1 small head (about 1¼ lb.) red cabbage, cored
¼ cup pine nuts
3 tablespoons extra-virgin olive oil
1 teaspoon cumin seed
1 teaspoon dry rosemary leaves
1 small package (3 oz.) cream cheese, cut into ½-inch cubes
Salt and pepper

Elegantly nestled in a leaf wrapper, cabbage mixture adds a colorful accent to dinner menu. Chunks of cream cheese and pine nuts are added just before serving.

Fill a 5- to 6-quart pan with 2½ inches water; add ⅓ cup vinegar. Bring liquid to a boil over high heat.

Place cabbage in pan and turn often until 6 outer leaves are limp enough to remove without tearing, 1 to 2 minutes; peel off leaves as they loosen. Set whole leaves aside; then finely slice inner cabbage with a knife or food processor.

Discard liquid from pan. Place pan over medium-high heat, add pine nuts, and stir often until nuts are golden, 2 to 4 minutes; set aside. Add oil, cumin, and rosemary to pan; stir until cumin darkens, about 30 seconds. Add sliced cabbage and remaining vinegar and cook, stirring often, until cabbage is very wilted, 4 to 5 minutes. Gently mix in cream cheese, keeping chunks whole.

Lay each whole leaf cupped side up on a plate. Spoon equal amounts of cheese mixture in each. Sprinkle nuts on cabbage. Add salt and pepper to taste. Makes 6 servings.

PER SERVING: 170 calories, 3.9 g protein, 8.3 g carbohydrates, 15 g fat, 16 mg cholesterol, 53 mg sodium

SWEET & BITTER MUSTARD GREENS

¾ pound mustard greens (tough stems trimmed), rinsed
3 tablespoons extra-virgin olive oil
1 large onion, thinly sliced
¾ cup golden raisins
1 tablespoon minced fresh marjoram or 1 teaspoon dry marjoram leaves
Salt and pepper

Set aside 6 mustard green leaves, each 6 to 7 inches long. Finely chop remaining greens.

Support a steaming rack (or cake rack) about ¾ inch above the bottom of a 10- to 12-inch frying pan. Fill pan with ½ inch water. Bring to a boil over high heat.

Lay whole leaves on rack, cover, and steam just until slightly limp, about 30 seconds. Lift from pan and set aside.

Discard liquid from pan. Add oil, onion, raisins, and marjoram; cook over medium heat, stirring often, until onion tastes sweet, about 15 minutes. Stir in chopped greens; cook, stirring, until greens are very wilted, about 2 minutes.

Place each whole leaf flat on a plate. Mound an equal amount of raisin mixture on top of each leaf. Season to taste with salt and pepper. Makes 6 servings.

PER SERVING: 138 calories, 2.4 g protein, 19 g carbohydrates, 7.2 g fat, 0 mg cholesterol, 16 mg sodium

MINTED LETTUCE & PEA CUPS

1 small head (5 oz.) red-leaf lettuce
2 tablespoons butter or margarine
1 package (10 oz.) frozen petite peas, thawed
¼ cup chopped fresh mint or 1½ tablespoons dry mint leaves
2 teaspoons grated lemon peel
Salt and pepper

Separate lettuce leaves, rinse, and set aside 6, each 6 to 7 inches long. Cut remaining leaves into fine slivers.

Melt butter in a 10- to 12-inch frying pan over medium-high heat. Add slivered lettuce and peas; stir often until lettuce wilts, about 2 minutes. Stir in mint and lemon peel.

Lay each whole leaf on a plate. Mound equal amounts of pea mixture on top of each. Add salt and pepper to taste. Makes 6 servings.

PER SERVING: 70 calories, 2.6 g protein, 6.4 g carbohydrates, 4.1 g fat, 10 mg cholesterol, 105 mg sodium

Tart, Torte & Turnover . . . the Quick Way

EASY AS PIE, *you can take purchased unbaked pie shells and create three showy desserts. Look for rolled-out pastry, sold folded or in pans (both work fine), in your market's refrigerated or freezer section. If pastry is frozen, let thaw. If in pans, turn out and pat flat.*

ALMOND APPLE TURNOVER

- 2 **unbaked purchased 9-inch pie shells**
- 1 **can (12½ oz.) almond filling**
- 3 **large (about 1½ lb. total) Golden Delicious apples, cored, peeled, and sliced ¼ inch thick**
- 1 **teaspoon grated lemon peel**
- 1 **tablespoon lemon juice**
- 1 **large egg**
- ¼ **cup coarsely chopped almonds**

Lay 1 pie shell flat on a 12- by 15-inch baking sheet. Spread almond filling evenly over pastry up to ½ inch of rim. Arrange apples on almond filling, mounding slices slightly in center; sprinkle with lemon peel and juice. Brush pastry rim with water.

Gently lay remaining pie shell over apples, patting and easing to align edges of top and bottom shells. Press pastry rim to seal, then flute. Cut 8 evenly spaced slashes, each about 2 inches long, through top pie shell.

Beat egg to blend, then brush generously onto pastry; reserve remaining egg for other uses. Sprinkle almonds evenly over pastry. Bake in a 350° oven until medium golden brown, 35 to 40 minutes. Let cool on pan about 15 minutes, then, supporting with 2 wide spatulas, transfer turnover to a platter (if it starts to crack, ease and slide from pan to platter). Cut into wedges. Makes 8 to 10 servings.

PER SERVING: 344 calories, 4 g protein, 45 g carbohydrates, 17 g fat, 27 mg cholesterol, 281 mg sodium

CHOCOLATE STRAWBERRY TORTE

- 1 **unbaked purchased 9-inch pie shell**
- 1 **package (6 oz.) semisweet chocolate baking chips**
- ¼ **cup whipping cream**
  About ¾ cup berry-flavored liqueur such as blackberry, raspberry, or black raspberry
  About 1½ cups strawberries, rinsed and hulled
  About 3 cups vanilla ice cream

Lay pie shell flat on a 12- by 15-inch baking sheet. Fold edge under ½ inch, and flute to form a slight rim. With a fork, prick pie shell at about 1-inch intervals. Bake in a 425° oven until light golden brown, 12 to 15 minutes; cool on a rack. Use, or wrap and store up to 2 days.

Meanwhile in a double boiler over hot but not simmering water (or in a bowl nestled over hot water), combine chocolate and cream; stir until chocolate is smoothly melted. Remove from heat; mix in 2 tablespoons liqueur. Pour chocolate mixture onto pie shell and spread smoothly up to fluted rim.

Cut berries lengthwise into thin slices. Arrange slices on chocolate, overlapping, about 1 inch in from rim. (If made ahead, cover and let stand up to 4 hours.)

Cut torte into wedges and top each with about a ⅓-cup scoop of ice cream. Offer remaining liqueur to pour onto ice cream to taste. Makes 8 servings.

PER SERVING: 386 calories, 4 g protein, 45 g carbohydrates, 123 g fat, 31 mg cholesterol, 202 mg sodium

CARAMEL PEAR & WALNUT TART

- 1 **unbaked purchased 9-inch pie shell**
- 3 **small firm-ripe pears such as Anjou or Bartlett, each about 2½ inches in diameter**
  About 1 tablespoon lemon juice
- 1 **tablespoon butter or margarine**
- ¾ **cup coarsely chopped walnuts**
- ⅔ **cup sugar**
- ⅔ **cup whipping cream**

Lay pie shell in a 9-inch tart pan with a removable bottom. Fold pastry edge down into pan and press flush with pan rim. With a fork, prick bottom of pie shell about 15 times. Bake in a 400° oven until medium golden brown, about 15 minutes. Cool on a rack. Remove pan rim and slide pastry onto a plate.

Peel pears, cut in half lengthwise, and core. Brush fruit with lemon juice to reduce darkening. Lay pears cut side down. Beginning about ½ inch from stem end of each pear half, cut lengthwise through pear at ¼-inch intervals. Set pear halves, cut side down with stem end toward center, in pie shell, evenly spaced.

Melt butter in a 10- to 12-inch frying pan over medium heat. Add walnuts and stir often until a little darker brown, about 10 minutes; drain the nuts on paper towels. Wipe pan clean.

Add sugar and heat until it melts and turns a light caramel color; shake pan frequently to mix unmelted sugar into the liquid as it forms. Add cream and stir until smooth. Stir in walnuts. Immediately pour caramel mixture over pears, covering the fruit completely. Let stand until caramel cools slightly, at least 10 minutes, or up to 3 hours. Cut into wedges between pear halves. Makes 6 servings.

PER SERVING: 475 calories, 4 g protein, 51 g carbohydrates, 35 g fat, 35 mg cholesterol, 237 mg sodium

Handsome fresh pear tart begins with a pastry shell. Carefully slice pear halves; top fruit with buttery chopped walnuts and caramel glaze.

Chocolate Cherry Cake

THE DISTINCTIVE CONTRAST *of tart, dried sour cherries and rich, dark chocolate sets off this handsome dessert, created by Fran Bigelow, a Seattle chocolate master.*

The pitted cherries resemble fat raisins; look for them in markets that stock a wide assortment of dried fruits, and in fancy food shops and health food stores.

Soak cherries in kirsch, then fold them into a velvety chocolate mousse used to fill the cake's thin layers. Coat the cake with melted chocolate.

FRAN'S CHOCOLATE CHERRY CAKE

> Chocolate cake (recipe follows)
> Chocolate cherry filling (recipe follows)
> 1 cup whipping cream
> 8 ounces bittersweet or semisweet chocolate, finely chopped

With serrated knife, cut cake into 4 rectangles, each 3¾ by 10 inches. Also, cut heavy cardboard into a 3¾- by 10-inch rectangle. With 2 wide spatulas, carefully lift 1 cake layer onto cardboard and set on a metal rack. Gently spread evenly with ⅓ of filling to within ¼ inch of edges. Top with second layer, aligning with first; spread with ½ remaining filling. Top with third layer; spread with remaining filling. Top with last layer. Cover and chill until filling is firm, at least 1 hour.

In a 1- to 1½-quart pan, bring cream to boil over high heat. Remove from heat and stir in chocolate until melted; let cool 10 minutes. Place cake on a rack set in a rimmed pan. Starting at 1 end and working steadily toward the other, cover cake completely with warm chocolate in a slow, even, single pour. (If needed, use a spatula to touch up sides.) Let cake stand at room temperature until glaze is set, at least 1 hour. With 2 spatulas, transfer cake on cardboard to platter; serve. If made ahead, chill cake until firm, then cover airtight with a foil tent (do not touch cake); chill up until next day.

Cut cake into ¾-inch-thick slices; wipe knife between cuts. Serves 12 to 14.

PER SERVING: 525 calories, 5.6 g protein, 45 g carbohydrates, 39 g fat, 197 mg cholesterol, 122 mg sodium

Chocolate cake. Butter a 10- by 15-inch baking pan. Line pan with waxed paper.

Glossy sheen of poured dark chocolate cloaks layers of cake supported on cardboard; inside is a sour cherry and cream filling. Serve with espresso.

In a 1- to 1½-quart pan, stir 8 ounces chopped **bittersweet** or semisweet **chocolate** with ½ cup (¼ lb.) **butter** or margarine over low heat until melted; set aside.

In a bowl, beat 5 **large egg yolks** (reserve whites) on high speed with a mixer until very thick. Stir in 2 tablespoons **all-purpose flour** and chocolate; mix well. With clean beaters, whip reserved **egg whites** in a deep bowl on high speed until foamy. Gradually add ¾ cup **sugar,** beating at high speed until whites hold stiff, moist peaks. Fold whites gently but thoroughly into chocolate mixture.

Pour batter into prepared pan and spread evenly. Bake in a 350° oven until cake feels firm in center when lightly touched, 20 to 25 minutes. Let cool 30 minutes, then invert onto a sheet of foil; carefully peel waxed paper off cake. Use cake; if made ahead, seal in foil and store at room temperature up until next day.

Chocolate cherry filling. Mix 3 ounces finely chopped **dried pitted sour cherries** and ½ cup **kirsch** (cherry liqueur); let stand until fruit softens, about 1 hour. Drain; reserve liquid for other uses.

In a 1- to 1½-quart pan, stir 8 ounces chopped **bittersweet** or semisweet **chocolate** and 2 tablespoons **butter** or margarine over low heat until melted. Let cool to room temperature; beat in 2 **large egg yolks,** 2 tablespoons **sugar,** and cherries.

Beat 1 cup **whipping cream** until it holds soft peaks. Gently fold into chocolate mixture. Use at once.

More April Recipes

OTHER ARTICLES IN THE APRIL *issue feature a pair of vegetable marmalades to serve as a relish with meats or toast, and a main-dish salad inspired by a popular Mexican snack.*

TOMATO-CURRANT MARMALADE

An extra touch of sugar brings out the natural sweetness of this relish, which is good with simply cooked meats, poultry, fish, or buttered toast. It will keep well for up to a week.

- 1 tablespoon salad oil
- 1 small dried hot red chili
- ½ teaspoon *each* cumin seed and mustard seed
- 1 can (14½ oz.) pear-shaped tomatoes
- ½ cup currants
- ½ small unpeeled orange, finely chopped
- ¼ cup sugar
- 1 tablespoon white wine vinegar

In a 2- to 3-quart pan, combine oil, chili, cumin, and mustard seed. Cook on medium-high heat until seeds start to pop, 3 to 4 minutes. Stir in tomatoes and their liquid, currants, orange, sugar, and vinegar. Bring to a boil, stirring to break tomatoes into small pieces. Boil uncovered, stirring often, until reduced to 1½ cups, about 10 minutes. Use hot or at room temperature. If made ahead, cover and chill up to 1 week. Makes 1½ cups.

PER TABLESPOON: 26 calories, 0.3 g protein, 5.4 g carbohydrates, 0.6 g fat, 0 mg cholesterol, 28 mg sodium

ONION-FENNEL MARMALADE

Slow cooking transforms sliced onions and fennel into this golden relish. Serve hot or at room temperature with meat or poultry.

- 1½ pounds (2 large heads) fennel, stalks cut off and bases trimmed
- 2 medium-size onions, sliced crosswise
- ⅓ cup olive oil
- 1 or 2 beef bouillon cubes
- 1 tablespoon hot water

Rinse and drain fennel heads, then slice crosswise.

In a 10- to 12-inch frying pan on medium-low heat, combine sliced fennel, onion, and olive oil. Cover and cook until onion and fennel are very soft and golden, about 1½ hours; stir occasionally.

Mash bouillon cubes with water; stir into vegetables. Stir mixture, uncovered, over medium-high heat until moisture is nearly evaporated, about 5 minutes. Serve hot or at room temperature. If made ahead, cover and chill up to 5 days. Makes 2 cups.

PER TABLESPOON: 24 calories, 0.2 g protein, 0.8 g carbohydrates, 2.2 g fat, 0 mg cholesterol, 38 mg sodium

CANARDITA SALAD

A popular Mexican snack, carnitas, gets a new twist in this recipe. Crisp, juicy carnitas ("little meats") are most commonly made with pork and eaten with soft, warm corn tortillas.

In this version, duck (canard in French) gets cooked the same way pork is prepared for carnitas. Long, low, moist heat tenderizes the meat, then high heat quickly gives it a brown finish. As it does with pork, this process enhances duck's rich succulence.

For this main-dish salad, scatter the duck over cool greens, sweet pineapple, and avocado. Spoon a tart-hot tomatillo salsa over the salad to dress it.

- 1 duck (5 to 5½ lb.)
- 1 teaspoon dry thyme leaves
- 1 teaspoon cumin seed, crushed
- 1 small yellow onion, thinly sliced
- 2 cloves garlic, pressed or minced
  Fresh cilantro (coriander) sprigs
- 12 cups lightly packed bite-size pieces green-leaf lettuce, washed and crisped
- 1 firm-ripe avocado (about 10 oz.), peeled, pitted, and sliced
- 1¼ pounds peeled and cored pineapple, cut into 1-inch chunks (about 3 cups)
- 1 small red onion, thinly sliced
  Salsa dressing (recipe follows)
  Salt and pepper

Remove duck neck and giblets; reserve giblets for other uses. Rinse duck inside and out and pat dry. Trim off lumps of fat. Place duck and neck in a 12- by 15-inch roasting pan. Sprinkle duck inside and out with thyme and cumin. Place yellow onion and garlic in duck cavity. Cover pan tightly. Bake in a 350° oven until meat is very tender when pierced, about 2½ hours.

Remove duck from oven, uncover, and cool. Pour off fat and juices; reserve for another use if desired. Remove meat and skin from bones. Discard bones, skin, and lumps of fat. Tear meat into

coarse shreds. (If made ahead, cool, cover, and chill until the next day. Reheat, covered, in a 350° oven until hot, about 15 minutes. Then uncover and continue.) Return duck shreds to pan and bake, uncovered, in a 450° oven, stirring once, until meat is lightly browned, about 10 minutes. Transfer to a dish. Garnish with cilantro.

In a large bowl, mix lettuce, avocado, pineapple, and red onion. Mound lettuce mixture on dinner plates. Add warm duck, salsa dressing, and salt and pepper to taste. Makes 6 servings.

PER SERVING: 314 calories, 25 g protein, 18 g carbohydrates, 17 g fat, 84 mg cholesterol, 79 mg sodium

Salsa dressing. Pull husks from 1 pound **tomatillos** and discard. Wash fruit and place in an 8- to 9-inch-wide baking pan. Bake, uncovered, in a 350° oven until soft, about 30 minutes. Cool.

In a food processor or blender, whirl tomatillos, ½ cup **lime juice**, ½ cup lightly packed coarsely chopped **fresh cilantro** (coriander), and 2 tablespoons **water** until smooth. Stir in 3 to 6 tablespoons minced **fresh hot chili** (such as jalapeño) and **salt** to taste. Pour into a bowl. Serve, or cover and chill up to 3 hours. Makes about 3 cups.

PER ½ CUP: 25 calories, 1.2 g protein, 4.9 g carbohydrates, 0.4 g fat, 0 mg cholesterol, 3.9 mg sodium

Warm, shredded duck and tart salsa go on salad greens. Serve with flour tortillas.

SPICY ZUCCHINI BRAN MUFFINS

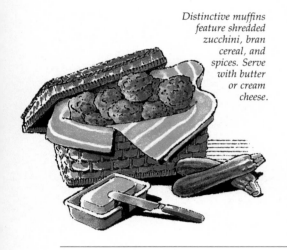

Distinctive muffins feature shredded zucchini, bran cereal, and spices. Serve with butter or cream cheese.

  2 **cups bran flake cereal**
  1 **cup shredded zucchini**
  ¾ **cup milk**
  1 **large egg**
  ½ **cup sugar**
  ⅓ **cup salad oil**
  1½ **cups all-purpose flour**
  2½ **teaspoons baking powder**
  1½ **teaspoons ground cinnamon**
  ½ **teaspoon ground ginger**

In a large bowl, stir together bran cereal, zucchini, milk, egg, sugar, and oil; set aside and let stand until cereal softens slightly, 2 to 4 minutes.

Meanwhile, in a small bowl mix flour, baking powder, cinnamon, and ginger.

Add flour mixture to bran mixture and stir just until combined.

Evenly divide batter among 12 well-greased muffin cups, 2½-inch size. Bake in a 375° oven until muffins are browned on top and firm to touch, about 30 minutes. Remove from pans. Serve hot, or cool on racks and serve warm or at room temperature. To store, wrap airtight and chill up to 1 week; freeze for longer storage. Makes 12.—*Maureen W. Valentine, Seattle.*

PER MUFFIN: 182 calories, 3.5 g protein, 27 g carbohydrates, 7.2 g fat, 25 mg cholesterol, 163 mg sodium

CHICKEN-BROCCOLI QUICHE WITH ALMONDS

Pour milk and egg mixture into crust filled with chicken, broccoli, and cheese; top with almonds and bake.

  ½ **pound broccoli, rinsed**
  3 **large eggs**
  1 **cup milk or half-and-half (light cream)**
  ¼ **teaspoon *each* ground nutmeg and pepper**
  1 **cup finely chopped cold cooked chicken**
  1 **cup (¼ lb.) shredded gruyère or Swiss cheese**
  1 **baked 9-inch pie shell**
  2 **tablespoons sliced almonds**

Peel broccoli stalks. Thinly slice stalks; cut flowerets into about ¾-inch pieces.

Place a steamer rack at least 1 inch above bottom of a 2- to 3-quart pan. Add 1 inch water; set broccoli on rack. Cover and steam over high heat until broccoli is tender when pierced, about 5 minutes. Let broccoli cool.

Meanwhile, beat eggs, milk, nutmeg, and pepper to blend. Mix broccoli, chicken, and cheese and spread in pie shell. Pour egg and milk mixture over chicken; sprinkle with almonds. Bake in a 350° oven until center barely jiggles when gently shaken, about 45 minutes. Let stand at least 15 minutes, then cut into wedges. Makes 6 servings.—*Elizabeth Petersen, Ashland, Ore.*

PER SERVING: 365 calories, 20 g protein, 18 g carbohydrates, 24 g fat, 184 mg cholesterol, 332 mg sodium

PASTA SALAD WITH ASPARAGUS & TOFU

Basil and parmesan dressing fragrantly seasons salad of short pasta tubes, cooked asparagus, and tofu.

  ½ **pound regular tofu, drained and cut into ½-inch cubes**
     Basil dressing (recipe follows)
  1 **pound asparagus, tough ends removed**
  6 **ounces dry mostaccioli or penne**

Add tofu to dressing. Set aside for at least 15 minutes or up to 1 hour.

Rinse and peel asparagus. Cut diagonally into 1½-inch pieces. In a 5- to 6-quart pan, bring 3 quarts water to boiling. Add asparagus; cook, uncovered, until tender when pierced, about 4 minutes. Transfer asparagus with a slotted spoon to ice water. Drain when cool.

Add pasta to boiling water and cook until barely tender to bite, about 15 minutes. Drain; rinse with cold water until cool. Drain pasta, and mix with asparagus and tofu. Makes 6 servings.—*Linda Strader, Amado, Ariz.*

Basil dressing. Mix together ½ cup **seasoned rice wine vinegar** (or ½ cup white wine vinegar and 2 teaspoons sugar), ¼ cup grated **parmesan cheese,** 3 tablespoons minced **fresh basil leaves** or 1 tablespoon dry basil leaves, 3 tablespoons **olive oil,** 1 tablespoon **Dijon mustard,** and 1 clove **garlic,** minced or pressed.

PER SERVING: 249 calories, 10 g protein, 31 g carbohydrates, 10 g fat, 2.6 mg cholesterol, 142 mg sodium

CHAYOTE WITH SPICED LAMB FILLING

- 3 chayotes (about ¾ lb. each)
- 1 pound ground lean lamb
- 1 medium-size onion, minced
- 4 cloves garlic, minced or pressed
- ½ teaspoon *each* ground allspice and coarsely ground pepper
- ⅛ teaspoon ground cloves
- ⅓ cup raisins
- 1 can (6 oz.) tomato paste
- 2 tablespoons dry red wine
  Sour cream (optional)

In a 4- to 5-quart pan over high heat, bring 2 quarts of water to a boil and add chayotes. Cover and simmer until chayotes are tender when pierced, about 40 minutes; cool. Cut chayotes in half lengthwise and scoop out pulp, leaving ½-inch-thick shells. Chop pulp.

In a 10- to 12-inch frying pan over medium-high heat, add lamb, onion, garlic, allspice, pepper, and cloves; stir until meat is well browned, about 15 minutes. Stir in chayote pulp, raisins, tomato paste, and wine.

Spoon filling into chayote halves and place in a 9- by 13-inch baking dish. Cover tightly and bake in a 350° oven until filling is hot, about 25 minutes. Offer sour cream to add to taste. Makes 6 servings. — *Shirley Henderson, Piedmont, Calif.*

PER SERVING: 209 calories, 17 g protein, 23 g carbohydrates, 6.6 g fat, 53 mg cholesterol, 282 mg sodium

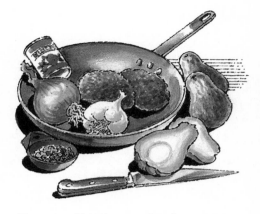

Chayote, a mild-tasting, pear-shaped squash, is boiled, filled with ground lamb mixture, then baked.

KOREAN BEAN SPROUT & PORK STIR-FRY

- 2 tablespoons soy sauce
- ⅓ cup sake or dry sherry
- 1 teaspoon cornstarch
- 4 green onions, ends trimmed
- ½ pound boneless lean pork, such as loin or leg
- 3 tablespoons sesame seed
- 2 tablespoons peanut or salad oil
- 1 tablespoon minced fresh ginger
- ¾ pound bean sprouts (about 4 cups)

Stir together soy sauce, sake, and cornstarch; set aside. Thinly slice 2 of the green onions; set aside.

Thinly slice pork into 2-inch strips.

To a wok or 12-inch frying pan over high heat, add sesame seed; stir until toasted, about 2 minutes; remove from pan and set aside. To pan add 1 tablespoon oil; when oil is hot, add ginger and sprouts. Stir-fry just until sprouts are hot; scoop onto a serving plate.

Add 1 more tablespoon oil to pan; when hot, add pork. Stir-fry until meat browns on edges, about 5 minutes. Pour in soy mixture and sesame seed. Stir until sauce boils; pour meat mixture onto sprouts. Garnish with sliced and whole onions. Serves 2. — *Lila K. Pang, Lanikai, Hawaii.*

PER SERVING: 463 calories, 33 g protein, 22 g carbohydrates, 29 g fat, 68 mg cholesterol, 1,117 mg sodium

Stir-fried pork, seasoned Korean-style, tops hot bean sprouts for a quick meal for two. Serve with warm sake.

LIME CUSTARD SQUARES

- ¾ cup plus 2 tablespoons all-purpose flour
- ⅓ cup sweetened shredded dry coconut
- ⅓ cup powdered sugar
- ⅓ cup (⅙ lb.) butter or margarine
- 3 large eggs
- 1 cup granulated sugar
- ¼ cup lime juice
- 1 teaspoon grated lime peel
- ¼ teaspoon baking powder

In a bowl, combine ¾ cup flour, coconut, ¼ cup powdered sugar, and butter; rub with your fingers to make coarse crumbs. Evenly press crumbs in an 8-inch-square pan. Bake in a 350° oven until light gold, about 20 minutes.

Meanwhile, with an electric mixer on high speed, beat eggs with granulated sugar until well mixed. Add lime juice, lime peel, 2 tablespoons flour, and baking powder; blend until smooth.

Pour egg mixture onto crust. Bake until top is golden and feels firm when lightly touched, about 20 minutes. Dust with remaining powdered sugar. Let cool. Cut pastry into 2-inch squares and lift from pan with a spatula. Makes 16 pieces. — *Roxanne E. Chan, Albany, Calif.*

PER PIECE: 139 calories, 1.9 g protein, 21 g carbohydrates, 5.4 g fat, 62 mg cholesterol, 63 mg sodium

Golden pastry flavored with coconut is base for a tart lime filling. Bake, cool, cut, and serve.

RANDALL RICHARDSON LEARNED *how to cook these brochettes while serving with the Peace Corps in Morocco. Khemisset is a village between Fez and the Moroccan capital, Rabat. When Richardson traveled between the two cities, he piled out of the bus along with the other passengers to enjoy Khemisset's famous liver brochettes. They are highly seasoned with onion, cumin, and chili powder and are far more interesting than just about anything else one can find at a bus stop.*

The seasonings could equally well be attributed to Mexico. Indeed, the blending of American chili peppers and Mediterranean cumin is a striking example of international cooperation.

KHEMISSET BROCHETTES

    1   pound sliced calf's liver, cut about
        ½ inch thick
    1½ teaspoons ground cumin
    1   teaspoon chili powder
    1   tablespoon finely chopped onion
    2   tablespoons olive oil or salad oil
    ¾   cup tomato-based chili sauce
    4   pocket bread rounds (optional)
        Thinly sliced green onions,
        including tops
        Salt

Trim off and discard membrane and any tubes from liver. Rinse liver, pat dry, and cut into 1-inch squares. Combine 1 teaspoon cumin with chili powder,

chopped onion, and oil. Add liver pieces and mix to coat evenly. Cover and chill 2 hours or up until next day, stirring several times. Combine remaining ½ teaspoon cumin with chili sauce. If made ahead, cover and chill up until next day.

Thread liver pieces, keeping slightly apart, on slender metal skewers. Place on a grill 4 to 6 inches above a solid bed of hot coals (you can hold your hand at grill level for only 2 to 3 seconds). Cook, turning often, until brown on all sides but still pink in the center (cut to test), 4 to 5 minutes total.

If desired, cut pocket bread rounds in half and stuff liver into the pockets. Offer seasoned chili sauce, sliced green onions, and salt to add to taste. Makes 4 servings.

PER SERVING: 289 calories, 24 g protein, 21 g carbohydrates, 12 g fat, 342 mg cholesterol, 817 mg sodium

Camarillo, Calif.

TO GEORGE LANG, *the historian of Hungarian cooking as well as its poet, what is usually served as goulash in this country shouldn't happen to a Rumanian. To the purist, gulyas boasts only beef, onions, and lard or bacon. Although many additions are permissible — tomato, dumplings, potato, or paprika, for instance — many other ingredients are not.*

Much as we respect Lang, we must remember he speaks as a high priest, and that many of us belong to a different denomination. We Low-Church types, Glen Fulcher included, reserve the right to add spaghetti to our potluck creations and still call them goulash.

And since the walls are down, Chef Fulcher takes a second heretical step. Instead of the permissible tomatoes, he adds prepared barbecue sauce. There are many to choose from, so pick one you like. And remember, they are usually a little sweet.

GLEN'S GOULASH, BARBECUE-STYLE

    1   pound ground lean beef
         Salad oil (optional)
    ¾   pound mushrooms, sliced
    2   medium-size onions, chopped
    1   medium-size green bell pepper,
         stemmed, seeded, and chopped
    1   teaspoon dry oregano leaves
    8   ounces dry spaghetti
    1¼   cups tomato-based barbecue sauce
         Chopped parsley

In a 5- to 6-quart pan over medium heat, stir ground beef often until browned and crumbly, about 15 minutes. (If needed, add 2 tablespoons oil.) Discard all but 2 tablespoons fat. Add mushrooms,

"He learned how to cook these brochettes at a bus stop in Morocco."

onions, green pepper, and oregano; stir often until onion is limp, about 10 minutes.

Meanwhile, bring about 4 quarts water to boiling on high heat in a 5- to 6-quart pan. Add spaghetti and boil, uncovered, until tender-firm to bite, 10 to 12 minutes. Drain pasta well and add to beef mixture along with barbecue sauce. Stir and cook until hot. Pour onto a platter and garnish with parsley. Makes 6 servings.

PER SERVING: 398 calories, 20 g protein, 40 g carbohydrates, 17 g fat, 51 mg cholesterol, 470 mg sodium

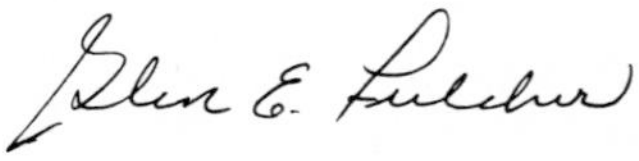

Glen E. Fulcher

Seattle

N O ONE HAS HONORED *corned beef and cabbage more than Jiggs, the central figure in* Bringing up Father. *Jiggs, a wealthy man of humble origins, strove valiantly to indulge his low-born taste for corned beef—but his sharp-eyed, sharp-tongued wife, Maggie, had loftier standards.*

Jiggs is gone, and corned beef is no longer scorned beef. Cooked with care, it's most flavorful (Walter Johns even uses the simmering broth for soup). In a self-deprecatory vein, he calls it Wally's Swill—swill being hog food. Hogs should be so lucky.

WALLY'S SWILL

1	corned beef brisket, 5 to 6 pounds
½	cup cider vinegar
6	whole cloves
2	cloves garlic
12	black peppercorns
3	dry bay leaves
1	tablespoon salad oil
1	large onion, chopped
2	cups thinly sliced carrots
2	cups thinly sliced celery
½	cup pearl barley
2	large thin-skinned potatoes (about 1 lb. total), peeled and cubed
2	tablespoons coarsely chopped fresh basil or 1 teaspoon dry basil leaves
2	large firm-ripe tomatoes, peeled, cored, and chopped
3	cups finely shredded cabbage
2	teaspoons Worcestershire
	Pepper (optional)

Rinse corned beef well and put in a 10- to 12-quart pan. Add about 6 quarts water. Bring to a boil over high heat, and cook for 5 minutes; drain. Repeat this step 3 or 4 times or until water has no salty taste.

To drained meat, add 3 quarts water, vinegar, cloves, 1 garlic clove, peppercorns, and 2 bay leaves. Bring to a boil, cover, reduce heat, and simmer until corned beef is very tender when pierced, 3 to 3½ hours. Let cool in broth. If made ahead, cover and chill up until next day.

Skim or lift off fat. Pour broth through a fine strainer into a large bowl. Trim fat from meat and discard. Cut enough meat into ½-inch cubes to make 2 to 3 cups; put remaining meat on a platter. Cover both meats and keep cold.

Rinse pan. Mince or mash remaining clove garlic. Add to pan along with oil and onion. Cook over medium-high heat, stirring often, until onion is limp. Add broth, carrots, celery, barley, potatoes, basil, and remaining bay leaf. Cover and simmer for 1 hour.

With a slotted spoon, lift out 4 cups of the vegetables; mash and return to pan. Add the diced corned beef, tomatoes, cabbage, and Worcestershire. Bring to a boil; cover and simmer until all the vegetables are very tender when pierced, about 10 minutes longer. Ladle into bowls; add pepper to taste. If you like, reserve large section of corned beef to slice for another meal. Makes 16 servings, about 1-cup size.

PER SERVING: 318 calories, 20 g protein, 14 g carbohydrates, 20 g fat, 97 mg cholesterol, 1,144 mg sodium

Walter J. Johns

Phoenix

T HE TORTE AND ITS RELATIVES—*tarts, tartes, tourtes, tortas, tortillas—have different meanings in different cuisines. The spectrum encompasses fruit pies and meat pies; thin, excruciatingly rich cakes in Germany, Austria, and Hungary; deep, heavy cheesecakes in Italy; meat, fish, or fowl pies in England; omelets in Spain; thin breads in Mexico; and so on. Other relatives—quiche, pissaladière, and pizza, for instance—have their own names. Most (but not all) are flat, and most (but again not all) have crusts that contain a filling.*

Confronted with this smörgåsbord of names, Steve Harrison turned away and toyed with the idea of calling his creation a "quizza," a combination quiche-and-pizza, but finally decided to let us name it. We call it Two-Cheese Torte and recommend it as a great luncheon dish.

Refreshing elements include almonds in the base and basil as a seasoning.

TWO-CHEESE TORTE

2	tablespoons olive oil
1	medium-size onion, chopped
¼	pound mushrooms, sliced
½	cup dry white wine
1	teaspoon dry basil leaves
⅛	teaspoon pepper
½	cup blanched almonds
3	large eggs
⅓	cup baking mix
¼	cup milk
1	cup (4 oz.) shredded gruyère cheese
¼	cup grated parmesan cheese

Heat oil in a 10- to 12-inch frying pan over medium heat. Add onion and stir often until limp, then add mushrooms and stir often for 3 minutes. Stir in the wine, basil, and pepper; stir frequently until nearly all the liquid is evaporated and mushrooms are lightly browned. Remove from heat and set aside.

In a blender or food processor, whirl almonds until finely chopped. Add eggs, baking mix, and milk; whirl until well blended, about 15 seconds.

Pour into a greased 9-inch pie pan. Spoon onion mixture evenly over batter, then evenly sprinkle with gruyère and parmesan cheeses. Bake in a 350° oven until top is golden brown and filling jiggles only slightly in center when pan is gently shaken, about 25 minutes. Let cool 10 minutes, then cut into wedges. Serves 4 to 6.

PER SERVING: 307 calories, 16 g protein, 9 g carbohydrates, 24 g fat, 160 mg cholesterol, 297 mg sodium

Stan R. Harrison

Portola Valley, Calif.

April Menus

SPRING'S BURGEONING PRODUCE *selection makes its way into this month's meals. Two can collaborate on the Mediterranean dinner highlighting artichokes and Swiss chard. For breakfast, a mountain of strawberries tucks into a big scone. Try cheese sandwiches and seasonal vegetables for lunch or quickly prepared supper.*

MEDITERRANEAN TROUT DINNER

Trout & Chard with Pine Nuts, Orange & Bay

Artichokes   Lemon Mayonnaise

Barbera or Côtes du Rhône

Iced Tea

Onions, seasoned with orange, bay leaves, and pine nuts, fill trout and flavor Swiss chard. Serve with a medium-bodied California coastal Barbera or French Côtes du Rhône; either provides a fine balance for the fish and its accompaniments.

Homemade mayonnaise, though it might seem difficult to make, goes together in a snap. Prepare it first, then trim the artichokes and start them steaming. Fix the trout and chard next, cooking the greens just before the fish come out of the oven.

TROUT & CHARD WITH PINE NUTS, ORANGE & BAY

- 1 **large orange**
- ¾ **cup pine nuts**
- 3 **tablespoons olive oil**
- 6 **small (about 1½-in.-long) dry bay leaves**
- 1 **large onion, sliced**
- 4 **whole boned trout, about ½ lb. each**
- ½ **pound Swiss chard (discolored stem ends trimmed), sliced crosswise**

Grate colored peel from orange; set aside. Cut off and discard remaining peel and membrane. Thinly slice fruit crosswise; set aside.

In a 10- to 12-inch frying pan over medium heat, shake nuts often until golden, 4 to 8 minutes. Pour out and set aside. Add 2 tablespoons oil and bay leaves to pan; cook until leaves turn gold, about 30 seconds. Add grated orange peel and onion; stir often until

Shared efforts—from stuffing boned trout and trimming artichokes to cooking Swiss chard and making blender mayonnaise—get dinner on the table in short order.

onion is limp, about 15 minutes. Mix in pine nuts.

Using half of onion mixture and 4 bay leaves, evenly stuff trout cavities (place 1 leaf in each fish); fasten shut with toothpicks. Brush trout all over with remaining oil. Place in a 9- by 13-inch baking dish. Bake in a 400° oven until fish is no longer translucent in thickest part (cut to test), about 18 minutes. Remove toothpicks.

Meanwhile, scrape remaining onion mixture from pan and set aside. Add ¼ inch water to pan and bring to a boil over high heat. Stir in chard, cover, and simmer until it wilts, about 3 minutes; drain any liquid. Stir in reserved onion mixture. Serve fish with chard and orange slices. Makes 4 servings.

PER SERVING: 473 calories, 35 g protein, 16 g carbohydrates, 33 g fat, 76 mg cholesterol, 181 mg sodium

LEMON MAYONNAISE

In a blender or food processor, whirl 2 tablespoons **lemon juice,** 1 teaspoon **Dijon mustard,** and 1 **large egg yolk** until blended. With motor running, gradually add ½ cup **olive oil** until incorporated. Add **salt** to taste. Serve, or chill, covered, up to 1 week. Makes ⅔ cup.

PER TABLESPOON: 103 calories, 0.3 g protein, 0.3 g carbohydrates, 11 g fat, 27 mg cholesterol, 16 mg sodium

STRAWBERRY SCONE BREAKFAST

Strawberry Scone
Spiced Steamed Milk
Soft-cooked Eggs
Coffee

Cinnamon-flavored milk whirls to a quick froth in the blender. Pour some over wedges of berry-filled scone, and mix some with coffee for cafe au lait. If you like, dust mugs of cafe au lait with unsweetened or sweetened cocoa.

Start coffee brewing, then stir up the scone. While it bakes, heat milk, cook eggs, and prepare strawberries. At the last minute, buzz milk in the blender.

Giant "sandwich" is a 9-inch breakfast scone filled with sliced strawberries; serve wedges with hot cinnamon-spiced milk and mugs of cafe au lait.

STRAWBERRY SCONE

> About 3 cups all-purpose flour
> About ¾ cup sugar
> ½ teaspoon baking powder
> 1 teaspoon baking soda
> 2 teaspoons grated lemon peel
> ½ cup (¼ lb.) butter or margarine
> 1 cup buttermilk
> 6 cups strawberries, rinsed and drained
> Spiced steamed milk (recipe follows)

In a food processor or large bowl, whirl or stir 3 cups flour, ¾ cup sugar, baking powder, soda, and lemon peel. Cut butter into chunks and whirl or cut in with a pastry blender until fine crumbs form. Add buttermilk and whirl or stir just until evenly moistened.

Scrape dough onto a lightly floured board and knead 10 turns. Pat into a 9-inch round, then place in a greased 9-inch-diameter cake pan. Sprinkle lightly with sugar. Bake in a 400° oven until deep golden, about 35 minutes.

Meanwhile, hull strawberries, slice, and stir in a bowl with sugar to taste, about 1 tablespoon.

Turn scone out of pan. Serve warm or, if made ahead, let cool on a rack, then store airtight up to 1 day. Slice scone horizontally, then carefully lift off top, supporting with 2 wide spatulas. Fill scone with strawberries, replace top, and cut into wedges. Offer wedges in bowls with steamed milk to pour over them. Serves 8.

PER SERVING WITHOUT STEAMED MILK: 391 calories, 6.7 g protein, 64 g carbohydrates, 13 g fat, 32 mg cholesterol, 281 mg sodium

SPICED STEAMED MILK

In a 3- to 4-quart pan, warm 6 cups **milk** and 3 **cinnamon sticks** (each about 3 in. long) over medium-low heat until steaming, stirring often, 20 to 25 minutes. Lift out and discard cinnamon. Ladle ⅓ of milk at a time into a blender and whirl until very frothy; pour into a pitcher. Makes about 8 cups.

PER CUP: 113 calories, 6 g protein, 9 g carbohydrates, 6.1 g fat, 26 mg cholesterol, 90 mg sodium

BROILED SANDWICH SUPPER

Mustard Seed–Havarti Sandwich
Horseradish Crème Fraîche
Edible-Pod Peas   Asparagus
Bananas with Anisette
Mineral Water

Horseradish, blended with crème fraîche or sour cream, seasons elements of this easy meal.

Since the sandwiches take just a few minutes to cook, ready other components of the meal first. Make the horseradish sauce, then steam about ⅓ pound each of peas and asparagus. Serve them warm, or chill in water to enjoy cold. For dessert, pour a splash of anisette (or fruit syrup for children) over sliced bananas.

(Continued on next page)

MUSTARD SEED–
HAVARTI SANDWICH

- 8 slices whole-grain bread, each about 3 by 5 inches
- 1 tablespoon melted butter or margarine
- 4 thin slices red onion
- ⅔ pound havarti cheese, thinly sliced
- 1 tablespoon mustard seed
- 4 large slices tomato
- 2 cups lightly packed watercress sprigs, rinsed and crisped
  Horseradish crème fraîche (recipe follows)

Place bread on a 12- by 15-inch baking sheet. Broil about 4 inches below heat until bread is golden, about 2 minutes. Turn over and lightly streak top of each piece of bread with butter. Place an onion slice on each of 4 pieces of bread; brush onion tops with remaining butter. Broil until bread is golden, about 1½ minutes. Remove bread pieces with onion from pan and set aside.

Arrange cheese equally over remaining bread and sprinkle mustard seed on top. Broil until cheese melts, 3 minutes.

Place 1 cheese and 1 onion bread on each of 4 plates. Lay 1 tomato slice on each onion slice, then put watercress on top. Add horseradish crème fraîche to taste. Makes 4 servings.

PER SERVING WITHOUT HORSERADISH CRÈME FRAÎCHE: 435 calories, 24 g protein, 30 g carbohydrates, 25 g fat, 86 mg cholesterol, 876 mg sodium

HORSERADISH CRÈME FRAÎCHE

Stir 2 tablespoons **prepared horseradish** and ½ cup **crème fraîche** or sour cream. Makes about ⅔ cup.

PER TABLESPOON: 42 calories, 0.3 g protein, 0.6 g carbohydrates, 4.4 g fat, 16 mg cholesterol, 7.4 mg sodium

MAY

Seasoned Boiled Artichokes & Steeped Shrimp (page 106)

Spring is a time for traditional celebrations. Mark your own special event in elegant style with one of our big, beautiful cakes; you'll find directions scaled to fit an intimate group or a crowd. For informal gatherings, enjoy a hands-on feast of artichokes and shrimp or savor colorful, quick-cooking skewered entrées hot off the grill. If you'd like to add an international accent to your May meals, you'll find spicy salads from India, couscous from North Africa, and a sweet bread ring from Italy.

Baking a Big, Beautiful Cake

A LARGE, ELEGANT CAKE *can provide a sumptuous finale to traditional spring celebrations. These tiered versions—designed by baker Carolyn Weil of Bette's Bakeshop in Berkeley—are lovely to look at and exceptionally good tasting.*

Sensitive to the needs of the home cook, Weil has scaled cake-baking directions to accommodate any size group. Her know-how is reflected in the recipes and charts that follow. With them, you can create a 6-inch birthday cake for 4 or a tiered extravaganza for 112.

She offers two flavors—a light sponge cake filled with a tart lemon curd and frosted with whipped cream, and a rich chocolate torte studded with raspberries and cloaked in dark chocolate.

Frosted flowers cascade down chocolate torte created by baker Carolyn Weil. She uses glass candlestick to elevate top layer.

TIME PLAN: BAKE, FILL, FROST

You can bake all the cake layers for either flavor up to 1 week ahead. Freeze them, unless you serve them within 3 days.

Two to three days before serving, make the lemon curd for the sponge cake or the ganache for the dense chocolate cake.

The next day, fill the lemon cake with the curd, then coat layers with the first round of cream. Hold in the refrigerator as long as overnight. For the chocolate cake, plaster the cake with a layer of cool, spreadable chocolate ganache. A final layer of warm ganache goes on when chocolate is firm—or cake can be chilled in this stage up to 2 days. Once the ganache is firm, layers can be stacked and held in the refrigerator up to overnight.

Frost flowers with sugar as early as the day before the party.

The day of the party, put the final coat of cream on the lemon cake. Stack cakes if tiered; they can be kept in the refrigerator up to 6 hours.

When a tiered cake is too large to fit in the refrigerator, consider completing each individual layer at home, then stack layers, pipe on trim, and garnish at the serving site. It's often safer to carry the large masterpiece in individual parts.

WHAT EQUIPMENT YOU'LL NEED

These cakes require round cake pans at least 2 inches deep. To make sure the larger pans will fit, measure your oven first. You'll find larger pans at cake-decorating supply stores (look in the yellow pages) or through mail-order catalogues.

Also available through cake supply specialists are doilies, hardboard rounds, corrugated cardboard rounds, cooking parchment (also sold in supermarkets, near the waxed paper), and ¼-inch wooden dowels (also sold in hardware stores). You can cut dowels with pruning shears.

Before you begin, make room in your refrigerator. Larger cake layers take up lots of space. Also, clean out strong-smelling foods; the cakes absorb odors readily.

HOW TO MULTIPLY THE RECIPES

First, determine the number of servings you'll need. A serving is a 2-inch square or wedge; plan for a few extras. Next, using the charts that follow, decide on the size and quantity of layers. Yield for each batch of batter varies slightly with type of mixer and baker's folding technique. Check chart for amount of batter required to fill pans.

Organize and measure your ingredients. We've limited the largest batch size (4 x basic recipe) to about 20 cups. You'll need at least a 6-quart bowl for that amount. This is more than enough to fill the largest pan.

When separating eggs, crack individually into a bowl in case a yolk should break; separate yolk and white, then add to those already separated.

For maximum volume, don't whip more than 6 egg whites at a time (you don't need to rinse bowl and beaters after each round). You can, however, combine all the egg yolk mixture in a single bowl if you have one large enough. Add whites, as whipped, to yolk mixture.

LEMON SPONGE CAKE

For amounts, pan sizes, and baking times, refer to charts on page 103.

Butter the bottom of a round cake pan or pans. Line bottom with cooking parchment or with waxed paper. Butter paper and dust with flour.

In a bowl (2 to 3 qt. for 1 x recipe), stir together **extra-large egg yolks, butter, vanilla,** and **lemon peel.** Set aside.

Measure **extra-large egg whites, cream of tartar, sugar,** and **cake flour.** In a large bowl of an electric mixer at high speed, beat 6 whites (about ⅞ cup) and ¼ teaspoon of the cream of tartar until mixture will hold very soft peaks. Gradually add 1 cup sugar, beating until completely dissolved (rub whites between fingers to see if mixture feels smooth) and whites hold stiff, shiny peaks. Add whites to yolk mixture and sift 1 cup flour over whites; gently fold in. Repeat to whip remaining whites, and add remaining flour.

Spread batter into cake pans, filling them about ¾ full. Bake in a 350° oven until tops spring back when lightly touched. Bake on only 1 oven rack at a time if layer is larger than 10 inches.

Set cakes on racks to cool. Cut around edges of cakes to release. Invert layers onto matching-size corrugated cardboard rounds. Peel off paper. If made ahead, wrap airtight and freeze up to 1 week.

With a long serrated knife, cut each layer in half horizontally (step 1 on page 102); as a cutting guide, push toothpicks around cake sides to mark. Brush off loose crumbs. Lift off top half. Spread cut surface with **lemon curd** (recipe follows) to within ½ inch of cake edge, using the amount specified for layer size. Replace top layer, cut side down, on filling. Repeat with remaining layers.

Make about ⅓ of the total amount of **sweetened cream** (recipe follows). With a long, thin spatula, spread top and sides of cakes with a thin, smooth layer of cream, using all (step 2). Chill in refrigerator until cream is firm, at least 40 to 60 minutes. If made ahead, cover, once cream is set, and chill until the next day.

Whip another ⅓ of the total amount of sweetened cream needed and frost cakes with a second layer of cream, using all. If made ahead, chill up to 2 hours.

To assemble tiered cakes, set largest layer on a slightly larger hardboard, another corrugated cardboard round, or a flat plate covered with a large doily.

Plunge a ¼-inch wood dowel straight down through a spot where you intend to set next layer. (We arranged dowels so layers aligned at edge of cake; this requires less skill than centering layers.) Mark dowel so it is ⅛ to ¼ inch taller than layer. Remove from cake and cut dowel at the mark with pruning shears. Cut additional dowel lengths (number depends on size of layer; use 4 or 5 for a 12-inch layer).

Insert the dowel pieces into the cake layer several inches apart (step 3); these will support the next (smaller) layer.

Lay a piece of plastic wrap slightly smaller than the next layer on top of the dowels. Position that layer on the plastic (step 4). If you are aligning the layers off-center, near the circumference, set in about ½ inch from edge of layer below; this leaves room for decoration to be piped on later. Repeat for remaining layers.

Lemon slices, lacy fern leaves, and fresh roses bedeck cream-frosted lemon-curd-filled sponge cake. Three tiers, arranged off-center, serve about 65 at couple's reception.

Slice **lemons** (see chart on page 103 for number) as thin as possible and remove seeds. Gently press slices around side of each cake layer; if slice is taller than cake, trim on 1 edge to desired height and place with cut edge down.

Make remaining ⅓ of sweetened cream, and spoon into a pastry bag fitted with a ¼- to ⅜-inch decorative tip. Pipe cream around base of each layer (step 5). Serve, or keep assembled cake in a cool place up to 2 hours; chill up to 8 hours. Decorate with **fresh nontoxic flowers,** plain or frosted (recipe follows).

To serve, lift off top layer if you want to reserve it for the honorees. Remove plastic wrap and dowels. Next, cut a circle 2 inches in from side of cake's top layer. Slice this outside ring into 2-inch wedges and serve. Cut another circle, 2 inches in from cut edge; slice cake into 2-inch wedges and serve. Repeat until you have a 3- or 4-inch section left in center, then cut into wedges. Lift off cardboard. Repeat to serve each layer. —*Carolyn Weil, Berkeley, Calif.*

PER SERVING: 292 calories, 4.9 g protein, 27 g carbohydrates, 19 g fat, 225 mg cholesterol, 50 mg sodium

(Continued on next page)

Lemon curd. (See chart on facing page for proportions and total amounts.) In a pan (1 to 1½ qt. for 1 x recipe, 2 to 3 qt. for 4 x recipe), whisk together **extra-large egg yolks, extra-large whole eggs, sugar,** minced **lemon peel,** and **lemon juice.** Add **unsalted butter.**

Stir over medium-low heat until mixture thickly coats a metal spoon, about 8 minutes for 1 x recipe, about 20 minutes for 4 x recipe. Pour into a bowl and cover surface of curd with plastic wrap. Chill until cold, at least 1 hour or up to 3 days.

Sweetened cream. (See chart at right for proportions and total amounts.) In a bowl, beat **whipping cream** on high speed with a mixer or whisk until softly whipped. Add **sugar** and **vanilla.** Beat until cream holds stiff peaks.

Frosted flowers. Select blossoms of **nontoxic, pesticide-free flowers** such as roses, orchids, or alstroemeria (Peruvian lily). Trim stems, leaving 1 inch. Gently rinse blossoms (avoid bruising) and drain, inverted, in a single layer on paper towel until dry. With a fine soft brush, gently coat petals with slightly beaten **egg white** (1 extra-large white will coat 8 blossoms, 2-in. size). Sprinkle with **superfine** or regular granulated **sugar** to coat petals. Dry on a wire rack at room temperature at least 2 hours or until the next day.

Lemon Sponge Cake Proportions

BATTER

	1 x recipe (5 to 7 cups)	2 x recipe (11 to 13 cups)	3 x recipe (17 to 19 cups)	4 x recipe (20 to 22 cups)
Extra-large eggs, separated	6	12	18	24
Unsalted butter or margarine, melted	½ cup (¼ lb.)	1 cup (½ lb.)	1½ cups (¾ lb.)	2 cups (1 lb.)
Vanilla	1 teaspoon	2 teaspoons	1 tablespoon	4 teaspoons
Minced lemon peel (yellow part only)	2 teaspoons	4 teaspoons	2 tablespoons	8 teaspoons
Cream of tartar	¼ teaspoon	½ teaspoon	¾ teaspoon	1 teaspoon
Sugar	1 cup	2 cups	3 cups	4 cups
Cake flour (stir before measuring)	1 cup	2 cups	3 cups	4 cups

SWEETENED CREAM

	1 x recipe (2 cups)	2 x recipe (4 cups)	3 x recipe (6 cups)	4 x recipe (8 cups)
Whipping cream	1 cup	2 cups	3 cups	4 cups
Sugar	1 tablespoon	2 tablespoons	3 tablespoons	¼ cup
Vanilla	½ teaspoon	1 teaspoon	1½ teaspoons	2 teaspoons

1 *Split layers with a long knife. Use toothpicks as a cutting guide to mark midpoint. Coat cut side with lemon curd.*

2 *Spread whipped cream over top and sides of cake in a thin, smooth layer. Chill until set; repeat with other layers.*

3 *Push dowels (cut ⅛ to ¼ inch taller than layer) into cake to support next layer. Cover area with plastic wrap.*

LEMON CURD

	1 x recipe (1 cup)	2 x recipe (2 cups)	3 x recipe (3 cups)	4 x recipe (4 cups)
Extra-large egg yolks	2	4	6	8
Extra-large whole eggs	1	2	3	4
Sugar	⅓ cup	⅔ cup	1 cup	1⅓ cups
Minced lemon peel (yellow part only)	1½ tablespoons	3 tablespoons	4½ tablespoons	6 tablespoons
Lemon juice	⅓ cup	⅔ cup	1 cup	1⅓ cups
Unsalted butter or margarine	2½ tablespoons	5 tablespoons	7½ tablespoons	10 tablespoons

PAN SIZES, BAKING TIMES, AMOUNTS NEEDED FOR ASSEMBLING

Pan size (round, 2 in. deep)	6 in. wide	8 in. wide	10 in. wide	12 in. wide	14 in. wide
Servings (about 2-in. piece)	4 to 6	12 to 14	22	28	40
Cups of batter	3	6	9	12	16
Baking time at 350°	30 min.	35 min.	45 min.	50 min.	55 min.
Lemon curd	½ cup	¾ cup	1 cup	1½ cups	2 cups
Sweetened whipped cream	1½ cups	2½ cups	4 cups	5½ cups	7 cups
Large lemons for garnish	½ to 1	1 to 1½	1½ to 2	2 to 2½	2½ to 3

4 *Set next layer (on cardboard round) on supports; align ½ inch from edge of base. Repeat with rest of layers.*

5 *Pipe whipped cream around base of each layer to join layers and hide cardboard rounds.*

BITTERSWEET CHOCOLATE TORTE

For proportions, pan sizes, and baking times, refer to charts on page 104.

Butter bottom of a round cake pan or pans at least 2 inches deep. Line bottom with cooking parchment or waxed paper. Butter paper and dust with flour.

In the top of a double boiler or large metal bowl, combine the chopped **bittersweet chocolate** and **unsalted butter** and set over simmering water. Stir until melted.

In a bowl (1½ to 2 qt. for 1 x recipe), beat **extra-large egg yolks** and ¾ of the total **sugar** at high speed with an electric mixer or whisk until pale yellow. Add **flour** and mix well. Add chocolate mixture; stir until blended.

Measure **extra-large egg whites, salt,** and **sugar.** In a large bowl of an electric mixer at high speed, beat 6 whites (about ⅞ cup) and ¼ teaspoon salt until foamy. Gradually add ¼ cup sugar, beating until mixture holds soft moist peaks. Add to yolk mixture; gently fold together to blend. Repeat to whip remaining whites.

Spread batter into prepared cake pans, filling about ⅔ full. Sprinkle **raspberries** evenly over the surface.

Bake in a 325° oven until a toothpick inserted in center of cake (not in a berry) comes out clean.

Meanwhile, if you plan to frost the cake the same day, make **chocolate ganache** (recipe follows). Pour ⅓ of the mixture into another bowl; set larger portion aside. Stir the small amount occasionally until cool (it should have the texture of whipped butter), about 2 hours for 2 cups.

When cake is done, let cool in pan on a rack (cake settles considerably as it cools). Press edges of cake down to make an evenly thick layer; or if needed, trim away edge to make top flat. To release, cut around sides of cake; invert onto matching-size corrugated cardboard round. Brush off crumbs. (If made ahead, wrap airtight and freeze up to 1 week.)

With a long, thin spatula, smoothly spread a thin layer of the chocolate ganache (from the small amount) over sides and top of each layer. Chill until firm, at least 1 hour or up to 2 days; cover when ganache is firm. Combine any leftover ganache with reserved ganache. Cover; hold the mixture at room temperature up to 2 days.

About 30 minutes before adding the second coat of ganache, set mixture over simmering water, stirring often, just until warm (about 100°), fluid, and the texture of heavy cream. If too hot and thin (it will melt first coat of ganache on cake), remove from water and let cool to about 100°, stirring occasionally.

Place 1 cake layer on a wire rack set in a larger rimmed pan; or, for large layer, set rack over 2 rectangular rimmed pans placed side by side.

Pouring in a continuous heavy stream, cover top and sides of layer completely with the liquid ganache; start at center, then move toward edge in a circular motion. Let stand until drips cease. Lift rack from pan, replace with another, and set another layer on it. Repeat until all layers are coated. Let stand until ganache firms, about 2 hours at room temperature, or 1 hour to the next day in the refrigerator. Scrape ganache drippings back into bowl. Let cool at room temperature until the texture of whipped butter; reserve to use for decorative borders.

For tiered cake, assemble as directed for lemon sponge cake (preceding); omit lemon slices and sweetened whipped cream.

Spoon reserved ganache into a pastry bag with a ⅜-inch decorative tip. Pipe a border around the base of each cake layer.

Serve cake, hold at cool room temperature up to 6 hours, or cover lightly and refrigerate until the next day. Just before serving, garnish with **nontoxic, pesticide-free flowers** or frosted flowers (recipe on page 102). Cut and serve cake as directed for lemon sponge cake (page 101).

PER SERVING: 406 calories, 6.5 g protein, 34 g carbohydrates, 32 g fat, 181 mg cholesterol, 81 mg sodium

Chocolate ganache. (See charts at right.) In the top of a double boiler or a metal bowl set over simmering water, combine chopped **bittersweet** or semisweet **chocolate** and **whipping cream,** stirring often until melted and blended.

Bittersweet Chocolate Torte Proportions

BATTER

	1 x recipe (5 to 7 cups)	2 x recipe (10 to 12 cups)	3 x recipe (15 to 17 cups)	4 x recipe (20 to 22 cups)
Bittersweet or semisweet chocolate, chopped	9 oz. (1½ cups)	1 lb. 2 oz. (3 cups)	1 lb. 11 oz. (4½ cups)	2 lb. 4 oz. (6 cups)
Unsalted butter or margarine	¾ cup (⅜ lb.)	1½ cups (¾ lb.)	2¼ cups (1⅛ lb.)	3 cups (1½ lb.)
Extra-large eggs, separated	6	12	18	24
Sugar	1 cup	2 cups	3 cups	4 cups
All-purpose flour	¼ cup	½ cup	¾ cup	1 cup
Salt	¼ teaspoon	½ teaspoon	¾ teaspoon	1 teaspoon

CHOCOLATE GANACHE

	1 x recipe (1½ cups)	2 x recipe (3 cups)	3 x recipe (4½ cups)	4 x recipe (6 cups)
Bittersweet or semisweet chocolate, chopped	½ lb. (1⅓ cups)	1 lb. (2⅔ cups)	1½ lbs. (4 cups)	2 lbs. (5⅓ cups)
Whipping cream	1 cup	2 cups	3 cups	4 cups

PAN SIZES, BAKING TIMES, AMOUNTS NEEDED FOR ASSEMBLING

Pan size (round, 2 in. deep)	6 in. wide	8 in. wide	10 in. wide	12 in. wide	14 in. wide
Servings (about 2-in. piece)	4 to 6	12 to 14	22 to 24	28	40
Cups of batter	2 to 2½	4 to 5	7½ to 8	9 to 10	15 to 16
Raspberries (rinsed and drained), for each pan	½ cup	⅔ cup	¾ cup	1 cup	1½ cups
Baking time at 325°	45 to 55 min.	50 to 60 min.	1 hour 5 min.	1 hour 10 min.	1 hour 15 min.
Ganache for 2 coats and trim	1½ cups	2 to 2½ cups	3 to 3½ cups	3½ to 4 cups	5 to 5½ cups

Party-Pretty Punches

FESTIVE CELEBRATIONS—*showers, weddings, anniversaries, graduations—are frequent events this time of year. And punches to sip are part of the scene.*

Here we offer three simple refreshments based on fresh and prepared fruit ingredients. Each can be tailored to various ages and tastes. Wine and stronger beverages are optional additions.

The first is a rosy mix of strawberries, guava drink, grapefruit concentrate, and sparkling wine or water. The next two have tropical flavors: one combines cantaloupe, mango, and passion fruit; the other is a frothy banana-citrus cooler.

STRAWBERRY-GUAVA PUNCH WITH SORBET

- 1 quart strawberries, rinsed and drained
- 1 quart strawberry sorbet or sherbet
- 1 can (6 oz.) frozen grapefruit juice concentrate
- 2 bottles (1½ qt. each) guava fruit juice drink
- 1 bottle (750 ml.) chilled sparkling wine or 1 bottle (1 pt. 12 oz.) chilled sparkling water

Place half of the berries (use the prettiest ones; keep hulls attached) on a flat pan without touching. Freeze until hard, about 1 hour; if done ahead, pack airtight when hard and freeze until the next day.

Put a 10- by 15-inch pan in the freezer. When cold, scoop sorbet into about 2-inch balls and place on the chilled pan. Freeze. If holding more than 1 hour, cover airtight and freeze up until the next day.

Hull remaining berries. In a blender or food processor, whirl berries with grapefruit concentrate until smoothly puréed. Pour into a 6- to 7-quart punch bowl. Add guava drink and sparkling wine; stir well. Add sorbet, then float frozen strawberries in punch. Ladle into punch cups or wide-mouth glasses; sip the liquid, and eat the sorbet and fruit with a spoon. Makes 18 cups, about 24 servings.—*Ruth E. Sheets, San Diego.*

PER SERVING: 145 calories, 0.5 g protein, 31 g carbohydrates, 0.2 g fat, 0 mg cholesterol, 12 mg sodium

Strawberry-guava punch effervesces when blended with sparkling wine or water. Frozen strawberries and sorbet scoops peek through pink foam.

CANTALOUPE, MANGO, PASSION FRUIT FIZZ

- 1 large (about 2 lb.) cantaloupe
- 1 medium-size (about ¾ lb.) ripe mango
- 5 to 6 ripe passion fruit (shells look shriveled) or 1 can (4½ oz.) passion fruit pulp
- 1 can (6 oz.) frozen tangerine juice concentrate
- 1 bottle (750 ml.) chilled Gewürztraminer and 1 bottle (about 1 qt.) chilled ginger ale (or omit wine and use 2 bottles ginger ale)
- Mint sprigs

Cut cantaloupe in half. Scoop out and discard seeds; cut off and discard rind. Cut melon into chunks and set aside.

Peel, pit, and cut mango into chunks; set aside. Cut passion fruit in half. Scoop out pulp and seeds with a spoon. To get rid of seeds, pour pulp (fresh or canned) into a fine strainer and rub through strainer into a bowl; discard seeds.

In a blender or food processor, combine passion fruit pulp, mango, and cantaloupe with tangerine concentrate; whirl until smoothly puréed. Pour purée into a 4- to 5-quart pitcher. Gently stir in wine and ginger ale. Pour into tall, slender glasses or wine flutes; garnish each with a sprig of mint. Makes 12 cups, about 16 servings.

PER SERVING: 99 calories, 0.6 g protein, 17 g carbohydrates, 0.2 g fat, 0 mg cholesterol, 11 mg sodium

BANANA-CITRUS COOLER

- 2 large ripe bananas, peeled, cut up
- ½ cup lime juice
- 1 can (12 oz.) frozen pineapple-orange-banana juice concentrate
- 1 bottle (1 pt. 12 oz.) chilled sparkling water
- 1¼ cups light rum (optional)
- Ice cubes
- 1 lime, thinly sliced

In a blender or food processor, smoothly purée bananas, lime juice, and concentrate. Pour into a 3-quart pitcher. Add water and rum. Stir down foam. Pour into ice-filled glasses; garnish with lime slices. Makes about 9 cups, 10 to 12 servings.

PER SERVING: 82 calories, 0.2 g protein, 21 g carbohydrates, 0.1 g fat, 0 mg cholesterol, 5.2 mg sodium

Take-it-Anywhere Spring Feast

FORGET THE FORKS *for this spring feast; all you need are fingers and napkins.*

You nibble on crisp carrots, radishes, and romaine spears. Strip artichokes leaf by leaf. Peel the shells from succulent, sweet shrimp and eat them plain, seasoned only by the highly spiced broth they cooked in. Or splash them with a refreshing vinegar, or dip them in flavored mayonnaise.

Dessert's as simple. Dunk fresh strawberries and biscotti into sweet or dry marsala.

HANDS-ON ARTICHOKE FEAST

Small Romaine Spears   Red Radishes
Baby Carrots
Seasoned Boiled Artichokes
& Steeped Shrimp
Mint-Ginger Vinegar
Seeded Mayonnaise
Crusty Bread   Butter
Dry Sauvignon Blanc
Sparkling Water
Strawberries   Biscotti   Marsala

You can easily tailor this meal to a group of any size. For each serving, prepare 2 or 3 pieces each of romaine, carrot, and radish. Also allow 1 big artichoke, 3 to 4 ounces shrimp, 1 to 2 ounces bread, 4 to 6 berries, and 1 or 2 cookies per person.

Clean and crisp the raw vegetables up to 1 day ahead. Shrimp and artichokes can be served warm, or make them ahead and serve cool. If you carry the meal to a site, keep foods cool en route in an insulated container. Sauces can be made ahead; add herbs to the vinegar shortly before serving to preserve color.

SEASONED BOILED ARTICHOKES & STEEPED SHRIMP

⅓ cup vinegar
1 tablespoon mustard seed
1 tablespoon cumin seed
2 teaspoons black peppercorns
8 thin slices (each the size of a quarter) fresh ginger
10 sprigs (each about 4 in.) fresh cilantro (coriander)
10 sprigs (each about 4 in.) fresh mint or 2 tablespoons dry mint leaves
2 tablespoons olive oil
8 large artichokes (4- to 4½-in. diameter, about ¾ lb. each)
2 pounds large shrimp (31 to 35 per lb.)

In an 11- to 12-quart pan, combine 5 quarts water, vinegar, mustard seed, cumin seed, peppercorns, ginger, cilantro, mint, and oil. Cover and bring to a boil over high heat.

Remove coarse outer leaves from artichokes and trim stems even with bases. With a sharp knife, cut off top third of each artichoke. With scissors, trim thorny tips off remaining leaves. Immerse artichokes in tap water and swish back and forth; shake out water. Place artichokes in the boiling water. Reduce heat, cover, and boil gently until bottoms are tender when pierced, 35 to 40 minutes. Lift out artichokes and drain.

Meanwhile, devein shrimp by inserting a toothpick between shell joints and under the vein that runs down shrimp's back; gently pull out vein. If vein breaks, repeat at another shell joint.

After you remove the artichokes from the pan, return water to boiling and add shrimp. Cover and remove from heat. Let steep until shrimp are pink, 2 to 3 minutes. Using a large strainer or slotted spoon, lift out shrimp and drain. Pour cooking liquid through a fine strainer; reserve seeds but discard ginger, mint sprigs (leave dry mint in), cilantro, and cooking liquid.

Serve shrimp and artichokes hot or cool. If made ahead, cool, cover, and chill up until the next day. Makes 8 servings.

PER SERVING: 202 calories, 23 g protein, 18 g carbohydrates, 5.4 g fat, 140 mg cholesterol, 246 mg sodium

MINT-GINGER VINEGAR

Mix 1½ cups **rice** or cider **vinegar,** 3 tablespoons **sugar** and 2 tablespoons minced **fresh ginger** until sugar dissolves. Up to 2 hours before serving, add 2 tablespoons minced **fresh** or dry **mint leaves** and 2 tablespoons minced **fresh cilantro.** Makes 1½ cups.

PER TABLESPOON: 8.5 calories, 0 g protein, 2.5 g carbohydrates, 0 g fat, 0 mg cholesterol, 0.2 mg sodium

SEEDED MAYONNAISE

Mix 2 cups **mayonnaise,** 3 tablespoons **lemon juice,** and reserved **seeds** from artichoke cooking water. Makes about 2 cups.

PER TABLESPOON: 101 calories, 0.2 g protein, 0.7 g carbohydrates, 11 g fat, 8.1 mg cholesterol, 79 mg sodium

Delectable shipboard picnic can be adjusted for groups of any size. All the foods are easy to transport and can be eaten with fingers.

Portable feast features big spring artichokes, moist shrimp cooked in their shells, and crisp vegetables to dip into a lean minted vinegar or a rich, seed-laced mayonnaise. Complete the meal with an equally simple dessert: fresh strawberries and biscotti dunked into sweet or dry marsala.

Ultimate Skewering...Beef, Fish, or Chicken

FOR SUMMER BARBECUING, *skewers make tiny, quick-cooking pieces of food easy to handle on the grill and attractively organized at the table. In this sampler of recipes, we offer hearty beef with corn, Yugoslavian-style fish with a fresh relish, and a Japanese version of chicken and vegetables.*

SKEWERED BEEF & CORN

- 4 pounds boneless chuck roast
  Unsalted meat tenderizer
  (optional)

Pineapple-wine marinade
(recipe follows)

- ¼ cup (⅛ lb.) butter or margarine, melted
- ¼ cup salad oil
- 5 medium-size ears corn, husked and cut into 2-inch lengths
- 3 medium-size green bell peppers, stemmed, seeded, and cut into 1½-inch squares
- 2 large mild red onions, cut into 1½-inch pieces
- 1 medium-size pineapple (about 3½ lb.), peeled, cored, and cut into 1½-inch cubes

Cut meat across the grain into slices about 1½ inches thick; if desired, apply tenderizer according to package directions. Then cut meat into 1½-inch cubes and place in a large bowl.

Pour marinade over meat; stir to coat. Cover and chill at least 6 hours or until next day; stir occasionally.

Drain marinade from meat, reserving ⅓ cup. In a small bowl, stir together butter, oil, and reserved marinade.

On 8 long, sturdy metal skewers, thread meat alternately with corn (through cob), bell peppers, onions, and

Chunks of beef alternate with onion, bell pepper, corn, and pineapple on these sturdy skewers. You can use economical beef chuck or a more tender cut.

Firm-textured fish such as swordfish, halibut, and ling cod are easy to handle on skewers; small amounts of olive oil and garlic season fish well.

pineapple. Brush skewers with butter mixture, then place on a lightly greased grill 4 to 6 inches above a solid bed of hot coals (you can hold your hand at grill level only 2 to 3 seconds). Cook, turning and basting frequently with butter mixture. For medium-rare (cut to test), grill about 15 minutes. Makes 8 servings.

PER SERVING: 578 calories, 39 g protein, 35 g carbohydrates, 32 g fat, 138 mg cholesterol, 159 mg sodium

Pineapple-wine marinade. In a bowl, mix 1½ cups *each* **canned** or chilled packaged **pineapple juice** and **dry red wine,** 1½ tablespoons **minced onion,** 1½ teaspoons *each* **Worcestershire** and **dry thyme leaves,** ¾ teaspoon **dry mustard,** ¼ cup firmly packed **brown sugar,** ¼ teaspoon **pepper,** and 2 cloves **garlic,** minced or pressed.

YUGOSLAVIAN FISH SKEWERS

- 3 tablespoons olive oil
- 2 cloves garlic, minced or pressed
- ¼ teaspoon pepper
- 2 pounds firm-textured fish steaks, such as swordfish, halibut, turbot, or ling cod, skinned (if needed) and cut into 1- by 1½-inch chunks
  Salt
  Serbian tomato relish (recipe follows)

In a large bowl, combine oil, garlic, pepper, and fish; mix gently. Thread fish chunks equally on 6 sturdy metal skewers.

Place skewers on a well-greased grill 4 to 6 inches above a solid bed of hot coals (you can hold your hand at grill level only 2 to 3 seconds). Cook, turning several times, until fish flakes but still looks moist when prodded in thickest part, 10 to 12 minutes. Season to taste with salt and serve with relish. Makes 6 servings.

PER SERVING: 224 calories, 27 g protein, 0.4 g carbohydrates, 12 g fat, 53 mg cholesterol, 121 mg sodium

Serbian tomato relish. Stem, seed, and finely chop 1 *each* **small fresh** or canned **hot red, green, and yellow chilies.** Core, peel, and dice 2 large **tomatoes.** Finely chop 1 medium-size **onion.** Mix chilies, tomatoes, and onion with 1 teaspoon

sugar, 1 tablespoon **red wine vinegar,** and **salt** to taste. Cover and refrigerate for at least 20 minutes or until next day. Makes about 3 cups.

PER ½ CUP: 18 calories, 0.6 g protein, 4 g carbohydrates, 0.1 g fat, 0 mg cholesterol, 94 mg sodium

YAKITORI CHICKEN & VEGETABLES

- 2 tablespoons sesame seed
- 3 large whole chicken breasts (about 1½ lb. each), skinned, boned, and split in half
  Sherry-soy marinade (recipe follows)
- 6 medium-size Oriental eggplants
- 15 to 18 large fresh shiitake or common mushrooms

Toast sesame seed in a small frying pan over medium heat until golden, about 3 minutes; shake pan often. Set aside.

Rinse chicken and pat dry. Cut each breast half into 6 or 7 equal-size chunks, then place in a bowl. Pour ¼ cup of the marinade over chicken and mix gently; reserve remaining marinade. Cover and chill 1 to 8 hours.

Lift chicken from marinade and thread equally on 6 metal skewers. Set chicken aside; discard marinade in bowl.

Slash each eggplant lengthwise or crosswise in 4 or 5 places, making evenly spaced cuts ⅓ inch deep. Cut mushroom stems flush with caps.

Place eggplants on a lightly greased grill 4 to 6 inches above a solid bed of hot coals (you can hold your hand at grill level only 2 to 3 seconds). Cook, turning often, until eggplants are slightly charred and very soft when pressed, 30 to 35 minutes.

After eggplants have cooked for about 20 minutes, start cooking mushrooms and chicken. Dip mushrooms in reserved marinade, drain briefly, and set on grill. Cook about 5 minutes; turn over and continue to cook until softened and lightly browned, about 5 minutes longer. At the same time you lay mushrooms on grill, place chicken on grill and cook, turning occasionally until no longer pink in center (cut to test), 10 to 12 minutes.

Arrange skewers, mushrooms, and eggplants on 1 or 2 shallow platters. Pull each eggplant apart at slashes to expose flesh. Moisten chicken and vegetables with reserved marinade and sprinkle

with sesame seed. Offer any remaining marinade to add to taste. Makes 6 servings.

PER SERVING: 374 calories, 53 g protein, 15 g carbohydrates, 11 g fat, 138 mg cholesterol, 383 mg sodium

Sherry-soy marinade. Stir together ⅓ cup **dry sherry,** 3 tablespoons *each* **soy sauce** and **Oriental sesame oil,** and 1½ teaspoons minced **fresh ginger.**

Tender nuggets of marinated chicken breast have sesame seed garnish; grill mushrooms and eggplant beside meat.

Chats: Cool, Spicy Salads from India

IN INDIA, *a chat is more than small talk. It's a snack, appetizer, or salad, eaten anytime to excite and tease the palate.*

Serve chats—like these four spicy salads—together as a cool make-ahead buffet for summer. Their bold flavor combinations and lean calorie counts make them especially appealing. Accompany the salads with chewy bread rounds quickly shaped from purchased frozen bread dough.

Or offer each salad on its own, with nontraditional companions, for simple warm-weather meals.

Potato chunks and green beans bathed in cayenne, pepper, and cumin, and accented with mint, offer an explosion of flavors. Cucumber gets a lively boost from minced fresh chilies and a few shreds of coconut. Both salads make interesting partners to grilled meats, fish, or poultry.

Crab, dressed with fennel-scented tomato sauce and enlivened with cilantro, can serve as an elegant luncheon salad with the chewy bread rounds or crusty rolls.

Try a favorite street vendor's snack for lunch: sweet, juicy fruit sprinkled with cumin, cayenne, and pepper. Then add chopped hot chilies, ginger, mint, cilantro, and lemon juice to taste. The result is refreshingly cool and hot in the same bite; try it with cold cooked ham or chicken.

POTATO & GREEN BEAN CHAT

- ½ **pound green beans, ends trimmed**
- 6 **medium-size red thin-skinned potatoes (2 to 2½ lb. total)**
  Potato chat masala (recipe follows)
- ½ **teaspoon ground coriander**
- 1 **teaspoon mustard seed, crushed**
- ⅓ **cup hot water**
- ⅓ **cup chopped fresh mint leaves**
- ¼ **cup thinly sliced green onion**
- ¼ **cup lemon juice**
  Salt
  Mint sprigs

In a 5- to 6-quart pan, bring about 3 quarts water to boiling. Add beans and cook, uncovered, until tender to bite, about 5 minutes. Lift out beans with tongs and immerse in cold water.

Add potatoes to boiling water and simmer, covered, until tender when pierced, 25 to 30 minutes. Drain; let cool. Cut potatoes into 1-inch cubes and place in a large bowl. Mix chat masala, coriander, mustard seed, and hot water,

and pour over potatoes; mix lightly and let stand about 15 minutes, stirring occasionally.

Drain beans and cut into 1½-inch lengths. To potatoes, add beans, chopped mint, onion, lemon juice, and salt to taste. Mix gently and pour into a shallow bowl. (If made ahead, cover and chill up to 4 hours.) Garnish with mint sprigs. Makes 5 or 6 servings.

PER SERVING: 139 calories, 4 g protein, 31 g carbohydrates, 0.5 g fat, 0 mg cholesterol, 14 mg sodium

Potato chat masala. Mix 1 teaspoon **ground cumin**, ½ to ¾ teaspoon **cayenne** (or to taste), and ½ teaspoon **pepper**.

CUCUMBER & CARROT CHAT

- 3 **tablespoons coarsely or finely shredded unsweetened dry coconut**
- ¼ **cup white wine vinegar**
- 2 **teaspoons sugar**
- 1 **teaspoon mustard seed, crushed**
- 2 **medium-size cucumbers, ends trimmed, halved, seeded, and thinly sliced**
- 1 **large carrot, peeled and shredded**
- 2 **or 3 fresh jalapeño chilies, stemmed, seeded, and minced**
  Salt

Soak the coconut in ¼ cup water until soft, about 5 minutes. Drain well. In a large bowl, combine coconut, vinegar, sugar, and mustard seed; mix until sugar dissolves. Add cucumbers, carrot, jalapeños, and salt to taste; mix well. Pour into a serving dish. Serve, or cover and chill up to 4 hours. Makes 5 or 6 servings.

PER SERVING: 43 calories, 1 g protein, 7 g carbohydrates, 1.6 g fat, 0 mg cholesterol, 8.7 mg sodium

CRAB CHAT

- 2 **tablespoons salad oil**
- 1 **small onion, chopped**
- 1 **tablespoon minced fresh ginger**
- 2 **cloves garlic, pressed or minced**
- 2 **teaspoons paprika**
- ½ **teaspoon cayenne**
- ½ **teaspoon dry thyme leaves**
- 1 **teaspoon fennel seed, crushed**
- 5 **medium-size Roma-type tomatoes (about 1 lb. total), cored and chopped**
- 1 **pound shelled cooked crab**
- 3 **tablespoons lemon juice**

- ⅓ **cup chopped fresh cilantro (coriander)**
  Salt
  Iceberg lettuce leaves, washed and crisped
- 2 **green onions, ends trimmed and thinly sliced**
  Lemon wedges

In a 10- to 12-inch frying pan, combine oil, onion, ginger, and garlic. Stir often over medium heat until onion is limp, 4 to 5 minutes. Stir in paprika, cayenne, thyme, and fennel. Add half of the tomatoes. Simmer, uncovered, until sauce is reduced to a thick pulp, about 5 minutes. Stir in crab and lemon juice. Let mixture cool. (If made ahead, cover and chill up to 8 hours.)

Stir in about 1 cup of the tomatoes, cilantro, and salt to taste. Spoon onto a platter lined with lettuce. Garnish with the remaining tomatoes and onions. Squeeze lemon to taste onto salad. Makes 5 or 6 servings.

PER SERVING: 139 calories, 16 g protein, 4.8 g carbohydrates, 6.2 g fat, 76 mg cholesterol, 218 mg sodium

FRUIT SALAD CHAT

- 1 **large firm-ripe papaya (about 1 lb.), peeled, seeded, and sliced**
- 1 **small honeydew melon (about 1¾ lb.), peeled, seeded, and cut into thin wedges**
- 2 **large kiwi fruit (about 8 oz. total), peeled and thinly sliced**
- 2 **cups strawberries, hulled and rinsed**
- 2 **large lemons, cut in half**
  Fruit chat masala (recipe follows)
  Salt
- 1 **tablespoon minced fresh ginger**
- 1 **or 2 fresh jalapeño chilies, stemmed, seeded, and minced**
- ¼ **cup chopped fresh mint leaves**
- ¼ **cup chopped fresh cilantro (coriander)**

On a large platter, arrange papaya, honeydew, kiwis, strawberries, and lemons. (If made ahead, cover and chill up until the next day.) Sprinkle fruit with chat masala and salt to taste. Offer ginger, jalapeños, mint, and cilantro to add to salad to taste. Squeeze lemon to taste onto salad. Makes 5 or 6 servings.

PER SERVING: 89 calories, 1.5 g protein, 22 g carbohydrates, 0.6 g fat, 0 mg cholesterol, 12 mg sodium

Fruit chat masala. Mix 1 teaspoon **ground cumin**, ¼ to ½ teaspoon **cayenne** (or to taste), and ¼ teaspoon **pepper**.

Spicy Indian salads make cool summer meal served together; or offer individually. Top to bottom, enjoy crab with tomatoes, cucumbers and carrots, potatoes with green beans, and fruit with chilies, mint, and cilantro to add to taste.

CHEWY BREAD ROUNDS

1 loaf (1 lb.) frozen white or whole-
   wheat bread dough, thawed
1 tablespoon melted butter or
   margarine
2 teaspoons poppy seed

On a lightly floured board, cut the loaf crosswise into 6 equal pieces. On greased 12- by 15-inch baking sheets, press each piece of dough into a round about ¼ inch thick and 5 inches across. Space pressed rounds about 2 inches apart. Cover lightly with plastic wrap and let rise in a warm place until puffy, 20 to 25 minutes. Uncover and brush with melted butter. Sprinkle center of each round with equal portions of poppy seed.

Bake in a 375° oven until golden brown, about 20 minutes total; if using 1 oven, switch pan positions halfway. Serve warm. (If made ahead, cool, wrap airtight up to 1 day; reheat, lightly covered, in a 350° oven until warm, about 5 minutes.) Makes 6.

PER PIECE: 225 calories, 5.9 g protein, 36 g carbohydrates, 6.1 g fat, 8.6 mg cholesterol, 384 mg sodium

Cheese Combinations as Quick Appetizers

NEED AN APPETIZER *in a hurry? Cheese is a convenient answer. It's ready to eat, appeals to a wide range of tastes, and is easy to dress up for a custom-made look.*

Simple seasonings, shaping, or heating can transform a cheese, giving it a different flavor or texture. Here are three combinations that take only a few minutes to assemble. And you can make the first two a day ahead.

PESTO CHEESE SPREAD

Offer with crisp breadsticks, red bell pepper strips, and cucumber slices.

- ⅓ **cup pine nuts or slivered almonds**
- 8 **ounces (about 1 cup) ricotta cheese, at room temperature**
- 8 **ounces neufchâtel cheese (about 1 cup) or mascarpone, at room temperature**
- ⅓ **cup pesto, purchased or homemade**
  Salt

Place nuts in a 9-inch pie or cake pan and bake in a 350° oven until golden, 6 to 8 minutes; shake occasionally. Set aside.

Meanwhile, with a mixer or food processor, beat ricotta, neufchâtel, and pesto until well blended. Add salt to taste. Stir in half the nuts. (If made ahead, cover and chill until next day. To serve, let warm to room temperature for best flavor.) Mound cheese mixture on a plate. Sprinkle with remaining nuts. Makes about 2 cups, 10 to 12 appetizer servings.

PER TABLESPOON: 47 calories, 2.1 g protein, 0.1 g carbohydrates, 4.1 g fat, 9.4 mg cholesterol, 45 mg sodium.

PROSCIUTTO-TOPPED BRIE

Even firm brie melts smoothly when baked. If you let it stand, hold on a warming tray to keep cheese fluid. Offer crisp toasted baguette slices and celery sticks to eat with it.

- 1 **chilled firm-ripe round brie cheese (8 oz.), or a ½-pound wedge**
- 3 **tablespoons finely chopped drained dried tomatoes packed in oil**
- 1 **ounce thinly sliced prosciutto, slivered**
- 1 **tablespoon oil from dried tomatoes or olive oil**

Cut brie in half crosswise. Set 1 half, cut side up, in a buttered shallow baking dish just slightly larger than cheese. Evenly distribute chopped tomatoes over cut cheese. Place other half of cheese on top, cut side down. Mix prosciutto shreds with oil and mound over cheese. (If made ahead, cover and chill until the next day.)

Bake, uncovered, in a 350° oven until cheese is hot in center, 12 to 18 minutes. Serve hot. Makes 4 appetizer servings.

PER SERVING: 268 calories, 13 g protein, 1.8 g carbohydrates, 23 g fat, 61 mg cholesterol, 741 mg sodium.

CHÈVRE WITH MINT & CUMIN

Serve with toasted pumpernickel triangles and green bell pepper wedges.

- 1 **log or slice unripened chèvre cheese (8 to 12 oz.)**
- 3 **to 4 tablespoons extra-virgin olive oil**
- ½ **teaspoon cumin seed, crushed**
  About ¼ teaspoon cayenne
- 2 **tablespoons chopped fresh mint leaves**

Set cheese on a small plate. Drizzle olive oil over cheese. Sprinkle with cumin, cayenne to taste, and mint. Makes 4 to 6 appetizer servings.

PER SERVING: 198 calories, 7 g protein, 2.8 g carbohydrates, 18 g fat, 35 mg cholesterol, 233 mg sodium.

Pine nuts tumble over mounded ricotta and neufchâtel cheese mixture seasoned with pesto. Prepare it ahead and refrigerate overnight so flavors can mellow; serve at room temperature. Crunchy breadsticks, cucumber slices, and wide strips of red bell pepper make good scoopers.

Fast & Light Soups

A LIGHT TOUCH *with seasonal vege-tables highlights their flavors in these quick soups that are easy on the waistline.*

Each soup starts with lean chicken broth as the base. In the first recipe, tiny carrots, potatoes, and green onions simmer with thyme and lemon. Two kinds of peas—edible pod, and ones to shell—go in the second soup; tarragon is the seasoning. Cooked watercress takes on a smokiness in the third soup, slimmer than its classic counterpart, with just enough sour cream—or yogurt—for a smooth texture.

BABY VEGETABLE SOUP

- 6 to 8 green onions, ends trimmed
- 1 tablespoon fresh thyme leaves, or 1 teaspoon dry thyme leaves
- 2 teaspoons grated lemon peel
- 1 tablespoon butter or margarine
- 1 quart regular-strength chicken broth
- 12 small (1½-in.-diameter, about 1 lb.) thin-skinned potatoes; or use 3½ cups 1-inch chunks thin-skinned potatoes
- ⅓ pound baby carrots (without tops; about 4 in. long), ends trimmed; or use 1½ cups thinly sliced carrots

Thinly slice green and white parts of onions separately. In a 3- to 4-quart pan over medium heat, stir white part of onions, thyme, and lemon peel in butter until onions are limp, 3 to 5 minutes.

Add broth and potatoes. Bring to a boil over high heat, then cover and simmer until potatoes are tender when pierced, 10 to 12 minutes. Add carrots and simmer until tender to bite, about 2 minutes. Stir in green onions and ladle into bowls. Makes 7 cups, enough for 4 servings.

PER SERVING: 169 calories, 5.2 g protein, 27 g carbohydrates, 4.7 g fat, 7.8 mg cholesterol, 104 mg sodium

PEA & PEA POD SOUP

- 1 medium-size onion, minced
- 1 tablespoon minced fresh tarragon leaves, or 1 teaspoon dry tarragon leaves
- 2 tablespoons butter or margarine
- 6 cups regular-strength chicken broth
- 2 cups shelled fresh peas or frozen petite peas
- ¾ pound edible-pod peas, ends and strings pulled off

In a 3- to 4-quart pan over medium heat, cook onion and tarragon in butter until onion is very limp, 12 to 15 minutes; stir frequently.

Add broth and shelled fresh peas. Bring to a boil over high heat and cook until peas are just tender to bite, 2 to 5 minutes. (If using frozen peas, just bring broth to boiling.)

Add edible-pod peas and bring to a boil. Serve at once; green color fades if soup stands. Makes 9½ cups, enough for 6 servings.

PER SERVING: 136 calories, 6.9 g protein, 14 g carbohydrates, 5.7 g fat, 10 mg cholesterol, 98 mg sodium

CREAM OF WATERCRESS SOUP

- 1 quart regular-strength chicken broth
- 1 quart watercress sprigs, rinsed and drained well
- ½ cup sour cream or unflavored yogurt
  Pepper

In a 3- to 4-quart pan, bring broth to a boil over high heat. Add watercress, cover, and simmer until it is tender to bite, 2 to 3 minutes. In a blender, smoothly purée a portion at a time with sour cream. Season to taste with pepper. Serve warm. Or cover and chill up to 1 day and serve cold. Makes 5½ cups, enough for 4 servings.

PER SERVING: 96 calories, 4 g protein, 3.1 g carbohydrates, 7.6 g fat, 13 mg cholesterol, 83 mg sodium

Fresh ingredients show off in simple soups (from top): baby carrots and potatoes; peas and pea pods with onion; and watercress. Serve for lunch or supper with sandwiches or simply cooked meats, fish.

An East-West Meal: Chinese Chicken Sandwich

ASIA AND THE WEST UNITE *in this stylish sandwich. Cured in salt and fragrant spices, chicken for the filling bakes to moist succulence. A choice of Chinese or Western breads and condiments lets diners tailor each sandwich to taste.*

The sandwich is prepared in two steps. Start the simple curing process on the chicken at least a day before you serve; rub breast or thigh pieces with salt, sugar, and spices, then chill overnight. Next, bake the chicken briefly, then slice it to serve with assorted breads and spreads.

Look for the unfilled Chinese baked or steamed buns at Asian bakeries, or use more readily available soft dinner rolls. The hoisin sauce and Chinese five spice can be found in many supermarkets and Oriental groceries.

CHINESE CHICKEN SANDWICH

> **Dry-cured chicken (directions follow)**
> **About 1 tablespoon salad oil**
> **Condiments (suggestions follow)**
> 16 **Chinese baked or steamed buns or any soft dinner rolls, split in half**

Place dry-cured chicken in a single layer in a 10- by 15-inch baking pan and brush lightly with salad oil. Bake in a 350° oven until no longer pink in thickest part, about 20 minutes for breasts, 20 to 30 minutes for thighs. Let cool. Slice thighs or breasts crosswise into ¼-inch-thick pieces.

Arrange chicken and condiments on a platter and in bowls. Offer bread from a basket. Let guests assemble sandwiches as they like. Makes 16 sandwiches; allow 2 per person. Makes 8 servings.

PER SANDWICH WITHOUT CONDIMENTS: 327 calories, 27 g protein, 32 g carbohydrates, 9.2 g fat, 97 mg cholesterol, 552 mg sodium

Style your own chicken sandwich with dry-cured roast chicken, soft buns, and a choice of condiments: orange slices, lettuce, cilantro, green onion, hoisin sauce, mustard, and mayonnaise.

Dry-cured chicken. Combine 1 tablespoon **Chinese five spice** (or ½ teaspoon *each* ground allspice, crushed anise seed, ground cinnamon, ground cloves, and ground ginger), 2 teaspoons **salt,** 1 teaspoon **sugar,** and ½ teaspoon **pepper.** In a glass, ceramic, or stainless steel bowl, coat 2 pounds **skinned and boned chicken thighs or breasts** with the salt mixture; cover and chill overnight.

Thoroughly rinse chicken under cold running water, rubbing lightly to release salt; drain and pat chicken dry (cover and chill up to 1 day, if desired).

Condiments. Offer about ⅓ cup *each* **hoisin sauce, Dijon mustard, mayonnaise,** thinly sliced **green onion,** and **cilantro** (coriander) **sprigs;** 3 large **oranges** (peel and white membrane cut off, fruit sliced crosswise); and 16 small **iceberg lettuce leaves** (rinsed and crisped).

"Drumsticks" & Speedy Scaloppine—with Turkey Parts

TURKEY PARTS *cut the big birds down to everyday size. Turkey thighs, at around $1.50 a pound, and wings, at less than $1 a pound, are particularly good values.*

Boned, skinned, and pounded thighs make a Chinese version of quick-cooking scaloppine. The wings, cut apart and baked with a crusty coating, turn into "drumsticks" to munch hot or cold.

Turkeys come in all sizes; so do parts. You can use weight as the guide for the thighs, but for wings, buy the amount specified.

SICHUAN TURKEY THIGHS SCALOPPINE

> About 2½ pounds turkey thighs
> 3 tablespoons soy sauce
> 2 tablespoons Sichuan chili sauce or Chinese hot bean paste (or pepper to taste)
> 3 tablespoons olive or salad oil
> 2 tablespoons minced shallots
> 1 tablespoon *each* minced garlic and fresh ginger
> ⅓ cup water

Rinse thighs and pat dry. Lay skin side down. With a short, sharp knife held against bone, cut and scrape meat free in a large, neat piece. (If part of back is attached to thigh, cut meat free from it, too.) Pull off skin; if desired, save skin and bone for other uses, such as broth.

Cut thigh meat into 6 to 8 equal pieces. Lay any small scraps of meat in center of big pieces. Place each piece between sheets of plastic wrap. With a flat mallet, firmly but gently pound meat until it is about ⅛ inch thick. If done ahead, wrap airtight and chill up until next day.

Mix soy sauce and chili sauce; rub on turkey (keep small bits in place on larger ones). Set aside.

In a 10- to 12-inch frying pan over medium-high heat, stir 1 tablespoon oil, shallots, garlic, and ginger just until shallots are golden, about 3 minutes. Remove from pan with a slotted spoon. Add more oil to pan; fill with 1 layer of turkey. Cook until edges turn white, about 2 minutes. Turn and cook until

meat is no longer pink in center (cut to test). Remove from pan; keep warm. Repeat to cook remaining turkey. Add water and shallot mixture to pan; stir to loosen pan drippings and pour over turkey. Makes 6 servings. — *Kimberly Scharf, Santa Barbara, Calif.*

PER SERVING: 236 calories, 30 g protein, 3.4 g carbohydrates, 11 g fat, 110 mg cholesterol, 708 mg sodium

OVEN-FRIED TURKEY WINGS WITH CRISP CORNMEAL CRUST

> 4 to 6 turkey wings (about 5 lb. total)
> 1¼ cups yellow cornmeal
> 2 tablespoons paprika
> 1 tablespoon dried marjoram leaves
> 1 teaspoon pepper
> 1 large egg
> 2 tablespoons water
> About 5 tablespoons melted butter or margarine
> Salt

Rinse wings and pat dry. With your hands, force each joint open until it snaps, then cut wings apart at joints. Cut through the midsection of each wing (the part with 2 bones) and through the joints. You can cook wing tips, or reserve them for other uses, such as broth.

On a sheet of waxed paper, mix cornmeal, paprika, marjoram, and pepper.

In shallow pan, beat egg and water to blend. Coat wing pieces in egg, then coat with cornmeal mixture (pat on lightly for extra-thick crust). Lay pieces slightly apart in an oiled 10- by 15-inch baking pan. Bake pieces in a 400° oven for 15 minutes, then drizzle evenly with melted butter. Continue baking until thickest part of meat at bone on the largest piece is no longer pink (cut to test), about 25 minutes longer. Serve wings hot or cool, adding salt to taste. Serves 4 to 6.

PER 8-OUNCE SERVING: 194 calories, 11 g protein, 15 g carbohydrates, 10 g fat, 84 mg cholesterol, 90 mg sodium

Big and little parts of turkey wings, oven-fried and crusty with cornmeal, make servings for different-size appetites.

Couscous with Chicken or Shellfish

BEST KNOWN *as the national dish of Algeria, Morocco, and Tunisia, couscous is also the name of the pellet-shaped semolina pasta that is integral to the dish, in which it's steamed slowly to softness.*

However, couscous (the pasta) really needs no cooking; it swells to edible tenderness after simply sitting for a few minutes in hot liquid. It makes a fast finish for these two whole-meal combinations. One pairs the pasta with roast chicken and vegetables, the other with shellfish.

You can buy packaged couscous (sometimes incorrectly marketed as a grain) in most supermarkets, or in bulk in Middle Eastern or specialty food stores.

COUSCOUS WITH ROASTED CHICKEN & VEGETABLES

- 1 **broiler-fryer chicken (3½ to 4 lb.) Pepper**
- 1 **small head (about 1 lb.) fennel, base trimmed and coarse stalks cut off; reserve green leaves**
- 2 **tablespoons olive oil**
- 1 **small head garlic**
- 4 **medium-size zucchini (about 1½ lb. total), ends trimmed, cut into 1-inch-thick slices**
- 2 **large carrots (about ¾ lb. total), peeled and cut into 1-inch-thick slices**
- 1 **large red bell pepper, stemmed, seeded, and cut into chunks**
- 1 **large red onion, cut into eighths**
- 3 **cups regular-strength chicken broth**
- 2 **cups couscous Salt**

Remove giblets from chicken; reserve for other uses. Rinse chicken and pat dry; pull off and discard lumps of fat. Place bird, breast up, on a rack in a 9- by 13-inch metal pan. Sprinkle liberally with pepper.

Rinse trimmed fennel and cut into 1-inch chunks. Reserve feathery tops.

Pour oil into a 10- by 15-inch pan. Place fennel, garlic, zucchini, carrots, bell pepper, and onion in pan; turn vegetables to coat with oil. Bake chicken and vegetables in a 400° oven until vegetables are soft and edges begin to blacken, and chicken is browned and thigh is no longer pink at bone (cut to test), 1 to 1¼ hours. Switch pan positions halfway through baking.

Separate garlic into cloves; set aside. Coarsely chop vegetables; set aside. Tip bird to drain juices from body cavity into pan. Put chicken on a platter; keep warm.

Skim and discard fat from pan. Add broth to pan and bring to a boil over high heat. Squeeze garlic from peel into pan. Stir in couscous and vegetables. Cover, remove from heat, and let stand until liquid is absorbed, about 5 minutes. Spoon couscous around chicken; garnish with reserved fennel and season to taste with salt. Serves 4 or 5.

PER SERVING: 674 calories, 50 g protein, 60 g carbohydrates, 26 g fat, 123 mg cholesterol, 240 mg sodium

SHELLFISH COUSCOUS

- 6 **slices bacon (about ⅓ lb.), cut into ½-inch-wide pieces**
- ¾ **pound large shrimp (31 to 35 per lb.), shelled and deveined**
- ¾ **pound bay scallops, rinsed**
- 1 **cup dry vermouth**
- 2½ **cups regular-strength chicken broth**
- ½ **cup orange juice**
- 2 **cups couscous**
- ¼ **cup dried tomatoes packed in oil, drained and slivered**
- ⅔ **cup minced chives**
- 2 **large oranges, peel and white membrane cut off if desired, and fruit thinly sliced**

In a 4- to 5-quart pan over medium heat, stir bacon often until crisp; transfer to paper towels to drain. Discard all but 2 tablespoons fat from pan. Turn heat to medium-high and add shrimp and scallops. Stir often until fish is opaque in center (cut to test), about 5 minutes. With slotted spoon, set fish aside; keep warm.

To pan, add vermouth; boil, uncovered, on high heat until liquid is reduced by half. Add broth and orange juice; bring to a boil. Stir in couscous, tomatoes, and ⅓ cup chives. Cover, remove from heat, and let stand until liquid is absorbed, about 5 minutes. Mound couscous on a platter. Spoon shellfish onto couscous, then sprinkle with bacon and remaining chives. Arrange orange slices around couscous or serve in a bowl. Serves 5 or 6.

PER SERVING: 443 calories, 28 g protein, 55 g carbohydrates, 12 g fat, 98 mg cholesterol, 541 mg sodium

Roast chicken is flanked by couscous laced with chopped vegetables. Bake vegetables in the oven with the meat.

Mixing Your Own Grains

THE HONEST, WHOLESOME *flavor of whole grains makes them enjoyable eating; their high fiber and carbohydrate content make them good for you. A generous variety of grains has long been routine stock in health-food stores. Now even supermarkets feature packaged grain blends intended for anything from cereal to pilaf.*

You can also make your own grain mix. Here we've assembled a blend that capitalizes on the different tastes and textures of eight whole grains (also called berries or kernels): brown rice, buckwheat, millet, oats, pearl barley, rye, triticale, and wheat. Sesame seed is an optional ingredient that adds a delicate crunch.

When you get to know the different grains, you might try adjusting the proportions, tailoring your grain mix to taste.

You can keep the mix on hand, scooping out a cup or so at a time to serve hot as a dinner grain or breakfast cereal, to cook and chill for a salad, or to bake in a hearty custard for breakfast or dessert.

MULTIGRAIN MIX

- 1½ cups oat groats (uncut oats)
- 1½ cups long-grain brown rice
- 1 cup whole-grain rye
- 1½ cups whole-grain whole wheat
- 1 cup whole-grain triticale
- 1 cup whole-grain buckwheat
- 1 cup pearl barley
- 1 cup millet
- 1 cup sesame seed (optional)

Mix together oats, rice, rye, whole wheat, triticale, buckwheat, barley, millet, and sesame seed. Use, or store up to 3 months in an airtight container in a cool, dry place. Makes 10½ cups, about 4¼ pounds.

HOT COOKED MULTIGRAIN MIX

In a 2- to 3-quart pan on high heat, bring 2½ cups **water** or regular-strength chicken broth to a boil.

To liquid, add 1 cup **multigrain mix** (recipe precedes). Cover, reduce heat to simmering, and cook until grains are tender to bite, about 25 minutes; drain.

As a grain dish, season to taste with **salt, pepper,** and **butter** or margarine (optional); as a cereal, serve with **milk** or light cream (half-and-half) and **brown sugar,** sugar, or maple syrup. Makes about 2⅓ cups, 4 or 5 servings.

PER SERVING, UNSEASONED: 105 calories, 3.5 g protein, 20 g carbohydrates, 3 g fat, 0 mg cholesterol, 1.2 mg sodium

MULTIGRAIN SALAD

- About 4⅔ cups hot cooked multigrain mix (recipe precedes; double proportions and use a 3- to 4-qt. pan)
- Vinaigrette dressing (recipe follows)
- 1 *each* medium-size green and yellow bell peppers, stemmed, seeded, and finely chopped
- ⅓ cup chopped green onion
- 1 large firm-ripe tomato, cored and finely chopped
- 1 medium-size cucumber, peeled and finely chopped
- Salt and pepper

Let cooked grain mix cool. In a bowl, mix grains with dressing, bell peppers, green onion, tomato, cucumber, and salt and pepper to taste. Serve, or cover and chill up until next day. Makes about 9 cups, 6 servings.

PER SERVING: 305 calories, 6.6 g protein, 38 g carbohydrates, 18 g fat, 0 mg cholesterol, 81 mg sodium

Vinaigrette dressing. In a small bowl, combine ⅓ cup *each* **salad oil** and **white wine vinegar,** 1 clove **garlic** (minced or pressed), 1 tablespoon **Dijon mustard,** and 1½ teaspoons **dry oregano leaves** or 1 tablespoon chopped fresh oregano leaves.

MULTIGRAIN CUSTARD

- 2 tablespoons butter or margarine
- 1 medium-size tart apple
- ⅓ cup firmly packed brown sugar
- 4 large eggs
- 2 cups milk
- 1 teaspoon vanilla
- ½ teaspoon ground cinnamon
- ¼ teaspoon ground nutmeg
- 2½ cups cooked multigrain mix (recipe precedes)
- ⅓ cup raisins

In a shallow 1½-quart baking dish, melt butter in a 350° oven; this takes 2 to 3 minutes. Core and thinly slice apple; stir

into melted butter. Set aside 1 tablespoon sugar; mix remainder with apple and bake, uncovered, until apple is slightly softened, about 15 minutes.

Meanwhile, in a bowl mix the 1 tablespoon sugar to blend with eggs, milk, vanilla, cinnamon, and nutmeg.

In baking dish, scatter grains and raisins over apple, then pour egg mixture evenly over grains. Return dish to oven and bake until the center does not jiggle when dish is gently shaken, 35 to 40 minutes. Let stand at least 10 minutes. Serve hot or cool. Makes 6 servings.

PER SERVING: 309 calories, 9.9 g protein, 43 g carbohydrates, 13 g fat, 204 mg cholesterol, 131 mg sodium

MULTIGRAIN PILAF

- 2 tablespoons butter or margarine
- 1 large onion, finely chopped
- 1 large carrot, finely chopped or shredded
- 1 clove garlic, minced or pressed
- ⅓ cup chopped parsley
- 1 cup multigrain mix (recipe precedes)
- 2¼ cups regular-strength chicken broth (or part water)
- ¾ teaspoon *each* dry basil leaves and dry oregano leaves
- Salt and pepper

In a 3- to 4-quart pan over medium-high heat, combine butter, onion, carrot, garlic, and parsley; stir often until vegetables are soft, about 10 minutes. Add multigrain mix and stir until grains are slightly toasted, about 5 minutes.

Add broth, basil, and oregano. Bring to a boil on high heat. Cover, reduce heat, and simmer until grains are tender to bite, about 25 minutes; drain. Season to taste with salt and pepper. Makes 2¾ cups, 4 or 5 servings.

PER SERVING: 182 calories, 5.3 g protein, 26 g carbohydrates, 8.5 g fat, 12.4 mg cholesterol, 81 mg sodium

A Sweet Bread Ring from Italy

IN THE WALLED MEDIEVAL TOWN of *Lucca in northern Italy,* buccellato—*sweet, anise-scented bread*—is the local specialty.

Studded with raisins soaked in grappa *(a clear Italian brandy), this shiny, richly browned bread is served plain or toasted for breakfast, or soaked in a strawberry-marsala sauce for dessert.*

BUCCELLATO

- ½ **cup raisins**
- ¼ **cup grappa, or sweet or dry marsala**
- 1 **package active dry yeast**
- 1½ **tablespoons anise seed**
- ¾ **cup warm milk (110°)**
- ½ **cup (¼ lb.) butter or margarine, at room temperature**
- ½ **cup sugar**
- 5 **large eggs**
- 1 **teaspoon *each* vanilla and grated orange peel**
- ½ **teaspoon *each* anise extract and salt**
  About 4¾ cups all-purpose flour

Combine raisins and grappa; let stand for 30 minutes.

In a small bowl, stir yeast and anise seed into milk. Let stand until yeast softens, about 5 minutes. In a large bowl, using a heavy spoon or an electric mixer, beat the butter and sugar until light and fluffy. Add 4 eggs, 1 at a time, beating well after each addition; stir in vanilla, orange peel, anise extract, and salt. Add yeast mixture, grappa drained from raisins, and 4½ cups flour; mix until evenly moistened.

To knead with a dough hook, beat at high speed until dough pulls cleanly from sides of bowl, 10 to 12 minutes; add a little flour if required.

To knead by hand, scrape dough onto a lightly floured board and knead until smooth and elastic, about 15 minutes; add as little flour as possible to stop sticking.

Stir in raisins and place dough in a greased bowl; turn over to grease top.

Cover dough, kneaded by either method, with plastic wrap. Let dough rise in a warm place until doubled in size, about 1 hour. Knead briefly with dough hook or by hand on a lightly floured board to expel air; add a little flour, as required, to clean bowl (if using dough hook) or prevent sticking.

Divide dough in half. Shape each half into a 20-inch-long rope. Place each rope on a greased 12- by 15-inch baking sheet; join ends of each and pinch to seal. Cover lightly with plastic wrap and let rise in a warm place until puffy, 25 to 30 minutes. Beat remaining egg to blend. Remove plastic; brush egg lightly over dough. Bake in a 350° oven until richly browned, 25 to 35 minutes. (If using 1 oven, switch pan positions after 15 minutes.)

Serve warm or cool. For longer storage, wrap airtight and freeze up to 1 month. Makes 2 rings, each about 1⅓ pounds.

PER OUNCE: 95 calories, 2.4 g protein, 14 g carbohydrates, 3 g fat, 37 mg cholesterol, 57 mg sodium

BUCCELLATO WITH STRAWBERRIES

Spoon equal portions **strawberry-marsala sauce** (recipe follows) on each of 6 dessert plates. Cut **buccellato** (recipe precedes) in 18 to 24 slices ⅜-inch-thick each; toast if desired. Lay 3 or 4 slices in sauce on each plate. If desired, serve with **sweetened whipped cream** and whole **strawberries** to garnish. Serves 6.

PER SERVING: 205 calories, 4 g protein, 33 g carbohydrates, 4.8 g fat, 56 mg cholesterol, 87 mg sodium

Strawberry-marsala sauce. In a blender or food processor, whirl until smoothly puréed 2½ cups stemmed and hulled **strawberries,** 6 tablespoons **sweet** or dry **marsala,** and 2 tablespoons **sugar.**

For dessert, serve raisin-studded slices of buccellato in strawberry–marsala sauce. The sweet, anise-scented bread originated in the medieval town of Lucca in northern Italy.

More May Recipes

OTHER ARTICLES IN THE MAY *issue fea-tured a colorful vegetable salad from Spain and individual pavlova desserts topped with fresh fruits.*

VEGETABLES IN JEREZ SAUCE

Spain's sherry capital lends its name to this salad. Simply steam vegetables, then add a thyme vinaigrette.

- 1 **medium-size head (about 1 lb.) fresh fennel, base trimmed**
- 2 **cups *each* cauliflowerets, diagonally sliced carrots, and red bell pepper cut into 1-inch pieces**
- 1 **can (about 1 lb.) yellow hominy, drained and rinsed**
  Jerez sauce (recipe follows)
- 1 **green onion (optional)**
  Salt and pepper

Cut fennel head lengthwise into sixths. Trim off leaves and tough stems.

Place a steaming rack in a 5- to 6-quart pan. Add ½ inch water to pan and bring to a boil over medium-high heat. Put fennel pieces on rack, cover, and cook 5 minutes. Add remaining vegetables in sequence, arranging them separately and cooking covered: cauliflower for 2 minutes, then carrots for 1 minute, then bell pepper. Cook until all vegetables are tender-crisp to bite, 4 to 7 minutes longer.

Separately lift vegetables from pan, arranging fennel, carrots, and bell pepper on a platter. Combine cauliflower with hominy; add to platter. Evenly spoon sauce over vegetables. Serve; or let cool, cover, and chill up to 1 day. Trim ends of onion; use it to garnish salad. To serve, mix vegetables with sauce. Add salt and pepper to taste. Serves 6 to 8.

PER SERVING: 190 calories, 2.5 g protein, 15 g carbohydrates, 14 g fat, 0 mg cholesterol, 222 mg sodium

Jerez sauce. In a bowl, mix ¼ cup **sherry vinegar** or wine vinegar, ½ cup **olive oil**, and 1 teaspoon **dry thyme leaves** with ¼ cup sliced **green onions**.

INDIVIDUAL PAVLOVAS WITH A FRUIT RAINBOW

Flavorful fruits color these upside-down, individual pavlova desserts.

Traditionally, Australia's pavlova is one large meringue, spread with whipped cream and served with kiwi fruit. Here, a pink foam of whipped cream and puréed berries goes beneath each golden, crisp

A sprinkling of raspberries and a fan of papaya slices embellish single-serving pavlova meringue resting on berry cream. Spoon seed-dotted kiwi–passion fruit sauce on top.

meringue. More berries, orange papaya slices, and green kiwi–passion fruit sauce complete the spectrum of tastes and hues.

  Berry cream (recipe follows)
  Individual meringues (recipe follows)
- 1 **medium-size ripe papaya (about 1 lb.), peeled, seeded, and thinly sliced lengthwise**
- ¾ **cup raspberries or hulled, thinly sliced strawberries**
  Kiwi–passion fruit sauce (recipe follows)

Spread equal portions of berry cream into 5-inch-wide pools on 6 dessert plates.

Place a meringue on cream on each plate. Arrange equal amounts of papaya and raspberries on or beside meringues. Offer sauce to ladle onto portions. Makes 6 servings.

PER SERVING: 321 calories, 4.5 g protein, 50 g carbohydrates, 13 g fat, 44 mg cholesterol, 54 mg sodium

Berry cream. In a blender or food processor, whirl 1½ cups **raspberries** or hulled strawberries with 1½ tablespoons **sugar** until smoothly puréed. In a bowl, beat 1 cup **whipping cream** until stiff.

Fold in berry purée. If made ahead, cover and chill up to 24 hours.

Individual meringues. In large bowl of an electric mixer, beat 4 **large egg whites** at high speed until foamy. Gradually add ¾ cup **sugar**, beating until meringue holds stiff, moist peaks. Beat in 1 teaspoon **vinegar** and 1 tablespoon **cornstarch**. Evenly space 6 equal mounds of meringue on a greased 12- by 15-inch baking sheet.

Bake in a 250° oven until pale golden and firm when gently pressed, 55 to 60 minutes. Let cool completely on baking sheet on a rack. Slide a wide spatula under meringues to loosen. If made ahead, store airtight up to 24 hours.

Kiwi–passion fruit sauce. Peel 3 large **kiwi fruit** (about ¾ lb. total); quarter and whirl in a blender or food processor until smoothly puréed. Halve 3 ripe **passion fruit** (about ⅓ lb. total); scoop seeds into blender (or omit passion fruit and use 1 more kiwi). Whirl just to blend.

If sauce is made ahead, cover and chill up to 24 hours.

Brown sugar topping bakes on top of apples and rhubarb for brunch or dessert.

STREUSEL-TOPPED RHUBARB & APPLES

- 3 medium-size Golden Delicious apples, peeled, cored, and cut into ¾-inch chunks
- 1 tablespoon lemon juice
- 1 pound rhubarb (ends trimmed), sliced ¼ inch thick
- ⅓ cup granulated sugar
- ¾ cup whole-wheat flour
- ¾ cup firmly packed brown sugar
- ¼ cup sweetened or plain toasted wheat germ
- ½ teaspoon ground cinnamon
- ½ teaspoon ground nutmeg
- ½ cup (¼ lb.) butter or margarine
- ⅓ cup slivered almonds

In a large bowl, stir together the apples, lemon juice, sliced rhubarb, and granulated sugar. Scrape fruit mixture into a buttered 9-inch round or square baking pan.

In a small bowl, mix flour, brown sugar, wheat germ, cinnamon, and nutmeg. With your fingers, rub in butter until mixture forms coarse crumbs. Stir in almonds; spoon mixture evenly over fruit.

Bake in a 350° oven until fruit is very tender when pierced, 55 to 60 minutes. Serve in bowls with milk and cream, if desired. Makes 6 to 8 servings.—*Laura Getschmann, Bremerton, Wash.*

PER SERVING: 336 calories, 4 g protein, 50 g carbohydrates, 15 g fat, 31 mg cholesterol, 127 mg sodium

---

Frying pan meal combines eggs, cheese, hot or mild sausage, vegetables.

WESTERN SUPPER SCRAMBLE

- 1 pound hot or mild Italian sausages, casings removed
- 1 russet potato (about ½ lb.), scrubbed and cut into ½-inch cubes
- 1 large red or green bell pepper, stemmed, seeded, and cut into ½-inch pieces
- 1 large yellow onion, chopped
- ¼ cup water
- 5 large eggs, beaten to blend
- ½ cup shredded cheddar cheese
  Sour cream or unflavored yogurt
  Sliced green onions

In a 10- to 12-inch nonstick frying pan over medium-high heat, break up sausage with a spoon and cook with potato, stirring occasionally, until sausage starts to brown, 10 to 15 minutes.

Add bell pepper, yellow onion, and water; continue cooking, stirring gently a few times, until potato is tender when pierced, about 15 minutes. Reduce heat to medium.

Push sausage mixture to half of pan; pour eggs into other half. Cook eggs, stirring occasionally, until set to your liking. Sprinkle cheese over eggs. Serve with sour cream and green onions to add to taste. Makes 4 to 6 servings.— *Karin Andersen, Irvine, Calif.*

PER SERVING: 410 calories, 19 g protein, 11 g carbohydrates, 32 g fat, 296 mg cholesterol, 673 mg sodium

---

Stir-fry celery, cabbage, jicama, and seasonings; add turkey and marinade.

CHINESE STIR-FRIED TURKEY

- ¾ pound (3 cups) shredded cooked turkey or chicken
  Marinade (recipe follows)
- 2 tablespoons salad oil
- 1½ tablespoons minced fresh ginger
- 2 cloves garlic, thinly sliced
- 3 small dried hot red chilies
- 2 cups shredded cabbage
- 3 stalks celery, sliced diagonally
- 1 cup 1-inch pieces green onion
- 1½ cups peeled, julienned jicama

Mix turkey and marinade; cover. Chill at least 30 minutes or until next day.

Add oil to wok or 10- to 12-inch frying pan over medium-high heat. When hot, add ginger, garlic, and chilies; stir-fry until garlic is golden, about 1½ minutes. Add cabbage, celery, onion, and jicama; stir-fry until celery is barely tender-crisp to bite, about 3 minutes. Add turkey mixture; stir until sauce boils vigorously. Serves 4.—*Dorothy Zopf, Arroyo Seco, N. Mex.*

PER SERVING: 320 calories, 29 g protein, 17 g carbohydrates, 15 g fat, 66 mg cholesterol, 986 mg sodium

Marinade. In a small bowl, mix 1 cup **regular-strength chicken broth;** 2 tablespoons *each* **cornstarch, soy sauce, oyster sauce** (or more soy), and **dry sherry** (or more broth); 1 tablespoon **Oriental sesame oil;** and ½ teaspoon *each* **ground cinnamon** and **anise seed.**

Tofu & Spinach Manicotti

1 medium-size onion, chopped
3 stalks celery, chopped
2 cloves garlic, minced or pressed
2 teaspoons dry oregano leaves
2 tablespoons olive oil
2 cans (15 oz. each) unsalted or regular tomato purée
1 cup dry red wine
1 cup water
1 pound soft tofu, rinsed and drained
1 package (10 oz.) thawed frozen chopped spinach, squeezed dry
12 dry manicotti shells (about 6 oz. total)
½ cup shredded mozzarella cheese

In a 10- to 12-inch frying pan over medium-high heat, stir onion, celery, garlic, and oregano in oil often until onion is limp, about 8 minutes. Add purée, wine, and water. Cover and simmer 25 minutes; stir often.

Mix tofu and spinach well. Stuff manicotti with this mixture. Spread 1¾ cups of the tomato sauce in a 9- by 13-inch pan. Set manicotti in sauce; cover with remaining sauce.

Bake, covered, in a 375° oven until pasta is tender when pierced, about 50 minutes. Sprinkle with cheese. Serves 6. —*Marilynn Harvey, San Francisco.*

PER SERVING: 347 calories, 17 g protein, 49 g carbohydrates, 11 g fat, 7.4 mg cholesterol, 125 mg sodium

Baked manicotti shells have lean, flavorful filling of spinach and tofu.

Mushroom Pâté

⅓ pound fresh mushrooms, such as common, shiitake, or a combination
⅓ cup minced onion
¼ cup (⅛ lb.) butter or margarine
1 tablespoon dry sherry or regular-strength chicken broth
1 small package (3 oz.) cream cheese, cut into chunks
¼ cup minced parsley
Raw vegetables and crackers or small toast rounds

Rinse mushrooms, drain, and coarsely chop. In a 10- to 12-inch frying pan over medium heat, cook mushrooms and onion in butter, stirring often, until mushrooms are browned, about 15 minutes. Mix in sherry.

In a bowl, beat cream cheese and parsley until thoroughly mixed. Stir in mushroom mixture.

Spoon the pâté into a small crock or bowl and serve; or cover and refrigerate up to 3 days, then bring to room temperature before serving. Offer mushroom pâté to spread on vegetables and crackers. Makes 1 cup, enough for 6 to 8 servings.—*Roxanne Chan, Albany, Calif.*

PER SERVING: 96 calories, 1.4 g protein, 2 g carbohydrates, 9.5 g fat, 27 mg cholesterol, 92 mg sodium

Quickly prepared mushroom spread is good on crisp raw vegetables, crackers.

Chewy Dried Fruit Bars

½ cup (¼ lb.) butter or margarine
¾ cup firmly packed brown sugar
½ cup molasses
1 large egg
1 teaspoon ground cinnamon
½ teaspoon baking soda
¼ teaspoon *each* ground ginger and ground cloves
1 cup all-purpose flour
¾ cup whole-wheat flour
1 cup chopped walnuts
1 cup chopped dried fruit (such as apricots, figs, pitted dates, apples)

In the large bowl of an electric mixer, beat butter, sugar, and molasses until smooth. Add egg and beat until well combined. Stir in cinnamon, soda, ginger, and cloves; then stir in all-purpose and whole-wheat flours, nuts, and dried fruit until evenly moistened.

Spread dough in a greased 10- by 15-inch rimmed baking pan. Bake in a 350° oven until cooky begins to pull from pan sides, about 25 minutes.

Let cool in pan on a rack, then cut into 24 equal bars. Serve, or store airtight up to 3 days. Makes 24 bars.—*Donna Higgins, Halfway, Ore.*

PER BAR: 157 calories, 2.2 g protein, 22 g carbohydrates, 7.2 g fat, 22 mg cholesterol, 63 mg sodium

Tuck moist cooky bars into lunch boxes, or pack in a knapsack for a hike.

CHICKEN BREAST is a very mild, lean protein. Most people find it good for gussying up because it displays seasonings well. Take Chicken Kiev, for instance, a delicate preparation in which the flattened breast is wrapped around butter.

It was Chicken Kiev that inspired John Stevenson to invent the following dish. Stevenson likes basil, grows a lot of it, and is always searching for new ways to use it. Of course, he is familiar with pesto, and it seemed logical to use this richly oleaginous mixture in place of butter.

CHICKEN BREASTS WITH PARMESAN PESTO

- 3 whole chicken breasts (about 1 lb. each)
- 1 cup lightly packed fresh basil leaves
- ¾ cup freshly grated parmesan cheese
- ¼ cup olive oil
- 1 small clove garlic
- 1½ tablespoons *each* butter or margarine and olive oil
  About ⅓ cup all-purpose flour
  Basil sprigs

Bone, skin, and split chicken breasts. Place each piece between plastic wrap and firmly pound with a flat mallet until each portion is about ¼ inch thick. Cover and chill while you make the pesto.

In a blender or food processor, combine basil, cheese, oil, and garlic; whirl until a thick paste.

Spoon pesto equally onto each chicken piece. Roll up to enclose pesto; secure each roll with a toothpick.

In a 12- to 14-inch frying pan, melt butter in oil over medium-high heat. Dip each chicken roll in flour, shake off excess, and add to pan. Cook, turning as needed, until golden brown on all sides and meat is opaque in center (carefully cut to test), 6 to 8 minutes total.

Transfer to a serving dish and garnish with basil sprigs. Makes 6 servings.

PER SERVING: 380 calories, 40 g protein, 6.3 g carbohydrates, 21 g fat, 103 mg cholesterol, 354 mg sodium

John H. Stevenson

Bellevue, Wash.

CHESTER CARR, *known as Copper to his children and grandchildren, favors his progeny with recipes of his devising. At 83, he is still a fountain of recipes, but he perfected his Copper's Green Chili Enchiladas 40 years ago. David Cothrun, a son-in-law, sends Mr. Carr's recipe to us from Taft, California.*

None of the ingredients is a surprise, but their proportions make the dish a winner—especially because of the generous use of green chilies and jalapeños. This is not exactly spa food, but Cothrun has tried to hold the calorie line by using very lean beef and blotting the tortillas. He also recommends a careful hand with the salt.

COPPER'S GREEN CHILI ENCHILADAS

- 2 pounds ground very lean beef
  Salad oil
- 3 large onions, chopped
- 4 large cloves garlic, minced or pressed
- 2 cans (7 oz. each) diced green chilies
- 1 can (1 lb.) stewed tomatoes
- 1 tablespoon dry oregano leaves
- 2 teaspoons ground cumin
- ½ teaspoon pepper
- 2 to 3 fresh jalapeño chilies, seeded and minced
- 16 corn tortillas (6- to 7-in. size)
- 1 pound longhorn cheddar cheese, shredded
- 1 cup thinly sliced green onions (ends trimmed), including tops
  Salt
  About 1 cup sour cream
  About 1 cup prepared salsa

In an 8- to 10-quart pan over medium-high heat, crumble meat and stir often until well browned, about 25 minutes; add 1 tablespoon oil if meat is too lean to brown well. Lift meat from pan with a slotted spoon and set aside. To drippings in pan add onions and garlic; stir often until onion is limp, about 10 minutes. Return meat and any juices to pan, then add green chilies, tomatoes and their liquid, oregano, cumin, pepper, and jalapeño chilies. Stir to free browned bits in pan, then bring mixture to a boil over high heat. Simmer, uncovered, until nearly all the liquid is gone, stirring often. If made ahead, cool, cover, and chill up to 3 days; reheat to continue.

For the enchiladas, pour about ¼ inch oil into a 10- to 12-inch frying pan on medium-high heat. When the oil is hot, fry 1 tortilla at a time, turning as needed, until crisp, 30 to 45 seconds. Lift out and drain in paper towel–lined pans; keep warm until all tortillas are fried.

To assemble each enchilada, place 1 hot tortilla on each of 8 dinner plates. Quickly top each tortilla with about ½ cup chili, about ¼ cup cheese, and 1 tablespoon green onion. On each serving, make another layer of tortilla, chili, cheese, and green onion.

Accompany with salt, sour cream, and salsa to add to taste. Makes 8 servings.

PER SERVING: 911 calories, 42 g protein, 43 g carbohydrates, 65 g fat, 157 mg cholesterol, 1,182 mg sodium

Chester D. Carr

Roswell, New Mexico

"Stevenson likes basil, grows a lot of it, and is always searching for new ways to use it."

MOST CIVILIZATIONS *have based their diets on some cereal crop, with wheat and rice the most important of these. The Japanese and Chinese usually take their rice steamed or boiled, and they don't mind if it's somewhat sticky. Near Easterners and people from North Africa prefer their rice fluffy, and often blend it with broth to make pilafs. The people of India prepare especially complex rice dishes called* pulaos. *Bud Lawhead's Lemon Ginger Rice may draw its inspiration from one of these.*

Lemon and ginger give this rice a character hovering between a flavor and a perfume—one perceived less on the tongue than in a mysterious hinterland somewhere between the throat, the nose, and the ethmoid sinuses. One medium that delivers the ginger shows the chef's touch of originality, inspiration, or perhaps (if it was all he had on hand) desperation.

LEMON GINGER RICE

1 cup *each* diet or regular ginger ale
   and water
1 cup long-grain white rice
1 tablespoon grated lemon peel
½ teaspoon ground ginger
2 tablespoons untoasted wheat
   germ
   Salt

In a 2- to 3-quart pan, bring ginger ale and water to a boil over high heat. Stir in rice, lemon peel, and ginger; cover and turn heat to low. Cook until rice is tender to bite and liquid is absorbed, about 20 minutes. Remove from heat and fluff rice with a fork, then mix in the wheat germ and season to taste with salt. Makes 4 or 5 servings.

PER SERVING: 147 calories, 3 g protein, 32 g carbohydrates, 0.5 g fat, 0 mg cholesterol, 15 mg sodium

Hollywood, Calif.

LAMB IS PROBABLY *the most widely available meat in the world, and charcoal open fires and skewers the most available cooking devices. It is not surprising, therefore, that barbecued lamb is to be found, in some guise, wherever animals are raised for food. Kebabs, satays, souvlaki, shashlik—all are variations on one theme:* chunks of meat, marinated or not, threaded on skewers with or without vegetables and grilled over hot coals. Shashlik is the Russian version, traditionally prepared with a white wine marinade. Don Reid prefers red wine in his treatment.*

SHASHLIK

2 pounds boneless lean lamb, fat
   trimmed off and meat cut into
   1-inch cubes
1 small onion, chopped
¼ cup salad oil
1 dry bay leaf
1 clove garlic, minced or pressed
1 tablespoon Worcestershire
¼ teaspoon pepper
2 tablespoons chopped parsley
1 teaspoon dry oregano leaves
1 cup dry red wine
1 pound small onions (about 1-in.
   diameter)
2 medium-size red bell peppers,
   stemmed, seeded, and cut into
   1-inch squares
   Salt and pepper

Place lamb cubes in a heavy plastic bag; set in a bowl. Add to bag the chopped onion, oil, bay leaf, garlic, Worcestershire, pepper, parsley, oregano, and wine. Seal bag and rotate to distribute marinade. Chill 2 to 24 hours, turning bag over several times.

Meanwhile, put whole onions in a 3- to 4-quart pan. Cover with water, bring to a boil on high heat and simmer 5 minutes; drain and peel onions. If made ahead, cover and chill up to 24 hours.

Drain lamb; reserve marinade. Alternately and equally thread lamb, bell pepper squares, and onions onto 6 to 8 metal skewers, each at least 14 inches long.

Lay skewers on a grill 4 to 6 inches above a solid bed of hot coals (you should be able to hold your hand at grill level for only 2 to 3 seconds). Cook, basting often, and turn as needed until meat is evenly browned but still pink in the center (cut to test), 8 to 10 minutes. Offer salt and pepper to add to taste. Makes 6 to 8 servings.

PER SERVING: 260 calories, 22 g protein, 6.8 g carbohydrates, 16 g fat, 77 mg cholesterol, 98 mg sodium

Idaho Falls, Idaho

IF YOU ARE UNSURE *of the pronunciation of ragout, just remember the sensible, phonetic, Italian spelling:* ragu. *The word stems from the French* ragoûter, *meaning to revive the taste of. This origin hints that ragouts were originally devised to deal with leftovers or the less desirable cuts of meat. Certainly British literary people regarded ragouts with derision, attributing British success at empire building to the easy availability of good plain roast beef. The civilized French ignored such jingoism and went on developing their complex and splendid cuisine.*

Rodney Garside's Veal Ragout is essentially a simple dish, but it tastes complex. The sauce does wonders for rice or noodles.

VEAL RAGOUT

2   pounds boned veal shoulder
3   tablespoons salad oil
1   large onion, chopped
2   cloves garlic, minced or pressed
3   tablespoons all-purpose flour
1¾ cups or 1 can (14 oz.) regular-
    strength chicken broth
2   tablespoons catsup
1   teaspoon dry basil leaves
½   pound mushrooms, about 1½-inch
    diameter, quartered
    Hot cooked rice
    Salt and pepper

Trim and discard any excess fat from meat, then cut meat into about 1-inch cubes. Pour oil into a 4- to 5-quart pan over medium-high heat. When oil is hot, add meat, a portion at a time, and stir often until browned. As meat is cooked, set aside with a slotted spoon.

Add onion and garlic to pan, and stir often until onion is limp, about 10 minutes. Reduce heat to medium, mix in flour, and stir until it is lightly browned. Whisk in broth, then return meat and any juices to pan along with catsup and basil. Bring to a boil, then reduce heat and simmer for 1 hour. Stir in mushrooms, cover, and continue to cook until meat is very tender when pierced, about 30 minutes longer. Accompany stew with hot rice; season to taste with salt and pepper. Makes 4 to 6 servings.

PER SERVING: 372 calories, 32 g protein, 9 g carbohydrates, 23 g fat, 107 mg cholesterol, 180 mg sodium

Tuolumne, Calif.

May Menus

STRATEGIES TO SIMPLIFY *meals work in these May menus, getting the cook into and out of the kitchen fast.*

Packing for a bike picnic is easy because the filling for sandwiches is a well-seasoned grain salad that doesn't need to be kept cold as you travel.

A more hassle-free way of baking pan-cakes guarantees success to even the most inexperienced cook. You might try it on Mother's Day and treat the honoree to a pancake pizza.

Combining salad and entrée streamlines cooking and serving. Broil a marinated chicken breast and set on bed of crisp greens for a salad entrée.

Spoon yogurt over spiced lentils in pocket bread for picnic sandwiches. For dessert, eat dried apricots with chunks of halvah (sesame confection).

At the picnic site, scoop spicy lentil salad into pocket bread halves. Eat cherry tomatoes and cucumber spears out of hand.

Make the lentil mixture up to a day ahead and pack in a leakproof container. For best color, add the celery and onions no more than 2 hours before serving.

For a quick pick-me-up, bring along a chunk of halvah (sweet ground sesame confection) to eat on dried apricot halves. You'll find the candy at Middle Eastern delicatessens, or in some supermarkets' candy or international food section. If you can't find it, you might bring along some honey-roasted peanuts or other sesame or nut candy.

SPICED LENTIL POCKET BREAD SANDWICHES

1 cup (7 oz.) lentils
1 dry bay leaf
1 small dried hot red chili
1 teaspoon cumin seed
⅓ cup olive oil
3 tablespoons wine vinegar
1 clove garlic, pressed or minced
½ cup thinly sliced green onion
1 cup chopped celery
   Salt and pepper
4 pocket bread rounds (6-in. diameter), cut in half
   Yogurt sauce (recipe follows)

Sort through lentils and discard any debris or rocks. Rinse, drain, and place in 3- to 4-quart pan with 1 quart water, bay leaf, chili, and cumin seed. Bring to a boil, cover, and simmer until lentils are just tender to bite, about 40 minutes. Drain. Let cool. If desired, discard chili.

In a large bowl, mix together oil, vinegar, and garlic; add lentils and mix gently together. If made ahead, cover and chill up until the next day. Up to 2 hours before serving, add onion, celery, and salt and pepper to taste. If desired, transport in an insulated chest.

To serve, scoop about ½ cup of the lentil mixture into each pocket bread half and add yogurt mixture to taste. Makes 8 sandwiches, 4 servings.

PER SERVING: 490 calories, 18 g protein, 63 g carbohydrates, 19 g fat, 0 mg cholesterol, 397 mg sodium

Yogurt sauce. Mix 1 cup **unflavored yogurt,** 2 tablespoons chopped **fresh mint leaves,** and 2 tablespoons **golden raisins.** Serve; if made ahead, cover and chill up until the next day. Transport in a thermos. Makes 1¼ cups.

PER TABLESPOON: 9.9 calories, 0.6 g protein, 1.5 g carbohydrates, 0.2 g fat, 0.7 mg cholesterol, 8.0 mg sodium

---

PANCAKE PIZZA FOR BREAKFAST

Pancake Pizza
Butter   Maple Syrup
Sliced Bananas
Canadian Bacon Slices
Orange Juice   Coffee

Instead of cooking individual pancakes on top of the range, bake a pizza-size one in the oven. Cut into wedges and offer butter, maple syrup, and bananas to add to taste.

While the pancake bakes, brown the bacon, slice the bananas, and make coffee.

PANCAKE PIZZA

    2 **large eggs**
 1¾ **cups milk**
    2 **tablespoons salad oil**
    1 **teaspoon maple flavoring**
    2 **cups regular or complete pancake
        mix, plain or buckwheat flavor**
  ¾ **cup granola cereal**
  ¾ **cup pecan halves**

In a bowl, beat eggs, milk, oil, and maple flavoring to blend. Add pancake mix and beat until smooth. Coat the inside of a 14-inch pizza or 10- by 15-inch baking pan with a nonstick cooking spray, or oil generously. Pour batter into pan. Sprinkle evenly with granola and pecans.

Offer wedges of pecan- and granola-topped oven-baked pancake pizza instead of individual pancakes.

Bake on the bottom rack of a 425° oven until a toothpick inserted in center comes out clean, 12 to 15 minutes. Cut into wedges and serve. Makes 6 pizza servings. —*Desiree Witkoski, Long Beach, Calif.*

PER SERVING: 429 calories, 11 g protein, 49 g carbohydrates, 22 g fat, 101 mg cholesterol, 709 mg sodium

---

HOT & COLD SALAD PLATE

Chicken on Cool Greens
Herb Bread Batons
**Cantaloupe Wedges
with Orange Liqueur**
Sauvignon Blanc or Iced Tea

A mustard vinaigrette marinates the chicken and dresses the greens in this hot- cold entrée salad. Serve with toasted baguette batons.

Marinate the chicken at least 30 minutes while the greens crisp in the refrigerator. If you're in a hurry, purchase ready-to-use salad or mesclun mix available in some supermarkets and specialty produce stores. Broil the chicken; when it's done, briefly toast the herb bread.

For a light, refreshing dessert, pour a little orange, almond, or hazelnut liqueur into the cavities of small cantaloupe halves. Garnish with a few toasted nuts.

(Continued on next page)

CHICKEN ON COOL GREENS

- ⅓ cup salad oil or olive oil
- 3 tablespoons white wine vinegar
- 1 tablespoon Dijon mustard
- 1 clove garlic, pressed or minced
- ¼ cup minced shallots
- 4 boneless chicken breast halves, (each 4 to 6 oz.)
- 12 cups (about ¾ lb.) bite-size pieces washed and crisped mixed salad greens (such as curly endive, leaf lettuce, arugula, butter lettuce, escarole)

 Salt and pepper

Mix the oil, vinegar, mustard, garlic, and shallots. Combine ¼ cup of the dressing with the chicken in a plastic bag; seal bag and turn chicken in dressing to coat. Set in a bowl and chill at least 30 minutes or up until the next day.

Discard chicken marinade. Place chicken, skin side down, on a rack in a 10- by 15-inch broiler pan. Broil about 4 inches from heat, turning when about half done, until chicken is white in thickest part (cut to test), 12 to 15 minutes total.

Shortly before chicken is cooked, mix greens with the remaining dressing. Divide salad equally between 4 dinner plates. Set a chicken breast half (whole or sliced) on each bed of greens. Add salt and pepper to taste. Makes 4 servings.

PER SERVING: 312 calories, 28 g protein, 5.4 g carbohydrates, 20 g fat, 66 mg cholesterol, 198 mg sodium

HERB BREAD BATONS

- 1 baguette (8 oz.)
- ¼ cup olive oil
- 2 tablespoons minced fresh marjoram leaves or thyme leaves, or 1 teaspoon dry marjoram leaves or dry thyme leaves

If baguette is short and wide (about 4 in. wide), cut loaf lengthwise into quarters. If loaf is long and thin (1½ to 2 in. wide), cut it in half crosswise and lengthwise to make 4 pieces.

Mix oil with herbs. Brush cut sides of baguette with seasoned oil. Place breadsticks, cut sides up, on a 12- by 15-inch baking sheet and broil 4 inches from heat until toasted, about 2 minutes. Serve hot. Makes 4 servings.

PER SERVING: 284 calories, 5.2 g protein, 32 g carbohydrates, 15 g fat, 1.7 mg cholesterol, 329 mg sodium

JUNE

Fresh Mozzarella and Tomatoes with Basil (page 131)

Warm, lazy summer days
demand meals that are easy on the cook. For leisurely outdoor
entertaining, we suggest a simplified Indonesian rice table,
featuring skewers of beef cooked on the grill. To give an
evening picnic a new twist, serve a hearty hot soup
accompanied by cheese and rustic bread. Other June features
present the latest information on gas barbecues, show you
how to make fresh mozzarella at home, and provide ideas for
enjoying the season's bounty of fruits and vegetables.

127

Indonesian Rice Table

A LIVELY INTERPLAY of *tastes, textures, and colors characterizes our simplified version of Dutch-Indonesian* rijsttafel, *or rice table. This menu, a complete meal for eight, keeps the essence of the original with only a fraction of the work.*

Start with a cool salad of brown rice. You add fruit, grilled beef satay, a curried dressing with a touch of chili heat, shrimp crackers, and nuts with dried fruit.

Dutch colonists in what is now Indonesia created the rijstafel known to many Westerners. Based on the native rice table meal, traditionally a part of religious celebrations, it was expanded into a show of up to 50 side dishes with rice.

Here, you combine elements into just a few dishes. Nearly everything can be prepared in advance.

Shrimp crackers lend an agreeable crunch and delicate fish flavor to the menu. These small disks are sold in international foods stores; fried, they expand.

INDONESIAN RICE SALAD SUPPER

Brown Rice Table
Beef Satay
Curried Peanut Dressing
Shrimp Chips
Raisins, Cashews & Coconut
Guava Nectar

For a condiment, mix equal portions of cashews, raisins, and dry coconut.

BROWN RICE TABLE

- 2 tablespoons salad oil
- 2 cloves garlic, minced or pressed
- 1 medium-size onion, minced
- 2 cups long-grain brown rice
- 5 cups regular-strength beef broth
- 2 dry bay leaves
- 2 slices fresh ginger (each the size of a quarter)
- 1½ teaspoons pepper
- 4 cups thinly sliced cabbage
- 2 cups finely shredded carrots
  Cilantro dressing (recipe follows)
  Fruits and vegetable (directions follow)
  Beef satay (recipe follows)
  Curried peanut dressing (recipe follows)

To a 5- to 6-quart pan over medium-high heat, add oil, garlic, onion, and rice. Stir until rice is opaque, about 5 minutes. Stir in broth, bay leaves, ginger, and pepper. Bring to a boil, then cover and simmer until all the liquid is absorbed, about 50 minutes. Using a fork, scrape rice into a 10- by 15-inch rimmed pan. Let cool completely; remove bay leaves and ginger.

Meanwhile, mix cabbage with carrots. (At this point, you can cover and chill rice, cabbage mixture, dressing, and fruits and vegetable separately up to 2 hours.)

Add dressing to cabbage and carrots; using 2 forks, gently combine with rice.

Mound rice mixture in the center of a large platter. Surround rice with beef satay and fruits and vegetable. Offer curried peanut dressing to add to taste. Makes 8 servings.

PER SERVING: 447 calories, 6 g protein, 66 g carbohydrates, 19 g fat, 0 mg cholesterol, 30 mg sodium

Cilantro dressing. Mix together ½ cup minced **fresh cilantro** (coriander), ¼ cup minced **fresh mint leaves**, ½ cup *each* **lime juice** and **salad oil**, and 2 teaspoons **sugar**.

Fruits and vegetable. Diagonally slice 2 medium-size firm-ripe peeled **bananas.** (If fruits and vegetable are to be made ahead, peel and slice bananas just before serving.) Rinse, hull, and halve 4 cups **strawberries.** Cut 2 medium-size ripe **papayas** into wedges and scoop out seeds. (Or use 2 ripe mangoes; slice fruit from pit and cut fruit into bite-size pieces.) Diagonally slice 1 large **European-style cucumber.**

BEEF SATAY

If your grill space is small, cook the beef in successive batches.

- 3 pounds boned beef sirloin or tenderloin (fat trimmed), cut into 1-inch chunks
  Satay sauce (recipe follows)

Place beef in a bowl and mix with sauce. If made ahead, cover and chill up to 24 hours. Thread beef evenly on 16 slender (10- to 14-in.-long) bamboo or metal skewers; reserve sauce.

Place beef on a lightly greased grill 4 to 6 inches above a solid bed of medium

coals (you should be able to hold your hand at grill level only 4 to 5 seconds). Cook for 4 minutes. Brush with reserved sauce, turn, and brush again. Continue to cook until beef is done to your liking (cut to test), 4 to 6 minutes longer for medium-rare. Serves 8.

PER SERVING: 450 calories, 31 g protein, 5 g carbohydrates, 33 g fat, 107 mg cholesterol, 594 mg sodium

Satay sauce. In a small bowl, mix ⅓ cup **lemon juice;** ¼ cup **soy sauce;** 2 tablespoons **molasses;** 1 tablespoon **salad oil;** 3 cloves **garlic,** minced or pressed; and 2 teaspoons **ground coriander.**

CURRIED PEANUT DRESSING

- 1 cup thinly sliced green onions
- 2 cloves garlic, minced or pressed
- 1½ tablespoons minced fresh ginger
- 1 tablespoon salad oil
- 1½ teaspoons curry powder
- 1½ cups water
- ⅔ cup chunk-style peanut butter
- 2 tablespoons lemon juice
- 1 tablespoon *each* soy sauce and firmly packed brown sugar
- ¾ teaspoon crushed dried hot red chilies

In a 1½- to 2-quart pan over medium heat, combine onions, garlic, and ginger with oil. Stir often until vegetables begin to brown, 8 to 10 minutes.

Add curry powder and stir for 1 minute. Add water, peanut butter, lemon juice, soy sauce, brown sugar, and chilies; stir until mixture boils and thickens. Serve warm or at room temperature. If made ahead, cover and chill up to 2 days. Return to room temperature to serve; thin with water, if desired. Makes 2½ cups.

PER TABLESPOON: 31 calories, 1 g protein, 1.5 g carbohydrates, 2.5 g fat, 0 mg cholesterol, 47 mg sodium

SHRIMP CHIPS

- 2 to 4 cups salad oil
- 8 ounces dried shrimp chips (also called shrimp crackers)

In a wok or 5- to 6-quart pan, heat 1 inch oil to 375° on a thermometer. Add a few shrimp chips at a time and cook until puffy and lightly browned, 30 to 60 seconds. Lift out and let drain on paper towels. If made ahead, store airtight up to 3 days. Makes 8 servings.

NUTRITION INFORMATION NOT AVAILABLE

Cascades of fruit, cucumber, and skewered beef surround a mound of brown rice seasoned with cabbage, carrots, and herbs. Together they make a colorful dinner salad dressed with curry sauce and lime. Enjoy with shrimp crackers and guava nectar.

Make Your Own Fresh Mozzarella

A RARE TREAT, *genuinely fresh mozzarella is remarkable for its delicate, clean flavor and tender texture. To appreciate it at its best—within a few hours of making—you can produce your own fresh mozzarella.*

Michael Chiarello, chef at Tra Vigne in St. Helena, California, perfected his technique through repetition, and, even though your first batch or two probably won't match his for looks, the taste will be comparable. Cheesemaking is a multiple-day procedure. Plan to set aside several hours, mostly devoted to watching a thermometer, and then wait at least another day for the curd to ripen. This recipe yields up to 3 pounds of cheese, probably more than you can use at once; for meal-size servings, shape portions of it on different days.

The Italians call fresh mozzarella pasta filata, meaning spun paste, because you literally stretch it. Don't mistake this kind for the aged cheese on pizzas.

Be sure to follow steps carefully, especially sterilizing, to ensure freshest flavors.

FRESH MOZZARELLA

Rennet, tablets or liquid, is found in pharmacies and health-food stores.

- 3 **cups whipping cream**
- 1¾ **gallons plus 1 cup nonfat milk (29 cups total)**
- ¼ **rennet tablet or 1 teaspoon liquid rennet**
- ¼ **cup cool water (about 70°)**
- ½ **cup freshly opened buttermilk Brine (directions follow)**

Before you begin, sterilize all tools and containers by pouring boiling water over them or immersing them in boiling water. During the cheesemaking process, have boiling water on hand to pour over tools—spoons and thermometer in particular—*each time* you return them to the milk mixture. This prevents certain bacteria from affecting the cheese's flavor.

To make the curd, pour cream and nonfat milk into a 3- to 4-gallon pan; stir with a metal spoon to mix. Place pan on lowest heat until milk is 90°, stirring occasionally and checking temperature often; if liquid is cold, this may take up to 1 hour. But be patient, since higher cooking temperatures are harder to control.

As the milk heats, combine the rennet and cool water in a small bowl. Let the mixture stand until completely dissolved, about 15 minutes; you may need to crush the tablet with the back of a spoon. (Or mix liquid rennet with water in a bowl.)

When the milk reaches 90°, add buttermilk and stir thoroughly with a spoon. Ladle out any butter lumps.

Slowly pour rennet mixture in a spiraling pattern over milk, stirring. Continue to stir for 3 to 5 minutes, using an up-down circular motion to distribute the rennet evenly.

Keep the milk at 90° until it forms a clot firm enough to hold its shape in a spoon, 30 to 45 minutes; check tempera-

Fresh Mozzarella
Step by Step

1 *Scooped into spoon, rennet-thickened milk clot has right firmness if it holds its shape.*

2 *Cut clot in a crosshatch pattern with knife to form small curds and release whey.*

3 *Spoon curds into a cheesecloth-lined colander and let whey drain away.*

4 *Slice drained curd after it meets "stretch test" (see text) in hot water.*

5 *Ladle hot water over curd, let stand to soften, push together.*

6 *Roll flowing, melted cheese under from an end to make smooth balls; don't pat top.*

7 *Perfect, smooth balls come with practice; rough-looking cheeses still taste good.*

ture about every 5 minutes, removing mixture from heat intermittently, if needed. As you check the temperature, insert the thermometer gently to avoid breaking clot more than necessary.

Next, to create crosshatch pattern and to release clear-colored whey, cut through solid clot to pan bottom with a long knife. First cut clot across, then at right angles for ½-inch squares. Then cut diagonally, holding knife at a 45° angle; turn pan at right angles and repeat. Let curds stand on low heat at 90° for 15 minutes longer (remove pan occasionally, if necessary, to keep temperature from fluctuating), then stir with a slotted spoon for 30 seconds.

From this point on, you need clean but not sterilized equipment. Quickly line a large colander with at least 2 layers of cheesecloth, edges overlapping rim; set in a sink with an open drain. Ladle curds into colander. Let stand until curds stop dripping, about 1 hour.

To protect cheese's flavor, place colander in a large pan; cover airtight with plastic wrap. Chill until curd is ready to shape (see below), 1 to 4 days. Each day, replace cheesecloth and discard whey.

Testing the curd. To determine when curd is ready to shape, cut off a small ¼-inch slice and cover with hot water (170° to 180°). If after 15 to 30 seconds the slice begins to soften and melt and, when held by 1 end, the piece stretches from its own weight, it's ready. If the slice doesn't stretch but tears, chill remaining curd, testing daily, up to 4 days. If curd still won't melt—milk got too hot or sufficient acidity did not develop—slice and cover with hot water (170° to 180°), stirring. Drain, rinse with cold water, drain again. Season with salt; eat like cottage cheese.

Shaping the curd. Divide the ready curd in 4 equal portions; let the number of portions you want to use come to room temperature. Cover and chill remaining curd in cloth-lined colander until you want to shape it—no more than 5 days from when you started.

Working with 1 curd portion at a time, trim off and discard any dried-looking bits. Cut curd into ¼-inch-thick slices and put into a large bowl. Pour about 1 quart hot water (170° to 180°) over slices to cover; let stand ½ to 1 minute to warm and begin to melt. With the back of a large spoon, gently push slices together

For a memorable first course, present slices of fresh mozzarella and ripe tomatoes with chopped basil; extra-virgin olive oil drenches them all. With patience, you can make the cheese at home; its shiny surface comes from gentle handling.

and lift them from beneath, also on spoon back, so the weight of the cheese makes it stretch. Repeat lifting cheese along the length to stretch it; don't let rope fold back onto itself.

When cheese is flowing softly, as shown at left, step 6, lift 1 end of the rope from the water and roll it under itself to form a smooth-surfaced ball 1 to 2 inches thick; pinch from rope and drop into brine. Working quickly, repeat to shape rest of cheese; if handled too slowly or roughly, cheese looks uneven—but it's fine to eat. Keep cheese in brine 5 to 15 minutes to flavor (saltiness depends on length of time in brine); lift from brine.

For tenderest texture and most delicate flavor, rinse and serve at once; or keep cold, covered, no more than 4 hours. Flat to bitter flavors develop when cheese is past its prime, although it is safe to eat.

Repeat to shape remaining cheese. Makes 2½ to 3 pounds, depending on how long the curd drains before shaping.

PER OUNCE, ESTIMATED ONLY: 60 calories, 4 g protein, 1 g carbohydrates, 4.5 g fat, 15 mg cholesterol, sodium varies with time in brine

Brine. In a corrosion-resistant bowl, make enough brine to cover cheese, using ½ cup **salt** for each 1 quart **water.**

The Gas Barbecue

WHEELED UP by the back door or built into a patio, the gas barbecue has taken on the role of an outdoor kitchen appliance. It combines labor-saving convenience with the timeless appeal of back-yard cooking.

Whether you're shopping for a gas barbecue or want to make better use of the one you have, it's helpful to understand how these units operate—and how they differ from the familiar charcoal-fired kind.

Prices run from around $150 to well over $500—considerably more than the cost of most charcoal grills. For that investment, the gas models offer certain advantages: no need to build and ignite a charcoal fire, speedier heat-up time, stove-like temperature controls, predictable cooking results, and no ashes to clean up.

How else do these units differ from charcoal grills? Their heat output and pattern vary by model, not by how you lay the fire, and cooking is best done with the hood closed. Many people notice flavor differences, which are a matter of personal preference.

Our report incorporates Sunset tests of various sizes and types to help you evaluate gas barbecues' capabilities and features. Ultimately, the choice depends on how and what you want to cook.

Small-size gas barbecue is best for lean, quick-cooking foods, such as chicken breasts.

HOW A GAS BARBECUE WORKS

Whether built into a counter, standing on a fixed pedestal, or mounted on a rolling cart, all gas models work basically the same way.

The container is a rectangular firebox with a hinged hood shaped like either a box or a barrel. The inside of the firebox resembles an upside-down broiler: the heat concentration comes from below, and the position of the heat source is fixed.

At the bottom of the firebox, gas lines (one to each burner) feed in fuel—either liquid propane from a refillable tank mounted below the barbecue or natural gas from a permanent hookup.

Once ignited, gas flames reach upward through burners, whose number and configuration vary by manufacturer and model (see drawings on page 135). Stove-like controls let you regulate the flames.

Above the burners is a heat distributor. It collects the burners' heat and radiates it upward and outward, diffusing heat more evenly than raw flames do.

For 25 years, the commonest heat-distribution setup has been a cast-iron grate supporting natural lava rock. More recent alternatives for lava rock are manufactured ceramic or pumice briquets, charcoal-impregnated clay briquets, solid metal plates, and bar grids of heat-retentive steel or cast iron replacing both rock and grate.

Food cooks on a grill above the heat distributor. Some barbecues have grill supports at two or three heights, so—as with oven racks or an adjustable grill on a charcoal barbecue—you can vary the distance between heat and food.

FUEL & BTUs

Heating capacity of gas barbecues is rated in British thermal units (BTUs); one BTU is the amount of heat required to raise the temperature of 1 pound of water 1°. Models on the market claim BTU outputs ranging from 24,000 to 44,000. For barbecues of comparable size, the BTU ratings do not vary significantly from one manufacturer to another.

A higher BTU rating does *not* mean a barbecue cooks more evenly or more efficiently. You use a barbecue's maximum BTU output only when you set all burners on high—something you rarely do, except to heat it up. Just figure that a higher BTU rating indicates a shorter heating-up time before cooking can begin. More BTUs mean you're likely to get better browning on a steak, though BTUs really have nothing to do with how evenly the cooking surface is heated.

In a gas barbecue, there is no difference between the heat performance of liquid propane and that of natural gas. (Bottled propane is under higher pressure and therefore burns hotter than natural gas; to compensate, manufacturers engineer natural gas barbecues to release more fuel into a burner.) Note: barbecues are made for *either* liquid propane *or* natural gas. *Never use one kind of fuel in a barbecue meant for the other.* Call your gas company for details on bringing a gas line to your barbecue area.

Cooking time provided by a 5-gallon tank of propane depends on your barbecue's BTU output, how many burners you use, and whether you cook over high or low heat. Expect 20 to 30 hours of use from one tank. A refill costs $6 to $10; look under Gas—Propane in the Yellow Pages. Use your bathroom scale to weigh your tank empty and again filled, then reweigh it—before a party, for instance—to make sure your supply is adequate.

With a natural gas hookup to a barbecue, you are assured a ready supply of fuel any time; it will cost 13 to 25 cents an hour.

HOW DO GAS BARBECUES COOK?

It's easier to understand gas grilling if you view it as a technique closely related to oven cooking as well as to conventional charcoal barbecuing. The gas heat source can be adjusted so it is under the food for direct-heat cooking, or (depending on the design of the unit) around the food or to one side for indirect-heat cooking.

Unlike a charcoal barbecue, a gas barbecue has its heat effectiveness reduced dramatically when it is used open. But when closed to contain the heat, it can work well for both direct-heat and indirect-heat cooking (as in a kettle-type charcoal barbecue).

For maximum operating efficiency, open the barbecue hood only to tend foods. But dripping fat may cause flare-ups, particularly with direct-heat cooking; pay close attention to see if this starts to be a problem (sometimes you can even hear the flaming).

To cook over direct heat, turn on both (or all) burners to use the entire grill surface. Turn on only one burner if you're going to need just a small cooking area.

For indirect-heat cooking, you turn on all burners to heat the barbecue, then turn off the burner or burners directly beneath the food when you begin to cook. You get best results when heat is balanced around the food.

A distinct advantage of gas barbecues over charcoal ones is the faster heat-up period and the control you have over changing temperatures. It takes about 15 minutes for the heat distributor to absorb and diffuse enough heat to cook foods either quickly or slowly. Regular charcoal barbecues take about 30 minutes to heat up so cooking can begin (however, starter-impregnated charcoals ignite faster).

WHAT DETERMINES THE HEAT PATTERN?

You can arrange regular charcoal to make any pattern of heat you want. Gas barbecues have less flexibility. Several factors affect their heat pattern: burner shape, the heat distribution material and its evenness (both across the grill and vertically), the distances between burners and heat distributor, and the distance between heat distributor and grill.

To see how much heat the units produced and how the heat was distributed, we evaluated a representative group of two- and three-burner gas barbecues. An independent technician with industrial heat-sensing equipment assisted us.

We set all burners on high and heated the barbecues for 15 minutes. The maximum temperature at grill level ranged from 600° on some units to about 800° on others, depending on the burner configuration and the distance between the burner and the grill. We found that smaller units had less even grill temperatures than larger ones.

Larger gas barbecue model with ample grill and hood space can hold big turkeys and roasts. It cooks larger cuts of meat efficiently using indirect heat.

On small barbecues, foods that work best are thin, very lean or fat-free, and quick-cooking, such as skinned chicken breast, lean firm-textured fish, fat-trimmed red meats, and vegetables.

Burner shape. This determines the pattern of the heat. Hottest spots on each unit's grill are at the center (where gas jets are usually closest together) and directly over the burners' perimeter. Next-hottest areas are across the back of the grill. The coolest area is across the front of the grill; at any point where the firebox is perforated, such as at a match

hole, you have significant heat loss. The temperature across the entire grill drops rapidly whenever the hood is lifted.

Heat distributor. The shape, size, and distribution of the material affect the heating pattern. We tested five types of heat distributors: lava rock, pumice briquets, charcoal-impregnated clay briquets, metal bar grids, and solid metal plates.

A regular pattern or solid spread of material is best for even heating. But flares from dripping fat tend to be more troublesome on barbecues with a solid

A Look at Gas Barbecue Anatomy...Basic Features & Extras

Hood

Distance from grill to closed hood limits height of food you can cook—from thin steaks to turkey. Grease will quickly darken a hood window (you may still see flashes of fat flare up).

Handle

Full-width handle is well balanced, easy to use for right- or left-handed cooks. Check that handle attachment won't loosen or can be tightened. Wooden handles won't get hot.

Grill

Stainless steel and chrome wire are lighter to lift; cast iron holds heat best. Some grills lift out in sections. Porcelain enamel coatings make cleaning easier.

Burners

Usually stainless steel. Gas jets dot burners' edges. In two-burner barbecues, H-shape is popular; each half of H is separate burner with separate heat control.

Shelves

Usually project at sides, sometimes front. May fold down, or be removable.

Burner controls

Knobs like ones on gas range. Childproof models lock into low, medium, high; ones that turn in continuous range let you control heat to finer degree. Knobs that project out from firebox stay comfortable to touch.

Wheels

One pair lets portable models move, but can be awkward. Casters opposite (not fixed legs) make it easier; need to lock for stability. *Never* move operating unit.

Temperature gauge

Seldom accurate. At best, gives rough average interior temperature—but may not correspond to settings of burner controls.

Heat distributor

Soaks up heat of burner flames, radiates and diffuses it to cook food on grill. Traditional: natural lava rocks on a grate. New: smooth ceramic and pumice briquets or metal grids and plates.

Firebox

Kind of food you want to cook—hamburgers, leg of lamb, large fish—determines cooking space and firebox size you need. Units are cast aluminum, stainless steel, porcelainized steel, or cast iron (heaviest to move). Wall thickness indicates construction quality.

Ignition

Produces spark to start burners. Follow barbecue directions precisely; may need a few tries.

Match hole

Should be easy to reach for manual lighting if igniter fails. Also is useful view port to check for healthy flames—blue with yellow tip.

Fuel gauge

Measures tank weight. Can register empty when not, or the opposite. To double-check fuel level, unmount tank and weigh on bathroom scale.

Liquid propane tank

Standard 5-gallon tank weighs 18 to 20 pounds empty, 37 to 40 full—hard to heft. Tank mount should be easy to reach. Best kind is end-of-barbecue bracket that holds tank collar with a wing nut. You couple tank valve to barbecue hose. Carefully follow barbecue directions for handling, connecting fuel.

Grease collection

Below opening in firebox floor, you need to provide receptacle for dripping fat. Simplest is wire hook to hold an empty can; best is bracket for disposable aluminum-foil tray. Don't believe that all fat will burn off inside barbecue.

arrangement of heat distributors, and less of a problem if fat can drip past the heat distributor and be collected below the flames.

Because lava rocks are irregularly shaped, they create a less even heat pattern than manufactured briquets or heating bars do. The lava is most prone to flare-ups because it catches dripping fat in its pits and crevices. The rock never really wears out, but gets pretty messy, or even rancid; two to five years' use is average. You can prolong use by burning off the clogged fat occasionally. Just turn rocks over and keep the barbecue on high until they stop smoking.

Replacement rocks cost about $7 for an 8-pound bag, enough to cover about 400 square inches. Make sure rocks are big enough that they won't fall through the grate.

Mass-produced ceramic and pumice briquets have uniform size and shape (round, square, or pyramid), which help distribute heat evenly (like an even layer of charcoal briquets in a charcoal barbecue). These cost about $12 a box, enough to cover about 300 square inches. As their smooth surfaces get coated with fat, you can turn them over and burn the fat off the same way you clean lava rock. Theoretically, these briquets will stay fresh longer than lava rock.

Charcoal-impregnated clay briquets cost about $7 for a 7-pound bag, enough to cover about 250 square inches. The first few times you heat them, they emit a charcoal aroma.

For heat-retentive steel or cast-iron bar grids, best guesses place their life span at five to six years (when corrosion will necessitate replacing them). However, they haven't been on the market long enough for anyone to know for sure.

The steel or cast-iron plates come in 18- or 21-inch lengths and are 6 inches wide (but can overlap to adjust to the width of the barbecue). They are tented over an accompanying angled support. A set costs about $30.

What Type of Burner?

These eight burner types are typical of what you'll find. Models with more than two burners use multiples of a bar design. Flame pattern follows burner perimeter; burner shape shows you where to expect hottest areas of grill. The greater a burner's perimeter, the more even the heating pattern is likely to be. Only small units have oval type (shortest perimeter). Burner controls allow you to change the heat pattern for direct or indirect cooking.

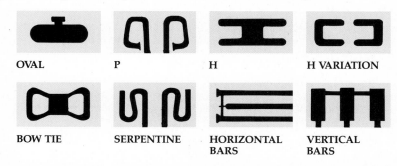

OVAL   P   H   H VARIATION

BOW TIE   SERPENTINE   HORIZONTAL BARS   VERTICAL BARS

Vertical distances. The smallest barbecues have only 1⅛ inches between burners and heat distributor and 1¾ inches between heat distributor and grill. Larger barbecues have 1¾ to 2¼ inches between burners and heat distributor and 3½ or more inches between heat distributor and grill.

On the bigger barbecues, the space between the burner, heat distributor, and cooking grill allows the heat to spread out more evenly and cook more effectively, giving results more comparable to those achieved with charcoal.

What About Smoke & Flavor?

People like grilling because it can give foods good color and flavor. The key to the flavor of the cooked food is the source of the smoke.

Flavorful smoke comes from moist wood chips or chunks that smolder and give off a sweet, fragrant aroma. To use wood chips in gas barbecues, follow the manufacturer's instructions.

In charcoal barbecues, the vapors given off by burning charcoal briquets or mesquite charcoal also provide some flavor, but taste-tests have demonstrated that most people can't tell them apart, despite mesquite's mystique. However, our tasters could distinguish charcoal-cooked foods from gas-cooked foods—unless wood chips or charcoal flavor–impregnated clay briquets were used in the gas barbecues.

Flare-ups can create smoke that imparts a charred or burned taste. They also blacken food surfaces, making it difficult to judge doneness. To avoid flare-ups, minimize fat or sauces dripping onto the heat distributor or burner: trim fat from foods before cooking and baste carefully.

It's harder to control flare-ups when you're cooking over direct heat. Just remember to keep a careful watch on the barbecue when you cook, lift foods from the grill if drips flare, leave the hood open until flames burn off, and then return foods to the grill.

A Summer Meal that Travels Well: Soup, Bread & Cheese

JUST GOOD SOUP, *bread, cheese, fresh berries, and wine make up this menu. To celebrate summer's warm evenings and their clear vistas, we suggest bringing the simple meal outdoors to enjoy on the deck or patio, or in a park. The components go together quickly and travel well.*

Beans and ham hocks form the base of the soup, which you can cook ahead. At serving time, stir in the mustard greens and herb sauce. To make the rustic-looking loaf, roll out thawed frozen bread dough and sprinkle it with rolled oats, polenta, and sesame seed. Cut and stretch the dough into a freeform cloud shape, then bake. Serve seasoned goat cheese to spread on the bread.

For dessert, offer the season's best berries with cream and wine.

VISTA DINNER PARTY

**Bean & Greens Soup
Goat Cheese with Caraway & Mint
Cloud Bread
Chardonnay or Pinot Noir
Berries with Cream &
Late-harvest White Wine**

If you'll be transporting the meal to a location more than a few minutes from home, chill the soup completely, then pack it in a cooler. Also keep cold the ready-to-serve mustard greens, green sauce, cheese (pack seasonings separately), berries, cream, and white wines.

At site, heat soup to boiling over a portable burner or camp stove, season cheese, and set out berries to lose their chill.

BEAN & GREENS SOUP

2	large onions, chopped
3	stalks celery, chopped
3	cloves garlic, minced or pressed
½	cup chopped parsley
1	dry bay leaf
2	tablespoons salad oil
1	cup dry Great Northern beans, sorted of debris and rinsed
2	pounds meaty smoked ham hocks, cracked
1½	quarts water
2	quarts regular-strength chicken broth
½	pound mustard greens (stems trimmed), rinsed, drained, and thinly sliced
	Green sauce (recipe follows)

In a 6- to 8-quart pan over medium heat, cook the onions, celery, garlic, parsley, and bay in oil, stirring, until vegetables are very limp, 15 to 20 minutes. Add beans, ham hocks, water, and broth. Bring to a boil over high heat, then cover and simmer until beans are very tender to bite, about 2¼ hours.

Lift ham hocks from pan, let cool, then pull meat and fat from bones. Discard fat and bones. Tear meat into shreds and return to pan. (At this point, you can let soup cool, cover, and chill up to 3 days.)

Skim and discard fat from broth. Bring soup to a boil over high heat, either on a cooktop or a portable burner; hold at a low simmer. Ladle soup into bowls; add mustard greens and green sauce to taste. Makes 6 servings, each about 2½ cups.

PER SERVING: 357 calories, 25 g protein, 31 g carbohydrates, 15 g fat, 43 mg cholesterol, 1,102 mg sodium

Green sauce. In a blender or food processor, whirl until smooth 1½ cups *each* lightly packed, rinsed, drained **watercress sprigs** and **basil leaves;** 1 small clove **garlic;** ½ cup **extra-virgin olive oil;** and ½ cup grated **parmesan cheese.** Makes ¾ cup.

PER TABLESPOON: 101 calories, 1.7 g protein, 1.4 g carbohydrates, 10 g fat, 2.6 mg cholesterol, 65 mg sodium

GOAT CHEESE WITH CARAWAY & MINT

10	or 11 ounces unripened goat cheese, such as Montrachet
3	tablespoons extra-virgin olive oil
1	tablespoon chopped fresh mint
1	teaspoon caraway seed

Place cheese on a plate. Drizzle evenly with oil; sprinkle with mint and caraway. Serve, or let stand up to 2 hours. Serves 6.

PER SERVING: 233 calories, 8.8 g protein, 3.5 g carbohydrates, 21 g fat, 44 mg cholesterol, 291 mg sodium

CLOUD BREAD

	All-purpose flour
1	loaf (1 lb.) frozen white or whole-wheat bread dough, thawed
1	large egg, beaten to blend
⅓	cup regular rolled oats
¼	cup polenta or yellow cornmeal
2	tablespoons sesame seed

Sprinkle a 12- by 15-inch sheet of foil with flour. Roll dough on foil to make an irregular oval that measures about 9 by 13 inches.

Brush dough top and sides with beaten egg, reserving a little. Combine oats, polenta, and sesame; pat half of this mixture onto the dough. Carefully flip dough onto the center of a greased 12- by 15-inch baking sheet. Brush dough top with more egg; pat on rest of oat mixture.

With a razor blade or small sharp knife, make 2-inch slashes through dough in about 8 places. Pat and stretch slightly to form your version of a cloud. Cover loosely with plastic wrap and let rise in a warm place until puffy, 25 to 30 minutes.

Mist dough all over with water, then bake, uncovered, in a 375° oven for 5 minutes. Mist, then repeat 5 minutes later. Continue to bake until bread is deep golden, about 30 minutes total.

Lift bread from pan and serve warm or cool. When cool, wrap it airtight and keep up to 2 days; freeze to store longer. Makes 1 loaf (about 1 lb.).

PER OUNCE: 105 calories, 3.2 g protein, 17 g carbohydrates, 2.4 g fat, 19 mg cholesterol, 141 mg sodium

Simple dessert blends raspberries, strawberries, cream, and late-harvest wine.

Fresh mustard greens go limp and tender in hot bean-and-ham soup; a watercress-basil sauce provides additional seasoning. Accompany with cloud-shaped bread and mild goat cheese topped with olive oil, caraway, and mint.

All-Idaho Picnic

To some Sun Valley residents, *the best way to welcome summer's plenty is to take a walk and gather edible wild plants along the way. Afterward, they enjoy their harvest in a picnic that highlights these and other native foods.*

Bill McDorman, an experienced naturalist, collects wild greens for a salad. Caterer Selene Islams uses local potatoes in a salad laced with dill, while smoked Idaho trout flavors her cheese salad. A vinaigrette flavors cultivated mushrooms, and a mustard dressing cloaks garden-grown baby beets.

Mr. McDorman also brings his specialty, tangy sourdough scones, made with hundred-year-old starter. Jelly and cheese accompany the scones. For a quicker bread choice, buy crusty rolls.

Adapt this meal for spring or summer dining, in the fields or on the patio.

Wash and crisp greens; add dressing just before serving. The other salads can be prepared ahead. Make the scones in the morning, thaw frozen ones, or buy rolls.

Novices should use cultivated greens for the salad. But if you know wild greens, or have experienced guidance, you can look for greens and flowers in the field—or your garden—so long as you don't forage where pesticides or other toxins may be present. Never experiment on your own.

This salad uses cultivated greens in place of wild ones. Many taste similar to those found in the wild. Cultivated sorrel, watercress, mint, dandelion, mustard, and shallots have flavors reminiscent of their untamed ancestors. Good-tasting weeds such as lamb's-quarters, Bermuda buttercup, and sour dock have a mild acidity.

WILD GREEN SALAD

12 **cups bite-size greens (spinach, sorrel, watercress, fresh mint leaves, young dandelion leaves, or mustard greens; choose several kinds), washed and crisped, tough stems removed**

Gathering wild greens and flowers, this experienced naturalist selects the makings for salad. Other picnic dishes, prepared ahead, take advantage of Idaho's bounty of local trout, potatoes, and other regional ingredients. Tangy sourdough scones are served with a choice of jelly or cheese.

1 cup thinly sliced celery
2 tablespoons thinly sliced shallots
½ cup edible flowers or petals (Bermuda buttercup, calendula, nasturtium, mustard, radish, sunflower), optional
⅓ cup salad oil
2 tablespoons lemon juice
Salt and pepper

In a large bowl, combine greens, celery, shallots, and flowers. Mix oil and lemon juice; pour over salad and mix. Add salt and pepper to taste. Makes 6 servings.

PER SERVING: 131 calories, 2.1 g protein, 4.8 g carbohydrates, 12 g fat, 0 mg cholesterol, 50 mg sodium

POTATO SALAD WITH DILL

2 pounds medium-size red thin-skinned potatoes
Dill sauce (recipe follows)
Salt and pepper
Red bell pepper slivers (optional)

In a 5- to 6-quart pan, bring about 3 quarts water to a boil. Add potatoes, cover, and boil gently until tender when pierced, 25 to 30 minutes; drain. When cool, cut into ¼-inch-thick slices.

Mix sauce and potatoes with salt and pepper to taste. Serve, or cover and chill up to 1 day. Top with bell pepper. Serves 6.

PER SERVING: 254 calories, 3.1 g protein, 28 g carbohydrates, 14 g fat, 0 mg cholesterol, 39 mg sodium

Dill sauce. Mix 6 tablespoons **salad oil,** ¼ cup **dry white wine,** 2 tablespoons **white wine vinegar,** 3 tablespoons minced **fresh dill** or 1 tablespoon dry dill weed, 2 tablespoons minced **green onion,** and 1 teaspoon **Dijon mustard.**

MUSHROOMS WITH GARLIC VINAIGRETTE

1½ pounds mushrooms
1 cup thinly sliced green onions
Garlic vinaigrette (recipe follows)
Salt and pepper
3 green onions, ends trimmed

Rinse mushrooms, drain, and trim base of stems. Thinly slice mushrooms and mix in a salad bowl with sliced onions, vinaigrette, and salt and pepper to taste. Garnish with whole onions. Serve, or cover and chill up to 4 hours. Makes 6 servings.

PER SERVING: 174 calories, 3.9 g protein, 7.6 g carbohydrates, 15 g fat, 46 mg cholesterol, 92 mg sodium

Garlic vinaigrette. In a small bowl, combine 3 tablespoons **tarragon vinegar;** 1 tablespoon **Dijon mustard;** 1 large **egg;** 1 clove **garlic,** pressed or minced; ½ teaspoon **white pepper;** ½ teaspoon **dry mustard;** and ½ teaspoon **dry tarragon leaves.** Whisk in 6 tablespoons **salad oil.**

SMOKED TROUT SALAD

½ pound smoked trout, boned, skinned, cut into ½-inch strips
½ pound jarlsberg cheese, cut into julienne strips
2 cups red or green seedless grapes
2 cups thinly sliced celery
Sherry mayonnaise (recipe follows)
Salt
1 tablespoon canned green peppercorns, rinsed and drained

Combine trout, cheese, grapes, and celery. Add mayonnaise; mix gently. Add salt to taste. Pour into serving bowl; sprinkle with peppercorns. Serve, or cover and chill up to 1 day. Serves 6.

PER SERVING: 376 calories, 13 g protein, 9.6 g carbohydrates, 30 g fat, 38 mg cholesterol, 533 mg sodium

Sherry mayonnaise. Mix ¾ cup **mayonnaise,** 3 tablespoons **sherry** or wine **vinegar,** and 1 tablespoon **Dijon mustard.**

BEETS WITH HONEY MUSTARD DRESSING

3 pounds tiny (1-in.-wide) beets, scrubbed; or 2 cans (1 lb. each) whole beets, drained and rinsed
Honey mustard dressing (recipe follows)
Salt and pepper

Cut off beet tops, leaving about 1 inch attached (reserve some tops for garnish, if desired). In a 5- to 6-quart pan, bring about 2 quarts water to a boil. Add beets, cover, and simmer until tender when pierced, about 20 minutes; drain. When cool, rub off skins and trim tops. (Omit this step for canned beets. Cut canned beets in half if larger than 1 in.)

Combine beets, dressing, and salt and pepper to taste; mix. Serve, or cover and chill until the next day. Garnish with beet tops. Makes 6 servings.

PER SERVING: 229 calories, 3.9 g protein, 26 g carbohydrates, 13 g fat, 45 mg cholesterol, 166 mg sodium

Honey mustard dressing. In a blender container, mix 1 teaspoon **dry mustard** with 1 teaspoon **water;** let stand 15 minutes. Add 1 **large egg yolk,** 2 teaspoons **honey,** and 1 tablespoon **lemon juice;** blend. With motor turned on, add ⅓ cup **salad oil** in a steady stream. Turn motor off; stir in 2 tablespoons thinly sliced **chives** or green onions.

SOURDOUGH SCONES

1 cup sourdough starter (see page 138 of the May 1988 *Sunset*)
About 6½ cups all-purpose flour
1¼ cups warm water (110°)
1 package active dry yeast
2 large eggs
2 tablespoons sugar
Salad oil
½ teaspoon salt

In a large bowl, combine starter, 1½ cups flour, and 1 cup water; stir until smooth. Cover and let stand in a warm place until bubbly and sour smelling, 12 to 24 hours. Soften yeast in remaining ¼ cup water. Add to the bubbly sponge mixture. Stir in eggs, sugar, 2 tablespoons oil, and salt. Add 5 more cups flour.

With a dough hook, beat dough on low speed until moistened. Then beat on high speed until dough cleans sides of bowl, about 2 minutes; if still sticky, add flour, 1 tablespoon at a time.

With a heavy spoon, stir dough until moistened. Scrape out onto a floured board and knead until smooth, about 5 minutes; add flour, as required, to prevent sticking. Return to a greased bowl.

Cover dough with plastic wrap and let rise in a warm place until doubled, about 1 hour. Punch dough down and knead with dough hook or on a floured board to expel bubbles. Divide dough into 20 equal portions. Pat each to a thickness of ½ inch. Place about 1 inch apart on floured 12- by 15-inch baking sheets. Cover lightly with plastic wrap. Let stand in a warm place until puffy, about 20 minutes.

Meanwhile, in a wok or 5- to 6-quart pan, heat about 1 inch oil to 350° on a thermometer. Add dough pieces, 2 or 3 at a time. Cook, turning often, until golden, 3 to 4 minutes. Lift out with a slotted spoon; drain on paper towels. Repeat with remaining dough. Serve hot or cool, or store airtight up to 6 hours. Or freeze up to 2 weeks, then thaw to serve. Makes 20.

PER PIECE: 213 calories, 5.7 g protein, 36 g carbohydrates, 4.7 g fat, 28 mg cholesterol, 68 mg sodium

Cooking Squid Abalone-style

WITH ITS MILDLY SWEET FLAVOR, *squid is often compared to abalone. The similarity is most apparent when squid tubes are quickly pan-fried with a crumb coating—the way abalone is typically prepared. But unlike abalone, squid is affordable.*

Both shellfish are mollusks, but squid conceals its shell in the hood or mantle as a thin, transparent quill or cuttlebone. Before frying, the hoods—or tubes (cleaned squid without tentacles)—must be cut and tenderized to keep them from curling up in the pan.

Most squid available in the West is from the California coast, primarily Monterey and San Pedro. It's harvested almost year-round and is always available, since much of the catch is frozen. Imported squid is also sold here, usually as frozen tubes. A giant Mexican species is available as tenderized thick steaks, but it shouldn't be used in this recipe since it requires different handling.

California squid are small, ranging from 7 to 12 whole squid per pound. If you buy squid whole, you must clean them first. You can also buy cleaned tubes, usually measuring 4 to 5 inches long; imported squid tubes may be a little larger.

To clean whole squid, *gently pull on the body (mantle or hood) to separate it from the head (with eyes and tentacles); discard heads or clean to use for other preparations. With a sharp knife or scissors, slit tube lengthwise and scrape out the quill and viscera inside. With your fingers, pull off and discard fins and thin speckled membrane covering tube; rinse tube well.*

If you buy cleaned tubes, simply cut them open lengthwise (see step 1), and rinse away any remaining outside membrane or inside viscera.

To tenderize squid, *place each split tube, membrane side up, on a board (if tubes are over 4½ in. wide, cut in half). Using a sharp knife, make ¾-inch-deep cuts at about 1-inch intervals all around tube perimeters. With a textured side of a metal tenderizing mallet, pound tubes gently and evenly until they are paper-thin; start in the center of each tube and gradually work all the way out and over edges, being careful to avoid tearing. If done ahead, cover and chill until the next day.*

If you don't have a tenderizing mallet, use a single-edge razor blade to score the

3 *Using a textured mallet, pound tubes gently until paper-thin.*

1 *With scissors, first slit tubes from base to tip; lay tubes flat, with the outside surfaces up.*

4 *Fry crumb-coated squid steaks until they're lightly browned.*

2 *With a sharp knife, make ¾-inch-deep cuts at 1-inch intervals all around tube perimeters.*

membrane side of each piece at about ½-inch intervals, making a crosshatch pattern; be careful not to cut through meat.

SQUID STEAKS, ABALONE-STYLE

      2 **large eggs**
    ¼ **cup milk**
      1 **cup fine dry bread crumbs**
    1½ **tablespoons grated parmesan cheese**
      1 **tablespoon finely chopped parsley**
      2 **pounds whole squid or 1 pound squid tubes (hoods or mantles), cleaned and tenderized (directions precede)**
         About ½ cup olive oil or salad oil

In a shallow bowl, beat eggs and milk to blend. On waxed paper, mix crumbs, cheese, parsley. Dip each piece of squid in egg mixture, drain briefly, then coat with crumb mixture, shaking off excess; set aside in a single layer on waxed paper.

Place a 10- to 12-inch frying pan with about 2 tablespoons oil (⅛ in. deep) over medium-high heat until oil ripples when pan is tilted. Add squid, without crowding, and cook until browned, about 30 seconds on each side. Remove from pan and keep warm. Continue until all are cooked; add oil as needed. Serves 4 to 6.—*Christine Trigale, Monterey, Calif.*

PER SERVING: 332 calories, 17 g protein, 15 g carbohydrates, 22 g fat, 271 mg cholesterol, 207 mg sodium

Blending Vegetables for Special Flavor Effects

IN THE SAME WAY *you blend herbs and spices for seasoning, you can mix various vegetables to get specific flavor effects, as in these three dishes. The baked ratatouille is a mellow blending of four vegetables with just a whisper of oil. Corn, chilies, and bell peppers balance each other in the oven casserole. Bold cauliflower complements mild zucchini in a salad; they share a garbanzo dressing.*

OVEN RATATOUILLE

   1   **small (about 1 lb.) eggplant**
   4   **medium-size zucchini (about 1 lb. total)**
1½   **pounds firm-ripe Roma-style tomatoes**
   1   **large onion, chopped**
   1   **cup finely chopped fresh or ⅓ cup dry basil leaves**
   1   **tablespoon olive oil**
       Salt and pepper

Trim ends off eggplant and zucchini. Cut eggplant in ½- by 2-inch sticks; cut zucchini in ½-inch slices. Core and quarter tomatoes. Mix vegetables, onion, basil, and oil in a deep 3- to 4-quart baking dish.

Cover dish tightly and bake in a 400° oven for 2 hours. Uncover and bake until eggplant is creamy to bite and juices are reduced by about ⅔, about 20 minutes; baste vegetables occasionally. Add salt and pepper to taste. Serve hot, at room temperature, or chilled; if made ahead, cover and chill up to 1 week. Makes 6 to 8 servings.

PER SERVING: 68 calories, 2.8 g protein, 12 g carbohydrates, 2 g fat, 0 mg cholesterol, 12 mg sodium

HIGH-DESERT CORN CASSEROLE

   5   **fresh jalapeño or serrano chilies**
   2   **tablespoons salad oil**
   1   **medium-size onion, chopped**
   1   **medium-size red bell pepper, stemmed, seeded, and minced**
   4   **cups fresh or thawed frozen corn kernels**
   1   **cup small-curd cottage cheese**
   2   **large eggs**
   1   **tablespoon cornstarch**
       Salt and pepper
   1   **cup (4 oz.) shredded cheddar cheese**

Stem, seed, and chop 3 of the chilies. Put in a 10- to 12-inch frying pan with salad oil, onion, and bell pepper. Cook over medium-high heat, stirring often, until onion is limp and pepper is tender to bite; add 2 cups of corn and stir until hot.

Meanwhile, in a food processor or blender, combine remaining 2 cups corn, cottage cheese, eggs, and cornstarch; purée until smooth, about 2 minutes.

Remove cooked vegetables from heat and stir the puréed mixture into them; season to taste with salt and pepper. Scrape into a shallow 10-inch round or oval baking dish or pan. Sprinkle cheddar cheese over vegetables. (If made ahead, cover and chill up to overnight.)

Bake in a 375° oven until mixture puffs in center and cheese begins to brown at edges, about 30 minutes. Garnish with whole chilies. Serves 8.—*Sandra Atkinson, San Ramon, Calif.*

PER SERVING: 214 calories, 11 g protein, 19 g carbohydrates, 12 g fat, 87 mg cholesterol, 224 mg sodium

CAULIFLOWER & ZUCCHINI WITH TAHINI

   1   **medium-size (about 1 lb.) cauliflower**
   4   **medium-size zucchini (1 lb. total)**
       Tahini sauce (recipe follows)
       Parsley sprigs
       Lemon slices
       Salt

Break cauliflowerets from core; discard core and leaves. Trim zucchini ends and discard. Cut zucchini into ½-inch slices.

In a 4- to 5-quart pan over high heat, bring 3 quarts water to boiling. Add cauliflowerets; cook, uncovered, until tender when pierced, 6 to 8 minutes. Lift out with a slotted spoon, drain, and put on a platter.

Add zucchini to boiling water and cook, uncovered, until tender when pierced, 4 to 6 minutes. Drain and immerse in cold water until cool; drain and put on platter with cauliflower. If made ahead, cover and chill up to overnight; drain off any liquid that accumulates on platter. Serve vegetables at room temperature.

Pour tahini sauce over vegetables. Garnish with parsley and lemon; add salt to taste. Makes 8 servings.—*Katy El Tawil, San Mateo, Calif.*

PER SERVING: 152 calories, 5.8 g protein, 15 g carbohydrates, 9 g fat, 1.8 mg cholesterol, 124 mg sodium

Tahini sauce. Drain and reserve liquid from 1 can (8¾ oz.) **garbanzos.** In a blender, whirl beans, ½ cup *each* **unflavored yogurt** and **lemon juice**, ½ cup **canned tahini**, ½ teaspoon **ground cumin**, and 1 clove **garlic** until smoothly puréed. Add a little bean liquid to make sauce pourable; add **salt** and **pepper** to taste. Serve, or cover the sauce and chill it up to 1 week; stir before using.

For ratatouille, cut up eggplant, onion, tomatoes, and zucchini and add fresh basil. Bake mixture of vegetables and herb to develop mellow, rich flavor.

Fresh Figs for Dessert or Breakfast

WHILE FIG VARIETIES *vary in sweetness, intensity of flavor, and color, they aren't always identified in the market. For the cook, this is no problem, since varieties can be used interchangeably.*

Here we pair the fruit, raw or cooked, with the tart coolness of either fresh Italian mascarpone (purchased or made at home) or sour cream. Try the dishes for breakfast or dessert.

Among the dark-skinned figs are 'Mission' and 'Brown Turkey' ('San Piero'). Showy 'Osborn Prolific' is yellow-green heavily streaked with violet. Greenish white to green figs include 'Conadria', 'Kadota', and 'King'.

Remember that harvested figs don't ripen further, and as they mature, they tend to split. Choose plump-looking (not shriveled) fruit with no signs of spoilage. They should give easily to gentle pressure. Firm figs taste dry.

Here's a great choice for a summer dessert: fresh figs are halved, drizzled with orange liqueur, then paired with smooth mascarpone cheese and toasted pine nuts.

FIGS WITH ORANGE LIQUEUR & MASCARPONE

- 8 medium-size ripe figs (¾ to 1 lb.)
- 2 tablespoons orange-flavored liqueur, or 1 tablespoon thawed frozen orange juice concentrate
- ¾ to 1 cup mascarpone cheese (recipe follows) or purchased mascarpone
    Toasted pine nuts (directions follow)
    Mint sprigs (optional)

Rinse and drain figs. Trim tip off stem, if desired. Cut fruit vertically in half. Arrange 4 halves on each of 4 dessert plates. Drizzle fruit with liqueur (or brush lightly with orange concentrate).

In the center of each plate, mound about ¼ cup mascarpone (if desired, shape into a cone with a small spatula). Sprinkle cheese with pine nuts; garnish plates with mint. To eat, spread cheese and nuts onto figs. Use a fork or pick up to eat. Makes 4 servings.

PER SERVING: 268 calories, 2.4 g protein, 21 g carbohydrates, 19 g fat, 67 mg cholesterol, 27 mg sodium

Mascarpone cheese. Heat 2 cups **whipping cream** to lukewarm (90° to 100°) and pour into a bowl. Stir in 3 tablespoons **buttermilk** (freshly opened) and cover with plastic wrap. Hold at room temperature 24 to 36 hours, until mixture is the consistency of a soft yogurt (thickening is faster on hot days).

Line a colander with clean muslin cloth or several layers of cheesecloth; set colander in a sink. Pour cream mixture into cloth; let drain about 10 minutes. Fold cloth over cream mixture, then set colander on a rack in a rimmed pan, arranging so rack is at least 1 inch above pan bottom. Enclose whole unit with plastic wrap, making airtight. Let stand in refrigerator until most liquid has drained out of cream, at least 36 or up to 48 hours.

Scoop mascarpone from cloth to use; if made ahead, put mascarpone in an airtight container and chill up to 1 week. Makes about 1½ cups.

PER TABLESPOON: 59 calories, 0.5 g protein, 0.6 g carbohydrates, 6.2 g fat, 22 mg cholesterol, 8.7 mg sodium

Toasted pine nuts. In a 6- to 8-inch frying pan over medium heat, frequently shake 1 tablespoon **pine nuts** until golden, about 5 minutes. Let cool; if made ahead, cover and chill up to 1 week.

BAKED WHOLE FIGS

- 8 medium-size ripe figs (¾ to 1 lb.), rinsed and drained
    About ¼ cup sour cream or mascarpone (see preceding recipe)
- 1 lime, cut into 8 wedges
- 2 to 3 tablespoons honey

Rinse figs and set stems up and slightly apart in an 8- or 9-inch-square pan. Bake, uncovered, in a 350° oven until figs swell from the heat and skins are taut, about 20 minutes.

Gently spoon 2 figs onto each of 4 dessert plates or small bowls. Accompany with sour cream, lime, and honey to add to taste. Makes 4 servings.

PER SERVING: 131 calories, 1.2 g protein, 27 g carbohydrates, 3.2 g fat, 6.3 mg cholesterol, 9.3 mg sodium

BAKED APPLES & FIGS WITH CASSIS

- 2 medium-size Granny Smith or Gravenstein apples
- 1 tablespoon lemon juice
- 6 medium-size ripe figs (½ to ¾ lb.)
- ¼ cup cassis (currant-flavored liqueur) or black raspberry-flavored liqueur
- 1 tablespoon sugar
- 2 teaspoons butter or margarine
    About ⅓ cup mascarpone (recipe precedes) or sour cream

Peel, core, and thinly slice apples. Overlap slices in a shallow 9-inch-wide baking dish. Drizzle fruit with lemon juice. Rinse figs and cut off stems. Thinly slice figs crosswise and place fruit evenly over apples. Pour liqueur over fruit, sprinkle with sugar, and dot with butter in small pieces.

Bake, uncovered, in a 400° oven until juices bubble vigorously, about 15 minutes. Spoon into small bowls and top with mascarpone. Makes 4 servings.

PER SERVING: 233 calories, 1.2 g protein, 31 g carbohydrates, 11 g fat, 35 mg cholesterol, 33 mg sodium

More June Recipes

OTHER JUNE ARTICLES *feature a dessert of juicy peaches topped with pralines and a hearty brunch entrée from Mexico.*

PEACHES & PRALINES

Caramelized sugar works two ways to dress up fresh peaches or nectarines: first, it sweetens a rum-cream sauce you serve with the fruit; second, it turns pecans into crackly pralines you scatter on top.

How to caramelize sugar. *In an 8- to 10-inch frying pan over medium-high heat, warm sugar until it melts and turns a light caramel color; shake pan frequently to mix dry sugar into the liquid that forms. Watch carefully to avoid burning.*

- ⅓ cup sugar
- ¼ cup whipping cream
- 2 tablespoons rum or brandy
- 3 medium-size ripe peaches (peeled, if desired) or nectarines, pitted and sliced
  Pralines (recipe follows)

Caramelize sugar as directed above. At once, add cream, stirring until sauce is smooth. Remove from heat; stir in rum. Use warm or let cool. If made ahead, chill in a covered container up to 1 week. To reheat, stir in pan over low heat just until warm. Spoon peaches onto 4 dessert plates. Pour sauce over fruit; top with pralines. Serves 4.

PER SERVING: 411 calories, 2.6 g protein, 50 g carbohydrates, 23 g fat, 28 mg cholesterol, 50 mg sodium

Pralines. In an 8- to 10-inch frying pan over medium heat, combine 1 tablespoon **butter** or margarine and ¾ cup **pecan halves;** stir until nuts darken slightly, about 10 minutes. Drain on paper towels.

Wipe pan clean; add 6 tablespoons **sugar** and caramelize as directed above. At once, stir in nuts and 1½ teaspoons **butter** or margarine. Immediately pour nuts onto a sheet of foil, pushing them apart with a spoon; let cool. Break nuts apart. Serve, or store airtight up to 1 week.

HUEVOS CON FRIJOLES NEGROS Y PLATANOS
(Eggs with Black Beans & Plantains)

One of the traditional Mexican dishes you can make with ease uses fresh plantains (or green-tipped bananas), canned black beans, homemade chili sauce, and domestically produced Mexican cheese (or parmesan).

Refried black beans (recipe follows)
- 8 fried eggs
  Fried plantains (recipe follows)
  Red chili purée (recipe follows)
- ⅓ cup grated or crumbled cotija cheese or parmesan cheese
  Lime wedges

Spoon beans equally onto 8 warm plates and top each portion with an egg; arrange plantains alongside. Add chili purée to taste; then sprinkle with cheese. Offer lime to squeeze over individual servings. Makes 8 servings.

PER SERVING WITHOUT RED CHILI PURÉE: 737 calories, 25 g protein, 66 g carbohydrates, 43 g fat, 277 mg cholesterol, 1,368 mg sodium

Refried black beans. In a 4- to 5-quart pan, cook 12 slices diced **bacon** over medium-high heat until fat is melted. Add 1 large **onion,** chopped; cook, stirring often, until limp, about 5 minutes.

Drain 4 cans (about 1 lb. each) **black beans,** reserving about ½ cup of the **bean liquid.** Mash beans with a heavy spoon or potato masher and add to pan. Cook over low heat, stirring often, until hot, moistening mixture with reserved bean liquid as necessary. Season to taste with **salt.** Keep warm.

Fried plantains. Peel 3 large ripe **plantains** (skins should be almost black) or 4 large, firm, green-tipped bananas. Cut into ¼-inch-thick diagonal slices.

Pour **salad oil** to a depth of 1 inch into a 10- to 12-inch frying pan and heat to 375° on a thermometer. Drop plantain slices, several at a time, into hot oil and cook, turning as needed, until golden brown, 2 to 3 minutes.

Meanwhile, line a 12- by 15-inch baking sheet with paper towels. With a slotted spoon, transfer plantains as cooked to pan; keep warm in a 150° oven.

Red chili purée. Arrange about 9 (3 oz. total) **dried New Mexico** or California **chilies** on a 12- by 15-inch baking sheet. Bake in a 300° oven until chilies smell toasted, about 4 minutes. Let cool slightly. Discard stems and seeds.

In a 3- to 4-quart pan, combine chilies, 2 cups **water,** 1 small chopped **onion,** and 2 cloves **garlic;** cover and bring to a boil over high heat. Cover and simmer until chilies are very soft, about 30 minutes. Let cool. In a blender or food processor, purée chili mixture; rub purée

A hearty start, the Yucatán way, combines eggs, black beans, cotija cheese, fried plantains, and mild chili sauce.

through a fine strainer and discard residue. If made ahead, cover and chill up to a week. Makes about 2 cups.

PER TABLESPOON: 9 calories, 0.3 g protein, 2 g carbohydrates, 1 g fat, 0 mg cholesterol, 1 mg sodium

Zesty mustard vinaigrette dresses chef's salad topped with kiwi fruit and pear.

Fruit Chef's Salad

3 quarts bite-size pieces red-leaf lettuce, rinsed and crisped
1 large Asian pear or 2 Bartlett pears (about ¾ lb. total)
2 large kiwi fruit (about ½ lb. total), peeled and thinly sliced crosswise
1 large carrot, peeled and shredded
¼ pound provolone cheese, cut into julienne strips
¼ pound cooked ham, cut into julienne strips
  Mustard dressing (recipe follows)
  Salt and pepper

Place lettuce in a large salad bowl. Quarter pear, core, and cut in thin wedges. Arrange pear, kiwi fruit, carrot, cheese, and ham in neat mounds over greens. Pour mustard dressing over salad and mix lightly together. Add salt and pepper to taste. Makes 4 entrée servings. — *Carole Van Brocklin, Port Angeles, Wash.*

PER SERVING: 449 calories, 17 g protein, 33 g carbohydrates, 30 g fat, 36 mg cholesterol, 701 mg sodium

Mustard dressing. Mix ⅓ cup **salad oil**, 3 tablespoons **cider vinegar,** 1 tablespoon **honey,** 2 teaspoons **dry mustard,** and 1 clove **garlic,** pressed or minced. Use or, if made ahead, cover and chill up to 2 days. Makes ½ cup.

Wheat pilaf, scented with cinnamon, accompanies lamb.

Spiced Bulgur with Apple

2 tablespoons salad oil
1 medium-size onion, chopped
1 clove garlic, pressed or minced
2 teaspoons minced fresh ginger
1 cup bulgur (cracked wheat)
¼ teaspoon ground cinnamon
1½ cups regular-strength chicken broth
1 small red apple
¼ cup golden raisins
  Salt
¼ cup chopped salted roasted pistachios

In a 3- to 4-quart pan, combine oil, onion, garlic, and ginger. Cook over medium heat, stirring often, until onion is limp, about 5 minutes. Add bulgur; cook, stirring, until lightly toasted, about 3 minutes. Stir in cinnamon and broth; bring to a boil on high heat. Reduce heat, cover, and simmer until the bulgur is tender to bite, about 10 minutes.

Meanwhile, core and finely dice apple; stir with raisins into pilaf. Add salt to taste. Spoon into a bowl. Garnish with pistachios. Makes 4 to 6 servings. — *J. Hill, Sacramento, Calif.*

PER SERVING: 218 calories, 4.6 g protein, 34 g carbohydrates, 8 g fat, 0 mg cholesterol, 16 mg sodium

Sauté vegetables to go on toast; top with cheese, onion relish.

Zucchini Toast

1 tablespoon butter or margarine
¾ pound mushrooms, thinly sliced
5 small zucchini (1 lb. total), ends trimmed, thinly sliced
6 slices whole-grain bread
6 slices (1 oz. each) jack cheese
  Salt and pepper
  Red onion relish (recipe follows)

In a 10- to 12-inch frying pan, cook butter, mushrooms, and zucchini over high heat, stirring often, until mushrooms are lightly browned, 12 to 15 minutes.

Meanwhile, place bread on a wire rack on a 12- by 15-inch baking sheet. Bake in a 400° oven until firm and golden, about 15 minutes. Spoon an equal portion of vegetables on each piece of toast and drape a cheese slice over vegetables. Bake until cheese melts, about 5 minutes longer. Transfer sandwiches to plates and offer salt, pepper, and onion relish. Makes 6 sandwiches. — *Sarah Majoros, Honolulu.*

PER SERVING: 322 calories, 17 g protein, 28 g carbohydrates, 17 g fat, 46 mg cholesterol, 446 mg sodium

Red onion relish. Thinly slice 1 small **red onion.** Soak in ice water to cover for 15 minutes; drain. Add 2 tablespoons **red wine vinegar,** 1 tablespoon **sugar,** ½ teaspoon **dry basil leaves,** and ¼ teaspoon **crushed dried hot red chilies.** Mix to coat onion.

JICAMA BURRITO BUNDLES

- 4 flour tortillas (10 in. wide)
- 2 tablespoons salad oil
- 1 large onion, chopped
- 1 small red bell pepper, stemmed, seeded, and chopped
- 1 cup chopped peeled jicama
- 1 teaspoon cumin seed
- 1½ cups cooked long-grain brown rice
- ⅓ cup chopped fresh cilantro (coriander)
- 1½ cups (6 oz.) shredded cheddar cheese
- Salt
- Salsa

Stack tortillas and wrap in foil. Place packet in oven as it preheats to 400°.

Bake until tortillas are warm, about 10 minutes.

Meanwhile, in a 10- to 12-inch frying pan, stir oil, onion, pepper, jicama, and cumin over high heat until vegetables begin to brown, 8 to 10 minutes. Remove from heat. Stir in rice, cilantro, cheese, and salt to taste.

Place ¼ of the mixture in center of each tortilla. Fold tortilla's sides and ends to enclose filling; place, seam side down, in a 10- by 15-inch baking pan. Brush lightly with water. Bake in a 400° oven until crisp, about 30 minutes. Serve with salsa. Serves 4.—*Christine Hanover, Lewiston, Calif.*

PER SERVING: 464 calories, 17 g protein, 50 g carbohydrates, 22 g fat, 45 mg cholesterol, 477 mg sodium

Square burrito, filled with vegetables and rice, crisps in the oven; serve with salsa.

OVEN-BARBECUED CHICKEN

- 3 tablespoons firmly packed brown sugar
- 1 tablespoon cornstarch
- ¾ cup pineapple juice
- 3 tablespoons catsup
- ¼ cup cider vinegar
- 1 tablespoon chili powder
- 1 teaspoon ground ginger
- ⅛ teaspoon ground allspice
- 1 tablespoon soy sauce
- 2 cloves garlic, pressed or minced
- 1 broiler-fryer chicken (about 3½ lb.), cut up

In a 1- to 1½-quart pan, mix sugar and cornstarch. Stir in pineapple juice, cat-sup, vinegar, chili powder, ginger, all-spice, soy sauce, and garlic. Cook, stirring, over high heat until sauce boils.

Reserve chicken neck and giblets for other uses, if desired. Rinse chicken and pat dry; set, skin side down, in a foil-lined 10- by 15-inch baking pan. Brush ½ of the sauce over chicken.

Bake in a 400° oven for 25 minutes. Turn chicken over and brush with remaining sauce. Continue baking until skin is well browned and meat is not pink at thigh bone (cut to test), 25 to 30 minutes longer. Transfer to a platter. Makes 4 servings.—*Betty Jane Morrison, Lakewood, Colo.*

PER SERVING: 516 calories, 49 g protein, 24 g carbohydrates, 24 g fat, 154 mg cholesterol, 557 mg sodium

Pineapple-chili baste flavors and glazes chicken as it bakes.

RICOTTA CUSTARD

- 1 pound (about 2 cups) ricotta cheese
- 1 cup half-and-half (light cream)
- 3 large eggs, separated
- ½ cup sugar
- ¼ teaspoon almond extract
- ½ teaspoon grated lemon peel
- ¼ cup sliced almonds
- 3 cups sliced strawberries, sweetened to taste

In a blender, combine ricotta cheese, half-and-half, egg yolks, 6 tablespoons sugar, and almond extract. Whirl until ricotta feels smooth. Stir in lemon peel.

In a bowl, beat egg whites until foamy.

Gradually add 2 tablespoons sugar, beating until stiff, moist peaks form. Fold in cheese mixture. Pour into a buttered 1½- to 2-quart shallow baking dish.

Set dish in a larger shallow baking pan. Place in a 350° oven. Fill outer pan with 1 inch boiling water. Bake 20 minutes. Sprinkle custard with nuts. Continue baking until center feels set when gently touched, 10 to 15 minutes longer. (Custard will form sauce on bottom.) Serve custard warm or cool with berries. Serves 8.—*Roxanne Chan, Albany, Calif.*

PER SERVING: 250 calories, 11 g protein, 20 g carbohydrates, 15 g fat, 143 mg cholesterol, 87 mg sodium

Ricotta custard forms sauce on bottom as it cooks; serve with strawberries.

ORIGINALLY DEVISED as a gourmet's dinner for a back-country pack trip, *Chateau Sierra Chicken* called for preparation in advance. The chicken roulades were shaped, then frozen and transported, well insulated, to the first night's campsite, where they were unwrapped and cooked over a fire. We present a somewhat more elaborate version here, for diners who prefer to have a floor under their feet. The basic chicken preparation is the same, but a pan sauce of broth, drippings, wine, and sour cream makes for additional richness.

CHATEAU SIERRA CHICKEN

- **2 whole chicken breasts (about 1 lb. each), skinned, boned, cut in half**
- **2 to 3 ounces mozzarella cheese, shredded**
- **3 tablespoons butter or margarine**
- **1 clove garlic, minced or mashed**
- **2 teaspoons chopped parsley**
- **3 tablespoons dry white wine**
- **¼ cup all-purpose flour**
- **¼ teaspoon paprika**
- **¼ teaspoon pepper**
- **½ cup regular-strength chicken broth**
- **½ cup sour cream**
  Salt

Place each piece of chicken between sheets of plastic wrap. With a flat mallet, pound until chicken is about ⅜ inch thick. Top each piece with ¼ of the cheese, 1 teaspoon of the butter, ¼ of the garlic, ¼ of the parsley, and 1 teaspoon of the wine. Roll chicken to enclose filling, and secure with toothpicks.

In a paper or plastic bag, combine flour, paprika, and pepper. Coat chicken pieces with flour mixture; shake off excess. Reserve flour mixture.

In a 10- to 12-inch frying pan over medium heat, melt the remaining butter; add chicken pieces. Turn often until evenly browned on all sides. Add broth; cover, reduce heat, and simmer until chicken is no longer pink in center (cut to test), 6 to 8 minutes. With a slotted spoon, transfer chicken to a warm platter; keep warm.

Blend remaining wine with 1 teaspoon of the reserved flour; mix with sour cream, then whisk mixture into pan juices. Stir over high heat until sauce just comes to a boil. Pour sauce over chicken. Add salt to taste. Makes 4 servings.

PER SERVING: 375 calories, 39 g protein, 8 g carbohydrates, 20 g fat, 133 mg cholesterol, 260 mg sodium

C. A. Johnson

Ridgecrest, Calif.

THE CENTRAL ASIAN STEPPES *that gave us the Huns, the Tatars, and the Mongols also gave us garlic, which has extended its empire to lands of which Genghis Khan never even dreamed. Garlic invaded Europe and the Near East early; it was well known to the ancient Egyptians as well as to the Greeks and Romans. The last peoples to submit were the British, the Scandinavians, and their descendants, who were overcome by Trojan horse–like tactics—the garlic sneaking in while hidden in ethnic foods of nearly every kind.*

We are all comfortable now with garlic as a seasoning, but it is still uncommon as

"Chateau Sierra Chicken was originally devised as a gourmet's dinner for a back-country pack trip."

a principal ingredient, as it is in Trent Anderson's sopa de ajo (garlic soup). Slow sautéeing modifies the garlic's native assertiveness, leaving the soup with just a hint of the warm flavor.

SOPA DE AJO

- 1 head garlic
- 1½ tablespoons salad oil
- 6 cups or 1 large can (49½ oz.) regular-strength chicken broth
- ¼ teaspoon Oriental sesame oil (optional)
- 3 tablespoons *each* finely chopped red bell pepper and green onions with tops
  Fresh cilantro (coriander) leaves

Peel garlic; thinly slice cloves. In a 10- to 12-inch frying pan over medium-low heat, combine oil and garlic. Stir often until garlic is golden brown, about 10 minutes.

Meanwhile, pour broth into a 4- to 5-quart pan. Bring to a boil over high heat. When garlic is done, ladle about ½ cup of the broth into the frying pan and stir to free any browned bits, then pour garlic mixture back into broth. Cover and simmer for 30 minutes to blend flavors. Add sesame oil, bell pepper, and green onions and cook until hot, 2 to 3 minutes.

Ladle into small bowls, adding 2 or 3 cilantro leaves to each. Makes 5 or 6 first-course servings, about 1-cup size.

PER SERVING: 80 calories, 3 g protein, 5.8 g carbohydrates, 4.9 g fat, 0 mg cholesterol, 56 mg sodium

Novato, Calif.

PORK CHOPS HAVE ALWAYS BEEN *the people's meat. Back when a chicken every Sunday was a distant dream, one could still reasonably hope for pork chops. Indeed, the word pork has populist overtones when it refers to political favors, construction contracts, or the placement of military bases. The term pork chop itself has such a staccato, rifle-fire sort of reverberation it seems fitting that a celebrated Korean War battle took the name of Pork Chop Hill. Who ever heard of a Filet Mignon Hill?*

Pork, because of the way it is now produced, is leaner than it used to be. And when surface fat is trimmed away, even marbled, succulent cuts like shoulder chops are proportionately leaner. Pork is also a rich source of vitamin B_1. The real reason for eating pork, though, is the flavor. In James Hensinger's Country Casserole, both flavor and texture are notably enhanced by chicken broth, steak sauce, green chilies, and slow cooking. The addition of potatoes and carrots makes this a genuine one-dish meal.

COUNTRY CASSEROLE

- 4 shoulder pork chops, each about ¾ inch thick (about 1¾ lb. total)
- 6 tablespoons all-purpose flour
- ½ teaspoon pepper
- 2 tablespoons salad oil
- 1 can (10½ oz.) condensed chicken broth
- 3 tablespoons prepared steak sauce
- ½ cup water
- 1 large can (7 oz.) diced green chilies
- 2 medium-size (about 1 lb. total) russet potatoes, scrubbed and cut into ⅛-inch slices
- 1 large onion, sliced
- 4 medium-size carrots, cut into 2-inch lengths

Trim and discard excess fat from pork chops. In a plastic or paper bag, combine flour and pepper. Shake chops in flour mixture, then shake off excess. Reserve flour mixture.

Pour oil into a 10- to 12-inch frying pan over medium-high heat. When oil is hot, add chops and brown well. Lift out and set aside. Add remaining flour mixture to pan and stir until flour is golden brown, then whisk in smoothly the broth, steak sauce, and water; stir until boiling rapidly. Mix in chilies and remove from heat.

In a greased 8- by 12-inch baking dish, arrange in layers half the potatoes, half the onion, and half the carrots. Lay pork chops on carrots and layer the remaining potatoes, onion, and carrots on top of the meat. Pour the hot sauce evenly over vegetables. Cover and bake in a 350° oven for 1½ hours, then uncover and continue baking until meat and potatoes are very tender when pierced, 25 to 30 minutes. Makes 4 servings.

PER SERVING: 479 calories, 36 g protein, 39 g carbohydrates, 20 g fat, 98 mg cholesterol, 1,118 mg sodium

Aurora, Colo.

June Menus

JUNE STARTS THE FEAST *of fresh treasures from gardens and farms throughout the West. These menus set the pace for the months that follow, as the summer harvest continues.*

The first meal—a chicken with roasted potatoes and a roasted vegetable sauce— comes right out of the oven. It's a perfect Sunday dinner, although simple steps make it workable for midweek, too.

Golden apricots, poached and in jam, create a breakfast quick enough for any morning but special enough for guests.

The main foods of the third meal are grilled over hot coals.

SUNDAY CHICKEN DINNER

**Roast Chicken & Potatoes
with Vegetable Purée**
Red & Green Bell Pepper Salad
Black Ripe or Oil-cured Olives
Raspberry Ginger Fizzes
Raspberries

Roasted under the chicken, carrots and onions make a mellow sauce for the bird. Tender raspberries mingled with ginger ale are a fizzy refresher.

As chicken and vegetables bake, cut bell peppers into large chunks and dress with olive oil and lemon juice. Scatter black olives over salad, or serve them separately.

To make raspberry ginger fizzes, drop berries into glasses of chilled ginger ale, and muddle slightly to release their flavor. Serve as an apéritif, with the meal, or for dessert. To convert fizzes to dessert sodas, add a scoop of vanilla ice cream.

ROAST CHICKEN & POTATOES WITH VEGETABLE PURÉE

- ¼ **cup (⅛ lb.) butter or margarine**
- 1¼ **pounds thin-skinned potatoes (1½- to 2-in. diameter), scrubbed and cut in half**
- 1 **small onion, cut in half**
- 1 **small carrot, quartered**
- 1 **teaspoon minced fresh or ½ teaspoon dry rosemary**
- ½ **cup garlic cloves**
- 1 **broiler-fryer chicken (4 to 4½ lb.)**
- ¾ **to 1 cup regular-strength chicken broth**
  Salt and pepper

Chicken roasted with potatoes, garlic, and rosemary makes a good outdoor meal; vegetables thicken sauce. Serve crisp bell peppers and olives as salad, raspberries for dessert.

Place butter, potatoes (cut side down), onion, carrot, rosemary, and garlic in a 9- by 13-inch pan. Discard excess fat from chicken. Rinse chicken, pat dry, and set on vegetables. Bake in a 400° oven until chicken is no longer pink at thigh bone (cut to test), about 1 hour. Brush chicken with pan juices after the first 30 minutes.

Supporting chicken with 2 forks, tilt it to drain juices from cavity into the pan. Place chicken, potatoes, and half the garlic on a platter; keep warm.

Scrape onion, carrot, remaining garlic, and juices into a food processor or blender; whirl to purée smoothly, adding enough broth to make a pourable sauce; serve from a small bowl. Carve chicken and serve meat and vegetables with the puréed sauce; add salt and pepper to taste. Makes 4 servings.

PER SERVING: 922 calories, 62 g protein, 34 g carbohydrates, 59 g fat, 263 mg cholesterol, 360 mg sodium

APRICOT BOUNTY BREAKFAST

**Eggs Cooked in the Shell
Poached Fresh Apricots
or Fresh Apricots
Apricot Jam Sticks   Hot Herb Tea**

Breaking the nighttime fast doesn't need to be complicated to be special. Here, cream cheese and apricot jam warm and flow together inside crackling tortilla cases; the assembly takes about 5 minutes, the baking 15. Fresh apricots, poached or served au naturel, are a refreshing complement to the jam sticks.

If you want warm poached apricots, start them after the jam sticks are baking. Just barely cover with water, add sugar or honey to taste, and bring to a boil, then simmer gently just until the fruit is thoroughly heated—5 minutes or so.

Serve eggs cooked hard or soft in the shell. Brew a pot of fragrant herb tea to serve with the meal.

Crackling-crisp baked flour tortillas are dusted with sugar, filled with jam and cheese. Serve with poached apricots, eggs in the shell, and hot herb tea.

APRICOT JAM STICKS

    4 flour tortillas (7-in. diameter)
    1 small package (3 oz.) cream cheese
    ¼ cup apricot jam
    1 tablespoon milk
    1 tablespoon sugar

Cut tortillas in half. Cut cream cheese into 8 portions; shape each portion into a log about 5 inches long.

Place cream cheese and jam on the cut edge of each tortilla, dividing equally. Roll tortilla around cheese and jam to enclose; place seam down in a 10- by 15-inch baking pan. Brush rolls with milk, then sprinkle equally with sugar.

Bake in a 450° oven until tortillas are golden, 12 to 13 minutes. Remove from pan—they stick if allowed to cool. Serve warm. Makes 4 servings.

PER SERVING: 213 calories, 3.8 g protein, 30 g carbohydrates, 9.5 g fat, 24 mg cholesterol, 207 mg sodium

STEAK DINNER FROM THE GRILL

**Grilled Beef Steaks
Scorched Corn & Chili Salsa
Grilled Crookneck Squash
Inner Romaine Leaves
with Minced Onion
Baguettes
Sliced Peaches
Almond Macaroons
Candied Ginger
Iced Guava Nectar with Lime Slices**

Corn, charred lightly to develop a sweet, smoky taste, is the base of a warm salsa seasoned with chilies. The corn shares the grill with steak and crookneck squash, which are enlivened by the salsa.

Choose the cut of beef you like—from lean flank to tender rib-eye steak; allow 4 to 6 ounces for a serving. Cuts about 1 inch thick take 10 to 12 minutes to cook to the rare stage.

Cut crookneck squash (plan about ¼ lb. for a serving) in half lengthwise so it browns better; brush with olive oil to keep moist. Start the corn first, then add the meat and squash to the grill. They can finish cooking as you cut corn from the cob to complete the salsa. If the squash finishes cooking before the meat, remove it from the grill and serve warm or at room temperature.

Fashion a salad with romaine, mild onions, and an oil-and-vinegar dressing.

Slice fresh peaches for dessert; serve with cookies and candied ginger. Offer fruit nectar to sip.

(Continued on next page)

Scorched Corn & Chili Salsa

2 medium-size ears corn

1 small ripe tomato, stemmed, cored, seeded, and finely diced

1 medium-size fresh Anaheim (California) chili, stemmed, seeded, and finely diced

2 cloves garlic, minced

2 tablespoons lime juice

1 tablespoon ground New Mexican or California chilies
   Salt

Remove and discard husks and silks from corn. Place corn on a grill 4 to 6 inches above a solid bed of hot coals (you can hold your hand at grill level only 2 to 3 seconds). Grill until lightly browned on all sides, turning as needed.

Remove corn from barbecue and cut kernels off cob.

In a bowl, mix corn kernels, tomato, diced chili, garlic, lime juice, ground chili, and salt to taste. Serve, or cover and chill up to 1 day. Makes 2 cups, 4 servings.

PER SERVING: 54 calories, 2.1 g protein, 12 g carbohydrates, 0.8 g fat, 0 mg cholesterol, 11 mg sodium

Grilled Prawns & Spinach Salad (page 152)

Outdoor entertaining takes the spotlight for informal summer gatherings. The July issue features shellfish entrées for special friends—lobster tails and giant prawns cooked on the barbecue. For a simple supper, serve grilled pork and poultry in hot sandwiches. Enjoy summer's superb produce in artistic salads, satisfying soups, vegetable casseroles, and even catsup. Our show-stopping dessert is an elegant fruit taco—mixed fruits in a sugary cooky shell, presented in a bright pool of berry purée.

Shellfish Spectacular

SHOW OFF WITH SHELLFISH *on the barbecue. Guests will rave as giant prawns and lobster tails sear on the grill. Their succulent, sweet flesh needs little adornment in order to make dramatic presentations.*

Prawns are actually just large shrimp. Buy them according to size; the seafood industry calls them either colossal (10 to 15 per lb.) or extra-colossal (fewer than 10 per lb.). Since market labels vary, ask for them by count per pound.

The tails of spiny lobsters are often sold frozen. Split them to grill evenly.

These shellfish have price tags to match their size. Large prawns range from $15 to $18 per pound. Lobster tails range from $19 to $23 a pound. You may need to order them ahead.

Simple duo: tomato slices and skewered prawns, both basted with basil oil.

GRILLED PRAWNS & TOMATOES WITH BASIL OIL

- 1 to 1¼ pounds colossal (10 to 15 per lb.) or extra-colossal prawns (8 to 10 per lb.)
- ¼ cup extra-virgin olive oil
- 1 clove garlic, pressed or minced
- 2 tablespoons minced fresh basil or 1 teaspoon dry basil
- 3 large firm-ripe tomatoes (about 8 oz. each), cored and cut crosswise into ½-inch-thick slices
- 4 large romaine leaves, washed and crisped
  Salt and pepper
  Fresh basil sprigs (optional)

Peel and devein prawns. Thread equal portions of prawns on each of 4 skewers. Mix the oil, garlic, and minced basil. Brush prawns and tomatoes with basil oil.

Place prawns and tomatoes on a grill 4 to 6 inches above a solid bed of hot coals (you can hold your hand at grill level only 2 to 3 seconds). Cook, brushing tomatoes and prawns with basil oil and turning them once, until prawns are just opaque in thickest part (cut to test) and tomatoes are hot, about 6 minutes total for both.

Place 1 romaine leaf on each of 4 dinner plates. Place tomatoes on romaine; set prawns alongside. Drizzle prawns and tomatoes with remaining basil oil. Add salt and pepper to taste. Garnish with basil sprigs. Makes 4 servings.

PER SERVING: 251 calories, 20 g protein, 8.3 g carbohydrates, 16 g fat, 140 mg cholesterol, 150 mg sodium

GRILLED PRAWNS & SPINACH SALAD

- 1 to 1¼ pounds colossal (10 to 15 per lb.) or extra-colossal prawns (8 to 10 per lb.)
- ¼ cup dry sherry
- ¼ cup rice vinegar or cider vinegar
- 2 tablespoons Oriental sesame oil
- 1 tablespoon minced fresh ginger
- 2 teaspoons sugar
- 1 teaspoon soy sauce
- 1 teaspoon finely shredded orange peel
- 3 small oranges (about 1 lb. total)
- 3½ quarts bite-size pieces spinach leaves (about 10 oz.), rinsed and crisped
- 1 large red bell pepper, stemmed and cut into thin slivers
  Salt and pepper

Peel prawns and devein. To butterfly, cut down back of each prawn almost but not completely through; rinse and pat dry.

Mix sherry, vinegar, oil, ginger, sugar, soy sauce, and peel. Combine 2 tablespoons of mixture with shrimp; cover and chill at least 30 minutes or up to 1 hour. Reserve remaining mixture. Cut peel and membrane off oranges. Thinly slice fruit crosswise, then cut slices in half crosswise. In a large bowl, combine oranges, spinach, and bell pepper. Cover and chill up to 1 hour.

Spread shrimp out flat on grill over solid bed of hot coals (you can hold your hand at grill level only 2 to 3 seconds); cook, turning once, until opaque in thickest part (cut to test), about 3 minutes total.

Add shrimp and reserved dressing to spinach mixture; mix lightly. Place equal portions on 4 dinner plates. Add salt and pepper to taste. Makes 4 servings.

PER SERVING: 233 calories, 21 g protein, 18 g carbohydrates, 8.9 g fat, 140 mg cholesterol, 265 mg sodium

SAGE-BUTTERED LOBSTER TAILS

- 4 spiny lobster tails (8 to 10 oz. each), thawed if frozen
- 4 medium-size crookneck squash (about ¾ lb. total), ends trimmed
- ¼ cup (⅛ lb.) butter or margarine, melted
- 1 teaspoon grated lemon peel
- 2 tablespoons lemon juice
- 2 tablespoons minced fresh sage or 1 teaspoon dry sage leaves
  Fresh sage sprigs (optional)
  Lemon wedges
  Salt and pepper

With kitchen scissors, cut off fins and sharp spines along sides of each tail. Set tail, shell side down, on a board; with a heavy knife, split tail in half lengthwise, using a hammer or mallet to force knife through shell. Rinse lobster and pat dry.

Starting about ½ inch from the stem end, cut each squash lengthwise 3 or 4 times at about ¼-inch intervals, leaving attached at stem end. Gently fan slices out slightly.

Mix butter, lemon peel, lemon juice, and minced sage. Reserve ½ of the butter mixture. Place lobster, shell side down, on a grill 4 to 6 inches above a solid bed of medium-hot coals (you can hold your hand at grill level only 3 to 4 seconds). Set squash on grill, gently fanning out slices.

Grill split spiny lobster tails alongside fans of crookneck squash for a seafood dinner. Baste both lobster and squash with sage-flavored butter during cooking.

Brush lobster and squash with ½ of the sage butter. Cook squash 3 minutes; gently turn over with a wide spatula, brush with more butter and cook until tender when pierced, about 3 more minutes. Cook lobster tail 5 minutes, then turn over and continue cooking until just opaque in thickest part (cut to test), about 2 minutes longer. Place lobster and squash on dinner plates, drizzle reserved butter over lobster, and garnish with sage sprigs and lemon wedges. Add salt and pepper to taste. Makes 4 servings.

PER SERVING: 242 calories, 27 g protein, 5.7 g carbohydrates, 13 g fat, 121 mg cholesterol, 594 mg sodium

Picture-Perfect Salads

S PLASHY WITH COLOR *and rich with tex-ture, these three salads are each picture pretty without being fussy. You simply let nature take its course.*

The first salad plays upon the inherent good looks of raw vegetables, artfully arranged to feature color, shape, and texture. The second weaves fat strands of pasta around bright broccoli and dark shiitake mushrooms. The third salad emphasizes the contrast of warm and cool colors in an elegant arrangement of reds and greens. Each salad is a palette not only of colors, but also of flavors.

VEGETABLE STILL LIFE WITH SAUCE

About 2 pounds assorted vegetables, rinsed or scrubbed— such as baby carrots with tops; inner celery stalks with leaves; baby bok choy, whole or cut into

halves lengthwise; radishes with tops; fennel, sliced lengthwise; European cucumber, sliced
2 small green bell peppers
Green herb sauce (recipe follows)

Remove all but the prettiest leaves on vegetables with tops. If made ahead, wrap damp vegetables (including tops) in paper towels, then enclose in a plastic bag and chill up to 4 hours.

Cut bell peppers in half crosswise. From each cut side, slice off pieces of pepper until you have a cup about 1 inch deep. Cut out and discard seeds from stem end. Rinse peppers; if prepared ahead, put in bag with other vegetables.

Fill pepper cups equally with sauce; set 1 on each plate. Arrange assorted vegetables around sauce for dipping. Serves 4.

PER SERVING: 319 calories, 3 g protein, 14 g carbohydrates, 29 g fat, 16 mg cholesterol, 275 mg sodium

Green herb sauce. In a food processor or blender, purée ½ cup *each* Italian parsley and sliced green onions with 2 table-spoons olive oil. Mix with ½ cup mayon-naise and salt and pepper to taste; if made ahead, cover and chill up until next day.

BROCCOLI BUDS ENTWINED WITH PASTA

2 ounces dried shiitake mushrooms
8 ounces dry long pasta tubes, about ⅛ inch thick, such as macaroni or bucatini
Oriental dressing (recipe follows)
1 pound broccoli flowerets

Put shiitake mushrooms in a small bowl. Cover with boiling water; let stand until mushrooms are soft, about 20 minutes. Lift from water and squeeze dry. Cut off

Garden-fresh look is easily achieved with tiny vegetables and simply cut larger ones. Herb-laced dipping sauce is in bell pepper cup; you can eat the pepper, too.

Cool bed of pasta swirls around mushrooms and broccoli; Oriental flavors spark dressing.

and discard tough stems; place mushrooms in a large bowl.

Meanwhile, in a 5- to 6-quart pan, bring 4 quarts water to boiling over high heat. Add pasta and cook, uncovered, until tender to bite, about 25 minutes. Drain and pour into bowl with mushrooms. Pour dressing over pasta; mix gently but thoroughly. Cover and chill at least 1 hour or until next day; mix several times.

In the pan, bring 3 to 4 quarts water to a boil on high heat. Add broccoli and cook, uncovered, until tender to bite, about 5 minutes. Drain; immerse at once in ice water until cold. Drain again. If made ahead, cover and chill up until next day. Mix broccoli with pasta; mound onto 4 to 6 dinner plates. Makes 4 to 6 servings.

PER SERVING: 250 calories, 8 g protein, 43 g carbohydrates, 6 g fat, 0 mg cholesterol, 533 mg sodium

Oriental dressing. Mix ⅓ cup **seasoned rice vinegar** (or ⅓ cup rice vinegar and 2 teaspoons sugar), 3 tablespoons **soy sauce,** 1 tablespoon **salad oil,** 2 teaspoons *each* **Oriental sesame oil** and **hot chili oil.**

AVOCADO FANS WITH RED PEPPER PAINT

- 2 **large firm-ripe avocados**
- 2 **tablespoons lemon juice**
  Red pepper paint (recipe follows)
- 2 **cups washed and crisped arugula, watercress sprigs, or mâche**
- 2 **medium-size lemons, cut zigzag into halves**
- 1 **teaspoon paprika (optional)**

Cut avocados in half lengthwise; pit, then peel. Lay cut side flat. Cut each avocado into ¼-inch-wide slices from base to ½ inch from top end. With a wide spatula, transfer each half to a dinner plate; press slices gently from 1 side to fan. Coat with lemon juice.

Pour or spread ¼ of the pepper paint beside each avocado half. Cluster arugula beside avocado. Dip zigzag edges of lemon in paprika and put 1 half on each plate; squeeze on juice to taste. Serves 4.

PER SERVING: 305 calories, 4 g protein, 13 g carbohydrates, 29 g fat, 33 mg cholesterol, 40 mg sodium

Red pepper paint. In a blender or food processor, smoothly purée 1 jar (7 oz.) **roasted red peppers,** ½ cup **regular-strength chicken broth,** and ¼ cup **dry white wine.** Pour into a 10- to 12-inch frying pan and boil over high heat, stirring often, until reduced by half, about 5 minutes. Stir in ½ cup **whipping cream** and bring to a boil; let cool. Serve at room temperature or cold. If made ahead, cover and chill up until next day.

Gold-red purée of canned roasted peppers sets off two-tone greens of fanned avocado slices. Sprigs of nippy arugula complement flavors.

Fruit Taco

NOT YOUR TYPICAL TACO, *this twist makes the quintessential Mexican snack an elegant dessert. Fresh summer fruits fill a thin cooky or sugary tortilla shell.*

Make the taco shells out of thin, almond-flavored cookies, shaping them when still warm. For a quicker alternative, drape sugar-coated tortillas over a mold and bake; their shape firms as they cook.

Present fruit-filled tacos in a pool of berry purée. Don't worry if the tacos crack apart on the first forkful—one Spanish translation for the word taco is "mess."

FRUIT TACOS

    6 taco cookies or sugared tortillas (recipes follow)
    Fruit filling (recipe follows)
    Berry purée (recipe follows)
    Softly whipped cream, sweetened to taste, or sour cream (optional)

Set 1 cooky or tortilla on each of 6 dessert plates. Holding shell with open side up, spoon equal portions of filling into each shell; then lay 1 side of shell on plate. Spoon equal portions of purée around each taco. Serve at once. Offer whipped cream to add to taste. Break off pieces of taco to eat with fruit. Makes 6 servings.

PER SERVING WITH COOKY SHELL: 388 calories, 4.8 g protein, 54 g carbohydrates, 18 g fat, 133 mg cholesterol, 182 mg sodium

PER SERVING WITH TORTILLA SHELL: 407 calories, 3.3 g protein, 63 g carbohydrates, 18 g fat, 41 mg cholesterol, 299 mg sodium

Taco cookies. Drape a piece of foil over a form (such as a 2-by-4, book, or wedge of crumpled foil) that stands 3 to 6 inches high, at least 7 inches long, 1 to 1½ inches wide at top, and 1 to 3 inches wide at base. If you shape more than 1 shell at a time, use several forms or a longer one.

In a bowl, beat together 2 **large eggs,** ½ cup **sugar,** ½ cup (¼ lb.) **melted butter** or margarine, 2 tablespoons **water,** 1½ teaspoons **vanilla,** and ¾ teaspoon **almond extract.** Stir in ⅔ cup **all-purpose flour** until smoothly blended.

Use a 12- by 15-inch baking sheet with a nonstick surface; or coat a 12- by 15-inch baking sheet with a nonstick cooking spray; or grease, then flour pan. In the center of pan, pour ¼ cup batter. With back of spoon, spread batter into a 7-inch-diameter circle of uniform thickness.

Bake in a 325° oven until edges are browned and cooky is richly golden, 18 to 20 minutes (underbaked cookies won't hold shape when cool; if they collapse, return to oven, bake a few minutes, and reshape). If using 2 pans, switch pan positions halfway through cooking.

Quickly lift hot cooky with a wide spatula, then center over foil-draped mold. At once, gently press cooky around mold to form shell (see picture below); let lower edges flare out slightly. Let cool on form until firm. Use or store

airtight in a rigid container up to 1 week. Makes 6.

Sugared tortillas. Drape foil over a non-flammable form such as a wedge of foil (see taco cookies, preceding, for form dimensions). Set 1 or 2 foil-draped forms, spaced 3 to 4 inches apart, on a foil-lined 12- by 15-inch baking sheet.

In a 9-inch-diameter cake pan, mix ¾ cup **sugar** and 1½ teaspoons **ground cinnamon.** Brush both sides of 6 **flour tortillas** (7 in. diameter), 1 or 2 at a time, lightly with **melted butter** (about ½ cup total), then turn in cinnamon sugar to coat both sides. Drape center of tortilla over top of form.

Bake in a 500° oven until tortilla is crisp and golden brown, 4 to 6 minutes. Remove from form and cool on rack. Repeat with remaining tortillas. Save remaining cinnamon sugar for another use, if desired. Use tortillas, or store airtight in a rigid container up to 1 week. Makes 6.

Fruit filling. In a large bowl, mix any of the following fresh fruits to make 4 cups: whole **blueberries,** rinsed and drained; whole **raspberries,** rinsed and drained; sliced **strawberries;** sliced peeled **peaches;** sliced **nectarines;** or sliced firm-ripe **plums.** Gently mix in 1 tablespoon **lemon juice** and **sugar** to taste. If made ahead, cover and chill up to 30 minutes.

Berry purée. Rinse and drain 2 cups **raspberries** or hulled strawberries. In a blender or food processor, whirl berries until smoothly puréed. If desired, force purée through a fine strainer; discard seeds.

In a 1- to 1½-quart pan, stir 3 tablespoons **sugar** with 1 teaspoon **cornstarch.** Blend in purée. Stir over high heat until sauce boils and thickens. Add ¼ cup **berry-flavor** or orange-flavor **liqueur,** 1 tablespoon **lemon juice,** and more sugar to taste, if needed. Cool, cover, and chill until cold, at least 1 hour or up to 1 day. Makes 1⅓ cups.

With the back of a spoon, evenly spread batter into a 7-inch circle.

Shape hot cooky over foil-draped form (here, a 2-by-4) to give it a taco shape.

Elegant dessert version of a Mexican taco translates to a sweet curve of cooky spilling over with colorful summer fruits in a pool of berry purée. Taco cookies, fruit filling, and purée can be prepared ahead, but dessert is assembled just before serving.

Beyond Nibbling: How to Cook with Pistachios

DISTINGUISHED *by their slightly flowery flavor and golden green color, California-grown pistachios have become widely available. Although they make fine nibbling, they also make an inviting, attractive choice as a nut to cook with.*

For a noteworthy appetizer, try pistachios in a topping for baked mushrooms or zucchini slices. Mixed with bread crumbs, the nuts make a tender crust for oven-fried fish. Or melt sugar and spices with them for a sweet tidbit.

Glazed with melted sugar and fragrant with cinnamon and mace, these pistachios are crisp, crunchy sweets. Nuts can be stored in an airtight container for up to a week.

PISTACHIO-TOPPED MUSHROOMS OR ZUCCHINI

20 mushrooms (about 1½-in. caps), or 2 zucchini (about 6 in. long)
About 3 tablespoons olive oil
1 small onion, minced
2 garlic cloves, minced or pressed
2 teaspoons mustard seed
1 large egg
About ¾ cup shelled salted pistachios
¾ cup shredded jack cheese

Rinse and drain mushrooms. Carefully break stems out of caps. Mince stems. (Or rinse zucchini, trim off ends, and cut each diagonally into 10 equal slices.)

In a 10- to 12-inch frying pan, combine mushroom stems (omit for zucchini), 1 tablespoon oil, onion, garlic, and mustard seed. Stir often over medium-high heat until liquid evaporates and onions are slightly browned, about 5 minutes; let cool. Stir in egg, ½ cup chopped pistachios, and cheese.

Meanwhile, generously brush vegetables with oil. Set mushrooms, cup side down, (or zucchini slightly apart) in a 10- by 15-inch rimmed baking pan. Bake in a 400° oven until golden and liquid evaporates, about 10 minutes; after 5 minutes, turn vegetables over. Remove from oven; turn temperature to 325°.

Spoon filling equally into caps or onto zucchini slices. Top each piece with 1 or 2 whole pistachios. Bake vegetables until filling is tinged golden brown, about 15 minutes. Pick up to eat. Makes 20.

PER MUSHROOM: 73 calories, 2.8 g protein, 2.4 g carbohydrates, 6 g fat, 17 mg cholesterol, 27 mg sodium

PER ZUCCHINI SLICE: 68 calories, 2 g protein, 2 g carbohydrates, 6 g fat, 17 mg cholesterol, 27 mg sodium

PISTACHIO-CRUSTED FISH FILLETS

½ cup shelled salted pistachios, finely chopped
⅓ cup fine dry bread crumbs
¼ cup minced parsley
½ teaspoon pepper
1 large egg
4 skinned and boned white-flesh fish fillets (about 4 oz. each), such as sole or orange roughy
¼ cup (⅛ lb.) butter or margarine
2 green onions (ends trimmed), thinly sliced
1 tablespoon drained capers
Lime or lemon wedges (optional)
Salt

On a sheet of waxed paper or foil, mix nuts with crumbs, parsley, and pepper.

In an 8- to 9-inch-wide pan, beat egg to blend. Dip fillets, 1 at a time, in egg to coat. Drain briefly, and press each side of the fillet into the nut mixture to coat well. Lay fillets well apart in a greased 10- by 15-inch pan.

Melt butter in a 6- to 8-inch frying pan over medium heat. Add onions and capers, and stir just until onions are brighter green. Holding onions and capers back with a spoon, pour butter evenly over fish.

Bake in 450° oven until fish is opaque in center of thickest part (cut to test), about 10 minutes. With a wide spatula, transfer fillets to 4 dinner plates and top equally with onion and caper mixture. Offer lime wedges to squeeze onto fish; add salt to taste. Makes 4 servings.

PER SERVING: 353 calories, 28 g protein, 11 g carbohydrates, 22 g fat, 154 mg cholesterol, 345 mg sodium

SWEET SPICED PISTACHIOS

1 cup shelled salted pistachios
¼ cup sugar
½ teaspoon *each* ground cinnamon and ground mace or ground nutmeg

In a 10- to 12-inch frying pan over medium heat, shake the pistachios frequently until they're hot and golden, about 5 minutes. Sprinkle sugar, cinnamon, and mace over nuts; stir until sugar melts and coats nuts with a glossy finish, about 5 minutes. Pour the pistachio mixture onto a sheet of foil. When cool, break the nuts apart and serve, or store airtight up to 1 week. Makes about 1½ cups.

PER TABLESPOON: 39 calories, 1 g protein, 3.4 g carbohydrates, 2.6 g fat, 0 mg cholesterol, 0.4 mg sodium

Sandwiches Hot off the Grill

FRESH FROM THE BARBECUE, *these lean sandwiches cook in minutes. Start with thin pieces of turkey or pork; grill, then pile onto toasted bread with a zippy relish.*

GRILLED TURKEY ON SESAME BUN

1¼ to 1½ pounds boned, skinned turkey breast slices (¼ in. thick)

3 tablespoons olive oil

2 tablespoons lemon juice

6 sliced sesame sandwich buns or hamburger buns

6 large butter lettuce leaves, washed and crisped

1 large firm-ripe tomato, cored and cut crosswise into 6 slices

Salt and pepper

Lemon-herb mayonnaise (recipe follows)

Coat turkey slices with oil and lemon juice. If done ahead, cover and chill up to 4 hours.

Place turkey on a grill 4 to 6 inches above a solid bed of hot coals (you can hold your hand at grill level only 2 to 3 seconds). Cook, turning once, until meat is white in center (cut to test), 2 to 3 minutes total. Set buns, cut sides down, on cooler part of grill and cook just until lightly toasted, about 30 seconds.

To assemble sandwiches, place 1 lettuce leaf, ⅙ of the turkey, and 1 tomato slice on bottom half of each bun. Add salt and pepper to taste. Top turkey with equal portions of the lemon-herb mayonnaise and top half of bun. Makes 6 sandwiches.

PER SERVING: 431 calories, 26 g protein, 24 g carbohydrates, 26 g fat, 72 mg cholesterol, 374 mg sodium

Lemon-herb mayonnaise. Mix together ½ cup **mayonnaise**, 1 tablespoon minced **fresh marjoram leaves** or 1 teaspoon dry marjoram leaves, and ½ teaspoon grated **lemon peel**.

GRILLED PORK ON RYE

8 boneless center-cut pork loin chops (½ in. thick), about 1 pound total

¼ cup coarse-grain mustard

2 tablespoons olive oil

8 slices rye bread

1 cup (4 oz.) shredded fontina cheese

Red cabbage relish (recipe follows)

Trim surface fat off chops. Place meat between sheets of plastic wrap and pound evenly with a flat mallet to make ⅛ inch thick. Coat pork with ½ of the mustard and all of the oil. If made ahead, cover and chill until the next day.

Place pork on a grill 4 to 6 inches above a solid bed of hot coals (you can hold your hand at grill level only 2 to 3 seconds). Cook, turning once, until meat is white in center (cut to test), 2 to 3 minutes total. Remove from grill; keep warm.

Place bread on cooler part of grill and cook until toasted on 1 side, about 30 seconds; turn over and cover 4 slices toasted bread with equal portions of cheese. Continue cooking until bottom is toasted, about 30 seconds longer.

Set each slice of the plain toast on a warm dinner plate. Spread with remaining mustard. Set 2 slices of pork on each piece of toast. Mound equal portions of cabbage relish on each sandwich. Set cheese-topped bread slice alongside. Eat either as an open-faced or closed sandwich. Makes 4 servings.

PER SERVING: 613 calories, 35 g protein, 34 g carbohydrates, 38 g fat, 110 mg cholesterol, 486 mg sodium

Red cabbage relish. In a bowl, mix 2 tablespoons **cider vinegar**, 1 tablespoon **olive oil**, 2 teaspoons **honey**, and ½ teaspoon **caraway seed**. Add 1 cup finely shredded **red cabbage** and ½ cup finely chopped **Golden Delicious apple**. Mix lightly and add **salt** and **pepper** to taste. Serve, or cover and chill up to 4 hours. Makes about 1½ cups.

Quickly grill slices of turkey breast, slide them into a sesame bun, and top with garnishes and a dollop of lemon-herb mayonnaise.

Quail or Rabbit from the Freezer Section

DOMESTICALLY REARED *rabbit and quail are dining delicacies found fresh at the meat counter occasionally, but with surprising frequency in the freezer.*

Rabbit is very lean, and its flavor most resembles chicken breast; richer quail tastes more like chicken thighs. Both take well to distinctive seasonings.

Roquefort or bleu d'Auvergne are traditional cheeses with the French-style rabbit, but any blue cheese will work.

Balsamic vinegar flavors and glazes the quick-cooking, pan browned quail.

RABBIT IN BLUE CHEESE-MUSTARD SAUCE

- 3 tablespoons olive oil
- 1½ tablespoons *each* fresh thyme leaves and savory leaves, or 1½ teaspoons *each* of the dry herbs
- 2 fresh or dry bay leaves, crumbled
- 1 fryer rabbit (2½ to 3 lb.), cut up
- ½ cup Dijon mustard
- ½ cup water
- ½ cup half-and-half (light cream)
- ½ cup crumbled blue cheese

In a 9- by 13-inch metal pan, stir together oil, thyme, savory, and bay leaves. Add rabbit and turn to coat evenly. Cover and chill at least 1 hour or until next day.

In a bowl, stir mustard and water until smooth. Turn rabbit over, then spread top of meat with half of mustard mixture. Bake, uncovered, in a 375° oven for 20 minutes. Turn meat over and spread other side with remaining mustard mixture. Continue to bake, basting once or twice, until meat is no longer pink in thickest part (cut to test), 25 to 30 minutes more.

Lift rabbit from pan to a platter and keep warm. Place pan over medium-high heat and boil, stirring, until juices are reduced to ½ cup, about 8 minutes. Add half-and-half; whisk until bubbling. Add all but 2 tablespoons cheese and whisk until melted. Pour sauce over rabbit; sprinkle with remaining cheese. Makes 4 or 5 servings.

PER SERVING: 428 calories, 42 g protein, 5.4 g carbohydrates, 25 g fat, 137 mg cholesterol, 996 mg sodium

QUAIL WITH ROSEMARY & BALSAMIC VINEGAR SAUCE

- 8 quail (about 4 oz. each)
- ¼ cup (⅛ lb.) butter or margarine
- ¾ cup regular-strength beef broth
- ½ cup balsamic vinegar
- 1 tablespoon fresh rosemary leaves, or 1 teaspoon dry rosemary leaves
  Rosemary sprigs (optional)

Rinse quail and pat dry. Melt 2 tablespoons butter in a 10- to 12-inch frying pan over medium-high heat. Add birds and brown lightly on all sides, about 10 minutes. Breast meat should be red and moist at the bone; to check, cut from just above wing joint to breastbone. Lift birds into a serving dish; keep warm.

To pan, add broth, vinegar, and rosemary. Over high heat, boil, uncovered, until reduced to ½ cup, about 5 minutes. Add remaining butter; stir constantly over medium heat until smoothly blended. Pour sauce over birds and garnish with rosemary sprigs. Makes 4 servings.

PER SERVING: 401 calories, 30 g protein, 17 g carbohydrates, 30 g fat, 31 mg cholesterol, 203 mg sodium

Blue cheese-mustard sauce moistens herb-flavored baked rabbit. To complete the meal, serve with little boiled potatoes and poached leeks.

Vegetable Casseroles

SATISFYING VEGETABLES STAR *in three oven-baked casseroles sturdy enough to satisfy the heartiest appetite. In the first, glistening eggplant skins make a sleek shell for eggplant slices and herb-seasoned tomato filling.*

The second offering is fila pastry pie. Fila sheets sandwich a thick layer of onions, olives, and feta cheese.

The vegetable gratin features sliced carrots, potatoes, and turnips baked until tender beneath a blanket of gruyère cheese.

MOLDED VEGETABLE MOUSSAKA

To accompany, butter and toast split pita bread rounds and make a salad of romaine lettuce and pine nuts.

- 2 **eggplants (about 1 lb. each), stems trimmed**
- ¼ **cup olive oil or salad oil**
  Tomato filling (recipe follows)
  Ricotta custard (recipe follows)
- 1 **thin orange slice (optional)**
  Parsley sprig (optional)

Cut eggplants lengthwise into quarters. With a grapefruit knife, cut centers of eggplant from skin, making skin sections about ½ inch thick. Cut center sections crosswise into ½-inch-thick slices.

Brush 2 baking pans, 10- by 15-inch size, with olive oil. Arrange slices and eggplant shells, cut side down, in a single layer in pans. Brush tops of eggplant with remaining oil. Bake, uncovered, in a 450° oven until eggplant feels very soft when pressed, 20 to 30 minutes; slide a spatula under pieces to release from pan.

To assemble, fit eggplant skins, purple side down and narrow ends to the center, closely together in an oiled 9-inch-diameter cheesecake pan with removable bottom. Press ends flush with pan rim. Spoon half the tomato filling evenly into pan. Lay eggplant slices on filling; top with remaining tomato mixture.

Pour custard over filling. Put casserole in a 10- by 15-inch pan in a 375° oven; bake until center of custard jiggles only slightly when gently shaken, 35 to 45 minutes. Let cool 10 minutes. Run a knife around pan edge. Invert a flat plate on pan. Hold pan and plate together; invert. Remove pan. Garnish with orange and parsley. Serve hot or at room temperature, cut into wedges. Makes 4 to 6 servings.

PER SERVING: 361 calories, 18 g protein, 20 g carbohydrates, 23 g fat, 118 mg cholesterol, 308 mg sodium

Tomato filling. In a 10- to 12-inch frying pan on medium heat, stir 1 cup chopped **onion** with 1 tablespoon **olive oil** or salad oil until onion is limp and slightly golden, 10 to 12 minutes. Add 1½ pounds firm-ripe **Roma-type tomatoes**, cored and chopped, and ½ teaspoon *each* **dry marjoram leaves** and **dry thyme leaves**. Stir on high heat until tomatoes fall apart to make a sauce, 8 to 10 minutes. Stir in ¼ cup *each* grated **parmesan cheese** and chopped **parsley**, and ¼ pound shredded **jarlsberg cheese**. Use, or cover and chill up to 1 day. Add **salt** and **pepper** to taste.

Ricotta custard. In a bowl, whisk together 1 cup **ricotta cheese**, ¼ cup grated **parmesan cheese**, 2 large **eggs**. Blend in ½ cup **milk**. Use, or cover and chill up to 1 day.

ONION & FETA BAKLAVA

Serve with mixed green salad (mesclun), artichokes, olives, and pistachios.

- ½ **pound fila dough, thawed if frozen**
- ½ **cup (¼ lb.) butter or margarine, melted**
  Onion-feta filling (recipe follows)

Lay fila out flat. If needed, cut through stack to make 8- by 12-inch pieces. Cover with plastic wrap to prevent drying.

Butter an 8- by 12-inch pan. Lay a sheet of fila in pan. Brush lightly with ½ to 1 teaspoon butter. Top with another piece of fila; repeat layering and buttering until half the fila is used. Spread filling over top layer. Continue to layer fila on filling, buttering each sheet.

With a sharp knife, cut through pastry to pan, making 6 or 8 wedges. If made ahead, cover and chill up to 1 day. Bake, uncovered, in a 400° oven until golden, 40 to 50 minutes. Serve hot, warm, or at room temperature. Serves 6 to 8.

PER SERVING: 412 calories, 12 g protein, 25 g carbohydrates, 30 g fat, 155 mg cholesterol, 629 mg sodium

Onion-feta filling. In a 10- to 12-inch frying pan, melt 2 tablespoons **butter** or margarine on medium heat. Add 2 cups chopped **onion**; 2 cloves **garlic**, minced or pressed; and ¼ teaspoon *each* **dry marjoram leaves**, **dry rosemary leaves**, and **dry thyme leaves**. Stir often until onion is golden, about 15 minutes.

In a bowl, mix onions with ½ pound *each* crumbled **feta cheese** and **neufchâtel cheese**, 2 large **eggs**, 3 table-

spoons **milk**, and ¼ cup pitted **niçoise olives** or chopped pitted black ripe olives. Use, or cover and chill up to 1 day.

SUMMER VEGETABLE GRATIN

As a variation, use only 1 vegetable instead of 3; you need 2 pounds total. Serve with a salad of watercress, thinly sliced fennel, and chopped roasted hazelnuts.

- 2 **medium-size carrots (about 8 oz.), peeled**
- 3 **medium-size thin-skinned potatoes (about 1 lb. total), scrubbed**
- 2 **small turnips (about 8 oz. total), peeled**
- 1 **teaspoon dry thyme leaves or dry tarragon**
- 1 **cup whipping cream**
- ¼ **pound gruyère or Swiss cheese, shredded**
  Rye croutons (directions follow)
  Salt

Making ⅛-inch-thick slices, cut the carrots diagonally and the potatoes and turnips crosswise.

To make individual casseroles, divide each vegetable into 4 equal portions. Next, layer the portions in 4 shallow, 2-cup-size gratin dishes or casseroles.

To make a single large casserole, layer the vegetables in a shallow 2- to 2½-quart baking dish.

Sprinkle vegetables with thyme; pour cream over them. Cover loosely with foil. Bake in a 375° oven for 1 hour. Remove foil; sprinkle vegetables with cheese.

Bake, uncovered, until vegetables are very tender when pierced, about 20 minutes longer. Remove from oven and let stand about 5 minutes so vegetables can absorb extra liquid. Serve hot with croutons; add salt to taste. Makes 4 servings.

PER SERVING: 416 calories, 13 g protein, 30 g carbohydrates, 28 g fat, 98 mg cholesterol, 171 mg sodium

Rye croutons. Trim crusts from 4 slices **Russian** or Jewish **rye bread**. Blend 1 to 2 tablespoons **butter** or margarine with 1 clove minced **garlic**. Spread 1 side of bread slices with butter. Put bread, buttered side down, in a single layer in a 10- to 12-inch frying pan. Cook, uncovered, on medium-high heat until butter sizzles. Remove from pan, cut each piece into 4 triangles, and serve hot. Makes 16.

PER PIECE: 41 calories, 1.3 g protein, 7.6 g carbohydrates, 0.9 g fat, 2.1 mg cholesterol, 88 mg sodium

Cooking with Fresh Black-eyed Peas

WELL KNOWN IN DRIED FORM, *black-eyed peas are less familiar fresh. But the mild, green-bean flavor of the fresh peas deserves a try. Buy them at Asian markets and some produce stores, or get them at many farmers' markets and farms selling U-pick produce.*

Three quick recipes give you several ways to try them: in a marinated salad, in a spicy soup, and as a snack.

Since ancient times, black-eyed peas have been a staple in the cuisines of Southeast Asia, India, and Africa. As immigration from those areas has increased in the West, so has the supply of black-eyed peas. California is now the major U.S. producer of both fresh and dried forms.

This member of the cowpea family grows in many colors, each with a different name, but the black-eyed is the most available to us. (One popular cousin, the Chinese long bean, is eaten as a pod.)

Plan on buying about 1¾ pounds of peas to get 2 cups shelled.

Black-eyed peas and other light components—vegetables, rice, and broth—combine to make California Hopping John, a hearty soup.

FRESH BLACK-EYED PEA SALAD

- ¾ cup regular-strength chicken broth
- 2 cups shelled fresh black-eyed peas
- ½ cup (about 2 oz.) matchstick-size slivers of cooked ham
- 3 tablespoons salad oil
- 3 tablespoons red wine vinegar
- 1 tablespoon minced fresh or 1 teaspoon dry tarragon leaves
- 1 teaspoon sugar
  Salt and freshly ground pepper
  Butter lettuce leaves, rinsed and crisped

In a 2- to 3-quart pan, bring broth to a boil over high heat. Add peas; cover and simmer until peas are tender to bite, about 12 minutes. Drain peas and let cool.

In a bowl, stir peas with ham, oil, vinegar, tarragon, and sugar; add salt and pepper to taste. Spoon pea mixture on lettuce-lined salad plates. Makes 4 servings.

PER SERVING: 225 calories, 10 g protein, 19 g carbohydrates, 12 g fat, 8.4 mg cholesterol, 227 mg sodium

CALIFORNIA HOPPING JOHN

- 1 medium-size onion, chopped
- 2 cloves garlic, minced or pressed
- 2 tablespoons salad oil
- 1 teaspoon ground cumin
- 1 large can (7 oz.) diced green chilies
- 1 canned chipotle chili in adobo sauce or dry chipotle chili; or 2 large fresh jalapeño chilies, cut in half
- ½ cup long-grain brown rice
- 2 cups shelled fresh black-eyed peas
- 3 cups regular-strength chicken broth
- 3 large ripe tomatoes, peeled, cored, and chopped
  Pepper

In a 4- to 5-quart pan over medium-high heat, cook onion and garlic in oil, stirring often, until onion is limp, about 10 minutes. Add cumin; stir for 1 minute. Add green and chipotle chilies, rice, peas, and broth. Bring to a boil over high heat, cover, and simmer for 25 minutes.

Add tomatoes and their juices. Continue to simmer, covered, until rice is tender to bite, about 10 minutes more.

Remove chipotle or jalapeños. Season to taste with pepper. Makes 2 quarts, 4 to 6 servings.

PER SERVING: 206 calories, 7.9 g protein, 32 g carbohydrates, 6.2 g fat, 0 mg cholesterol, 241 mg sodium

BLACK-EYED PEAS TO MUNCH

- ¾ to 1 cup salad oil
- 2 cups shelled fresh black-eyed peas
  Salt

Pour ¼ inch of oil into an 8- to 10-inch frying pan. Place over medium-high heat until oil is very warm. Add peas, immediately cover pan, and fry, shaking pan often, until peas are golden, 9 to 12 minutes (lift lid to check—carefully; peas spatter). Remove pan from heat; let stand, covered, until any popping stops, about 1 minute.

With slotted spoon, lift hot peas to paper towels to drain. Add salt to taste. Serve warm or cool; if made ahead, store the cool peas airtight up to 1 week. Makes 1½ cups.

PER TABLESPOON: 36 calories, 1.1 g protein, 2.9 g carbohydrates, 2.3 g fat, 0 mg cholesterol, 0.8 mg sodium

Make Your Own Catsup

THE UBIQUITOUS CONDIMENT *for the all-American hamburger and fries, catsup is easy to create at home. You simply purée fruit and seasonings, then boil the mixture down to thicken it and concentrate flavor.*

Today, catsup's main ingredient is usually ripe tomatoes, but in the past it was often made from other kinds of fruit, vegetables, or even fish. Here we offer a traditional tomato-based catsup and an old-fashioned plum version. Both draw on your garden's late-summer bounty.

You can store the catsups in the refrigerator for up to a month. If you want to preserve them longer, see directions below for canning.

CALIFORNIA CATSUP

  6 pounds ripe Roma-type tomatoes, cored and chopped
  1 large onion, chopped
  2 tablespoons chopped garlic
1½ cups cider vinegar
  1 cup sugar
  1 teaspoon ground coriander
  ½ to ¾ teaspoon cayenne
  ½ teaspoon ground mace or nutmeg
  ¼ teaspoon ground cinnamon
  1 dry bay leaf
    About 1¼ teaspoons salt

In a blender or food processor, combine tomatoes, onion, and garlic, a portion at a time, and whirl until smoothly puréed. Pour mixture through a fine strainer set over a 5- to 6-quart pan, stirring and pressing to push mixture through. Discard any residue left in strainer. To pan, add vinegar, sugar, coriander, cayenne, mace, cinnamon, and bay leaf.

Boil gently, uncovered and stirring often, until mixture is thick and reduced to about 4 cups, 1½ to 2 hours (adjust heat to maintain a gentle boil; if mixture splatters out of pan, lower heat). Add salt to taste. Remove and discard bay leaf. Serve warm or cool. To store, cool, cover, and chill up to 1 month. Or process as directed at right. Makes about 2 pints.

PER TABLESPOON: 22 calories, 0.4 g protein, 5.4 g carbohydrates, 0.1 g fat, 0 mg cholesterol, 46 mg sodium

Tomatoes or plums—with onion, garlic, vinegar, and spices—are base for two tangy homemade catsups. Refrigerated, catsup can be stored for up to a month.

To process for canning. Fill clean, hot, sterilized half-pint or pint canning jars to within ¼ inch of rim. Wipe jar rims clean. Cover with hot, sterilized lids; screw on bands. Place jars on a rack in a canning kettle half-full of hot water. Add more hot water, if needed, to cover jars by 1 inch. Cover pan and simmer for 20 minutes.

Lift out jars, set on a towel, and let cool. Test the seal by pressing each lid. If lid stays down, the seal is good. If it pops when pressed, store jar in refrigerator up to 1 month.

PLUM CATSUP

Serve this sweet and tangy sauce with smoked or fresh pork, chicken, or duck.

Follow recipe for **California catsup** (preceding), omitting tomatoes. Use 6 pounds ripe **tart red plums,** pitted. Decrease **cider vinegar** to 1 cup. Increase the **sugar** to 1½ cups. Add 1½ teaspoons ground **ginger.** Boil gently, uncovered, until thick and reduced to about 6 cups, 1½ to 2 hours. Makes 3 pints.

PER TABLESPOON: 28 calories, 0.2 g protein, 6.9 g carbohydrates, 0.2 g fat, 0 mg cholesterol, 29 mg sodium

Stir cucumber-based gazpacho with green onion swizzle sticks.

WHITE GAZPACHO

1 **medium-size European cucumber (about 1 lb.)**
2 **cups unflavored yogurt**
2 **tablespoons lemon juice**
1 **clove garlic, peeled**
2 **cups regular-strength chicken broth**
1 **cup water**
2 **tablespoons minced fresh cilantro (coriander)**
2 **tablespoons thinly sliced green onions**
6 **whole green onions, ends trimmed; or 6 cucumber spears, each 4 to 6 inches**

Peel and coarsely chop the whole cucumber. In a blender or food processor, whirl chopped cucumber, yogurt, lemon juice, and garlic (if using a blender, add about ½ cup of the chicken broth). Pour mixture into a storage container, about 2-quart size, and stir in chicken broth and water. Cover and chill at least 2 hours, or up to 1 day.

Stir in minced cilantro. Pour mixture into a serving bowl or pitcher; top with sliced green onions. To serve, ladle or pour into bowls or glasses with whole green onions or cucumber spears. Makes 1 quart, 4 servings. — *Lynne French, Aptos, Calif.*

PER SERVING: 109 calories, 8 g protein, 14 g carbohydrates, 2.6 g fat, 6.8 mg cholesterol, 115 mg sodium

Simple dressing and chopped onion flavor refreshing potato salad.

POTATO SALAD WITH OREGANO VINAIGRETTE

2 **pounds (about 7 medium-size) red thin-skinned potatoes**
⅓ **cup olive oil or salad oil**
¼ **cup white wine vinegar or lemon juice**
1 **tablespoon fresh or 1½ teaspoons dry oregano leaves**
1 **tablespoon minced parsley**
  Salt and pepper
⅓ **cup diced red onion**
  Fresh oregano sprigs (optional)

In a 4- to 5-quart pan, cover potatoes with at least ½ inch water. Cover pan and bring to a boil on high heat; reduce heat to simmering. Cook until potatoes are tender when pierced, about 30 minutes. Drain and let potatoes stand until cool enough to touch; peel and cut into about ½-inch chunks.

Meanwhile, in a serving bowl, blend olive oil, vinegar, oregano, and parsley. Add warm potatoes and mix gently; add salt and pepper to taste. Mound diced red onion in center of salad, then garnish with oregano sprigs. Serve at room temperature, or cover and hold up to 4 hours. Mix onion with potatoes before serving. Makes about 1 quart, 4 to 6 servings. — *Jackie Tieger, Buena Park, Calif.*

PER SERVING: 233 calories, 3.1 g protein, 28 g carbohydrates, 12 g fat, 0 mg cholesterol, 12 mg sodium

Baked roll encloses jack cheese; serve with meat sauce.

CHEESE-&-EGG ROLL

¼ **pound Italian sausage, chopped**
1¾ **cups purchased marinara sauce**
  Roulade (recipe follows)
½ **pound jack cheese, shredded**
  Fresh basil or parsley sprigs

In a 2- to 3-quart pan on medium-high heat, brown sausage; stir often. Stir in sauce and bring to a boil; keep warm.

Invert warm roulade onto waxed paper; gently peel paper from top. Sprinkle the cake with cheese. Supporting underneath with the paper, lift from a narrow end and roll cake snugly around cheese. Set roll, seam down, on an ovenproof platter. Bake in a 325° oven until cheese melts, 10 to 15 minutes. Garnish with basil; slice and serve with sauce. Makes 4 to 6 servings. — *Laura Getschmann, Bremerton, Wash.*

PER SERVING: 360 calories, 20 g protein, 13 g carbohydrates, 25 g fat, 320 mg cholesterol, 858 mg sodium

Roulade. Line a 10- by 15-inch pan with waxed paper. With a mixer, whip 6 **large egg yolks** until thick. Smoothly blend ⅓ cup *each* **all-purpose flour** and **water;** beat into egg yolks.

With clean beaters, whip 6 **large egg whites** until they hold soft peaks. Fold yolks into whites. Spread evenly in pan. Bake in a 325° oven until cake is lightly browned, about 15 minutes.

PASTA IN ITALIAN GARDEN SAUCE

- 1 **medium-size carrot, diced**
- 1 **stalk celery, diced**
- 3 **cloves garlic, minced**
- 3 **tablespoons butter or olive oil**
- 2½ **pounds (2 qt.) Roma-type tomatoes, cored, chopped**
- 1 *each* **medium-size zucchini and crookneck squash, diced**
- 1 **teaspoon dry oregano leaves**
  Salt and pepper
- ½ **pound dry linguine or pasta twists, cooked and hot**
  Grated parmesan cheese

In a 10- to 12-inch frying pan on medium-high heat, cook carrot, celery, and garlic in butter until garlic begins to brown slightly, stirring occasionally. Add tomatoes; cover and cook on high heat, stirring occasionally, until most of the liquid is evaporated (reduced to about 4 cups), about 10 minutes. Add squash and oregano. Cover and simmer until squash is just tender when pierced, about 10 minutes longer; stir often. Add salt and pepper to taste.

Mix hot pasta and vegetable sauce in a serving bowl. Sprinkle with about 2 tablespoons parmesan cheese; offer additional cheese to add to taste. Makes 4 servings. —*Robyn Dunne, Atascadero, Calif.*

PER SERVING: 364 calories, 11 g protein, 60 g carbohydrates, 11 g fat, 23 mg cholesterol, 127 mg sodium

Lots of tomatoes—plus squash, celery and garlic— make sauce for linguine.

CALYPSO CALAMARI SALAD

- 1 **pound (25 to 30) cleaned squid mantles (tubes), cut into ½-inch-wide rings**
- ½ **cup minced celery**
- ¼ **cup sweetened or unsweetened shredded dry coconut**
- ⅓ **cup salad oil**
- 3 **tablespoons lime juice**
- 2 **tablespoons minced fresh California (Anaheim) green chili**
- 2 **green onions, ends trimmed, minced**
  Salt and pepper
- ½ **pound spinach, stemmed, washed well, and drained**
- 1 **large ripe papaya**

In a 4- to 5-quart pan, bring 2 quarts water to boiling. Stir in squid. Drain at once and rinse with cold water to cool; drain again.

In a bowl, combine squid, celery, coconut, oil, lime juice, chili, onions, and salt and pepper to taste.

Arrange spinach on a platter. Peel papaya, cut in half, scoop out seeds; thinly slice and arrange on spinach. With a slotted spoon, remove squid from dressing and mound onto center leaves; pour dressing over spinach and fruit. Makes 4 servings. —*Roxanne E. Chan, Albany, Calif.*

PER SERVING: 340 calories, 20 g protein, 19 g carbohydrates, 21 g fat, 264 mg cholesterol, 113 mg sodium

Squid rings bathed in coconut dressing top papaya slices and spinach.

HONEY BLUEBERRY CHEESECAKE

  Whole-wheat crust (recipe follows)
- 1 **pound cream cheese**
  About ⅔ cup honey
- 2 **large eggs**
- 2 **teaspoons vanilla**
- 2 **cups sour cream**
- 1 **to 2 cups blueberries, rinsed and drained**
  Mint leaves

Press crust over bottom of a 9-inch-diameter pan with removable bottom.

Beat cream cheese and ⅓ cup honey until mixed. Beat in eggs and vanilla. Pour mixture into pan. Bake in a 325° oven until center is set when pan is jiggled, about 25 minutes. Stir sour cream with ¼ cup honey; spread evenly over cake. Return to oven to set cream, 5 to 6 minutes. Cool 2 hours, or cover and chill up to 1 day. Run a knife around pan edge; remove rim. Set cake on a platter; top with berries and mint. Serves 12. —*Amy Olson, Veronica, Ore.*

PER SERVING: 403 calories, 6.7 g protein, 32 g carbohydrates, 29 g fat, 118 mg cholesterol, 199 mg sodium

Whole-wheat crust. With your fingers or in a food processor, rub or whirl ¾ cup **whole-wheat flour**, ⅓ cup *each* **brown sugar** and **butter** or margarine, and ¼ cup **sesame seed** until mixture sticks together.

Honey-laced cheesecake has whole-wheat crust, blueberries on top.

DRY SOUP (sopa seca) *is no longer surprising to students of Mexican cooking; they know it as a sort of stew or casserole based on rice, pasta, or tortillas.*

Spain can counter with a liquid salad—the well-known gazpacho. Most people consider gazpacho to be a cold soup, but a look at the list of ingredients is enough to affirm its credentials as a salad.

Eric Lie makes it by emptying a veritable cornucopia of vegetables into the blender—cucumbers, tomatoes, and bell peppers—and whirling them with Bloody Mary mix. The last, a chili-seasoned tomato juice cocktail, is his great contribution; most gazpachos use plain tomato juice and bring mere refreshment, while Lie's brings exaltation. Try this soup for a nourishing, stimulating, and satisfying luncheon appropriate to a day when you're saving room for a noble dinner.

GAZPACHO PICANTE

- 2 **medium-size cucumbers**
  About 2 pounds firm-ripe tomatoes, or 1 large can (28 oz.) tomatoes
- 2 **medium-size red or green bell peppers, stemmed, seeded, and chopped**
- 4 **cups ½-inch cubes French bread without crust**
- ¼ **cup** *each* **red wine vinegar and olive oil**
- 1 **bottle (1 qt.) chili-seasoned tomato cocktail**
- 1 **small onion, minced**
- 2 **cloves garlic, minced or pressed**
  Croutons (directions follow)
- 1 **cup thinly sliced green onions (ends trimmed), including tops**
  Salt and liquid hot pepper seasoning

Peel and coarsely chop the cucumbers. Peel, core, and coarsely chop the tomatoes (or use canned tomatoes and their liquid).

"For gazpacho, he empties a veritable cornucopia of vegetables into the blender."

In a blender, smoothly purée, a portion at a time, the cucumbers, tomatoes and their juices, half the bell peppers, bread, vinegar, oil, and tomato cocktail. As puréed, pour into a large bowl. Stir in the minced onion and garlic. To serve cold, pour into bowls and add 2 or 3 ice cubes to each; or cover and chill at least 2 hours or until next day (whisk before serving).

Offer remaining bell peppers, croutons, and green onions in individual bowls to add to soup to taste, along with salt and liquid hot pepper seasoning. Makes 6 servings, each about 2-cup size.

PER SERVING: 414 calories, 8.6 g protein, 52 g carbohydrates, 20 g fat, 1.6 mg cholesterol, 887 mg sodium

Croutons. Trim and discard crusts from 4 to 6 slices **French bread,** then cut bread into ½-inch cubes. Pour ¼ cup **olive oil** into a 10- to 12-inch frying pan over medium heat. When hot, add bread cubes and stir gently until golden brown. Drain on paper towels. If made ahead, let cool, then package airtight and hold at room temperature up to 2 days.

Eric I. Lie

Edmonds, Wash.

When we eat veal, at least the so-called better cuts, we are likely to pay a good price for it. But Jordan Paine finds ground veal just as delicate in flavor, much less costly, and a fine starting point for his Veal Mushroom Patties.

VEAL MUSHROOM PATTIES

- 2 tablespoons *each* salad oil and butter or margarine
- 1 small onion, minced
- 1 clove garlic, minced or pressed
- ¼ pound mushrooms, minced
- ½ teaspoon dry thyme leaves
- 3 tablespoons minced parsley
- 1 small firm-ripe tomato, cored, peeled, seeded, and minced
- ¼ teaspoon pepper
- 1 pound ground veal
- ¼ pound cooked ham, minced
- ⅓ cup fine dry bread crumbs
- 1 large egg
- ¾ cup regular-strength beef broth

In a 10- to 12-inch frying pan, melt half the butter in half the oil over medium heat. Add onion, garlic, mushrooms, thyme, and parsley; stir often until mushrooms are lightly browned. Add tomato and pepper and continue stirring until mixture is almost dry. Transfer to a large bowl and let stand until lukewarm. Meanwhile, rinse and dry frying pan.

To vegetable mixture add veal, ham, crumbs, and egg. Mix well with your hands or a fork. Shape mixture into 6 patties, each about 1 inch thick.

In the frying pan over medium heat, melt remaining butter in remaining oil. When hot, add patties and cook, turning once, until meat is no longer pink in center (cut to test) and well browned on both sides, about 15 minutes total.

Transfer patties to a platter, and discard fat in pan. Over high heat, add broth to pan; stir to free browned bits

and boil until liquid is reduced by about half. Pour over patties. Makes 6 servings.

PER SERVING: 288 calories, 21 g protein, 7 g carbohydrates, 19 g fat, 121 mg cholesterol, 430 mg sodium

Scottsdale, Ariz.

What you might buy under the name sea bass can really be any of several fish species that come in all sizes and vary in oil content and texture. Yet all are mild in flavor, and any will perform well as the star in Edward W. Fisher's Sea Bass with Wine Sauce. Its crab topping and the wine-flavored sauce with capers make it a good candidate for a dinner party dish.

SEA BASS WITH WINE SAUCE

- ¼ cup (⅛ lb.) butter or margarine
- 1½ teaspoons dry fines herbes mix or ½ teaspoon *each* dry thyme leaves, dry marjoram leaves, and dry tarragon leaves
- 1 tablespoon *each* minced onion and parsley
- ¼ cup minced celery
- 1 cup soft white bread crumbs
- ½ pound cooked shelled crab
- 1½ to 2 pounds boned and skinned sea bass
  Wine sauce (recipe follows)
  Paprika
  Parsley sprigs

"Sea bass can really be several fish species that come in all sizes."

Melt butter in a 10- to 12-inch frying pan over medium heat. Add fines herbes, onion, minced parsley, and celery and stir often until slightly browned, about 5 minutes. Stir in the bread crumbs and crab; set aside.

Rinse fish and pat dry, then cut into 4 to 6 equal portions. Lay fish in a buttered 8- by 12-inch baking dish. Evenly top fish with wine sauce. Cover and bake in a 425° oven until fish is opaque but still moist-looking in thickest part (cut to test), about 20 minutes if fish is 1½ inches thick, less time if pieces are thinner. Uncover casserole, mound crab mixture on fish; baste crab with some of the pan sauce, then sprinkle generously with paprika. Bake 5 minutes longer; garnish with parsley sprigs. With a spatula, transfer fish to plates and spoon sauce onto each portion. Makes 4 to 6 servings.

PER SERVING: 324 calories, 32 g protein, 10 g carbohydrates, 17 g fat, 124 mg cholesterol, 409 mg sodium

Wine sauce. Melt 2 tablespoons **butter** or margarine in a 1- to 1½-quart pan over medium heat. Add 2 tablespoons **all-purpose flour** and stir until bubbly. Mix in 1 tablespoon minced **onion,** 1 small clove **garlic** (minced or pressed), 1 teaspoon **sugar,** and 1½ cups **milk.** Stir on medium-high heat until boiling rapidly.

Remove from heat and stir in 2 tablespoons *each* **cognac** or brandy and **dry white wine,** and 1 tablespoon drained **capers.** Season to taste with **salt** and **pepper.**

Long Beach, Calif.

July Menus

WITH SUMMER IN FULL SWING, *here are three quick-to-cook meals that make generous use of plentiful fresh produce while keeping kitchen duties at a minimum.*

Poultry stars in each. For the Mexican brunch, chicken goes into salsa-topped enchiladas you can make ahead. Chicken wings make a spicy (mild to fiery) contribution to a Fourth of July picnic. Add ground turkey to an economical stir-fry.

MEXICAN BRUNCH

Enchiladas with Green Chili Salsa
Crenshaw Melon Wedges
Hibiscus Iced Tea

Popular Mexican flavors come together in these chicken-filled enchiladas served over purchased refried beans. The refreshing salsa uses tart tomatillos.

You can make enchiladas and hibiscus tea ahead (check ingredients of herbal teas for a blend with hibiscus flowers). While enchiladas heat, slice melon.

ENCHILADAS WITH GREEN CHILI SALSA

- Salad oil
- 12 corn tortillas (6-in. diameter)
- Chicken filling (recipe follows)
- 3 cups (¾ lb.) shredded jack cheese
- 1 large can (30 oz.) refried beans, heated
- Green chili salsa (recipe follows)
- 12 green onions, ends trimmed

To a 10- to 12-inch frying pan over medium-high heat, add ¼ inch oil. When oil is hot, cook tortillas, 1 at a time, turning once, just until limp and slightly blistered, about 10 seconds. Add more oil as needed. Drain tortillas on paper towels.

Working quickly while tortillas are warm, spoon about 2 tablespoons of the chicken filling down center of each tortilla. Tightly roll tortilla around filling.

Place tortillas, seam down, in a 9- by 13-inch baking dish or pan. Sprinkle cheese over tortillas and cover with foil (if made ahead, chill up until next day). Bake in a 350° oven until hot in center, about 30 minutes.

Spoon heated beans equally onto 6 dinner plates. With a wide spatula, lift 2 enchiladas onto each portion of beans; top enchiladas with salsa. Garnish each plate with 2 green onions. Serves 6.

PER SERVING: 675 calories, 34 g protein, 58 g carbohydrates, 41 g fat, 81 mg cholesterol, 1,161 mg sodium

Chicken filling. Mix together 1½ cups shredded **cooked chicken;** 1 large **onion,** minced; ¼ cup minced **fresh cilantro** (coriander); 1 tablespoon **chili powder;** and 3 cloves **garlic,** minced or pressed.

Green chili salsa. Discard hulls from ¼ pound **fresh tomatillos.** Rinse tomatillos and mince. Mix with 1 small **cucumber,** peeled and minced; 1 small can (4 oz.) **diced green chilies;** and ¼ cup **lime juice.** Serve, or cover and chill up until next day.

HIBISCUS ICED TEA

- 8 cups water
- 24 bags herbal tea containing hibiscus flowers
- ½ cup sugar
- ¼ cup lime juice
- 1 lime, cut crosswise into thin slices

In a 3- to 4-quart pan over high heat, bring water to a boil. Add tea bags, sugar, and lime juice.

Remove from heat and let stand, covered, until cool (or chill). Discard bags. Pour tea into ice-filled glasses; top with lime slices. Makes about 8 cups.

PER 1-CUP SERVING: 52 calories, 0 g protein, 15 g carbohydrates, 0 g fat, 0 mg cholesterol, 24 mg sodium

JULY 4TH CELEBRATION

Independence Day Pizzas
Fiery Chicken Wings   Corn on the Cob
Blueberry Pie with
Strawberries & Cream
Fruit Sparklers

Cheer on the holiday with spicy chicken wings and chili-topped pizzas. Serve with fruit sparklers and follow with a patriotic red, white, and blue(berry) pie.

You can toast muffins ahead, then add toppings to broil when ready to serve. Cook corn at the same time. For drinks, fill glasses with equal portions of sparkling mineral water and fruit juice.

For Mexican brunch, nestle chicken and cheese enchiladas on warm refried beans; top generously with tomatillo-cucumber salsa. Serve with melon and iced tea.

INDEPENDENCE DAY PIZZAS

6 **English muffins**
1 **small yellow bell pepper, stemmed, seeded, and thinly sliced**
½ **cup thinly sliced onion**
2 **cups (½ lb.) shredded Swiss cheese**
1 **small fresh California (Anaheim) green chili, stemmed, seeded, and thinly sliced**

Split English muffins in half and lay, cut side up, on a 12- by 15-inch baking sheet. Broil 4 to 6 inches from heat until lightly toasted, then turn muffins over and toast other side, about 4 minutes total.

Next, with cut sides up, evenly cover each half with bell pepper, onion, cheese, and chili. Return to broiler until cheese melts, about 4 minutes. Makes 12.

PER PIECE: 138 calories, 7.3 g protein, 14 g carbohydrates, 5.6 g fat, 10 mg cholesterol, 280 mg sodium

FIERY CHICKEN WINGS

5 **pounds chicken wings**
Fiery sauce (recipe follows)

Rinse chicken wings and pat dry. Cut apart at joints; reserve wing tips for other uses. Line 2 baking pans, each 10 by 15 inches, with heavy foil. Evenly divide wing pieces between pans.

In a 400° oven, bake wings uncovered; every 10 minutes, gently stir wings to loosen them from foil. When wings are golden, about 40 minutes total, pour sauce over them and turn to coat evenly.

Continue to bake until sauce is bubbling and edges of wings are lightly browned, about 30 minutes longer; turn wings once or twice. Eat hot, or let cool and serve at room temperature. Serves 4 to 6.

PER SERVING: 484 calories, 39 g protein, 18 g carbohydrates, 28 g fat, 120 mg cholesterol, 486 mg sodium

Fiery sauce. Stir together ½ cup **catsup,** ¼ cup *each* **vinegar** and **honey,** and up to 2 tablespoons **liquid hot pepper** seasoning (adjust heat to taste).

(Continued on next page)

Celebrate the Fourth of July in an outdoor picnic to please all ages. Menu features muffin mini-pizzas, spicy chicken wings, and corn on the cob.

SUMMER STIR-FRY

Summer Turkey Stir-fry
Seedless Grapes
Brownie Ice Cream Bars   **Chardonnay**

Ground turkey (or ground chicken) is the lean choice for this stir-fried combination.

Add water to the bulgur, then cut vegetables. For dessert bars, press a small scoop of ice cream between two brownies.

SUMMER TURKEY STIR-FRY

- 1 cup bulgur (cracked wheat)
- 2 cups boiling water
- 2 tablespoons olive or salad oil
- 3 cloves garlic, minced or pressed
- 1 pound ground turkey or chicken
- 2 cups thinly sliced carrots
- 2 small zucchini, ends trimmed, thinly sliced
- 1 tablespoon minced fresh ginger
  Cooking sauce (recipe follows)
- ½ cup thinly sliced green onions

In a bowl, mix together bulgur and boiling water; set aside until most of the liquid is absorbed, about 1 hour; drain.

Place a wok or 10-inch frying pan over high heat. Add 2 tablespoons oil, garlic, and turkey; stir-fry until lightly browned, crumbling meat with spoon, about 5 minutes. Scoop out turkey and set aside. To pan, add carrots, zucchini, ginger, and ⅓ cup water; stir to free browned bits. Cover and cook vegetables until they are tender to bite, about 5 minutes; stir often. Boil, uncovered, until nearly all the liquid evaporates. Add turkey and sauce; stir until boiling.

Spoon bulgur onto plates; top equally with turkey and sprinkle with green onions. Serves 4. —*Mrs. L. K. Ross, Elk Grove, Calif.*

PER SERVING: 456 calories, 26 g protein, 46 g carbohydrates, 19 g fat, 76 mg cholesterol, 650 mg sodium

Cooking sauce. Mix ½ cup regular-strength **chicken broth,** 2 tablespoons **soy sauce,** and 1 tablespoon **cornstarch.**

AUGUST

Tomato Explosion (page 176)

Celebrate summer with a
salute to the Pacific—our Hawaiian appetizer party offers a
colorful array of Asian, South Pacific, and Portuguese foods
representing the Islands' ethnic diversity. Celebrate the
harvest by enjoying fresh vegetables and flavorful fruits at
their peak—and by quickly cooking some in our easy
chutneys. Celebrate the imagination and vitality of today's
Western cooks by sampling such treats as two-tone summer
soups, breakfast salads, and frosty-cold coffee coolers.

Pupu Party

A MELTING POT *of Asian, South Pacific, and Portuguese cultures, Hawaii offers an exciting mix of foods. Island supermarkets, delicatessens, and ethnic stores sell a tremendous variety of these foods ready to serve, making it easy for locals as well as travelers with minimal kitchens to put together an impromptu pupu (Hawaiian appetizer) party.*

In the Islands, buy a selection of foods you'd like to try. Many take no cooking, while some require reheating or grilling. Set them out for guests to sample.

On the Mainland, choices may be more limited. But you can make many of the favorites yourself and supplement with ready-made purchases from the market.

ISLAND OR MAINLAND PUPU PARTY

Chinese Barbecued Spareribs
Sushi with Pickled Ginger
Teriyaki Beef Sticks or Hawaiian Jerky
Pickled Maui Onions   Kim Chee
Hawaiian Seasoned Tuna
Papaya & Portuguese Sausage Skewers
Tropical Fruits
Guava Wine Cooler
Pineapple Rum Punch

To expand this menu for more than 10 to 12, include other store-bought items. Ready-to-eat nibbles include taro chips or Hawaiian potato chips, macadamia nuts, toasted coconut chips, Japanese rice crackers, and lomi lomi salmon.

Most foods can be eaten out of hand or with wooden picks or chopsticks.

The pickled onions and kim chee can be made weeks ahead.

Marinate the meats and assemble the sausage skewers up to a day in advance. On party day, make the sushi up to 8 hours ahead; also prepare the tuna. About 1 hour before serving, bake the ribs and light the briquets for the skewered meats. Add sparkling water to punches just before serving. For fruit, offer pineapple, papaya, mango, coconut, or guava.

CHINESE BARBECUED SPARERIBS

- ¾ cup sugar
- ½ cup soy sauce
- 3 tablespoons hoisin sauce
- 2 tablespoons dry sherry
- 1 tablespoon minced fresh ginger
- 1 rack pork spareribs, 3 to 4 pounds (have meatman saw ribs in half crosswise)

In a 12- by 17-inch pan, combine sugar, soy, hoisin, sherry, and ginger. Lay ribs in pan and coat with soy mixture. Cover and chill, turning occasionally, at least 4 hours or up to overnight.

Lift ribs from marinade and put in a foil-lined 12- by 17-inch roasting pan. Bake, uncovered, in a 350° oven until meat is browned and no longer pink at bone (cut to test), 1 to 1¼ hours. To serve, cut between rib bones. Makes 10 to 12 appetizer servings. — *Reynold Choy, Honolulu.*

PER SERVING: 237 calories, 14 g protein, 15 g carbohydrates, 13 g fat, 54 mg cholesterol, 855 mg sodium

SUSHI WITH PICKLED GINGER

Various forms of sushi are sold. Some are wrapped in nori or stuffed in fried tofu cases. For a simpler version, press the rice into compact shapes and top with pickled ginger (buy in Japanese markets).

- 1½ cups short-grain white rice
  About ½ cup seasoned rice vinegar (or 2 tablespoons sugar and salt to taste dissolved in ½ cup white wine vinegar)
- 1 tablespoon thinly sliced or shredded pickled ginger, drained

In a 2- to 3-quart pan, rinse rice with water until water runs clear; drain. Add 1¾ cups water to rice. Cover and bring to a boil over high heat. Reduce heat to low and cook without stirring until all water is absorbed, about 15 minutes.

Stir in 3 tablespoons vinegar. Spread rice in a 10- by 15-inch pan. Cool rice quickly to room temperature, turning often. Press about 2 tablespoons of rice into 1- by 2-inch ovals; dip hands into remaining vinegar as needed to prevent sticking. Place ginger on top of rice. (If made ahead, cover tightly and hold at room temperature up to 8 hours.) Makes 22 pieces, 10 to 12 appetizer servings.

PER SERVING: 102 calories, 1.7 g protein, 23 g carbohydrates, 0.1 g fat, 0 mg cholesterol, 10 mg sodium

(Continued on page 174)

Mainland-style party features fruit, crackers, coconut, Sushi with Pickled Ginger, Papaya and Portuguese Sausage Skewers, Teriyaki Beef Sticks, Chinese Barbecued Spareribs, Kim Chee, Hawaiian Seasoned Tuna, and Pickled Maui Onions.

Island visitors sample Hawaiian specialties from local markets and delicatessens for easy appetizer party on Waikiki balcony. At home, you can prepare favorites yourself.

TERIYAKI BEEF STICKS

In Hawaii, thin slices of marinated beef are sold for teriyaki beef. For a quick appetizer, cut slices into about 1-inch-wide strips, thread on skewers, and grill.

- ¼ **cup soy sauce**
- 2 **tablespoons sugar**
- 1 **tablespoon minced fresh ginger**
- 2 **cloves garlic, pressed or minced**
- 2 **tablespoons dry sherry**
- 2 **tablespoons salad oil**
- 1 **pound boneless lean beef steak, such as sirloin or top round, about 1 inch thick**

In a bowl, mix soy, sugar, ginger, garlic, sherry, and oil. Trim off and discard excess fat from beef. Cut meat across the grain in ¼-inch-thick slices. Mix meat with soy marinade. Cover and chill at least 2 hours or up to overnight.

Weave thin wooden skewers in and out of meat slices, so meat lies flat. (If made ahead, cover and chill up to overnight.) Cook on a grill 3 to 4 inches above a solid bed of hot coals (you can hold your hand at grill level only 2 to 3 seconds), turning meat until brown on both sides, 5 to 7 minutes. Makes 12 sticks, 10 to 12 appetizer servings.

PER SERVING: 77 calories, 8.8 g protein, 1.5 g carbohydrates, 3.7 g fat, 25 mg cholesterol, 190 mg sodium

HAWAIIAN JERKY
(Pipikaula)

Hawaiian beef jerky is moister than its Mainland counterpart, because it's dried in large pieces.

- 1 **flank steak (1½ to 2 lb.)**
- ½ **cup soy sauce**
- 1 **tablespoon Hawaiian or coarse salt**
- ¼ **cup firmly packed brown sugar**
- 3 **cloves garlic, pressed or minced**
- 2 **tablespoons minced fresh ginger**
- ¼ **teaspoon crushed dried hot red chilies**

Trim fat from meat; cut steak in half lengthwise. In a large bowl, stir together soy, salt, sugar, garlic, ginger, and chilies. Add meat and mix to coat pieces well; cover and chill, turning occasionally, 6 hours or up to overnight. Lift meat from marinade (do not pierce meat) and place on wire racks set in 10- by 15-inch rimmed pans. Place in a 150° to 200° oven and bake until meat is firm and dry and no longer has a raw texture in thickest part (cut to test), 8 to 10 hours. Cool meat and thinly slice across grain to serve. Wrap airtight and refrigerate up to 1 week. Makes about 1 pound jerky, enough for 10 to 12 appetizer servings.

PER SERVING: 120 calories, 11 g protein, 2.9 g carbohydrates, 6.9 g fat, 30 mg cholesterol, 562 mg sodium

PICKLED MAUI ONIONS

- 2 medium-size Maui or other mild white onions, cut into 1-inch chunks; separate the layers
- 1½ cups water
- ¾ cup distilled white vinegar
- ⅓ cup sugar
- 3 cloves garlic, crushed
- 2 small dried hot red chilies
- 1 tablespoon salt

Place onions in wide-mouth 1-quart (or slightly larger) jar. In a 1- to 2-quart pan, bring water, vinegar, sugar, garlic, chilies, and salt to boiling. Pour over onions; put leakproof lid on jar. Let onions cool, then chill at least 3 days or up to 1 month; turn jar over occasionally. Pour into a bowl; serve with toothpicks. Makes 1 quart.

PER ½-CUP SERVING: 36 calories, 0.5 g protein, 8.7 g carbohydrates, 0.1 g fat, 0 mg cholesterol, 413 mg sodium

KOREAN KIM CHEE

- 2 pounds napa cabbage
- 1½ cups water
- ⅓ cup salt
- ½ to 1 teaspoon cayenne
- ½ teaspoon crushed dried hot red chilies
- 2 to 3 cloves garlic, minced
- ⅓ cup thinly sliced green onion

Cut cabbage into 1-inch squares. Mix cabbage, water, and salt; let stand 1 hour. Drain cabbage and squeeze out liquid. Mix cabbage, cayenne, chilies, garlic, and green onion. Pack in a wide-mouth 1-quart jar. Cover and chill at least 3 days or up to 1 month. Spoon into a bowl and serve with toothpicks. Makes 1 quart.

PER ½-CUP SERVING: 21 calories, 15 g protein, 4.3 g carbohydrates, 0.3 g fat, 0 mg cholesterol, 834 mg sodium

HAWAIIAN SEASONED TUNA (Ahi Poke)

Bite-size pieces of seafood (here, ahi, or tuna) are mixed with zesty seasonings and seaweed to make poke (poe-key). Ugo, an edible seaweed available in Japanese markets, adds texture to the fish mixture. Omit it, if desired.

Freezing kills parasites in raw fish. Ask the fishmonger if the tuna has been previously frozen. If not, wrap airtight and freeze at 0° or below at least 3 days; thaw in refrigerator.

- 1 tablespoon sesame seed
- 1 tablespoon salad oil
- 1 teaspoon minced fresh ginger
- ¼ to ½ teaspoon crushed dried hot red chilies
- 2 tablespoons soy sauce
- ¼ cup minced green onion
- 2 tablespoons Japanese salted seaweed (*ugo*), rinsed well, drained, and chopped (optional)
- 1 pound fresh raw tuna (such as ahi)

In a 6- to 8-inch frying pan over low heat, cook sesame seed in oil just until seed is golden, 2 to 3 minutes. Remove from heat and stir in ginger. Let cool. Stir in chilies, soy, onion, and seaweed. Trim off and discard any skin, dark portions, or tough membranes from tuna. Cut tuna into ½-inch cubes. Mix fish with sesame mixture. (If made ahead, cover and chill up to 4 hours.) Serve with wooden picks or chopsticks. Makes 10 to 12 appetizer servings.

PER SERVING: 58 calories, 9.2 g protein, 0.6 g carbohydrates, 1.9 g fat, 17 mg cholesterol, 186 mg sodium

PAPAYA & PORTUGUESE SAUSAGE SKEWERS

Hawaiian-style Portuguese sausage (linguisa) is hotter and spicier than most Mainland linguisa, but either kind complements papaya.

- 1 to 1¼ pounds linguisa sausage
- 1 large firm-ripe papaya, peeled, seeded, and cut into 1-inch chunks
  Lime wedges

Prick sausages all over with a fork. In a 10- to 12-inch frying pan, bring about 1 inch of water to boiling. Add sausages, cover, and simmer until they are hot throughout, 5 to 8 minutes. Lift out and let cool. Cut sausages into ½-inch-thick diagonal slices.

On a thin wooden skewer, impale a piece of sausage, a piece of papaya, and another piece of sausage; repeat for remaining skewers. (If made ahead, cover and chill up to overnight.) Grill 3 to 4 inches above a solid bed of hot coals (you can hold hand at grill level only 2 to 3 seconds) until meat is lightly browned on both sides, about 5 minutes. Serve with lime to squeeze over each serving. Makes 16 to 20 skewers, 10 to 12 appetizer servings.

PER SERVING: 91 calories, 5.2 g protein, 4.7 g carbohydrates, 5.9 g fat, 21 mg cholesterol, 117 mg sodium

GUAVA WINE COOLER

In a 3-quart pitcher or bowl, mix 2 cans (12 oz. each) cold canned **guava nectar** and 1 bottle (750 ml.) cold **white Zinfandel**. Just before serving, mix in 1 bottle (25 oz.) cold **sparkling water**. Add **ice** to cool. Makes 12 servings, 6-ounce size.

PER SERVING: 79 calories, 0.4 g protein, 9.9 g carbohydrates, 0.1 g fat, 0 mg cholesterol, 6.9 mg sodium

PINEAPPLE RUM PUNCH

In a blender, whirl until smooth 1 can (12 oz.) thawed **pineapple juice concentrate**, 1 can (12 oz.) thawed **frozen coconut milk** (optional), 1½ cups **light rum** or sparkling water, and ⅓ cup **lime juice**. Pour into a 3-quart pitcher and stir in 3 cups **sparkling water**. Add **ice** to cool. Makes 12 servings, 6-ounce size.

PER SERVING: 130 calories, 0.5 g protein, 16 g carbohydrates, 0 g fat, 0 mg cholesterol, 2.4 mg sodium

The Tomato Explosion

TAKE YOUR PICK. *It's tomato time again, and the harvest choices—from your garden or in the market—are stunningly varied. Big beefsteak types share space with cherry tomatoes as small as currants. Ripe tomatoes can be green (tomatillos), yellow-green, yellow, orange, or red—and round, oval, or shaped like tiny pears.*

Here, these four recipes make the most of this varied ensemble to create impact with both flavor and appearance.

You'll get the best flavor when you use vine-ripened fruit, but your best chance of getting vine-ripened fruit is to grow tomatoes yourself.

In second place is market fruit that's been properly handled. Tomatoes grow to maximum size, then ripen. If picked full-size and firm-green, the fruit matures well at 60° to 75° (the warmer the temperature, the quicker the ripening; loosely enclose tomatoes in a paper bag to speed the pro-cess). If immature full-size fruit is chilled to 55° or lower, ripening halts, and even though the tomato will change color and look ripe, the texture is not succulent, and the flavor incomplete.

When you buy tomatoes, ask how they've been stored and buy only fruit that hasn't been refrigerated; keep unripe fruit at room temperature. When fruit is fully ripe, chill to slow spoilage, and use within a day or two.

Golden tomato and orange slices create a simple, flavorful union. Unusual salad also features thin slices of red onion, diced golden bell pepper, salt-cured olives, and a garnish of fresh basil. Balsamic vinegar is drizzled over each salad just before serving.

Potpourri of tiny tomatoes—red, green, and gold—combines with lime and cilantro for a refreshing salad.

Firm, meaty but mild Roma-type tomatoes take well to salty prosciutto and sharp bite of anchovies; enjoy with toast.

Asian seasonings and a garnish of purple basil leaves give thick slices of ripe beefsteak-type tomatoes an exotic air.

GOLDEN GARDEN SALAD

    4 medium-size (about 1½ lb. total)
       ripe yellow tomatoes
    2 large (about 1½ lb. total) oranges
    1 medium-size yellow bell pepper,
       stemmed, seeded, and diced
    ½ small red onion, thinly sliced
    1 to 2 tablespoons minced fresh
       basil leaves
    ¼ cup balsamic or wine vinegar
       Basil sprigs
       Salt-cured olives (optional)
       Salt and freshly ground pepper

Rinse and core tomatoes; cut into thin slices, arranging equally on 6 salad plates or placing all on a platter.

With a sharp knife, cut off and discard peel and white membrane from oranges. Cut fruit crosswise into thin slices; beside tomatoes, equally arrange orange slices, diced bell pepper, and onion slices.

Sprinkle salads with minced basil and drizzle vinegar evenly over tomatoes and oranges. Garnish with basil sprigs and olives. Add salt and pepper to taste. Makes 6 servings.

PER SERVING: 64 calories, 1.6 g protein, 16 g carbohydrates, 0.4 g fat, 0 mg cholesterol, 8.8 mg sodium

MULTICOLORED SOUTHWEST TOMATO SALAD

    3 pounds (10 to 12 cups) ripe cherry
       tomatoes (red, yellow, yellow-
       green, orange); include some
       ½ inch or less in diameter
   10 medium-size tomatillos (about
       1-in. diameter), husks removed,
       rinsed, cored, and thinly sliced
    1 fresh jalapeño chili, stemmed,
       seeded, and minced

    ½ cup lightly packed fresh cilantro
       (coriander) leaves
    ¼ cup lime juice
       Lime wedges
       Salt and pepper

Stem cherry tomatoes; rinse and drain. For tomatoes larger than ¾-inch diameter, cut in half. Place tomatoes in a bowl with tomatillos, chili, cilantro, and lime juice. Mix gently. Accompany with lime wedges, and add salt and pepper to taste. Makes 8 to 10 servings.

PER SERVING: 26 calories, 1.2 g protein, 5.6 g carbohydrates, 0.3 g fat, 0 mg cholesterol, 8.8 mg sodium

ROMA TOMATOES & PROSCIUTTO SALAD

    3 tablespoons red wine vinegar
    1 clove garlic, minced or pressed
    1 tablespoon chopped parsley
    ½ cup extra-virgin olive oil
    2 ounces thinly sliced prosciutto or
       cooked ham, slivered
    ¾ pound Roma-type tomatoes,
       rinsed, cored, and diced
    ¼ cup thinly sliced green onions
    6 large butter lettuce leaves, washed
       and crisped
    1 can (2 oz.) anchovies rolled with
       capers, well drained
       Salt and freshly ground pepper

For dressing, mix vinegar, garlic, parsley, and all but 1 tablespoon oil; set aside.

Pour remaining oil into an 8- to 10-inch frying pan over medium-high heat. When hot, add prosciutto; stir often until crisp, 3 to 4 minutes. With a slotted spoon, transfer prosciutto to a bowl.

To the bowl, add tomatoes, onions, and dressing; mix gently. Line 6 salad plates with lettuce, then spoon salad equally onto leaves; garnish with anchovies. Add salt and pepper to taste. Serves 6.

PER SERVING: 208 calories, 4.5 g protein, 3.7 g carbohydrates, 21 g fat, 9.5 mg cholesterol, 470 mg sodium

SLICED BEEFSTEAK TOMATOES WITH GINGER-BASIL VINAIGRETTE

    ½ cup salad oil
    ¼ cup tarragon or white wine
       vinegar
    1 tablespoon lemon juice
    1 tablespoon *each* minced fresh
       ginger and minced fresh purple
       (or green) basil
    1 clove garlic, minced or pressed
    ½ teaspoon Chinese five spice
       (or ¼ teaspoon *each* anise seed,
       ground cinnamon, and ground
       cloves)
    ¼ teaspoon dry mustard
    4 large (about 2½ lb. total)
       beefsteak-type tomatoes
       Fresh purple (or green) basil
       sprigs
       Salt and pepper

Mix oil, vinegar, lemon juice, ginger, basil, garlic, five spice, and dry mustard. Let stand 10 to 15 minutes; if made ahead, cover and chill up to 3 days. Stir to use.

Rinse, core, and thickly slice tomatoes; put on a platter. Pour half the vinaigrette over the tomatoes; reserve balance to add to individual portions to taste. Garnish with basil sprigs. Season to taste with salt and pepper. Makes 6 to 8 servings.

PER SERVING: 152 calories, 1.4 g protein, 7.2 g carbohydrates, 14 g fat, 0 mg cholesterol, 12 mg sodium

Two-Tone Summer Soups

SPLASHING VIBRANT COLORS *and flavors side-by-side create these dramatic-looking, delectable, and simple fruit soups. Offer them for brunch or dessert, and stage the show at the table or gently carry the two-tone bowls in from the kitchen.*

You start with colorful fresh fruit purées from the blender or food processor. We suggest three combinations of six different fruits. Poured into bowls, mixtures hold their own territory; they don't bleed because they have similar consistencies—though as you eat they'll swirl prettily together, blending their tastes.

Try our pairings or your own preferences. You could also multiply combinations or experiment with different seasonal fruits.

GREEN & GOLD MELON SOUP

> **Honeydew melon soup (recipe follows)**
> **Cantaloupe soup (recipe follows)**
> **Sour cream (optional)**
> **Mint sprigs**

Pour honeydew and cantaloupe soups into separate small pitchers. With a pitcher in each hand, simultaneously and gently pour soups into a soup bowl (use 1½- to 2-cup size; wide bowls create the most dramatic effect). Allow 1 to 1⅓ cups soup total for each portion. Repeat to fill remaining bowls. Top each serving with a dollop of sour cream and a mint sprig. Makes 6 to 8 servings.

PER SERVING: 101 calories, 1.4 g protein, 26 g carbohydrates, 0.4 g fat, 0 mg cholesterol, 23 mg sodium

Honeydew melon soup. In a food processor or blender, smoothly purée 5 cups chopped **honeydew melon.** Add ⅓ cup **lime juice** (in blender, add juice while puréeing fruit) and 2 tablespoons **sugar.** Serve, or cover and chill up until next day. Just before serving, stir in 2 teaspoons minced **fresh mint leaves.** Makes 1 quart.

Cantaloupe soup. In a food processor or blender, smoothly purée 5 cups chopped **cantaloupe.** Add ⅓ cup **lemon juice** (in blender, add juice while puréeing fruit) and 2 tablespoons **sugar.** Serve, or cover and chill up until next day; stir before using. Makes 1 quart.

CACTUS PEAR & TREE PEAR SOUP

> **Red prickly pear or raspberry soup (recipe follows)**
> **Tree pear soup (recipe follows)**
> 6 to 8 star anise (optional)

Pour prickly pear and tree pear soups into separate small pitchers. With a pitcher in each hand, simultaneously and gently pour soups into a soup bowl (use 1½- to 2-cup size; wide bowls create the most dramatic effect), allowing 1 to 1⅓ cups soup total for each portion. Repeat to fill remaining bowls. Top each portion with 1 star anise. Makes 6 to 8 servings.

PER SERVING: 260 calories, 3.1 g protein, 64 g carbohydrates, 2 g fat, 0 mg cholesterol, 27 mg sodium

Red prickly pear or raspberry soup. If using **red prickly pear fruit** (also called cactus pears or tunas), you will need about 5 pounds despined fruit. Wear rubber gloves because of hidden needles. To clean the fruit, cut each piece in half lengthwise; use a small knife to pull outer layer (including peel) from fruit, which separates easily. Discard the outer layer. In a food processor, smoothly purée cactus pears or 4 cups rinsed and drained raspberries, then pour into a fine strainer over a bowl. Firmly rub pulp into bowl; discard seeds (or rub fruit through a food mill and discard seeds; don't use a blender, which will pulverize seeds).

To prickly pear purée, add ⅓ cup **lemon juice** and 2 tablespoons **sugar.** To raspberry purée, add 1 cup orange juice, ⅓ cup lemon juice, and ⅓ cup sugar. Serve, or cover and chill up until next day; stir purée before using. Makes about 5 cups.

Tree pear soup. Drain and save 1½ cups syrup from 2 cans (1 lb. each) **pears in extra-light syrup;** discard remaining syrup. In a 1- to 2-quart pan, combine syrup and 1 **star anise** or 1 teaspoon anise seed. On high heat, bring syrup to

a boil; cover and simmer very gently for flavors to blend, about 10 minutes; remove star anise. In a food processor or blender, smoothly purée pears, then add syrup (in blender, add syrup as fruit purées). Add ¼ cup **lemon juice** and 1 tablespoon **sugar.**

Serve, or cover and chill up until next day; stir before using. Makes 1 quart.

STRAWBERRY & PEACH SOUP

> **Strawberry soup (recipe follows)**
> **Peach soup (recipe follows)**
> **Black peppercorns**

Pour strawberry and peach soups into separate small pitchers. With a pitcher in each hand, simultaneously and gently pour soups into a soup bowl (use 1½- to 2-cup size; wide bowls create the most dramatic effect), allowing 1 to 1⅓ cups soup total for each portion. Repeat to fill remaining bowls. Sprinkle a few peppercorns onto each portion. Serves 6 to 8.

PER SERVING: 121 calories, 1.5 g protein, 30 g carbohydrates, 0.5 g fat, 0 mg cholesterol, 4.2 mg sodium

Strawberry soup. In a 1- to 2-quart pan, bring 1 cup **dry red wine,** such as Cabernet Sauvignon, and ½ teaspoon **black peppercorns** to a boil on high heat. Boil gently, uncovered, until wine is reduced to ½ cup; discard peppercorns.

In a food processor or blender, smoothly purée 6 cups rinsed, drained, and hulled **strawberries** (in blender, add wine to fruit). Pour wine, purée, and ¼ cup **sugar** into a fine strainer over a bowl. Rub purée into bowl; discard seeds. Serve, or cover and chill up until next day; stir before using. Makes about 3½ cups.

Peach soup. In food processor or blender, smoothly purée 1 quart peeled, chopped **peaches.** Add about ¾ cup **orange juice** to thin soup to same consistency as strawberry soup (in blender, add juice when puréeing), 3 tablespoons **lemon juice,** and 2 tablespoons **sugar.** Serve, or cover and chill up until next day; stir soup before using. Makes about 3½ cups.

Fresh fruits, each whirled to a smooth purée in blender or food processor, are the simple beginnings for these festive soups. Partners are pale pears with magenta-hued prickly pears, orange cantaloupe with green honeydew melon, and peaches with strawberries.

Quick & Cool Breakfast Salads

WHEN THE WEATHER SIZZLES, *depart from the traditional and start the morning with a refreshingly cool salad that won't weigh you down. If you wake up late, consider the salads as brunch or lunch.*

Try sweet cantaloupe filled with yogurt-dressed couscous, succulent pineapple and kiwi bathed in basil-perfumed lime juice, or crisp greens with juicy grapes and warm cheese. Accompany any of the salads with whole-wheat toast triangles, breadsticks, or crusty rolls.

COUSCOUS IN CANTALOUPE

- 1⅓ cups regular-strength chicken broth
- ¾ teaspoon ground coriander or curry powder
- ½ cup couscous
- 1 large (3½ to 4 lb.) cantaloupe
- 1 cup unflavored yogurt
- ⅓ cup chopped roasted peanuts
- ¼ cup golden raisins
- 2 tablespoons minced fresh mint
  Fresh mint sprigs (optional)
  Lemon wedges (optional)

In a 1½- to 2-quart pan, bring broth and coriander to a boil over high heat. Stir in couscous until evenly moistened. Cover pan and remove from heat; let stand until broth is absorbed, about 5 minutes. Remove lid and let cool.

Meanwhile, cut cantaloupe lengthwise into quarters; scoop out and discard seeds.

Mix cooled couscous with yogurt, peanuts, raisins, and minced mint. Spoon equal portions of couscous into cavity of each cantaloupe wedge. Garnish with mint sprigs and lemon. Makes 4 servings.

PER SERVING: 300 calories, 12 g protein, 50 g carbohydrates, 7.9 g fat, 3.4 mg cholesterol, 80 mg sodium

For a fast, refreshing breakfast, team pineapple, kiwi fruit, Canadian bacon, and basil-lime-honey dressing. Buy peeled and cored fresh pineapple to speed preparation time.

PINEAPPLE-HAM PLATE WITH BASIL HONEY

- 1 tablespoon salad oil
- 6 ounces thinly sliced Canadian bacon
- ¼ cup lime juice
- 2 tablespoons honey
- 1 tablespoon minced fresh basil or 1½ teaspoons dry basil leaves
- 1 peeled and cored pineapple (about 2½ lb.)
- 2 medium-size (½ lb. total) kiwi fruit
  Fresh basil sprigs (optional)

In a 10- to 12-inch frying pan, combine oil and bacon. Cook over medium-high heat, turning once, until lightly browned, 3 to 4 minutes total.

Meanwhile, mix the lime juice, honey, and minced basil. Cut the pineapple crosswise into about ⅓-inch-thick slices. Peel kiwi fruit and cut crosswise into ¼-inch-thick slices. Lay equal portions of the pineapple, kiwi, and bacon on 4 dinner plates. Spoon lime juice mixture over fruit and meat. Garnish with basil sprigs. Makes 4 servings.

PER SERVING: 303 calories, 11 g protein, 53 g carbohydrates, 7.8 g fat, 21 mg cholesterol, 608 mg sodium

BROILED CHEESE & FRUIT PLATE

- 3 tablespoons salad oil
- 2 tablespoons raspberry vinegar or red wine vinegar
- 2 teaspoons honey
- 1 cup seedless grapes, rinsed
- 1 medium-size Asian pear or Bartlett pear, quartered, cored, and thinly sliced
- 1 piece (4 oz.) firm-ripe brie cheese, cut into 2 equal-size pieces
- 4 cups (4 oz.) bite-size pieces butter lettuce, rinsed and crisped

In a large bowl, mix oil, vinegar, and honey. Add grapes and pear; stir to coat.

Place cheese pieces slightly apart in an 8- or 9-inch pie pan. Brush cheese with about 1 tablespoon of the dressing from the fruit mixture. Broil about 4 inches from heat until cheese is warm and begins to melt around edges, 1 to 2 minutes.

Add lettuce to fruit; mix and place salad on 2 dinner plates. With a wide spatula, transfer a piece of hot cheese onto each salad. Makes 2 servings.

PER SERVING: 479 calories, 13 g protein, 28 g carbohydrates, 37 g fat, 57 mg cholesterol, 361 mg sodium

Steaming Fish in the Microwave

THIN PIECES OF FISH *steam to moist succulence in just minutes in a microwave. Heat penetrates their slim profiles quickly and evenly.*

For light, lean, and flavorful results, complement the fish with bright seasonings: orange, ginger, and cilantro with seabass; fresh salsa with trout; lemon and capers with sole.

Each of these recipes cooks in about 2 minutes and serves 1 or 2 people. For more servings duplicate recipe, cooking each dish separately.

MICROWAVE-STEAMED BASS WITH GINGER

½	pound white seabass fillets (1 to 1½ in. thick)
1	tablespoon orange juice
2	teaspoons soy sauce
1	teaspoon fine shreds fresh ginger
½	teaspoon fine shreds orange peel
	Fresh cilantro (coriander) sprigs
	Orange wedges

Cut fillets crosswise into 1-inch-wide strips. To butterfly fish, cut down the center length of each strip almost all the way through, then open out flat.

Set butterflied fish pieces on a 9- to 10-inch nonmetal plate and drizzle evenly with orange juice and soy. Sprinkle ginger and orange peel evenly over fish. Cover with plastic wrap.

Place dish in a microwave oven and cook at full power (100 percent) until fish is slightly translucent but still moist in thickest part (cut to test), 2 to 3 minutes. Garnish with cilantro and squeeze orange over fish to taste. Serves 1 or 2.

PER SERVING: 118 calories, 21 g protein, 1.6 g carbohydrates, 2.3 g fat, 47 mg cholesterol, 421 mg sodium

MICROWAVE-STEAMED TROUT WITH SALSA

1	cleaned whole boneless trout (8 oz.), head removed
1	small firm-ripe tomato, cored and diced
1	tomatillo (1-in. diameter), husk removed, cored, and diced
1	green onion, ends trimmed, thinly sliced
½	to 1 teaspoon minced fresh hot chili
	Salt and pepper
	Lime wedges

Shreds of orange peel and fresh ginger season thin, butterflied fillets of seabass; two pieces cook in about 2 minutes. Garnish fish with cilantro sprigs and orange wedges.

Rinse trout and pat dry. Lay fish open, skin down, on a 9- to 10-inch nonmetal dinner plate. Cover with plastic wrap and cook in a microwave oven at full power (100 percent) until fish is slightly translucent but still moist in thickest part (cut to test), 1½ to 2½ minutes.

Meanwhile, mix the tomato, tomatillo, and onion; stir in chili to taste. Mound mixture over cooked fish. Add salt, pepper, and lime to taste. Makes 1 serving.

PER SERVING: 213 calories, 26 g protein, 8.9 g carbohydrates, 8.1 g fat, 66 mg cholesterol, 68 mg sodium

MICROWAVE-STEAMED SOLE WITH CAPERS

½	pound sole fillets
1	teaspoon lemon juice
1	tablespoon thinly sliced chives
½	teaspoon finely shredded lemon peel
½	teaspoon drained capers
⅛	teaspoon crushed dried hot red chilies
	Lemon wedges
	Salt and pepper

Rinse fish and pat dry. On a 9- to 10-inch nonmetal plate, place fish in a single layer, overlapping thin edges. Drizzle with lemon juice and sprinkle with chives, lemon peel, capers, and chilies. Cover with plastic wrap and cook in a microwave oven at full power (100 percent) until fish is slightly translucent but still moist in thickest part (cut to test), 1½ to 2 minutes. Season with lemon, salt, and pepper to taste. Serves 1 or 2.

PER SERVING: 105 calories, 21 g protein, 0.3 g carbohydrates, 1.4 g fat, 55 mg cholesterol, 111 mg sodium

Feasting on Corn

READY TO PLUCK *from your garden or priced to move at the supermarket, corn is at its sun-ripened best this month. Make it the focus of a simple feast.*

Seasoned butters flavor the corn, as well as bread and grilled lamb chops. For a light alternative to the butters, rub lime wedges on corn or squeeze onto lamb, followed by a sprinkle of salt and a touch of chilies.

When you husk corn in the somewhat untypical fashion we picture below, the ears look something like golden comets.

Provide plenty of damp hand towels, paper napkins, or disposable hand wipes.

CORN COMET SUPPER

Corn Comets   Cherry Tomatoes
Grilled Lamb Rib Chops
Seasoned Butters
Sourdough Bread
Basket of Frozen Fruit Ices on Sticks
Watermelon Chunks

Choose at least 3 butters; all can be made ahead. For each serving, allow ½ to ¾ cup cherry tomatoes (about ¼ lb.), 2 or 3 small lamb rib chops cut ½ to ¾ inch thick (about ½ lb. per person), 2 or 3 slices bread, a fruit ice on a stick, and 1 or 2 chunks of melon.

About 45 minutes before serving, ignite charcoal briquets for the lamb and bring water to boiling for the corn. The corn can cook and hold in hot water while chops grill, or they can cook simultaneously.

CORN COMETS

16 **to 20 medium-size ears of corn**
   Lime wedges
   Salt and pepper
   Paprika
   Crushed dried hot red chilies
   Seasoned butters (suggestions follow)

Pull off and discard coarse outer layer of corn husks, then gently peel back the thinner inside husks but do not detach from cob. Pull off and discard corn silk and rinse corn under cool running water. You can husk corn as much as 4 hours ahead (however, if corn is just harvested, you may not want to wait to cook it); cover corn with cool damp towels.

In a covered 10- to 12-quart kettle, bring 4 quarts water to a boil over high heat. Insert corn, tips down and husks up, into the pan, supporting ears vertically with each other. Cook until corn is hot and kernels look slightly darker yellow, about 10 minutes (husks will stick out of pan). Serve, or remove kettle with corn from heat and let corn stand in water to keep hot up to 20 minutes.

Lift ears by their husks from water, drain briefly, and arrange, husks up, in a bowl. To eat, rub corn with lime wedges and sprinkle with salt and pepper, paprika or chilies, or a combination of these. Or spread with seasoned butters. Makes 8 to 10 servings, 2 ears each; or 5 to 7 servings, 2 or 3 ears each.

PER 5-INCH EAR, UNBUTTERED: 77 calories, 2.7 g protein, 17 g carbohydrates, 1 g fat, 0 mg cholesterol, 14 mg sodium

SEASONED BUTTERS

Make flavored butters from basic recipe; spread them on corn, lamb, and bread.

Basic butter. Combine **butter** or margarine, at room temperature, and **seasonings** (suggestions follow) in a food processor with a metal blade or in a bowl. Process, pushing mixture from container sides with a rubber spatula, or mix with a fork until well blended. Serve each butter in a small dish at room temperature. If made ahead, let stand in a cool place up to 4 hours, or cover and chill up to 3 days, then bring to room temperature.

Pesto butter. Combine ½ cup (¼ lb.) **butter** or margarine, ½ cup lightly packed, finely chopped **fresh basil leaves** (or 1½ tablespoons dry basil), and ¼ cup grated **parmesan cheese,** following directions for basic butter, preceding. Makes about ½ cup. —*Sandy Kelso, Lebanon, Ore.*

PER TABLESPOON: 115 calories, 1.3 g protein, 0.6 g carbohydrates, 12 g fat, 33 mg cholesterol, 164 mg sodium

Horseradish butter. Combine ½ cup (¼ lb.) **butter** or margarine, 1 teaspoon **prepared horseradish,** and 1 tablespoon **Dijon mustard,** following directions for basic butter, preceding. Makes about ½ cup. —*Lamar Parker, Tempe, Ariz.*

PER TABLESPOON: 104 calories, 0.1 g protein, 0.3 g carbohydrates, 12 g fat, 31 mg cholesterol, 173 mg sodium

Olive cream butter. Instead of butter, combine 2 small packages (3 oz. *each*) **cream cheese,** 1 small can (4½ oz.) drained **chopped black ripe olives,** and 1 small jar (2 oz.) drained **diced pimientos,** following directions for basic butter, preceding. Makes about 1¼ cups.

PER TABLESPOON: 42 calories, 0.7 g protein, 4.3 g carbohydrates, 4.3 g fat, 9.4 mg cholesterol, 74 mg sodium

Bacon-and-egg butter. In a 6- to 7-inch frying pan over medium heat, cook 4 slices **bacon** until crisp; drain on paper towels. Combine ½ cup (¼ lb.) **butter** or margarine, bacon (if mixing by hand, crumble bacon first), and 2 hard-cooked **large eggs** (if mixing by hand, rub eggs through a fine wire strainer), following directions for basic butter, preceding. Makes about ½ cup.

PER TABLESPOON: 140 calories, 2.6 g protein, 0.2 g carbohydrates, 14 g fat, 102 mg cholesterol, 184 mg sodium

Make corn on the cob the heart of a summer feast; serve with grilled lamb chops, and a selection of seasoned butters to complement both.

Shortcut Chutneys

Traditionally cooked long *and slowly, chutneys are sweet-tart preserves of fruit and vegetables flavored with exotic spices. Here, we short-cut the concept, using fresh fruits and vegetables, and quickly cooking them with complex seasonings. Serve these light condiments in generous portions with meats, poultry, or fish from the barbecue.*

Eggplant & Apricot Chutney

> 1 small globe eggplant (about ¾ lb., or ¾ lb. Asian eggplant)
> 3 medium-size ripe apricots
> 2 tablespoons olive oil or salad oil
> 2 cloves garlic, minced or pressed
> 1 teaspoon curry powder
> ¼ to ½ teaspoon crushed dried hot red chilies
> 1 cup regular-strength chicken broth
> ¼ cup firmly packed brown sugar

Remove stem of eggplant and discard; cut eggplant into ½-inch cubes. Halve and pit apricots; cut fruit in ½-inch pieces.

In a 10- to 12-inch frying pan over medium-high heat, cook eggplant in oil until lightly browned, 4 to 8 minutes; turn with a spatula as needed. Add garlic, curry, and chilies, and cook 1 to 2 minutes longer.

Add ⅓ cup broth; cover pan and simmer 2 to 3 minutes. Add another ⅓ cup broth, stir, then cover pan and cook until eggplant is very soft when pressed. Remove lid, add remaining broth and sugar, and boil until liquid is almost gone.

Stir in apricots and serve warm or at room temperature. If made ahead, cover and chill up to overnight. Makes about 3 cups.

Per ¼ Cup: 54 calories, 0.7 g protein, 8 g carbohydrates, 2.5 g fat, 0 mg cholesterol, 7.2 mg sodium

Spiced Fresh Peach Chutney

> 2 medium-size (about ¾ lb.) firm-ripe peaches
> 1 cup seedless grapes
> 2 tablespoons honey
> 2 teaspoons Dijon mustard
> 1 tablespoon salad oil
> 1 small onion, chopped
> ¼ cup raisins
> 1 tablespoon mustard seed
> ½ teaspoon ground allspice

Peel and pit peaches; cut into ½-inch pieces and mix with grapes, honey, and mustard; set aside.

In a 10- to 12-inch frying pan on medium-high heat, combine oil, onion, raisins, mustard seed, and allspice. Cook, stirring often, until onion is golden and raisins are plump, 5 to 8 minutes. Mix gently with fruit. Serve warm or at room temperature. If made ahead, cover and chill up to overnight. Makes about 2 cups.

Per ¼ Cup: 83 calories, 0.9 g protein, 16 g carbohydrates, 2.4 g fat, 0 mg cholesterol, 39 mg sodium

Pineapple, Ginger & Orange Chutney

> 2 medium-size (about 1 lb.) oranges
> ⅓ cup minced fresh ginger
> ⅓ cup sugar
> 1½ cups ½-inch chunks pineapple
> ¾ cup seeded and chopped thin-skinned European cucumber

With a vegetable peeler, pare only orange part of peel from oranges. Cut peel into long, very thin slivers.

Cut off and discard remaining peel and white membrane from each orange. Holding fruit over a bowl, cut parallel to membrane to release segments. Squeeze juice into bowl; discard membrane.

In a 1½- to 2-quart pan, combine orange peel and ginger. Add 2 cups water and bring to a boil, uncovered, over high heat; drain. Add 2 cups more water and repeat.

To the peel and ginger, add orange juice drained from fruit, 1 cup water, and sugar. Bring to a boil on high heat and cook uncovered, stirring occasionally, until liquid has almost cooked away, about 10 minutes; watch carefully near the end to avoid scorching.

Meanwhile, add pineapple and cucumber to orange segments.

When boiling syrup is reduced (fruit peel should look translucent, though bubbles may make it hard to see), stir in 2 tablespoons water to thin the mixture, then pour over fruit in bowl. Mix gently. Serve warm or at room temperature. If made ahead, cover and chill up to overnight. Makes about 3 cups.

Per ¼ Cup: 45 calories, 0.3 g protein, 11 g carbohydrates, 0.1 g fat, 0 mg cholesterol, 0.7 mg sodium

Spoon ginger-flavored chutney of orange and pineapple chunks onto grilled steak.

From Old Finland: The Queen's Cake

A SWEET BERRY-FILLED DESSERT, referred to as the Queen's cake, comes to us from an area of eastern Finland known historically as Karelia. Since World War II, most of this vast region has been a part of the Soviet Union. The Finns, however, have held fast to Karelian ways and cooking.

A rich, rather dense dough made with two types of flour—all-purpose and potato—encases a berry filling. Potato flour is available among the specialty foods in most supermarkets; or use cornstarch.

This dessert comes from Kati Kaapro of the Majurska Café in the old town and fortress in Lappeenranta, Finland.

THE QUEEN'S CAKE

½ cup (¼ lb.) butter or margarine, at room temperature
½ cup granulated sugar
1 teaspoon vanilla
2 large eggs
1 teaspoon grated lemon peel
2 cups all-purpose flour
½ cup potato flour or cornstarch
1 teaspoon *each* baking powder and baking soda
   Fresh berry filling (recipe follows)
1 tablespoon powdered sugar

In a large bowl, beat butter and sugar with an electric mixer until smooth and fluffy. Beat in vanilla, eggs, and lemon peel until well blended. In a small bowl, combine all-purpose and potato flours, baking powder, and baking soda; add to the butter mixture and stir to mix thoroughly.

Press ⅔ of dough evenly into a well-buttered and floured 8-inch-diameter cake pan with a removable bottom. Top evenly with berry filling.

To make the decorative topping, roll remaining dough, a section at a time, into ½-inch-diameter ropes. Make first rope 8 inches long and lay across center of cake. Make 2 slightly shorter ropes and place them equidistant from each other on 1 side of center rope. Repeat with 2 more dough strips on other side of center rope. Reroll scraps as needed. Place 5 ropes at right angles to the first set. Press dough ends against pan rim.

Bake the cake on the bottom rack in a 350° oven until dough is richly browned, 40 to 45 minutes. Let cool in pan on a rack for 30 minutes, then run a knife between cake and pan side; remove pan rim. Slide a spatula between cake and pan bottom to release, but leave in place. Set cake on a platter and sprinkle the top with powdered sugar. Serve in wedges either warm or at room temperature. Makes 8 or 9 servings.

PER SERVING: 319 calories, 4.6 g protein, 49 g carbohydrates, 12 g fat, 88 mg cholesterol, 260 mg sodium

Fresh berry filling. Rinse ⅔ cup *each* (2 cups total) **blackberries, blueberries,** and **raspberries,** or all of 1 kind; drain well. Mix 3 tablespoons **sugar** with 1 tablespoon **quick-cooking tapioca;** add to berries along with 2 teaspoons **lemon juice;** stir gently to mix well.

Beneath its golden lattice of buttery cake, a sweet-tart filling of plump blueberries, blackberries, and raspberries peeks through. Powdered sugar is sprinkled over just before serving. Berry-filled cake comes from eastern Finland.

Coffee Coolers

O N A HOT AFTERNOON, *try a cooler of good, frosty-cold coffee in an icy glass. Flavor with liqueur, frozen banana, frozen milk, or ice cream.*

Vary the intensity of the double-strength coffee by the amount of water you use.

COFFEE FLOAT

> Double-strength coffee
> (recipe follows)
> 1½ cups ice cubes
> ¼ cup coffee-flavor liqueur
> (optional)
> 2 or 3 scoops vanilla ice cream
> (1 to 1½ cups total)

Pour the hot double-strength coffee over ice in a pitcher. When ice is almost melted, add liqueur, if desired. Pour into 2 or 3 tall glasses, filling to within 1½ inches of top. Add a scoop of ice cream to each glass. Makes 2 or 3 servings.

PER SERVING: 94 calories, 1.8 g protein, 11 g carbohydrates, 4.8 g fat, 20 mg cholesterol, 43 mg sodium

Double-strength coffee. Measure ½ cup finely ground regular or decaffeinated **espresso** or other dark **roast coffee** into a cone lined with a paper coffee filter. Pour 1½ to 2 cups hot **water** (190° to 195°) through filter into a glass measure.

Or put grounds in filter-plunger pot, add water, let stand 2 to 3 minutes, then push plunger. Makes 1⅛ to 1⅔ cups.

COFFEE BANANA RUM SLUSH

> 2 small ripe bananas (10 oz. total)
> Double-strength coffee (see coffee float recipe, preceding; use ½ of the amounts given)
> 1 cup milk
> 2 to 3 tablespoons firmly packed brown sugar
> 2 to 5 tablespoons rum (optional)
> Ground cinnamon

Peel bananas and cut into about ½-inch slices. Place slices slightly apart in an 8- to 9-inch cake pan. Cover and freeze until banana is frozen, at least 2 hours or up to 1 week. Cover and chill coffee until cold, at least 30 minutes.

In a blender or food processor, combine banana, coffee, and milk. Whirl until puréed; add sugar and rum to taste. Pour into chilled glasses and sprinkle with cinnamon. Makes 2 or 3 servings.

PER SERVING: 142 calories, 3.4 g protein, 27 g carbohydrates, 3 g fat, 11 mg cholesterol, 45 mg sodium

FROZEN CAPPUCCINO

> 1 cup milk
> Cold double-strength coffee (see coffee float recipe, preceding)
> Sugar
> Unsweetened cocoa (optional)
> Ground cinnamon (optional)

Pour milk into ice-cube tray and freeze until solid, at least 4 hours or up to 1 week (cover when solid).

In a blender or food processor, combine cold coffee and frozen milk cubes; whirl until smoothly blended. Pour into chilled glasses. Add sugar to taste. Sprinkle with cocoa and cinnamon, if desired. Makes 2 or 3 servings.

PER SERVING: 54 calories, 2.9 g protein, 4.6 g carbohydrates, 2.7 g fat, 11 mg cholesterol, 44 mg sodium

MOCHA FRAPPÉ

> Double-strength coffee (see coffee float recipe, preceding)
> 1⅓ cups ice cubes
> 2 cups chocolate ice cream
> Chocolate-covered coffee beans or crushed coffee beans (optional)

Pour hot coffee over ice cubes and let stand until coffee is cold and most of the ice has melted. If made ahead, cover and chill until the next day.

In a blender or food processor, combine coffee and ice cream; whirl until smoothly blended. Pour into chilled glasses. Garnish each glass with the coffee beans, if desired. Makes 3 servings.

PER SERVING: 183 calories, 3.4 g protein, 22 g carbohydrates, 9.6 g fat, 40 mg cholesterol, 81 mg sodium

Whirled in a blender to a frothy float, double-strength coffee and frozen milk combine in refreshing Frozen Cappuccino. Add sugar, cocoa, and cinnamon to taste.

Dried tomatoes and olives flavor egg-and-bread breakfast casserole.

TOMATO OLIVE STRATA

About 8 slices firm white bread
2 **cups (½ lb.) shredded jack cheese**
¼ **cup drained dried tomatoes packed in oil, minced**
1 **small can (2¼ oz.) sliced ripe olives, drained**
5 **large eggs**
2½ **cups milk**
½ **teaspoon pepper**

Butter a 7½- to 8- by 11-inch baking dish. Line the bottom with a layer of bread, cut to fit. Make another layer of bread to fit on top, then lift out top layer and set aside.

Sprinkle half the cheese over the bread in dish. Scatter tomatoes and olives on top of cheese. Cover with reserved bread and sprinkle with remaining cheese.

Beat eggs to blend with milk. Pour over cheese, moistening entire surface, then sprinkle with pepper. Cover with plastic wrap; chill at least 4 hours or until next day. Bake, uncovered, in a 350° oven until edges of strata are lightly browned and center is firm when gently touched, about 50 minutes. Cool 10 minutes, then cut strata into squares. Makes 4 to 6 servings. —*Jeanne Cissna, Eureka, Calif.*

PER SERVING: 423 calories, 21 g protein, 26 g carbohydrates, 26 g fat, 277 mg cholesterol, 797 mg sodium

---

A refreshing shrimp salad spills over tomatoes and watercress.

SHRIMP & CUCUMBER TOMATO SALAD

1 **small (about 8 oz.) cucumber**
1 **pound shelled cooked tiny shrimp**
½ **cup thinly sliced green onion, including some of the tops**
2 **tablespoons minced fresh cilantro (coriander)**
½ **cup reduced-calorie or regular mayonnaise**
About 2 cups washed and crisped watercress
4 **medium-size firm-ripe tomatoes, cored and cut into quarters**
1 **lemon, cut into 8 wedges**
Salt and pepper

Cut peel from cucumber and discard. Cut cucumber in half lengthwise. Scoop out and discard seeds. Finely dice the cucumber and mix with shrimp, green onion, and cilantro. If made ahead, cover and chill up to 2 hours.

Mix cucumber salad with mayonnaise just before serving. Arrange a bed of watercress with tomato quarters and lemon wedges on 4 salad plates. Spoon salad mixture equally onto the watercress and tomatoes. Add salt and pepper to taste. Makes 4 servings. —*Betty Cornelison, Portland.*

PER SERVING: 233 calories, 26 g protein, 13 g carbohydrates, 9.7 g fat, 231 mg cholesterol, 498 mg sodium

---

Cook broccoli with rice; season with chili powder, raisins, nuts.

BROCCOLI WITH PINE NUTS & RICE

⅓ **cup pine nuts or slivered almonds**
1 **tablespoon olive or salad oil**
½ **cup long-grain white rice**
¼ **cup golden raisins**
1½ **teaspoons chili powder**
2 **cups regular-strength chicken broth**
About 1¼ pounds broccoli

In a 10- to 12-inch pan over medium-high heat, stir pine nuts until lightly toasted, about 4 minutes; set nuts aside.

To pan, add oil, rice, raisins, and chili powder. Stir until rice is opaque, about 3 minutes. Add broth, mix, and bring to a boil; then cover and simmer until rice is barely tender to bite, about 15 minutes.

Meanwhile, cut flowerets off broccoli and reserve. Trim and discard tough ends of stalks; thinly slice tender sections of stalks and reserve.

After the rice has cooked 15 minutes, drop broccoli on top of rice. Cover pan and cook until broccoli is just tender to bite, about 10 minutes more. Gently stir together broccoli and rice mixture; pour onto a platter and sprinkle with pine nuts. Makes 4 servings. —*Jane Cross, Albuquerque.*

PER SERVING: 256 calories, 9.7 g protein, 35 g carbohydrates, 11 g fat, 0 mg cholesterol, 73 mg sodium

FILIPINO EGGPLANT FRITTATA

- 1 tablespoon sesame seed
- 2 teaspoons minced fresh ginger
- 2 tablespoons *each* soy sauce, vinegar, and dry white wine
- ½ teaspoon cornstarch
- 1 pound Asian eggplants
- 2 tablespoons salad oil
- 3 large eggs, beaten to blend

In a 10- to 11-inch nonstick frying pan over medium heat, toast sesame seed, about 5 minutes; stir often. Pour out seeds and save. Mix ginger, soy, vinegar, wine, and cornstarch; set aside.

Thinly slice eggplants crosswise; discard stems. Add oil and eggplant to frying pan. Stir often over medium heat until eggplant is very soft when pressed, about 25 minutes. Pour eggs over eggplant; cover and cook until eggs are set, about 4 minutes.

Lay a rimless 12- by 15-inch baking sheet over pan; holding together, invert frittata onto sheet. Slide frittata back into frying pan. Cook, uncovered, until lightly brown on bottom, about 1 minute. Slide frittata onto a plate.

Add ginger mixture to pan; stir until boiling, then pour over frittata. Sprinkle with sesame seed. Serves 2. — *Sonia Ottusch, Malibu, Calif.*

PER SERVING: 339 calories, 13 g protein, 19 g carbohydrates, 24 g fat, 411 mg cholesterol, 1,143 mg sodium

Small rounds of eggplant form base of frittata; top with ginger sauce.

BEEF & CUCUMBER STIR FRY

- ¾ pound boneless lean beef, such as top sirloin
- 2 tablespoons dry sherry
- 1 tablespoon soy sauce
- 3 cloves garlic, minced or pressed
- 1 large (about 12 oz.) cucumber
- 3 tablespoons salad oil
- 1 can (15 oz.) baby corn, drained, or 16 fresh baby corn ears, husked
- 2 green onions, ends trimmed, thinly sliced

Thinly slice meat across the grain. In a bowl, mix sherry, soy sauce, and garlic; stir in meat and set aside.

Peel cucumber; cut in half lengthwise. Discard seeds; cut each half in thirds, then into thick sticks.

Place a wok or 12-inch frying pan on high heat. When hot, add 1 tablespoon oil and half the meat mixture. Stir-fry until meat is slightly tinged with brown. Pour meat into a bowl; repeat to cook remaining meat.

Add the last tablespoon of oil to pan; when hot, add cucumber and corn. Stir-fry until vegetables are hot, about 4 minutes. Add meat, any juices, and onions; stir until hot, 1 to 2 minutes. Makes 4 servings. — *Regina Albright, Las Vegas.*

PER SERVING: 252 calories, 22 g protein, 8.7 g carbohydrates, 14 g fat, 49 mg cholesterol, 314 mg sodium

Stir-fry lean beef with baby corn, onion, cucumber, and garlic.

TORTILLA TURTLES

- 6 large (10-in.-diameter) flour tortillas
  Salad oil
- ½ cup sugar
- 1½ teaspoons ground cinnamon
  About ½ pound caramels (about 1 cup), unwrapped
- 1 package (6 oz.) or 1 cup semisweet chocolate baking chips
- ⅓ cup whipping cream

Cut tortillas into quarters. Pour ¼ inch oil into a 10- to 12-inch frying pan on high heat. When oil is hot, cook tortilla pieces, a few at a time without crowding, until crisp and lightly browned; turn to cook evenly. Drain on paper towels.

In a large paper or plastic bag, mix together sugar and cinnamon. Add 3 or 4 tortilla pieces at a time and gently rotate bag to coat. Mound tortillas on a wide platter.

In a 1- to 2-quart pan, combine caramels, chocolate, and cream. Stir often over medium-low heat until mixture melts smoothly. Drizzle about ½ the sauce over tortillas; pour extra sauce in a bowl for adding to taste. Eat warm. Serves 8 to 10. — *Barbara Keenan, Fort Morgan, Colo.*

PER PIECE WITH SAUCE: 148 calories, 1.5 g protein, 22 g carbohydrates, 6.8 g fat, 3.8 mg cholesterol, 75 mg sodium

Drizzle caramel-chocolate sauce over sweet tortillas.

WHY IS BREAKFAST *like the weather? The answer is, of course, that everybody talks about it but nobody (well, almost nobody) does anything about it. The difference is that something can be done about breakfast, as Art Hornik so artfully proposes with his Breakfast Scramble.*

The basic concept is the Bauernfrühstück, the German farmers' breakfast, which scrambles eggs with potatoes and (when it's available) left-over meat, usually ham or bacon. Hornik adds to this foundation a colorful blend of green onion and red bell pepper, then enlivens the flavor with liquid hot pepper seasoning, dill weed, and lemon pepper. The result is an omelet exciting enough to arouse your early-morning appetite and sturdy enough to carry you through to a late lunch.

ART HORNIK'S BREAKFAST SCRAMBLE

     2 tablespoons butter or margarine
  1½ cups diced cooked red thin-
        skinned potatoes
     ½ to 1 cup finely diced cooked
        chicken, beef, ham, or sausage
     2 tablespoons thinly sliced green
        onion, including tops
     ¼ cup diced red bell pepper
     6 large eggs
     2 tablespoons water
     ⅛ teaspoon liquid hot pepper
        seasoning
     ¼ teaspoon lemon pepper or pepper
     ¼ teaspoon dry dill weed
        Salt
        Sour cream

Melt butter in a 10- to 12-inch frying pan over medium-high heat; add potatoes. Turn occasionally with a spatula until lightly browned, about 5 minutes. Reduce heat to medium-low and scatter chicken, onion, and bell pepper over potatoes; let cook about 1 minute.

Meanwhile, beat eggs to blend with water, hot pepper seasoning, lemon pepper, and dill weed. Pour egg mixture

"The basic concept is the German farmers' breakfast, which scrambles eggs with potatoes and left-over meat."

over potatoes. When edges begin to set, lift with spatula to let uncooked egg flow underneath; repeat until eggs are set as you like. Spoon mixture onto plates; season to taste with salt and sour cream. Serves 4.

PER SERVING: 251 calories, 15 g protein, 12 g carbohydrates, 16 g fat, 442 mg cholesterol, 235 mg sodium

Arthur Hornik

Fresno, Calif.

SOME CHEFS FREELY ADMIT *that they are the best cooks since the days of Escoffier. Others are "born to blush unseen and waste their sweetness on the desert air," as Thomas Gray wrote of the rose. Fortunately, some of the latter have loyal offspring who see to it that their creations come to the attention of Chefs of the West. One such is Pat Naughten, who sends in her father's recipe for Dr. Bob's Pasta. Of the scores of ways to blend seafood with pasta, Dr. Robert Naughten's scallop and pine nut sauce is remarkable for its simplicity and elegance.*

DR. BOB'S PASTA

     ¼ cup pine nuts
     ¼ cup olive oil
     3 cloves garlic, minced or pressed
     1 pound scallops, rinsed, drained,
        and thinly sliced
     ½ cup regular-strength chicken broth
     ½ cup madeira
     ¼ cup minced parsley
     8 ounces dry pasta such as capellini
        (angel hair), vermicelli, or
        fettuccine
        Salt and pepper
        About ¾ cup freshly grated
        parmesan cheese

In a covered 5- to 6-quart pan, bring 3 quarts water to boiling over high heat.

Meanwhile, in a 10- to 12-inch frying pan over medium heat, stir nuts just until lightly browned, about 4 minutes; pour out and set aside. Add oil to pan; when hot, add garlic and scallops and stir just until scallops are opaque, about 2 minutes. Lift out scallops with a slotted spoon and set aside.

Turn heat to high; add broth and madeira to pan. Boil until juices are reduced by ⅓, then add scallops and parsley and mix gently until hot; keep warm.

When water boils, add pasta and boil, uncovered, until just tender to bite, 3 to 6 minutes; drain well. Pour pasta into a wide serving bowl; pour scallop mixture onto pasta and sprinkle with nuts. Lift with 2 forks to mix, seasoning to taste with salt, pepper, and ¼ cup of the cheese; offer remaining cheese to add to individual portions. Makes 4 or 5 servings.

PER SERVING: 465 calories, 20 g protein, 42 g carbohydrates, 20 g fat, 42 mg cholesterol, 429 mg sodium

Robert N. Naylor

Los Gatos, Calif.

THE COOKS OF INDIA *use yogurt (often with cucumbers) to soothe palates inflamed by the heat of curries. Combining the vexation and the remedy, S.M. Estvanik blends yogurt with curry spices and citrus juices to make Hyderabadi Spareribs. The flavors don't cancel each other out but collaborate to make a complex and delicious marinade. Honey added to the last bastings helps develop a rich color.*

HYDERABADI SPARERIBS

- 1 cup unflavored yogurt
- 1 teaspoon *each* grated orange peel and lemon peel
- ¼ cup orange juice
- 2 tablespoons lemon juice
- 1 tablespoon crushed dried hot red chilies
- ½ teaspoon *each* chili powder and ground cumin
- 3 cloves garlic
- ¼ cup packed parsley
- ¼ cup catsup
  About 4 pounds pork spareribs, trimmed of excess fat
- 2 tablespoons honey

"The cooks of India use yogurt to soothe palates inflamed by curries."

In a blender or food processor, combine yogurt, orange peel, lemon peel, orange juice, lemon juice, crushed chilies, chili powder, cumin, garlic, parsley, and catsup. Whirl until smoothly puréed.

Place ribs in a large, heavy plastic bag; pour in yogurt mixture, then seal bag and rotate to coat meat with marinade. Set bag in a pan and chill 3 hours or until next day, turning bag over occasionally.

In a barbecue with a lid, ignite 50 charcoal briquets on firegrate. When briquets are lightly covered with gray ash, about 30 minutes, push half the coals to each side of the grate; add 5 briquets to each side. Place a metal drip pan or foil in the center of the grate and set cooking grill 4 to 6 inches above coals. Lift meat from marinade and drain briefly.

Place ribs, meatiest side up, on grill directly above drip pan. Cover barbecue and close dampers about halfway, to maintain low heat. Cook ribs, brushing with marinade and turning occasionally, for 45 minutes. Stir honey into remaining marinade; brush onto ribs. Continue to cook ribs, covered, brushing with honey mixture until all is used and meat at bone in a thick section is no longer pink (cut to test), 15 to 20 minutes longer. Cut ribs apart. Makes 4 or 5 servings.

PER SERVING: 647 calories, 44 g protein, 17 g carbohydrates, 44 g fat, 174 mg cholesterol, 312 mg sodium

Seattle

THERE IS LITTLE NEED TO SHOUT *the praises of stir-fry cooking; to do so would be preaching to the choir. It is enough to say that it preserves the color and flavor of the ingredients, that it takes relatively little time, and that it encourages experimentation. Phillip Roullard uses fresh tuna instead of the more usual pork or chicken. Chinese five spice is the mystery ingredient.*

STIR-FRIED TUNA FOR TWO

- 1 teaspoon cornstarch
- 2 tablespoons *each* water, dry sherry, and soy sauce
- 1 tablespoon sesame seed
- 2 tablespoons salad oil
- 1 clove garlic, minced or pressed

"Stir-fry cooking preserves the color and flavor of the ingredients."

- 1 tablespoon minced fresh ginger
- 2 cups cauliflowerets, cut into ¼-inch-thick slices
- ½ teaspoon Chinese five spice (or ¼ teaspoon *each* ground cinnamon and ground allspice)
- ½ cup diced red bell pepper
- 4 green onions, ends trimmed, cut into 1-inch lengths
- ½ pound tuna, such as ahi, cut into ¼-inch-thick slices
- ½ teaspoon Oriental sesame oil

In a small bowl, stir together cornstarch, water, sherry, and soy; set aside.

In a wok or 10- to 12-inch frying pan over high heat, shake sesame seed until golden, about 3 minutes; pour sesame seed from pan and set aside.

To pan, add 1 tablespoon salad oil; when oil is hot, add garlic and ginger, then cauliflower; stir-fry until cauliflower is tender-crisp when pierced, 3 to 4 minutes. Add five spice, bell pepper, and green onions; stir-fry just until onion is bright green, about 1 minute. With a slotted spoon, ladle mixture into a bowl. Add remaining oil to pan; lay slices of tuna in a single layer in pan. After 30 seconds, turn slices and cook about 30 seconds longer. Lift tuna, as cooked, from pan. Pour the cornstarch mixture into pan and stir until boiling. Add vegetables, tuna, and sesame oil; mix gently until hot. Spoon onto dinner plates and sprinkle with sesame seed. Makes 2 servings.

PER SERVING: 230 calories, 21 g protein, 10 g carbohydrates, 12 g fat, 34 mg cholesterol, 727 mg sodium

Phillip C. Roullard

San Diego

August Menus

GARDENS AND MARKETS *burst their seams in August, overflowing with summer's finest vegetables and fruits. Make good use of them in this month's meals.*

Grill marinated vegetables alongside chicken legs for a patio dinner.

For a centerpiece relish to take on a picnic, bake a panful of vegetables until their textures and flavors meld together.

And for a simple lunch or dinner, cut sweet corn off the cob to make chowder.

GRILLED VEGETABLE SUPPER

Marinated Cucumbers (optional)
Grilled Vegetables & Chicken with Toasted Sesame Sauce
Vinegared Rice
Iced Tea (optional)
Litchi & Raspberry Float

Cook vegetables and chicken legs on the grill. Serve with a spicy toasted sesame sauce. Consider the litchi float a refreshing apéritif, wine cooler, or dessert.

You can make the sesame sauce up to 2 days in advance. Marinate the vegetables and chicken up to 2 hours ahead. Ignite the briquets about 1 hour before serving.

While the briquets heat, cook about 1½ cups medium-grain white rice. Serve rice hot or sushi-style (mix cooked rice with 3 tablespoons seasoned rice vinegar—or 3 tablespoons white wine vinegar mixed with 4 teaspoons sugar and salt to taste; serve cool). For a salad, dress sliced cucumbers with vinegar and sugar to taste.

GRILLED VEGETABLES & CHICKEN WITH TOASTED SESAME SAUCE

½ cup dry sherry or sake
2 tablespoons soy sauce
1 tablespoon Oriental sesame oil or salad oil
4 whole (about 2¼ lb. total) chicken legs
8 green onions, ends trimmed
4 small (about ¾ lb. total) crookneck squash, ends trimmed, cut in half lengthwise
8 large fresh or soaked dry shiitake mushrooms (stems removed) or large common mushrooms
Sesame sauce (recipe follows)

Combine sherry, soy sauce, and oil. Mix half of the liquid with the chicken, the remaining half with the vegetables. If made ahead, cover and chill both mixtures up to 2 hours.

Place chicken on a grill 4 to 6 inches above a solid bed of medium-hot coals (you can hold your hand at grill level only 3 to 4 seconds). Turn chicken often and extinguish flare-ups with a water spray. Cook chicken 5 minutes. Add vegetables to grill. Brush chicken and vegetables occasionally with remaining marinade and turn as needed to brown evenly.

Cook until onions are lightly browned, 5 to 10 minutes; mushrooms are lightly browned, 10 to 15 minutes; squash is tender when pierced, about 20 minutes; and chicken is no longer pink at bone (cut to test), 20 to 25 minutes total. Remove from grill as done and keep warm. Serve with sesame sauce. Makes 4 servings.

PER SERVING: 392 calories, 35 g protein, 16 g carbohydrates, 21 g fat, 116 mg cholesterol, 631 mg sodium

Sesame sauce. In an 8- to 10-inch frying pan, cook ½ cup **sesame seed** over medium-low heat, shaking pan often, until golden, 10 to 12 minutes.

In a blender, whirl hot sesame seed and 3 tablespoons **salad oil** until a fine paste forms. Add ¼ cup **water**, 2 tablespoons **lemon juice**, 2 tablespoons minced **fresh ginger**, 2 tablespoons **soy sauce**, 1 tablespoon **sugar**, 1 clove **garlic**, and ⅛ teaspoon **cayenne**. Whirl until smooth. If made ahead, cover and chill up to 2 days. To serve, warm to room temperature and thin with water if too thick to pour. Makes ⅞ cup.

PER TABLESPOON: 62 calories, 1 g protein, 2.6 g carbohydrates, 5.5 g fat, 0 mg cholesterol, 148 mg sodium

LITCHI & BERRY FLOAT

1 can (11 or 20 oz.) litchis or longans, chilled
1 cup raspberries, rinsed and drained
3 cups chilled White Zinfandel, Gewürztraminer, Chenin Blanc, or Johannisberg Riesling
Ice cubes
Lime wedges (optional)

In each of 4 tall glasses, place equal portions of litchis with their syrup, berries, and wine. Add ice and lime. Sip liquid, eat fruit with a spoon. Makes 4 servings.

PER SERVING: 191 calories, 0.6 g protein, 20 g carbohydrates, 0.3 g fat, 0 mg cholesterol, 35 mg sodium

Meal from the grill includes marinated chicken legs and vegetables served with plain or tangy rice. Spoon toasted sesame sauce over all.

Scoop eggplant and pepper relish onto lettuce leaves or bread chunks.

Make the caponata up to a week ahead. Rinse and crisp the lettuce leaves at least 30 minutes before leaving home.

Most of this lunch tastes best when served at room temperature, but keep lettuce and water cool in an ice chest.

CAPONATA

- 2 medium-size (about 2 lb. total) eggplants, stems trimmed
  Salt
- 2 medium-size (about ¾ lb. total) zucchini, ends trimmed
- 2 large (1 lb. total) red or yellow bell peppers, stemmed and seeded
- 1 large onion
- 2 large (about 1 lb. total) ripe tomatoes, cored and diced
- ½ cup wine vinegar
- 2 teaspoons sugar
- 1 dry bay leaf
- ½ cup Greek or green ripe olives
- ¼ cup olive oil

Cut eggplant into 1-inch cubes. Sprinkle with 1½ teaspoons salt. Let stand for about 20 minutes. Rinse lightly, drain, and pat dry. Cut zucchini into ½-inch slices. Thinly slice peppers and onion. Place eggplant, zucchini, peppers, and onion in a 12- by 17-inch roasting pan.

In a blender or food processor, whirl tomatoes, vinegar, and sugar until tomatoes are puréed. Add tomato mixture, bay leaf, olives, and oil to vegetables; mix to blend.

Bake in a 400° oven, stirring every 20 to 30 minutes until vegetables are very soft when pressed and most of the liquid evaporates, 1½ to 2 hours. Add salt to taste. Cool and serve at room temperature. If made ahead, cover and chill up to 1 week. Makes about 6 cups, 6 servings.

PER SERVING: 214 calories, 4 g protein, 23 g carbohydrates, 14 g fat, 0 mg cholesterol, 414 mg sodium

(Continued on next page)

Brimming bowl of vegetable relish takes center stage at picnic. Scoop olive-studded mixture onto lettuce leaves or crusty bread; salami, cheese, fruit complete the meal.

SUMMER SOUP & SANDWICH LUNCH

Caribbean Corn Chowder
Grilled Cheese & Onion Sandwiches
Lemonade
Papaya Sundaes

Chunky with lots of vegetables, this lean corn chowder is delicious hot or at room temperature. Serve with warm grilled cheese sandwiches for a lunch or supper.

While the soup cooks or cools, make the sandwiches. Tuck thinly sliced red onion and münster or jack cheese between pieces of buttered rye bread; brown on a hot griddle or in a frying pan and serve.

For the fruit sundaes, fill papaya halves with vanilla ice cream and lime sorbet. Garnish with lime wedges.

CARIBBEAN CORN CHOWDER

    2 tablespoons salad oil
    1 large onion, chopped
    1 large red bell pepper, stemmed, seeded, and chopped
    3 large (about 8 oz. total) fresh Anaheim or California green chilies, stemmed, seeded, and chopped
 5½ cups regular-strength chicken broth
    2 tablespoons minced fresh or 1 teaspoon dry tarragon leaves
  ¼ teaspoon pepper
    5 large (3½ lb. total) ears corn, husks and silk removed
       Salt
       Fresh tarragon sprigs (optional)

In a 5- to 6-quart pan, combine oil, onion, bell pepper, and chilies. Stir over high heat until onion is soft, 6 to 8 minutes. Add broth, tarragon, and pepper. Cover and bring to a boil over high heat.

Cut corn kernels off cob. Add corn to broth. Cover and simmer until corn is hot, about 5 minutes. Add salt to taste. Serve hot or cool; if made ahead, cover, and chill up to 1 day. Reheat, if desired. Ladle into bowls and garnish with tarragon sprigs. Makes 6 servings.

PER SERVING: 171 calories, 6.1 g protein, 24 g carbohydrates, 7.2 g fat, 0 mg cholesterol, 66 mg sodium

SEPTEMBER

Baked-Tomato Spaghetti (page 201)

Savor the riches of the end-
of-summer harvest season with our selection of edible
pleasures collected in Italy. Uncomplicated yet memorable,
these dishes let the inherent flavors of ripe vegetables and
fruits shine through. Sweet-tart European-style plums also
take the September spotlight, both as an accent to meats and
in handsome desserts. Other articles feature showmanship
with big shrimp, low-fat main dishes, a special soup from
Shanghai, and a main-dish Southwest salad.

Celebrating the Harvest Italian-style

THIS TIME LAST YEAR, *we were in Italy. From Milan to Rome, market stalls glowed with the rich colors of vegetables and fruits from the end-of-summer harvest. And in homes, trattorias, restaurants, and inns, good cooks paid tribute to the harvest with dishes that were simple, forthright, and, like late summer's lemon gold light, memorable.*

Since home garden and commercial crops in the Western United States are very similar to the produce available in Italy's Mediterranean climate, we decided to duplicate or adapt some of the recipes we collected in our sojourn, to celebrate our own harvest here in the West. On the following pages, we invite you to share the results.

The Italian way with foods is surprisingly quick and easy—often using just a few ingredients, and uncomplicated seasonings. The premise is straightforward: you use the freshest ingredients and treat them with respectful simplicity, letting their inherent goodness shine through.

Our Italian food adventure begins with a pizza party on the patio of a villa. It concludes with a barbecue supper from Florence, featuring spaghetti with fresh, herb-baked tomatoes and a mixed grill of assorted meats and mushrooms.

Along the way, we savor the season's just-harvested vegetables and delight in early fall fruits—sweet treasures from the trees and vines of the countryside.

We pay special tribute to the grape: for its own fresh sweetness and, made into Italian wines, for its way of enhancing other foods (see page 202 for an overview of the wines).

Everyone loves individual pizzas, especially when they're baked in a brick oven.

**TUSCAN VILLA
PIZZA PARTY**

Raw Vegetables with Olive Oil & Salt
(recipe on page 197)
Prosciutto   Salami   Cheese
Mixed Green Salad
Tomato-Cheese Pizza
Red Onion Frittata *(recipe on page 196)*
Tomato Frittata *(recipe on page 197)*
Zucchini Frittata *(recipe on page 197)*
Buttered Carrots
Pizza with Grapes *(recipe on page 199)*
Chianti   Sparkling Water

Tommaso Montesi Righetti invites friends over for pizza on his patio. As he cooks individual pizzas in a wood-fueled outdoor oven, guests nibble at a centerpiece of raw vegetables. He also offers prosciutto, salami, cheese, and several different vegetable frittatas. Dessert is a flat bread somewhat like pizza except it is sweet and savory, topped with wine grapes, rosemary, and olive oil.

Make the dough and sauce for the pizzas first. While the dough rises, cook the frittatas; they can be served at room temperature. Bake the grape pizza while you eat the tomato pizza—or bake the dessert pizza first and serve at room temperature.

TOMATO-CHEESE PIZZA

1½ pounds (about 7 large) ripe Roma-type tomatoes, cored and cut into chunks; or 1 can (14½ oz.) pear-shaped tomatoes

3 tablespoons olive oil
Pizza dough (recipe follows), or 2 loaves (1 lb. each) frozen white bread dough, thawed

¼ cup minced fresh or 2 tablespoons dry oregano leaves

1 pound mozzarella cheese, thinly sliced

¼ cup grated parmesan cheese
Salt and pepper

In a blender or food processor, whirl tomatoes (include liquid with canned tomatoes) until coarsely puréed. In a 3- to 4-quart pan, bring tomatoes to a boil.

(Continued on page 196)

At Rome's oldest market, Piazza Campo dei Fiori, Daniela Sentuti inspects vegetables. Her father, Renato, shops here at dawn for his nearby restaurant, Papà Giovanni.

On the patio near the wood-fueled brick oven, host Tommaso Montesi Righetti and friends begin bountiful meal with Tomato-Cheese Pizza. Menu also includes mixed green salad, vegetables, cold meats, several different vegetable frittatas, and a dessert pizza topped with wine grapes.

Eggs bind vegetables together to form tomato, zucchini, and onion frittatas. Cut omelet-like frittatas into wedges and serve hot or at room temperature.

purpose flour; mix to blend. Beat with an electric mixer until dough is elastic and stretchy, 3 to 5 minutes. Stir in 1⅓ cups more flour.

To knead with a dough hook, beat dough until it is smooth, elastic, and cleans sides of bowl, 5 to 7 minutes; if dough is sticky, add flour, 1 tablespoon at a time.

To knead by hand, scrape dough onto a floured board and knead until smooth and springy, 5 to 10 minutes. Place in an oiled bowl; turn dough over to oil top.

Cover bowl with plastic wrap. Let rise in a warm place until doubled, about 45 minutes. Punch dough down and knead lightly on a floured board.

ITALIAN WAYS WITH VEGETABLES

Italians savor some vegetables raw in salads and antipasto, embellished only with a fruity, extra-virgin olive oil. Cooked vegetables are used in omelet-like frittatas or as a filling for crêpes.

RED ONION FRITTATA

For a light meal, serve a frittata with salad and a glass of Orvieto or Gavi.

- 3 tablespoons olive oil
- 2 medium-size (1 lb. total) red onions, sliced into ¼-inch-thick rings
- 1 tablespoon red wine vinegar
  Salt and pepper
- 6 large eggs
- 2 tablespoons water

Pour 2 tablespoons oil into an 11- to 12-inch frying pan with sloping sides and a nonstick finish. Add onions and vinegar; stir often over medium-high heat until lightly browned, 8 to 10 minutes. Add salt and pepper to taste.

Meanwhile, beat eggs and water to blend. With a slotted spoon, add cooked onions to eggs, stirring. Reduce heat to medium-low; add remaining oil to pan. Pour egg mixture into pan, evenly distributing onions. Cook without stirring until egg mixture is set about ¼ inch around outer edge. With a wide spatula, lift some of the egg mixture from sides of pan, all the way around, tipping pan to let uncooked portion flow to pan bottom. Continue cooking until eggs are almost set on top and golden brown on bottom, 10 to 15 minutes.

Lower heat and boil gently, uncovered, until sauce thickens and reduces to about 1 cup, 25 to 40 minutes.

Lightly brush 3 baking sheets, each 12 by 15 inches, with oil. Divide dough in 6 equal balls. Put 2 balls on each pan; pat and stretch each into a 7-inch round. Brush dough with oil. Let rise, uncovered, in a warm place until slightly puffy, 15 to 30 minutes.

Bake in a 450° oven for 5 minutes. (If you have only 1 oven, shape 4 pizzas and bake 2 pans at 1 time; shape remaining dough and let rise while those bake.) Spread ⅙ of the tomato sauce over each crust to within ½ inch of edges. Place ⅙

of the oregano, mozzarella, and parmesan on each crust. Drizzle with remaining oil.

Bake in a 450° oven, switching pan positions halfway, until well browned and crusty on the bottom, 10 to 12 minutes longer. Serve hot. Add salt and pepper to taste. Makes 6 servings.

PER SERVING: 608 calories, 26 g protein, 65 g carbohydrates, 28 g fat, 62 mg cholesterol, 538 mg sodium

Pizza dough. In a large bowl, sprinkle 1 package **active dry yeast** over 1½ cups **warm water** (110°) and let stand for 5 minutes to soften.

Stir in ½ teaspoon **salt** and 1 tablespoon **olive oil.** Add 2¼ cups **all-**

Invert over pan a rimless 12- by 15-inch baking sheet or flat rimless plate somewhat wider than pan. Holding pan and baking sheet together, turn frittata out onto baking sheet. Slide frittata, browned side up, back into pan. Cook to lightly brown bottom, 2 to 5 minutes, then slide out onto a serving plate (if difficult, invert frittata, in the same manner as before, onto a serving plate). Cut into wedges and serve hot or at room temperature. Makes 6 servings.

PER SERVING: 160 calories, 7.1 g protein, 6.2 g carbohydrates, 12 g fat, 213 mg cholesterol, 65 mg sodium

TOMATO FRITTATA

Follow recipe for **red onion frittata** (preceding), except omit onion and vinegar; use 1¼ pounds (about 6 large) firm-ripe **Roma-type tomatoes,** cored and coarsely chopped. Cook tomatoes over high heat, shaking pan occasionally, until most of liquid evaporates, 5 to 10 minutes. Add to beaten eggs. If desired, garnish frittata with **tomato** slices. Makes 6 servings.

PER SERVING: 152 calories, 7.1 g protein, 4.7 g carbohydrates, 12 g fat, 213 mg cholesterol, 71 mg sodium

ZUCCHINI FRITTATA

Follow recipe for **red onion frittata** (preceding), except omit onion and vinegar; use 3 medium-size **zucchini** (about 1 lb., ends trimmed), thinly sliced. Cook zucchini over high heat, stirring often, until edges brown, about 10 minutes. Add to beaten eggs. If desired, sprinkle frittata with grated **parmesan cheese.** Makes 6 servings.

PER SERVING: 145 calories, 7.1 g protein, 2.8 g carbohydrates, 12 g fat, 213 mg cholesterol, 65 mg sodium

CORTI'S CRESPELLE WITH SPINACH

Fresh basil-tomato sauce blankets spinach-filled crêpes. Sip a young Dolcetta or Valpolicella with them.

2⅓ **pounds (about 12 large) ripe Roma-type tomatoes, cored and cut into chunks; or 1 large can (28 oz.) pear-shaped tomatoes**
1 **cup fresh or 2 tablespoons dry basil leaves**

1 **pound spinach, stems trimmed and leaves shredded, rinsed, and drained; or 1 package (10 oz.) frozen chopped spinach, thawed About 2 cups (1 carton, 15-oz. size) ricotta cheese**
2 **large eggs Crêpes (recipe follows)**
½ **cup grated parmesan cheese Salt and pepper**

Purée tomatoes in a blender or food processor (a portion at a time, if necessary). In a 2- to 3-quart pan, combine tomatoes and basil. Bring to a boil, then boil gently, uncovered, until sauce is reduced to 2 cups, 30 to 50 minutes. As sauce thickens, lower heat and stir often.

In a 5- to 6-quart pan, cook fresh (not frozen) spinach over high heat, stirring, until wilted, 1 to 2 minutes. Drain and cool. Squeeze excess water out of fresh or frozen spinach. In a bowl, beat together ricotta and eggs. Stir in spinach.

Down center of each crêpe, place an equal portion of spinach filling; roll to enclose. Cut crêpes crosswise into about 2-inch lengths. Set crêpes in a single layer in a buttered 10-inch quiche dish or shallow 1½- to 2-quart baking dish. Sprinkle crêpes with ½ of the parmesan cheese. Spoon tomato sauce over crêpes and sprinkle with remaining cheese. If made ahead, cover and chill until the next day. Bake, uncovered, in a 375° oven until hot in center, 30 to 40 minutes. Add salt and pepper to taste. Makes 6 servings.

PER SERVING: 301 calories, 20 g protein, 21 g carbohydrates, 16 g fat, 154 mg cholesterol, 352 mg sodium

Crêpes. In a blender, combine ⅔ cup **milk,** 1 **large egg,** 6 tablespoons **all-purpose flour,** 2 tablespoons grated **parmesan cheese;** whirl until blended.

Set a 7-inch crêpe pan (or a frying pan with a bottom that measures 7 in. across) over medium-high heat. For each crêpe, put about ¼ teaspoon **butter** or margarine in pan; swirl to coat pan bottom. Add 3 tablespoons batter all at once and swirl to coat flat part of pan bottom. Cook until crêpe appears dry and edge is lightly browned; turn over to lightly brown other side. Turn out onto a plate. Repeat, stacking as cooked. Makes 6.

Giulio Corti serves his grandmother's version of crespelle—plump spinach-filled crêpes with fresh basil-tomato sauce.

RAW VEGETABLES WITH OLIVE OIL & SALT

For a no-cook appetizer, dip crisp raw vegetables into a small bowl of extra-virgin olive oil, salted to taste. The presentation can be as simple as one young artichoke, to break apart for a single serving. Or try a large bowl or basket overflowing with vegetables as an edible centerpiece for a party. Serve with a chilled Frascati, Galestro, or Soave.

Raw vegetables (choices follow)
Extra-virgin olive oil
Salt

Present cold, crisp vegetables in a bowl or basket, or on a plate. Offer each diner a small bowl for mixing olive oil and salt to taste. To eat, break off a piece of vegetable and dip in oil mixture. For each serving, allow about 6 ounces of vegetables and about 1 tablespoon of oil.

PER SERVING: 170 calories, 2.3 g protein, 12 g carbohydrates, 14 g fat, 0 mg cholesterol, 60 mg sodium

Vegetables. Rinse or scrub and drain vegetables. Use small **artichokes** (tough outer bracts removed; eat tender base of bracts, and trimmed heart); **bell peppers** (from base end, cut peppers vertically almost to stem end in 6 to 8 sections; pull off sections to eat); baby **carrots** (or larger carrots partially cut into 3-in. sections to break off); **celery** stalks; **fennel** (ends trimmed; pull off sections to eat); **green onions** (ends trimmed); **radishes** (rinsed, some leaves trimmed); or small **summer squash** (partially cut through in ½- to 1-in. sections; break off pieces to eat).

Classic pairing of raw vegetables and olive oil is called pinzimonio. You break off pieces of vegetable to dip in bowl of extra-virgin olive oil seasoned with salt.

ZUCCHINI CARPACCIO

At Borgo Antico on Florence's Piazza Santo Spirito, tiny raw zucchini are cut into paper-thin rounds, then piled on a bed of pungent greens. Parmesan cheese, olive oil, and pepper go on top. A chilled Gavi or Orvieto suits the dish well.

- 4 cups (about 3 oz.) arugula or watercress sprigs, rinsed and crisped
- 4 small (about 10 oz. total) zucchini, ends trimmed, rinsed
- 2 to 3 ounces parmesan cheese
  About 6 tablespoons extra-virgin olive oil
  Salt and pepper

Place equal portions of arugula on each of 4 salad plates. Slice the zucchini as thinly as possible, using a vegetable slicer, truffle or cheese slicer, food processor, or knife. Mound equal portions of zucchini on the arugula. Using a truffle or cheese slicer, cut thin shavings of cheese to distribute equally over zucchini. Add olive oil and salt and pepper to taste to each serving. Makes 4 first-course servings.

PER SERVING: 248 calories, 6.4 g protein, 2.8 g carbohydrates, 25 g fat, 9.7 mg cholesterol, 238 mg sodium

TOAST WITH FRESH TOMATO PASTE

The flavor of fresh tomatoes is concentrated in an uncooked paste to spread on toast. Sip cooled Tocai.

- 1 pound (about 7 large) ripe Roma-type tomatoes, cored and chopped
- ⅓ cup chopped red onion
- 2 tablespoons chopped fresh or 1 tablespoon dry basil leaves
- ¼ cup olive oil
- 6 slices (3½ by 5 in. and about ½ in. thick) crusty Italian or French bread
  Salt and pepper

Place about ⅔ of the tomatoes in a clean towel. Wring and squeeze tightly to remove juice and crush tomatoes. Reserve crushed tomatoes. Mix chopped tomatoes with onion, basil, and 2 tablespoons oil.

Carpaccio usually means paper-thin slices of raw beef. This reinvention substitutes zucchini (cut with a truffle slicer) for meat.

Brush both sides of bread lightly with remaining oil; place in a single layer on a 12- by 15-inch baking sheet. Broil about 5 inches from heat until golden on both sides, 2 to 4 minutes total; turn once.

Spread toast equally with crushed tomatoes. Mound equal portions of chopped tomato mixture on paste. Add salt and pepper to taste. Serve at once. Makes 6.

PER SERVING: 177 calories, 3.4 g protein, 20 g carbohydrates, 9.4 g fat, 0.3 mg cholesterol, 172 mg sodium

FALL FRUITS: GRAPES IN PIZZA, WITH SAUSAGES; PEARS IN WINE

In early fall, the grape crush begins. New vintages brighten the glass, and grapes and other fall fruits appear in many seasonal specialties.

PIZZA WITH GRAPES

One unusual use of wine grapes is in a flat bread seasoned with rosemary and glistening with olive oil and sugar. (We substitute seedless table grapes for harder-to-find

wine grapes.) Serve at lunch, for dessert, or as a snack. If you like, accompany it with fontina cheese and a chilled young Chianti or Bardolino.

> 2 **tablespoons olive oil**
>   **Pizza dough (see tomato-cheese pizza recipe, page 194); or 2 loaves (1 lb. each) frozen white bread dough, thawed and kneaded together**
> 2 **cups (about 11 oz.) red seedless grapes, rinsed and patted dry**
> 2 **tablespoons fresh or dry rosemary leaves**
> 2 **tablespoons sugar**
>   **Salt (optional)**

Rub a 10- by 15-inch pan with 1 tablespoon olive oil. On a floured board, roll dough into a rectangle about ½ inch thick. Fold rectangle over to support; transfer to pan. Unfold dough; press and stretch to fit pan. If dough is too elastic, let rest about 5 minutes, then continue. Brush dough with 1 tablespoon olive oil. Let stand, uncovered, in a warm place until slightly puffy, about 15 minutes. Evenly sprinkle grapes, rosemary, and sugar over dough. Lightly sprinkle with salt, if desired.

Bake on the bottom rack of a 450° oven until well browned and crusty, 25 to 35 minutes. Serve warm or cool. Makes 12 to 16 servings.

PER SERVING: 145 calories, 3.2 g protein, 27 g carbohydrates, 2.9 g fat, 0 mg cholesterol, 70 mg sodium

Fresh chopped tomatoes go over fresh tomato paste spread on oil-anointed toast. The only embellishments are basil, olive oil, and onion.

Wine grapes bake on pizza dough with rosemary, olive oil, and a little sugar. The result is sweet and savory, crusty and chewy.

SAUSAGE WITH GRAPES

Winemaker Paola di Mauro from Marino, south of Rome, cooks grapes with sausages. Serve with potatoes, salad, or cooked spinach. Accompany with a Chianti or Barbera or, if you can find it, di Mauro's own white Marino or red Colle Picchione.

> 8 **mild Italian sausages (1⅓ to 1½ lb. total)**
> 1 **cup water**
> 1 **quart (about 1½ lb.) green seedless grapes, rinsed**
> 1 **small cluster green seedless grapes**

Prick sausages with a fork and place in a 10- to 12-inch frying pan. Add water. Bring to a boil, cover, and simmer 10 minutes. Drain water and fat from pan. Add the 1 quart grapes to pan; cover and

Wine-glazed pear stands tall as a fresh fruit dessert. Its elegant appearance belies the simplicity of its preparation. Serve fruit warm or cool with wine-enhanced juices.

simmer until grapes are soft, about 10 minutes. Uncover and cook over high heat, turning sausages and stirring grapes occasionally. As liquid reduces, lower heat to medium; stir often until sausages are well browned and grapes are soft and lightly browned, 15 to 20 minutes. Transfer sausages to platter and spoon grapes over them. Garnish with cluster of grapes. Makes 8 servings.

PER SERVING: 239 calories, 12 g protein, 16 g carbohydrates, 15 g fat, 43 mg cholesterol, 510 mg sodium

WINE-GLAZED BAKED PEARS

  8 **firm-ripe medium-size (about 4½ lb. total) Bosc or Bartlett pears**
1⅓ **cups dry red wine**
 ½ **cup sugar**

Trim bottoms of pears if needed so they can stand up. Set pears upright in a shallow 2- to 2½-quart baking dish or pan (they should fit snugly). Pour wine over pears; sprinkle with half the sugar.

Bake in a 425° oven for 45 minutes. Baste pears with pan juices and sprinkle with remaining sugar. Continue baking, basting occasionally with pan juices (if most juice evaporates and pears begin to brown before they're tender, add a few tablespoons of water; you should have about ½ cup pan juices when done). Bake until pears are tender when pierced and richly browned, 15 to 30 minutes longer. Serve warm or cool. Makes 8 servings.

PER SERVING: 188 calories, 1 g protein, 49 g carbohydrates, 0.9 g fat, 0 mg cholesterol, 2.1 mg sodium

FLORENTINE MIXED GRILL

Baked-Tomato Spaghetti
Florentine Mixed Grill
Mixed Green Salad
Wine-glazed Baked Pears
(recipe above)
Chianti Classico Riserva

Although Benedetta and Fabio Picchi are professional chefs, they cook very simply at home, taking great care in selecting quality ingredients.

At their Florence restaurant, Cibrèo, Signor Picchi serves an antipasto of tomato halves baked with olive oil, garlic, and parsley. The long baking partially dries the

tomatoes, intensifying their sweetness. At home, he mixes these sweet and flavorful tomatoes with spaghetti and fresh basil.

Grilled meats, particularly beef, are a specialty around Florence. He cooks a mixed grill of steak, pork ribs, Cornish game hen, and mushrooms on a rack in his fireplace, but a covered barbecue works just as well.

Salad is a colorful mixture of tender greens, yellow bell pepper, fresh basil leaves, onion, and radishes, dressed with wine vinegar and extra-virgin olive oil.

The dessert has three ingredients. You pour red wine over whole pears, sprinkle with sugar, and bake until richly glazed.

While meat marinates, bake tomatoes and pears in the same oven. Start the barbecue or fire about 1 hour before you plan to serve. Assemble salad and chill. When meat is almost done, cook the pasta. The meat can rest while you enjoy the first course.

BAKED-TOMATO SPAGHETTI

- 12 **medium-size (about 1¾ lb. total) firm-ripe Roma-type tomatoes**
  Salt and pepper
- 3 **to 6 cloves garlic, minced**
- ½ **cup chopped parsley**
- ½ **cup olive oil**
- 1 **pound dry spaghetti**
- 2 **tablespoons butter or margarine, at room temperature**
- ½ **cup fresh whole or 2 tablespoons crumbled dry basil leaves**
  Grated parmesan cheese (optional)

Cut tomatoes in half lengthwise and set, cut sides up, in a 9- by 13-inch baking pan or dish. Sprinkle lightly with salt and pepper. Mix garlic, ⅓ cup parsley, and 2 tablespoons olive oil; pat mixture over cut sides of tomatoes. Drizzle 2 tablespoons oil over tomatoes. Bake in a 425° oven until browned on top (55 to 70 minutes; pan juices may become dark).

In a 5- to 6-quart pan, bring about 3 quarts water to a boil on high heat. Add spaghetti and cook, uncovered, until barely tender to bite, 8 to 9 minutes. Drain.

In a warm large serving bowl, combine butter, remaining parsley and oil, basil, and 4 tomato halves. Remove and discard most of the skin from the 4 halves; coarsely mash. Add pasta and mix. Add remaining baked tomatoes and pan juices. Gently mix, adding salt, pepper, and cheese to taste. Makes 9 cups, or 6 to 8 servings.

PER SERVING: 379 calories, 8.3 g protein, 48 g carbohydrates, 17 g fat, 7.8 mg cholesterol, 40 mg sodium

First course is spaghetti with oven-baked tomatoes, pungent garlic, and fresh basil.

FLORENTINE MIXED GRILL

- 1 **Cornish game hen (about 1½ lb.)**
- 1 **rack (about 2 lb.) baby back pork ribs, fat trimmed**
  Herb marinade (recipe follows)
- 1 **beef porterhouse steak (2½ to 3 lb.), cut 2 inches thick**
- 16 **large (3-in.-wide) fresh shiitake or common mushrooms, rinsed and drained**
- 1 **to 2 cloves garlic, cut in thin slivers (optional)**
  Herb oil (recipe follows)
  Salt and pepper

Cut lengthwise through breast of hen to split. Pull bird open; place skin side on board and press down firmly, cracking bone slightly to flatten. Pull off and discard fat; rinse hen and pat dry.

In a 9- by 13-inch pan, combine game hen, pork, and herb marinade; turn to

Chef Fabio Picchi cooks assorted meats—steak, pork ribs, Cornish game hen—and mushrooms on a fireplace grill. A covered barbecue works just as well.

Italian Wines with Our Italian Dishes

MANY ITALIAN WINES GO well with the simple dishes we've featured; here is a brief survey. Among domestic wines, good choices include dry Sauvignon Blancs, Chardonnays, Gamays, and Zinfandels made in a style that brings out fresh, immediate flavors and aromas (rather than wines with heavy body or complex taste).

WHITE WINES

Frascati tastes best young. Light in body and color, it's made from a blend of white grapes grown in Latium province's volcanic hills.

Galestro, from Tuscany, is a refreshing, fruity blend of grapes that's low in alcohol (10½ percent). It offers easy sipping with light foods.

Gavi, from the Piedmont, tastes dry and refined. Made from Cortese grapes, it may also be fizzy (*frizzante*) or sparkling (*spumante*).

Orvieto, from Umbria, can be made dry (*secco*) with a crisp finish and a pale straw color; it also is made as a sweet golden wine (*abboccato*).

Pinot Grigio, recently popular here, is crisp, dry, and slightly delicate to rich and full flavored. It's made in Friuli-Venezia Giulia, Trentino-Alto Adige, and the Veneto.

Soave is light and dry, with a faintly green, pale straw color. This popular wine is made southeast of Verona, in the Veneto.

Tocai has light to firm body, dryness with fruity overtones. It's a popular wine from the Friuli-Venezia Giulia.

RED WINES

Barbera and **Dolcetto** are both typical wines of the Piedmont. When from Asti, they are light and lively; those from Alba tend to be heavy and rather tannic.

Bardolino is either red or rosé (*chiaretto*). A refreshing, light-bodied wine, it's made from four grapes in the Veneto region.

Chianti ranges from light and fruity to

At the rooftop bar at the Mediterraneo Hotel in Rome, guests taste wines by the glass from Angelo Bettoja's cellar.

full and complex. It's made in Tuscany from a blend of red grapes with a little white. Vintages aged at least three years are *riserva;* those from the historic area are *classico.*

Rosso Cònero, from the Marches, is a delicious well-rounded red made from the Montepulciano d'Abbruzzo grapes.

Valpolicella, from the Veneto, is refreshing, with some depth.

---

coat meat. Cover and chill, turning occasionally, at least 1 or up to 4 hours. Trim excess fat from steak.

Cut off and discard shiitake mushroom stems (trim stem ends of common mushrooms). Cut 3 or 4 slits in each shiitake cap and tuck a thin sliver of garlic in each slit (omit garlic for common mushrooms). Brush mushrooms with herb oil.

Place game hen, bone side down, beside pork and steak on a grill 4 to 6 inches above a solid bed of medium-hot coals (you can hold your hand at grill level only 3 to 4 seconds).

Cover barbecue; open vents. Cook 10 minutes. Uncover, and turn meats, basting with remaining marinade. Add mushrooms to grill. Turn foods as needed to brown evenly. Cook hen and pork until no longer pink at bone in thickest part (cut to test), 20 to 25 minutes total; steak until done to your liking (cut to test), 15 to 20 minutes for medium rare; mushrooms until browned on all sides, 10 to 15 minutes. Transfer foods to a platter; carve meats. Add salt and pepper to taste. Serves 8.

PER SERVING: 492 calories, 44 g protein, 4.1 g carbohydrates, 33 g fat, 142 mg cholesterol, 122 mg sodium

Herb marinade. Mix ½ cup **lemon juice,** 1 tablespoon **olive oil,** 2 tablespoons chopped **fresh sage leaves** or 2 teaspoons dry sage leaves, 1 tablespoon minced **lemon peel** (yellow part only), and 3 **bay leaves.**

Herb oil. Mix 3 tablespoons **olive oil,** 1 tablespoon chopped **fresh mint leaves** or dry mint, 2 teaspoons minced **fresh oregano** or 1 teaspoon dry oregano leaves.

Cooking with European-style Plums

DEEP PURPLE-BLUE, *European-style plums are mild-mannered when raw but take on a full, rich taste when cooked.*

Now, during their peak season, is the time to make the most of these prune plums. Try them in savory dishes; the plums have a sweet-tart flavor that accents smoked pork chops and more elaborate Peking-inspired duck salad. The warm salad uses prune plums to make a fresh version of Chinese plum sauce to go with the duck—home roasted, or available barbecued from a Chinese market.

You'll also want to try prune plums in desserts like lattice-topped pie accented with orange and port, and kuchen flavored with almond paste.

Known by many variety names, such as Italian, President, and Empress, these plums are distinguished from Japanese-style ones by their bluer (as opposed to red) skin, elongated (instead of round) shape, and sweeter flavor. It is European-style plums that are dried to make prunes.

California and the Northwest states grow the bulk of the fresh prune plum crop. Italian is the predominant variety, but you can use any type in these recipes.

WARM PEKING DUCK SALAD

    1   Chinese barbecued duck (2 to
        2½ lb.), or roasted duck (recipe
        follows)
    8   prune plums (about ½ lb.)
    1   small head (½ to ¾ lb.) escarole,
        leaves rinsed and crisped
        Won ton strips (recipe follows)
    ¼   cup sliced green onions
    ⅔   cup fresh cilantro (coriander)
        sprigs
        Plum sauce (recipe follows)

Strip skin and fat off duck in large pieces; discard fat. Cut skin into thin strips. Pull meat off carcass; shred meat. Halve plums, pit, and cut halves into segments attached at one end. Reserve 4 large escarole leaves. Stack remaining leaves and thinly slice crosswise. If made ahead, cover each component separately and chill up until next day.

Place duck skin in a 10- to 12-inch frying pan over medium heat and stir often until skin is deep brown, 8 to 10 minutes; halfway through cooking, spoon out and discard fat. Drain skin on paper towels.

On each of 4 dinner plates, place 1 large escarole leaf, then arrange equal amounts of shredded escarole, duck

Dark, oval prune plums' greenish gold centers change to amber when very ripe.

meat, skin, won ton strips, green onions, and cilantro. Place plums alongside, fanning segments. Offer sauce. Makes 4 entrée servings.

ESTIMATED PER SERVING WITH CHINESE DUCK: 379 calories, 16 g protein, 26 g carbohydrates, 26 g fat, 58 mg cholesterol, 129 mg sodium

Roasted duck. From 1 small **duck** (about 4 lb.), pull off and discard lumps of fat; reserve any giblets for other uses. Pierce skin all over with a fork or slender metal skewer. Combine ½ teaspoon *each* **ground ginger** and **ground cinnamon** and ¼ teaspoon *each* **ground nutmeg** and **pepper.** Rub bird inside and out with spices.

Place duck, breast up, in a V-shaped rack in a 12- by 15-inch roasting pan. Insert a meat thermometer into thickest part of thigh. Cover pan tightly with foil. Bake in a 400° oven until thermometer reaches 175°, about 45 minutes. Uncover and siphon off fat. Remove thermometer.

Combine 1 tablespoon *each* **honey** and **soy sauce;** brush half of it over top of duck. In a 475° oven, roast duck until skin is deep brown, about 10 minutes. Turn duck over; repeat basting and browning. If made ahead, cool, cover, and chill up to 1 day.

ESTIMATED PER SERVING: 683 calories, 38 g protein, 5.3 g carbohydrates, 56 g fat, 174 mg cholesterol, 374 mg sodium

Won ton strips. Stack 14 **won ton wrappers** (about 3 in. square). Cut into ½-inch-wide strips; separate pieces. In a 10- to 12-inch frying pan, heat ¼ inch **salad oil** over medium heat until a won ton strip added to oil browns quickly. Add remaining strips; cook until golden, turning once, 1 to 2 minutes. Lift from oil with a slotted spoon; drain on paper towels. If made ahead, store airtight up to 1 day.

Plum sauce. Halve and pit ½ pound (about 8) **prune plums.** Place in a 1- to 2-quart pan with ⅓ cup **water,** 3 tablespoons **honey,** 2 tablespoons *each* **soy sauce** and **cider vinegar,** 1 teaspoon *each* **ground ginger** and grated **lemon peel,** ½ teaspoon **ground cinnamon,** ¼ teaspoon **anise seed,** and ⅛ teaspoon *each* **cayenne** and **ground cloves.**

Boil, covered, until plums mash easily, about 8 minutes. Whirl smooth in a blender; serve warm. If made ahead, cool, cover, and chill until next day; reheat.

PER TABLESPOON: 16 calories, 0.2 g protein, 4.3 g carbohydrates, 0 g fat, 0 mg cholesterol, 86 mg sodium

(Continued on next page)

East-West salad includes escarole, Chinese duck meat and skin, crisp won ton strips, plum fans, and warm plum sauce.

Cascading plums in light lemon-and-honey sauce dress up smoked pork chop. Entrée goes together quickly.

Polka-dot kuchen contrasts plums skin up and skin down; cake with crisp crust rises around them. Serve with ice cream.

SMOKED PORK CHOPS WITH PRUNE PLUMS

      4 smoked pork chops, each about
         ¾ inch thick and ⅓ pound
    ⅔ cup regular-strength beef broth
    1½ teaspoons finely shredded lemon
         peel
      3 tablespoons lemon juice
      2 tablespoons honey
    ⅛ teaspoon crushed dried hot red
         chilies (optional)
     12 prune plums (about ¾ lb.)
      2 teaspoons cornstarch

Trim and discard fat from pork chops. In a 10- to 12-inch frying pan over medium-high heat, brown chops on both sides, about 10 minutes. Stir all but 2 tablespoons broth with lemon peel and juice, honey, and chilies; add to chops. Cover and simmer for 5 minutes.

Meanwhile, halve and pit plums. Add fruit to frying pan; cover and simmer until plums are hot, 2 to 3 minutes. With a slotted spoon, lift chops and plums to plates and keep warm. Stir remaining broth with cornstarch. Add to broth in pan; stir over high heat until liquid boils. Pour over meat and fruit. Serves 4.

PER SERVING: 283 calories, 24 g protein, 27 g carbohydrates, 9.4 g fat, 60 mg cholesterol, 1,520 mg sodium

ALMOND PRUNE PLUM KUCHEN

    ¾ cup (⅜ lb.) butter or margarine
    ¾ cup sugar
    ⅓ cup (2½ oz.) almond paste
      4 large eggs
      1 cup all-purpose flour
    ¾ cup rolled oats
     10 prune plums (about ⅔ lb.), halved
         and pitted
         Vanilla ice cream (optional)

In a large bowl of an electric mixer, beat butter with ½ cup of the sugar and almond paste. Add eggs, 1 at a time, beating well after each. Stir in flour and oats. Spread batter in a buttered 7- to 8-by 11-inch baking dish.

Arrange plum halves in rows of 4 across dish, alternating rows of fruit cut side up and cut side down. Press plums slightly into batter. Sprinkle kuchen with remaining sugar. Bake in a 375° oven until cake pulls from pan sides, 40 to 45 minutes. Cut into rectangles and serve warm or cool with ice cream. If made ahead, let kuchen cool, then cover and hold at room temperature up to 2 days. Serves 8.

PER SERVING: 419 calories, 7.4 g protein, 47 g carbohydrates, 23 g fat, 184 mg cholesterol, 212 mg sodium

PORT & PRUNE PLUM PIE

    4½ cups quartered and pitted prune
         plums (about 1¾ lb. whole fruit)
      1 cup sugar
    ¼ cup quick-cooking tapioca
      3 tablespoons port
      2 teaspoons *each* grated orange peel
         and vanilla
    ½ teaspoon ground nutmeg
         Pastry for a double-crust 9-inch
         pie
      1 large egg, lightly beaten

In a large bowl, stir plums, sugar, tapioca, port, peel, vanilla, and nutmeg. Let stand at least 15 minutes or up to 1 hour for tapioca to soften; stir occasionally.

On a lightly floured board, roll half of pastry into a 12-inch circle; ease into a 9-inch pie pan. Fill with plum mixture. On floured board, roll out remaining pastry into a 10-inch square. With a pastry wheel or knife, cut into 8 equal strips.

Arrange pastry strips on top of pie in a lattice pattern. Fold bottom crust over lattice, making flush with rim of pan. Flute edge. Brush pastry (not the filling) with egg.

Set pan in a foil-lined 10- by 15-inch pan (pie bubbles as it cooks). Bake in a 400° oven until pastry is golden and filling is bubbling in center, about 1 hour. Serve wedges warm or cool. If made ahead, let cool, then cover and chill up to 2 days. Serves 6 to 8.

PER SERVING: 426 calories, 4.3 g protein, 68 g carbohydrates, 16 g fat, 34 mg cholesterol, 286 mg sodium

Ruby-colored cooked plums juice up beneath pie's golden lattice crust; the raw purple-blue fruit changes color when heated. Plum filling has subtle accents of grated orange peel, ground nutmeg, and port. Serve pie in generous wedges warm or at room temperature.

Sizzling Shrimp

S IZZLED IN HOT OIL, *shrimp brown crisp and succulent in golden crusts.*

For show-off presentations, start with big, plump shrimp to fry. Stuff a triangle of cheese into a slit in each shrimp, wrap with bacon, and coat with crumbs. Or dip butterflied shrimp in a coconut batter, then coconut shreds, and brown.

CHEESE-FILLED SHRIMP

12	colossal-size shrimp (15 per lb.)
2	ounces jack cheese
6	slices bacon, cut in half crosswise
	About ⅓ cup fine dry bread crumbs
	Salad oil
	Tomato-based cocktail sauce

Peel shrimp (leave shell on tail, if desired) and devein. Starting about ¼ inch from head end, cut along back of each shrimp to make a pocket about ¾ inch deep and 1½ inches long. In center of slit, make a ¼-inch cut through shrimp.

Cut cheese into 1-inch triangles about ½ inch thick. Tuck 1 point of the triangle into the ¼-inch cut. Tightly wrap a half-slice of bacon around shrimp to enclose cheese. Impale a slender wooden skewer through tail end of shrimp and then through bacon and cheese. If made ahead, cover and chill up until next day.

Coat shrimp in crumbs. In a deep 3- to 4-quart pan, heat about 2 inches oil until it reaches 350° on a thermometer. Cook 3 or 4 shrimp at a time, turning if needed, until golden and cheese begins to melt, about 1½ minutes.

Drain shrimp on paper towel–lined pans in a 150° oven, up to 20 minutes. Serve hot, offering cocktail sauce as a dip. Makes 6 to 12 appetizer servings, or 3 or 4 entrée servings. —*Leonard Cohen, Avila Beach, Calif.*

PER SHRIMP: 88 calories, 7.3 g protein, 1.4 g carbohydrates, 5.8 g fat, 44 mg cholesterol, 124 mg sodium

COCONUT SHRIMP

Look for coconut milk and panko (Japanese-style coarse bread crumbs) at Asian markets or some supermarkets.

12	colossal-size shrimp (15 per lb.)
1	tablespoon dry sherry
⅛	teaspoon curry powder
¾	cup all-purpose flour
2	teaspoons cornstarch

Wrap jack cheese-filled shrimp tightly with bacon, then skewer; coat shrimp in crumbs and brown in hot oil. Dip cooked shrimp in cocktail sauce.

½	teaspoon baking powder
½	cup canned or thawed frozen coconut milk (or ½ cup milk plus ½ teaspoon coconut extract)
2	to 3 tablespoons water
1½	cups shredded sweetened dry coconut
¾	cup panko or coarse fresh bread crumbs
	Salad oil
	Salt and pepper
	Mango chutney

Peel shrimp (leave shell on tail, if desired) and devein. To butterfly shrimp, cut a slit almost completely through each back. Mix sherry, curry powder, and shrimp. Cover and chill 30 minutes or up until next day.

In a bowl, mix ½ cup flour, cornstarch, and baking powder. Stir in coconut milk and enough water to make a smooth, thin batter.

On waxed paper, mix the shredded coconut and panko. Put remaining ¼ cup flour on another piece of waxed paper.

In a 4½- to 5-quart pan, heat about 1 inch salad oil to 350° on a thermometer. Lay shrimp flat, coat in plain flour, batter, then in panko mixture. Fry 3 or 4 shrimp at a time, turning until golden, about 1½ minutes. Drain on paper towel–lined pans in a 150° oven for up to 30 minutes. Skim oil often to remove any browned bits.

Add salt and pepper to taste. Serve hot with chutney as a dip. Makes 6 to 12 appetizer servings, or 3 or 4 entrée servings. —*Conrad Nanaka, Kapaa, Kauai, Hawaii.*

PER SHRIMP: 157 calories, 6.5 g protein, 13 g carbohydrates, 9 g fat, 38 mg cholesterol, 93 mg sodium

Low-Fat Main Dishes

WHOLESOME MAIN DISHES *with less than 30 percent of their calories coming from fat are not only highly recommended, but easy to achieve. Simply start with foods low in fat, add little or no fat, and include a good balance of complex carbohydrates. Here, poached chicken with couscous applies these principles to the letter, as do shrimp and apples mixed into pasta, and toasted rice with beans.*

For a hearty yet wholesome entrée, pour lean apricot-mustard poaching liquid over cooked chicken breasts and couscous, then sprinkle with minced basil; serve with lime.

APRICOT–DIJON MUSTARD CHICKEN

- 1 can (12 oz.) apricot nectar
- 3 tablespoons Dijon mustard
- 3 whole (about 3½ lb. total) chicken breasts, split, boned, and skinned
- 2¼ cups regular-strength chicken broth
- 1¾ cups (10-oz. package) couscous
- 2 tablespoons minced fresh basil leaves
  Fresh basil sprigs, rinsed and drained
- 2 limes, each quartered

In a 10- to 12-inch frying pan, combine apricot nectar and mustard. Over high heat bring mixture to a boil. Lay chicken breasts, smooth side down, in apricot mixture. Cover pan, reduce heat, and simmer until breasts are no longer pink in thickest section (cut to test), 15 to 18 minutes; turn breasts over after 10 minutes.

Meanwhile, in a 2- to 3-quart pan over high heat, bring broth to a boil and stir in couscous. Remove from heat, cover, and let sit 5 minutes.

Stir couscous with a fork to fluff; pour onto a platter. Lift breasts onto couscous; cover with foil and keep warm. Boil apricot liquid on high heat, lid slightly ajar, until reduced to 1 cup, about 5 minutes. Pour sauce over breasts, then sprinkle with minced basil. Garnish with basil sprigs and accompany with lime wedges to add to taste. Serves 6.

PER SERVING: 385 calories, 7 percent of which come from fat, 41 protein, 48 g carbohydrates, 3 g fat, 86 mg cholesterol, 350 mg sodium

ORIENTAL PASTA RISOTTO

- 3½ cups regular-strength chicken broth
- ½ cup seasoned rice vinegar (or ½ cup rice or other white vinegar with 2 teaspoons sugar)
- ½ teaspoon grated lemon peel

- ½ to ¾ teaspoon crushed dried hot red chilies
- 1½ cups tiny dry pasta shapes, such as rice or stars
- 1 medium-size apple, such as Gravenstein or Golden Delicious
- ½ pound shelled cooked tiny shrimp

In a 4- to 5-quart pan on high heat, bring broth, ⅓ cup vinegar, lemon peel, and chilies to a boil; add pasta. Reduce heat and boil gently, uncovered, stirring often until much of the liquid is absorbed by the pasta and the mixture is like a thick, hot cereal, 10 to 15 minutes.

Meanwhile, rinse apple, cut in eighths, core wedges, then thinly slice each wedge crosswise. Mix slices with remaining vinegar and set aside until pasta is cooked. Stir apple mixture and shrimp into hot pasta; ladle into bowls. Serves 4.

PER SERVING: 392 calories, 7 percent of which come from fat, 23 g protein, 67 g carbohydrates, 3 g fat, 111 mg cholesterol, 176 mg sodium

HERBED BROWN RICE WITH BEANS

- 1 cup long-grain brown rice
- 1 teaspoon olive or salad oil
- 3 cups regular-strength chicken broth
- 2 medium-size (about ¾ lb. total) onions, diced
- 1 pound mushrooms, rinsed and thinly sliced
- 2 cloves garlic, minced or pressed
- 1 tablespoon *each* dry basil leaves, dry oregano leaves, and dry marjoram leaves

- 2 dry bay leaves
- 2 large (about 1 lb. total) firm-ripe tomatoes
  About 1 cup nonfat unflavored yogurt
- 1 can (15 oz.) white kidney beans (cannellini), drained and rinsed
- ⅓ cup chopped green onion
- 12 warm corn tortillas (6-in. size), optional

In a 9- to 10-inch-square baking pan, bake rice, uncovered, in a 350° oven until golden brown, about 40 minutes; shake pan occasionally. Set rice aside.

In a 10- to 12-inch frying pan, combine oil, ½ cup broth, onions, mushrooms, garlic, basil, oregano, marjoram, and bay leaves. Cook, covered, over medium heat until mushrooms are juicy and onions are translucent, about 15 minutes. Uncover and stir often until liquid has evaporated.

To pan, add rice and remaining broth. Bring to a boil over high heat; reduce heat and simmer, covered, until rice is tender to bite, about 25 minutes.

Meanwhile, rinse, core, and dice tomatoes. Put tomatoes and yogurt separately in 2 small bowls.

Mix rice and beans in a bowl; top with green onion. Serve with tomato and yogurt; accompany with tortillas. Serves 6.

PER SERVING: 281 calories, 10 percent of which come from fat, 13 protein, 53 g carbohydrates, 3 g fat, 0.8 mg cholesterol, 317 mg sodium

Shanghai Four-Thread Soup

S AVORY, CLEAR BROTH *surrounds a mushroom-capped island of shredded meat and vegetables in this special soup from Shanghai. To present, break apart the island, separating the strands of flavor.*

To mold the island, pack shreds of chicken, pork, ham, and bamboo shoots into a small bowl and steam them.

SHANGHAI FOUR-THREAD SOUP

1 large (about 2½-in.-wide) dry shiitake mushroom

6 cups regular-strength chicken broth

¼ cup dry sherry

4 slices fresh ginger (each about the size of a quarter)

2 green onions, ends trimmed

1 pork loin chop (3 to 4 oz.), ⅓ to ½ inch thick

1 chicken breast half (5 to 6 oz.)

2 ounces thinly sliced cooked ham

⅓ to ½ cup canned sliced bamboo shoots, drained

2 teaspoons Oriental sesame oil or salad oil

Soak mushroom in hot water until soft, about 20 minutes.

In a 3- to 4-quart pan, combine broth, sherry, ginger, and onions. Bring to a boil. Add pork and chicken; cover, remove from heat, and let stand 4 minutes. Lift out meats and let cool.

Remove bones, fat, and any skin from pork and chicken. Return bones to broth; discard fat and skin. Continue simmering broth, covered, for about 30 minutes; if made ahead, cool, cover, and chill until next day. Reheat to continue.

Meanwhile, cut pork, ham, and bamboo shoots in very thin slivers about 3 inches long. Tear chicken into thin shreds. Separately mix pork with half the oil and chicken with other half.

Squeeze water out of mushroom; remove and discard tough stem. Place mushroom, top down, in the center of an oiled, deep 1- to 1½-cup bowl. Arrange chicken, ham, pork, and bamboo shoots, each in a quarter of the bowl, tightly packing the best-looking shreds against the sides. After sides are arranged, fill center of bowl in a random fashion with remaining shreds, packing tightly. Cover bowl tightly with foil. If made ahead, chill until next day.

Set bowl on a rack over about 1 inch of water in a 5- to 6-quart pan. Cover pan and bring to a boil; boil until meat in center of bowl feels hot and firm when pressed, 14 to 20 minutes.

Invert cake from bowl into a 2- to 3-quart soup tureen. Skim fat from broth and discard; pour broth through a fine strainer into tureen. At the table, break up steamed cake with a ladle or knife. Ladle some of the meat, vegetables, and broth into each bowl. Makes 6 servings.

PER SERVING: 103 calories, 10 g protein, 3.8 g carbohydrates, 4.8 g fat, 2 mg cholesterol, 213 mg sodium

At the table, break apart mushroom-capped island of shredded meat and vegetables to release strands of flavor into clear chicken broth.

Southwest Salad

A QUICK START *for this main-dish vege-table salad comes from canned black-eyed peas. With flavor overtures suggestive of the Southwest, the salad is a simple combination of lettuce, sliced tomatoes, and seasoned peas. But when it's paired with crisp toasted triangles of homemade cornbread, it becomes suitable fare for luncheon guests.*

Just about every step has make-ahead options.

SOUTHWESTERN SALAD

- 1 can (15 oz.) black-eyed peas, drained
- ½ cup finely chopped red onion
  Southwest dressing (recipe follows)
- 1½ pounds (about 2 heads) butter lettuce, rinsed and crisped
- 4 large (about 2 lb. total) firm-ripe tomatoes, cored and cut into 12 equal slices
  About ½ cup salted and roasted pumpkin seeds (optional)
  Toasted cornbread triangles (recipe follows)
  Salt and pepper

In a bowl, mix peas and onion with dressing. If made ahead, chill up to 4 hours.

Select 8 large lettuce leaves and arrange equally on 4 dinner plates. Tear remaining leaves into bite-size pieces and mound equally on whole leaves. Evenly arrange pea mixture and tomatoes on plates of lettuce, then sprinkle with a few pumpkin seeds. Place several cornbread triangles on each plate. Offer remaining pumpkin seeds and cornbread in separate containers. Season salads to taste with salt and pepper. Makes 4 servings.

PER SERVING WITHOUT CORNBREAD TRIANGLES: 404 calories, 9.1 g protein, 32 g carbohydrates, 30 g fat, 0 mg cholesterol, 353 mg sodium

Southwest dressing. Mix ½ cup **extra-virgin olive oil,** 6 tablespoons **red wine vinegar,** 1 teaspoon **chili powder,** and ½ teaspoon *each* **cumin seed** and **crushed dried hot red chilies.** If made ahead, cover and chill up to 3 days.

Toasted cornbread triangles. In a bowl, stir together ½ cup **all-purpose flour,** ½ cup **yellow cornmeal,** 2 tablespoons

sugar, ½ teaspoon **baking powder,** and ⅛ teaspoon **salt.**

In a small bowl, beat to blend 1 **large egg** and ¾ cup **buttermilk.** Add to dry ingredients and mix until evenly moistened. Pour batter into an oiled 9-inch-square baking pan. Bake in a 350° oven until firm to touch in the center, about 20 minutes.

Let cool in pan; if made ahead, cover and keep up to 1 day.

Slide a spatula around and under bread to free it from pan. Hold an inverted 12- by 15-inch baking sheet on top of the pan; flip over to release bread onto sheet. Cut bread into 9 equal squares, then cut each square diagonally in half.

Melt 1 tablespoon **butter** or margarine; brush half of it over cornbread. Broil cornbread about 4 inches from heat until browned, about 2 minutes. With a spatula, turn triangles over and brush with remaining butter. Broil until lightly browned, about 2 minutes. Serve hot.

PER PIECE: 46 calories, 1.3 g protein, 7.5 g carbohydrates, 1.1 g fat, 17 mg cholesterol, 48 mg sodium

In main-dish vegetable salad, salted pumpkin seeds reinforce Southwest flavors of black-eyed peas and ripe tomatoes. Serve salad with toasted cornbread triangles.

Broiled lamb chops, glazed by mint-based sauce, are served with remaining sauce.

MARY'S MINTED LAMB CHOPS

- 3 tablespoons mint jelly
- 2 tablespoons wine vinegar
- 1 tablespoon soy sauce
- 1 tablespoon salad oil
- 2 tablespoons minced fresh mint or dry mint leaves
- 2 teaspoons Dijon mustard
- ¼ teaspoon pepper
- 1 clove garlic, minced or pressed
- 4 loin lamb chops (about 2 lb. total), about 2 inches thick
  Fresh mint sprigs
  Salt

In a 1- to 1½-quart pan, stir jelly over low heat just until melted, about 3 minutes. Remove from heat and stir in vinegar, soy sauce, oil, minced mint, mustard, pepper, and garlic.

Set lamb chops on a rack in a 12- by 14-inch broiler pan. Generously brush jelly mixture over top of chops. Broil about 4 inches from heat until browned, about 10 minutes. Turn over and brush with more mint sauce. Continue cooking until done to your liking, 8 to 10 minutes longer for medium-rare. Transfer to plate and garnish with mint sprigs. Offer any remaining mint sauce to spoon over chops. Add salt to taste. Makes 4 servings. —*Lois Dowling, Tacoma, Wash.*

PER SERVING: 591 calories, 32 g protein, 11 g carbohydrates, 45 g fat, 140 mg cholesterol, 413 mg sodium

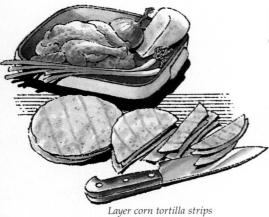

Layer corn tortilla strips with chicken, cheese, and onion for enchilada casserole.

CHICKEN YOGURT ENCHILADA BAKE

- ¼ cup (⅛ lb.) butter or margarine
- ¼ cup all-purpose flour
- 2 cups regular-strength chicken broth
- 1 cup unflavored yogurt
- 1 can (7 oz.) diced green chilies
- 12 corn tortillas (6-in. size)
- 2 cups (about 9 oz.) bite-size pieces cooked chicken
- 1 small onion, chopped
- 2 cups (8 oz.) shredded jack cheese
- ¼ cup thinly sliced green onions

In a 1½- to 2-quart pan, melt butter over medium heat. Add flour and stir until bubbly. Whisk in broth; stir until boiling. Remove from heat; mix in yogurt and chilies. Cover the bottom of a 9- by 13-inch baking dish with ⅓ of the sauce.

Quickly dip tortillas in water. Drain briefly and cut into 1-inch strips. Scatter ½ of the tortillas over sauce, then cover evenly with all the chicken and chopped onion, ⅔ of the cheese, and ⅓ of the sauce. Top with remaining tortillas, sauce, and cheese. Cover dish and bake in a 400° oven until hot in center, 30 to 35 minutes. Sprinkle with green onions. Makes 6 servings. —*Bette Rehner, Denver.*

PER SERVING: 488 calories, 30 g protein, 36 g carbohydrates, 26 g fat, 94 mg cholesterol, 670 mg sodium

Spinach shreds, tomato wedges, shrimp lend color to this lean rice soup.

RICE & SPINACH SOUP

- 1½ quarts regular-strength chicken broth
- 1 large onion, chopped
- ⅓ cup medium-grain white rice
- 2 cloves garlic, minced or pressed
- 2 small dried hot red chilies
- 1 quart (4 oz.) lightly packed rinsed spinach leaves
- 1 medium-size firm-ripe tomato
- ¼ pound tiny shelled cooked shrimp
- 2 tablespoons lime juice
  Lime wedges (optional)

In a 3- to 4-quart pan, combine the broth, onion, rice, garlic, and chilies. Cover and bring to a boil over high heat. Simmer, covered, until rice is very tender to bite, 20 to 30 minutes.

Meanwhile, cut spinach into thin shreds. Core tomato and cut into about ¾-inch-wide wedges. Stir spinach, tomato, and shrimp into simmering broth. Simmer, uncovered, just until spinach wilts and tomato is hot, about 1 minute. Stir in lime juice; ladle into bowls. Offer lime wedges to add to taste. Makes 6 servings. —*Mollie Minus, Milwaukie, Ore.*

PER SERVING: 107 calories, 8.1 g protein, 14 g carbohydrates, 2 g fat, 37 mg cholesterol, 114 mg sodium

Braised Romaine with Bacon

1 medium-size head (about 1 lb.)
   romaine lettuce
2 slices bacon, cut in thin slivers
1 small onion, thinly sliced
3 tablespoons water
   Lemon wedges
   Salt and pepper

Cut romaine in quarters lengthwise.
Rinse gently between leaves; drain.

In a 10- to 12-inch frying pan, cook
bacon over medium-high heat, stirring
often until crisp, 4 to 6 minutes. With a
slotted spoon, lift out bacon and set
aside. Add onion to pan and stir often
until onion is lightly browned, about 5
minutes. Remove onion from pan with
slotted spoon and set aside.

Lay lettuce quarters, cut side down, in
pan over medium-high heat. Add water
and cover pan. Cook until lettuce is
wilted and lightly browned on bottom,
about 3 minutes. Transfer lettuce to platter. Spoon bacon and onion across lettuce and garnish with lemon wedges.
Add salt and pepper to taste. Makes 4
servings. —*Ida Cooke, Coburg, Ore.*

PER SERVING: 120 calories, 3.5 g protein, 3.4 g carbohydrates, 10 g fat,
12 mg cholesterol, 131 mg sodium

*Crisp bacon and sautéed
onion march across braised
quarters of romaine.*

Kasha Salad with Fruit

2 tablespoons salad oil
1 cup roasted whole kasha
   (buckwheat) kernels, or bulgur
1½ cups regular-strength chicken
   broth
¾ cup chopped dried apricots
1 medium-size red apple, cored and
   diced
¼ cup chopped roasted cashews
¼ cup raisins
   Orange vinaigrette (recipe follows)
   Butter lettuce leaves, rinsed and
   crisped
   Orange wedges

In a 2- to 3-quart pan, combine oil and
kasha. Stir over medium heat until

lightly toasted, 3 to 4 minutes. Add
broth. Cover pan and cook over low heat
just until kasha is tender to bite and liquid is absorbed, 10 to 15 minutes; do not
stir. Remove lid and let cool, about 30
minutes; do not stir. Add apricots,
apple, cashews, raisins, and vinaigrette;
mix gently. Spoon into lettuce-lined
bowl. Garnish with orange wedges.
Makes 6 servings. —*Roxanne Chan,
Albany, Calif.*

PER SERVING: 348 calories, 4.9 g protein, 47 g carbohydrates, 17 g fat,
0 mg cholesterol, 18 mg sodium

Orange vinaigrette. Mix 1 teaspoon
grated **orange peel**, ½ cup **orange juice**,
¼ cup **salad oil**, 1 tablespoon **cider vinegar**, and 1 teaspoon **honey**.

*Offer orange-scented kasha
and fruit salad with cold
cooked ham or poultry.*

Carrot & Zucchini Chocolate Cake

2 cups all-purpose flour
2 cups sugar
½ cup unsweetened cocoa
1 teaspoon *each* baking powder,
   baking soda, and ground
   cinnamon
½ teaspoon *each* ground nutmeg,
   ground allspice, and salt
1½ cups shredded carrots
1½ cups shredded zucchini
1 package (6 oz.) semisweet
   chocolate baking chips
1 cup salad oil
4 large eggs
   Powdered sugar

In a large bowl, mix flour, sugar, cocoa,
baking powder, baking soda, cinnamon,
nutmeg, allspice, and salt. Stir in carrots,
zucchini, and chocolate chips. In a small
bowl, beat oil to mix with eggs; add to
dry mixture and stir to moisten well.

Spread batter in an oiled 9- by 13-inch
baking dish or pan. Bake in a 325° oven
until a toothpick inserted in center
comes out clean, 50 to 55 minutes. Cool
on a rack. Sprinkle generously with
powdered sugar and cut into squares. If
made ahead, cover and store up to 2
days. Serves 12. —*Mary Sutton, Spokane,
Wash.*

PER SERVING: 480 calories, 5.8 g protein, 61 g carbohydrates, 26 g fat,
71 mg cholesterol, 223 mg sodium

*For a pretty pattern, sift
powdered sugar over
leaves on cake.*

NOT FOR NOTHING *are Scots called canny. For openers, they discovered the virtues of oats as human health food a long time before the rest of us. More than two centuries ago, Dr. Samuel Johnson described oats in his famous dictionary as a grain eaten by horses in England and by men in Scotland. Loyal Scot James Boswell, his biographer, was quick to inform Johnson that such a diet was responsible for the fine horses of England and the fine men of Scotland.*

Medical research has finally caught up with Boswell, and oats are experiencing a renaissance in our diets. Fortunately, we don't have to eat oats merely out of duty to our vascular and digestive systems; their flavor and texture are substantial, and in Robert House's waffles they truly justify those much-abused terms "nutty" and "crunchy."

OAT BRAN–BUTTERMILK WAFFLES

- 1 cup oat bran
- 1 cup whole-wheat flour
- ½ teaspoon *each* baking powder and baking soda
- 1 large egg
- ¼ cup salad oil, or melted and cooled butter or margarine
- 1 cup buttermilk
- 1 cup milk
  Butter or margarine
  Syrup

In a bowl, stir together oat bran, flour, baking powder, and soda. In another bowl, beat egg and oil to blend with buttermilk and milk; add liquids to dry ingredients and stir until evenly moistened.

In an oiled waffle iron heated to medium-high, add enough batter to fill about half full. Cover and bake until waffle no longer steams and is crisp and golden, 4 to 5 minutes. Lift out waffle and season to taste with butter and syrup. Repeat to bake remaining waffles. Makes 3 waffles, each 9 inches square.

PER WAFFLE: 511 calories, 18 g protein, 53 g carbohydrates, 26 g fat, 106 mg cholesterol, 358 mg sodium

Robert B. House

Mount Vernon, Wash.

GORDON LECKENBY *has come up with a new way to package chicken in an edible container: instead of stuffing a tomato, an avocado, or a puff-pastry case, he uses half an acorn squash, previously baked tender. The shell holds a stir-fried medley of chicken and vegetables. Diced jicama adds refreshing crunch, while Sichuan peppercorns enliven the flavor and make your tongue tingle with a strange (but not painful) sensation.*

CHICKEN IN A SQUASH SHELL

- 2 small (about 1 lb. each) acorn squash
- 1 tablespoon salad oil
  About 1 pound boned, skinned chicken breasts, cut into ½-inch cubes
- ½ cup finely diced red bell pepper
- ½ cup finely diced jicama
- 1 small onion, finely chopped
- 2 small firm-ripe tomatoes, peeled, cored, and finely diced
- 1 teaspoon Sichuan peppercorns, coarsely ground, or ½ teaspoon pepper
  Soy-ginger sauce (recipe follows)
- ¼ cup chopped green onion
  Sour cream

Cut squash in half lengthwise and scoop out seeds. Place squash, cut side down, in an oiled 9- by 13-inch pan. Bake, uncovered, in a 400° oven until tender when pierced, 30 to 40 minutes.

About 15 minutes before squash is done, pour oil into a 10- to 12-inch frying pan over medium-high heat. When oil is hot, add chicken and stir-fry until lightly browned and white throughout (cut to test). Remove from pan with a slotted spoon. Add to pan bell pepper, jicama, onion, tomatoes, and peppercorns; stir-fry 5 minutes. Add sauce; stir until boiling; add chicken and any juices. Keep warm.

Place each squash half in an individual bowl, then fill equally with chicken mixture. Add green onion and sour cream to taste. Makes 4 servings.

PER SERVING: 280 calories, 30 g protein, 30 g carbohydrates, 5.5 g fat, 66 mg cholesterol, 611 mg sodium

Soy-ginger sauce. In a small bowl, stir together 2 tablespoons *each* **soy sauce** and **dry sherry,** ¾ cup **regular-strength chicken broth,** 1 tablespoon firmly packed **brown sugar,** 1 teaspoon finely minced **fresh ginger,** and 1 tablespoon **cornstarch.**

Gordon Leckenby

Seattle

"The Scots discovered the virtues of oats a long time before the rest of us."

"Reconnoitering the refrigerator, he found only a dispirited cauliflower."

Soak mushrooms in hot water to cover until soft, about 25 minutes. Lift from water and squeeze dry; cut off and discard mushroom stems. Thinly slice mushrooms; set them aside.

Trim tough end from cauliflower stem and discard, then cut head in quarters and thinly slice; set aside.

Set a wok or 12-inch frying pan over high heat; add oil. When oil is hot, add beans, garlic, and ginger; stir-fry to heat, about 30 seconds. Add cauliflower and 3 tablespoons water; stir-fry to mix well, then cover and cook, stirring often, until cauliflower is barely tender to bite, about 7 minutes. Add water, 1 tablespoon at a time, if needed to prevent sticking. Add mushrooms, oyster sauce, chicken broth, and cornstarch mixture. Stir until boiling. Garnish portions with cilantro sprigs. Makes 4 to 6 servings.

PER SERVING: 71 calories, 2.1 g protein, 5.4 g carbohydrates, 5 g fat, 0 mg cholesterol, 306 mg sodium

Cary Yoshio Mizobe

Gardena, Calif.

"His Hamburger-on-a-Stick shows an intuitive grasp of a fundamental principle."

In a large mixing bowl, combine the beef, eggs, soy sauce, matzo meal, and pepper. Mix well, then shape into 8 cylinders, each 5 inches long. Roll each cylinder in cornflake crumbs to coat evenly. If made ahead, lay on a platter, cover with plastic wrap, and chill up to 4 hours.

Run a metal skewer (at least 7 in.) lengthwise through the center of each cylinder. Using a wide spatula to support meat, place each cylinder on a grill 4 to 6 inches above a solid bed of hot coals (you should be able to hold your hand at grill level for only 2 to 3 seconds).

Cook, turning with spatula, until evenly browned and done to your liking (cut to test), about 10 minutes for medium rare. Push meat off skewers into hot dog buns. Add condiments, as desired. Makes 8 servings.

PER SERVING: 429 calories, 27 g protein, 35 g carbohydrates, 19 g fat, 175 mg cholesterol, 506 mg sodium

Condiments. Offer a choice of **catsup, mustard, pickle relish,** and minced **onion.**

Jeremy

Menlo Park, Calif.

F OR GENERATIONS, *Asian cooks have put fermentation to work for them in wonderful ways never dreamed of in the West. One result is fermented black beans, whose dark, mysterious flavor Cary Yoshio Mizobe has in turn put to work in his own inventive way.*

As he tells it, he returned home from work late one night too bushed to shop. But, in reconnoitering the refrigerator, he found only a dispirited cauliflower there. Somehow he conjured up fermented black beans and an odd collection of other ingredients to create the following dish, which resembles cauliflower to the same degree that a Hepplewhite chair resembles a tree.

CAULIFLOWER WITH MUSHROOMS IN SPICY BLACK BEAN SAUCE

- 2 **large dried shiitake mushrooms**
- 1 **small head (about 1½ lb.) cauliflower**
- 2 **tablespoons Oriental sesame seed oil**
- 2 **tablespoons salted fermented black beans, rinsed and coarsely chopped**
- 3 **cloves garlic, minced or pressed**
- 1½ **tablespoons minced fresh ginger**
- 1¼ **tablespoons oyster sauce**
- ½ **cup regular-strength chicken broth**
- 1 **teaspoon cornstarch blended with 1 tablespoon water**
  Fresh cilantro (coriander) sprigs

G ENIUS ASSERTS ITSELF EARLY *in music and mathematics, possibly because both depend on inborn abilities for abstract thought and quick perception of pattern and order. Genius in those arts that depend on extended observation of the real world, however, shows itself much later. Hence, child novelists are inconceivable, and so, for the most part, are child chefs.*

But Jeremy Kermit, age five, may be breaking new ground. His Hamburger-on-a-Stick shows an intuitive grasp of a fundamental principle in creative cooking—that of preparing a familiar ingredient in a new way.

HAMBURGER-ON-A-STICK

- 2 **pounds ground lean beef**
- 3 **large eggs**
- 1 **tablespoon soy sauce**
- ½ **cup matzo meal or fine dry bread crumbs**
- ¼ **teaspoon pepper**
  About ½ cup cornflake crumbs
- 8 **hot dog buns**
  Condiments (suggestions follow)

September Menus

BUSINESS AND PLEASURE *settle into busy routines that signal the end of summer. Preserve your energy with these meals designed to keep cooking not only at a minimum, but also at less busy times of the day.*

This platter salad is ideal for one of September's classic scorchers.

Braise the boneless roast early in the day. Serve it as part of a whole-meal salad; moisten zucchini and chewy wheat berries with a low-fat dressing from meat juices.

To make sundaes, spoon ripe plums poached in a little water or red wine and sugar over vanilla ice cream; crumble a few gingersnaps over the fruit.

COOL PORK PLATTER WITH ZUCCHINI & WHEAT BERRIES

- 1 to 1½ tablespoons salad oil
- 1 boned, fat-trimmed, rolled, and tied pork loin roast, 1½ to 2 pounds
- 1½ cups regular-strength chicken broth
- 1 piece (about 1 oz.) ginger, thinly sliced
- ½ cup sake or dry white wine
- ¼ cup soy sauce
- 1 clove garlic, minced or mashed
- ½ cup chopped green onions
- ½ cup lemon juice
  Steamed zucchini (directions follow)
  Cooked wheat berries (directions follow)
  Lettuce leaves, rinsed and crisped
- 1 lemon, cut into wedges

To a 5- to 6-quart pan on medium high heat, add oil. When hot, add pork and brown well, 10 to 15 minutes. Drain fat from pan and discard. Add broth, ginger, sake, soy, garlic, and onions. Cover and simmer gently until a thermometer inserted into the center of the meat registers 155° to 160°, about 40 minutes.

Thinly sliced braised pork loin goes with zucchini and plump wheat berries in this hearty salad for outdoor dining. Braising juices make a wonderful, low-fat dressing.

Lift meat from pan and set on a platter; let cool. If made ahead, cover and chill up to 2 days; use cold or at cool room temperature.

Ladle and discard fat and ginger from pan juices; if made ahead, cover and chill up to 2 days. Add lemon juice to pan juices and pour into a small bowl; serve at cool room temperature.

Thinly slice meat and overlap on platter. Mound zucchini and wheat berries beside meat, garnishing with lettuce leaves and lemon wedges. Season portions to taste with dressing. Makes 6 servings.

PER SERVING: 417 calories, 37 g protein, 39 g carbohydrates, 13 g fat, 72 mg cholesterol, 856 mg sodium

Steamed zucchini. Trim the ends from 6 small (about 1½ lb. total) **zucchini;** cut into ½-inch slices. In a wok or 5- to 6-quart pan, place a rack at least 1 inch above boiling water; put zucchini on rack. Cover and steam until zucchini is just barely tender when pierced, about 5 minutes. Immediately immerse zucchini in ice water; when cool, drain well. If made ahead, cover and hold at room temperature for up to 4 hours; or cover and chill up until the next day. Serve at room temperature.

Cooked wheat berries. In a 5- to 6-quart pan, combine 1½ cups **wheat berries** and 3 cups **regular-strength chicken broth.** Bring to a boil on high heat, then reduce heat, cover, and simmer until tender to bite, about 1½ hours. Drain well (reserve broth for soups or other uses) and let cool; serve warm or at room temperature. If made ahead, cover and chill up until the next day; serve at room temperature.

INDIAN-SUMMER LUNCHEON

Golden Pepper, Pasta & Orange Salad
Sliced Tomatoes
French Bread Jarlsberg Cheese
Grapes Nectarines
Lemonade Dry Chenin Blanc

Re-create the golden light of Indian summer with this menu that uses yellow bell peppers and yellow tomatoes. If you can't find them in your market, enjoy ripe red versions of either.

Broil the peppers and cook the pasta ahead of time. Layer the salad ingredients on a wide platter to show off their color, then mix just before serving.

GOLDEN PEPPER, PASTA & ORANGE SALAD

  4 **medium-size (about 2 lb. total) yellow or red bell peppers**

  2 **large (about 1¼ lb. total) oranges**

4½ **cups cool cooked pasta such as gnocchi-shape, shells, or penne**

 ¼ **cup extra-virgin olive oil**

 ¼ **cup balsamic or red wine vinegar**

  2 **teaspoons hot chili oil (optional)**

  1 **small (about 6 oz.) red onion, thinly sliced**

 ¼ **cup finely chopped fresh basil leaves**

     Fresh basil sprigs, rinsed and drained (optional)

     Salt

Cut peppers in half lengthwise. Lay cut side down in a foil-lined 10- by 15-inch pan. Broil 2 to 3 inches from heat until skins are charred, about 10 minutes. Let stand, draped with foil, until cool enough to touch. Pull off and discard skin, stems, and seeds. Cut peppers into thin strips.

With a knife, cut peel and white membrane from oranges. Holding each orange over a small bowl, cut between segments to release fruit; squeeze juice from membrane into bowl.

In a large bowl, mix pasta, olive oil, vinegar, and chili oil. Mound pasta onto a platter or in a bowl and top with peppers, onions, and oranges (including juice). Sprinkle with chopped basil; garnish with basil sprigs. Mix salad, and season with salt to taste. Serves 6.

PER SERVING: 316 calories, 7.3 g protein, 50 g carbohydrates, 10 g fat, 0 mg cholesterol, 4.5 mg sodium

(Continued on next page)

Golden bell peppers, orange segments, onions, and basil combine in this cold pasta salad; accompany with red or yellow sliced tomatoes, bread, cheeses and fruit.

WEEKEND BRUNCH

Scrambled Eggs with Mushrooms
Cantaloupe & Honeydew Wedges
Biscuits with Cream Cheese Hearts
Cranberry Sparklers
Espresso or Spice Tea

Cinnamon sugar and cream cheese dress up refrigerated biscuits for this lazy meal.

Sauté mushrooms, then add eggs, scrambling them while the biscuits bake. To make the sparklers, pour equal amounts of chilled cranberry juice cocktail and sparkling mineral water into individual glasses.

BISCUITS WITH CREAM CHEESE HEARTS

⅓ cup sugar
1 teaspoon ground cinnamon
¼ teaspoon almond extract
3 tablespoons butter or margarine, melted
1 small package (3 oz.) cream cheese, cut into 10 equal pieces
¼ cup chopped almonds
1 package (11 oz., 10 pieces) refrigerated biscuits

In a small bowl, combine sugar and cinnamon. In another small bowl, combine almond extract and butter. Dip each piece of cheese in butter, then roll in cinnamon-sugar mixture; lay pieces side-by-side on waxed paper. Mix almonds with remaining cinnamon-sugar mixture.

Separate the biscuits and pat each into a 3-inch round. Place a piece of cream cheese in the center of each biscuit, fold dough over to completely enclose cheese, then pinch dough edges to seal. Dip filled biscuit in butter, then roll in cinnamon-sugar mixture.

Place each biscuit, seam side down, in an ungreased 2½-inch muffin cup. Bake in a 375° oven until rich golden brown, about 15 minutes. Remove from pan immediately and let cool about 10 minutes; serve warm. (Cover and chill any leftovers up until next day; wrap in foil and reheat in a 350° oven until warm, about 20 minutes.) Makes 10.

PER BISCUIT: 192 calories, 3.6 g protein, 22 g carbohydrates, 10 g fat, 19 mg cholesterol, 331 mg sodium

OCTOBER

Harvest Sheaf Loaf (page 218)

Invigorating autumn days
lure you outdoors this month. What better way to enjoy brisk
October weather than with a potluck tailgate picnic before the
football game? For a more elegant gathering, we suggest a
festive dinner featuring game birds. Readers share their
favorite muffin recipes, and we present a half dozen rated
outstanding by Sunset taste panels. Other articles feature
main-dish fish salads, hearty grain and legume dishes,
homemade cereal mixes, and fragrant apple cakes.

Harvest Loaf

SHAPED LIKE A WHEAT SHEAF, *this free-form loaf serves as an edible centerpiece for a harvest meal. The slender stalks get crisp like breadsticks; the plumper ears turn into small, crusty rolls.*

Cutting and snipping with knife and scissors give the wheat-flecked yeast dough its textured surface. Form a quadrilateral of dough, then follow the steps shown below to form stalks and heads of grain.

HARVEST SHEAF LOAF

    1 package active dry yeast
 1¼ cups warm water (about 110°)
    1 tablespoon molasses
  ¾ teaspoon salt
    3 tablespoons butter or margarine,
        at room temperature
  ⅔ cup whole-wheat flour
  ⅓ cup untoasted wheat germ
 2¼ to 2¾ cups all-purpose flour
    1 large egg
    1 tablespoon milk
        Kosher salt (optional)

Sprinkle yeast over water in a large bowl; let stand about 5 minutes to soften. Stir in molasses, salt, and butter. Beat in whole-wheat flour and wheat germ.

To knead with a dough hook, set at low speed and gradually beat in 2¼ cups of the all-purpose flour until moistened. Then beat on high speed until dough pulls cleanly from side of bowl, 3 to 5 minutes. If dough is sticky, add more flour, 1 tablespoon at a time.

To knead by hand, use a heavy spoon to gradually stir in 2¼ cups of the all-purpose flour until blended. Turn out onto a floured board and knead until smooth and elastic, about 10 minutes, adding as little flour as possible to prevent sticking. Place dough in greased bowl; turn over to grease top.

Either way, cover bowl with plastic wrap; put in warm place until dough doubles, about 1 hour. Punch down; knead briefly on floured board to release air.

Pinch off a 2-inch-thick dough ball; roll into a 14-inch-long rope. Lay rope across center width of a greased 12- by 15-inch baking sheet. Form remaining dough into a quadrilateral about 10 inches long, 6 inches wide across top, 3 inches wide across bottom. Set dough atop rope; press onto pan to adjust size and even thickness.

With a knife, score dough from top to bottom at 5 equal intervals. Following scored marks, cut through dough to pan (see bottom left picture); *do not cut through center where dough rope lies.*

Spread strips apart at top so they don't stick together.

On bottom section, twist each strip, stretching slightly to reach 1 to 2 inches beyond pan's bottom edge. Flare strips at base, fitting snugly against edge of baking sheet. Tie dough rope loosely over sheaf.

Turn pan so top section faces you. Starting 1 inch in from dough rope, snip strip ⅔ of the way through at a 45° angle to top of dough; repeat at 1-inch intervals (see picture, below). Lift and turn each snipped section alternately to opposite sides. Repeat for each strip.

Cover sheaf loosely with plastic wrap and let rise in a warm place until puffy, 20 to 30 minutes. Beat egg and milk to blend. Brush dough with egg mixture; sprinkle lightly with kosher salt.

Bake in a 400° oven until bread is golden brown, 25 to 30 minutes. Transfer to rack to cool. Serve warm or cool. If made ahead, cool, wrap airtight, and store at room temperature up to 8 hours, or freeze up to 1 week. Thaw and reheat, uncovered, in 350° oven until warm, 5 to 10 minutes. Break off pieces to eat. Makes 1 loaf (about 1½ lb.), about 12 servings.

PER OUNCE: 90 calories, 2.8 g protein, 15 g carbohydrates, 2.3 g fat, 18 mg cholesterol, 100 mg sodium

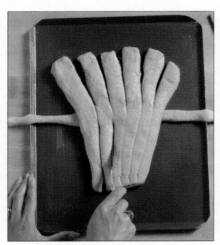

Score and cut quadrilateral of dough into 6 strips; don't cut through center. Slightly fan strips apart at top.

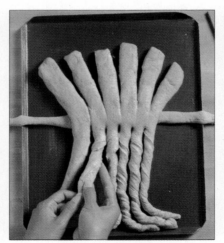

Twist and pull lower half of each strip to extend 1 to 2 inches beyond baking sheet. Curve 3 strips to each side, snug onto pan.

Snip top strips at equal intervals, tilting scissors at 45° angle into top of dough. Turn cut sections to opposite sides.

Ruggedly handsome bread looks and tastes like wheat. Shape yeast dough by hand, then cut and snip with knife and scissors to give its distinctive shape. Slim, vertical stalks bake into crisp breadsticks, while plumper ears turn into small, crusty rolls. Break off chunks to eat with soup.

Before-the-Game Picnic

MUCH MORE *than a simple picnic, tailgating is like car camping for the day. By using your vehicle to carry insulated containers, dishes, utensils, and even a barbecue, you can present an outdoor meal with flourishes of indoor dining.*

Chilled Escarole Soup
Brie   French Bread
Grilled Chicken Breasts & Sausages
Rustic Roasted Vegetable Salad
Tomato Salad
Pea & Pastina Salad
Breadsticks   Rolls   Mustards
Cannoli Torta
Football Cookies   Grapes   Peaches
Dry Sauvignon Blanc   Mineral Water

To ease preparation, treat the menu as a potluck, with guests bringing different dishes. Each recipe specifies how the food can be transported, and each has make-ahead steps.

Bring a grill to cook boned and skinned chicken breasts and assorted sausages (allow a total of 4 to 5 ounces for a serving) to go with the salads. Also bring tomatoes to slice and season at the picnic.

Start with soup, cheese, and bread while meats cook. If you want football cookies, make a favorite recipe in football shapes, then add lacings with purchased white icing in a tube.

CHILLED ESCAROLE SOUP

1   **medium-size onion, finely chopped**
1   **tablespoon olive oil**
1   **pound (about 2 heads) escarole, rinsed, drained, and chopped**
2   **cups unflavored yogurt or sour cream (or half of each)**
8   **cups chilled regular-strength chicken broth**

Portable barbecue grills quick-cooking boned chicken breasts and browns plump sausages.

In a 10- to 12-inch frying pan, stir onion often in oil over medium-high heat until onion is limp, 4 to 5 minutes. Add escarole and stir until wilted, 6 to 8 minutes. In a blender, smoothly purée escarole mixture with yogurt. Mix with broth. Cover and chill until cold, at least 3 hours or up until next day. Transport in a thermos jug. Pour into cups to sip. Makes 10 to 12 servings.

PER SERVING: 63 calories, 4 g protein, 5.4 g carbohydrates, 2.8 g fat, 2.3 mg cholesterol, 70 mg sodium

RUSTIC ROASTED VEGETABLE SALAD

To minimize cleanup, cook the vegetables in sequence in foil-lined pans; it goes faster if you have more than 1 oven.

6   **medium-size (about 2½ lb. total) zucchini, ends trimmed**
    About ½ cup olive oil
3   **large (2½ to 3 lb. total) red onions**
    About ¼ cup balsamic or red wine vinegar
10 **Asian eggplants (about 4 oz. each), stems trimmed**
3   **medium-size (about 1½ lb. total) yellow bell peppers**
    Herb dressing (recipe follows)
    Salt and pepper

Cut zucchini lengthwise into about ¼-inch-thick slices. Line 2 pans, 10 by 15 inches each, with foil; brush foil with oil. Arrange zucchini in a single layer in pans; brush lightly with oil. Bake, uncovered, in a 500° oven until browned, 35 to 40 minutes. Slide foil with zucchini off pans; let cool. Line pans with more foil; oil foil.

Cut onions crosswise into about ½-inch-thick slices; arrange slices in a single layer in pans. Brush generously with vinegar, then brush lightly with oil. Bake in a 500° oven until well browned on edges, 30 to 35 minutes. Slide foil with onions off pans; let cool. Line pans with more foil; oil foil.

Cut eggplants lengthwise into ⅜-inch-thick slices; arrange in a single layer in pans (you may need to fill 1 pan twice). Brush lightly with oil. Bake at 475° until browned and very soft when pressed, 25 to 30 minutes. Slide foil with eggplant off pans; let cool. Line pans with foil; do not oil.

Cut peppers in half lengthwise; place skin up in pans. Broil 2 to 3 inches from heat until charred, about 10 minutes. Remove from oven and drape with more foil; let cool. Pull off and discard skin, stems, and seeds; tear peppers into 1-inch strips.

To transport, pack into individual containers and carry at room temperature (keeps up to 4 hours; or cover and chill up until next day). Arrange vegetables on a large platter, pour dressing over them; add salt and pepper to taste. Makes 10 to 12 servings.

PER SERVING: 215 calories, 3.6 g protein, 18 g carbohydrates, 16 g fat, 0 mg cholesterol, 0.8 mg sodium

Herb dressing. In a jar, combine ⅓ cup **olive oil**, ⅓ cup **balsamic vinegar** or red wine vinegar, ¼ cup chopped **fresh chives** or green onion, and 2 teaspoons chopped **fresh oregano** or 1 teaspoon dry oregano leaves. Cover; if made ahead, let stand up to 4 hours; carry at room temperature.

TOMATO SALAD

    ¼ cup lightly packed fresh basil
       leaves, chopped; or 2 tablespoons
       dry basil leaves
    ¼ cup olive oil
    ¼ cup balsamic or red wine vinegar
    3 to 4 pounds (about 6 large) ripe
       tomatoes
       Fresh basil sprigs (optional)
       Salt and pepper

Mix chopped basil, oil, and vinegar; put in a small covered jar (hold up to 4 hours). Rinse tomatoes and transport, uncut, with dressing at room temperature. Carry basil sprigs in an insulated chest.

At the picnic, core tomatoes and slice about ½ inch thick onto a large platter; pour basil dressing over them. Garnish with basil sprigs, and add salt and pepper to taste. Makes 10 to 12 servings.

PER SERVING: 65 calories, 1.1 g protein, 5.5 g carbohydrates, 4.7 g fat, 0 mg cholesterol, 9.3 mg sodium

PEA & PASTINA SALAD

    ¾ pound (about 1½ cups) small dry
       pasta stars, or about 1 pound
       (2 cups) dry rice pasta
       Lemon dressing (recipe follows)
    4 cups (20 oz.) frozen petite peas
       Salt and pepper

In a 6- to 8-quart pan, bring 4 quarts water to a boil over high heat. Stir in pasta and cook, uncovered, until barely tender to bite, 6 to 7 minutes. Drain, rinse with cold water, and drain again.

In a large bowl, mix pasta with lemon dressing. If made ahead, cover and chill

Set up in eucalyptus grove, pregame tailgate picnic—of salads, grilled meats, torta—was a potluck menu. Each dish has make-ahead steps and was easy to transport.

up until next day. Transport, covered, in an insulated chest, along with peas in a plastic bag.

To serve, stir thawed peas into salad. Add salt and pepper to taste. Makes 10 to 12 servings.

PER SERVING: 192 calories, 5.8 g protein, 28 g carbohydrates, 6.5 g fat, 0 mg cholesterol, 67 mg sodium

Lemon dressing. In a small bowl, combine ⅓ cup *each* **olive oil** and **white wine vinegar**, 1 teaspoon **ground nutmeg**, 2 tablespoons grated **lemon peel**, and 5 tablespoons **lemon juice**.

(Continued on next page)

CANNOLI TORTA

1 cup whipping cream

2¾ cups (1 large container, 15 oz., and 1 small container, 8 oz.) ricotta cheese

About 1 cup shelled, salted pistachios, chopped

2 tablespoons orange-flavor liqueur

2 tablespoons rum

3 tablespoons powdered sugar

½ cup finely chopped semisweet chocolate

Fresh candied orange peel (directions follow)

Press-in pastry (directions follow)

About ½ cup finely grated semisweet chocolate

In a bowl, whip cream until it holds soft peaks. In another bowl, combine cheese, ½ cup pistachios, liqueur, rum, sugar, chopped chocolate, and candied peel with syrup. Mix well; fold in whipped cream. If made ahead, cover and chill 2 hours or up until next day; carry in an insulated chest.

At picnic, remove pan rim from pastry. Mound filling onto pastry, top with grated chocolate, and garnish with remaining pistachios. Cut into wedges. Makes 10 to 12 servings.

PER SERVING: 473 calories, 12 g protein, 36 g carbohydrates, 32 g fat, 88 mg cholesterol, 137 mg sodium

Fresh candied orange peel. With vegetable peeler, pare orange part of peel from 2 medium-size **oranges;** ream juice from fruit. With a knife, cut the peel into very thin shreds.

In a 1½- to 2-quart pan over high heat, bring peel and 1 cup water to a boil; drain. Repeat step. Add juice and ⅓ cup **sugar.** Boil, uncovered, stirring occasionally, until syrup is reduced to 2 to 3 tablespoons, 10 to 15 minutes. Remove from heat; stir in 2 tablespoons **rum.** If made ahead, cover and chill up to 1 week.

Press-in pastry. Combine 1½ cups **all-purpose flour,** ½ cup (¼ lb.) **butter** or margarine, and 2 tablespoons **sugar.** Whirl in a food processor or rub with fin-

gers until fine crumbs form. Whirl or stir in with a fork 1 **large egg** until dough holds together.

Press dough on bottom (not sides) of an 11-inch tart pan with removable rim. Bake in a 300° oven until golden brown, 40 to 45 minutes. Let cool; cover airtight. If made ahead, keep pastry up until next day; carry at room temperature.

Paper plates, supported in sturdy baskets, comfortably hold ample lunch with cup of puréed soup to sip. Cleanup is speedy.

Football cookies add to the party spirit. Use a favorite shortbread or gingerbread cooky dough, then add ball lacings with icing in a tube.

Festival Fall Dinner with Wild or Farm-Grown Fowl

ON OPENING DAY *of pheasant season, Emily and Peter Schott (assisted by a crew and a well-rigged trailer kitchen) serve this elegant multi-course game dinner to two dozen special guests on the banks of the Boise River in Idaho.*

But the Schotts' festive dishes aren't limited to the hunter's kitchen; they work just as well in tamer conditions and for smaller parties.

For an easy start, buy farm-grown fresh or frozen quail, pheasant, and mallard ducks. You may need to place a special order—in some cases, weeks in advance. Try deluxe supermarkets, poultry or meat specialty stores, or game farms. Some of the farms will ship frozen or chilled birds, and some mail-order food catalogs also offer them. (The Schotts, chef-owners of Peter Schott's New American Cuisine Restaurant, use farm birds for this meal. Since they like to age the meat briefly, wild birds shot on opening day aren't usable until 3 or 4 days later.)

These specialty birds are relatively expensive. Quail range from $1 to $3 each. Pheasant cost $4 to $8 per pound, mallards $4 to $7 per pound. Shipping adds more to the costs.

You can capture the essence of this extravaganza at home, featuring 1 kind of game bird to serve a party of 8. If you have a cooking team, you might produce all the dishes. Each poultry choice makes 8 servings; increase the leek and cabbage dishes proportionately with every increase of the poultry entrée.

Start the meal with a stand-up presentation of cheese paired with raw vegetables and accompanied by champagne. Next, you might serve soup to sip from mugs—a light broth or creamed mixture. If you have help, you could sit down to soup, then to a second course of the leeks.

Choose quail, pheasant, or duck as the menu focus. The braised red cabbage complements any of them. You can also bake small apples (top each with currant jelly) and Idaho potatoes to serve with the birds. A full-bodied, mellow Cabernet Sauvignon, Zinfandel, or Merlot is a good wine selection to accompany this meal.

Dessert might be as simple as fresh pears and nuts, or as elaborate as the Schotts' two-tone chocolate mousse.

You can make the leeks and their dressing, the cabbage, and the dessert 1 to 2 days ahead. Several hours before serving, start the mushroom sauce for the pheasants or marinate the ducks. When cooking the birds, take care to keep them slightly underdone as directed, or they will get dry and stringy. Reheat cabbage to serve.

If you don't want to prepare this whole menu, you can use the dishes singly, incorporating them into one of your own favorite menus. The sweet-tart braised cabbage goes well with roast pork, chicken, or grilled sausages. Offer the leeks as a light lunch or as a fancy appetizer salad to start an elegant dinner.

QUAIL IN RASPBERRY SAUCE

16	quail (each about 4 oz.)
2	to 3 tablespoons salad oil
⅓	cup sugar
½	cup raspberry vinegar or red wine vinegar
2	cups regular-strength chicken broth
1½	tablespoons cornstarch
1½	tablespoons water
1	cup fresh or partially thawed, frozen, unsweetened raspberries
2	tablespoons brandy
2	tablespoons lemon juice
	Salt and white pepper

Rinse birds and pat dry; save necks and giblets for another use.

Pour 2 tablespoons oil into a 10- to 12-inch frying pan over medium-high heat. Add birds, a few at a time (do not crowd), and brown all over, about 5 minutes per bird; add oil as needed. Arrange birds, breast up and slightly apart, on a rack in a 12- by 17-inch roasting pan.

Roast birds in a 400° oven until breasts are still red and moist in center but not wet-looking (cut into breast just above wing joint to test), 12 to 15 minutes. Place on a platter if needed; keep warm in a 150° oven up to 30 minutes. Reserve roasting juices.

Meanwhile, to the frying pan add sugar and 1 tablespoon vinegar. Cook over medium-high heat until sugar liquefies and turns a golden caramel color, 3 to 5 minutes. While stirring, add remaining vinegar; simmer, stirring, until caramel dissolves, about 2 minutes.

Add broth and quail roasting juices; boil, uncovered, until reduced by ½, about 15 minutes.

Mix cornstarch and water; stir into sauce. Stir until boiling. Add raspberries, brandy, lemon juice, and salt and pepper to taste. Pour over birds. Makes 8 servings.

PER SERVING: 458 calories, 40 g protein, 12 g carbohydrates, 27 g fat, 0 mg cholesterol, 121 mg sodium

PHEASANTS & CHANTERELLES

2	pheasants (each 2 to 2½ lb.)
2	tablespoons salad oil
1	cup *each* coarsely chopped onion, carrot, and celery
10	dry juniper berries
6	whole cloves
1	clove garlic, pressed or minced
1	teaspoon minced fresh sage, or ¼ teaspoon dry rubbed sage
	About 3 cups water
4	slices (4 oz. total) salt pork or bacon
	Mushroom sauce (recipe follows)

Rinse pheasants and pat dry. Remove necks; reserve giblets for another use.

Put oil in a 10- to 12-inch frying pan; place pan over medium-high heat. Add birds and necks; cook, turning to brown all sides, about 10 minutes.

Place browned birds, breast up, on a rack in a 12- by 15-inch roasting pan. To frying pan with necks add onion, carrot, celery, juniper berries, cloves, garlic, and sage; cook over medium heat, stirring often, until onion is limp. Add 3 cups water. Boil, uncovered, until liquid is reduced by ½, 10 to 15 minutes. Pour mixture through a fine strainer and measure; you need 1 cup broth. As necessary, return broth to pan and boil until reduced to 1 cup, or add water to make 1 cup; reserve broth for mushroom sauce, following. Discard vegetables and necks and skim the fat from the broth.

Drape birds with salt pork. Roast in a 400° oven, brushing often with pan juices, until breast meat at bone is white with a touch of pink but no longer wet and soft (cut to the bone parallel to wing joint to test), 30 to 40 minutes.

As the birds cook, prepare the mushroom sauce. When pheasants are done, pour any pan juices into the mushroom

Mushroom sauce. In the same frying pan used to brown pheasants, melt 2 tablespoons **butter** or margarine over medium-high heat. Add ¾ teaspoon minced **garlic,** 1 tablespoon minced **shallot,** and 3 cups (9 oz.) **chanterelles** or thinly sliced common mushrooms. Cook, stirring often, until mushrooms are lightly browned and liquid evaporates, about 5 minutes. Stir 2 tablespoons **all-purpose flour** into pan. Smoothly stir in 1 cup **dry white wine** and **reserved broth** (from pheasant recipe). Boil, uncovered, stirring often, until reduced by ⅓, about 5 minutes. Add ½ cup **whipping cream** and bring to a boil. Add **salt** and **white pepper** to taste.

GRILLED MALLARD DUCKS WITH SOY

    4 mallard ducks (each 2 to 2½ lb.)
    3 cloves garlic, pressed or minced
    ¾ cup light soy sauce
    ¼ teaspoon crushed dried hot red
       chilies
    2 lemons, cut into wedges
    ½ cup canned lingonberries
       About 2 cups watercress sprigs,
       rinsed and crisped

Cut ducks in half lengthwise with poultry shears, or use a hammer to pound a heavy knife through bone. Remove backbones. Cut off wings at upper joints.

On each duck half, start at edge of breast and slide a small, sharp knife parallel to the bone, cutting meat free from breast and back bones. Then cut thigh from body so you end up with boned body meat with a leg attached. Trim off any loose skin flaps. If breast fillets fall free, reserve.

Reserve wings and carcass bones for broth. Rinse duck halves and pat dry.

Place duck halves in a large plastic bag set in a dish or pan. Add garlic, soy, and chilies. Seal bag and turn to coat meat well. Cover and chill, turning often, at least 30 minutes or up to 2 hours.

Lay duck halves out flat, skin down, on a grill 4 to 6 inches above a solid bed of medium-hot coals (you can hold your hand at grill level only 3 to 4 seconds).

Lean mallard duck halves, marinated in mixture of soy sauce, garlic, and crushed chilies, grill over hot coals; turn frequently until cooked to a juicy rare stage.

sauce. Remove salt pork from pheasant. With poultry shears or a heavy knife with a hammer to pound it through the bone, cut each pheasant in half lengthwise along backbone and through the breastbone. Cut halves crosswise to make quarters. Place on platter. Spoon sauce onto birds. If needed, keep warm in a 150° oven up to 30 minutes. Makes 8 servings.

PER SERVING: 583 calories, 46 g protein, 5.5 g carbohydrates, 41 g fat, 37 mg cholesterol, 326 mg sodium

Cook, turning often to brown evenly and avoid burning and flares, until breast is still red and moist in the center of the thickest part (cut to test) but no longer wet-looking, about 20 minutes. Place on a platter; if needed, keep warm in a 150° oven up to 30 minutes. Garnish duck with lemon, lingonberries, and watercress. Makes 8 servings.

ACCURATE NUTRITIONAL DATA NOT AVAILABLE. Estimated 580 calories per serving.

POACHED LEEKS WITH VALENCIA DRESSING

8 leeks (about 1½-in. diameter), about 2½ pounds total
8 small fuchsia-colored salad savoy or radicchio leaves
¾ pound tiny shelled cooked shrimp
Valencia dressing (recipe follows)

In a 5- to 6-quart pan bring about 3 quarts water to boiling. Meanwhile, trim roots and tough dark green tops from leeks. Cut leeks in half lengthwise. Wash leeks thoroughly, gently rinsing between layers. If leeks tend to separate, tie each half at its midpoint with a cotton string. Drop leeks into boiling water and simmer, uncovered, until tender when pierced, 6 to 8 minutes. Drain and immerse in ice water. When cool, drain thoroughly. Remove strings. If made ahead, cover and chill up to the next day.

On each of 8 salad or dinner plates, place 2 leek halves; beside them arrange equal portions salad savoy leaves and shrimp, then top with dressing. Makes 8 servings.

PER SERVING: 240 calories, 11 g protein, 19 g carbohydrates, 15 g fat, 83 mg cholesterol, 115 mg sodium

Valencia dressing. Combine ⅓ cup finely chopped **white onion,** ⅓ cup finely chopped **red bell pepper,** ⅓ cup **cider vinegar,** ¼ cup **extra-virgin olive oil,** ¼ cup **salad oil,** 2 tablespoons **honey,** ½ teaspoon minced **garlic,** and ¼ teaspoon **cayenne.** Mix well. Cover and chill at least 4 hours or up until next day. Makes 1½ cups.

BURGUNDY APPLE CHESTNUT CABBAGE

2½ pounds (1 large head) red cabbage
2 cups dry red wine
⅓ cup lemon juice
½ cup firmly packed brown sugar
2 Red Delicious apples (1 lb. total), quartered, cored, and thinly sliced
¼ cup (⅛ lb.) butter or margarine
1 large onion, finely chopped
1 dry bay leaf
1 cup regular-strength chicken broth
1 can (10 oz. drained weight) chestnuts in water, drained
Salt and white pepper

Core and cut cabbage into ¼-inch-wide strips. In a large bowl, combine cabbage, wine, lemon juice, sugar, and apples. Mix well. If made ahead, cover and let stand up to overnight.

In a 6- to 8-quart pan, melt butter over medium-high heat until bubbly. Add the onion and cook, stirring, until light gold, about 5 minutes. Add cabbage mixture, bay leaf, and broth. Simmer, covered, until cabbage wilts, 10 to 15 minutes. Uncover and boil gently, stirring occasionally, until cabbage is very tender when pierced, 45 to 50 minutes. (If made ahead, cool, cover, and chill until the next day; reheat to continue.) If liquid remains in pan, boil, uncovered, until it evaporates, stirring occasionally. Stir in chestnuts. Simmer, stirring occasionally, until chestnuts are hot, about 5 minutes. Add salt and pepper to taste. Serves 8.

PER SERVING: 217 calories, 3.1 g protein, 39 g carbohydrates, 6.9 g fat, 16 mg cholesterol, 97 mg sodium

TWO-TONE CHOCOLATE MOUSSE

Dark mousse (recipe follows)
White mousse (recipe follows)
Custard sauce (recipe follows)
¾ cup chopped salted pistachios
2 to 3 cups raspberries, rinsed and drained
Whipped cream (optional)

Line a 4- by 8-inch loaf pan with plastic wrap. Spread ½ of the dark mousse in bottom of pan. Chill until firm, about 30 minutes. Spread all of white mousse evenly on dark mousse. Chill until firm, about 30 minutes. If remaining dark mousse has firmed, stir over hot water until fluid but not hot (if overheated, let cool); spread over white mousse. Cover and chill until firm, at least 4 hours or up to 3 days.

Invert layered mousse onto a board or platter; remove plastic. With a thin, sharp knife, cut mousse into 12 to 14 equal slices; wipe blade between cuts. Lay slices on dessert plates. (If done ahead, cover and chill up until next day.) Pour an equal amount of custard onto each plate. Garnish equally with pistachios, berries, and whipped cream. Makes 12 to 14 servings.

PER SERVING: 403 calories, 5.9 g protein, 35 g carbohydrates, 27 g fat, 152 mg cholesterol, 41 mg sodium

Dark mousse. In the top of a double boiler, combine 10 ounces **semisweet** or bittersweet **chocolate,** chopped; ⅔ cup **whipping cream;** and ¼ cup (⅛ lb.) **unsalted butter** or margarine. Stir over simmering water just until smooth. Remove from heat. Stir in until smooth 2 **large egg yolks,** ⅔ cup sifted **powdered sugar,** and ¼ cup **rum.**

White mousse. In the top of a double boiler, combine 6 ounces **white chocolate,** chopped; 2 tablespoons **whipping cream;** and 2 tablespoons **unsalted butter** or margarine. Stir over simmering water just until melted and smooth. Remove from heat. Stir in until smooth 1 **large egg yolk** and 1 tablespoon **rum.** Cool to lukewarm.

Custard sauce. In a 1½- to 2-quart pan, scald 2 cups **milk.** In a double boiler top, mix 1 **large egg,** 2 **large egg yolks,** and ⅓ cup **sugar.** Add milk and stir over simmering water until custard thickly coats a metal spoon, 10 to 15 minutes. Remove from heat. Add 2 tablespoons **rum** or orange-flavored liqueur and 1 teaspoon **vanilla.** Cool, cover, and chill up to 2 days.

The Big Muffin Tasting

AMONG RECIPES *most frequently shared by our readers are ones for muffins. Here are a half-dozen rated as outstanding by Sunset taste panels. They range from tender and sweet to dense and wholesome, and use a variety of flours, cereals, fresh and dried fruits, and spices.*

To reheat muffins, place in a single layer on a flat pan or sheet of foil; cover with foil. Bake in a 350° oven until warm, 15 to 18 minutes.

HEAVENLY PUMPKIN GEMS

- 2 cups all-purpose flour
- 1 tablespoon baking powder
- 1 teaspoon ground cinnamon
- ¼ teaspoon ground nutmeg
- ¼ teaspoon ground ginger
- ¼ teaspoon salt (optional)
- ½ cup salad oil, or butter or margarine (¼ lb.) at room temperature
- ½ cup plus 2 tablespoons sugar
- 2 large eggs
- 1 cup canned pumpkin
- ½ cup sour cream
- 2 small packages (3 oz. each) cream cheese, each cut into 6 cubes
- 3 tablespoons apricot preserves
- ¼ cup sliced almonds

In a large bowl, mix together flour, baking powder, cinnamon, nutmeg, ginger, and salt. In another bowl, beat oil and the ½ cup of sugar until blended. Add the eggs, pumpkin, and sour cream and beat until thoroughly mixed. Stir pumpkin mixture into the dry ingredients just until moistened (batter will be stiff).

Spoon batter into 12 paper-lined 2½-inch muffin cups, filling halfway. Place 1 cheese cube in the center of each cup; top cubes equally with preserves. Completely cover cheese and jam with remaining batter. Sprinkle muffin tops with almonds and remaining sugar. Bake in a 400° oven until well browned, about 45 minutes. Remove from pan and cool at least 10 minutes. If made ahead, wrap airtight and chill up until the next day; freeze to store longer (thaw wrapped). To reheat, follow preceding directions. Makes 12. —*Ayako Hill, Sacramento.*

PER MUFFIN: 312 calories, 5.2 g protein, 33 g carbohydrates, 18 g fat, 55 mg cholesterol, 166 mg sodium

PEANUT BUTTER–BANANA BRAN MUFFINS

- 1 cup whole-wheat flour
- 1 cup bran cereal (not flakes)
- 2 teaspoons baking powder
- ¼ teaspoon salt (optional)
- ½ cup salad oil, or butter or margarine (¼ lb.) at room temperature
- ½ cup firmly packed light brown sugar
- 2 large eggs
- 1 cup mashed very ripe bananas (about 2 medium-size)
- ½ cup chunk-style peanut butter
- ½ cup milk

In a small bowl, mix together flour, bran cereal, baking powder, and salt.

In a large bowl, beat oil with sugar to blend. Add eggs, bananas, and peanut butter and beat until well mixed; add milk. Stir dry ingredients into liquids just until moistened.

Spoon batter equally into 12 greased or paper-lined 2½-inch muffin cups. Bake in a 350° oven until well browned, about 30 minutes; remove from pan. If made ahead, let cool, then wrap airtight and hold at room temperature up until the next day; freeze to store longer (thaw wrapped). To reheat, follow preceding directions. Makes 12.—*Karen Yamaguchi, Chula Vista, Calif.*

PER MUFFIN: 265 calories, 6.4 g protein, 29 g carbohydrates, 16 g fat, 37 mg cholesterol, 207 mg sodium

BLUEBERRY MUFFINS

After adding blueberries to batter, work quickly and handle as little as possible. Otherwise, the baking soda may turn the berries green (a harmless reaction).

- 1½ cups whole-wheat flour
- 1½ cups all-purpose flour
- 1 cup plus 2 tablespoons firmly packed light brown sugar
- ¼ teaspoon salt (optional)
- 2 teaspoons baking soda
- 4 teaspoons baking powder
- 1 tablespoon ground cinnamon
- 2 large eggs
- 1½ cups buttermilk
- ¼ cup salad oil, or butter or margarine (⅛ lb.) melted and cooled
- 2 cups blueberries, fresh or unsweetened frozen (unthawed)

In a large bowl, stir together whole-wheat flour, all-purpose flour, 1 cup of the sugar, salt, baking soda, baking powder, and cinnamon. In another bowl, beat eggs to blend with buttermilk and oil. Add to the dry ingredients and stir just to moisten. Add blueberries, and stir briefly and gently to mix through batter.

Spoon batter equally into 12 greased or paper-lined 2½-inch muffin cups (cups will be very full). Sprinkle tops with remaining brown sugar. Bake in a 375° oven until tops are well browned, about 35 minutes. Remove from pan and let cool 5 minutes. If made ahead, let cool, wrap airtight, and hold at room temperature up until next day; freeze to store longer (thaw wrapped). To reheat, follow preceding directions. Makes 12. —*Kathy English, Salt Lake City.*

PER MUFFIN: 265 calories, 5.9 g protein, 48 g carbohydrates, 6.2 g fat, 37 mg cholesterol, 331 mg sodium

HOMESTEAD BRAN MUFFINS

This batter keeps up to 2 weeks in the refrigerator, so you can have fresh, hot muffins any time you like. (If batter is made ahead, be sure to stir it before using.) Although you can bake muffins on demand, you can also store them using the procedure given in preceding recipes.

- 3 cups bran cereal (not flakes)
- ¾ cup boiling water
- 3 tablespoons thawed frozen orange juice concentrate
- ½ cup salad oil
- 2 large eggs
- 2 cups buttermilk
- 2½ cups all-purpose flour
- 1½ cups sugar
- 2½ teaspoons baking soda
- 1 cup dried currants
- ½ cup finely chopped walnuts

In a large bowl, combine 1 cup bran cereal, water, orange juice concentrate, and oil; stir to mix. Add eggs and buttermilk; mix well. In a small bowl, mix remaining bran, flour, sugar, baking soda, and currants. Add to liquid mixture and stir until evenly moistened. If made ahead, cover batter and chill up to 2 weeks.

Spoon batter equally into 24 greased or paper-lined 2½-inch muffin cups; sprinkle evenly with nuts. Bake in a 350° oven until well browned, about 30 minutes. Remove from pan. Makes 24. —*Janice Condit, Placerville, Calif.*

PER MUFFIN: 213 calories, 4.7 g protein, 37 g carbohydrates, 7.2 g fat, 18 mg cholesterol, 211 mg sodium

SPICY APPLE MUFFINS

1¾ cups all-purpose flour
2 teaspoons baking powder
1 teaspoon baking soda
1 teaspoon ground cinnamon
¼ teaspoon ground allspice
⅛ teaspoon ground nutmeg
¼ cup granulated sugar
¼ cup firmly packed brown sugar
¼ teaspoon salt
1 large egg
1 cup nonfat milk
⅓ cup salad oil
1 large tart apple (such as Granny Smith or Newtown Pippin), peeled, cored, and finely diced

In a small bowl, mix together the flour, baking powder, soda, cinnamon, allspice, nutmeg, granulated sugar, brown sugar, and salt. In a large bowl, beat egg, milk, oil, and apple to blend. Add the dry ingredients and stir just to moisten.

Spoon batter equally into 12 greased or paper-lined 2½-inch muffin cups. Bake in a 350° oven until well browned, 30 to 35 minutes. Remove from pan and let cool 5 minutes. If made ahead, cool, then wrap airtight and hold at room temperature up until next day; freeze to store longer (thaw wrapped). To reheat, follow preceding directions. Makes 12. —*Doris M. Rogers, Port Orchard, Wash.*

PER MUFFIN: 174 calories, 3.1 g protein, 26 g carbohydrates, 6.6 g fat, 18 mg cholesterol, 202 mg sodium

CALIFORNIA BREAKFAST MUFFINS

¾ cup oat bran
¾ cup quick-cooking rolled oats
¼ cup toasted wheat germ
1 cup all-purpose flour
1 tablespoon baking powder
2 large eggs
½ cup unsweetened applesauce
½ cup honey

Sunset taste panel evaluates muffins made from reader-submitted recipes. Behind, visiting tour group watches through test kitchen windows.

½ cup salad oil
⅓ cup milk
1½ cups grated carrots (about 2 large)
¾ cup raisins
½ cup sliced almonds

In a small bowl, mix together oat bran, rolled oats, wheat germ, flour, and baking powder. In a large bowl, beat to blend eggs, applesauce, honey, oil, milk, carrots, raisins, and almonds. Add the dry ingredients and stir just until moistened.

Spoon batter equally into 12 greased or paper-lined 2½-inch muffin cups. Bake in a 375° oven until well browned, about 35 minutes. Remove from pan and cool 5 minutes. If made ahead, let cool, cover, and hold at room temperature up until next day; freeze to store longer (thaw wrapped). To reheat, follow preceding directions. Makes 12. —*Liane Farber, San Mateo, Calif.*

PER MUFFIN: 289 calories, 6.2 g protein, 38 g carbohydrates, 13 g fat, 36 mg cholesterol, 128 mg sodium

Main-Dish Salads with Warm Fish

APPEALINGLY EASY, *these main-dish salads combine warm fish, crisp vegetables, and authoritative seasonings.*

ORIENTAL STIR-FRIED SHARK SALAD

- 3 tablespoons salad oil
- 1 to 1¼ pounds boned, skinned shark or halibut, in 1-inch chunks
- 1 tablespoon minced fresh ginger
- 2 cups thin, diagonal slices celery
- 4 cups (½ lb.) edible-pod peas, ends and strings removed
- 1 package (3 oz.) dry ramen noodles (omit seasoning packet)
- 2 tablespoons *each* Oriental sesame oil and soy sauce
- ¼ cup seasoned rice vinegar
- ½ cup cilantro (coriander) sprigs

Place 2 tablespoons salad oil in a wok or 10- to 12-inch frying pan over medium-high heat. Add fish and ginger; stir-fry until fish is slightly translucent but still moist in center (cut to test), 4 to 6 minutes. Lift from wok; set aside.

Add remaining salad oil, celery, and peas to wok. Stir-fry until vegetables are tender-crisp to bite, 4 to 5 minutes. Remove from heat. Gently stir in fish, noodles (break into bite-size pieces), sesame oil, soy, vinegar, and cilantro. Serves 4.

PER SERVING: 423 calories, 29 g protein, 26 g carbohydrates, 23 g fat, 58 mg cholesterol, 660 mg sodium

ITALIAN-STYLE GRILLED FISH SALAD

- 2 large oranges
- 6 cups lightly packed arugula or watercress sprigs, rinsed and crisped
    About 16 slices plain melba toast
- 1 small red onion, thinly sliced
- ½ cup oil-cured black olives or drained small black ripe olives
- ⅓ cup *each* red wine vinegar and olive oil
- 2 teaspoons fresh or ¾ teaspoon dry thyme leaves
- 2 teaspoons anchovy paste
- ¼ teaspoon pepper
- 1 to 1¼ pounds boned and skinned swordfish or wahoo (also called ono), cut into 1-inch chunks

Grate 1 teaspoon peel from oranges; set aside. Cut off and discard remaining peel and white membrane; thinly slice fruit crosswise. On 4 dinner plates, arrange equal amounts of arugula, then alternate slices of toast, onion, and orange on greens. Scatter olives over salads.

In a bowl, mix grated peel, vinegar, oil, thyme, anchovy, and pepper. Thread fish on 8 slender skewers, each about 10 inches long; brush sparingly with dressing.

Place fish on a lightly-greased grill 4 to 6 inches above a solid bed of hot coals (you can hold your hand at grill level only 2 to 3 seconds). Cook, brushing once or twice with dressing, until fish is slightly translucent but still moist in center (cut to test), about 5 minutes; turn once. Put skewers on plates; spoon remaining dressing onto salads. Serves 4.

PER SERVING: 468 calories, 24 g protein, 28 g carbohydrates, 30 g fat, 1.7 mg cholesterol, 725 mg sodium

HOT & COOL CURRIED FISH & RICE

- 1 small head (¾ lb.) romaine lettuce, cored, rinsed, and crisped
- 1 cup sliced green onions
- 1 large red bell pepper, stemmed, seeded, and finely chopped
- 2 tablespoons salad oil
- 2 teaspoons curry powder
- 1½ cups unflavored yogurt
- ⅓ cup water
- 2½ cups cooked white or brown rice
- 4 Chilean sea bass fillets (1¼ to 1½ lb. total), each ¾ to 1 inch thick

Finely slice ⅓ of the lettuce. Arrange remaining whole leaves on a platter; mound shreds over half of leaves.

In a 10- to 12-inch nonstick frying pan over medium-high heat, stir onions and bell pepper in half the oil until onions are limp, 8 to 10 minutes. Add curry powder; stir 1 minute. Put vegetables in a bowl and mix with yogurt and water; set aside 1¼ cups. Stir remaining yogurt mixture with rice, then mound rice on shredded lettuce.

Add remaining oil to pan over medium-high heat. Add fish; cook, turning once, until slightly translucent but still moist in center (cut to test), 6 to 7 minutes. Place fish on whole lettuce leaves. Spoon reserved yogurt sauce on fish. Serves 4.

PER SERVING: 420 calories, 35 g protein, 42 g carbohydrates, 12 g fat, 63 mg cholesterol, 165 mg sodium

Pea pods, noodles, shark, and sesame dressing make an Oriental stir-fry. Assemble and prepare ingredients before you start to cook; stir-frying takes only minutes.

Pairing Grains, Legumes, or Nuts for Main Dishes

NATURE HAS A CLEVER TRICK. *If you pair certain grains, legumes, or nuts, they form complete proteins that rival those from animal sources. Here, polenta (corn) and beans, brown rice and peanuts, and barley and lentils not only make flavorful alliances, but also form well-balanced main dishes.*

POLENTA SALAD WITH WHITE BEANS

2 tablespoons olive or salad oil
2 medium-size onions, diced
4 cloves garlic, minced or pressed
2¾ cups regular-strength chicken broth
1 cup polenta or yellow cornmeal
2 cans (15 oz.) white kidney beans (cammelli), drained and rinsed
  Basil dressing (recipe follows)
2½ cups thinly sliced carrots
  Fresh basil sprigs (optional)
  Salt and pepper

In a 4- to 5-quart straight-sided pan, combine oil, onion, and garlic. Stir often over medium heat until onion is sweet-tasting and golden, about 20 minutes. Add 2 cups broth and bring to a boil over high heat.

Meanwhile, in a bowl, mix polenta with the remaining ¾ cup broth. Gradually stir polenta mixture into boiling broth. Reduce to simmer; stir with a long spoon for about 15 minutes (polenta thickens quickly but needs more cooking to be stiff enough). Smooth surface of polenta and let cool in pan until firm, at least 1 hour (or cover and chill up until next day).

In a large bowl, gently mix beans with basil dressing; set aside up to 4 hours.

In a 10- to 12-inch frying pan, bring 1 inch of water to a boil over high heat. Add carrots; simmer, uncovered, until tender to bite, about 8 minutes. Drain and let cool. Mix carrots with beans.

Run a knife around rim of polenta; invert polenta onto a board and cut into ¾-inch chunks. Add to vegetables in bowl; mix salad gently. Garnish with basil sprigs; season to taste with salt and pepper. Serves 6.

PER SERVING: 374 calories, 12 g protein, 50 g carbohydrates, 15 g fat, 0 mg cholesterol, 535 mg sodium

Basil dressing. Mix together ½ cup minced **fresh basil leaves** or ¼ cup dry basil leaves, ⅓ cup **cider vinegar**, ¼ cup **olive** or salad **oil**, and 1 teaspoon **pepper**.

WILD SPANISH RICE

½ cup wild rice
2 cups regular-strength chicken broth
2 tablespoons salad oil
1 medium-size red onion, chopped
2 cloves garlic, minced or pressed
1 cup long-grain brown rice
2½ cups tomato juice
1 medium-size green bell pepper
2 medium-size (6 oz. total) firm-ripe Roma-style tomatoes
¾ cup pimiento-stuffed Spanish-style green olives, cut in halves
½ cup roasted, salted peanuts

Pour wild rice into a fine strainer and rinse under running water. Put rice and broth in a 10- to 12-inch frying pan and bring to a boil over high heat. Cover and simmer until rice is tender to bite, about 45 minutes. Drain, reserving broth. Set broth and rice aside (if made ahead, cover and chill up until next day).

To pan, add oil, onion, garlic. Stir often over medium heat until onion is golden, 10 to 12 minutes. Add brown rice and stir on high heat until rice begins to turn opaque, about 3 minutes. Add tomato juice and reserved broth. Bring to boiling on high heat; cover and simmer until rice is tender to bite, about 50 minutes.

Meanwhile, stem and seed bell pepper and core tomatoes; dice both vegetables.

When brown rice is tender, add wild rice, bell pepper, tomato, olives; stir to mix. Pour immediately onto a platter; sprinkle with peanuts. Makes 4 to 6 servings.

PER SERVING: 331 calories, 9.7 g protein, 45 g carbohydrates, 14 g fat, 0 mg cholesterol, 852 mg sodium

BARLEY, LENTIL & EGGPLANT CASSEROLE

2 medium-size eggplants (about 2 lb. total), stems trimmed
⅓ cup olive or salad oil
¾ cup lentils
¾ cup pearl barley
5 cups regular-strength chicken broth
1 tablespoon dry oregano leaves
1 cup thinly sliced green onion
⅓ cup minced fresh mint or 3 tablespoons dry mint
1 teaspoon pepper
½ pound mozzarella cheese, shredded
  Fresh mint sprigs

Cut eggplants into ¾-inch cubes and distribute equally in 2 baking pans, each 10 by 15 inches. Mix equal portions of oil with eggplant. Bake in a 425° oven until very soft when pressed, about 40 minutes. Every 15 minutes, turn eggplant with a spatula and alternate pan positions.

Meanwhile, sort lentils, removing any debris. Rinse and drain lentils and barley. In a 3- to 4-quart pan, bring broth to a boil; add lentils, barley, and oregano. Cover and simmer until barley and lentils are tender to bite, about 25 minutes; drain and reserve broth (if made ahead, cover and chill lentil mixture, broth, and eggplant until next day).

Mix lentil mixture and 1 cup reserved broth with eggplant, sliced onion, minced mint, pepper, and half the cheese. Pour into a 9- by 13-inch baking dish, leveling, then sprinkle with remaining mozzarella. Bake, covered, in a 425° oven until hot, about 30 minutes. Serve hot or warm; garnish with mint sprigs. Serves 6.

PER SERVING: 456 calories, 21 g protein, 45 g carbohydrates, 22 g fat, 30 mg cholesterol, 206 mg sodium

Your Own Cereal Mixes, Ready & Waiting

HOMEMADE CEREALS, *rich in fiber from wholesome ingredients, are not only convenient; they give a good start to the day.*

Here, we present two distinctive breakfast cereals. The first cereal is a toasted mix. The second is a moist blend of oatmeal and fruit you can refrigerate up to 1 week.

BANANA-SWEETENED GRANOLA

Serve granola with milk or yogurt and fresh fruit; or eat dry as a crunchy snack.

- ½ **cup bulgur (cracked wheat)**
- 1 **cup boiling water**
- 1 **cup mashed ripe banana (about 2 medium-size)**
- ½ **cup nonfat milk**
- ¼ **cup salad oil**
- 1 **tablespoon vanilla**
- 4 **cups regular rolled oats**
- 1½ **cups bran cereal**
- 1 **cup *each* sweetened flaked dry coconut and blanched almonds**
- ½ **cup *each* toasted wheat germ and sunflower seed**
- ¼ **cup sesame seed**

Granola, sweetened with ripe banana then baked crisp, contains (from left) almonds, sunflower and sesame seeds, bran cereal, coconut, bulgur, oats, and wheat germ.

In a small bowl, mix together bulgur and boiling water; set aside until most of the liquid is absorbed, about 1 hour.

In a large bowl, beat banana with milk, oil, and vanilla until well mixed. Add oats, bran cereal, coconut, almonds, wheat germ, sunflower seed, sesame seed, and bulgur with liquid.

Evenly divide cereal mixture between 2 baking pans, each 10 by 15 inches; spread in an even layer. Bake in a 300° oven until mixture is crisp and golden, about 1½ hours; stir every 20 minutes. Let cool. Serve, or package airtight and keep up to 1 month. Makes about 8 cups. —*Jeanne Cissna, Eureka, Calif.*

PER ½-CUP SERVING: 293 calories, 9.6 g protein, 35 g carbohydrates, 15 g fat, 0.1 mg cholesterol, 91 mg sodium

MUESLI, SACRAMENTO-STYLE

- 2 **medium-size Golden Delicious apples, rinsed and drained**
- 1 **cup pitted prunes**
- 1¾ **cups water**
- 2 **cups regular rolled oats**
- 2 **tablespoons *each* honey and lemon juice**
- ½ **teaspoon ground cinnamon**
  Toppings (optional; choices follow)

Core apples and cut into chunks. In a blender or food processor, whirl apples, prunes, and water until fruit is minced; scrape container sides often. Pour mixture into a bowl; stir in oats, honey, lemon juice, and cinnamon. Cover airtight and chill at least overnight or up to 1 week.

Spoon muesli into small bowls and add toppings of your choice. Makes about 5 cups. —*Eleanor Reynolds, Sacramento.*

PER ½-CUP SERVING: 135 calories, 3 g protein, 30 g carbohydrates, 1.2 g fat, 0 mg cholesterol, 2 mg sodium

Toppings. To vary each serving, offer toppings such as chopped **nuts** (almonds, pecans, walnuts, or peanuts), sliced **fruit** (banana, pineapple, oranges, or strawberries), whole **berries,** and **dairy products** (milk, or unflavored or flavored yogurt).

Stamina-building breakfast of moist, uncooked oatmeal is topped with fruit and nuts. When covered tightly and refrigerated, prepared mixture will keep up to a week.

Fragrant & Fruity Fall Cakes

AUTUMN'S FAVORITE FRUIT *enhances these simple cakes. In the first, sliced green apples bake on a rich butter cake and are later crowned with an almond toffee topping. Chunks of apple, raisins, and pecans stud the moist spice cake; for a lavish touch, offer maple-flavored cream with this cake.*

ALMOND TOFFEE APPLE CAKE

- ¾ cup (⅜ lb.) butter or margarine
- 1 cup sugar
- 2 large eggs
- 2 cups all-purpose flour
- 2 teaspoons baking powder
  About ¾ pound (1 large or 2 small) Granny Smith or Newtown Pippin apples, cored, quartered, and thinly sliced
  Almond topping (recipe follows)

In a large bowl, beat butter and sugar until creamy. Add eggs, 1 at a time, beating until blended. Add flour and baking powder; mix until blended.

Spread batter in a greased 2-inch-deep, 9-inch-diameter cake pan with removable rim. Place apples on batter, overlapping slightly. Bake in 350° oven until cake top is lightly browned in center and springs back when touched, 50 to 60 minutes.

Just before cake is done, prepare almond topping. Spread hot topping over hot cake and return to oven. Bake until topping is browned, 15 to 20 minutes longer.

Cool in pan about 10 minutes, cut around pan sides to free topping from pan, and remove rim. Serve warm or cool. If made ahead, cool, cover, and let stand at room temperature until the next day. Cut into wedges. Makes 12 servings.—*Mia Flink, Daly City, Calif.*

PER SERVING: 401 calories, 5.1 g protein, 42 g carbohydrates, 22 g fat, 82 mg cholesterol, 259 mg sodium

Almond toffee topping. In a 1- to 1½-quart pan, melt 6 tablespoons **butter** or margarine over medium heat. Stir in ½ cup **sugar** and 1 tablespoon **all-purpose flour;** stir until blended and bubbly. Stir in 1 cup **sliced almonds.** Use hot.

Overlapping apple slices form a juicy layer of fruit between rich, buttery cake and chewy almond toffee; topping is spread over hot cake just before baking is done.

SPICED APPLE PECAN CAKE

- ¾ cup raisins
- 2 tablespoons rum or brandy
- 1 cup (½ lb.) butter or margarine, at room temperature
- 1 cup sugar
- 3 large eggs
- 3 cups all-purpose flour
- 1½ teaspoons baking soda
- ½ teaspoon ground nutmeg
- ½ teaspoon ground cinnamon
- ½ teaspoon salt
- ¼ teaspoon ground ginger
- ¼ teaspoon ground allspice
- ¼ teaspoon ground mace
- 3½ cups (about 1 lb.) coarsely chopped Granny Smith or Newtown Pippin apples
- 1 cup chopped pecans
- 12 pecan halves
  Maple cream (recipe follows), optional

Mix raisins and rum; set aside.

In a large mixing bowl, beat butter and sugar until light and creamy. Add eggs, 1 at a time, beating until blended.

Stir together flour, soda, nutmeg, cinnamon, salt, ginger, allspice, and mace. Add to butter mixture, ½ at a time, mixing to blend. Stir in raisins and rum, apples, and chopped pecans just until well distributed.

Spread batter into a buttered and floured 2-inch-deep, 10-inch-diameter cake pan with removable rim; arrange pecan halves over top. Bake in a 325° oven until a toothpick inserted in center comes out clean, about 1 hour. Cool in pan on a rack. Remove rim; serve warm or cool. (If made ahead, cool, cover, and chill up to 2 days; warm to room temperature to serve.) Cut into wedges and offer maple cream to spoon over each piece. Serves 12.

PER SERVING WITHOUT MAPLE CREAM: 455 calories, 6.2 g protein, 56 g carbohydrates, 24 g fat, 82 mg cholesterol, 368 mg sodium

Maple cream. In a bowl, beat 1 cup **whipping cream** until soft peaks hold. Add 2 tablespoons **maple syrup,** beating briefly just to blend. Makes 1¾ cups. Serve immediately.

PER TABLESPOON: 29 calories, 0.2 g protein, 1.2 g carbohydrates, 2.6 g fat, 9.5 mg cholesterol, 3 mg sodium

More October Recipes

OTHER ARTICLES IN THE OCTOBER *issue feature hot soups, a new version of tamale pie, swordfish steaks with salsa, and a lively beverage combining grape and lemon juice.*

CREAMY POTATO WATERCRESS BISQUE

Substantial enough to serve as a meal-in-a-bowl with bread and cheese, this puréed soup also makes a festive starter for holiday dinners. Add chopped ham for contrasting color and flavor.

   3 cups regular-strength chicken
       broth
   2 large thin-skinned potatoes (about
       1 lb. total), peeled and cut into
       1-inch chunks
   2 cups lightly packed watercress
       sprigs, rinsed and drained
   1 cup sour cream
   3 green onions, ends trimmed and
       thinly sliced
       Salt and white pepper
   ¼ pound thinly sliced cooked ham,
       chopped

In a 3- to 4-quart pan, bring chicken broth and potatoes to a boil over high heat; reduce heat, cover, and simmer until the potatoes are tender when pierced, 15 to 20 minutes.

Smooth bisque owes its velvety texture to sour cream, its assertiveness to green onions. Top with ham for added flavor and substance.

Reserve 4 of the most attractive watercress sprigs. In a blender or food processor, whirl remaining watercress, sour cream, onions, and broth mixture, a portion at a time, until puréed. Season to taste with salt and pepper.

Return soup to pan and stir over medium heat just until hot. Ladle soup into wide, shallow bowls. Top each serving with a mound of ham and a watercress sprig. Makes 4 servings.

PER SERVING: 284 calories, 13 g protein, 23 g carbohydrates, 16 g fat, 42 mg cholesterol, 1,223 mg sodium

ITALIAN VEGETABLE SOUP WITH EGGS

This colorful, quick-cooking soup gains substance and flavor from eggs poached in the broth. The recipe comes originally from Italy.

   1 small onion, diced
   3 cloves garlic, minced or mashed
   2 tablespoons olive oil
   1 pound thin-skinned red potatoes,
       scrubbed and diced
   2 medium-size (about ½ lb. total)
       carrots, peeled and thinly sliced
   7 cups regular-strength chicken
       broth
   1 can (8 oz.) tomato sauce
   1 package (10 oz.) frozen peas
   6 large eggs
   ½ cup chopped parsley

In a 5- to 6-quart pan, cook the onion and garlic in oil over medium heat, stirring occasionally, until the onion is soft and slightly browned, about 10 minutes.

Add the potatoes, carrots, broth, and tomato sauce. Simmer, covered, until the potatoes are just tender when pierced, about 20 minutes.

Stir in peas. Heat broth to just below simmering. Gently break the eggs, 1 at a time, into the soup, spacing them so they don't run into each other. Cook until eggs are set to your liking, 3 to 5 minutes for soft yolks. With a slotted spoon, gently transfer each egg to a soup bowl. Divide the soup equally among the bowls and sprinkle parsley over the top. Makes about 11 cups, 6 servings.—*Stella Jensen, Antioch, Calif.*

PER SERVING: 284 calories, 14 g protein, 30 g carbohydrates, 12 g fat, 274 mg cholesterol, 433 mg sodium

INTERNATIONAL TAMALE PIE

This untraditional version of tamale pie abounds with international overtones. Instead of the typical filling of ground beef, you'll taste Mediterranean and Middle Eastern influences in the layers of cumin-flavored ricotta cheese custard and roasted onion, bell peppers, and eggplant. Easy-to-use tortillas replace the cornmeal mush used to encase the pie in more standard versions.

   2 large (about 2 lb.) red onions,
       thinly sliced
   4 medium-size (about 1 lb.) red bell
       peppers, stemmed, seeded, and
       cut into quarters
   2 medium-size (about 2 lb. total)
       eggplants, stemmed and cut into
       ½- by 3-inch strips
   6 tablespoons olive oil
   3 cloves garlic, minced or pressed
       About 2 cups (15-oz. container)
       ricotta cheese
   6 large eggs
   1 cup (about 4 oz.) grated parmesan
       cheese
 1½ teaspoons ground cumin
   1 teaspoon ground coriander
   ½ teaspoon ground nutmeg
       Salt and pepper
  12 corn tortillas (6-in. size)
   1 cup purchased salsa (optional)

In a pan at least 2 inches deep and about 12 by 15 inches in diameter, mix onions, peppers, eggplants, oil, and garlic. Bake in a 425° oven until vegetables are well browned and eggplant is soft when pressed, about 40 minutes; stir often. Let stand until cool enough to handle. Pull off and discard skin from red pepper quarters. Cut peppers into thin strips and mix with vegetables. If made ahead, cover and chill up to 2 days.

In a bowl, combine ricotta, eggs, parmesan, cumin, coriander, nutmeg; beat until well mixed. Add salt and pepper to taste.

Oil or butter a 9- by 13-inch baking dish or a shallow 3-quart oval casserole. Line dish bottom with 2 tortillas, then tear 2 more tortillas into large pieces to fill in gaps. Spoon ⅓ of the vegetables evenly over the tortillas. Spoon ⅓ of the cheese mixture in dollops over the vegetables, spreading gently to cover. Make another layer of tortillas, using 2 whole and 2 torn into pieces.

Repeat layers of vegetables, cheese

mixture, and tortillas, ending with vegetables and cheese mixture. If made ahead, cover and chill up until next day.

Bake, uncovered, in a 350° oven until edges are well browned, 40 to 45 minutes (50 minutes if chilled). Let stand 20 minutes, then spoon out portions. Offer salt, pepper, and salsa to add to taste. Serves 8 to 10. —*Robyn Raymer, Albany, Calif.*

PER SERVING: 379 calories, 18 g protein, 32 g carbohydrates, 22 g fat, 157 mg cholesterol, 326 mg sodium

SWORDFISH STEAKS WITH SALSA

A vivid sauce of tomatoes, chile, and cilantro lends Mexican zest to pan-fried swordfish. To complete the fiesta, also serve black beans and sliced avocadoes, topped with sour cream.

    4 swordfish steaks (about 2 lb. total)
    2 tablespoons salad oil
    2 cloves garlic, minced or pressed
    1 fresh jalapeño chili, stemmed, seeded, and minced
    5 firm-ripe Roma-style tomatoes, cored, seeded, and diced
    ½ cup packed fresh cilantro (coriander) leaves, chopped

Rinse fish and pat dry. Heat oil in a 10- to 12-inch frying pan over medium-high heat. Add fish and cook, turning once, until well browned and just opaque in center when cut, about 7 minutes total. Transfer to a platter; keep warm.

Add garlic and chili to pan and cook, stirring, until fragrant, about 30 seconds. Add tomatoes and cilantro; stir until hot. Spoon over fish. Makes 4 servings.

PER SERVING: 349 calories, 46 g protein, 3 g carbohydrates, 16 g fat, 89 mg cholesterol, 209 mg sodium

PINK GRAPE-LEMONADE

This pink lemonade comes naturally by its modest blush and sweetness. Red grapes puréed with lemon juice are the source of the color and flavor. The purée is pressed from the skins, then thinned with water. Although you could more accurately call this beverage pink grapeade, it needs lemon juice to provide tang. Green grapes make an equally flavorful beverage, but the drink turns brown quickly.

Sautéed swordfish steaks topped with cilantro-spiked tomato-chili sauce can be on the table in less than 25 minutes.

In Guerrero, Mexico, wild red grapes are prepared in much the same fashion to make a drink called sangre de Baco *(literally, blood of Bacchus).*

Even if you make more than 1 batch, whirl 1 recipe at a time in the blender.

    ½ cup lemon juice
    6 cups stemmed seedless red grapes, rinsed (about 2 lb.)
      About 2½ cups water

In a blender, combine lemon juice and ¼ cup of the grapes; whirl until crushed. With motor on, add remaining grapes, a handful at a time, until puréed.

Pour purée, a portion at a time, into a fine strainer placed over a bowl; with a rubber spatula, firmly press purée into container. Discard pulp as it accumulates. Stir enough water into juice to make 1½ quarts. Pour lemonade into a pitcher, then into ice-filled glasses; or cover tightly and chill up to 2 days (stir before pouring). Makes 1½ quarts, 4 to 6 servings.

PER 1-CUP SERVING: 100 calories, 1 g protein, 27 g carbohydrates, 0.6 g fat, 0 mg cholesterol, 7.3 mg sodium

Wholesome waffles, with apple slices in the batter, bake crisp and brown.

WHEAT GERM WAFFLES

- 1 **medium-size apple, peeled, cored, and cut into ⅛-inch slices**
- 4 **teaspoons lemon juice**
- ¼ **cup firmly packed brown sugar**
- ½ **teaspoon ground cinnamon**
- 1⅓ **cups all-purpose flour**
- ½ **cup toasted wheat germ**
- ⅓ **cup quick-cooking rolled oats**
- 2 **teaspoons baking powder**
- 1 **teaspoon baking soda**
- 1 **large egg**
- 2 **cups milk**
- ½ **cup salad oil, or melted butter or margarine**
  Butter or margarine
  Maple syrup or powdered sugar

Mix apple slices with lemon juice, brown sugar, and cinnamon; set aside.

Mix flour, wheat germ, oats, baking powder, and soda. In a large bowl, beat egg, milk, and oil to blend; add dry ingredients, stirring until evenly moistened. Gently stir in apple mixture.

To an oiled waffle iron heated to medium-high, add 1 cup batter; push apple slices so they don't overlap. Cover and bake until waffle is crisp and golden; lift out. Repeat to bake remaining waffles. Serve with butter and syrup to taste. Makes 4, each 9 inches square.— *Alura Nielsen, Kirkland, Wash.*

PER SERVING: 638 calories, 15 g protein, 68 g carbohydrates, 35 g fat, 70 mg cholesterol, 502 mg sodium

---

Curry enriches flavor of carrot soup made hearty with broccoli, rice.

CURRIED CARROT-PEANUT SOUP

- 1 **pound (about 4 large) carrots**
- 6 **cups regular-strength chicken broth**
- ½ **cup finely chopped onion**
- ¼ **cup cream-style peanut butter**
- 1 **clove garlic, pressed or minced**
- 2 **tablespoons curry powder**
- ¼ **cup short- to long-grain white or brown rice**
- 2 **cups small broccoli flowerets (about 6 oz.)**

Slice carrots; put in a 4- to 5-quart pan with 3 cups of the broth. Cover, bring to a boil, then simmer rapidly over medium-high heat until carrots are very tender when pierced, 25 to 30 minutes. Drain, reserving liquid.

Whirl carrots in a blender or food processor until smoothly puréed. Return the purée to the pan and stir in the reserved liquid, remaining broth, onion, peanut butter, garlic, curry powder, and rice. Cover, bring to a boil, then simmer gently over medium-low heat until rice is very tender to bite, 30 to 40 minutes; stir occasionally. Add broccoli and cook just until tender when pierced, about 5 minutes. Serves 6.— *Mary Sims, Albany, Calif.*

PER SERVING: 175 calories, 7.9 g protein, 21 g carbohydrates, 7.6 g fat, 0 mg cholesterol, 138 mg sodium

---

Avocado, chilies, onions, bacon, cheese colorfully top baked chicken breasts.

CHICKEN BREASTS WITH CHEESE & CHILIES

- 4 **boned and skinned chicken breast halves (about 1½ lb. total)**
- 1 **cup (4 oz.) shredded jack cheese**
- 1 **can (4 oz.) diced green chilies**
- ½ **cup chopped green onions, including tops**
- 4 **slices crisply cooked bacon, crumbled**
- 1 **medium-size firm-ripe avocado, peeled, pitted, and chopped**
- 1 **cup sour cream (optional)**

Lay breasts in an 8- by 12-inch pan; cover tightly with foil. Bake in a 350° oven for 15 minutes.

Meanwhile, mix cheese and chilies. Cover each breast equally with mixture, patting to hold in place. Sprinkle chicken evenly with green onion and crumbled bacon.

Return to oven and bake, uncovered, until chicken is white in center of thickest piece (cut to test) and cheese melts, about 10 minutes. Scatter avocado over chicken; serve with sour cream to taste. Makes 4 servings. — *Sherda Bailey, McCall, Idaho.*

PER SERVING: 421 calories, 50 g protein, 6.3 g carbohydrates, 21 g fat, 129 mg cholesterol, 542 mg sodium

PASTA WITH GORGONZOLA SAUCE

- 1 tablespoon butter or margarine
- 2 cups (½ lb.) sliced mushrooms
- ¾ cup half-and-half (light cream)
- 5 ounces gorgonzola or cambozola blue cheese, crumbled
- ¾ cup regular-strength chicken broth
- 10 ounces dry spinach fettuccine
- ½ pound shelled cooked tiny shrimp
- 2 tablespoons minced parsley

In an 8- to 10-inch pan, melt butter over medium-high heat. Add mushrooms and stir often until browned, 8 to 10 minutes. Add half-and-half, cheese, and broth. Stir over medium heat until cheese melts—do not boil; keep warm.

Meanwhile, bring about 3 quarts water to boiling in a 5- to 6-quart pan on high heat. Add pasta and cook, uncovered, until tender to bite, about 7 minutes; drain. In pan, combine pasta, sauce, and shrimp. Lift with 2 forks until pasta absorbs most of liquid, 4 to 5 minutes. Pour onto a platter; sprinkle with parsley. Serves 6. —*Jolanda Kuster, Leavenworth, Wash.*

PER SERVING: 374 calories, 22 g protein, 37 g carbohydrates, 15 g fat, 152 mg cholesterol, 457 mg sodium

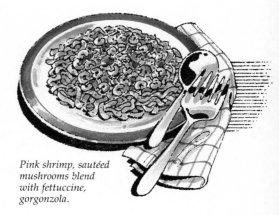

Pink shrimp, sautéed mushrooms blend with fettuccine, gorgonzola.

MICROWAVE SQUASH BAKE

- 1 medium-size onion, minced
- 1 teaspoon olive oil
- 1½ pounds yellow pattypan or crookneck squash, ends trimmed, thinly sliced
- 1 can (14½ oz.) pear-shaped tomatoes, drained and coarsely chopped
  Toasted herb crumbs (recipe follows)

Mix onion and oil in a shallow oval (about 8- by 12-in.) microwave-safe container and cover loosely with plastic wrap. Cook on full power (100 percent) in a microwave oven for 3 minutes.

Mix squash with onion; cover and cook on full power for 5 minutes. Mix in tomatoes; cover and cook on full power until squash is tender to bite, about 5 minutes longer. Uncover and sprinkle with crumb topping. Serves 4. —*Leslie Cohen, Santa Monica, Calif.*

PER SERVING: 133 calories, 4.2 g protein, 19 g carbohydrates, 5.6 g fat, 0.3 mg cholesterol, 228 mg sodium

Toasted herb crumbs. Whirl 1½ cups soft **white bread** cubes in a blender to form fine crumbs. In an 8- to 10-inch frying pan, stir crumbs with 1 tablespoon **extra-virgin olive oil** and ½ teaspoon *each* **dry basil leaves** and **dry oregano leaves** over medium-high heat until golden brown, about 10 minutes.

Microwave-cooked squash has garden-fresh taste.

PEARS FANDANGO

- About 2 pounds (about 4 large) ripe pears, such as Anjou, Bosc, or Comice
- 1 tablespoon butter or margarine
- ¼ cup firmly packed light brown sugar
- ¼ cup rum, Cointreau, or thawed frozen orange juice concentrate
- 1 teaspoon grated lemon peel
- 3 tablespoons lemon juice
- 1 pint to 1 quart vanilla ice cream

Peel, core, and thinly slice pears. In a 10- to 12-inch pan over medium-high heat, melt butter. Add pears and cook until slices are lightly browned, about 20 minutes. Add sugar, rum, lemon peel, and juice. Boil on high heat until sauce is thick enough to cling lightly to fruit, 2 to 3 minutes; keep warm.

Divide ice cream among 6 individual bowls; spoon pears and sauce equally onto ice cream and serve immediately. Makes 6 servings. —*Adrienne Sweeney, Kaneohe, Hawaii.*

PER SERVING: 225 calories, 2.2 g protein, 41 g carbohydrates, 7.2 g fat, 25 mg cholesterol, 62 mg sodium

Mangoes fandango. Follow directions above, but instead of pears, use about 2 pounds (about 2 medium-size) ripe **mangoes,** peeled and cut into chunks.

Simmered with butter and sugar, pears go over ice cream.

I F YOU SHOULD ENCOUNTER *the term* Val d'Auge *describing a chicken or veal selection on your menu, try the dish; it is prepared with cream, apples, and apple cider or apple brandy. The Valley of the Auge is a district of Normandy noted for its apples and apple products. John Martinelli is not a Norman, but he does come from Watsonville—one of California's noted apple-growing districts—where he produces apple juice and cider.*

Martinelli uses cider, along with cream soup, to simmer his pheasant. The moist heat and rather slow cooking tenderize the bird, which can be tough—especially if it's been flushed from the field and is not in its first blush of youth.

PHEASANT IN WATSONVILLE CREAM

- 1 **pheasant (about 2½ lb., thawed if frozen), cut into quarters**
- 3 **tablespoons all-purpose flour**
- 1 **can (10¾ oz.) condensed cream of mushroom soup**
- 1 **can (10¾ oz.) condensed cream of chicken soup**
- ½ **cup apple cider**
- 1 **tablespoon Worcestershire**
- ½ **finely chopped onion**
- 3 **cloves garlic, minced or pressed**
- ¼ **pound mushrooms, thinly sliced**
- ¾ **teaspoon paprika**

Rinse pheasant and pat dry. In a shallow 2- to 2½-quart casserole, stir together the flour, mushroom soup, chicken soup, cider, Worcestershire, onion, garlic, mushrooms, and paprika. Push pheasant down into sauce, and spoon some of the sauce over the meat.

Cover and bake in a 350° oven for 1 hour. Uncover and continue to bake until thigh is tender when pierced, 35 to 40 minutes longer. Baste frequently during baking.

Serve pheasant from the casserole, or transfer to a platter. Skim off and discard any fat; serve sauce in a small bowl to add to taste. Makes 4 servings.

ESTIMATED PER SERVING: 442 calories, 60 g protein, 23 g carbohydrates, 3.3 g fat, 6.9 mg cholesterol, 1,357 mg sodium

John Martinelli

Watsonville, Calif.

F IRE IN THE BELLY *is a term much used by newspapers and publicists to refer to that burning competitiveness deemed necessary to win an election or a Super Bowl. In such cases, fire in the belly is considered the cause of an action. But when it comes to chili recipes, it becomes an effect as well. Fierce competitiveness and supreme self-confidence characterize the chili-head, who will defend the superiority*

"He uses apple cider and slow cooking to tenderize his pheasant."

"Fierce competitiveness characterizes the chili-head."

of his recipe (and deride all others) with a crusader's zeal. It is no surprise, then, that R.J. Pujolar calls his formula Best in the West Venison Chili.

With ¼ cup of chili powder and 1 jalapeño, this is a moderately hot stew that should appeal to all but the most partisan fanciers of no-beans chili. Of course, you could always leave out the beans—since no chili recipe, however perfected, cannot be improved by some individual tinkering.

BEST IN THE WEST VENISON CHILI

- 3 tablespoons salad oil
- 2 pounds boneless venison, trimmed and cut into ¼-inch cubes
- 1 large onion, chopped
- 1 medium-size green bell pepper, stemmed, seeded, and chopped
- 3 cloves garlic, minced or pressed
- 1 fresh jalapeño chili, stemmed, seeded, and minced
- 1 large can (15 oz.) tomato sauce
- 1 can (28 oz.) tomatoes
- ¼ cup chili powder
- 1 teaspoon sugar
- 1 can (about 28 oz.) red kidney beans, drained
  Salt

Pour oil into a 5- to 6-quart pan over medium-high heat. When hot, add venison, a portion at a time, and brown well, stirring often. Then stir in onion, green pepper, garlic, and jalapeño. Stir often until onion is limp, about 10 minutes. Add tomato sauce, tomatoes (break up with a spoon) and their liquid, chili powder, and the sugar.

Stirring often, bring to a boil. Cover, reduce heat, and simmer until venison is very tender to bite, about 1 hour and 45 minutes; stir occasionally. Stir in beans and simmer until hot, about 10 minutes longer. Season to taste with salt. Makes about 10 cups, 7 or 8 servings.

PER SERVING: 329 calories, 32 g protein, 28 g carbohydrates, 11 g fat, 73 mg cholesterol, 969 mg sodium

[signature: Ralph J. Pujolar]

San Francisco

JACK-O'-LANTERNS *are fall reminders of harvest, and of pumpkins turning golden in the fields. Bill Bissell, however, ignores seasonal sentimentality and puts pumpkin to work at any time of the year. With unabashed bravado, he waves the can opener and produces Pumpkin and Oat Cake, a not-too-sweet bread. It's ideal for breakfast, but it can also fill hunger chinks at other times of the day.*

To the canned pumpkin add the other ingredients—including rolled oats, wheat germ, raisins, walnuts—to the predictable flour, sugar, and other basic elements of cake making, and the result is a product (to quote Donald Barthelme) "absolutely bursting with minimum daily requirements." It boasts another virtue, too, in that it freezes well if you don't finish it in a few days.

PUMPKIN & OAT CAKE

- 2¾ cups all-purpose flour
- 1½ cups sugar
- 1¼ cups regular rolled oats
- ½ cup untoasted wheat germ
- 2 teaspoons baking powder
- 2 teaspoons ground allspice
- 2 teaspoons baking soda
- 1 teaspoon *each* ground nutmeg and ground cinnamon
- ¼ teaspoon salt
- ¾ cup salad oil
- 1 cup milk
- 3 large eggs
- 1 can (1 lb.) pumpkin
- 1 cup chopped walnuts
- 1 cup raisins

In the large bowl of an electric mixer, stir together the flour, sugar, oats, wheat germ, baking powder, allspice, baking soda, nutmeg, cinnamon, and salt until well combined. In another bowl, mix well the oil, milk, eggs, and pumpkin. Pour oil mixture into dry ingredients and beat at medium speed for 1 minute. Add walnuts and raisins and mix just until blended.

Spoon batter into 2 greased and flour-dusted 5- by 9-inch loaf pans. Bake in a 350° oven until a toothpick inserted in the center comes out clean, 55 to 65 minutes. Let cool in pans for 10 minutes, then turn out onto racks and let cool completely. If made ahead, wrap airtight and chill up to 5 days. Freeze to store longer. Makes 2 loaves, each about 2 pounds.

PER 1-OUNCE SERVING: 97 calories, 1.9 g protein, 13 g carbohydrates, 4.4 g fat, 13 mg cholesterol, 54 mg sodium

[signature: Bill Bissell]

Walnut Creek, Calif.

"Ignore seasonal sentimentality and put pumpkin to work."

October Menus

WITH THE CHANGING SEASON, *meals begin to move indoors. For brunch, we present a homey, oven-baked pancake for six that is intriguing enough to offer guests. For cool evenings, consider a hot meatball soup with a Mexican lilt or a vegetable curry you can serve with or without meat; both go together easily.*

ONE-PANCAKE BREAKFAST

Puffy Pear Pancake
Crisp Bacon
Iced Orange Juice   Café Vanilla

The light, airy texture of this tender pancake contrasts pleasantly with the warm, buttery pears that nestle in it. Before serving, you invert the baked pancake onto a plate; the fruit then becomes the decorative topping.

Get the pancake in the oven, then brown the bacon, make the coffee, and squeeze the orange juice.

Allow about 1 pound bacon for 6 people. To make café vanilla, mix equal amounts of hot milk flavored with vanilla (about ½ teaspoon vanilla to 3 cups milk) and strong coffee.

PUFFY PEAR PANCAKE

1 teaspoon anise seed (optional)
2 tablespoons butter or margarine
3 large (1¼ to 1½ lb. total) ripe Bartlett or Anjou pears, peeled, cored, cut in half lengthwise
5 large eggs, separated
½ cup sugar
½ teaspoon vanilla
¼ cup all-purpose flour

Place an 8- to 10-inch frying pan with ovenproof handle over medium heat. Add anise seed and butter. When butter melts, add pears; cook until fruit is lightly browned on both cut and rounded sides, about 10 minutes; turn pears over occasionally. When pears are browned, turn cut side down and space evenly apart in pan; remove from heat but keep warm.

Meanwhile, in a large bowl, whip egg whites on high speed until foamy, then whip in sugar. Continue beating until whites hold stiff peaks. With unwashed beaters, beat yolks in another bowl until double in volume, then stir in vanilla

For a weekend breakfast, serve this souffléed oven pancake topped with glazed pears. Place fruit cut side down in pan, top with batter, and bake; invert pancake to serve.

and flour; beat until well mixed. Stir about ¼ of the whites into yolks, then fold yolk mixture gently into whites.

Pour egg mixture over warm pears, pushing batter down between fruit with a slender spatula. Cook over medium heat until pancake is dark gold on bottom (lift a corner with a spatula to check). Then bake pancake in a 300° oven until the top is dark gold color and the center is set (cut to test), about 15 minutes.

With a knife, loosen pancake from pan sides. Place a large plate (slightly wider than frying pan) over the pan; invert pancake and lift off frying pan. Cut into 6 wedges. Makes 6 servings.

PER SERVING: 233 calories, 6.2 g protein, 34 g carbohydrates, 8.4 g fat, 187 mg cholesterol, 92 mg sodium

*Cilantro is the aromatic flavor that recurs
throughout this menu.*

*While meatballs bake, simmer the broth.
For a salad, sprinkle pineapple wedges with
minced fresh cilantro and basil; diners can
sprinkle lightly with kosher or other coarse-
textured salt and lime. Also dot warm
garlic bread with chopped cilantro and
grated parmesan cheese; broil if you want
to toast bread.*

*For dessert, lightly dust ground cin-
namon on scoops of coffee ice cream.*

ALBÓNDIGAS SOUP

    1 large onion, slivered
    2 cloves garlic, minced or mashed
 1½ teaspoons ground cumin
    1 tablespoon salad oil
    1 can (about 14 oz.) pear-shaped
       tomatoes
 2½ quarts regular-strength beef broth
       Meatballs (recipe follows)
   ¼ cup chopped fresh cilantro
       (coriander)
    1 or 2 limes, cut into wedges

In a 5- to 6-quart pan on medium heat,
combine onion, garlic, cumin, and oil.
Stir often until onion is golden, 10 to 15
minutes. Add tomatoes and their liquid,
breaking them up. Add broth; cover and
bring to boiling on high heat. Add meatballs; if meat is cool or chilled, simmer
gently, uncovered, until hot in center,
about 10 minutes. Stir cilantro into soup.
Ladle soup into bowls and squeeze in
lime juice to taste. Makes 3½ quarts, 6 to
8 servings. —*Josephine Caporicci, Hay-
ward, Calif.*

PER SERVING: 248 calories, 14 g protein, 15 g carbohydrates, 15 g fat,
41 mg cholesterol, 370 mg sodium

Meatballs. In a bowl, mix together ¾
pound *each* **ground lean beef** and **bulk
pork sausage,** ½ cup **cooked white rice,**

*Mexican-style soup features baked meatballs—or albóndigas—in a cumin-spiced
broth. Wedges of pineapple with cilantro and lime make a refreshing salad.*

¼ cup *each* **all-purpose flour** and **water,**
and 1 teaspoon **ground cumin.** Shape
mixture into 1- to 1½-inch balls and place
slightly apart in a 10- by 15-inch pan.
Bake in a 450° oven until well browned,
about 15 minutes. Loosen from pan with
a wide spatula, then transfer with a

slotted spoon to soup, preceding; discard fat.

If made ahead, transfer meatballs to a
shallow bowl and let stand up to 1 hour.
Or you can cover and refrigerate up until
the next day.

(Continued on next page)

MAHARAJA'S SUPPER

Okra Curry
Grilled Lamb Chops
Basmati or White Rice
Toasted Pocket Bread
Lemon Lassie

Seasoned as a curry, okra, a popular vegetable in India, does not develop its slippery texture when cooked this way. Fresh okra is available year-round, but you may find it more readily available frozen.

The meat is optional, as the menu is quite satisfying with just the curry and rice. Have all the ingredients ready for the curry before you start to cook; if you do not have all the spices, simply substitute curry powder.

Lassie is an Indian yogurt beverage made with equal parts ice water and yogurt. Here we use lemon-flavor yogurt.

OKRA CURRY

¼ cup (⅛ lb.) **butter or margarine**
2 medium-size (about ¾ lb. total) **onions, slivered**
2 tablespoons **minced fresh ginger**
   Curry spices (directions follow) or 2 tablespoons **curry powder**
1¼ pounds **okra**, stem ends trimmed off and cut into 1-inch pieces, or 1 package (1¼ lb.) frozen sliced okra
1 medium-size firm-ripe **tomato**, cored and chopped
   Salt

Melt butter in a 10- to 12-inch frying pan over medium-high heat. Add onion, ginger, and curry spices. Stir often until onion is slightly browned, 10 to 15 minutes. Add okra; stir often until it is tender when pierced, about 10 minutes. Mix with chopped tomato, and add salt to taste. Makes 3 or 4 main-dish servings, 5 or 6 side-dish servings.

PER MAIN-DISH SERVING: 185 calories, 3.9 g protein, 17 g carbohydrates, 12 g fat, 31 mg cholesterol, 134 mg sodium

Curry spices. Mix together 1½ teaspoons **ground turmeric**, 1 teaspoon *each* **ground cumin** and **ground coriander**, ¼ teaspoon *each* **ground cinnamon** and **cayenne**, and ⅛ teaspoon *each* **ground cardamom** and **ground cloves**.

Petite Pumpkins with Spiced Squash (page 247)

Thiis month we launch the festive season with Thanksgiving in the Pilgrim tradition— a menu based on ingredients native to the New World. For a light-hearted party, we gather with friends to salute the season's new wine. You'll find uses both edible and decorative for autumn's delightful petite pumpkins. We show off the Western nut harvest in a trio of handsome dessert tarts. Holiday gifts to prepare in advance include colorful ribbon pasta and international seasoning mixes.

A Really American Thanksgiving

MAKING GOOD USE *of the produce and game they found in the New World, the Pilgrims celebrated the first Thanksgiving with a menu based on indigenous ingredients. Americans still use this menu as the basis for their own holiday meals. This year we expand on nearly 370 years of tradition by including a broader range of native ingredients, from both North and South America.*

These foods, mainstays of dishes to go with the turkey (cook it the way your family likes best), include corn, cranberries with chilies, green beans and jicama, sunflower seed, quinoa with wild rice, and two kinds of potatoes.

For dessert, rich ice cream parfaits blend native flavors of pumpkin or vanilla with chocolate, caramel, or caramelized goat's milk. They're eaten with pine nut cookies. A prickly pear fruit punch is served as an apéritif or throughout the meal.

NATIVE THANKSGIVING FOR 12

Green Bean & Jicama Salad
Sunflower Flatbread
Roast Turkey   Giblet Gravy
Wild Rice & Quinoa Dressing
Roasted Sweet & White Potatoes
Scorched Corn Pudding
Cranberry Chili Relish
Pumpkin or Vanilla Ice Cream Parfaits
Pine Nut Cookies
Prickly Pear Punch

If you have only one oven, you'll need to juggle a bit to have all foods ready to serve at once. To help, most dishes have steps that can be done 1 to 2 days ahead.

On Thanksgiving, bake the bread and partially bake the potatoes early in the morning. When the turkey comes from the oven (buy a 12- to 14-lb. bird, larger if you want leftovers), drape it with foil and keep it in a warm place for 30 minutes to 1 hour; juices will have time to settle into the meat while you make the gravy.

Meanwhile, bake the dressing and corn pudding (which were assembled ahead), and finish baking the potatoes. If you want the bread warm, reheat it for just a few minutes in the oven.

The ice cream parfaits come straight from the freezer, and the made-ahead cookies still taste fresh 2 days after baking.

GREEN BEAN & JICAMA SALAD

- ¾ pound green beans, ends and strings removed
- 1 pound jicama, peeled and rinsed
- 6 tablespoons white wine vinegar
- ⅓ cup olive oil or salad oil
- 1 tablespoon Dijon mustard
- 1 teaspoon dry oregano leaves
- ⅔ cup thinly slivered red onion
  Salt and pepper
  Watercress sprigs, rinsed and crisped

Rinse beans and cut into julienne strips with a food processor, French bean cutter (the grate found on the end of many vegetable peelers), or a knife. Bring about 2 quarts water to boiling in a 3- to 4-quart pan on high heat. Immerse beans in water and cook, uncovered, just until tender-crisp to bite, about 1 minute. Drain and at once immerse beans in ice water. When cool, drain.

Meanwhile, cut jicama into very thin matchstick-size strips.

In a small bowl or jar, mix 5 tablespoons of the vinegar, oil, mustard, and oregano.

If made ahead, wrap beans and jicama airtight separately; cover dressing. Chill vegetables and dressing up to 2 days. Mix onion, remaining 1 tablespoon vinegar, and 1½ cups cold water; let stand at least 20 minutes or up until next day. Drain onions and mix with beans, jicama, and dressing; add salt and pepper to taste. Mound in a serving bowl; if made ahead, cover and chill up to 2 hours. Garnish with watercress. Makes 12 servings.

PER SERVING: 80 calories, 1 g protein, 6 g carbohydrates, 6.1 g fat, 0 mg cholesterol, 41 mg sodium

SUNFLOWER FLATBREAD

- 1½ pounds thawed frozen white bread dough
- 2 tablespoons olive oil
- ½ cup crumbled cotija cheese or freshly grated parmesan cheese
- ½ cup packed coarsely chopped fresh cilantro (coriander)
- ¼ cup salted toasted sunflower seed
  Coarse salt

Cut dough into 6 equal pieces. On a lightly floured board, roll each piece into a 7- to 8-inch round. Lightly coat 3 baking sheets, 12- by 15-inch size, with some of the olive oil. Place 2 rounds of dough

well apart on each pan, then brush dough with remaining oil.

Sprinkle rounds equally with cheese, then cilantro and sunflower seed. Also sprinkle lightly with salt. Cover lightly with plastic wrap and let rise in a warm place until puffy, about 20 minutes.

Bake in a 475° oven until deep golden brown, 8 to 10 minutes. Serve warm. If made ahead, let cool on racks, wrap airtight, and freeze up to 5 days. To reheat, thaw wrapped, then return to unoiled pans and bake, uncovered, in a 350° oven until crust is crisp, 3 to 5 minutes. Makes 6 rounds, 12 servings.

PER SERVING: 201 calories, 5.6 g protein, 28 g carbohydrates, 7.5 g fat, 5.5 mg cholesterol, 349 mg sodium

WILD RICE & QUINOA DRESSING

- 1½ cups wild rice
- ¾ cup quinoa or ½ cup long-grain white rice
- 2 pounds hot or mild bulk pork sausage
- ¼ cup chili powder
- ¼ cup distilled white vinegar
- ⅓ cup packed chopped fresh cilantro (coriander)
  Salt

Pour rice into a fine strainer and rinse well under running water; put in a bowl. In the same strainer, rinse quinoa under running water; rub grain to wash well and remove any bitter natural residue that may be present.

In a 6- to 8-quart pan, bring 5½ cups water to boiling on high heat. Add rice; cover and simmer 30 minutes. Add quinoa. Cook, covered, until grains are just tender to bite, 10 to 15 minutes longer; drain well.

Meanwhile, break sausage into about ½-inch chunks into a 10- to 12-inch frying pan; sprinkle with chili powder. Cook on high heat, stirring often, until meat is lightly browned and no longer pink in center (break apart a chunk to test), about 7 minutes. Add vinegar, stirring to free browned bits in pan.

Add sausage mixture and cilantro to grains; mix lightly with a fork, add salt to taste, and spoon into a buttered shallow 3-quart casserole. If made ahead, cover and chill up to 2 days. Bake, uncovered, in a 350° oven until hot in center and lightly browned, about 25 minutes (40 minutes if chilled). Serves 12.

PER SERVING: 435 calories, 13 g protein, 25 g carbohydrates, 32 g fat, 52 mg cholesterol, 538 mg sodium

(Continued on page 244)

Roast Turkey

Sunflower
Flatbread

Roasted Sweet
and White
Potatoes

Green Bean
and Jicama
Salad

Cranberry
Chili Relish

Scorched Corn
Pudding

Quinoa and
Wild Rice
Dressing

Foods of the New World flank a plump, juicy Thanksgiving turkey. Green beans, corn, chilies, cranberries, and potatoes are familiar ingredients. Quinoa and wild rice —also indigenous to North and South America—may still seem exotic fare.

All the elements of a traditional Thanksgiving are on the table: turkey, cranberries, bread, sweet and white potatoes; the change is in the seasonings.

ROASTED SWEET & WHITE POTATOES

¼ cup (⅛ lb.) *each* butter or margarine and olive oil

2 pounds *each* sweet potatoes and russet potatoes, peeled and cut into 1-inch chunks

1 large onion, cut into eighths

8 cloves garlic, cut into halves

½ cup hazelnuts, coarsely chopped
   Salt

Put butter, oil, sweet potatoes, russet potatoes, onion, and garlic in a 10- by 15-inch baking pan at least 2 inches deep.

Bake on bottom rack of a 475° oven for 30 minutes; stir with a wide spatula after 15 minutes—vegetables near rim of pan begin to brown quickly. (If made ahead, let stand, uncovered, up to 4 hours.) Mix in nuts. Bake, stirring occasionally, until potatoes are very tender when pierced and are tinged with brown, about 15 minutes (20 minutes if cooled). Add salt to taste. Serves 12.

PER SERVING: 224 calories, 3.1 g protein, 28 g carbohydrates, 12 g fat, 10 mg cholesterol, 52 mg sodium

SCORCHED CORN PUDDING

For an attractive presentation, you can line the casserole with cornhusks, tips rising above the rim. First, select enough dry husks (available in 1-lb. bags in some supermarkets and Mexican markets; leftovers keep indefinitely) to line the casserole. Discard silks, cover husks with boiling water, and let stand about 30 minutes to soften. Drain and pat dry.

3 packages (10 oz. each, 7 cups total) frozen corn kernels

3 tablespoons butter or margarine

¼ cup all-purpose flour

2¼ cups milk

5 teaspoons sugar

¼ teaspoon pepper

¼ teaspoon cayenne
   Salt

3 large eggs

In a 12- to 14-inch nonstick frying pan on high heat, stir corn frequently until about ¼ of the kernels are tinged with brown, about 15 minutes. Add butter; when melted, stir in flour. Remove from heat and stir in milk, sugar, pepper, cayenne, and salt to taste. In a small bowl, beat eggs to blend, then stir into corn mixture. If made ahead, cover and chill up until next day.

Pour pudding into a buttered shallow 2½-quart casserole (if desired, line with husks in a single layer, as described preceding). Bake, uncovered, in a 350° oven until center feels firm when lightly pressed, about 40 minutes (50 minutes if chilled). Makes 12 servings.

PER SERVING: 151 calories, 5.5 g protein, 21 g carbohydrates, 6.2 g fat, 67 mg cholesterol, 70 mg sodium

CRANBERRY CHILI RELISH

2 cups fresh or thawed frozen cranberries

1 large (about 8 oz.) tart apple, peeled, cored, and minced

3 tablespoons sugar

2 tablespoons minced fresh cilantro (coriander)

2 tablespoons lime juice

1 fresh small hot chili (such as jalapeño or serrano), stemmed, seeded, and minced
   Salt

Whirl cranberries in a food processor until finely chopped, or grind through a food chopper with a fine blade. In a bowl, combine cranberries, apple, sugar, cilantro, lime juice, chili, and salt to taste. Serve, or cover and chill up to 3 days. Makes 2 cups, 12 servings.

PER SERVING: 31 calories, 0.1 g protein, 7.9 g carbohydrates, 0.1 g fat, 0 mg cholesterol, 0.7 mg sodium

PUMPKIN OR VANILLA ICE CREAM PARFAITS

Alternate in tall stemmed glasses (such as parfait, champagne, or pilsner) layers of **pumpkin** or vanilla bean **ice cream,** and **cajeta** (Mexican caramelized goat's milk, found in Mexican markets and some supermarkets) or your favorite caramel sauce or chocolate sauce (homemade or purchased). Repeat until glasses are filled as you like. To decorate (optional), tuck a long **cinnamon stick** into each glass. If made ahead, cover and put in the freezer up to 2 days. Remove from freezer about 10 minutes before serving.

PER SERVING OF ⅔ CUP ICE CREAM AND 3 TABLESPOONS SAUCE: 447 calories, 7.4 g protein, 64 g carbohydrates, 18 g fat, 67 mg cholesterol, 175 mg sodium

PINE NUT COOKIES

- 1 cup (½ lb.) butter or margarine, at room temperature
- 1 cup powdered sugar
- 2 teaspoons vanilla
- 2 teaspoons anise seed
- 2 cups all-purpose flour
- 1 cup pine nuts

In a bowl, cream together butter, ⅓ cup of the sugar, vanilla, and anise seed. Mix in flour and pine nuts. Shape dough into 1 tablespoon–size balls, pressing firmly so balls hold their shape.

Place balls about 1 inch apart on 2 ungreased 10- by 15-inch baking pans. Bake in a 275° oven until edges are light golden brown, 35 to 40 minutes. Switch pan positions halfway through baking.

While cookies are still warm, transfer all to 1 pan and place close together without touching. Evenly sift remaining sugar over them.

Serve cool; if made ahead, cover airtight and hold at room temperature up to 3 days; freeze to store longer. Makes about 3½ dozen, 12 servings.

PER COOKY: 90 calories, 1.4 g protein, 8 g carbohydrates, 6.3 g fat, 12 mg cholesterol, 45 mg sodium

PRICKLY PEAR PUNCH

- Prickly pear purée (directions follow) or 1 quart chilled cranberry juice cocktail
- 2 bottles (750 ml. each) chilled brut champagne or sparkling wine
- 1 to 2 quarts chilled sparkling water

Pour fruit purée into a pitcher. Present with chilled wine and water. Mix by the glass, filling each about ⅓ full of purée. Then slowly add enough wine or water

He splashes sparkling wine or water into yellow-green prickly pear purée. The pears' delicate sweet taste is a bit like melon.

to fill glass to rim. Makes about 12 servings.

PER ⅓ CUP PURÉE AND ⅔ CUP BRUT CHAMPAGNE: 149 calories, 1.2 g protein, 17 g carbohydrates, 0.7 g fat, 0 mg cholesterol, 14 mg sodium

Prickly pear purée. Cut in half lengthwise 5 pounds despined **green** or red **prickly pear fruit** (also called cactus pears or tunas); there may be hidden stickers, so wear rubber gloves.

With a small knife, pull outer layer including peel from soft fruit (they separate easily); discard outer layer. In a food processor, purée fruit, then pour into a fine strainer over a bowl. Firmly rub pulp into bowl and discard seeds (or rub pulp through a food mill and discard seeds; don't use a blender, which pulverizes seeds). Blend purée with ⅓ cup **lemon juice** and 2 tablespoons **sugar.** Cover and chill at least 2 hours or up until next day. Makes 1 quart.

New World flavors—pumpkin and vanilla—go into rich, layered ice cream parfaits. Offer sugar-dusted pine nut cookies to go with the dessert.

Pint-size Pumpkins

PARADE THESE PETITE PUMPKINS *across your Thanksgiving table for a festive harvest look. Not only are they decorative containers but they are also edible (including skin, if tender). Fill their centers with relish, vegetables, or custard.*

Use either miniature pumpkins (such as Jack Be Little or Munchkin), or the small golden mottled squash called Sweet Dumpling. Bake or steam either kind until tender, scoop out seeds, and fill with a favorite filling. They reheat well if made ahead.

COOKED PETITE PUMPKIN SHELLS

Rinse 8 **miniature pumpkins** (Jack Be Little or Munchkin) or Sweet Dumpling squash (each 6 to 8 oz.). Pierce deeply with a knife or sharp fork several times.

To bake. Set pumpkins in a 9- by 13-inch baking pan. Bake, covered, in a 375° oven until pumpkins are tender when pierced, 45 to 60 minutes.

To steam. Set pumpkins (a few at a time, if they don't all fit) on a rack above about 1 inch water in a wok or 5- to 6-quart pan. Cover pan and bring water to a boil; steam until pumpkins are tender when pierced, 15 to 20 minutes.

Let cool and, when comfortable to touch, cut out tops about 2 inches wide with a small, sharp knife; set tops aside. With a small spoon, scoop seeds from pumpkins and discard. If made ahead, cover and chill up until the next day. Makes 8 cooked pumpkin shells.

PUMPKIN PIE IN A PUMPKIN

- 2 large eggs
- 1 can (16 oz.) pumpkin
- ¾ cup firmly packed brown sugar
- 1½ teaspoons ground cinnamon
- ½ teaspoon ground ginger
- ¼ teaspoon ground allspice
- ¼ teaspoon salt (optional)
- ⅔ cup half-and-half (light cream)
- ½ cup orange juice
- 8 cooked petite pumpkin shells (directions precede)
  Lightly sweetened, softly whipped cream (optional)
  Shreds of orange peel (optional)

In a bowl, beat eggs to blend with pumpkin, sugar, cinnamon, ginger, allspice, and salt. Stir in half-and-half and juice. Fill shells almost to the rim with pumpkin filling.

To bake. Place the pumpkin shells in a 9- by 13-inch baking pan. Bake, uncovered, in a 350° oven until filling does not jiggle in center when gently shaken, 20 to 25 minutes. You do not need to reheat lids.

To steam. Place filled pumpkins (a few at a time, if they don't all fit) on a rack above about 1 inch water in a 5- to 6-quart pan or wok. Lids do not need to be reheated.

Drape foil over pumpkins to prevent condensation from dripping into filling. Cover pan and bring water to a boil.

Traditional pumpkin pie filling bakes inside an edible pumpkin shell for festive holiday dessert. As you eat the filling, scoop some soft meat to eat with it.

Sweet Dumpling squash holds piquant apricot chutney to eat with turkey. Colorful condiment and edible container can be cooked ahead.

Steam until filling does not jiggle in center when gently shaken, 15 to 20 minutes.

Gently transfer pumpkins to a dish. Serve warm or cool. If made ahead, cool, cover, and chill up to 1 day. Garnish each pumpkin with whipped cream and orange peel. Set lids alongside, if desired. Makes 8 servings.

PER SERVING: 196 calories, 4.7 g protein, 39 g carbohydrates, 3.9 g fat, 61 mg cholesterol, 35 mg sodium

PETITE PUMPKINS WITH APRICOT CHUTNEY

  1 tablespoon salad oil
  1 large onion, chopped
  1 tablespoon minced fresh ginger
  1 tablespoon mustard seed
  1 teaspoon curry powder
  ⅛ teaspoon cayenne
  2 cups (12 oz.) coarsely chopped dried apricots
  ⅔ cup golden raisins
  ½ cup cider vinegar
  ⅓ cup sugar
    Salt
  ⅓ cup chopped fresh cilantro (coriander)
  8 cooked petite pumpkin shells (directions precede)

In a 3- to 4-quart pan, combine oil, onion, and ginger; stir over medium-high heat until onion is faintly browned, 8 to 10 minutes. Add mustard seed, curry powder, and cayenne; stir over low heat until spices are fragrant, 1 to 2 minutes. Add apricots, raisins, vinegar, and

sugar; cover and cook over low heat, stirring occasionally, until liquid is absorbed, about 7 minutes. Add salt to taste. If made ahead, cool, cover, and chill up to 3 days. Stir in cilantro before serving.

Fill warm or cool pumpkin shells to the rim with warm or cool apricot chutney. Set lids on top or alongside. Makes 8 servings.

PER SERVING: 248 calories, 4.4 g protein, 59 g carbohydrates, 2.6 g fat, 0 mg cholesterol, 8.6 mg sodium

PETITE PUMPKINS WITH SPICED SQUASH

  3 pounds banana squash
  ¼ cup (⅛ lb.) butter or margarine, at room temperature
  2 tablespoons maple syrup or honey
  1 teaspoon ground coriander
  ¼ teaspoon ground nutmeg
    Salt
  8 cooked petite pumpkin shells (directions precede)

Place banana squash cut side down in a 9-inch-square pan. Bake, covered, in a 375° oven until squash is tender when pierced, 45 to 55 minutes.

Meanwhile, beat together butter, syrup, coriander, and nutmeg. Scoop cooked squash from shell into a food processor or bowl; add ½ the spiced butter. Whirl or mash squash until smooth. Add salt to taste. Fill pumpkins almost to rim with squash mixture. If made ahead, cover and chill pumpkins and remaining butter up until next day.

To bake. Set pumpkins in a 9- by 13-inch baking dish or pan; lids do not need to be reheated. Cover pan and bake in a 350° oven until hot in center, 20 to 45 minutes.

To steam. Set pumpkins directly on a rack, a few at a time if they don't all fit, over about 1 inch water in a 5- to 6-quart pan or wok. Drape foil over pumpkins so condensation does not drip into squash. Pumpkin lids do not need to be reheated. Cover pan and bring water to a boil. Steam until squash is hot in center, 12 to 15 minutes.

Carefully transfer pumpkins to a dish. Mound remaining spiced butter equally on each filled shell. Set lids on pumpkins or alongside. Serve hot. Makes 8 servings.

PER SERVING: 175 calories, 3.3 g protein, 32 g carbohydrates, 6.1 g fat, 16 mg cholesterol, 67 mg sodium

Puréed banana squash, laced and topped with spiced butter, fills baked pumpkin shells. Cook petite pumpkins separately, fill with spiced squash, and reheat to serve.

Very Nutty Tarts

E ND A HOLIDAY FEAST *with any of these desserts based on Western nuts. The shape, texture, and flavor of each nut variety gives these tarts their distinctive character.*

Try a thin pound cake–textured torte laced with toasted pine nuts. Caramel-coated pecans fill a ground nut crust for an ultrarich version of pecan pie. Bind roasted hazelnuts and almonds in a honey batter and pour over glazed apricots in a buttery crust.

PINE NUT TORTE

Vin santo, used in the ricotta sauce, is a medium-dry Italian dessert wine made from dried grapes.

- 1¼ **cups pine nuts or slivered almonds**
- ¾ **cup (⅜ lb.) butter or margarine (at room temperature)**

Sugar-dusted pine nut torte, created by Florentine baker Giulio Corti, goes with spiked cherries and a creamy ricotta sauce.

- 1½ **cups powdered sugar (plus 1 to 2 tablespoons for dusting)**
- 4 **large eggs**
- 1 **teaspoon vanilla**
- 1⅔ **cups all-purpose flour**
  Ricotta sauce (recipe follows)
  Spiked cherries (recipe follows) or orange slices (peel and membrane removed)

Place nuts in a 9-inch pie or cake pan. Bake in a 350° oven until golden, about 10 minutes; shake pan occasionally.

In a bowl, beat the butter and 1½ cups sugar until creamy. Add the eggs, 1 at a time, beating well at each addition. Mix in vanilla. Add flour; mix until blended. Stir in the nuts. Spread batter into a buttered and floured 11-inch tart pan with removable rim.

Bake torte in a 350° oven until pale gold, 30 to 35 minutes. Remove from oven and dust top generously with powdered sugar. Cool in the pan on a rack. If made ahead, cool, cover, and store airtight up until the next day. Remove pan rim; cut torte into wedges. Offer ricotta sauce and spiked cherries to spoon over each serving. Makes 12 servings.

PER PLAIN SERVING: 310 calories, 6.9 g protein, 30 g carbohydrates, 19 g fat, 102 mg cholesterol, 30 mg sodium

Ricotta sauce. Whirl 1 cup (1 carton, about 8 oz.) **ricotta cheese** in a blender until smooth. In the top of a double boiler, whisk together 2 **large egg yolks,** ¼ cup **sugar,** and ⅓ cup **vin santo** (or sweet marsala or cream sherry), and ¼ teaspoon **almond extract.** Whisk over simmering water just until mixture thickens, 2 to 3 minutes. Whisk in ricotta cheese. Serve warm or cool. If made ahead, cover and chill up to 2 days. Makes 1⅓ cups.

PER TABLESPOON: 35 calories, 1.5 g protein, 3.3 g carbohydrates, 1.3 g fat, 22 mg cholesterol, 14.3 mg sodium

Spiked cherries. Drain 1 jar or can (17 oz.) **dark sweet cherries.** Return cherries to a jar and add ½ cup **vodka** and ¼ cup **cherry-flavored liqueur** (kirsch). Put lid on jar and invert several times. Chill at least until next day or up to 1 month, turning jar over occasionally. Makes about 2 cups.

PER 2 TABLESPOONS: 47 calories, 0.2 g protein, 6.3 g carbohydrates, 0 g fat, 0 mg cholesterol, 1 mg sodium

PECAN CARAMEL TART

- 1¾ **cups pecan halves**
- ¾ **cup water**
- ¾ **cup sugar**
  About 7 tablespoons whipping cream
  Baked nut crust (recipe follows)
  Chocolate sauce (recipe follows)

Place nuts in a 9-inch pie or cake pan. Bake in a 350° oven until golden beneath skin, 8 to 10 minutes; shake occasionally.

Meanwhile, in a 1½- to 2-quart pan, stir together water and sugar. Cook over medium-low heat, without stirring, until water turns clear, 12 to 15 minutes. Wash sugar crystals from pan sides with a wet brush as mixture boils. Increase heat to high and boil, uncovered, until syrup turns golden brown, 5 to 7 minutes. Remove from heat and gradually stir in 7 tablespoons cream (it will splatter) until blended. Sauce should be consistency of corn syrup. If too thick, add a little more cream; if too thin, stir over low heat until thicker.

Gently mix nuts into warm caramel. Pour into crust and push nuts to arrange evenly; let cool. Drizzle warm chocolate sauce over tart. Cool until chocolate is firm. If made ahead, cover and store at room temperature up to 2 days. Cut into wedges. Makes 10 to 12 servings. —*Fran Bigelow, Seattle.*

PER SERVING: 427 calories, 5.9 g protein, 25 g carbohydrates, 36 g fat, 28 mg cholesterol, 66 mg sodium

Baked nut crust. Whirl 2 cups **walnuts** in a blender or food processor until finely ground but not powdery; remove from blender. Add ½ cup **blanched almonds** and 3 tablespoons **sugar** to blender or processor and whirl until powdery.

In a bowl, beat 6 tablespoons **butter** or margarine until fluffy. Add 1 teaspoon **vanilla** and the ground nuts; mix just until the dough holds together. Press dough over bottom and sides of 9-inch tart pan with removable rim. Bake in a 350° oven until golden, 20 to 25 minutes. Use warm or cool.

Chocolate sauce. In a 1- to 1½-quart pan, stir 2 tablespoons *each* **whipping cream** and chopped **semisweet chocolate** over low heat just until smooth. Use warm.

Apricot Nut Tart

1 cup (6 oz.) dried apricots

⅔ cup dessert wine such as orange muscat or late-harvest Johannisberg Riesling, or orange juice

½ teaspoon grated orange peel

⅔ cup honey

1 cup whole hazelnuts

1 cup blanched almonds

3 large eggs

1 teaspoon vanilla

2 tablespoons butter or margarine, melted

Butter pastry (recipe follows)

Whipped cream (optional)

In a 1- to 1½-quart pan, combine apricots, ⅓ cup wine, orange peel, and 2 tablespoons honey. Simmer, uncovered, over low heat, gently stirring occasionally, until apricots are soft and liquid is absorbed, 20 to 25 minutes.

Meanwhile, place hazelnuts and almonds in 2 separate 9-inch pie or cake pans. Bake in a 350° oven until nuts are golden, about 10 minutes; shake occasionally. Place hazelnuts in a towel; rub to remove as much skin as possible. Discard skin.

In a bowl, mix eggs, remaining wine and honey, vanilla, and butter until blended. Stir in nuts.

Press butter pastry over bottom and sides of an 11-inch tart pan with removable rim. Distribute apricots evenly in pastry. Pour nut mixture over fruit, arranging nuts evenly over top.

Bake tart on the bottom rack of a 350° oven until golden brown all over, 45 to 50 minutes. Cool in the pan on a rack. If made ahead, cool, cover, and store at room temperature up until next day. Remove pan rim. Cut tart in wedges; offer cream to add to taste. Serves 10 to 12.

PER SERVING: 432 calories, 8.4 g protein, 45 g carbohydrates, 26 g fat, 97 mg cholesterol, 120 mg sodium

Butter pastry. In a food processor or a bowl, mix 1⅓ cups **all-purpose flour** and ¼ cup **sugar**. Add ½ cup (¼ lb.) **butter** or margarine, cut into small pieces; whirl (or rub with your fingers) until mixture forms fine crumbs. Add 1 **large egg yolk;** whirl (or mix with a fork) until dough holds together.

Almonds and hazelnuts in honey batter nearly hide layer of wine-poached apricots. Serve the baked tart with the same kind of wine used in cooking the fruit.

Colorful Ribbon Pasta

A S PRETTY AS RIBBON CANDY, *colorful ribbon pasta is simple to make—once you understand the technique.*

This artfully structured pasta comes from Patrizio Sacchetto of the Blue Fox restaurant in San Francisco. Under his tutelage, we found it fun to create—and a great homemade holiday gift.

Before you start, consider the following questions:

DO I NEED SPECIAL TOOLS?

You'll need a pasta machine to roll the stiff doughs to uniform thickness. A food processor is invaluable; a blender is handy, too.

Boil ribbon pasta just until tender to bite. Fresh pasta holds intense color; dry pasta fades slightly.

IS MULTICOLORED PASTA HARD TO MAKE?

No, but it takes time—and patience, too. The basic process is simple. Making vegetable purées (for color) and doughs takes the most time, but doughs can be made ahead; they also freeze well.

DO I NEED SPECIAL INGREDIENTS?

You need semolina flour. Widely available in well-stocked supermarkets and fancy food stores, this specially milled wheat flour comes in a range of textures. The kind you need for our recipes can range from coarser than all-purpose flour through gritty like fine cornmeal. These all work well. Semolina doughs are stiff to work with but have a springier texture when cooked than do plain wheat-flour pastas. You can use semolina flour liberally to keep doughs from sticking without adding the gumminess that regular wheat flour gives.

WHAT DOES RIBBON PASTA TASTE LIKE?

The purées add color but little taste. A few hot ribbons make an elegant serving. See page 252 for suggestions.

WHAT ARE THE STEPS?

First make plain and colored pasta doughs, then knead until supple. Divide doughs into easy-to-use portions. Cut 1 portion of each color and 1 portion of the plain pasta into fettuccine-width strands. Roll a wide strip of uncolored pasta to form the base (plain pasta shows off the colored stripes best). Use water to "glue" the strands onto the wide, plain strip. Roll this striped sheet through the pasta machine to make it evenly thick and squeeze the layers firmly together. Then cut into ribbons. Repeat, using remaining dough.

RIBBON PASTA

1 **recipe plain pasta dough for stripes and base (recipe on opposite page)**

1 **recipe green pasta dough for stripes (recipe on page 252)**

1 **recipe magenta pasta dough for stripes (recipe on page 252)**

1 **recipe orange pasta dough for stripes (recipe on page 252)**

About 4 cups (1½ lb.) semolina flour for rolling out pasta

Too pretty to eat? A bundle of colorful dried ribbon pasta makes a welcome gift for a cook.

Kneading the dough. Using 1 batch of dough at a time (plain, green, magenta, orange), flatten to about ⅜ inch thick, dust liberally with flour, and feed through pasta machine rollers at widest setting 10 to 12 times; fold dough in half lengthwise each time, and flour. When ready to use, dough will feel as smooth and supple as well-cured leather. Fold up finished strips and wrap airtight in plastic wrap or bags. Repeat to knead all batches of dough (total: 5 plain, 1 *each* of colored).

To make stripes. Cut 1 folded batch plain dough and each batch of colored dough into quarters. As you work, use 1 quarter at a time and keep remaining dough wrapped.

Flatten 1 quarter plain dough to about ⅜ inch thick and dust liberally with flour. Feed dough through rollers, at widest setting, several times; fold in half each time, repeating until dough is width of roller. Narrow roller spacing 1 notch and feed dough through again; repeat until you reach next-to-narrowest setting.

To create fettuccine-width strands, feed dough through the cutter setting closest to ¼ inch. As strands emerge, swish entire length in a generous amount of flour to prevent sticking; lay strands out straight or loosely swirl. Keep them in an airtight container or bag. Repeat with the remaining quarters of green, magenta, and orange dough.

To make base strip. Cut each of remaining 4 batches of plain dough into thirds (12 portions); set aside for bases, keeping in airtight containers or bags. Flatten 1 portion about ⅜ inch thick and dust liberally with flour. Feed dough several times through rollers at widest setting; fold in half each time, repeating until dough strip is the width of the rollers. Progressively reduce roller spacing to next-to-narrowest setting; roll strip through, taking care to keep sides straight. Lay strip flat on a well-floured board. Trim ends to make a neat rectangle about 6 by 20 inches. Cover strip with plastic wrap. Store scraps in an airtight container or bag.

To glue stripes to base. Uncover base strip and brush water down a long side. Lay a strand of colored pasta on base piece, aligning neatly against edge. Repeat, alternating remaining colors and the plain pasta strands on base. If a strand is too short, gently stretch or butt another same-color strand up to it. Return all scraps, as accumulated, to airtight containers or bags, segregating them by color.

When base is covered with stripes, coat liberally with flour on all sides. Lift gently and feed through rollers at widest setting or roll lightly with a rolling pin. Feed strip through rollers at next-to-narrowest setting (pasta will lengthen). Trim ends straight. Cut crosswise into 8-inch pieces. Cut resulting rectangles lengthwise into 1½-inch-wide ribbons. Separate ribbons.

As each base strip is filled, make another. As ribbons of pasta are used, roll another batch. (If you need to stop during this process, store remaining dough airtight in the refrigerator up to 2 days.) Reroll scraps and either make another multicolor sheet or cut into strands for fettuccine.

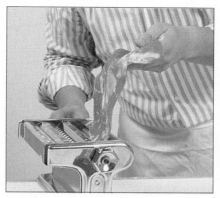

1 *Feed dough through rollers until it feels like soft Italian leather, then cut in ribbons.*

2 *On moistened sheet of plain dough, align ribbons of colored and plain pasta.*

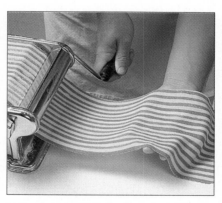

3 *Crank sheet with stripes through machine to weld pieces and make dough thinner.*

4 *Cut sheet with zigzag roller or knife into wide noodles.*

Use any extra fettucine strands as suggested on page 252; save colorful scraps to add to clear broth.

Storing. To store pasta fresh, generously flour pieces and wrap airtight in bunches of 1 to 2 dozen ribbons; chill up to 3 days or freeze up to 1 month (thaw to cook).

Or dry pasta: lay ribbons flat in a single layer, colored side up, on wire racks or on a towel-lined flat surface. Let stand until pasta feels dry to touch and is rigid, 12 to 18 hours. Package airtight, 1 to 2 dozen pieces in a plastic bag. Handle gently. Store in a cool, dark place up to 2 months.

Makes about 240 pasta ribbons, each about 1½ by 8 inches, 7 to 7½ pounds when dry.

PER OUNCE: 128 calories, 4.7 g protein, 23 g carbohydrates, 1.7 g fat, 34 mg cholesterol, 15 mg sodium

PLAIN PASTA DOUGH

  15 **large eggs**
  10 **tablespoons regular-strength chicken broth or water**
  10 **teaspoons olive oil**
      About 10⅔ cups (about 4 lb.) semolina flour for pasta

In a food processor, whirl 3 eggs, 2 tablespoons broth, and 2 teaspoons oil to blend. With motor running, add 2 cups flour. Then add 2 to 3 more tablespoons flour until dough forms a ball and feels only slightly sticky.

Repeat steps to make 4 more batches of dough. If made ahead, put each batch in plastic bag; chill up to 2 days. Freeze to store longer. Makes about 6¼ pounds.

(Continued on next page)

COLORED PASTA DOUGH FOR STRIPES

The whimsical pasta on page 250 makes use of this dough, colored by vegetable purées. You can also use the dough to make fettuccine; mix the cooked strands with the basil cream sauce (recipe at right), or moisten them with extra-virgin olive oil or melted butter and season to taste with grated parmesan cheese, salt, and freshly ground pepper.

Knead, roll, and cut as on pages 250-251.

- 1 **large egg**
- 1 **teaspoon olive oil**
- 1 **recipe of vegetables for colored dough (directions follow)**
  About 1¾ cups (about 10 oz.) semolina flour for pasta

Put egg, oil, and vegetable in a blender; whirl until very smoothly puréed. Scrape purée into a food processor. (Or with beets and carrots, simply purée vegetables in a food processor with egg and oil.)

With motor running, pour in 1⅓ cups of the flour, then add 4 to 5 more table-spoons until dough forms a ball and is only slightly sticky to touch. If made ahead, put in a plastic bag and chill up to 2 days. Freeze to store longer. Repeat to make 1 batch of each color. Makes about 1¼ pounds of each dough.

Spinach for green dough. Cut stem ends from 1 pound **spinach;** discard ends and yellow leaves. Wash and drain green leaves. Bring about 3 quarts water to boiling in a 5- to 6-quart pan on high heat. Immerse leaves in boiling water until limp, 20 to 30 seconds. Drain and at once immerse leaves in ice water. When cool, drain well and squeeze out moisture. Lay spinach out on a towel; roll up in cloth and squeeze tightly. Coarsely chop spinach.

Beets for magenta dough. Select 2 stemmed **beets** with roots (¼ lb. each). Place on a sheet of foil and bake in a 375° oven until tender when pierced, about 1½ hours. Let cool. Pull off skin and discard. Coarsely chop beets and mix with 1 tablespoon **red wine vinegar.**

Carrots for orange dough. Peel and slice ½ pound **carrots** into a 2- to 3-quart pan. Boil on high heat, uncovered, in 2½ cups **regular-strength chicken broth** until carrots are very tender when pierced and liquid has evaporated, 25 to 30 minutes; watch closely toward end of cooking.

Served with a light cream sauce, multicolor pasta shows off its eye-catching hues. Use leaves of fresh basil to flavor sauce and garnish each serving.

RIBBON PASTA WITH BASIL CREAM

The wine vinegar helps preserve color of beet pasta during cooking.

- 3 **tablespoons wine vinegar**
- 2 **tablespoons butter or margarine**
- 2 **tablespoons minced shallots**
- 1 **cup whipping cream**
- 1 **cup regular-strength chicken broth**
- ½ **cup lightly packed fresh basil leaves**
- 8 **to 10 ounces fresh or 6 to 8 ounces dry ribbon pasta (20 to 24 pieces, recipe on page 250), or fettuccine made from plain or colored pasta dough**
  Fresh basil leaves
  Freshly grated parmesan cheese
  Salt and freshly ground pepper

In a 5- to 6-quart pan, bring 3 quarts water and vinegar to boil.

Also melt butter in a 5- to 6-quart pan over medium-high heat. Add shallots and stir until golden, about 2 minutes. Add cream and broth. Boil on high heat until reduced to 1 cup, about 10 minutes. Stir in basil leaves; keep warm.

Add pasta to boiling water on high heat. Boil gently, uncovered, until pasta is just barely tender to bite, 2 to 3 minutes for fresh, 7 to 11 minutes for dry (color fades slightly as it cooks); stir occasionally. Drain pasta. Quickly ladle the sauce equally onto 4 warm, rimmed dinner plates. Quickly lift pasta ribbons (use tongs and handle gently to avoid tearing), 1 at a time, and drape them in equal mounds on each plate; or mound the fettuccine equally onto plates. Garnish with basil leaves. Offer cheese, salt, and pepper to add to taste. Makes 4 first-course servings.

PER SERVING: 501 calories, 12 g protein, 51 g carbohydrates, 28 g fat, 150 mg cholesterol, 123 mg sodium

Toasts & Spreads, Italian Style

Toast in the west *generally means breakfast, but in Italy toast is crostini —presented as a snack or a first course. Here, three recipes offer appetizing mixtures to eat on toasted cornbread, baguette, or Italian or French bread.*

MUSHROOM PÂTÉ & CORNBREAD TOAST

    2 tablespoons butter or margarine
    1 pound mushrooms, chopped
    ¾ cup chopped shallots
    1 small carrot, peeled and chopped
    1 clove garlic, pressed or minced
       Salt and white pepper
       Cornbread toast (recipe follows)

In a 10- to 12-inch frying pan, stir butter, mushrooms, shallots, carrot, and garlic over high heat until liquid evaporates and mushrooms brown, 10 to 15 minutes. Purée mixture in a blender or food processor; add salt and pepper to taste. Spoon into a bowl. (If made ahead, cool, cover, and chill up until the next day.) Serve warm or at room temperature to spread onto toast. Makes 10 to 12 appetizer servings.

PER SERVING: 164 calories, 4.3 g protein, 22 g carbohydrates, 6.7 g fat, 34 mg cholesterol, 177 mg sodium

Cornbread toast. In a small bowl, mix 1 cup **all-purpose flour**, 1 cup **yellow cornmeal**, 1½ teaspoons **baking powder**, ½ teaspoon **baking soda**, and ½ teaspoon **salt** (optional). In a large bowl, mix 1 cup **buttermilk**, 1 **large egg**, and ¼ cup (⅛ lb.) melted **butter** or margarine. Add dry ingredients to milk mixture; stir until evenly moistened. Spread batter in a greased 8- to 9-inch-square pan.

Bake in a 400° oven until top springs back when lightly touched in center, 20 to 25 minutes. Cool in pan about 15 minutes, then invert onto rack and cool. If made ahead, store airtight until the next day. Cut bread into ½-inch-thick slices, then cut slices in thirds. Lay slices on a 12- by 15-inch baking sheet. Broil about 4 inches from heat, turning once, until browned on both sides, 5 to 7 minutes total.

TUNA MOUSSE WITH TOAST

    2 small packages (3 oz. each) cream
       cheese
    1 can (9¼ oz.) water-packed light
       tuna, drained
    ⅓ cup thinly sliced chives or green
       onions
       Salt and white pepper
       Toast (recipe follows)

Let cheese come to room temperature. In a food processor or blender, whirl cheese and tuna until smoothly blended, scraping container sides often. Stir in ¼ cup chives, and add salt and pepper to taste. Transfer mixture to a bowl. (If made ahead, cover and chill up until next day.) Sprinkle with remaining chives. Serve tuna mixture to spread on toast. Makes 12 to 14 appetizer servings.

PER SERVING: 112 calories, 7.3 g protein, 9.3 g carbohydrates, 4.8 g fat, 21 mg cholesterol, 189 mg sodium

Toast. Cut 1 slender **baguette** (8-oz. size) crosswise into ¼-inch-thick slices. Place slices in a single layer on wire racks on 12- by 15-inch baking sheets. Bake in a 350° oven until golden, 10 to 15 minutes. Serve warm or cool. If made ahead, store airtight up until next day.

FLORENTINE LIVER PÂTÉ WITH BROTH

    ⅔ cup medium-dry sherry
    1½ cups regular-strength chicken or
       beef broth
    2 tablespoons butter or margarine
    1 medium-size onion, finely
       chopped
    ¾ pound chicken livers or calf's liver
       (trimmed of tough membrane), cut
       into ½-inch chunks
    1 tablespoon minced anchovy fillets
    2 tablespoons chopped capers
       Salt and pepper
       Toast (recipe follows)
    2 tablespoons chopped parsley

In a 1- to 1½-quart pan, combine ½ cup sherry and broth. Bring to a boil and simmer, covered, about 30 minutes. (If made ahead, cool, cover, and chill until the next day. Bring to a boil.)

Meanwhile, in a 10- to 12-inch frying pan, combine butter and onion. Stir occasionally over medium heat until onion is faintly browned, 10 to 15 minutes. Add remaining sherry; boil, uncovered, until liquid evaporates, about 2 minutes. Reduce heat to medium and add liver, stirring often until liver is firm and slightly pink in center (cut to test), about 5 minutes. Add anchovies and capers.

Whirl liver mixture in a food processor just until coarsely puréed, or finely chop with a knife. Add salt and pepper to taste. (If made ahead, cool, cover, and chill up until the next day. To serve, stir in frying pan on medium heat or put in microwave oven to warm.)

Spoon warm pâté onto toast. Sprinkle with parsley. Put on rimmed plates or wide bowls; ladle hot broth over toast and eat with a knife and fork. Makes 8 first-course servings.

PER SERVING: 181 calories, 12 g protein, 21 g carbohydrates, 5.3 g fat, 196 mg cholesterol, 392 mg sodium

Toast. Follow recipe for **toast,** preceding, but instead of using a slender baguette, use 8 slices (each ½ inch thick, 3 by 5 in.) from a larger loaf of **Italian** or sweet French **bread.**

For an appetizer or snack, offer intensely flavored mushroom pâté warm or at room temperature to spread on rectangles of lightly toasted cornbread.

A Cassoulet to Celebrate the New Wine

THE THIRD THURSDAY *of November will once again be a day of good-humored high jinks in the world of wine. That's the day the French government releases the beaujolais nouveau. This triggers a flurry among oenophiles who want the first samples of these wines—which are only a month or so from the vine.*

Now American vintners have jumped into the act, bottling their own versions for early release. This is a chance to preview the quality of beaujolais wines of the same vintage that will be stored for aging. And the young wines have a fresh, fruity character with an appeal of its own.

So we propose that you gather a couple of dozen friends and build an informal wine tasting around a selection of domestic and imported beaujolais nouveau (about $5 to $8 a bottle) and a grand cassoulet.

DINNER WITH NEW WINE

Pacific Cassoulet
Orange Slaw with Balsamic Vinegar
Baguettes   Butter
Basket of Apples
Cambozola Cheese
Beaujolais Nouveau, Domestic
& French

The wine may take no time to reach the glass, but making the cassoulet takes some engineering that can be worked out in steps over 2 or more days. Mostly, the cassoulet activities take place on their own in the oven or a simmering pot, needing but an occasional check.

PACIFIC CASSOULET

2   pounds Great Northern beans
4   to 5 pounds lamb shanks, cracked
1   pound bone-in pork shoulder
    or butt
1   duck (4 to 5 lb.), thawed if frozen
1½ pounds sliced bacon
2   large onions, coarsely chopped
3   medium-size firm-ripe tomatoes,
    cored and coarsely chopped
2   large green bell peppers, cored,
    seeded, and coarsely chopped
4   quarts regular-strength chicken
    broth
1   cup canned tomato purée
2   large carrots, peeled
2   tablespoons chopped parsley
1   teaspoon dry thyme leaves

½   teaspoon dry rosemary leaves
1   dry bay leaf
10 cloves garlic, cut in half
1   bottle (750 ml.) beaujolais
    nouveau or dry white wine
1½ pounds garlic or Polish sausage
    Bread crumbs (directions follow)

Sort beans for debris, then rinse and place in an 8- to 10-quart pan; add 4 quarts water. Either bring to a boil, let stand 1 hour, and drain, or let stand in cold water overnight, then drain.

Meanwhile, cut lamb and pork off bones and into 2- to 3-inch chunks; reserve bones. Cut up duck; add neck; reserve giblets for other uses.

Line the bottom of 2 roasting pans, each about 2½ inches deep and 12 by 16 inches, with bacon. Evenly divide lamb, pork, bones, duck (skin up) onions, tomatoes, and bell peppers over the bacon. Bake in a 450° oven until duck skin and meats are lightly browned, about 30 minutes. After 15 minutes, turn meat in the melting fat to coat, then exchange pan positions.

On a 15-inch square of cheesecloth, lay roasted duck back (broken in half) and

neck; tie securely to enclose. Add to drained beans 3½ quarts broth, the duck in cheesecloth, duck wings, lamb and pork bones, tomato purée, carrots, parsley, thyme, rosemary, bay leaf, and garlic. Cover and bring to a boil on high heat, then simmer slowly until beans are very tender to bite, 2½ to 3½ hours. If liquid evaporates, exposing beans or bones before beans are cooked, add water to cover by at least ½ inch.

As beans cook, put contents of roasting pans in 1 pan. Add wine and remaining 2 cups broth. Cover tightly with foil. Bake in a 450° oven until meat pulls apart easily, 3 to 3½ hours.

About 20 minutes before the meat is done, add the sausage to roasting pan and cover tightly. When all the meats are cooked, use a slotted spoon to transfer contents of pan to a large bowl; set aside. Reserve pan with juices.

When beans are cooked, remove from heat. With a slotted spoon, lift out cheesecloth bag and bones and set aside to cool. Pull any meat off bones and put scraps in a bowl with baked meats; discard skin and bones. Chop carrots and add to meats. Partially cover meat bowl

Delicious complexity of cassoulet comes from its rich bounty of ingredients—sausage, duck, lamb, pork, beans, vegetables—flavored with herbs and wine.

with a lid and tip bowl to drain accumulated juices into roasting pan holding reserved meat juices.

Set a colander into the roasting pan. Pour beans into colander, draining liquid into meat juices. Pour beans into a bowl. Cover and chill meat and beans separately. Also cover and chill liquid in roasting pan until fat hardens, at least 8 hours. (To speed process, you can skim liquid fat from broth and proceed, but you will not get rid of as much fat.)

Lift hardened fat from roasting pan and discard. Place pan over high heat; when liquid is melted, measure. You need 4 cups. If you have more, boil and stir until reduced to 4 cups; if you have less, add water. Save liquid.

In the roasting pan or a same-size casserole, arrange half the beans in an even layer. Top with meats (except sausages), then top with remaining beans, then reduced juices. Nestle sausages into beans; if made ahead, cover and chill up until next day. Sprinkle with bread crumbs. Bake, uncovered, in a 350° oven until mixture is hot in center and crumbs are brown, 1 to 1½ hours. Serves 20 to 24.

PER SERVING: 504 calories, 31 g protein, 29 g carbohydrates, 29 g fat, 84 mg cholesterol, 442 mg sodium

Bread crumbs. Mix 1½ cups **unseasoned fine dry bread crumbs** with ⅓ cup minced **parsley** and 1 clove minced **garlic.**

ORANGE SLAW WITH BALSAMIC VINEGAR

About 3 pounds Savoy cabbage, rinsed and finely shredded

4 medium-size oranges

½ cup *each* balsamic vinegar and olive oil

2 cloves garlic, minced or pressed Salt and pepper

Place cabbage in a large bowl. With a knife, cut peel off oranges. Hold 1 orange at a time over bowl, and cut fruit segments from membrane into bowl. Squeeze juice from membrane into bowl; discard membrane.

Mix together vinegar, oil, and garlic. If made ahead, cover and chill salad and dressing separately up to 4 hours. Mix dressing with salad and add salt and pepper to taste. Makes about 6 quarts, 20 to 24 servings.

PER SERVING: 68 calories, 1.3 g protein, 6.6 g carbohydrates, 4.6 g fat, 0 mg cholesterol, 16 mg sodium

Toasted crumbs top cassoulet, a richly flavored make-ahead casserole to savor with cabbage salad and newly released beaujolais nouveau.

Handy Seasonings to Mix & Keep

A COUNTRY'S CUISINE *often distinguishes itself by the mix of herbs and spices used repeatedly in its dishes. By blending seasonings, you can reproduce some favorite international flavors. Here we give three choices—Italian, Mexican, and Scandinavian—and suggestions for using them.*

Keep one or more of the mixes on hand to simplify cooking. A collection of blends makes a good gift for someone setting up house, a beginner cook, or the busy professional. In airtight containers, mixes keep well up to 6 months. These contain no salt; add it to the finished dishes as you like.

ITALIAN

Oregano, basil, garlic, and often fennel are mainstay seasonings in Italian foods. We give recipes using a mix of them for a quick spaghetti sauce (try it with lasagna, too) or pizza.

For a more direct approach, sprinkle the mix on oiled or buttered chicken or turkey before roasting or onto meaty fish (such as swordfish) before broiling or grilling.

Or, for a minestrone touch, add it to plain bean or vegetable soup.

ITALIAN SEASONING MIX

- 2 **tablespoons dry rosemary leaves**
- ¾ **teaspoon fennel seed**
- ¼ **cup dry oregano leaves**
- ¼ **cup dry basil leaves**
- 1 **tablespoon *each* garlic powder and dry thyme leaves**

Whirl rosemary and fennel in a blender until powdered (or finely crush by hand). Stir in oregano, basil, garlic powder, and thyme. Use as suggested, preceding, or in the following recipes. Store airtight up to 6 months. Makes about ¾ cup.

MEXICAN

Chilies, cumin, coriander: these flavors are ubiquitous in favorite Mexican dishes (including burritos and enchiladas).

As you experiment with the blend, consider these uses: stir it into refried beans for a quick dip; heat it with beans (with or without meat) for quick chili; stir it into tomato soup, scrambled eggs, or rice pilaf; mix it with oil and vinegar to sprinkle on salad greens; or pat it onto beef steaks before grilling.

MEXICAN SEASONING MIX

- ¼ **cup chili powder**
- 2 **tablespoons *each* ground cumin, ground coriander, dry oregano leaves, and dry basil leaves**
- 1 **tablespoon *each* dry thyme leaves and garlic powder**
- ¾ **teaspoon cayenne**

Stir together chili powder, cumin, coriander, oregano, basil, thyme, garlic powder, and cayenne. Use as suggested, preceding, or in the following recipes. Store airtight up to 6 months. Makes about ⅞ cup.

SCANDINAVIAN

In Scandinavia, cooks season lightly, and the cool taste of dill is present year-round. Mixing dill with onion powder and lemon peel creates a refreshing blend.

Use the seasoning to flavor a quick appetizer dip or salad dressing (recipes on opposite page). Or sprinkle it on buttered fish or chicken, then bake or broil. You can also use it to add a distinctive flavor to hot cooked vegetables and seafood soups.

SCANDINAVIAN SEASONING MIX

- 6 **tablespoons dry dill weed**
- ⅓ **cup dry ground lemon peel**
- ¼ **cup onion powder**

Stir together dill, lemon peel, and onion powder. Use as suggested, preceding, or in the recipes on opposite page. Store airtight up to 6 months. Makes about ⅞ cup.

OTHER WAYS TO USE THE MIXES

To simplify cooking, use these international seasoning mixes to add traditional flavors to your favorite Italian, Mexican, and Scandinavian dishes.

MUSHROOM SPAGHETTI SAUCE

- 1 **tablespoon butter or margarine**
- ½ **pound mushrooms, thinly sliced**
- 1 **can (15 oz.) tomato sauce**
  About 1 tablespoon Italian seasoning mix (recipe precedes)
- 8 **ounces dry spaghetti**
  About ⅓ cup grated parmesan cheese

Melt butter in a 10- to 12-inch frying pan over medium-high heat. Add mushrooms and stir occasionally until liquid has evaporated and mushrooms are golden brown, about 12 minutes. To mushrooms, add tomato sauce and seasoning mix; cover and simmer about 20 minutes to blend flavors. Add more mix to taste, if desired.

In a 4- to 5-quart pan, cook spaghetti, uncovered, in 3 quarts boiling water until tender to bite, about 12 minutes. Drain pasta; pour into a bowl, add sauce, and lift with 2 forks to mix. Serve, adding cheese to taste. Makes 4 servings.

PER SERVING: 314 calories, 13 g protein, 54 g carbohydrates, 6 g fat, 13 mg cholesterol, 799 mg sodium

PEPPERONI-PEPPER PIZZA

- 1 **loaf (1 lb.) frozen white bread dough, thawed**
  Pizza sauce (recipe follows)
- 2 **cups (8 oz.) firmly packed shredded mozzarella cheese**
- ¼ **pound thinly sliced pepperoni sausage**
- 1 **jar (7 oz.) roasted red peppers, drained and chopped**

On a lightly floured board, roll dough to make an 11- by 16-inch rectangle. Fit into an oiled 10- by 15-inch baking pan; fold edges under to form a rim. Spread pizza sauce over dough. Sprinkle with cheese, pepperoni, and peppers.

Bake on lowest rack of a 400° oven until crust is brown on bottom (lift to check), about 25 minutes. Cut into rectangles. Makes 3 or 4 servings.

PER SERVING: 653 calories, 27 g protein, 67 g carbohydrates, 31 g fat, 72 mg cholesterol, 1,993 mg sodium

Pizza sauce. In 1½- to 2-quart pan, simmer, uncovered, 1 can (15 oz.) **tomato sauce** and 1 tablespoon **Italian seasoning mix** (recipe precedes) until reduced to 1¼ cups, about 15 minutes. Use hot or cool.

CHICKEN ENCHILADAS

- 1½ **cups (6 oz.) shredded mild cheddar cheese**
- 2 **cups cooked chicken chunks, torn into shreds**
- 1 **large can (7 oz.) diced green chilies, drained**
  Enchilada sauce (recipe follows)
- 8 **corn tortillas (6- to 7-in. size)**
  About ½ cup sour cream

Set ½ cup cheese aside. Mix together remaining cheese, chicken, and chilies.

Pour sauce into an 8- or 9-inch pan. Coat 1 tortilla with sauce, then set in a 9- by 13-inch pan. Spoon ⅛ of the chicken mixture down center of tortilla. Roll to enclose filling; place, seam side down, in pan. Repeat to fill remaining tortillas.

Pour remaining sauce evenly over enchiladas; sprinkle with remaining cheese. Bake enchiladas, tightly covered, in a 350° oven until hot in center (cut to test), about 15 minutes. Uncover; spoon sour cream on top. Makes 8 enchiladas, 4 servings.

PER ENCHILADA: 570 calories, 39 g protein, 44 g carbohydrates, 28 g fat, 120 mg cholesterol, 1,786 mg sodium

Enchilada sauce. In a 2- to 3-quart pan, combine 3 cans (8 oz. each) **tomato sauce** and 1½ tablespoons **Mexican seasoning mix** (preceding); bring to a boil, cover, and simmer 20 minutes. Taste; add more seasoning mix if you like. Use, or cover and chill up to 1 week. Makes 1¾ cups.

BEEF & BEAN BURRITO

- 1 **pound ground lean beef**
- 1 **can (8 oz.) tomato sauce**
  About 1 tablespoon Mexican seasoning mix (recipe precedes)
- 6 **flour tortillas (7- to 8-in. size)**
- 1 **can (15 oz.) refried beans**
- 1 **cup (4 oz.) shredded mild cheddar cheese**
- 2 **cups shredded iceberg lettuce**
  About ¾ cup prepared salsa
  About ½ cup sour cream

In a 10- to 12-inch frying pan over high heat, stir beef often until well browned. Pour off and discard fat. Add tomato sauce and 1 tablespoon seasoning mix, or more to taste; cook, uncovered, stirring often, until most of the liquid has cooked away, about 5 minutes.

Stack tortillas, wrap in foil, and bake in a 350° oven until warm, about 10 minutes.

At the same time, in a 2- to 3-quart pan over medium heat, stir the beans until hot.

Spoon ⅙ of the beans down center of 1 tortilla; top with ⅙ of the meat, cheese, and lettuce. Add salsa and sour cream to taste. Fold 1 end, then sides over filling to enclose. Repeat to make remaining burritos. Makes 6 burritos, 3 to 6 servings.

PER BURRITO: 463 calories, 26 g protein, 37 g carbohydrates, 23 g fat, 74 mg cholesterol, 884 mg sodium

Sprinkle Italian, Scandinavian, or Mexican seasoning mix (depending on your menu) onto chicken breasts before baking. Mixes are also good for seasoning cooked vegetables.

SCANDINAVIAN DIP

In a bowl, combine 1 cup **sour cream,** 1 tablespoon **Scandinavian seasoning mix** (recipe precedes), and **salt** to taste. Serve, or cover and chill up to 1 week. Offer as a dip for **crackers** and **raw vegetables** such as pieces of broccoli, carrot, or cucumber (about 6 cups total). Or serve with cooked fish. Makes 1 cup.

PER TABLESPOON: 32 calories, 0.5 g protein, 0.8 g carbohydrates, 3 g fat, 6.3 mg cholesterol, 7.9 mg sodium

SCANDINAVIAN SALAD DRESSING

Mix ½ cup **mayonnaise;** ½ cup **buttermilk,** unflavored yogurt, or sour cream; and 1 tablespoon **Scandinavian seasoning mix** (recipe precedes). Add **salt** to taste. Serve, or cover and chill up to 1 week. Ladle onto **salad greens;** allow 2 to 3 tablespoons for a serving. Makes 1 cup.

PER TABLESPOON: 53 calories, 0.4 g protein, 0.7 g carbohydrates, 5.5 g fat, 4.4 mg cholesterol, 47 mg sodium

NORDIC POTATO SOUP

Peel and dice 2 large (about 1⅓ lb. total) **thin-skinned potatoes** and 1 small **onion.** Put vegetables in a 4- to 5-quart pan with 3 cups **regular-strength chicken broth.** Cover and bring to a boil on high heat; simmer until potatoes are very tender when pierced, about 20 minutes. Stir 1 tablespoon **cornstarch** into ½ cup **whipping cream** until blended; mix with soup, 2 teaspoons (or more) **Scandinavian seasoning mix** (recipe precedes), and **salt** to taste; return to simmering. Makes about 5½ cups, 4 servings.

PER CUP: 238 calories, 5.6 g protein, 31 g carbohydrates, 11 g fat, 33 mg cholesterol, 60 mg sodium

Mystery Ingredient: Cocoa

NOT JUST FOR DESSERTS, *cocoa—used sparingly in these sauces for vegetables—adds a subtle depth and rich color.*

Mexican cooks have long employed chocolate in many dishes, where its presence is undetectable except as part of a grander complexity of flavors.

Although unsweetened cocoa, the defatted powder from chocolate, has a bitter bite, it mellows when paired with naturally sweet carrots or yams.

COCOA-GLAZED CARROTS & ONIONS

10 ounces fresh pearl onions (about 1-in. diameter), or 1 package (10 oz.) frozen pearl onions
1 pound baby or small carrots, peeled and ends trimmed
2 tablespoons butter or margarine

2 tablespoons lemon juice
1 tablespoon honey
1 tablespoon unsweetened cocoa
1 teaspoon grated fresh ginger

Place fresh onions in a bowl and cover with boiling water. Let stand 2 to 3 minutes; drain, then pull or slip skins off onions and discard. Also trim onions' root and stem ends.

Place fresh or frozen onions in a 10- to 12-inch frying pan. Barely cover with water and bring to a boil over high heat. Cover pan and simmer gently until the onions are tender when pierced, 8 to 15 minutes. Drain; pour onions from the pan and set them aside.

If using baby carrots, leave whole; cut small carrots diagonally into ¼-inch-thick slices. Put in frying pan used for onions, barely cover with water, and bring to a boil on high heat. Put lid on

pan and simmer gently until carrots are just tender when pierced, 7 to 10 minutes. Drain carrots and set aside.

In the frying pan, combine butter, lemon juice, honey, cocoa, and ginger. Stir over medium-high heat until smoothly blended. Add carrots and onions. Stir gently on high heat until sauce is thick enough to cling to vegetables, 2 to 3 minutes. Pour into a bowl. Makes 4 to 6 servings.

PER SERVING: 93 calories, 1.5 g protein, 14 g carbohydrates, 4.1 g fat, 10 mg cholesterol, 79 mg sodium

MAHOGANY YAMS WITH ORANGE

To help keep yam slices intact, use a wide spatula to turn them in the pan.

⅓ cup coarsely chopped pecans or walnuts
3 tablespoons butter or margarine
2 pounds yams or sweet potatoes, peeled and cut into ¼-inch slices
½ cup thawed frozen orange juice concentrate, or orange-flavor liqueur
¼ cup firmly packed light brown sugar
2 tablespoons lemon juice
1½ tablespoons unsweetened cocoa
1 teaspoon grated lemon peel
½ teaspoon ground cinnamon
¼ teaspoon ground nutmeg

In a 10- to 12-inch pan, cook pecans over medium-high heat, stirring often, until toasted, 2½ to 3 minutes. Pour nuts from pan and set aside.

Melt 1 tablespoon of the butter in frying pan over medium heat. Add as many yam slices as will fit in a single layer and cook until slices are lightly browned on bottom, 5 to 7 minutes. With a wide spatula, carefully turn slices over and cook until browned on bottom. Transfer with the spatula to a plate. Melt the remaining butter and repeat steps to cook the remaining yams.

Return cooked yams to pan along with orange juice, brown sugar, lemon juice, cocoa, lemon peel, cinnamon, and nutmeg. Turn yams with spatula until evenly coated with sauce. Gently simmer, covered, until yams are tender when pierced, about 15 minutes.

Uncover and cook over medium-high heat, turning yams often with spatula until sauce is thick enough to coat them. Spoon into a serving dish and sprinkle with pecans. Makes 8 servings.

PER SERVING: 241 calories, 2.5 g protein, 42 g carbohydrates, 7.7 g fat, 12 mg cholesterol, 56 mg sodium

Shiny, amber glaze gilds baby carrots and pearl onions. Ginger-accented glaze gets its rich color and mellow flavor from the sparing addition of unsweetened cocoa.

Millet—the Birdseed That's Good to Eat

RARELY EXPLORED *in the West beyond its roles in birdseed, baked goods, and soup, millet today—as it has for centuries—forms a significant part of the diet for people who live in India, Africa, and Japan. You can find this ancient grain in health-food stores and well-stocked supermarkets. It's particularly tasty as cereal, or in salad or pilaf.*

Mild millet has a pleasant but curious dry texture that is both fluffy and chewy; flavor is enhanced if the grain is toasted before cooking. Should you decide to experiment, millet takes well to any seasoning that goes with rice.

MILLET BREAKFAST CEREAL

- 1 **cup millet**
- 2½ **cups water**
- ⅓ **cup firmly packed brown sugar**
- 1 **teaspoon ground cinnamon**
   About 3 cups warm milk
- 1 **medium-size ripe banana, thinly sliced (optional)**

In a 10- by 15-inch baking pan, spread millet out in a thin layer. Bake in a 300° oven until millet smells and tastes toasted (chew a few grains; color does not change much), 15 to 20 minutes.

In a 1½- to 2-quart pan, combine millet and water. Bring to a boil over high heat, then cover and simmer until millet is tender to bite and liquid is absorbed, 20 to 25 minutes.

Meanwhile, mix together sugar and cinnamon.

Spoon millet into bowls; add to taste cinnamon sugar, milk, and banana slices. Makes 5 or 6 servings.

PER ½-CUP SERVING WITH 1 TABLESPOON SUGAR AND ½ CUP MILK: 261 calories, 7.2 g protein, 50 g carbohydrates, 5 g fat, 17 mg cholesterol, 66 mg sodium

MILLET SALAD

- ½ **cup slivered almonds**
- 1 **cup millet**
- 2½ **cups regular-strength chicken broth**
- ½ **cup chopped red onion**
- ¼ **cup fresh mint leaves, finely chopped; or 2 teaspoons dry mint leaves**
- ¼ **cup extra-virgin olive oil or salad oil**
- 1 **clove garlic, minced or pressed**
- ⅓ **cup lemon juice**
   Salt and freshly ground pepper

Hearty breakfast cereal is boiled millet, toasted first in oven to develop its nutty flavor. Serve with milk, banana, cinnamon sugar.

In a 1½- to 2-quart pan, stir nuts over medium-high heat until toasted, 7 to 8 minutes. Pour from pan and let stand. In pan, combine millet and broth and bring to a boil over high heat. Cover, reduce heat to simmer, and cook until millet is tender to bite and liquid is absorbed, about 25 minutes (do not stir). Fluff millet with a fork. Pour into a wide bowl to cool, stirring often to break up any lumps.

When millet is cool (allow at least 30 minutes), add almonds, onion, mint, oil, garlic, and lemon juice; mix well. Add salt and pepper to taste. Serve, or cover and chill up until next day. Makes 6 servings.

PER SERVING: 268 calories, 6.5 g protein, 27 g carbohydrates, 16 g fat, 0 mg cholesterol, 27 mg sodium

MILLET PILAF

- 1 **tablespoon butter or margarine**
- 1 **small onion, chopped**
- 1 **cup millet**
- 2½ **cups regular-strength chicken broth**
   Salt and pepper

In a 10- to 12-inch frying pan, melt butter over medium-high heat. Add onion; stir often until limp, about 3 minutes. Add millet and stir until it smells and tastes toasted (chew a few grains; color does not change much), about 5 minutes. Add broth slowly; cover and simmer until millet is tender to bite and liquid is absorbed, about 20 minutes. Stir with a fork to fluff; transfer to a serving dish. Season to taste with salt and pepper. Serves 6.

PER SERVING: 130 calories, 3.9 g protein, 23 g carbohydrates, 3.3 g fat, 5.2 mg cholesterol, 38 mg sodium

Dutch Pancakes

PANCAKE TIME *is any time in The Netherlands, where restaurants featuring this treat serve them throughout the day. Diners choose sweet or savory toppings to go over a plate-size pancake, which is much like a thick crepe. (One Amsterdam restaurant, The Pancake Bakery, offers 53 toppings—ranging from pineapple to an Indonesian vegetable combination.)*

At home, try one of the sweet toppings—syrup, apples, or cherries—over plain pancakes. For a savory version, top pancakes with Dutch cheese and ginger, or stir crumbled bacon into the batter.

Plate-size Dutch pancake is good any time of day. Sweet or savory topping choices include sautéed apple slices, cherry sauce, syrup, or thinly sliced Dutch cheese.

PLATE-SIZE DUTCH PANCAKES

To speed cooking, make pancakes in two pans at the same time.

    4 large eggs
  2½ cups milk
    ½ teaspoon salt (optional)
  1½ cups all-purpose flour
    8 teaspoons butter or margarine
       Fruit or maple syrup, or sautéed
       apples or cherry sauce (recipes
       follow)

In a blender, whirl eggs, milk, and salt, then add flour and whirl until smooth. Melt 1 teaspoon of the butter in a 10- to 12-inch frying pan over medium heat; swirl to coat. Pour ½ cup batter into pan; tilt pan to spread batter evenly over bottom.

Cook pancake until top looks dry and bottom is well browned, 1½ to 3 minutes. Loosen pancake with a wide spatula, then carefully flip over and cook until bottom is brown, 1 to 2 minutes longer. Keep warm. Repeat to make remaining pancakes, stirring batter. Serve with fruit or syrup. Makes 8 pancakes, 4 servings.

PER PANCAKE: 205 calories, 8 g protein, 22 g carbohydrates, 9.4 g fat, 158 mg cholesterol, 111 mg sodium

SAUTÉED APPLES

    1 tablespoon butter or margarine
    2 large Red Delicious apples, cored
       and thinly sliced
    ½ teaspoon grated lemon peel
    1 tablespoon lemon juice
    1 tablespoon sugar

Melt butter in a 10- to 12-inch frying pan over medium-high heat; add apples, lemon peel, lemon juice, and sugar. Cook, gently turning occasionally, until apples are tender to bite, about 7 minutes. If made ahead, keep the fruit warm in a 150° oven up to 1 hour. Makes 2 cups, 4 servings.

PER SERVING: 89 calories, 0.2 g protein, 17 g carbohydrates, 3.2 g fat, 7.8 mg cholesterol, 30 mg sodium

CHERRY SAUCE

In a 2- to 3-quart pan, mix 1 tablespoon **cornstarch** and 2 tablespoons **sugar.** Add 1 tablespoon **lemon juice** and ½ cup **water.** Stir in 3 cups pitted fresh or frozen **Bing cherries.** Stir mixture over medium-high heat until boiling; serve hot. Makes 2½ cups, 4 servings.

PER SERVING: 110 calories, 1.3 g protein, 26 g carbohydrates, 1.1 g fat, 0 mg cholesterol, 0.9 mg sodium

GOUDA & GINGER DUTCH PANCAKES

       Plate-size Dutch pancakes (recipe
       precedes)
    1 pound gouda cheese, thinly sliced
    ⅓ cup chopped preserved ginger in
       syrup
    ¼ cup minced parsley

Follow directions for pancakes. As each is cooked, slide onto an ovenproof dinner plate. Arrange ⅛ of the cheese in a single layer on top of each cake, then sprinkle with ⅛ of the ginger and parsley. Place in a 400° oven until cheese melts, 6 to 7 minutes. Makes 8 pancakes, 4 servings.

PER PANCAKE: 445 calories, 22 g protein, 32 g carbohydrates, 25 g fat, 223 mg cholesterol, 584 mg sodium

BACON DUTCH PANCAKES

Follow directions for **plate-size Dutch pancakes** (recipe precedes), stirring into batter ½ pound **bacon,** cooked and crumbled. Makes 8 pancakes, 4 servings.

PER PANCAKE: 251 calories, 10 g protein, 22 g carbohydrates, 13 g fat, 165 mg cholesterol, 238 mg sodium

Microwave Cooky-Candy

YOUNG COOKS *need only a little supervision to master these no-bake cooky confections from the microwave.*

A 2-quart glass measuring cup works well for the cooking because its handle stays cool to touch. If you use a bowl, wear oven mitts; the bowl gets hot.

JOHN'S OAT & PEANUT BUTTER COOKIES

- ¾ **cup sugar**
- ⅓ **cup (⅙ lb.) butter or margarine**
- ¼ **cup milk**
- ¼ **cup chunk-style peanut butter**
- 2⅓ **cups regular rolled oats**
- 1 **teaspoon vanilla**

In a 2-quart glass measuring cup or non-metal (microwave-safe) bowl, combine sugar, butter, and milk. Cook, uncovered, in microwave oven on full power (100 percent) for 2 minutes, then stir until butter is melted. Cook on full power until mixture bubbles; cook 30 seconds longer.

Stir in peanut butter until melted and well mixed. Stir in oats and vanilla. Drop mixture in about 1-tablespoon mounds onto waxed paper–lined 12- by 15-inch baking sheets, spacing slightly apart. Cool or chill until firm, 40 to 60 minutes. Serve, or store airtight up to 2 days. Makes 2 dozen. —*John Dollbaum, Oakland.*

PER COOKY: 90 calories, 1.8 g protein, 11 g carbohydrates, 4.3 g fat, 7.2 mg cholesterol, 40 mg sodium

SARA'S OAT, COCONUT & COCOA COOKIES

- ½ **cup light corn syrup**
- ¼ **cup granulated sugar**
- ¼ **cup (⅛ lb.) butter or margarine**
- ¼ **cup milk**
- 2 **tablespoons unsweetened cocoa**
- 2⅓ **cups regular rolled oats**
- ½ **cup sweetened shredded dry coconut**
  About ¼ cup powdered sugar

In a 2-quart glass measuring cup or non-metal (microwave-safe) bowl, combine syrup, sugar, butter, and milk. Cook, uncovered, in microwave oven on full power (100 percent) for 2 minutes, then stir until butter is melted. Cook on full power until mixture bubbles; cook 30 seconds longer. Stir in cocoa until well blended, then stir in oats and coconut; cool slightly.

Using your hands, roll about 1-tablespoon portions of dough into balls. Roll balls in powdered sugar. Place slightly apart on a plate. Cool or chill until firm, 40 to 60 minutes. Serve, or store airtight up to 4 days. Makes 2 dozen. —*Sara Reynolds, Chico, Calif.*

PER COOKY: 83 calories, 1.3 g protein, 13 g carbohydrates, 3 g fat, 7.2 mg cholesterol, 40 mg sodium

POLKA DOT GRANOLA DROPS

- ¼ **cup (⅛ lb.) butter or margarine**
- ¼ **cup milk**
- 2 **cups miniature marshmallows**
- 2 **cups granola cereal**
- ½ **cup multicolor candy-coated chocolate pieces**

In a 2-quart glass measuring cup or non-metal (microwave-safe) bowl, combine butter, milk, and marshmallows. Cook, uncovered, in microwave oven on full power (100 percent) for 2 minutes; stir until butter and marshmallows are melted. Cook on full power until mixture bubbles; cook 30 seconds longer.

Stir in granola. Cool mixture until warm to touch; stir in candy. Drop mixture in about 1-tablespoon mounds slightly apart on waxed paper–lined 12- by 15-inch baking sheets; lightly press each cooky so it will hold together. Cool or chill until firm, 40 to 60 minutes. Serve, or store airtight up to 4 days. Makes 2 dozen.

PER COOKY: 98 calories, 1.7 g protein, 12 g carbohydrates, 4.7 g fat, 6.3 mg cholesterol, 30 mg sodium

Sara's set to sample a polka dot granola drop. No-bake cooky confections are cooked briefly in the microwave. Extras will keep up to several days.

More November Recipes

OTHER ARTICLES FEATURE *a new "steam-stewing" technique to reduce fat in pot-roasted beef and a savory Yorkshire pudding dotted with roasted onions. November recipes also include rabbit braised with chilies, orange and lime juices; steamed fish topped with a flavorful sauce; and cranberry pudding cake to serve with ice cream.*

LIGHTENED-UP POT ROAST

If you've a hankering for pot roast but are concerned about fat in the marbled beef chuck, here's a technique that keeps the beef in the pot but gets rid of the fat. You remove all surface fat before rolling and tying the roast. Then a "steam-stewing" step eliminates hidden, intramuscular fat.

To steam-stew, you begin by cooking the meat in a little liquid rather than browning it in added fat. You then boil away the liquid, leaving the richly browned drippings and melted-off fat from within the meat; skim off and discard the fat.

Next, add the seasonings and more liquid and simmer the meat until tender. Fat continues to cook out of the meat during this step; again, you skim and discard it. You can cook vegetables with the meat, and also turn the dark, rich juices into a tasty, lean sauce.

- ⅓ **ounce (about ¼ cup) dried porcini mushrooms**
- 1 **boned beef chuck roast (3½ to 4 lb.), fat trimmed, rolled and tied**
- 2 **tablespoons Worcestershire**
- 1 **large (about ½ lb.) onion, chopped**
- 2 **cloves garlic, minced**
- 2 **cups regular-strength beef broth**
- 1 **cup dry red wine**
- 1 **can (6 oz.) tomato paste**
- 1½ **pounds small (about 1½-in.-diameter) thin-skinned red potatoes, scrubbed**
- 1½ **pounds carrots, peeled and cut into ½-inch-thick sticks**
- 2 **teaspoons cornstarch mixed with 1 tablespoon water (optional) Parsley sprigs**

In a small bowl, pour about ⅓ cup boiling water over mushrooms; let soak at least 20 minutes to soften.

In a 5- to 6-quart pan, combine meat, Worcestershire, and ½ cup water. Cover pan and bring to a gentle boil; let cook 30 minutes. Uncover and cook on high heat until liquid evaporates, leaving only fat and sticky browned drippings in pan;

during this step, turn meat to brown evenly on all sides. If meat starts to stick, stir 2 to 3 tablespoons water at a time into pan to release browned bits. Skim off and discard fat.

To pan, add onion and garlic, and stir on medium-high heat to glaze lightly with browned drippings, adding 1 to 2 tablespoons water. Add broth, wine, and tomato paste; bring to simmering.

Meanwhile, lift mushrooms from liquid, squeezing water from them into bowl. Chop mushrooms and add to pan. Pouring carefully to keep any grit in bowl, pour most of the soaking liquid into pan; discard residue.

Cover pan and simmer meat gently on low heat for 2 hours. Skim off and discard any fat on cooking liquid. Lay potatoes on and around meat; cook 20 minutes. Lay carrots on meat and potatoes. Continue simmering until meat and vegetables are all tender when pierced, 20 to 30 minutes longer.

With 1 or 2 slotted spoons, transfer vegetables and meat to a platter; keep warm. Skim and discard any fat on pan juices. If you want to thicken juices slightly, bring to a rolling boil, stirring in the cornstarch mixture.

Ladle a little of the sauce over meat to moisten; garnish platter with parsley. Pour remaining sauce into a small gravy boat or pitcher. Slice meat and serve alongside vegetables and sauce. Makes 8 to 10 servings.

PER SERVING: 320 calories, 26 g protein, 26 g carbohydrates, 12 g fat, 78 mg cholesterol, 290 mg sodium

YORKSHIRE PUDDING WITH ROASTED ONIONS

If the truth be known, Yorkshire pudding is actually a wide, bumpy popover. But sometimes the bumps get bigger, as they do in the old English country dish, toad-in-a-hole. In the authentic recipe, sausages poke above a crisp brown crust; in ours, the "toads" are roasted onions. It's a savory companion to a roast, or a splendid main course when served with a green salad.

You can begin the recipe a day ahead. Simply roast the quartered onions with the oil and balsamic vinegar until richly browned and naturally sweet. We use red onions because they look attractive, but white onions work as well.

Add batter to the pan of hot onions, then bake until golden and crisp. Serve pudding at once, before its crustiness softens.

- ¼ **cup balsamic or red wine vinegar**
- 1 **tablespoon extra-virgin olive oil**
- 4 **medium-size (about 2 lb. total) red onions**
- 1 **cup all-purpose flour**
- 2 **eggs**
- 1 **cup low-fat or whole milk**
- ¼ **cup (⅛ lb.) butter or margarine**

Mix vinegar and oil; set aside.

Peel onions and cut into quarters. In a 9- by 13-inch oval or rectangular baking dish, arrange onions evenly apart, with a flat side down. Brush quarters evenly with some of the vinegar mixture. Roast in a 500° oven until well browned, about 40 minutes; baste every 10 minutes with remaining vinegar mixture.

Remove from oven; with a wide spatula, gently loosen onions—be careful to keep quarters intact—and any browned bits in pan. If made ahead, let onions cool in pan, then cover and chill until next day. To continue, bring to room temperature.

In a bowl or a blender, beat or whirl flour and eggs to blend. Add milk, and beat or whirl until batter is smooth.

Dot onions with butter. Bake in a 375° oven until butter sizzles, about 5 minutes. Stir batter and pour it evenly around but not on top of the onions. Continue to bake until pudding is well browned on edges and puffed, 35 to 40 minutes. Serve hot, scooping onions and pudding from the dish. Makes 8 to 10 servings.

PER SERVING: 154 calories, 4.3 g protein, 17 g carbohydrates, 7.8 g fat, 57 mg cholesterol, 73 mg sodium

CHILI RABBIT WITH ORANGE

Delicately flavored rabbit takes well to the piquant-hot seasonings in this simple braised dish. The meat is notably lean.

- 2 **large (about 1¼ lb. total) oranges**
- 2 **tablespoons salad oil**
- 1 **fryer rabbit (2½ to 3 lb.), cut into serving-size pieces**
- 1 **cup orange juice**
- ½ **cup lime juice**
- 1 **can (4 oz.) diced green chilies**
- 1 **teaspoon cumin seed**
- 2 **teaspoons cornstarch mixed with 1 tablespoon water**
- 3 **cups hot cooked rice Salt**

Asian seasonings add pungency to pork and black bean sauce topping fillets of steamed fish; garnish with sliced almonds and baby corn. Serve with green beans.

Grate 1 tablespoon peel from oranges; set fruit and peel aside. Pour oil into a 10- to 12-inch frying pan over medium-high heat. Add rabbit (do not crowd pan) and brown well; as pieces are browned, remove from pan and set aside. Discard fat.

To pan, add orange peel, orange juice and lime juice, chilies, and cumin; stir browned bits free. Add rabbit; cover and simmer until meat is no longer pink at bone in thickest part (cut to test), 30 to 40 minutes.

Meanwhile, with a knife, cut peel and membrane from oranges. Thinly slice oranges and arrange on a platter. Lift rabbit onto platter; keep warm. Over high heat, boil pan juices until reduced to 1 cup. Stir cornstarch mixture into pan; when boiling, pour over rabbit. Accompany with rice, and season to taste with salt. Serves 4 to 6. —*Marian Chase, San Pedro, Calif.*

PER SERVING: 395 calories, 35 g protein, 39 g carbohydrates, 10 g fat, 98 mg cholesterol, 185 mg sodium

STEAMED FISH WITH PORK SAUCE

Ground pork and readily available Asian seasonings blend to make a richly flavored sauce to serve over steamed fish fillets.

2   **pounds firm-texture, white-flesh boned and skinned fish (such as halibut, cod, or grouper), about 1 inch thick**
¼   **pound ground lean pork**
2   **cloves garlic, minced or pressed**
2   **tablespoons salted fermented black beans (optional), rinsed, drained, and mashed**
1   **tablespoon grated fresh ginger**
1   **tablespoon soy sauce**
½   **cup dry sherry**
1   **tablespoon cornstarch**
1   **cup regular-strength chicken broth**
1   **green onion, ends trimmed, minced**
1   **jar (7½ oz.) baby corn (optional), drained**
2   **tablespoons sliced almonds**

Rinse fish, pat dry, and cut into 4 to 6 equal-size pieces. Place on a rack set over 1 inch of boiling water in a 5- to 6-quart pan or wok. Cover and boil on medium heat until fish is opaque but still looks moist and slightly translucent in thickest part (cut to test), about 10 minutes.

Meanwhile, in an 8- to 10-inch frying pan on high heat, stir pork until crumbled and lightly browned, 3 to 4 minutes. Add garlic, beans, ginger, soy, and sherry. Mix cornstarch, broth, and onion; add to pork. Stir until mixture boils; keep warm.

Arrange fish on a platter; pour sauce over fish. Garnish with corn and nuts. Serves 4 to 6. —*Roxanne Chan, Albany, Calif.*

PER SERVING: 318 calories, 49 g protein, 7 g carbohydrates, 9.1 g fat, 112 mg cholesterol, 448 mg sodium

CRANBERRY PUDDING CAKE

Beneath a tender layer of cake, cranberries with almonds bake tart and sticky-sweet in this easy, old-fashioned dessert. Ice cream is the perfect embellishment, particularly if the cake is warm.

2   **cups fresh or frozen cranberries**
½   **cup sliced almonds or chopped walnuts**
1   **cup sugar**
2   **large eggs**
¼   **cup (⅛ lb.) melted butter or margarine, at room temperature**
½   **cup all-purpose flour**
3   **to 4 cups vanilla ice cream (optional)**

Butter a 9-inch-diameter baking dish or casserole at least 2 inches deep. Mix cranberries and almonds in dish, then sprinkle with ½ cup sugar.

With an electric mixer, beat eggs, remaining sugar, and butter until thick and foamy. Stir in flour, beat to blend well, then pour over berries. Gently shake dish to settle batter evenly. Bake in a 325° oven until top is golden brown and springs back when lightly touched, about 45 minutes. Serve hot or at room temperature; if made ahead, cover when cool and hold at room temperature up until next day.

Scoop out portions of cake with fruit and put on dessert plates or in dessert bowls. Add ice cream, if desired. Makes 6 to 8 servings. —*Eileen Ritter, Sacramento.*

PER SERVING WITHOUT ICE CREAM: 242 calories, 3.7 g protein, 36 g carbohydrates, 10 g fat, 69 mg cholesterol, 76 mg sodium

For Thanksgiving or party prelude, offer warm, spiced apple cider-based eggnog.

CIDER EGGNOG

2   **large eggs**
2   **tablespoons firmly packed brown sugar or maple syrup**
3   **tablespoons dark rum (optional)**
1   **tablespoon lemon juice**
¼   **teaspoon *each* ground cinnamon and ground nutmeg**
¾   **to 1 cup whipping cream**
1   **quart apple cider or juice**

In a small bowl, whisk to blend eggs, brown sugar, rum, lemon juice, and ⅛ teaspoon *each* of the cinnamon and nutmeg.

In another bowl, whip cream on high speed of an electric mixer with the remaining ⅛ teaspoon cinnamon and nutmeg until cream holds soft peaks. If made ahead, cover egg and cream mixtures and chill up to 2 hours.

In a 2- to 3-quart pan, bring apple cider to boiling over high heat; remove from heat and quickly whisk egg mixture into cider. Pour into a serving bowl and pour cream onto the liquid. At once, ladle warm cider eggnog into punch cups. Makes 8 to 10 servings, ¾-cup size. —*Desiree Witkowski, Long Beach, Calif.*

PER SERVING: 125 calories, 1.7 g protein, 15 g carbohydrates, 6.7 g fat, 62 mg cholesterol, 23 mg sodium

Chicken thighs and onions roast in the oven with tart, sticky cranberry glaze.

CRANBERRY CHICKEN

1   **tablespoon butter or margarine**
1   **small onion, chopped**
3   **pounds chicken thighs (skin removed, if desired)**
⅔   **cup catsup**
⅓   **cup firmly packed brown sugar**
1   **tablespoon cider vinegar**
1   **teaspoon dry mustard**
1½   **cups fresh or frozen cranberries, rinsed**

Place butter and onion in a 10- by 15-inch baking pan. Roast onion, uncovered, in a 400° oven until pale gold, 10 to 15 minutes; stir occasionally. Push onion to 1 section of pan, then place thighs, side by side, in pan but not on onion. Bake, uncovered, 25 minutes longer.

In a bowl, stir together catsup, sugar, vinegar, mustard, and cranberries. Scoop browned onions out of pan and stir them into the cranberry mixture. Space chicken evenly in pan, then spoon cranberry mixture over thighs.

Bake until cranberry mixture is slightly caramelized and chicken is no longer pink at bone in thickest part (cut to test), about 20 minutes longer. Makes 8 servings. —*Carole Van Brooklin, Port Angeles, Wash.*

PER SERVING: 199 calories, 20 g protein, 18 g carbohydrates, 5 g fat, 84 mg cholesterol, 339 mg sodium

Savory eggplant spread makes tasty partner with roast lamb and pocket bread.

EGGPLANT HASH

2   **eggplants (2½ lb. total), stems trimmed, diced**
2   **medium-size onions, diced**
2   **teaspoons ground cumin**
1   **teaspoon paprika**
¼   **cup olive oil or salad oil**
2   **medium-size firm-ripe tomatoes**
¼   **cup chopped fresh cilantro (coriander)**
1   **tablespoon lemon juice**
    Salt

Divide eggplant and onion between 2 baking pans, 10- by 15-inch size.

Mix the cumin, paprika, and oil equally into each pan. Bake, uncovered, in a 400° oven until eggplant is brown on edges, about 30 minutes; stir once with a wide spatula.

Scrape vegetables into 1 pan. Return to oven; bake until eggplant is very soft when pressed, about 30 minutes. Core and dice tomatoes and mix with vegetables. Bake until tomatoes are soft, about 15 minutes more. Stir in cilantro and lemon juice; season to taste with salt. Serve at room temperature. Makes 1 quart, 6 to 8 servings. —*Leila Advani, Sunnyvale, Calif.*

PER SERVING: 105 calories, 1.9 g protein, 11 g carbohydrates, 7.1 g fat, 0 mg cholesterol, 9 mg sodium

Vegetable-Seafood Appetizers

Cucumbers with shrimp (recipe follows)
Endive with salmon (recipe follows)
Lemon wedges

Arrange cucumber and endive appetizers on a platter. If made ahead, cover and chill up to 2 hours. Accompany with lemon wedges. Makes 24 pieces, 8 to 12 servings. —*Gail Reiss, Mendocino, Calif.*

Cucumbers with shrimp. Peel 1 **European cucumber** (about 1 lb.) and cut into 12 equal rounds. Scoop and discard center of each piece, making ⅛- to ¼-inch-

thick shells. Mix ¼ pound **shelled cooked tiny shrimp** with ¼ cup **mayonnaise** and 2 tablespoons minced **fresh cilantro** (coriander). If made ahead, cover and chill separately up to 4 hours. Drain shells and fill with shrimp mixture.

Endive and salmon. Cut 8 to 12 large leaves from 2 or 3 heads rinsed and crisped **Belgian endive.** Cut ¼ pound thinly sliced **smoked salmon** into 8 to 12 pieces. Also cut thin **red onion** slices; separate to make 8 to 12 small rings. Lay a ring in each leaf; top with a piece of salmon.

PER PIECE CUCUMBER: 47 calories, 2.2 g protein, 1.1 g carbohydrates, 4.8 g fat, 21 mg cholesterol, 49 mg sodium

PER PIECE ENDIVE: 12 calories, 1.8 g protein, 0.2 g carbohydrates, 0.4 g fat, 2 mg cholesterol, 75 mg sodium

Two quick appetizers: cucumber cups with shrimp, endive and smoked salmon.

Farmhouse Zucchini Spoonbread

1 pound zucchini, ends trimmed, coarsely grated
2 teaspoons salt
1 cup all-purpose flour
¾ cup yellow cornmeal
2 teaspoons baking powder
1 cup buttermilk
2 large eggs
¼ cup (⅛ lb.) butter or margarine, melted
½ cup shredded cheddar cheese
¼ cup minced onion
2 tablespoons chopped green bell pepper (optional)

In a colander, mix zucchini with salt and crush gently with your hands; set aside 30 minutes to drain. Rinse well under cool running water. With your hands, squeeze as much moisture from squash as possible. Lay squash out on towels and pat dry.

In a large bowl, mix flour, cornmeal, and baking powder. Add buttermilk, eggs, and melted butter; whisk to blend well. Stir in zucchini, cheese, onion, and bell pepper. Pour mixture into a buttered 9-inch-square baking pan. Bake in a 425° oven until top is golden, about 30 minutes. Spoon onto plates. Makes 8 servings. —*Mrs. L.K. Ross, Sonora, Calif.*

PER SERVING: 224 calories, 7.7 g protein, 26 g carbohydrates, 10 g fat, 77 mg cholesterol, 396 mg sodium

Flecks of zucchini and bell pepper lace firm, moist spoonbread; enjoy warm.

Apple Cottage Pudding

1½ cups all-purpose flour
½ cup sugar
2 teaspoons baking powder
¼ teaspoon baking soda
1 large egg
½ cup milk
½ cup (¼ lb.) butter or margarine, melted
2 cups chopped tart green apple; or fresh or frozen cranberries, rinsed
Lemon sauce (recipe follows)

In a bowl, mix flour, sugar, baking powder, and baking soda. Add egg, milk, and butter and whisk together to blend smoothly. Stir in apple.

Pour batter into a buttered shallow 2-quart baking dish. Bake in a 400° oven until well browned, about 35 minutes. Spoon warm or cool pudding into bowls and top with the lemon sauce. Makes 8 servings. —*Laura Getschmann, Bremerton, Wash.*

PER SERVING: 382 calories, 4 g protein, 54 g carbohydrates, 17 g fat, 71 mg cholesterol, 310 mg sodium

Lemon sauce. In a 2- to 3-quart pan, blend ⅔ cup **sugar**, 2 tablespoons **cornstarch**, and 1⅓ cups **water**. Stir on high heat until boiling rapidly. Stir in 3 tablespoons **butter** or margarine and 3 tablespoons **lemon juice;** remove from heat. Use warm or cool.

Spoon apple pudding into bowls; drench with tart lemon sauce.

TRYING TO REPRODUCE *a dish that you have tasted in your favorite restaurant is sometimes frustrating, but it can be fun—even if you can't get a perfect match. The early attempts are nearly always edible (to some degree), and the process is instructive. You learn something about proportions and even more about which flavors supplement each other and which cancel each other.*

Kenneth Fitch's soup is the result of an attempt to duplicate the tortilla soup at a Mexican restaurant. How closely it succeeds we can't say, but it is hard to imagine a better flavor. The garlic is not assertive, submerging its voice into the choral blending of flavors; the cheese and tortilla strips lend body; and the tequila lends an air of mystery: can you taste it or not?

"The soup is the result of an attempt to duplicate the tortilla soup at a Mexican restaurant."

FITCH'S TIJUANA TORTILLA SOUP

 1 tablespoon salad oil, plus oil for frying
 1 large onion, chopped
 5 cloves garlic, minced or pressed
 2 small (about ½ lb. total) red thin-skinned potatoes, scrubbed and cubed
 2 quarts regular-strength chicken broth, or 1 large can (49½ oz.) plus 1 small can (14½ oz.) regular-strength chicken broth
 2 medium-size carrots, thinly sliced
 2 stalks celery, thinly sliced
 ½ cup diced red bell pepper
 2 tablespoons tequila
 ½ teaspoon *each* dry thyme leaves and ground cumin or cumin seed
 ¼ teaspoon rubbed sage
 1 dry bay leaf
 ¼ teaspoon pepper
 Liquid hot pepper seasoning
 ½ cup chopped fresh cilantro (coriander)
 6 to 8 corn tortillas (6-in. diameter), cut into ½- by 2-inch strips
 ¼ pound *each* jack cheese and sharp cheddar cheese, shredded
 Freshly made or purchased salsa

In a 5- to 6-quart pan on medium heat, combine 1 tablespoon oil, onion, and garlic. Stir often until onion is soft, about 10 minutes. Then add potatoes, broth, carrots, celery, bell pepper, tequila, thyme, cumin, sage, bay leaf, pepper, and hot pepper seasoning to taste. Bring

to a boil over high heat; reduce heat, cover, and boil gently until potatoes are tender when pierced, 15 to 20 minutes. Stir in cilantro.

Meanwhile, add about ¼ inch oil to a 10- to 12-inch frying pan over medium-high heat. When hot, add tortilla strips, a portion at a time, and stir until crisp, 45 to 60 seconds. Lift out with a slotted spoon and drain on paper towels. Repeat to cook remaining tortilla strips.

To serve, present tortilla strips, cheeses, and salsa in separate bowls. Add these elements to soup bowls as desired, then ladle soup into bowls. Makes 10 cups, 8 to 10 servings.

PER SERVING WITH TORTILLAS AND CHEESE: 225 calories, 9.6 g protein, 17 g carbohydrates, 13 g fat, 22 mg cholesterol, 221 mg sodium

Kenneth Fitch

Phelan, Calif.

NOT DISTINCTLY FLAVORED *itself, eggplant has the amazing ability to pick up, and often enhance, flavors from sauces or seasonings. It's a good mixer—a party vegetable. In consequence, it need not be ashamed to share billing with veal (or to go it alone) beneath a* parmigiana *sauce; or,*

with lamb, tomato, onion, and herbs, become the main dish in a Turkish feast.

S.M. Estvanik pairs eggplant with Italian sausage and tomato to dress a dish of fettuccine. Here the eggplant blends into and enriches the sauce without dissolving in it, becoming a pleasant and somewhat mysterious complication.

FETTUCCINE WITH EGGPLANT & SAUSAGE

 1 pound mild Italian sausage
 1 large onion, chopped
 2 cloves garlic, minced or pressed
 1 large (about ½ lb.) green bell pepper, stemmed, seeded, and chopped
 1 large (about 1¼ lb.) eggplant, stemmed and cut into ½-inch cubes
 1 can (about 14½ oz.) stewed tomatoes
 1 can (6 oz.) tomato paste
 1 teaspoon *each* dry oregano leaves and dry basil leaves
 About 9 ounces fresh fettuccine
 Freshly grated parmesan cheese
 Salt and pepper

Remove sausage casings and crumble meat into a 5- to 6-quart pan over medium heat. Stir frequently until meat is well browned, about 15 minutes. Discard all but about 1 tablespoon of the fat. Add onion, garlic, and bell pepper; stir often until onion is limp, about 8 minutes. Add eggplant and stir often for 2 to 3 minutes, then add the tomatoes and their liquid, tomato paste, oregano, and basil. Bring to a boil, then cover and simmer until eggplant mashes very easily when pressed, about 45 minutes.

Meanwhile bring about 3 quarts water to boil in a 5- to 6-quart pan over high heat. Add fettuccine and boil uncovered just until tender to bite, 7 to 8 minutes. Drain well and pour onto a rimmed platter. Spoon sauce onto pasta. Add parmesan cheese, salt, and pepper to taste to individual portions. Makes 4 to 6 servings.

PER SERVING: 394 calories, 20 g protein, 43 g carbohydrates, 18 g fat, 95 mg cholesterol, 935 mg sodium

Seattle

C ROSS BEEF BURGUNDY *with Chili con Carne and you get Braised Beef Tips Baumann, a robust stew that begins, like most stews, with beef chunks and onion. The Burgundian element comes from red wine, while Mexico and the Southwest furnish the seasonings—green chilies, chili powder, cumin, and oregano. The result, to adapt wine writers' terminology, is a stew that is rustic without being clownish, robust without being aggressive, with a long finish yet not conducive to dyspepsia.*

BRAISED BEEF TIPS BAUMANN

  2 tablespoons salad oil
2½ pounds fat-trimmed boneless beef chuck, cut into 1-inch cubes
  1 large onion, chopped
  1 large clove garlic, minced or pressed
  2 tablespoons catsup
  ½ cup dry red wine
  1 can (4 oz.) diced green chilies
  1 jar (2 oz.) sliced pimientos, drained
  2 tablespoons chili powder
  ½ teaspoon *each* pepper, dry oregano leaves, and ground cumin
  2 cups regular-strength chicken or beef broth
  4 to 6 cups hot cooked rice or wide egg noodles
    Chopped parsley

Pour oil into a 5- to 6-quart pan over medium-high heat. When hot, add meat, a portion at a time, and cook until well browned on all sides, 7 to 10 minutes total; as browned, lift out and put in bowl.

To pan, add onion and garlic; stir often until onion is faintly browned, about 10 minutes. Pour meat and any juices back into pan, then add catsup, wine, chilies, pimientos, chili powder, pepper, oregano, cumin, and broth; stir to mix well. Bring to a boil, cover, and simmer until meat is very tender when pierced, about 2 hours.

Drain off and measure juice; transfer meat to a rimmed platter and keep warm. If you have more than 2 cups juice, return to pan and boil on high heat until reduced to this amount. Pour juice over meat; mound rice beside meat and sprinkle both with parsley. Makes 4 to 6 servings.

PER SERVING: 551 calories, 41 g protein, 41 g carbohydrates, 24 g fat, 123 mg cholesterol, 368 mg sodium

Eugene P. Baumann

Gold Beach, Ore.

P ROBABLE DESCENDANTS *of an accidental meeting of mush and hot stones, the various American breakfast pancakes are a varied lot made of wheat flour, corn meal, buckwheat flour, or mixtures of the three. They may be Spartan, with a minimum of egg, or sybaritic, with extra egg, buttermilk, sour cream, and a host of adjuncts such as fruit, honey, jam, and syrup. William Craig's tend toward the sybaritic,*

"For the health-conscious he also throws in oats, oat bran, and fresh fruit."

but for the health-conscious he also throws in oats, oat bran, and fruit. These contemporary panaceas may not confer immortality, but they certainly complicate the texture in a delightful way.

Craig also likes to add the fruit while the cakes are cooking. We had some problems with sticking and preferred to add the fruit after the cakes were finished.

GRANDPA CRAIG'S PANCAKES

  1 cup all-purpose flour
  ½ cup yellow cornmeal
  ½ cup quick-cooking rolled oats
  ⅓ cup oat bran
  ¼ cup sugar
1½ teaspoons baking soda
  1 teaspoon baking powder
  ¼ teaspoon salt
  2 cups buttermilk
  ½ cup sour cream
  2 large eggs
  2 tablespoons melted butter or margarine
    Salad oil
    Maple syrup
    Fresh berries, or sliced peaches or bananas

In a large bowl, stir together flour, cornmeal, rolled oats, oat bran, sugar, soda, baking powder, and salt. In another bowl, beat to blend buttermilk, sour cream, eggs, and butter. Mix liquid ingredients into dry until well blended.

Heat an electric griddle to 375° or place a frying pan or griddle over medium-high heat until pan is hot enough to make a drop of water bounce and sizzle.

Brush griddle lightly with oil. For each pancake, pour about ¼ cup batter onto griddle, spacing cakes about 1 inch apart. Cook until bubbles appear, tops look dry, and bottoms are golden brown. Turn pancakes over and cook until golden brown on bottom.

Accompany pancakes with maple syrup and/or fresh fruit to add to taste. Makes about 20 pancakes, each about 4 inches in diameter.

PER PANCAKE: 102 calories, 2.6 g protein, 11 g carbohydrates, 5.1 g fat, 23 mg cholesterol, 131 mg sodium

William L. Craig

Los Altos, Calif.

November Menus

CALMING COUNTERBALANCES *to the bustle of activity during the holidays, homey foods are featured in this month's menus. Each dish is simple; some cook without attention while you handle other duties at home. Most have make-ahead steps you can juggle to fit your schedule.*

Versatile as well as easy, each of these meals can play a double role in your menu planning. Serve the soup and salad or the ham and casserole combinations for a weekend lunch or weekday dinner. The roast turkey breast brunch is equally suited to supper on a busy day.

If you are among those who believe that soup tastes better the second day, put this one on to simmer while you are having dinner the night before.

Delicately aromatic extra-virgin olive oil adds the final touch of flavor for this hearty all-vegetable soup. You also might like to drizzle a little of the oil over toasted rolls, Italian-style, instead of buttering them. Make the slaw up to 2 hours before the meal.

Buy gelato or ice cream and keep it ready in the freezer. To make quick warm chocolate sauce for the gelato, put your microwave to work. If this is an on-the-run meal for some family members, give them chocolate-coated ice cream bars to nibble as they travel.

WHITE BEAN & CORN SOUP WITH SAVORY

1 pound (2¼ cups) dry small white beans
2 quarts regular-strength chicken broth
2 teaspoons dry savory leaves or dry thyme leaves
1 can (28 oz.) pear-shaped tomatoes
1 can (17 oz.) cream-style corn
Pepper
Extra-virgin olive oil
Salt

Sort the beans to remove any debris; rinse and drain. To a 4- to 5-quart pan, add beans, broth, and savory. Bring to a boil over high heat; reduce heat, cover, and simmer until beans are tender to bite, about 1½ hours.

With a knife, cut through tomatoes, still in can, to make small pieces; add to soup along with corn and pepper to taste. Cover and simmer about 30 minutes longer to blend flavors. With spoon or potato masher, mash some of the beans to thicken soup slightly. If made ahead, let cool, cover, and chill up to 2 days; reheat to continue.

Ladle soup into wide bowls. Add a

Thick soup full of beans, corn, and tomatoes is a ready-and-waiting main dish for a busy week night. Serve it with fruity cabbage slaw, whole-wheat rolls, and milk.

small swirl of olive oil to taste to each portion and stir into soup as you eat. Season as desired with more pepper and salt. Makes 12 cups, 6 to 8 servings.

PER SERVING: 286 calories, 16 g protein, 52 g carbohydrates, 2.6 g fat, 0 mg cholesterol, 394 mg sodium

PEAR & RADISH CABBAGE SLAW

- ¼ **cup lemon juice**
- ¼ **cup honey**
- 2 **medium-size (about 1 lb. total) firm-ripe pears, such as Bartlett or Anjou**
- 4 **cups thinly shredded green cabbage**
- ¼ **cup slivered red radishes**
  Salt

In a salad bowl, mix together lemon juice and honey. Cut pears in quarters and trim away stem and core. Thinly slice fruit crosswise into bowl and mix gently to coat with dressing. Mound cabbage and radishes onto fruit. If made ahead, cover and chill up to 2 hours. Mix salad to serve, adding salt to taste. Makes 6 to 8 servings.

PER SERVING: 63 calories, 0.6 g protein, 16 g carbohydrates, 0.2 g fat, 0 mg cholesterol, 9.2 mg sodium

Turkey breast half is a convenient size for a family; dried fruits and cranberries bake along with it. Serve with rice pilaf and green beans topped with buttery almonds.

ROAST TURKEY BREAST BRUNCH

Roast Turkey Breast with Dried Fruits & Cranberries
Rice Pilaf
Green Beans with Butter–toasted Almonds
Apple-Ginger Mimosas
Apple Cider

Even though turkey has a guaranteed star appearance on Thanksgiving, convenient, easy-to-cook turkey parts can still be enjoyed at other meals. Here, tangy dried fruit complements the delicate flavor of moist baked breast.

Make a pilaf of rice from a favorite recipe; you could also start with a mix. Toast slivered almonds in butter and pour over hot cooked green beans. Winter-style mimosas use apple cider as their base. Put a piece of crystallized ginger in each glass, and fill equally with the cider and sparkling wine. Serve plain cider as a non-alcoholic alternative.

ROAST TURKEY BREAST WITH DRIED FRUITS & CRANBERRIES

- 1 **bone-in turkey breast half, 2½ to 3 pounds**
- 1 **pound (about 2 cups) dried peaches, apricots, pitted prunes, or figs, or a combination**
- 1 **cup regular-strength chicken broth**
- 1 **cup fresh or frozen cranberries**
- 1 **tablespoon firmly packed brown sugar**

Trim any fat off turkey and discard; rinse breast and pat dry. Lay skin up in a 9- by 13-inch pan; surround with dried fruit and pour broth over fruit. Tightly cover pan with foil. Bake in a 400° oven until a thermometer in center of thickest part of breast reaches 170°, about 1 hour. When breast has cooked 40 minutes, uncover it and add cranberries to the pan; baste breast with juices in pan 2 or 3 times as it cooks.

Lift breast onto a platter; with a slotted spoon, arrange fruit around meat. Add brown sugar to pan juices; boil over medium heat until sauce clings to back of spoon. Spoon over turkey and fruits. Makes 6 servings.

PER SERVING: 474 calories, 40 g protein, 53 g carbohydrates, 13 g fat, 111 mg cholesterol, 124 mg sodium

HARVEST SUPPER

Pan-browned Ham with Braised Fennel
Pumpkin & Apple Casserole
Curly Endive Salad
Gamay   Milk
Oatmeal Cookies

This simple meal abounds with fall flavors: ham, pumpkin, and apples.

Cooked ham needs only pan browning; use its drippings to quickly cook fennel. Canned pumpkin also speeds the making of the casserole. Crisp curly endive gives a nice texture to the salad. Buy or bake cookies to go with milk for dessert.

PAN-BROWNED HAM WITH BRAISED FENNEL

- **About 1 pound fennel**
- 2 **teaspoons olive oil or salad oil**
- 1 **slice (about 1 lb.) center-cut cooked ham**
- ⅓ **cup dry white wine or regular-strength chicken broth**
- ¼ **teaspoon pepper**

(Continued on next page)

Rinse fennel and trim off discolored base and any other discolored or bruised portions. Also cut off coarse stalks, reserving green leaves. Thinly slice fennel and chop enough leaves to make 2 to 3 tablespoons; reserve remaining leaves.

Pour oil into a 10- to 12-inch frying pan over medium-high heat; when hot, add ham and brown on both sides, about 5 minutes total. Transfer to a small platter, cover, and keep warm. Add sliced fennel to pan along with wine and pepper. Stir often, uncovered, on medium-high heat, until fennel is tender to bite and only 1 or 2 tablespoons liquid remain, about 5 minutes. Stir chopped leaves into fennel, then pour fennel and juices around ham. Garnish with fennel leaves. Cut ham into equal portions. Makes 4 servings.

PER SERVING: 203 calories, 25 g protein, 4.8 g carbohydrates, 8.6 g fat, 60 mg cholesterol, 1,469 mg sodium

PUMPKIN & APPLE CASSEROLE

- 2 medium-size (about 1 lb. total) sweet apples such as Golden Delicious, peeled, cored, chopped
- 1 medium-size onion, chopped
- ½ cup *each* diced carrot and celery
- 3 cloves garlic, minced or pressed
- 1 dry bay leaf
- 1 teaspoon *each* dry thyme leaves and dry basil leaves
- 1 tablespoon butter or margarine
- ½ cup regular-strength chicken broth
- 1 can (1 lb.) solid-packed pumpkin, or 2 cups cooked and mashed squash, such as banana or Hubbard squash
  Salt and pepper

In a 10- to 12-inch frying pan over medium-high heat, combine apple, onion, carrot, celery, garlic, bay leaf, thyme, basil, butter, and broth. Stir often until liquid has evaporated and apples and vegetables are tender to bite and tinged with brown, about 20 minutes; discard bay leaf. Stir pumpkin into apple-vegetable mixture, then spread into a shallow 1- to 1½-quart casserole. If made ahead, cover and chill up until next day.

Bake, uncovered, in a 400° oven until mixture is hot and top is faintly browned, about 25 minutes (35 minutes if chilled). Spoon from dish; add salt and pepper to taste. Serves 4.—*J. Hill, Sacramento.*

PER SERVING: 144 calories, 2.8 g protein, 28 g carbohydrates, 3.7 g fat, 7.7 mg cholesterol, 61 mg sodium

Gingerbread People 1989 (page 274)

Holiday ideas old and new add a festive air to our December issue. Two favorites from the 1960s—gingerbread people and Christmas bread—return in updated, revised versions. For seasonal entertaining, we offer an informal gathering featuring home-roasted chestnuts, a holiday dinner saluting the season's fresh citrus, and a simple yet traditional feast; you'll also find a trio of lean eggnogs. Add variety to winter meals with farm-raised salmon, colorful salads, and easy vegetable dishes.

Sunset Holiday Recipes: Family Traditions

FAMILY TRADITIONS ABOUND *during the holidays. Over the years, favorite* Sunset *recipes have become part of Christmas celebrations in many Western homes; some of them grace the table, some of them fill gift baskets, and some of them hang from the tree.*

It is, of course, almost inevitable that as those recipes become family custom, they are altered and adapted. Here, we share the traditions and updated recipes of two families. One makes jaunty personalized cookies. The other builds a rich, tree-shaped yeast bread.

NEARLY A QUARTER-CENTURY OF COOKIES

It was 24 years ago that Peggy and Tim Newman of Salt Lake City first made the gingerbread boys from our December 1965 issue. The seasonal ritual became a

December 1965

1967 *Elizabeth, Mark, Joyce, and John Newman pitch in to make gingerbread boys from recipe in 1965 article.*

1986 *Joyce introduces her new husband, Rich Littlewood, to family's cooky tradition.*

Gingerbread boy honors Mark's becoming an Eagle Scout in 1984.

Another family milestone: Hugging twosome celebrates parents' 25th anniversary in 1988. Gingerbread characters also depict family's diverse activities and interests.

family affair, with Mrs. Newman mixing the dough, the four children shaping the cookies, and Mr. Newman drawing faces and details with frosting.

Over the years, the Newmans' cutter, made from a strip of aluminum, evolved into a taller, slimmer model than the original *Sunset* pattern. (We've included the new shape on the next page.) The cookies began portraying the family's diverse activities—from Boy Scouts to ballet. And Mrs. Newman modified the recipe to make a lighter-colored cooky that showed up better on the tree.

THREE GENERATIONS OF CHRISTMAS BREAD

Bread shaped like a glittering Christmas tree brightened our pages in December 1967. "I've made it for our holiday breakfast ever since," says Florence Chisholm.

(Continued on next page)

December 1967

Building the tree, Mrs. Chisholm and daughter, Janet, follow our 1967 recipe.

Florence Chisholm offers Christmas bread to her son-in-law, Gordon Ruehl. Traditional yeast bread is now enjoyed by a third generation in Spokane.

1 *Mark off an inch-wide strip of aluminum and cut with tin snips. Gloves protect hands from sharp edges of metal.*

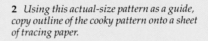

2 *Using this actual-size pattern as a guide, copy outline of the cooky pattern onto a sheet of tracing paper.*

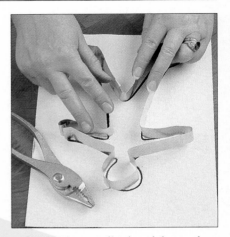

3 *Center strip at top of head; work down each side, bending aluminum strip to pattern. Overlap ends; hold with tape.*

"GINGER-KIDS": PERSONALIZE THESE COOKY PEOPLE

These cookies can hang on a tree for up to several days, in a dry place for several weeks. (Trees give off moisture, which may soften and weaken cookies.) Or give them as gifts; covered with plastic wrap, they last about a week. Steps for making the cutter are shown above, and given at the end of the recipe.

GINGERBREAD PEOPLE 1989

½ cup (¼ lb.) **butter or margarine**
1 cup firmly packed **light brown sugar**
2 teaspoons **baking soda**
1 teaspoon *each* **salt, ground allspice, ground cinnamon, ground cloves, and ground ginger**
1⅓ cups **light molasses**
⅔ cup **apple juice or water**
About 8 cups **all-purpose flour**
Purchased ornamental frosting, in tubes

In a large bowl of an electric mixer, beat together butter, sugar, soda, salt, and spices until creamy. Add molasses and juice; mix until blended. Stir in enough flour (about 7½ cups) to make a stiff dough. Cover tightly; chill at least 2 hours, or up to 4 days.

Roll out part of the dough at a time on a floured board to a thickness of ³⁄₁₆ inch (keep remaining dough covered). Cut out cookies (step 4, above); with cutter still in place, use a wide spatula to transfer each cooky and cutter to a lightly greased 12- by 15-inch baking sheet. Lift off the cutter. Place 1 cooky (or 2, widely spaced) on a sheet.

Adjust arms and legs to customize the figures. Use a sharp knife, scissors, or mat cutter to cut details—a hat or helmet, a skirt or scarf—from scraps of dough rolled to about ⅛ inch thick. For shirts or pants, use the appropriate part of the cutter as a pattern. For hair, press bits of dough through a garlic press. For even browning, the cooky—with all details in place—should be no thicker than ⅜ inch at any point.

Attach details, as shown in step 5. To make a hole for hanging, use a drinking straw to pierce a hole about ⅜ inch below the top of each cooky.

Bake in a 350° oven until firm and lightly browned on edges, 16 to 20 minutes. Let cool on baking sheet about 10 minutes, then transfer with a wide spatula to racks to cool completely. Decorate with frosting (step 6); let dry.

Store cookies in a single layer on trays or heavy cardboard covered with plastic wrap. Keep at room temperature for up to 1 week, or freeze up to 3 months. Makes about 16 cookies (3½ to 4 oz. each).

To hang the cookies, thread a piece of ribbon or yarn through the hole in each and tie to form a loop.

PER COOKY: 376 calories, 6.1 g protein, 74 g carbohydrates, 6 g fat, 15 mg cholesterol, 291 mg sodium

GOLDEN NUTMEG PEOPLE COOKIES

Look for golden syrup in markets that sell specialty foods. Or substitute light corn syrup.

Follow directions for **gingerbread people,** preceding, omitting allspice, cinnamon, cloves, ginger, and molasses. Into the creamed mixture, beat 1 tablespoon *each* **ground nutmeg** and **vanilla.** Then mix in 1⅓ cups (16-oz. can) **golden syrup** or light corn syrup.

PER COOKY: 390 calories, 6.1 g protein, 77 g carbohydrates, 6.1 g fat, 15 mg cholesterol, 304 mg sodium

MAKING THE CUTTER

You need a permanent felt-tip marker or china marker; a ruler; a piece of 6-inch-wide, 37-inch-long aluminum roof flashing (about 45¢ a foot at hardware stores and lumberyards); work gloves; tin snips (or old scissors); tracing paper; a pencil; a large nail; and masking tape.

With the marker, draw a line to mark off a 1-inch-wide strip the full length of the aluminum. Wearing gloves, cut the strip with tin snips—or an old pair of scissors (step 1, above). For extra safety (especially if children will be helping), cover sharp edges of aluminum with masking tape.

Trace the pattern, then bend strip as shown (step 3). Overlap ends where they join, and secure with tape; cut off extra metal. Refine shape; to make sharp loops, such as the thumb detail, bend the strip around the nail (optional).

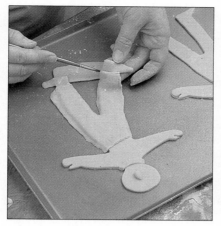

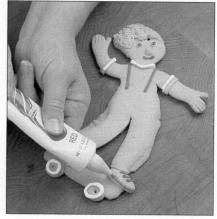

4 *Cut out cookies with cutter; transfer dough carefully to baking sheet. Allow space to add details and bend limbs.*

5 *To add detail (here, a skateboard), lightly moisten adjacent surfaces, then press gently to bond pieces.*

6 *Draw details such as face and shoes on baked cooky with ornamental frosting in a tube with a plain tip.*

CHRISTMAS-TREE BREAD: STACK ROUNDS LIKE SHINGLES

Serve this rich, fragrant yeast bread warm for your Christmas breakfast. Shape the tree by overlapping rounds of dough, fashioned with a doughnut cutter.

CHRISTMAS TREE BREAD 1989

1 package active dry yeast
1 cup warm (110°) water
¼ cup sugar
¾ teaspoon salt (optional)
1 large egg
About 3½ cups flour
¾ cup (⅜ lb.) cold butter or margarine
1 large egg yolk, beaten with 1 tablespoon water
Apricot glaze (directions follow)
About ¼ cup currant jelly

In the large bowl of an electric mixer, soften yeast in water, about 5 minutes. Add sugar, salt, whole egg, and ¾ cup of the flour. Beat on medium speed until smooth; set aside.

Put 2½ cups flour in another large bowl and add butter, cut in pieces. Using a pastry blender or 2 knives, cut in butter until pieces are the size of peas. Pour in yeast mixture and stir until flour is evenly moistened. Cover tightly and refrigerate at least 2 hours or up until next day.

Turn chilled dough out on a floured board and knead for 5 minutes, adding more flour as needed to prevent sticking. Return dough to bowl, cover, and let rest in refrigerator for about 30 minutes.

On a lightly floured board, roll chilled dough to a 16-inch circle. Using a floured 2¾-inch doughnut cutter (or round cooky cutter and a thimble), cut 25 rounds. Cut a 2¾-inch star with a cutter or knife; cut out center. Set all pieces aside; cover with plastic wrap.

Form dough trimmings into a smooth ball and roll into a rough triangle about ⅛ inch thick. (If dough is too elastic to roll out, cover and let rest about 20 minutes.) Using a sharp knife and ruler, trim to make a triangle 15 inches tall and 13 inches across base. Place on a lightly greased 14- by 17-inch baking sheet. Fold top 2 inches of triangle under. Shape tree trunk from dough trimmings rolled ¼ inch thick; press to back of triangle's base.

Arrange 6 rounds, overlapping slightly, across base of tree. Use 5 to make second row, 5 for third row, 4 for fourth row, 3 for fifth row, and 2 for top row. Place star on top. Set any leftover dough on pan.

Cover with plastic wrap and let rise slowly at room temperature until almost double, about 1½ hours. Brush gently with egg yolk mixture. Bake in a 325° oven until deep golden brown, about 40 minutes.

(If made ahead, let bread cool, then seal in foil and freeze up to 2 weeks. Reheat wrapped frozen bread in a 350° oven until warm, about 30 minutes.)

Brush hot bread gently with apricot glaze; let cool 10 minutes. Spoon about ¼ teaspoon currant jelly into center of each round. Serve bread hot or warm. Or cool on a rack, cover, and wrap airtight until next day. Makes 1 bread, about 2 pounds, 12 to 15 servings.

PER OUNCE: 114 calories, 1.8 g protein, 16 g carbohydrates, 4.8 g fat, 25 mg cholesterol, 47 mg sodium

Apricot glaze. Press ⅓ cup **apricot jam** through a fine strainer into a 1- to 2-cup pan. Stir jam over low heat until bubbly.

Glittering with ornaments of currant jelly, traditional tree-shaped yeast bread delights three generations for Christmas breakfast.

Chestnuts Roasting on an Open Fire

FROM THE DAYS OF DICKENS, *the aromatic popping of roasting chestnuts has evoked winter cheer. Roast the nuts over the traditional open fire or cook them in the oven for our hearthside party for a dozen.*

Your guests enjoy the scent and sound of the chestnuts roasting. Then they peel some nuts to eat plain or to splash with a sweet or savory sauce. To round out the menu, offer English cheeses with crackers, celery, fruit, mulled wine, and a classic Scottish Dundee cake.

ROASTED CHESTNUT PARTY FOR 12

Roasted Chestnuts
Tarragon-Riesling Sauce
Port Wine Syrup
Stilton Cheese
Sharp Cheddar Cheese
Assorted Crackers   Celery Sticks
Winter Fruit   Dundee Cake
Mulled Wine

You'll need a total of at least 1½ pounds of cheese (more, if you want a bountiful look) and about 1 pound of crackers. Also allow at least 1 piece of fruit and several celery sticks per person.

Chestnuts are easiest to peel when they're hot, so have a spot ready to rest the roasting pan—as well as hot pads and napkins to protect hands. You'll also need a container for shells. Be sure each nut is scored (see recipe below), and don't let any go directly into the fire: exploding chestnuts are messy and very hot.

The sauce and syrup both go well with the nuts; the syrup with port also complements Dundee or plain pound cake. Enjoy the mulled wine any cold evening.

ROASTED CHESTNUTS

With a small, sharp knife, cut an X through shell on a flat side of each of 4 pounds **chestnuts.** (If prepared ahead, chill nuts, covered, up until next day.) Cook nuts in batches, in either of the following ways.

On an open fire. Place 1 layer of nuts in a long-handled pan—a fireplace popcorn popper, fire-safe frying pan, or chestnut roaster (like a long-handled frying pan with holes in the bottom). Place over a low fire, balancing utensil on logs, and shake often until nuts are mealy in center when broken open, 30 to 35 minutes.

In an oven. Place nuts in a 10- by 15-inch rimmed baking pan. Roast in a 400° oven until nuts are mealy in the center when broken open, about 30 minutes.

To peel. Using thick napkins to protect hands, crack roasted nuts 1 at a time between hands; pull off shell and thin skin inside. Eat plain, or dip in (or, on small plates, drench with) **tarragon-Riesling sauce** or **port wine syrup** (recipes follow). Serves 12, about 5 nuts each.

PER PLAIN CHESTNUT: 59 calories, 0.8 g protein, 13 g carbohydrates, 0.5 g fat, 0 mg cholesterol, 0.5 mg sodium

TARRAGON-RIESLING SAUCE

1½ **cups fruity Johannisberg Riesling**
2 **teaspoons cornstarch**
1½ **teaspoons dry tarragon leaves**
¼ **teaspoon pepper**
½ **cup (¼ lb.) butter or margarine**

Mix 2 tablespoons wine with cornstarch; set aside. In a 1- to 2-quart pan, bring remaining wine, tarragon, and pepper to a boil over high heat. Boil, uncovered, until wine is reduced to 1 cup, 4 to 5 minutes.

Add cornstarch mixture and butter to wine; stir on medium heat until butter melts and sauce bubbles and thickens.

Pour sauce into a bowl and serve hot. (If made ahead, let cool, cover, and chill up to 3 days. Stir over medium heat until hot.) Makes 1½ cups, 12 servings.

PER TABLESPOON: 36 calories, 0.1 g protein, 0.4 g carbohydrates, 3.8 g fat, 10 mg cholesterol, 40 mg sodium

PORT WINE SYRUP

1 **bottle (750 ml.) port**
¾ **cup sugar**
1 **teaspoon grated lemon peel**

In a 4- to 5-quart pan, bring port and sugar to a boil over high heat. Boil, uncovered, for 8 minutes. Add peel; continue to boil until syrup is reduced to 1½ cups, 2 to 4 minutes longer.

Pour into a bowl and serve hot. (If made ahead, let cool, cover, and chill up

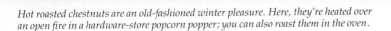

Hot roasted chestnuts are an old-fashioned winter pleasure. Here, they're heated over an open fire in a hardware-store popcorn popper; you can also roast them in the oven.

Warm chestnuts to peel are focus of casual winter buffet with cheese and crackers, celery, fruit, Dundee cake, mulled wine. Eat chestnuts plain or drizzle with sauce.

Sweet port syrup complements both chestnuts and Dundee cake.

to 1 week. Stir over medium heat until hot.) Makes 1½ cups, 12 servings.

PER TABLESPOON: 39 calories, 0.1 g protein, 10 g carbohydrates, 0 g fat, 0 mg cholesterol, 2.9 mg sodium

DUNDEE CAKE

   About 1 cup (½ lb.) butter or
   margarine
 1 tablespoon grated orange peel
 2 teaspoons grated lemon peel
 1 cup sugar
 5 large eggs
2¼ cups sifted cake flour
 1 teaspoon baking powder
 ½ cup *each* golden raisins, dark
   raisins, and dried currants
 ⅓ cup sliced almonds
   Port wine syrup (recipe on
   preceding page; optional)

With a mixer, beat 1 cup butter with orange and lemon peel and sugar until fluffy. Add eggs, 1 at a time; beat well after each.

Combine flour, baking powder, golden and dark raisins, and currants. Stir into butter mixture until smooth.

Generously butter a plain or fluted 9-inch (9-cup) tube cake pan; press almonds into butter. Evenly spread batter in pan.

Bake cake in a 325° oven until a toothpick inserted in center comes out barely clean, about 1¼ hours. Let cool 10 minutes, then turn cake out onto rack; cool completely. Serve cake, or store airtight up to 1 day. Freeze to store longer. Offer sauce to spoon onto thin slices. Serves 12 to 16.

PER SERVING WITHOUT SAUCE: 281 calories, 4.1 g protein, 35 g carbohydrates, 15 g fat, 117 mg cholesterol, 167 mg sodium

MULLED WINE

 2 large bottles (each 1½ l., 6¼ cups)
   dry red wine
 2 thin strips orange peel (colored
   part only), each about 10 inches
   long
12 cardamom pods, slightly crushed
 6 cinnamon sticks, each about
   3 inches long
 2 teaspoons whole allspice
 2 teaspoons whole cloves
   About ½ cup sugar

In a 5- to 6-quart pan, stir wine with peel, cardamom, cinnamon, allspice, cloves, and sugar to taste. Cover and place on medium-low heat until wine is steaming, about 20 minutes. Makes 12½ cups, 12 servings.

PER SERVING: 215 calories, 0.5 g protein, 13 g carbohydrates, 0 g fat, 0 mg cholesterol, 13 mg sodium

Merry Citrus: A Holiday Party Menu

A HARVEST OF CITRUS, *from her Los Angeles garden and elsewhere in the West, inspired Judy Hagmann's handsome holiday party menu with make-ahead steps. Each course, from salad to dessert, puts brightly colored citrus to work.*

WINTER CITRUS CELEBRATION

Grapefruit & Avocado Salad
with Tangerine Dressing

Grilled Quail in Citrus-Herb
Marinade with Oranges & Limes

Braised Red Cabbage
with Apricots & Lemon

Sweet Potatoes Baked in Jackets

Orange-Rum Cake with Kumquats

Cabernet Sauvignon   Espresso

If you want an early start, marinate the quail, cook the cabbage, crisp the salad greens, and make the cake (recipe on page 280) up to a day before the party.

Early in the day of the dinner, tie the quail legs; grilled birds will keep warm up to a half-hour in the oven. The baked sweet potatoes can keep warm with them.

You can segment the grapefruit several hours ahead; the avocado slices in the dressing hold their color well for at least 1 hour. Assemble salads just before serving.

GRAPEFRUIT & AVOCADO SALAD WITH TANGERINE DRESSING

1	large (about 1 lb.) ruby grapefruit
½	teaspoon grated tangerine peel
¼	cup tangerine juice
1	tablespoon honey
1	tablespoon lemon juice
2	large (about 10 oz. each) firm-ripe avocados
12	to 18 washed and crisped medium-size butter lettuce leaves
	Coarse salt

With a knife, cut peel and white membrane from grapefruit. Cut segments free from membrane into a bowl; squeeze juice from membrane into bowl. Add tangerine peel and juice, honey, and lemon juice. If made ahead, cover and hold up to 4 hours.

Peel, pit, and cut avocados into a total of 18 slices. If cut ahead, put slices in a shallow dish; pour grapefruit liquid over them; let stand up to 1 hour.

Classic partners, smooth avocado and tart-sweet grapefruit make a refreshing salad.

Arrange lettuce leaves on 6 salad plates. Top with alternating pieces of grapefruit and avocado; pour dressing equally over salads. Sprinkle lightly with salt. Makes 6 servings.

PER SERVING: 142 calories, 1.9 g protein, 13 g carbohydrates, 11 g fat, 0 mg cholesterol, 8.5 mg sodium

GRILLED QUAIL IN CITRUS-HERB MARINADE

Buying butterflied quail will save you some work.

12	quail (about ¼ lb. each)
	Citrus-herb marinade (recipe follows)
	Braised red cabbage with apricots and lemon (recipe follows)
1	or 2 medium-size oranges, peeled with a knife and sliced crosswise
2	limes, cut into wedges
	Salt and pepper

With poultry shears or kitchen scissors, cut parallel to each side of backbone on each quail; discard backbone. Open up birds and press to crack bones so they will lie flat. Rinse and pat dry.

In a large bowl, mix birds with marinade. Cover and chill at least 2 hours or up until the next day, turning quail occasionally. Lift from marinade, reserving liquid. Bring leg bones of each together at ends and tie with string.

Winter harvest of citrus brightens table centerpiece and stars in each course of the menu, from salad to dessert, for this holiday dinner.

Place quail on a grill 4 to 6 inches above a solid bed of hot coals (you should be able to hold your hand at grill level only 2 to 3 seconds). Cook, turning and basting often with marinade, until breasts are still red but not wet-looking at the bone (cut from wing joint into breast to test), 8 to 10 minutes. If made ahead, keep quail warm, uncovered, in a 150° oven for up to 30 minutes.

Transfer birds to a warm platter, along with cabbage, orange slices, and lime wedges. Squeeze one lime and add juice, salt, and pepper to taste. Makes 4 to 6 servings. —*Judy Hagmann, Los Angeles.*

PER SERVING WITHOUT CABBAGE: 487 calories, 40 g protein, 9 g carbohydrates, 32 g fat, 0 mg cholesterol, 335 mg sodium

Citrus-herb marinade. In a large bowl, mix ½ cup **brandy** or regular-strength chicken broth; ¼ cup *each* **lemon** and **orange juices;** 3 tablespoons *each* **Dijon mustard** and **extra-virgin olive oil;** 2 cloves **garlic,** minced or pressed; 1 teaspoon *each* grated **lemon** and **orange peels;** ½ teaspoon **freshly ground pepper;** 1 tablespoon chopped **fresh sage leaves** or 1 teaspoon rubbed sage; 3 **fresh rosemary sprigs** (each 3 in. long), or 1 teaspoon dry rosemary leaves; 12 **fresh thyme sprigs** (each 3 in. long) or 1 teaspoon dry thyme leaves; and 12 **fresh savory sprigs** (each 3 in. long) or 1 teaspoon dry savory leaves.

BRAISED RED CABBAGE WITH APRICOTS & LEMON

- 1 **cup chopped dried apricots**
- 2 **cups dry or fruity red wine**
- ½ **cup honey**
- 2 **tablespoons lemon juice**
- 1 **large head (2½ lb.) red cabbage, cored and finely sliced**

In a 5- to 6-quart pan over high heat, combine apricots, wine, honey, and lemon juice; bring to boiling. Cover and simmer 5 minutes. Add cabbage and stir often until wilted and most of the liquid is evaporated, about 15 minutes. If made ahead, let cool, cover, and chill up until next day. Boil uncovered, stirring often, until remaining liquid evaporates. Makes 6 servings.

PER SERVING: 196 calories, 3.7 g protein, 50 g carbohydrates, 0.6 g fat, 0 mg cholesterol, 29 mg sodium

(Continued on next page)

Brightly garnished with oranges and limes, entrée features grilled quail accompanied by tangy red cabbage and sweet potatoes baked in their jackets.

ORANGE-RUM CAKE WITH KUMQUATS

- ⅓ cup butter or margarine
- ¾ cup granulated sugar
- 1 tablespoon grated orange peel
- 2 large eggs
- 1 teaspoon baking powder
- ¼ teaspoon baking soda
- ¼ cup *each* orange juice and rum (or ½ teaspoon rum extract and ¼ cup water)
- 1¼ cups all-purpose flour
   Orange-rum syrup and candied orange peel (recipes follow)
   Powdered sugar and kumquats

With a mixer, beat butter, sugar, and grated peel until fluffy. Add eggs, 1 at a time, beating after each addition. Add baking powder and soda.

Mix juice and rum. Stir flour and juice mixture alternately into batter; beat to blend well.

Scrape batter into a heavily buttered and flour-dusted, deep, plain or decorative 6- to 10-cup tube cake pan or steaming mold. Bake in a 325° oven until cake pulls from pan sides, about 1 hour. Let cool in pan for 10 minutes, then run a small spatula between cake and pan sides. Invert cake onto rack to be sure it's loosened, then invert back into pan.

With a long, thin skewer, pierce cake to bottom at 1-inch intervals. Pour orange-rum syrup over warm cake. Let cool completely, at least 3 hours. Dip pan in hot water almost to rim; wipe pan dry, then invert cake out onto a plate. If prettier, you can turn the cake over. Serve, or cover and hold at room temperature up until next day. Spoon candied peel on top of cake; dust with powdered sugar. Accompany cake slices with kumquats. Makes 8 servings.

PER SERVING: 320 calories, 3.9 g protein, 50 g carbohydrates, 12 g fat, 81 mg cholesterol, 202 mg sodium

Orange-rum syrup. In a 1- to 2-quart pan, combine 2 tablespoons **butter** or margarine, ½ cup **sugar,** 1 teaspoon grated **orange peel,** and 2 tablespoons *each* **orange juice** and **light rum** (or use all juice). Stir over high heat until syrup boils and butter melts. Use while still warm.

Candied orange peel. With a vegetable peeler, pare colored part of peel from 1 small **orange;** cut peel into very thin shreds. Ream juice from fruit and save.

In a 1- to 1½-quart pan over high heat, cover peel generously with **water** and bring to a boil; drain. Repeat step. Add juice and 1 tablespoon **sugar.** Boil on high heat, stirring occasionally, until syrup is reduced to about 1 tablespoon, 2 to 4 minutes; remove from heat and let bubbles subside before checking. Let cool. If made ahead, chill, covered, up to 2 days.

Kumquats and freshly candied orange peel decorate moist orange-rum cake. You can make the dessert a day ahead, then garnish shortly before serving.

Traditional Holiday Dinner—Quick & Simple

STICKING TO THE *elements of a traditional holiday dinner, this menu updates the basic meat-starch-salad combination with some new flavors. It's an easy meal to put together for a dozen people. Ingredients are few and cooking steps minimal. With its simple preparation and wide flavor appeal, the menu could become a tradition itself.*

NEW HOLIDAY TRADITION

Prime Rib with Garlic & Herb Crust
Individual Yorkshire Puddings
Fennel Purée
Mixed Greens with Watercress Dressing
Tropical Fruits with Orange Liqueur
Cabernet Sauvignon or Champagne

Fresh accents enliven tradition-based dinner: prime rib with a garlic crust, individual Yorkshire puddings, fennel purée, and salad with a tangy watercress dressing.

To keep the day of your dinner as free as possible, do a few things a day ahead: purée the garlic for roast, make fennel purée, wash and crisp salad greens, and make the dressing.

Mix a variety of greens for the salad. Choose from tender red-leaf and butter lettuces, lacy frisée, spicy arugula, and bitter curly endive or chicory. (To serve 12, you'll need 12 to 14 cups washed and crisped bite-size pieces of greens, about ¾ lb. total.)

For dessert, decoratively arrange peeled slices of fresh pineapple, papaya, and kiwi fruit on plates. Douse fruit liberally with orange- or hazelnut-flavored liqueur.

After you remove the roast from the oven, increase the oven temperature to 400° and bake the puddings (no additional preheating needed). Puddings should be the last item to come to the table, since you want them as hot as possible.

PRIME RIB WITH GARLIC & HERB CRUST

1 center-cut beef standing rib roast (about 8 lb.)
2 large (½ lb. total) heads garlic
8 dry bay leaves

Cut off and remove strings and layer of surface fat on roast. Place meat, ribs down, in an 11- by 13-inch rimmed pan.

Peel garlic. In a food processor or blender, purée garlic. Pat purée evenly over top and sides of roast. Press bay leaves into garlic. Roast meat in a 350° oven until thermometer inserted through thickest part to the bone registers 120° for rare (about 16 minutes per lb.) or 130° for medium (about 18 minutes per lb.), 2 to 2½ hours total. Place roast on a platter and cover with foil; let stand at least 15 or up to 45 minutes before carving.

To carve, turn roast on a cut end and slice meat away from rack of bones. Cut bones apart and set aside for bone lovers; carve boneless meat across grain into thin slices. Makes 12 servings.

PER SERVING: 332 calories, 35 g protein, 5.9 g carbohydrates, 18 g fat, 101 mg cholesterol, 95 mg sodium

INDIVIDUAL YORKSHIRE PUDDINGS

3 tablespoons roast beef drippings (from prime rib, preceding) or melted butter or margarine
1¼ cups milk
3 large eggs
¾ cup all-purpose flour
½ teaspoon dry thyme leaves
½ teaspoon salt (optional)

Divide roast beef drippings evenly among 12 muffin cups (2½-in. diameter); rub drippings up sides of cups.

In a food processor or blender, whirl milk, eggs, flour, thyme, and salt to blend. Fill each muffin cup ⅔ full of batter. Bake in a 400° oven until puddings turn a rich golden brown, 40 to 45 minutes. Serve at once. Makes 12 servings.

PER PUDDING: 95 calories, 3.2 g protein, 7.3 g carbohydrates, 5.7 g fat, 61 mg cholesterol, 28 mg sodium

FENNEL PURÉE

3 pounds (about 2 large heads, stems trimmed) fennel, save feathery leaves
¼ cup (⅛ lb.) butter or margarine
Salt and pepper

Coarsely chop fennel heads; you should have about 2 quarts. In a covered 5- to 6-quart pan, cook fennel with butter on low heat until fennel is tender when pierced, about 45 minutes.

In a food processor or blender, purée fennel. Add salt and pepper to taste. (If made ahead, cover and chill up until next day.) Stir often on low heat to warm. Pour into a bowl. Top with feathery leaves. Makes 1 to 1½ quarts; serves 12.

PER SERVING: 49 calories, 1.2 g protein, 2.6 g carbohydrates, 3.9 g fat, 10 mg cholesterol, 130 mg sodium

WATERCRESS DRESSING

1 cup (1½ oz.) packed, rinsed and drained watercress leaves
¾ cup olive or salad oil
¼ cup lemon juice
1 teaspoon dry tarragon leaves

In a food processor or blender, finely chop watercress with oil, lemon juice, and tarragon; add salt and pepper to taste. If made ahead, cover and chill up until next day. Makes 1¼ cups.

PER TABLESPOON: 73 calories, 0.1 g protein, 0.3 g carbohydrates, 8.1 g fat, 0 mg cholesterol, 1.5 mg sodium

Smartly Dressed Holiday Salads

L ET HOLIDAY MEALS BEGIN *with a fine winter salad—dressed for the season with colorful and delicious ingredients. Winter fruit creates the main statement in two of our recipes.*

Serve sliced oranges and mixed greens topped with a jewel-toned cranberry vinaigrette. Or try red or yellow pear fans dressed with toasted nuts and raisins. Cloak shrimp, peas, and lettuce in a refreshing cilantro mixture, or drizzle romaine and endive with a pistachio and lemon dressing.

To accommodate your busy cooking schedule, you can rinse and crisp salad greens ahead. Three of the dressings can also be made in advance.

ORANGE & ONION SALAD WITH CRANBERRY VINAIGRETTE

1¼ cups fresh or frozen cranberries
⅓ cup sugar
4 large (about 2 lb. total) oranges
2 tablespoons salad oil
2 tablespoons red wine vinegar
3 quarts (about 1½ lb.) rinsed and crisped bite-size pieces butter lettuce, curly endive, or escarole (use butter and 1 or both of the other greens)
½ cup thinly sliced red onion rings
Salt and pepper

In a 1½- to 2-quart pan, stir together cranberries and sugar. Cover and cook on lowest heat, shaking pan occasionally, just until a few cranberries begin to burst, 8 to 15 minutes. Set aside.

Shred orange peel to make 1 teaspoon long, thin shreds. Ream 1 orange to make 3 tablespoons juice. Mix peel, juice, oil, vinegar; gently stir into cranberries. If made ahead, cover and chill up to 2 days.

Cut peel and white membrane from remaining oranges. Thinly slice oranges crosswise. In a large salad bowl combine orange slices, lettuce, and onion. Pour cranberry dressing over salad and mix. Add salt and pepper to taste. Serves 8.

PER SERVING: 126 calories, 1.9 g protein, 23 g carbohydrates, 3.8 g fat, 0 mg cholesterol, 4.7 mg sodium

Poached cranberries add ruby color and tart flavor to vinaigrette dressing for this colorful winter salad of sweet oranges, red onions, and crisp greens.

Cilantro-seasoned shrimp, tiny peas, and thinly sliced celery nestle in cups of red radicchio and green lettuce leaves.

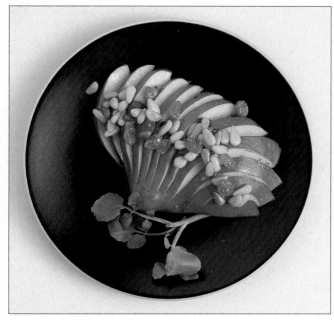

Browned pine nuts and plump golden raisins in sherry vinaigrette decorate fan of red pear slices. Garnish with watercress sprig.

GREEN & RED SHRIMP CUPS

  8 **large butter lettuce leaves, rinsed and crisped**
  8 **large radicchio leaves or medium-size butter lettuce leaves, rinsed and crisped**
  ½ **pound shelled cooked tiny shrimp**
1½ **cups thinly sliced celery**
  1 **package (10 oz.) frozen petite peas, thawed**
     Cilantro vinaigrette (recipe follows)
     Fresh cilantro (coriander) sprigs

On each of 8 salad plates, place 1 lettuce leaf; nest 1 radicchio leaf inside.

Mix the shrimp, celery, peas, and vinaigrette.

Spoon equal portions of the shrimp mixture into the radicchio cups. Garnish with cilantro sprigs. Makes 8 servings.

PER SERVING: 164 calories, 8.2 g protein, 5.5 g carbohydrates, 12 g fat, 58 mg cholesterol, 179 mg sodium

Cilantro vinaigrette. In a blender, combine ⅓ cup **salad oil,** 3 tablespoons **white wine vinegar,** ⅓ cup coarsely chopped **fresh cilantro** (coriander), 2 tablespoons **mayonnaise,** and 1 teaspoon **anchovy paste;** whirl until smooth. If made ahead, cover and chill up until next day. Makes about ½ cup.

PEAR FANS WITH RAISIN DRESSING

  3 **medium-size (about ⅓ lb. each) firm-ripe red or yellow Comice pears**
     Raisin dressing (recipe follows)
     Watercress sprigs, rinsed and crisped
     Salt and pepper

Cut pears in half lengthwise and remove cores. Starting about ½ inch from stem end, make cuts ¼ inch apart down length of pear.

Place pear half, cut side down, on a salad plate and press gently to fan out slices. Brush cut surfaces with dressing. Drizzle remaining dressing over pears. Tuck watercress around pears. Add salt and pepper to taste. Makes 6 servings.

PER SERVING: 187 calories, 2 g protein, 21 g carbohydrates, 13 g fat, 0 mg cholesterol, 26 mg sodium

Raisin dressing. Mix 3 tablespoons **salad oil,** 2 tablespoons **sherry** or cider **vinegar,** 4 teaspoons **honey,** 1 teaspoon **Dijon mustard,** and ½ teaspoon **anise seed.** If made ahead, cover and chill up until next day.

In a 6- to 8-inch frying pan, stir 1 tablespoon **salad oil** and ¼ cup **pine nuts** or slivered almonds over medium-low heat, until nuts begin to brown, about 5 minutes. Add ¼ cup **golden raisins** and stir until nuts and raisins are lightly browned, about 2 minutes. If made ahead, cool and store airtight up until next day. Mix nut and anise mixtures. Makes ⅔ cup.

ROMAINE & ENDIVE WITH PISTACHIO DRESSING

  2 **heads (about 5 oz. total) Belgian endive, rinsed and crisped**
12 **to 16 small (4 to 7 in. long, about 5 oz. total) inner leaves romaine lettuce, rinsed and crisped**
     Pistachio dressing (recipe follows)
     Lemon wedges (optional)
     Salt and pepper

On each of 4 salad plates, arrange endive and romaine leaves; drizzle with pistachio dressing. Garnish with lemon. Add salt and pepper to taste. Makes 4 servings.

PER SERVING: 221 calories, 2.2 g protein, 5.1 g carbohydrates, 22 g fat, 0 mg cholesterol, 70 mg sodium

Pistachio dressing. Mix ⅓ cup **avocado** or olive **oil,** 1 teaspoon finely shredded **lemon peel,** and 3 tablespoons **lemon juice.** Add ¼ cup chopped **salted pistachios** and 2 tablespoons minced **green onion.** Makes about ½ cup.

Festive, Potluck-Portable Vegetable Dishes

WITH THE LAST-MINUTE FLURRY needed to get the holiday dinner on the table, it's a welcome relief to cook the vegetables in advance, freeing both cook and kitchen for more timely duties.

These two vegetable choices—broccoli or baby bok choy—look festive, are potluck-portable, and can be prepared in advance. Serve them hot or at room temperature.

If you plan to reheat them, make sure the serving dish is appropriate to the method you choose. Use a good-looking shallow 3- to 4-quart baking dish in a conventional oven or a microwave-safe non-metal platter or casserole that will fit in a microwave oven.

To reheat in a conventional oven. Cover with foil and bake at 400° until hot, 20 to 30 minutes.

To reheat in a microwave oven. Cover with plastic wrap and cook at full power (100 percent), rotating dish ½ turn once, 4 to 7 minutes.

BROCCOLI WITH RED PEPPER & ONION

- 2 pounds broccoli
- 2 tablespoons olive oil
- 2 large onions (about 1¼ lb. total), thinly sliced
- 2 large red bell peppers (about 1 lb. total), stemmed, seeded, and thinly sliced
- 1 tablespoon drained capers
  Salt and pepper

Trim tough ends off broccoli. Peel broccoli stalks; cut lengthwise to make ⅓-inch-thick slices. Fill a 12-inch frying pan or a 5- to 6-quart pan with 1 to 1½ inches water; bring to a boil. Add ⅓ to ½ of the broccoli, and cook, turning over once, just until barely tender when pierced, 2 to 3 minutes. Lift out broccoli and immerse in ice water. Repeat with remaining broccoli; when cool, drain well. Arrange on a platter or shallow 3- to 4-quart baking dish.

Drain pan and dry. Add 2 tablespoons oil and onions. Stir often over medium-high heat for 5 minutes. Add peppers; stir often until edges are browned, 10 to 15 minutes. Stir in capers; spoon onto broccoli.

Serve warm. (If made ahead, cool, cover, and let stand up to 4 hours or chill until the next day; let warm to room temperature to serve. To reheat, see preceding directions.) Add salt and pepper to taste. Makes 8 servings.

PER SERVING: 90 calories, 3.5 g protein, 12 g carbohydrates, 4 g fat, 0 mg cholesterol, 49 mg sodium

BABY BOK CHOY WITH SESAME SOY

- 1 tablespoon sesame seed
- 8 medium-size heads baby bok choy (about 1½ lb. total)
  About 2 tablespoons Oriental sesame oil or salad oil
- 1 tablespoon minced fresh ginger
- 3 tablespoons dry sherry
- 3 tablespoons soy sauce
- ⅛ teaspoon crushed dried hot red chilies (optional)
- ¼ cup thinly sliced green onion

Stir sesame seed in a 10- to 12-inch frying pan over medium-low heat until golden, 3 to 5 minutes. Pour out of pan.

Cut heads of bok choy in half lengthwise. Rinse between leaves, keeping halves intact. Coat bottom of a 10- to 12-inch frying pan with 1½ teaspoons oil; set over medium-high heat. When pan is hot, lay bok choy, as many as will fit in a single layer, cut side down in pan. Add 2 tablespoons water. Cover and cook just until bok choy wilts, about 2 minutes. Lift out of pan, drain briefly, and arrange cut side up on a platter or shallow 3- to 4-quart baking dish. Empty pan. Repeat to cook remaining bok choy. (If made ahead, cool, cover, and let stand up to 4 hours or chill until the next day.)

Add 1 tablespoon oil and ginger to pan and stir over high heat until ginger is lightly browned, about 30 seconds. Add sherry and bring to a boil. Remove from heat and add soy and chilies. (If made ahead, cover sauce and store at room temperature up until the next day.)

Serve bok choy hot, at room temperature, or reheated (see preceding directions). Pour reserved sauce evenly over hot or cool vegetables. Sprinkle with onion and sesame seed. Serves 8.

PER SERVING: 55 calories, 1.9 g protein, 3.6 g carbohydrates, 4.1 g fat, 0 mg cholesterol, 442 mg sodium

Arrange blanched green broccoli around border of platter, then top with sautéed onions and red pepper strips. Vegetables keep their brilliant colors when reheated.

Leaner Eggnogs?

HOLIDAY CHEER WITH LESS GUILT *is what these eggnogs bring. By using low-fat or nonfat milk and far fewer eggs than traditional recipes call for, we've significantly lowered their fat and cholesterol content.*

Despite our cuts, these party drinks are so thick and rich-tasting that you won't miss the cream or extra eggs. For a festive touch, serve the nog in a pretty punch bowl and sprinkle the top with freshly grated nutmeg.

LEANER EGGNOG

This has the traditional taste of eggnog, with a lighter consistency.

- 4 large eggs, separated
- 1 cup sugar
- 2 quarts low-fat milk
- 1 tablespoon vanilla
- ¼ teaspoon ground nutmeg
- 1 cinnamon stick (about 3 in. long)
- 3 large egg whites
  About 1 cup rum or brandy (optional)

In the top of a 1½- to 2-quart double boiler, combine egg yolks with ½ cup of the sugar. Beat to blend, then add 1 quart milk; stir until well mixed. Add vanilla, ground nutmeg, and cinnamon stick. Place over simmering water; stir until mixture evenly coats a spoon, about 20 minutes. Remove from heat and discard cinnamon stick. Transfer mixture to a large bowl and stir in remaining milk. Cover and chill thoroughly, at least 4 hours or up to 2 days.

In a large bowl, beat egg whites (7 whites total) on high speed with an electric mixer until frothy. Gradually add the remaining ½ cup sugar, beating until whites hold stiff, moist peaks. Set aside about ½ cup of the meringue.

Add rum to taste to chilled custard; stir to mix in any spices that may have settled. Gently whisk the custard into the remaining meringue, about 1 cup at a time, just until smoothly blended. Transfer to a serving bowl and top with reserved meringue. Makes about 3 quarts, 16 servings (6 oz. each).

PER SERVING: 134 calories, 6.3 g protein, 19 g carbohydrates, 3.6 g fat, 62 mg cholesterol, 87 mg sodium

ALMOST EGGLESS NOG

The only eggs come from the frozen yogurt, which also gives a pleasant tang.

- 2 quarts frozen low-fat vanilla yogurt
- 1 quart low-fat milk
- 2 teaspoons vanilla
- 1 teaspoon ground cinnamon
- ½ teaspoon ground nutmeg
  About ¼ cup sugar (optional)
  About ½ cup rum or brandy (optional)

In a blender, whirl ½ the frozen yogurt, ½ the milk, and vanilla, cinnamon, and nutmeg until smoothly blended, about 1 minute. Pour into a chilled serving bowl. Whirl to smoothly blend remaining frozen yogurt and milk; stir into bowl. Add sugar and rum to taste. Makes 2¾ quarts, about 14 servings (6 oz. each).

PER SERVING: 166 calories, 5.9 g protein, 29 g carbohydrates, 2.5 g fat, 10 mg cholesterol, 35 mg sodium

GOLDEN APRICOT NOG

- ½ pound (1⅓ cups) dried apricots
- 1 cup water
- ¾ cup sugar
- 1 cinnamon stick (about 3 in. long)
  About 2 quarts nonfat milk
- 1 tablespoon vanilla
- ½ teaspoon ground nutmeg
- 4 large egg whites
  About ¾ cup rum or brandy (optional)

In a 1- to 2-quart pan, combine the apricots, water, ¼ cup of the sugar, and the cinnamon stick. Bring to a boil over high heat, then cover, reduce heat, and gently simmer until apricots are very tender when pierced, about 15 minutes; discard cinnamon. Let apricots cool at least 1 hour, then pour with liquid into a blender. Add 1 cup milk and whirl until mixture is smooth. Mix in a large bowl with 7 cups milk, vanilla, and nutmeg. Cover and chill at least 4 hours or up until next day.

Thick and creamy, nutmeg-dusted eggnog has lower fat and cholesterol than commercial dairy preparations. Though lighter, this beverage has the flavor of traditional rich eggnog.

In a large bowl, beat whites with an electric mixer on high speed until frothy. Gradually beat in remaining ½ cup sugar until whites hold stiff, moist peaks. Set aside about ½ cup meringue.

Gently whisk apricot mixture into remaining meringue in bowl until smoothly blended. Stir in rum to taste and enough more milk to thin to desired consistency. Pour into a serving bowl and float the reserved meringue on top of the liquid. Makes about 3½ quarts, about 18 servings (6 oz. each).

PER SERVING: 105 calories, 4.9 g protein, 21 g carbohydrates, 0.3 g fat, 2.2 mg cholesterol, 70 mg sodium

Cornhusks As Rustic Wrappers

LENDING A RUSTIC CHARM, *dry corn-husks make these foods look almost gift-wrapped.*

For an attractive fringe around a polenta, cheese, and corn torte, line a pan with husks before baking. (The husks also make it easier to remove the torte from the pan.) Or use husks to wrap caramels for candy purses.

Look for cornhusks in Mexican markets or some supermarkets. Stored airtight in a dry place, they keep almost indefinitely.

TRIPLE CORN TORTE

- **5** **to 7 dry cornhusks (8 to 10 in. long)**
- **2** **cups regular-strength chicken broth**
- **¾** **cup polenta or yellow cornmeal**
- **2** **tablespoons butter or margarine**
- **1** **small onion, chopped**
- **½** **teaspoon cumin seed**
- **1** **cup fresh or frozen corn kernels**
- **½** **cup shredded cheddar cheese**
- **1** **can (4 oz.) whole green chilies**
- **1** **small firm-ripe tomato, cored and cut into wedges**
  Prepared salsa (optional)

Separate husks and place in a large bowl. Cover with boiling water. Soak until pliable, about 10 minutes. Drain husks, pat dry, and tear into 2- to 3-inch-wide strips.

Butter a 7½- to 8-inch-diameter tart or cake pan with removable bottom. Line pan with husks, setting wide ends in center and overlapping slightly; pointed ends should extend over pan sides.

In a 2- to 3-quart pan, boil 1¼ cups broth. Mix remaining broth and polenta. With a long-handled spoon, stir polenta mixture into boiling broth. Cook, stirring, until thick (be careful: hot mixture splatters). Reduce heat to low; stir until polenta stops flowing after spoon is drawn across pan bottom, 3 to 5 minutes. Immediately pour hot polenta into husk-lined pan and quickly spread polenta in an even layer.

In a 10- to 12-inch frying pan, melt butter over medium-high heat. Add onion and cumin and stir often until onion is lightly browned, about 5 minutes. Stir in corn; heat until hot, about 3 minutes. Spread mixture evenly over polenta; sprinkle with cheese. Cut the chilies in half lengthwise and arrange, spoke-fashion, over cheese.

Soaked cornhusks bake under torte combining polenta, corn, chilies, and cheese; tomatoes garnish. Cut in wedges.

Bake in a 350° oven until husks are crisp and tart is hot, 10 to 15 minutes. Remove pan sides. Garnish with tomato. Cut into wedges. Add salsa to taste. Makes 3 or 4 entrée or 6 to 8 appetizer servings.

PER ENTRÉE SERVING: 270 calories, 8.6 g protein, 33 g carbohydrates, 12 g fat, 30 mg cholesterol, 350 mg sodium

CARAMEL–NUT CORNHUSK PURSES

- **18** **to 20 dry cornhusks (6 to 8 in. long)**
- **24** **whole blanched almonds**
- **2** **tablespoons melted butter or margarine**
- **24** **vanilla caramels, unwrapped**

Separate husks and place in a large bowl. Cover with boiling water. Soak until pliable, about 10 minutes.

Meanwhile, place nuts in a 10- by 15-inch pan. Bake in a 325° oven until golden, about 10 minutes. Remove from pan and set aside.

Drain husks and pat dry. Tear enough of them lengthwise into strips 3½ inches wide at base to make 24 pieces. Tear enough remaining husks lengthwise into ¼-inch-wide strips to make 24 ties.

Brush the center 3 inches of a wide piece of husk with butter. Set a caramel in the center; gently press nut into caramel. Gather ends of husk over caramel and secure with a cornhusk strip. Repeat with remaining caramels. Set wrapped caramels in a single layer in the 10- by 15-inch baking pan. Bake in a 325° oven until husks are dry and caramels are soft, 6 to 8 minutes. Serve warm or cool. Unwrap to eat. If made ahead, cool and store airtight up to 1 week. Makes 24.

PER PIECE: 52 calories, 0.6 g protein, 74 g carbohydrates, 2.5 g fat, 2.8 mg cholesterol, 31 mg sodium

Farm-Raised Salmon Is Here

BY WINTER, *the season for wild salmon is over in most parts of the West. If you yearn for fresh salmon now, farm-raised fish is the kind you're most likely to find.*

As part of the developing aquaculture industry, more and more salmon are being raised in ocean pens and land-based tanks in locations all over the world. Growers can control production and harvest to provide this fish fresh at times when most wild salmon is available only frozen.

Cook farmed salmon as you do wild fish, but don't be surprised if it has a milder flavor and softer texture.

SALMON FILLET WITH MUSTARD GLAZE

 1 **salmon fillet (1½ to 2 lb.)**
 2 **tablespoons Dijon mustard**
 1 **tablespoon olive oil**
 1 **tablespoon honey**
 ¼ **teaspoon grated lemon peel**
 1 **tablespoon lemon juice**
   Parsley sprigs
   Lemon wedges
   Salt and pepper

Rinse salmon fillet and pat dry. Place fillet, skin side down, on a piece of heavy-duty foil set in a rimmed 10- by 15-inch pan. With a pair of scissors, cut through foil around the fish; discard the foil rim. Mix the mustard, oil, honey, lemon peel, and lemon juice. Brush fish with all of the mustard mixture.

Broil fish about 5 inches from heat just until it looks slightly translucent and wet in thickest part (cut to test), 9 to 12 minutes. Lift foil to transfer fillet to a serving platter. Garnish with parsley and lemon wedges. Add salt and pepper to taste. Makes 4 to 6 servings.

PER SERVING: 198 calories, 23 g protein, 3.7 g carbohydrates, 9.8 g fat, 62 mg cholesterol, 201 mg sodium

SALMON PACKETS WITH GINGER

 6 **salmon fillets (6 to 8 oz. each)**
 12 **to 18 sprigs fresh cilantro (coriander)**
 2 **tablespoons soy sauce**
 2 **tablespoons dry vermouth**
 1 **tablespoon Oriental sesame oil (optional)**
 1 **tablespoon minced fresh ginger**

Rinse salmon and pat dry. On the center of each of 6 sheets of cooking parchment (each about 12 by 15 in.), set a piece of salmon. Place 2 or 3 sprigs of cilantro on each fillet. Mix soy, vermouth, sesame oil, and ginger; drizzle equal amounts of this mixture on each piece of fish.

Bring 2 opposite sides of parchment together and fold over twice. Fold ends over 2 or 3 times and tuck underneath fish. Place enclosed packets on a 12- by 15-inch baking sheet.

Bake in a 450° oven just until fish looks slightly translucent and wet in thickest part (cut a tiny slit through paper to test), 10 to 15 minutes. Transfer to dinner plates. Unwrap packets, tucking paper under fish. Makes 6 servings.

PER SERVING: 248 calories, 34 g protein, 1.3 g carbohydrates, 11 g fat, 94 mg cholesterol, 419 mg sodium

SALMON PACKETS WITH ROSEMARY

Follow recipe for **salmon packets with ginger** (preceding) except omit cilantro, soy, vermouth, sesame oil, and ginger. Mix 1 tablespoon *each* **extra-virgin olive oil** and **lemon juice**. Drizzle salmon pieces with equal amounts of the oil mixture. Lay 1 or 2 thin **lemon slices** and 1 sprig (3 in.) fresh **rosemary** (or sprinkle ⅛ teaspoon dry rosemary) over each fillet. Wrap and bake as directed. Add **salt** and **pepper** to taste. Makes 6 servings.

PER SERVING: 266 calories, 34 g protein, 2.1 g carbohydrates, 13 g fat, 94 mg cholesterol, 76 mg sodium

Whole salmon fillet broils in just minutes; mustard-honey glaze adds a tantalizing finish. Farmed salmon has a milder flavor and softer texture than wild salmon.

The Good Old Pressure Cooker

UNDER PRESSURE *to put good food on the table in a hurry? Consider the pressure cooker. Though it's been around for a long time and the cooking principles remain the same, it has recently undergone changes in style and operation.*

Foods do indeed cook faster in the above-boiling temperatures achieved under pressure. A microwave oven cooks small portions fast; with pressure cooking, the amount of food you cook does not affect the cooking time. (The results of the two methods are also, of course, very different.) Pressure cooking is particularly effective for foods that require long simmering, such as dried beans or firm-textured meats such as tongue; you save 25 to 50 percent of cooking time.

Newer models offer faster-acting pressure releases, so you need less liquid and can use a greater variety of foods. With older cookers, there was valid concern that a small bit of food, such as a grain of rice, might stick in the steam release valve and cause pressure safeties to open.

Pressure cookers come in a wide range of sizes, some as small as 2-quart, some large enough for canning. Our recipes use pans that are 4- to 6-quart in size.

First, read the instruction book for the pressure cooker you'll be using. Even though all pans are designed with safety features for releasing steam in the event of overheating, it's important to seat the lid properly and to understand how to regulate the heat, how to reduce the pressure, and how to release the lid.

General guidelines establish how full you can fill the pan, how much liquid must be present, and which foods you can cook. Of the following three recipes, the beans and tongue are appropriate for all models, but cook rice under pressure only if the manufacturer gives directions for doing so.

Once pressure is created by steam in the sealed pan, it is regulated by a gauge—and by the amount of heat applied. The two basic kinds of pressure controls indicate pressure changes in pound increments. One is a weight that jiggles to release pressure, making a noise. The other is an indicator that you must watch, with a marker that moves up and down.

At 5 pounds, the internal temperature is 228°; at 10 pounds, it's 240°; at 15 pounds,

it's 250°. In some models, steam is released before the pressure system comes into play; this may affect the cooking time slightly, and you may have to add liquid at the end to achieve the proper results, as in the risotto and beans.

How to build pressure. Seal lid and set pan on high heat until pressure is reached according to manufacturer's directions.

How to reduce pressure. Follow manufacturer's directions for regular or quick pressure release. For fast-cooking foods such as the rice, you should reduce pressure rapidly. Some pans have quick-release controls; some you set under cold running water with the gauge ajar.

SPEEDY RISOTTO

Check your pressure cooker manual to be sure rice can be cooked in it.

- 1 tablespoon olive or salad oil
- 1 small onion, chopped
- 1 tablespoon chopped oil-packed dried tomato
- ¼ cup dry white wine, such as Sauvignon Blanc or Fumé Blanc
- 1 cup medium-grain white (pearl) rice or arborio rice
- 1¾ cups regular-strength chicken broth
- ½ cup grated parmesan cheese

In 4- to 6-quart pressure cooker over high heat, combine oil, onion, and tomato. Cook, stirring often, until onion is limp, about 5 minutes. Add wine and boil, stirring often, until liquid evaporates. Stir in rice and broth. Secure lid. Place pan on high heat until gauge reaches 10 pounds or top ring (middle ring if gauge has 3 rings). Reduce heat to maintain 10 pounds pressure or hold top ring in place and cook for 7 minutes.

Reduce pressure quickly (see preceding). Open pan and stir cheese into rice; pour into a bowl. Makes 4 to 6 servings.

PER SERVING: 183 calories, 5.6 g protein, 26 g carbohydrates, 5.6 g fat, 5.2 mg cholesterol, 202 mg sodium

From pantry to table, flavorful bean casserole for eight pressure-cooks in under 2 hours.

BEEF TONGUE & POTATOES WITH CHIPOTLE ONION SAUCE

Use fresh tongue, not smoked or corned.

- 1 beef tongue, 3 to 3½ pounds, rinsed well
- 4 large onions, chopped
- 3 cups regular-strength chicken broth
- 1 canned chipotle chili in adobado sauce
- 16 small (about 2-in.-diameter) red thin-skinned potatoes, scrubbed

Place tongue, onions, broth, and chipotle in a 5- to 6-quart pressure cooker. Secure lid. Place pan on high heat until gauge reaches 15 pounds or bottom ring (see preceding). Reduce heat to maintain 15 pounds pressure or hold bottom ring in place and cook for 1½ hours.

Reduce pressure (see preceding). Remove lid and lift tongue onto an ovenproof platter; set aside. Lift out and discard chili.

Skim and discard any fat from cooking liquid, then add potatoes to pressure cooker; secure lid. Place pan on high heat until gauge reaches 15 pounds or bottom ring. Reduce heat to maintain 15 pounds pressure or hold bottom ring in place and cook for 6 minutes.

Pressure-cooked beans have same rich flavor, texture as beans baked for many more hours. They make a grand companion for baked ham.

Meanwhile, pull off and discard tough skin from tongue; trim off and discard any chunks of fat or bone from back of tongue; cover and keep meat warm in a 150° oven.

Reduce pressure quickly (see preceding) on potatoes. Using a slotted spoon, transfer potatoes to platter with tongue; cover and return to oven.

Boil tongue cooking liquid in pressure cooker on high heat, uncovered, until reduced to about 3 cups, about 20 minutes; stir occasionally.

Pour reduced sauce into a bowl. Slice tongue across the grain and serve meat and potatoes with the sauce. Makes 6 to 8 servings.

PER SERVING: 497 calories, 26 g protein, 42 g carbohydrates, 24 g fat, 124 mg cholesterol, 133 mg sodium

WESTERN PRESSURE-BAKED BEANS

Add molasses, catsup, and brown sugar after beans are cooked to make a sweet-tart sauce.

- 1 pound small white beans
- ¼ pound bacon, chopped
- 2 medium-size red onions, chopped
- ¼ cup mustard seed
- 2 tablespoons minced fresh ginger
- 1 tablespoon coriander seed
- 4 cloves garlic, minced or pressed
- 5 cups regular-strength chicken broth
- ⅓ cup light or dark molasses
- ⅓ cup catsup
- ¼ cup firmly packed brown sugar

Sort beans to remove debris; rinse, drain, and set aside. In a 4- to 6-quart pressure cooker over medium-high heat, cook bacon and onions, uncovered, until meat is browned, stirring often, about 15 minutes.

Add to pan the beans, mustard seed, ginger, coriander seed, garlic, and broth; stir to mix well.

Secure lid. Place pan on high heat until gauge reaches 15 pounds or bottom ring (see preceding). Reduce heat to maintain 15 pounds pressure or hold bottom ring in place, and cook beans for 1½ hours.

Reduce pressure (see preceding). Open pan and stir in molasses, catsup, and sugar. Cook on high heat, stirring often, until sauce is thick enough to cling to beans, about 5 minutes. If made ahead, let cool, cover, and chill up to 4 days; add about ½ cup water to beans and cook on medium-high heat, stirring often, until boiling. Makes about 1½ quarts, 8 to 10 servings.

PER SERVING: 245 calories, 10 g protein, 36 g carbohydrates, 7 g fat, 5.8 mg cholesterol, 160 mg sodium

For brunch, try whole-wheat coffee cake with a sweet cinnamon-nut center.

WHOLE-WHEAT COFFEE CAKE

1 cup (½ lb.) butter or margarine
1 cup firmly packed brown sugar
3 large eggs
2 teaspoons vanilla
3 cups whole-wheat flour
⅓ cup toasted wheat germ
1½ teaspoons *each* baking powder and baking soda
1½ cups buttermilk
Filling (recipe follows)

In large bowl of an electric mixer, beat butter, brown sugar, eggs, and vanilla until well blended. Stir together flour, wheat germ, baking powder, and soda. Alternately add flour mixture and buttermilk to butter mixture; blend well.

Generously butter a 12-cup plain or decorative tube cake pan. Spoon ⅓ of the batter evenly into pan and sprinkle with filling. Top with remaining batter. Bake in a 350° oven just until cake begins to pull from pan sides, about 55 minutes. Cool in pan 15 minutes, then invert onto a plate. Serve the coffee cake warm or at room temperature. Makes 10 to 12 servings. —*Linda Vozar, Jemez Springs, N.M.*

Filling. Mix ½ cup firmly packed **brown sugar,** ½ cup chopped **pecans,** and 2 teaspoons **ground cinnamon.**

PER SERVING: 415 calories, 7.9 g protein, 52 g carbohydrates, 21 g fat, 96 mg cholesterol, 369 mg sodium

---

ITALIAN SAUSAGE & PEA POD FETTUCCINE

1 pound hot Italian sausage, casings removed
1 medium-size onion, thinly sliced
3 cloves garlic, minced or pressed
1 small jar (2 oz.) minced pimientos
2 tablespoons minced fresh or 2 teaspoons dry basil leaves
1 cup milk or whipping cream
1 pound dry fettuccine
1 package (6 oz.) thawed frozen Chinese pea pods
½ cup grated parmesan cheese

In a 10- to 12-inch frying pan, crumble sausage. Stir with onion and garlic over

Hot-flavor Italian sausage, basil, and pea pods season sauce for fettuccine.

medium-high heat until sausage is browned, about 12 minutes. Spoon fat from pan and discard. To pan add pimientos, basil, and milk. Stir until simmering; keep warm.

Meanwhile, bring 3 quarts water to boiling in a 5- to 6-quart pan on high heat. Add pasta; cook, uncovered, just until tender to bite, about 8 minutes. Drain, then pour into a wide bowl.

Stir peas into meat mixture, then pour mixture over pasta; sprinkle sauce with cheese. Mix, lifting with 2 forks, until the pasta absorbs most of the sauce's liquid. Makes 5 or 6 servings. —*Sally Vog, Springfield, Ore.*

PER SERVING: 550 calories, 26 g protein, 62 g carbohydrates, 21 g fat, 125 mg cholesterol, 662 mg sodium

---

MICROWAVE SPAGHETTI SQUASH WITH GUACAMOLE

1 spaghetti squash (about 2½ lb.)
1 large firm-ripe avocado, peeled, pitted, cut into ¼-inch pieces
2 tablespoons lime juice
2 medium-size Roma-type tomatoes, cored and chopped
1 small green bell pepper, stemmed, seeded, and chopped
¼ cup *each* chopped green onion and minced fresh cilantro (coriander)
¼ teaspoon ground cumin
Salt
Fresh cilantro sprigs (optional)

Spaghetti squash shell cradles refreshing squash and avocado salad to eat on chips.

Cut squash in half lengthwise and scoop out seeds. Lay squash, cut sides down, in a 9- by 13-inch nonmetal dish. Cook on full power (100 percent) in microwave oven until squash strands pull easily from shell, 20 to 25 minutes.

With a fork, pull strands from shell halves into a bowl; let cool. Reserve the nicest squash half. If made ahead, cover and chill squash up until next day. To squash strands, add avocado, lime juice, tomatoes, bell pepper, onion, minced cilantro, cumin, and salt to taste. Mound in shell; garnish with cilantro sprigs. Serve as an appetizer or salad. Makes 8 cups. —*Roxanne Chan, Albany, Calif.*

PER ½ CUP SERVING: 47 calories, 0.8 g protein, 5.7 g carbohydrates, 2.7 g fat, 0 mg cholesterol, 12 mg sodium

GINGER CHICKEN & YAMS

2 tablespoons olive or salad oil
1 pound yams, peeled and cut into matchstick-size pieces
1 small red onion, cut into eighths, layers separated
1 pound boned and skinned chicken breasts, cut into bite-size pieces
2 tablespoons minced fresh ginger
Cooking sauce (recipe follows)
⅓ cup minced green onions

In a 10- to 12-inch frying pan or wok over medium heat, add 1 tablespoon oil, yam sticks, and onion. Stirring often, cook vegetables until just tender to bite, about 5 minutes. Spoon onto a platter; loosely cover, and keep warm.

Turn heat to high and add remaining tablespoon of oil to pan. When hot, add chicken and ginger. Stir-fry chicken until no longer pink in center (cut to test), about 4 minutes. Add vegetables and cooking sauce. Stir until the sauce boils. Add green onion and return mixture to platter. Serves 4.—*Cynthia Morrison, Bothell, Wash.*

Cooking sauce. Mix together 3 tablespoons *each* **soy sauce, dry sherry,** and **water,** 1 tablespoon firmly packed **brown sugar,** and 1½ teaspoons **cornstarch.**

PER SERVING: 335 calories, 29 g protein, 35 g carbohydrates, 8.3 g fat, 66 mg cholesterol, 857 mg sodium

Chicken stir-fry includes yams, cut into matchstick-size pieces, and tangy ginger.

BAKED BEEF STEW WITH CARROTS

2½ pounds boned beef chuck
2 medium-size onions, chopped
2 cups regular-strength beef broth
¼ cup red wine vinegar
2 teaspoons dry thyme leaves
1 teaspoon ground pepper
4 cups ¼-inch-thick carrot slices
About 6 cups hot mashed potatoes
Salt and pepper

Trim fat from meat and discard. Cut meat into 1-inch pieces and mix with onions in a shallow 3- to 3½-quart casserole. Bake in a 450° oven, uncovered, until meat and onions brown well, about 1 hour; stir occasionally.

Meanwhile, bring broth to a boil on high heat with vinegar, thyme, and pepper; add to browned meat and onions, stirring to free browned particles in casserole. Mix in carrots. Cover casserole tightly with foil and bake until meat is very tender when pierced, about 2 hours longer. If meat is still soupy, uncover and let cook until most of the liquid evaporates. Accompany with potatoes, and add salt and pepper to taste. Makes 6 to 8 servings.—*Natalie Haney, Roseville, Calif.*

PER SERVING: 385 calories, 25 g protein, 34 g carbohydrates, 17 g fat, 73 mg cholesterol, 568 mg sodium

Succulent beef stew with carrots bakes in the oven, goes with mashed potatoes.

BARBARA'S PUDDING IN A WOK

2 large eggs, separated
1 cup sugar
¼ cup (⅛ lb.) butter or margarine
¾ cup all-purpose flour
¼ cup unsweetened cocoa
2 teaspoons baking powder
½ cup Irish cream liqueur, or ½ cup whipping cream and 1 teaspoon brandy flavoring
½ cup coffee-flavored yogurt
1 cup whipped cream (optional)

With a mixer, whip egg whites until foamy. Gradually add ¼ cup sugar, beating until whites hold soft peaks.

In another bowl, beat together the remaining sugar, butter, and yolks. Mix flour, cocoa, and baking powder. Alternately add dry ingredients, liqueur, and yogurt to yolk mixture, beating smoothly; fold in egg whites. Scrape into a buttered 1½- to 2-quart soufflé or baking dish; cover with foil.

Set dish on a rack over 1 inch of water in a wok or 6- to 8-quart pan. Bring water to boiling, cover pan, and simmer over medium heat until pudding feels firm when lightly touched in the center, about 1 hour. Serve warm or at room temperature with whipped cream to taste. Serves 6 to 8.—*Barbara A. Colleary, Tempe, Ariz.*

PER SERVING: 274 calories, 4.3 g protein, 38 g carbohydrates, 12 g fat, 86 mg cholesterol, 196 mg sodium

Laced with flavors of chocolate, coffee, and Irish liqueur, pudding steams in a wok.

THE DUCK-FRUIT COMBINATION *is a historic one. The French serve duck with orange* (à l'orange *or, with orange and a number of other ingredients and considerably more fuss, as* bigarade) *or with cherries* (aux cerises *or* Montmorency). *The*

"The French serve duck with orange."

sweet-tart fruit complements the richness of the duck meat. (Persons of diminished sensibility would say that the fruit cuts the grease.) Dried fruit can perform the same function as oranges or cherries—and do so with considerable visual flair. To sweeten the deal, mixed dried fruit is a Western product, enabling you to garnish the bird and aid the economy at the same time.

DUCK IN FRUIT SAUCE À LA RICHARD

> 1 duck (about 5 lb.), thawed if frozen
> ¼ cup (⅛ lb.) butter or margarine
> ½ cup honey
> ¼ cup firmly packed brown sugar
> 1 package (8 oz.) mixed dried fruit
> Water
> Sweet-sour red cabbage (recipe follows)

Remove duck giblets; reserve for other uses if desired. Discard lumps of fat. Rinse duck inside and out; pat dry. Secure neck skin to back with a small metal skewer; bend wings akimbo.

With tines of a fork, prick duck skin all over, then place duck, breast down, on a rack in a deep 10- by 15-inch roasting pan. Roast in a 350° oven for 1 hour. Turn duck over and continue to cook for 45 minutes longer.

Meanwhile, melt butter in a 1- to 1½-quart pan over medium heat; stir in honey and brown sugar and cook until sugar is dissolved; set aside.

Put dried fruit in a 1- to 1½-quart pan, add 1⅓ cups water, and bring to a boil. Cover, remove from heat, and let stand until duck is ready.

After duck has cooked 1¾ hours, drain and discard all fat from roasting pan.

Reduce oven temperature to 300°. Continue to roast duck until meat at thigh bone is no longer pink (cut to test), about 45 minutes longer. Baste 3 or 4 times during the first 20 minutes with butter-honey mixture.

Lift duck onto a warm platter; discard fat in roasting pan. Pour butter-honey mixture into pan and stir on medium heat to free browned bits. Drain fruit and turn gently in roasting pan to warm slightly and mix with sauce. Spoon around duck on platter. Carve duck and serve fruit and duck with the red cabbage. Makes 4 or 5 servings.

PER SERVING: 1,071 calories, 41 g protein, 85 g carbohydrates, 66 g fat, 190 mg cholesterol, 244 mg sodium

Sweet-sour red cabbage. Core and finely shred 1 medium-size head (about 2 lb.) **red cabbage.** Put cabbage in a 5- to 6-quart pan with ½ cup **water,** ⅓ cup **cider vinegar,** 1 tablespoon *each* **granulated sugar** and firmly packed **brown sugar,** and ¼ teaspoon **pepper.** Cover, bring to a boil, then reduce heat and simmer, stirring occasionally, until cabbage is very tender to bite, about 40 minutes. Uncover and boil rapidly, stirring, until any liquid has evaporated. If made ahead, cover and chill up until next day. Stir, uncovered, on high heat to warm and cook away any accumulated liquid. Makes 4 cups.

Mike Shumaker

Newbury Park, Calif.

WESTERN CHEFS DON'T MIND *taking a lot of trouble with the food they prepare, but they like to have their trouble appreciated—hence the popularity of barbecuing, where the work shows. Behind-the-scenes detail can be less rewarding (unless the compliments are more effusive than usual). Lars Ryssdal, however, is one chef who doesn't mind the details; his Scallop Mousse Ravioli requires blending a scallop mousse, filling and cooking the ravioli, and then preparing a sauce.*

If you enjoy making pasta and have the appropriate tools and skills, by all means make your own. If you don't mind a shortcut, substitute prepared egg roll skins from the store, as we did. Most people won't notice the difference. The sauce, spiced with fragrant lime juice, cardamom, and cumin, is a splendid complement to the delicately flavored ravioli.

"If you enjoy making pasta, by all means make your own."

SCALLOP MOUSSE RAVIOLI

1 tablespoon butter or margarine
½ teaspoon dry tarragon leaves
2 medium-size shallots, chopped
¼ pound mushrooms, chopped
½ pound scallops, rinsed, drained, and cut into ½-inch chunks
5 teaspoons lime juice or raspberry vinegar
⅛ pound feta cheese
⅛ teaspoon pepper
Salt
3 or 4 egg roll wrappers (6 in. square)
1 large egg, beaten to blend
1 cup whipping cream
1 cup regular-strength chicken broth
¾ teaspoon ground cumin
½ teaspoon ground cardamom

In a 10- to 12-inch frying pan over medium heat, combine butter, tarragon, shallots, and mushrooms; stir often until mushrooms are lightly browned, about 10 minutes. Add scallops and 1 teaspoon lime juice; stir until scallops are opaque but still moist-looking in the center (cut to test), about 2 minutes.

Pour scallop mixture into a food processor or blender; add half the cheese and whirl until mixture is smoothly puréed; add pepper and salt to taste. Let cool. Rinse frying pan and set aside.

To assemble ravioli, lay 1 egg roll wrapper flat; keep remaining wrappers

covered with plastic wrap to prevent drying. Cut wrapper in half, then brush all 4 edges of each half with egg. Place ⅛ to ⅙ tablespoon scallop mixture near 1 end of each wrapper half. Fold other end over filling and press edges together to seal. Place filled wrappers on a baking sheet; cover with plastic wrap as you make remaining ravioli.

In a 5- to 6-quart pan, bring about 3 quarts water to boil on high heat.

Meanwhile, in the frying pan, combine cream, broth, remaining lime juice, cumin, and cardamom. Boil, uncovered, over high heat until mixture is reduced to about 1½ cups, about 5 minutes. Stir occasionally; keep warm.

Add ravioli to the boiling water; reduce heat to keep water just below an active boil and cook until wrappers are barely tender to bite, 5 to 6 minutes.

Lift ravioli from water with a slotted spoon, draining, and at once put 2 on each of 3 or 4 salad plates. Pour sauce equally over ravioli and crumble remaining cheese over the pasta. Makes 3 or 4 first-course servings.

PER SERVING: 346 calories, 17 g protein, 11 g carbohydrates, 27 g fat, 159 mg cholesterol, 338 mg sodium

Seattle

ONE TOPIC ON WHICH DINERS *do tend to be profuse in their praise is dessert. Even so, Chefs of the West remain largely —and mysteriously—untempted to abandon the barbecue grill, the casserole, or the stewpot and venture into the area of dessert. However, when one of our contributors does send in an applicable recipe, it's likely to be a blockbuster.*

Dan Perry Philpot's Truffles Sharon is a case in point. Composed significantly of chocolate and butter enriched (!) by sugar, egg, brandy, whipping cream, and walnuts, it is the sort of confection that haunts weight watchers' dreams—a recollection of Paradise Lost.

TRUFFLES SHARON

1 pound semisweet chocolate, chopped
1 cup (½ lb.) unsalted butter or margarine
¾ cup powdered sugar
1 large egg
1 tablespoon brandy
¼ cup chopped walnuts (optional)
⅔ cup whipping cream
About 25 walnut halves

Place ½ of the chocolate in the top of a double boiler. Set over hot, but not boiling, water and let stand until chocolate softens, then stir often until smoothly melted. Take great care that no moisture (including steam) comes in contact with chocolate; otherwise it will "seize" (harden). Remove chocolate from heat and let stand until cool but still liquid.

With a mixer, beat butter and sugar until smooth and fluffy, then beat in egg and brandy. Add liquid chocolate and beat until smooth; mix in chopped nuts.

Cover chocolate truffle mixture and chill until firm enough to hold its shape when scooped, 3 to 4 hours. Shape into generous 1-tablespoon-size balls; place balls as formed about 1 inch apart on a wire rack in a rimmed 10- by 15-inch pan. Cover and chill at least 30 minutes or up until next day.

Wash and dry double boiler top; put remaining chocolate and cream in it. Repeat steps to melt chocolate; let stand just until slightly warm. Remove truffles from refrigerator and uncover. Ladle chocolate over each truffle, guiding chocolate so it coats truffle sides. While chocolate is soft, nestle a walnut half on top of each truffle. When all the truffles are coated, chill just until chocolate coating is firm, at least 1 hour; save any leftover chocolate for snacking. Nest firm truffles individually in small paper cups. Serve chilled; if made ahead, wrap airtight and refrigerate up to 2 weeks. Makes about 2 dozen.

PER PIECE: 173 calories, 12 g protein, 12 g carbohydrates, 14 g fat, 30 mg cholesterol, 5.2 mg sodium

Salinas, Calif.

December Menus

HOLIDAY FESTIVITIES *crowd the calendar this month. To honor the season yet keep kitchen hours to a minimum, we suggest three special but simple menus.*

The first meal is a late-night supper for two, designed to be transportable so you can carry it on a tray to some cozy location once preparation is finished. The second is a leisurely weekend family dinner that relies on the oven to do most of the work–roasting both the meat and vegetable companions. The third is a quick-to-fix hearty breakfast with seasonal flavors of eggnog, rum, and cranberry.

LATE-NIGHT SUPPER FOR TWO

Cream of Fennel Soup
Prosciutto & Fontina Popovers
Mixed Salad Greens
Winter Pears   Parmesan Cheese
Chianti   Sparkling Water

After the children are tucked into bed, relax in front of a crackling fire with this light but satisfying supper.

Make the soup the day before or while the popovers are baking. For the salad, mix purchased mesclun or torn greens of your choice with oil and vinegar.

Serve imported aged parmesan cheese (called reggiano) and pears for dessert.

CREAM OF FENNEL SOUP

- 1 **large head (about 1 lb. with stems trimmed) fennel, rinsed; reserve feathery leaves**
- 1 **tablespoon butter or margarine**
- ¼ **cup minced shallots**
- 1¾ **cups, or 1 can (14½ oz.) regular-strength chicken broth**
- ¼ **teaspoon fennel seed**
- ⅛ **teaspoon ground white pepper**
- 2 **tablespoons whipping cream (optional)**

Trim base and any bruises from fennel; thinly slice.

In a 2- to 3-quart pan, melt butter over medium heat. Add fennel and shallots; cover and cook, stirring often, until vegetables are golden and juices have evaporated, about 15 minutes.

In a blender or food processor, smoothly purée vegetables, broth, fennel seed, pepper, and cream. Return to pan. (If made ahead, cover and chill up until next day.) Stir over medium heat until hot. Ladle into bowls; garnish with fennel leaves. Makes 2 servings.

PER SERVING: 124 calories, 4.9 g protein, 10 g carbohydrates, 7.4 g fat, 16 mg cholesterol, 291 mg sodium

PROSCIUTTO & FONTINA POPOVERS

- 1 **large egg**
- ½ **cup *each* all-purpose flour and milk**
- 1 **ounce prosciutto or cooked ham, chopped**
- ¼ **cup shredded fontina cheese**
- 1 **tablespoon minced green onion**

Heavily butter 4 muffin cups or heavy popover cups (each 2 to 2½ in. wide).

In a blender, smoothly mix egg, flour, and milk. Stir in the prosciutto, fontina, and green onion. At once, pour batter equally into buttered cups. Bake in a 375° oven until popovers are very well browned and firm to touch, about 50 minutes. Run a knife around edge of each popover to loosen; invert from cups. Serve hot. Makes 4.

PER POPOVER: 160 calories, 7.3 g protein, 14 g carbohydrates, 8.2 g fat, 77 mg cholesterol, 202 mg sodium

Quiet fireside supper for two features cream of fennel soup, crisp prosciutto and fontina popovers, and ripe pears served with aged parmesan cheese.

SUNDAY FAMILY SUPPER

Herb-roasted Chicken Breasts with Caramelized Onions & Sweet Peppers
Garlic Mashed Potatoes
Wilted Spinach
Praline-Caramel Ice Cream Parfaits
Dry Sauvignon Blanc   Milk

After a hectic weekend, gather the entire family for a leisurely supper.

Begin by roasting the vegetables, then cook potatoes. About 20 minutes before roasted vegetables are done, place chicken in same oven. Then mash potatoes, steam spinach, and prepare sauce for chicken.

For dessert, alternate layers of praline ice cream with purchased caramel sauce and toasted pecans in tall parfait glasses.

HERB-ROASTED CHICKEN BREASTS WITH CARAMELIZED ONIONS & SWEET PEPPERS

    6   chicken breast halves (about 3 lb.
        total), skinned
        Herb marinade (recipe follows)
    2   large (about 1¼ lb. total) onions,
        sliced crosswise
    2   large (about 2½ lb. total) *each* red
        and yellow bell peppers,
        stemmed, seeded, and slivered
    3   large (about 9 oz. total) heads
        garlic
    3   tablespoons olive oil
    ½   cup *each* regular-strength chicken
        broth and dry red wine

Rinse breasts; pat dry. Place in a 10- by 15-inch pan; brush with marinade. If done ahead, cover and chill up until next day.

Place onions, peppers, and garlic in a 12- by 17-inch pan; drizzle vegetables evenly with oil. Bake on the lower rack of a 450° oven for 45 minutes; stir occasionally. Place pan of chicken on upper rack of oven. Stir vegetables occasionally, until they are soft and edges are browned and the chicken is no longer pink in thickest part (cut to test), about 20 minutes longer. Transfer onions, peppers, and chicken to a platter; cover and keep warm. Reserve garlic for potatoes (recipe follows).

Skim any fat from chicken pan; add broth and wine. Bring to a boil on high heat, stirring to loosen browned bits.

Boil, uncovered, until reduced to ½ cup, 5 to 7 minutes. Spoon sauce over chicken. Makes 6 servings.

PER SERVING: 364 calories, 37 g protein, 17 g carbohydrates, 16 g fat, 86 mg cholesterol, 108 mg sodium

Herb marinade. Stir together 3 table-spoons **olive oil**, 1 tablespoon **balsamic** or red wine **vinegar**, 1½ teaspoons *each* **dry rosemary leaves** and **dry thyme leaves**, and ¼ teaspoon **coarsely ground pepper**.

GARLIC MASHED POTATOES

    5   large russet potatoes (about 3½ lb.
        total), peeled and cut into quarters
        Roasted garlic (reserved from
        preceding recipe)
    ½   cup warm milk
    ¼   cup (⅛ lb.) butter or margarine,
        melted
        Salt and pepper

Place potatoes in a 5- to 6-quart pan; cover with 1 inch water. Cover and bring to a boil on high heat. Boil gently until potatoes are tender when pierced, 20 to 25 minutes; drain well.

Meanwhile, cut garlic heads in half crosswise and squeeze soft garlic from peel into a large bowl; discard peel. Beat garlic with an electric mixer until smooth; add potatoes, milk, and butter. Continue beating just until potatoes are smoothly blended. Add salt and pepper to taste. Serves 6.

PER SERVING: 362 calories, 9.3 g protein, 62 g carbohydrates, 9.7 g fat, 26 mg cholesterol, 125 mg sodium

COUNTRY CHRISTMAS BREAKFAST

Golden Eggnog French Toast with Rum-spiced Apples
Oven-browned Sausage Links
Sparkling Cranapple Cider
Caffe Latte

Purchased eggnog flavors French toast and lends a seasonal touch to breakfast.

Allow ¾ to 1 pound pork sausage links for 4 people. Place meat in a 7- by 11-inch pan. Bake, uncovered, in a 350° oven until well browned, 35 to 40 minutes.

Meanwhile, prepare apples and French toast; keep warm. Brew coffee and heat milk. Just before mealtime, whirl the hot milk in a blender until foamy; add to coffee.

For Christmas breakfast, try eggnog-flavored French toast with spicy apple slices. Accompany with sausage links and creamy caffe latte.

GOLDEN EGGNOG FRENCH TOAST WITH RUM-SPICED APPLES

    2   tablespoons butter or margarine
    1   cup purchased eggnog
    ½   loaf (1-lb. size) day-old sourdough
        French bread, cut into 8 slices
        (about ½ in. thick)
        Rum-spiced apples (recipe
        follows)

Melt half the butter in a 10- to 12-inch fry-ing pan over medium heat. Meanwhile, pour eggnog into an 8- to 9-inch-wide cake or pie pan. Dip bread slices in egg-nog to coat both sides (do not soak); drain briefly and lay bread in frying pan. Cook about half of the slices at a time, turning as needed, until they are richly browned on both sides, 7 to 9 minutes total. Repeat to cook the remaining slices. Offer the rum-spiced apples to spoon onto individual portions. Makes 4 servings.

PER SERVING: 434 calories, 7.9 g protein, 68 g carbohydrates, 16 g fat, 62 mg cholesterol, 451 mg sodium

Rum-spiced apples. Peel, core, and thinly slice 3 large (about 1½ lb. total) **Golden Delicious apples.** Melt 1 table-spoon **butter** or margarine in a 10- to 12-inch frying pan on medium-high heat. Stir in 2 tablespoons **sugar,** ⅛ teaspoon **ground nutmeg,** and 2 tablespoons **rum,** if desired; add apples. Cook, stir-ring often, until fruit is just tender when pierced, about 5 minutes. Serve warm.

Articles Index

Index of Recipe Titles

General Index

Photographers

Victor Budnik: 108 (right), 109. Glenn Christiansen: 33 (top and bottom right), 193, 194, 195, 196, 197, 198, 199, 200, 201, 202, 248, 249, 271. Peter Christiansen: 1, 2, 4, 16, 37, 43, 50, 51, 58, 59, 64, 65, 67, 83, 87, 88, 91, 96, 97, 101, 102, 103, 112, 113, 114, 127, 131, 136, 137, 142, 148, 149, 154, 155, 156, 157, 159, 160, 162, 163, 168, 169, 179, 183, 185, 203, 204, 205, 208, 209, 214, 215, 220, 221, 222, 224, 228, 230, 239, 245 (top right), 254, 255, 257, 258, 261, 263, 269, 273, 274, 275, 278, 279, 280, 281, 282, 283, 284, 285, 286, 287, 294, 295. Mark Newman: 272. Don Normark: 85. Norman A. Plate: 8, 9, 18, 44, 62, 63, 72, 73, 78, 79, 80, 81, 84, 90, 105, 133, 141, 171, 176, 177, 182, 184, 207, 268, 288, 289. David Stubbs: 138. Darrow M. Watt: 5, 7, 10, 11, 12, 13, 14, 15, 17, 24, 25, 27, 30, 32, 33 (left), 40, 41, 42, 53, 54, 55, 56, 57, 60, 61, 66, 75, 76, 77, 82, 86, 89, 99, 100, 106, 107, 111, 115, 116, 118, 119, 124, 125, 129, 130, 132, 140, 151, 152, 153, 158, 173, 174, 180, 181, 190, 191, 206, 217, 218, 219, 227, 231, 238, 241, 243, 244, 245 (bottom left), 246, 247, 250, 251, 252, 253, 259, 260, 276, 277. Tom Wyatt: 108 (left). Nikolay Zurek: 143, 232, 233.